Crossing the Danger Water

Crossing the Danger Water

THREE HUNDRED YEARS OF AFRICAN-AMERICAN WRITING

Edited and with an Introduction by Deirdre Mullane

ANCHOR BOOKS
A DIVISION OF
RANDOM HOUSE, INC.
NEW YORK

FIRST ANCHOR BOOKS EDITION, OCTOBER 1993

Grateful acknowledgment is made for permission to reprint copyrighted material. Every reasonable effort has been made to trace the ownership of all copyrighted material included in this volume. Any errors that may have occurrec are inadvertent and will be corrected in subsequent editions, provided notification is sent to the publisher.

Acknowledgments for individual pieces appear on pages 757–59

Library of Congress Cataloging-in-Publication Data

Crossing the danger water : four hundred years of African-American writing / edited and with an introduction by Deirdre Mullane. — 1st Anchor Books ed.

p. cm.

Includes bibliographical references and index.

1. American literature—Afro-American authors. 2. Afro-Americans—Literary collections. 3. Afro-Americans—History. I. Mullane, Deirdre.

PS508.N3C73 1993

810.8′0896073—dc20 93-17194

CIP

ISBN 0-385-42243-1

www.anchorbooks.com

PRINTED IN THE UNITED STATES OF AMERICA

20

For N'Koumba,
who believes in the power of history

Editor's Acknowledgments

For the help and inspiration needed as this volume took shape, I would like to thank: Bob, Glen, and Matthew for their support; Laura De Flora, who provided materials from her collection; Jeff Golick, who helped with the preparation of the manuscript; the editors at Anchor Books who expressed interest in the project, Heidi Von Schreiner, Sallye Leventhal, and, especially, Deborah Ackerman, who edited the book as it took on ever greater dimensions; the New York Public Library and the Schomburg Center for Research in Black Culture; and the publishers and authors whose works are included here.

I teach the kings of their ancestors so that the lives of the ancients might serve them as an example, for the world is old but the future springs from the past.

—Mamadou Kouyaté, Mali griot
Sundiata: An Epic of Old Mali, *A.D. 1217–1237*

It has been called a great many names, and it will call itself by yet another name; and you and I and all of us had better wait and see what new form this monster will assume, in what new skin this old snake will come forth.

—Frederick Douglass
The Liberator, *May 26, 1865*

We'll cross the danger water

—"My Army Cross Over"

Contents

Introduction

This anthology represents an attempt to bring together writings—meant in the largest sense to include fiction, autobiography, poetry, letters, journalism, songs, court decisions, documents, and manifestos—that reflect the African-American experience of the last three centuries. Like any anthology, it is the product of competing priorities, the result of compromise between expected works and personal choice. When this process of selection is applied to works by African-American authors, one confronts as well the long tradition in which a single individual—Booker T. Washington, W. E. B. Du Bois, Martin Luther King, Malcolm X, Jesse Jackson—has been viewed as representative. Opinions are seen not as expressions of the thinking of a particular individual in specific circumstances, but rather as somehow typical, as if differences in education, temperament, and personal history are leveled by the shared experience of race.

There is, instead, a multitude of voices to be found in this volume, some clearly engaged in dialogue with each other. John B. Russwurm and Samuel E. Cornish clash over the subject of emigration. W. E. B. Du Bois responds here directly to Washington's "Atlanta Compromise." Langston Hughes rejects the academic poetry of Countee Cullen, Malcolm X analyzes the policy of nonviolent resistance. But while a great number of opinions are expressed here on a variety of topics, certain themes emerge nonetheless.

The definitive experience confronted by early African-American authors was the brutal reality of slavery. While some of the earliest writers seemed to rely on a just Providence for recompense in an afterlife, despite the careful selection by white clergymen of biblical texts on the subjects of servants and masters, few slaves proved to be true believers. Even those writers whose work is most infused with Christian sentiment, such as Phillis Wheatley, Jupiter Hammon, and Harriet Jacobs, exposed the hypocrisy of Christian slave masters. Others adapted Christian texts to their own purposes, as in the triumph of Old Testament figures in the African-American spirituals gathered here.

Early African-American essays and orations provide powerful evidence of a more muscular form of resistance. David Walker's *Appeal,* Henry Highland Garnet's "Call to Rebellion," and Frederick Douglass's oration on the Fourth of July sustain "one continual cry" against the institution of slavery. Their arguments are echoed in the published proceedings of political conventions and the articles and editorials from the nascent black press, which reached their highest pitch in the years just prior to the Civil War. Resistance often took more violent forms as well and the testimony of Nat Turner and others involved in armed revolts is also recounted here.

With oration, the slave narrative became the dominant form in early African-American literature. Within this genre, represented in this volume by Olaudah Equiano, Frederick Douglass, and Harriet Tubman, certain conventions were realized as the narrator recounted his or her experience in bondage, the escape, and the circumstances of life after slavery, often marginally better than life within it. The liberating potential of education forms a constant theme in these texts, which slave owners clearly recognized, imposing harsh penalties on any slave found reading or writing. The relationship between these narratives and the early works of African-American fiction, like Harriet Wilson's *Our Nig* and William Wells Brown's *Clotel*, and their uses in the present day are also explored, while the self-defining potential of autobiography continues to be an essential element in the writings of more recent authors like James Weldon Johnson, Richard Wright, James Baldwin, Malcolm X, and Maya Angelou. Beyond mere literacy, it remained to determine what the proper scope of a general education should include. Booker T. Washington touched off fierce debate with his assertion that "no race can prosper till it learns that there is as much dignity in tilling a field as in writing a poem," while W. E. B. Du Bois argues the importance of higher education for a "Talented Tenth."

Many of the writings in this volume exhibit a tension between the acknowledgment of a uniquely African-American heritage and the tendency toward assimilation, a conflict Du Bois termed a "twoness,—an American, a Negro; two souls, two thoughts, two unreconciled strivings; two warring ideals in one dark body." While James Weldon Johnson examines this "transition from one world into another" in *The Autobiography of an Ex-Coloured Man* and Richard Wright, in *Uncle Tom's Children*, acknowledges "the dual role which every Negro must play," Zora Neale Hurston jumps headfirst "into the crib of negroism." Various efforts to forge a cultural identity, from political and economic nationalism to the Black Arts Movement of the 1960s to rap's "hip-hop nation," are considered here.

Implicit in this debate is the relationship of the African-American diaspora to Africa herself and to other peoples of color around the world. Some of the earliest writers keenly felt profound dislocation upon being uprooted from Africa. Phillis Wheatley, whose surviving likeness depicts a young woman in European colonial dress, commented that should she return to Africa, "how like a Barbarian shou'd I look to the Natives." The pull of Africa to later generations is evident in the nineteenth-century colonization of Liberia, Marcus Garvey's efforts at economic interdependence, and Malcolm X's ties with African leaders as he framed African-Americans' demands for parity as an issue of human rights to be argued in the court of world opinion.

Several pieces in this volume touch on the obligation of African-Americans to perform military service in every war this country has waged. Some slaves were in fact emancipated for their service in the American Revolution, yet the companies of black troops that took up arms in the Civil War fought a constant struggle for fair treatment and equal pay. In the twentieth century,

American troops fighting abroad remained segregated, and several black veterans returning after World War I were lynched during the Red Summer of 1919 while still in uniform. The oral accounts included here of African-American soldiers who fought in Vietnam make clear that well into the twentieth century, these wars continued to be fought on two fronts.

Beyond these themes, the selection of pieces for this volume remained problematic. Some poems, speeches, and essays have become so much a part of our common culture that their inclusion seemed essential. That Langston Hughes's poem "I, Too" and Countee Cullen's "Heritage" are so well known does not diminish their power for readers coming to them for the first time. The prolific writers Zora Neale Hurston, Richard Wright, and James Baldwin are represented by some of their early, though accomplished, works, allowing the reader to discover their strong voices as their contemporary audiences did. Malcolm X, whose thinking was marked by a constant evolution, is viewed at major turning points along his intellectual and spiritual journey. While many commentators have written passionately about the riots in Los Angeles in the spring of 1992, the role of Representative Maxine Waters as a public figure in this debate made her opinions particularly meaningful. Certainly, the philosophies and talents of numerous writers are only partially represented, while many other important authors—Alexander Crummell and James Forten from the early eighteenth century; early black historians like George Washington Williams and Carter Woodson, and their heirs John Henrik Clark and John Hope Franklin; Wallace Thurman, Jessie Redmon Fauset, Arna Bontemps, and Nella Larsen of the Harlem Renaissance; Mary McLeod Bethune and Nannie Burroughs from the women's-club movement; new poets of the 1960s like Sonia Sanchez, Larry Neal, Don Lee, and Nikki Giovanni; and important contemporary essayists like Cornel West and Derek Bell—have been reluctantly omitted for reasons of space. Some contemporary authors are not included because permission for their work could not be obtained. The selection of pieces implies no judgment on the talent and significance of the writers omitted; rather, those that are included were chosen because they, in some particularly meaningful way, illustrated an essential aspect of the African-American experience, and some precedence has been given to older authors, whose works are not as widely available as those of contemporary authors.

Included here, too, are works of folklore and popular culture, from tales of strongmen like John Henry and Stagolee to the music of the spirituals, blues, and rap. The uses and limitations of folklore, dialect, and idiom are central to the work of Charles W. Chesnutt, Paul Laurence Dunbar, Zora Neale Hurston, Langston Hughes, and Alice Walker, to name only a few.

I have tried also to include pieces that are infrequently anthologized or are difficult to find. The possibility that African navigators may have reached the shores of the Americas in pre-Columbian times is not widely recognized, despite scholarly studies supporting this theory. It is surprisingly difficult to find, outside of libraries, basic documents like the Emancipation Proclamation, the Thirteenth and Fourteenth Amendments, executive orders and court rulings, and civil rights legislation. Though these documents were not written by African-Americans, their history and language provide a fuller understanding of African-American experience.

Some of the women whose works are included here may be less familiar than their male contemporaries, despite the greater interest in women's studies in the past several years. Perhaps even more than others of their sex, African-American women found their loyalties divided, nowhere more apparent than in the areas of education and female suffrage. To those who would argue, to use Du Bois's assertion, that "the Negro race, like all races, is to be saved by its exceptional men," women like Sojourner Truth and Anna Julia Cooper respond, "We wish not for the boys less, but for the girls more." This volume strives to provide African-American women with equitable space as well.

In all of these cases, I have tried to provide, briefly, a context for the particular selection. This volume can serve only as an introduction to its vast and complex subject and perspectives on many significant events in African-American history and culture have been necessarily omitted. Fortunately, many important works by African-American writers are coming back into print, and the reader is referred to the bibliography for suggestions for further reading.

Finally, I have attempted to highlight relationships among individual writers, and the connection between these writers and a larger tradition. For more than three hundred years, in the face of economic exploitation, peonage, lynching, prejudice, and denial of basic civil and human rights, African-American writers have collectively created a remarkable body of work, a rich and varied legacy that resonates powerfully today for all Americans.

Note to the Reader

The texts in this volume are reprinted with original spellings, punctuation, phrasing, etc., intact to preserve both the individual authors' styles and the tenor of the historical periods in which they were written. For the reader's convenience, works mentioned in the headnotes that are also included in this volume are cross-referenced with the symbol † .

The First Africans in North America

Although African-American history is often recounted from the arrival of twenty slaves in a Dutch man-of-war at Jamestown in 1619, Africans had traveled in the New World expeditions of the Spaniards Balboa, Cortés, Pizarro, and Coronado, and with the French in Canada and the Mississippi Valley. One of the most well known of these guides, Estevanico (c.1500–1539), served as interpreter and scout to the Spanish explorer Pánfilo de Narváez in Florida and the Gulf of Mexico in 1527. Captured by Native Americans, he managed to escape and wandered in the Southwest for several years before joining the expedition of Cabeza de Vaca into New Mexico and Arizona in 1539. As the first African the Zuni had ever seen, he was viewed as a god, and gifts of precious turquoise and other stones were bestowed upon him. For this, or for some other offense, he was killed by Zuni warriors.

Recent evidence suggests, though, that Africans may have visited the New World in pre-Columbian times as well. In *They Came Before Columbus,* Ivan Van Sertima documents how new archaeological findings, maritime studies, Spanish accounts of sitings of black-skinned peoples off the Isthmus of Darien and in Colombia and Peru, and African oral history all argue for an African "discovery" of the New World before the fifteenth-century Europeans.

IVAN VAN SERTIMA

They Came Before Columbus

"The implications of these discoveries can no longer be dismissed or ignored."

THESE SPANISH SIGHTINGS OF AFRICANS IN THE NEW WORLD and the later discovery by anthropologists of distinctive black settlements along the American seaboard (outside the mainstream of the post-Columbian slave complex) constitute only one strand of the evidence of pre-Columbian contact between Africa and America. An overwhelming body of new evidence is now emerging from several disciplines, evidence that could not be verified and interpreted before, in the light of the infancy of archaeology and the great age of racial and intellectual prejudice. The most remarkable examples of this evidence are the realistic portraitures of Negro-Africans in clay, gold and stone unearthed in pre-Columbian strata in Central and South America.

It has only been within the last decade, however, that this evidence has begun to filter down to the general public. When in 1862 a colossal granite head of a Negro was found in the Canton of Tuxtla, near the place where the most ancient of pre-Columbian statuettes were discovered, the historian Orozco y Berra declared in his *History of the Conquest of Mexico* that there was bound to be an important and intimate relationship between Mexicans and Africans in the pre-Columbian past. In his time, however, the Negroid heads could not be conclusively dated. We now know, without the shadow of a doubt, through the most modern methods of dating, that some of the Negroid stone heads found among the Olmecs and in other parts of Mexico and Central America are from as early as 800 to 700 B.C. Clearly American history has to be reconstructed to account for this irrefutable piece of archaeological data. Explanations, not excuses, have got to be found. The implications of these discoveries can no longer be dismissed or ignored. The time has come to disperse the cloud of silence and scepticism that has settled over this subject for a century.

A break in that cloud came about seven years ago with the work of Alexander Von Wuthenau. Fired by a passionate conviction that America was an inseparable part of the mainstream of world cultures before 1492 and excited by the vitality and sophistication of pre-Columbian art (so long neglected in the great art museums of the world), this art historian and lecturer carried out intensive diggings and investigations in Mexico. Out of his dedicated commitment emerged a wealth of visible witnesses to the pre-Columbian presence of Africans and others in the Americas. His book *The Art of Terracotta Pottery in Pre-Columbian South and Central America* broke new ground. It shattered conventional assumptions in the field of American art as well as history. But its favorable reception has only become possible because there has been a genuine change, however gradual, however slight, in the climate of prejudice that has long inhibited any serious scholarly inquiry into this matter. . . .

What Von Wuthenau has done is to open a door upon the photo gallery of the Americas. For, lacking the camera, the ancient and medieval Americans sought to capture for all time, in the art of realistic portraiture through the medium of clay, the significant figures of their respective generations. Africans move through all their major periods, from the time of the Olmec culture around 800 B.C., when they arise in massive stone sculptures, through the medieval Mexico of the Mayas, when they appear not only in terra-cotta portraits but on golden pectorals and on pipes, down to the late post-Classic period, time of the Conquest, when they begin to disappear as they disappeared all over the world until today, reemerging once more as significant figures.

A head from the post-Classic period stares at us across five centuries with a lifelike power and directness. This is clearly the type of African who came here in 1310 in the expeditionary fleet of Abubakari the Second of Mali. These men made a tremendous visual impression upon the Mixtecs, last of the great pre-Columbian potters, for this is one of their finest clay sculptures. It was found in Oaxaca in Mexico. Its realism is striking. No detail is vague, crudely wrought or uncertain. No stylistic accident can account for the undisputed Negro-ness of the features. From the full, vivid lips, the darkened grain of the skin, the prognathic bone formation of the cheeks, the wide nostrils, the generously fleshed nose, down to the ceremonial earring and the cotton cap Cadamosto noted on warrior boatmen on the Gambia, the American artist has deftly caught the face of the African.

The court tradition of Mali and documents in Cairo tell of an African king, Abubakari the Second, setting out on the Atlantic in 1311. He commandeered a fleet of large boats, well stocked with food and water, and embarked from the Senegambia coast, the western borders of this West African empire, entering the Canaries current, "a river in the middle of the sea" as the captain of a preceding fleet (of which only one boat returned) described it. Neither of the two Mandingo fleets came back to Mali to tell their story, but around this same time evidence of contact between West Africans and Mexicans appears in strata in America in an overwhelming combination of artifacts and cultural parallels. A black-haired, black-bearded figure in white robes, one of the representations of Quetzalcoatl, modeled on a dark-skinned outsider appears in paintings in the valley of Mexico, while the Aztecs begin to worship a Negroid figure mistaken for their Tezcatlipoca because he had the right ceremonial color. Negroid skeletons are found in this time stratum in the Caribbean. "A notable tale is recorded in the Peruvian traditions . . . of how black men coming from the east had been able to penetrate the Andes Mountains." Figures, like the one described above, return to prominence in American clay. We shall deal with this in subsequent chapters, but it is important to bear in mind that the Negroid terra cottas are scattered over several periods and bear witness, in conjunction with other evidence, that this was just one of several contacts between the two continents, joined throughout pre-Columbian history by a long but easily accessible and mobile waterway.

Onto this waterway Africans sometimes stumbled accidentally. This may account for some of the Negroid heads, which represent Africans appearing on the plateau of Mexico and other parts of Mesoamerica just before and after Christ. Here we see native American artists struggling in clay two thousand years ago to come to terms realistically with the alien physiognomy of the African. This struggle is not always successful. Prognathism or some other distinct Negro-African feature is sometimes deliberately overemphasized for effect, producing vivid but grotesque evocations. Nonetheless, the dense, close curl and kink of Negroid hair, the goatee beard, so uncommon to the hairless American Indian chin, and the heavy ear pendants, a popular West African feature, come through quite clearly. With respect to the latter, Cadamosto, the Portuguese explorer who visited the Senegambian border of Mali in 1450, notes "these peoples all have their ears pierced round with holes in which they wear various ear rings, one behind the other."

There may be some stylistic distortion in the Negroid head from the Mandingo contact period. The chin juts out with an exaggerated and primitive power. Strangely enough, it was regarded by the American Indians as a sacred face. It was venerated later by the Aztecs, simply because it was black, as their god Tezcatlipoca. Black gods and *gods with Negroid features* (for black is sometimes just a ceremonial color) may be found among the American Indians. Another black god is the god of jewelers, Naualpilli. The Negroid features of this god were sculpted in green stone by the Mexicans, while his kinky hair was cast in pure gold. There is also the god of traveling merchants, o Ek-chu-ah, who enters Mayan mythology in the wake of the Mandingo.

It is hard for many to imagine the Negro-African figure being venerated as a god among the American Indians. He has always been represented as the lowliest of the low, at least since the era of conquest and slavery. His humiliation as a world figure begins, in fact, with the coming of Columbus. It was in the very decade of his "discoveries" that the black and white Moors were laid low. The image of the Negro-African as a backward, slow and uninventive being is still with us. Not only his manhood and his freedom but even the memory of his cultural and technological achievements before the day of his humiliation seem to have been erased from the consciousness of history. . . .

We cannot see very far if we enter an ancient time with contemporary blinkers, even if our pathways into the past are illuminated by a hundred torches lit by the most recent archaeological discoveries. What is needed far more than new facts is a fundamentally new vision of history.

Olaudah Equiano
(1745–1797)

The impulse to compose a relation, or narrative, of the experience of slavery was uniquely felt by African-Americans in bondage. "No group of slaves anywhere, at any other period in history," writes the critic Henry Louis Gates, "has left such a large repository of testimony about the horror of becoming the legal property of another human being. . . . The narratives of ex-slaves are, for the literary critic, the very foundation upon which most subsequent Afro-American fictional and nonfictional narratives are based."

One of the earliest accounts of African life and the Middle Passage, Olaudah Equiano's 1789 *Narrative* forms a literary bridge from the Old World to the New. In it, Equiano recounts his noble Ibo parentage, his childhood and the customs of his native Benin (present-day Nigeria), his capture at age eleven by a hostile tribe, his transport by British slavers to the New World, and his remarkable travels as a servant to several British naval officers in the American colonies, Canada, and the West Indies before buying his own freedom from a Quaker merchant in Philadelphia on July 11, 1766. Upon gaining his independence, he left America for good, and later voyages took him to the Arctic, Turkey, and Central America.

Upon publication, Equiano's account was championed by a "constellation of worthies" and went through several popular editions. He later married Susanna Cullen, an Englishwoman, and devoted much of his final years to the cause of abolition, including publicizing the infamous case of the British slave ship *Zong,* in which 132 shackled slaves were thrown overboard, after which the owners made insurance claims for their loss. He died in London on March 31, 1797, without ever having seen Africa again. His only child, a daughter, died soon after.

Recounting his first exposure to books in his *Narrative,* Equiano writes, "I had often seen my master and Dick employed in reading; and I had a great curiosity to talk to the books as I thought they did, and so to learn how all things had a beginning. For that purpose I have often taken up a book, and have talked to it, and then put my ears to it, when alone, in hopes it would answer me; and I have been very much concerned when I found it remained silent." At the same time that it relates the details of an extraordinary life, Equiano's *Narrative,* like hundreds of later accounts, gives voice to the millions who endured the Middle Passage and the brutality of enslavement.

from *The Interesting Narrative of the Life of Olaudah Equiano, or Gustavus Vassa, the African*

"The first object that saluted my eyes when I arrived on the coast was the sea, and a slave ship, which was then riding at anchor, and waiting for its cargo."

CHAPTER II

The author's birth and parentage—His being kidnapped with his sister—Their separation—Surprise at meeting again—Are finally separated—Account of the different places and incidents the author met with till his arrival on the coast—The effect the sight of a slave ship had on him—He sails for the West Indies—Horrors of a slave ship—Arrives at Barbadoes, where the cargoe is sold and dispersed.

I hope the reader will not think I have trespassed on his patience, in introducing myself to him with some account of the manners and customs of my country. They had been implanted in me with great care, and made an impression on my mind, which time could not erase, and which all the adversity and variety of fortune I have since experienced, served only to rivet and record; for, whether the love of one's country be real or imaginary, a lesson of reason or an instinct of nature, I still look back with pleasure on the first scenes of my life, though that pleasure has been for the most part mingled with sorrow.

I have already acquainted the reader with the time and place of my birth. My father, besides many slaves, had a numerous family, of which seven lived to grow up, including myself and a sister, who was the only daughter. As I was the youngest of the sons, I became, of course, the greatest favourite with my mother, and was always with her, and she used to take particular pains to form my mind. I was trained up from my earliest years in the art of war; my daily exercise was shooting and throwing javelins; and my mother adorned me with emblems, after the manner of our greatest warriors. In this way I grew up till I was turned the age of eleven, when an end was put to my happiness in the following manner:—When the grown people in the neighbourhood were gone far in the fields to labour, the children generally assembled together in some of the neighbours' premises to play; and some of us often used to get up into a tree to look out for any assailant, or kidnapper, that might come upon us. For they sometimes took those opportunities of our parents' absence, to attack and carry off as many as they could seize. One day, as I was watching at the top of a tree in our yard, I saw one of those people come into the yard of our next neighbour but one, to kidnap, there being many stout young people in it. Immediately on this I gave the alarm of the rogue, and he was surrounded by the stoutest of them, who entangled him with cords, so that he could not escape till some of the grown people came and secured him.

II. But alas! ere long it was my fate to be thus attacked, and to be carried off, when none of the grown people were nigh. One day, when all our people were gone out to their work as usual, and only I and my sister were left to mind the house, two men and a woman got over our walls, and in a moment seized us both; and without giving us time to cry out, or to make any resistance, they stopped our mouths and ran off with us into the nearest wood. Here they tied our hands, and continued to carry us as far as they could, till night came on, when we reached a small house, where the robbers halted for refreshment and spent the night. We were then unbound, but were unable to take any food; and being quite overpowered by fatigue and grief, our only relief was some sleep, which allayed our misfortune for a short time. The next morning we left the house and continued travelling all the day. For a long time we had kept the woods, but at last we came into a road which I believed I knew. I had now some hopes of being delivered; for we had advanced but a little way before I discovered some people at a distance, on which I began to cry out for their assistance; but my cries had no other effect than to make them tie me faster and stop my mouth; they then put me into a large sack. They also stopped my sister's mouth, and tied her hands; and in this manner we proceeded till we were out of sight of these people.

When we went to rest the following night, they offered us some victuals; but we refused it; and the only comfort we had was in being in one another's arms all that night, and bathing each other with tears. But alas! we were soon deprived of even the small comfort of weeping together. The next day proved one of greater sorrow than I had yet experienced; for my sister and I were then separated, while we lay clasped in each other's arms. It was in vain that we besought them not to part us; she was torn from me, and immediately carried away, while I was left in a state of distraction not to be described. I cried and grieved continually; and for several days did not eat any thing but what they forced into my mouth. At length, after many days' travelling, during which I had often changed masters, I got into the hands of a chieftain, in a pleasant country. This man had two wives and some children, and they all used me extremely well, and did all they could to comfort me; particularly the first wife, who was something like my mother. Although I was a great many days' journey from my father's house, yet these people spoke exactly the same language with us. This first master of mine, as I may call him, was a smith, and my principal employment was working his bellows, which were the same kind as I had seen in my vicinity. They were in some respects not unlike the stoves here in gentlemen's kitchens; and were covered over with leather, and in the middle of that leather a stick was fixed, and a person stood up and worked it, in the same manner as is done to pump water out of a cask with a hand pump. I believe it was gold he worked, for it was of a lovely bright yellow colour, and was worn by the women on their wrists and ankles.

I was there, I suppose, about a month, and they at length used to trust me some little distance from the house. I employed this liberty in embracing every opportunity to inquire the way to my own home: and I also sometimes, for the same purpose, went with the maidens, in the cool of the evenings, to bring pitchers of water from the springs for the use of the house. I had also remarked where the sun rose in the morning, and set in the evening, as I had travelled along: and had observed that my father's house was towards the rising of the sun. I therefore determined to seize the first opportunity of making my escape, and to shape my course for that quarter; for I was quite oppressed and weighed down by grief after my mother and friends; and my love of liberty, ever great, was strengthened by the mortifying circumstance of not daring to eat with the free-born children, although I was mostly their companion.

III. While I was projecting my escape, one day an unlucky event happened, which quite disconcerted my plan, and put an end to my hopes. I used to be sometimes employed in assisting an elderly woman slave to cook and take care of the poultry; and one morning, while I was feeding some chickens, I happened to toss a small pebble at one of them, which hit it on the middle, and directly killed it. The old slave having soon after missed the chicken, inquired after it; and on my relating the accident (for I told her the truth, because my mother would never suffer me to tell a lie) she flew into a violent passion, threatened that I should suffer for it; and, my master being out, she immediately went and told her mistress what I had done. This alarmed me very much, and I expected an instant flogging, which to me was uncommonly dreadful; for I had seldom been beaten at home, I therefore resolved to fly; and accordingly I ran into a thicket that was hard by, and hid myself in the bushes. Soon afterwards my mistress and the slave returned, and, not seeing me, they searched all the house, but not finding me, and I not making answer when they called me, they thought I had run away, and the whole neighbourhood was raised in the pursuit of me.

In that part of the country, as well as in ours, the houses and villages were skirted with woods, or shrubberies, and the bushes were so thick that a man could readily conceal himself in them, so as to elude the strictest search. The neighbours continued the whole day looking for me, and several times many of them came within a few yards of the place where I lay hid. I expected every moment, when I heard a rustling among the trees, to be found out, and punished by my master. But they never discovered me, though they often were so near that I even heard their conjectures, as they were looking about for me; and now I learned from them, that any attempt to return home would be hopeless. Most of them supposed I had fled towards home; but the distance was so great, and the way so intricate, that they thought I could never reach it, and that I should be lost in the woods. When I heard this I was seized with a violent panic, and abandoned myself to despair. Night too began to approach, and aggravated all my fears. I had before entertained hopes of getting home and had determined when it should be dark to make the attempt; but I was not convinced it was fruitless, and began to consider that, if possibly I could escape all other animals, I could not those of the human kind; and that, now knowing the way, I must perish in the woods. Thus was I like the hunted deer:

> Ev'ry leaf, and ev'ry whisp'ring breath
> Convey'd a foe, and ev'ry foe a death.

I heard frequent rustlings among the leaves, and being pretty sure they were snakes, I expected every instant to be stung by them. This increased my anguish, and the horror of my situation became now quite insupportable. I at length quitted the thicket, very faint and hungry, for I had not eaten nor drunk any thing all the day. I crept to my master's kitchen, from whence I set out at first, which was an open shed, and laid myself down in the ashes with an anxious wish for death to relieve me from all my pains. I was scarcely awake in the morning, when the old woman slave, who was the first up, came to light the fire, and saw me in the fire place. She was very much surprised to see me, and could scarcely believe her own eyes. She now promised to intercede for me, and went for her master, who soon after came, and, having slightly reprimanded me, ordered me to be taken care of, and not ill treated.

IV. Soon after this my master's only daughter and child by his first wife, sickened and died, which affected him so much that for some time he was almost frantic, and really would have killed himself, had he not been watched and prevented. However, in a small time afterwards he recovered, and I was again sold. I was now carried to the left of the sun's rising, through many dreary wastes and dismal woods, amidst the hideous roaring of wild beasts. The people I was sold to used to carry me very often, when I was tired, either on their shoulders or on their backs. I saw many convenient well-built sheds along the road, at proper distances, to accommodate the merchants and travellers. They lie in those buildings along with their wives, who often accompany them; and they always go well armed.

From the time I left my own nation I always found somebody that understood me till I came to the sea coast. The languages of different nations did not totally differ, nor were they so copious as those of the Europeans, particularly the English. They were therefore easily learned; and, while I was journeying thus through Africa, I acquired two or three different tongues. In this manner I had been travelling for a considerable time, when one evening, to my great surprise, whom should I see brought to the house where I was, but my dear sister? As soon as she saw me she gave a loud shriek, and ran into my arms. I was quite overpowered: neither of us could speak; but for a considerable time, clung to each other in mutual embraces, unable to do any thing but weep. Our meeting affected all who saw us; and indeed I must acknowledge, in honour of those sable destroyers of human rights, that I never met with any ill treatment, or saw any offered to their slaves, except tying them, when necessary, to keep them [from] running away.

When these people knew we were brother and sister, they indulged us to be together; and the man, to whom I supposed we belonged, lay with us, he in the middle, while she and I held one another by the hands across his breast all night; and thus for a while we forgot our misfortunes in the joy of being together. But even this small comfort was soon to have an end, for scarcely had the fatal morning appeared, when she was again torn from me for ever! I was now more miserable, if possible, than before. The small relief which her presence gave me from pain was gone, and the wretchedness of my situation was redoubled by my anxiety after her fate, and my apprehensions lest her sufferings should be greater than mine, when I could not be with her to alleviate them.

Yes, dear partner of all my childish sports! Sharer of my joys and sorrows; happy should I have ever esteemed myself to encounter every misery for you, and to procure your freedom by the sacrifice of my own! Though you were early forced from my arms, your image has been always rivetted in my heart, from which neither time nor fortune has been able to remove it: so that, while the thoughts of your sufferings have damped my prosperity, they have mingled with adversity and increased its bitterness. To that Heaven, which protects the weak from the strong, I commit the care of your innocence and virtues, if they have not already received their full reward, and if your youth and delicacy have not long since fallen victims to the violence of the African trader, the pestilential stench of a Guinea ship, the seasoning in the European colonies, or the lash and lust of a brutal and unrelenting overseer.

I did not long remain after my sister. I was again sold, and carried through a number of places, till, after travelling a considerable time, I came to a town called Tinmah, in the most beautiful country I had yet seen in Africa. It was extremely rich, and there were many rivulets which flowed through it, and supplied a large pond in the centre of the town, where the people washed. Here I first saw and tasted cocoa nuts, which I thought superior to any nuts I had ever tasted before; and the trees which were loaded, were also interspersed among the houses, which had commodious shades adjoining, and were in the same manner as ours, the insides being neatly plastered and whitewashed. Here I also saw and tasted, for the first time, sugar-cane. Their money consisted of little white shells, the size of the fingernail. I was sold for one hundred and seventy-two of these, by a merchant who lived at this place. I had been about two or three days at his house, when a wealthy widow, a neighbour of his came there one evening, and brought with her an only son, a young gentleman about my own age and size. Here they saw me; and, having taken a fancy to me, I was bought of the merchant, and went home with them. Her house and premises were situated close to one of those rivulets I have mentioned, and were the finest I ever saw in Africa: they were very extensive, and she had a number of slaves to attend her. The next day I was washed and perfumed, and when meal-time came, I was led into the presence of my mistress, and ate and drank before her with her son. This filled me with astonishment; and I could scarcely avoid expressing my surprise that the young gentleman should suffer me, who was bound, to eat with him who was free; and not only so, but that he would not at any time either eat or drink till I had taken first, because I was the eldest, which was agreeable to our custom. Indeed every thing here, and their treatment of me, made me forget that I was a slave. The language of these people resembled ours so nearly, that we understood each other perfectly. They had also the very same customs as well. There were likewise slaves daily to attend us, while my young master and I, with other boys, sported with our days, and bows and arrows, as I had been used to do at home. In this resemblance to my former happy state, I passed about two months; and now I began to think I was to be adopted into the family, and was beginning to be reconciled to my situation, and to forget by degrees my misfortunes, when all at once the delusion vanished; for, without the least previous knowledge, one morning, early, while my dear master and companion was still asleep, I was awakened out of my reverie to fresh sorrow, and hurried away even amongst the uncircumcised.

Thus, at the very moment I dreamed of the greatest happiness, I found myself most miserable; and it seemed as if fortune wished to give me this taste of joy, only to render the reverse more poignant. The change I now experienced was as painful as it was sudden and unexpected. It was a change indeed from a state of bliss to a scene which is inexpressible by me, as it discovered to me an element I had never before beheld, and of which till then had no idea; and wherein such instances of hardship and cruelty continually occurred, as I can never reflect on but with horror.

V. All the nations and people I had hitherto passed through resembled our own in their manners, customs, and language; but I came at length to a country, the inhabitants of which differed from us in all these particulars. I was very much struck with this difference, especially when I came among a people who did not circumcise, and who ate without washing their hands. They cooked their provisions also in iron pots, and had European cutlasses and cross bows, which were unknown to us; and fought with their fists among themselves. Their women were not so modest as ours, for they ate, drank, and slept with their men. But, above all, I was amazed to see no sacrifices or offerings among them. In some of those places the people ornamented themselves with scars, and likewise filed their teeth very sharp. They sometimes wanted to ornament me in the same manner, but I would not suffer them; hoping that I might sometime be among a people who did not thus disfigure themselves, as I thought they did. At last I came to the banks of a large river, covered with canoes, in which the people appeared to live, with their household utensils, and provisions of all kinds. I was beyond measure astonished at this, as I had never before seen any water larger than a pond or a rivulet: and my surprise was mingled with no small fear when I was put into one of these canoes, and we began to paddle and move along the river. We continued going on thus till night; and when we came to land, and made fires on the banks, each family by themselves, some dragged their canoes on shore, others cooked in theirs, and laid in them all night. Those on the land had mats, of which they made tents, some in the shape of little houses; in these we slept; and after the morning meal, we embarked again, and proceeded as before. I was often very much astonished to see some of the women as well as the men, jump into the water, dive into the bottom, come up again, and swim about. Thus I continued to travel, both by land and by water, through different countries and various nations, till at the end of six or seven months after I had been kidnapped, I arrived at the sea coast.

It would be tedious and uninteresting to relate all the incidents which befell me during this journey, and which I have not yet forgotten, or to mention the various lands I passed through, and the manners and customs of the different people among whom I lived: I shall therefore only observe, that in all the places where I was, the soil was exceedingly rich; the pumpkins, aedas, plantains, yams, &c. &c. were in great abundance, and of incredible size. There were also large quantities of different gums, though not used for any purpose; and every where a great deal of tobacco. The cotton even grew quite wild; and there was plenty of red wood. I saw no mechanics whatever in all the way, except such as I have mentioned. The chief employment in all these countries was agriculture, and both the males and females, as with us, were brought up to it, and trained in the arts of war.

The first object that saluted my eyes when I arrived on the coast was the sea, and a slave ship, which was then riding at anchor, and waiting for its cargo. These filled me with astonishment, that was soon converted into terror, which I am yet at a loss to describe, and much more the then feelings of my mind when I was carried on board. I was immediately handled and tossed up to see if I was sound, by some of the crew; and I was now persuaded that I had got into a world of bad spirits, and that they were going to kill me. Their complexions too, differing so much from ours, their long hair, and the language they spoke, which was very different from any I had ever heard, united to confirm me in this belief. Indeed such were the horrors of my views and fears at the moment, that if ten thousand worlds had been my own, I would have freely parted with them all to have exchanged my condition with the meanest slave in my own country. When I looked round the ship too, and saw a large furnace or copper boiling and a multitude of black people, of every description, chained together, every one of their countenances expressing dejection and sorrow, I no longer doubted of my fate; and, quite overpowered with horror and anguish, I fell motionless on the deck, and fainted. When I recovered a little, I found some black people about me, who I believed were some of those who brought me on board, and had been receiving their pay: they talked to me in order to cheer me, but all in vain. I asked them if we were not to be eaten by those white men with horrible looks, red faces, and long hair. They told me I was not: and one of the crew brought me a small portion of spiritous liquor in a wine glass; but, being afraid of him, I would not take it out of his hand. One of the blacks therefore took it from him and gave it to me, and I took a little down my palate, which, instead of reviving me, as they thought it would, threw me into the greatest consternation at the strange feeling it produced, having never tasted any such liquor before.

Soon after this the blacks who brought me on board went off, and left me abandoned to despair. I now saw myself deprived of all chance of returning to my native country, or even the least glimpse of gaining the shore, which I now considered friendly; and I even wished for my former slavery, in preference to my present situation, which was filled with horrors of every kind, still heightened by my ignorance of what I was to undergo. I was not long suffered to indulge my grief. I was soon put down under the decks, and there I received such a salutation in my nostrils as I had never experienced in my life: so that, with the loathsomeness of the stench, and with my crying together, I became so sick and low that I was not able to eat, nor had I the least desire to taste any thing. I now wished for the last friend, death, to relieve me; but soon, to my grief, two of the white men offered me eatables; and, on my refusing to eat, one of them held me fast by the hands, and laid me across I think, the windlass, and tied my feet, while the other flogged me severely. I had never experienced any thing of this kind before, and although, not being used to the water, I naturally feared that element the first time I saw it, yet nevertheless, could I have got over the nettings, I would have jumped over the side, but I could not; and besides the crew used to watch us very closely, who were not chained down to the decks, lest we should leap into the water. I have seen some of these poor African prisoners most severely cut for attempting to do so, and hourly whipped for not eating. This indeed was often the case with myself. In a little time after, amongst the poor chained men, I found some of my own nation, which in a small degree gave ease to my mind. I inquired of these what was to be done with us. They gave me to understand we were to be carried to these white people's country to work for them. I was then a little revived, and thought if it were no worse than working, my situation was not so desperate. But still I feared I should be put to death, the white people looked and acted, as I thought, in so savage a manner; for I had never seen among any people such instances of brutal cruelty: and this is not only shewn towards us blacks, but also to some of the whites themselves. One white man in particular I saw, when we were permitted to be on deck, flogged so unmercifully with a large rope near the foremast, that he died in consequence of it; and they tossed him over the side as they would have done a brute. This made me fear these people the more; and I expected nothing less than to be treated in the same manner. I could not help expressing my fearful apprehensions to some of my countrymen; I asked them if these people had no country, but lived in this hollow place, the ship. They told me they did not, but came from a distant one. 'Then,' said I, 'how comes it, that in all our country we never heard of them?' They told me, because they lived so very far off. I then asked, where their women were: had they any like themselves. I was told they had. 'And why,' said I, 'do we not see them?' They answered, because they were left behind. I asked how the vessel could go. They told me they could not tell; but that there was cloth put upon the masts by the help of the ropes I saw, and then the vessel went on; and the white men had some spell or magic they put in the water, when they liked, in order to stop the vessel. I was exceedingly amazed at this account, and really thought they were spirits. I therefore wished much to be from amongst them, for I expected they would sacrifice me; but my wishes were in vain, for we were so quartered that it was impossible for any of us to make our escape.

VI. While we stayed on the coast I was mostly on deck; and one day, to my great astonishment, I saw one of these vessels coming in with the sails up. As soon as the whites saw it, they gave a great shout, at which we were amazed; and the more so as the vessel appeared larger by approaching nearer. At last she came to an anchor in my sight, and when the anchor was let go, I and my countrymen who saw it, were lost in astonishment to observe the vessel stop, and were now convinced it was done by magic. Soon after this the other ship got her boats out, and they came on board of us, and the people of both ships seemed very glad to see each other. Several of the strangers also shook hands with us black people, and made motions with their hands, signifying, I suppose, we were to go to their country; but we did not understand them. At last, when the ship, in which we were, had got in all her cargo, they made ready with many fearful noises, and we were all put under deck, so that we could not see how they managed the vessel.

But this disappointment was the least of my grief. The stench of the hold, while we were on the coast, was so intolerably loathsome, that it was dangerous to remain there for any time, and some of us had been permitted to stay on the deck for the fresh air; but now that the whole ship's cargo were confined together, it became absolutely pestilential. The closeness of the place, and the heat of the climate, added to the number in the ship, being so crowded that each had scarcely room to turn himself, almost suffocated us. This produced copious perspiration, so that the air soon became unfit for respiration, from a variety of loathsome smells, and brought on a sickness among the slaves, of which many died, thus falling victims of the improvident avarice, as I may call it, of their purchasers. This deplorable situation was again aggravated by the galling of the chains, now become insupportable; and the filth of necessary tubs, into which children often fell, and were almost suffocated. The shrieks of the women, and the groans of the dying, rendered it a scene of horror almost inconceivable. Happily, perhaps, for myself, I was soon reduced so low here that it was thought necessary to keep me almost continually on deck; and from my extreme youth, I was not put in fetters. In this situation I expected every hour to share the fate of my companions, some of whom were almost daily brought upon deck at the point of death, and I began to hope that death would soon put an end to my miseries. Often did I think many of the inhabitants of the deep much more happy than myself; I envied them the freedom they enjoyed, and as often wished I could change my condition for theirs. Every circumstance I met with served only to render my state more painful, and heighten my apprehensions and my opinion of the cruelty of the whites. One day they had taken a number of fishes; and when they had killed and satisfied themselves with as many as they thought fit, to our astonishment who were on the deck, rather than give any of them to us to eat, as we expected, they tossed the remaining fish into the sea again, although we begged and prayed for some as well as we could, but in vain; and some of my countrymen, being pressed by hunger, took an opportunity, when they thought no one saw them, of trying to get a little privately; but were discovered, and the attempt procured for them some very severe floggings.

One day, when we had a smooth sea and moderate wind, two of my wearied countrymen, who were chained together, (I was near them at the time) preferring death to such a life of misery, somehow made through the nettings and jumped into the sea; immediately another quite dejected fellow, who on account of his illness was suffered to be out of irons also followed their example; and I believe many more would very soon have done the same, if they had not been prevented by the ship's crew, who were instantly alarmed. Those of us who were the most active were in a moment put down under the deck; and there was such a noise and confusion amongst the people of the ship as I never heard before, to stop her and get the boat out to go after the slaves. However, two of the wretches were drowned; but they got the other, and afterward flogged him unmercifully, for thus attempting to prefer death to slavery. In this manner we continued to undergo more hardships than I can now relate, hardships which are inseparable from this accursed trade. Many a time we were near suffocation from the want of fresh air, being deprived thereof for days together. This, and the stench of the necessary tubs, carried off many.

VII. During our passage I first saw flying fishes, which surprised me very much; they used frequently to fly across the ship, and many of them fell on the deck. I also now first saw the use of the quadrant. I had often with astonishment seen the mariners make observations with it, and I could not think what it meant. They at last took notice of my surprise: and one of them, willing to increase it, as well as to gratify my curiosity, made me one day look through it. The clouds appeared to me to be land, which disappeared as they passed along. This heightened my wonder; and I was now more persuaded than ever that I was in another world, and that every thing about me was magic. At last we came in sight of the island of Barbadoes, at which the whites on board gave a great shout, and made many signs of joy to us. We did not know what to think of this, but as the vessel drew nearer we plainly saw the harbour, and other ships of different kinds and sizes; and we soon anchored amongst them off Bridge Town. Many merchants and planters now came on board, though it was in the evening. They put us in separate parcels, and examined us attentively. They also made us jump, and pointed to the land, signifying we were to go there. We thought by this we should be beaten by these ugly men, as they appeared to us; and when soon after we were all put down under the deck again, there was much dread and trembling among us, and nothing but bitter cries to be heard all the night from these apprehensions, insomuch that at last the white people got some old slaves from the land to pacify us. They told us we were not to be eaten, but to work, and were soon to go on land, where we should see many of our country people. This report eased us much; and, sure enough, soon after we landed, there came to us Africans of all languages.

We were conducted immediately to the merchant's yard, where we were all pent up together like so many sheep in a fold, without regard to sex or age. As every object was new to me, every thing I saw filled me with surprise. What struck me first was that the houses were built with bricks in stories, and were in every other respect different from those I had seen in Africa; but I was still more astonished at seeing people on horseback. I did not know what this could mean; and indeed I thought these people full of nothing but magical arts. While I was in this astonishment one of my fellow prisoners spoke to a countryman of his about the horses, who said they were the same kind they had in their country. I understood them, though they were from a distant part of Africa, and I thought it odd I had not seen any horses there; but afterwards, when I came to converse with different Africans, I found they had many horses amongst them, and much larger than those I then saw.

We were not many days in the merchants' custody before we were sold after the usual manner, which is this:—On a signal given, such as the beat of a drum, the buyers rush at once into the yard where the slaves are confined, and make choice of that parcel they like best. The noise and clamour with which this is attended, and the eagerness visible in the countenances of the buyers, serve not a little to increase the apprehensions of the terrified Africans, who may well be supposed to consider them the ministers of that destruction to which they think themselves devoted. In this manner, without scruple, are relations and friends separated, most of them never to see each other again. I remember in the vessel in which I was brought over in, in the man's apartment, there were several brothers, who, in the sale, were sold in different lots; and it was very moving on this occasion to see their distress and hear their cries at parting. O, ye nominal Christians! might not an African ask you, "learned you this from your God, who says unto you, Do unto all men as you would men should do unto you? Is it not enough that we are torn from our country and friends, to toil for your luxury and lust of gain? Must every tender feeling be likewise sacrificed to your avarice? Are the dearest friends and relations now rendered more dear by their separation from the rest of their kindred, still to be parted from each other, and thus prevented from cheering the gloom of slavery, with the small comfort of being together, and mingling their sufferings and sorrows? Why are parents to lose their children, brothers their sisters, or husbands their wives? Surely this is a new refinement in cruelty, which, while it has no advantage to atone for it, thus aggravates distress, and adds fresh horrors even to the wretchedness of slavery."

1789

Early Slave Revolts

While it may be argued that no enslaved person, kept against his or her will, usually in extreme deprivation, dies a natural death, it is certainly true that many lost their lives trying to gain their freedom and that many others, often uninvolved in the insurrections, were drawn into the vortex of violence and repression that followed. The first slave insurrection in the New World took place in 1526 in either Virginia or South Carolina when one hundred Africans, brought by the Spanish explorer Lucas Vásquez de Ayllón, revolted after his death. The surviving Spaniards fled to Haiti, while the remaining Africans, according to Herbert Apetheker's *American Negro Slave Revolts,* formed the first permanent, nonnative settlement in the United States. In the British colonial period, soon after twenty enslaved Africans were brought to Jamestown, Virginia, the resistance began; numerous plots were reported in Virginia in 1663, 1687, 1709, 1710, 1722, 1723, and 1730.

Two of the most significant early revolts took place in New York. An African-American community was first established in the city in 1626 with the arrival of eleven African bondsmen, possibly captured sailors. Under the English, slavery became institutionalized and a slave market was established in 1709 at the base of Wall Street. The first major revolt, what the historian Benjamin Brawley called "in some ways the most important single event in the history of the Negro in the Colonial Period," took place soon after.

After midnight on April 6, 1712, about twenty-three slaves took a blood oath, set fire to the outhouse of Peter Vantilburg, and confronted white citizens, killing nine of them. The militia was called out and the perpetrators were caught and brought to trial; six preferred suicide. The report of Governor Robert Hunter to the British Lords of Trade on the affair boasts of the "exemplary punishment" made of the twenty-one executed slaves. Acknowledging a pattern that would often be repeated, the governor notes the irregular legal proceedings—partially brought on in this case "to gratify some private pique" between slaveholders—and that in the aftermath of the revolt "more have suffered than we can find were active in this bloody affair."

Three decades later, the city was again beset by turmoil. On March

18, 1741, several buildings, including a fort at the Battery, were burned, and rumors spread rapidly that a general insurrection was afoot. Though no plot was discovered, about a month later Mary Burton, an indentured white servant to John Hughson, was questioned regarding a supposed robbery at her master's house and was prodded into revealing that her master and three black men—Caesar, Prince, and Coffee—were involved in a plot to burn the city and overthrow the whites. "Confessions" were made on May 30, 1741, while two slaves were chained to stakes surrounded by a bloodthirsty mob. Immediately after, the men were burned alive. Eleven more slaves were burned, and eighteen hanged, as were Hughson, his wife, a white boarder, and a priest. About eighty slaves were transported out of the state, and a tax was levied to discourage further importation of slaves.

Other early plots were reported in East Boston in 1638, and in Boston in 1723—but the most notorious of the slave revolts[†] would not come until the early part of the nineteenth century.

Report of Governor Hunter on the New York Slave Conspiracy

". . . more have suffered than we can find were active in this bloody affair. . . ."

I MUST NOW GIVE YOUR LORDSHIPS AN ACCOUNT OF A BLOODY conspiracy of some of the slaves of this place, to destroy as many of the Inhabitants as they could. It was put in execution in this manner: when they had resolved to revenge themselves for some hard usage they apprehended to have received from their masters (for I can find no other cause), they agreed to meet in the orchard of Mr. Crook the middle of the Town—some provided with fire arms, some with swords and others with knives and hatchets. This was the sixth day of April; the time of meeting was about twelve or one o'clock in the night, when about three and twenty of them were got togeather. One Coffee and negroe slave to one Vantiburgh set fire to an out house of his Master's, and then repairing to the place where the rest were they all sallyed out togeather with their arms and marched to the fire. By this time, the noise of fire spreading through the town, the people began to flock to it; upon the approach of severall the slaves fired and killed them. The noise of the guns gave the allarm, and some, escaping their shot, soon published the cause of the fire, which was the reason that not above nine Christians were killed, and about five or six wounded. Upon the first notice, which was very soon after the mischeif was begun, I order'd a detachment from the fort under a proper officer to march against them, but the slaves made their retreat into the woods by the favour of the night. Having ordered centries the next day in the most proper places on the Island to prevt their escape, I caused, the day following, the Militia of this town and of the county of west Chester to drive the Island; and by this means and strick searches in the town, we found all that put the design in execution. Six of these having first laid violent hands upon themselves, the rest were forthwith brought to their tryal before ye Justices of this place who are authorized by Act of Assembly to hold a Court in such cases. In that Court were twenty seven condemned, whereof twenty one were executed; one being a woman with child, her execution by that means suspended. Some were burnt, others hanged, one broke on the wheele, and one hung a live in chains in the town, so that there has been the most exemplary punishment inflicted that could be possibly thought of, and which only this act of assembly could Justify. Among these guilty persons several others were apprehended and again acquitted by the Court for want of sufficient evidence. Among those was one Mars, a negroe man slave to one Mr Regnier, who was to his tryall and acquitted by the Jury—the Sheriffe the next day moving the Court for the discharge of such as were or should be soe acquitted, by reason hee apprehended they would attempt to make their excape; but Mr Bickley, who yn executed the office of the Atter: Generall, for Mr Rayner opposed his motion, telling the Court that at that time, none but Mars being acquitted, the motion could be only intended in his favour, against whom he should have some thing further to object, and therefore prayed he might not be discharg; so the sheriff did not obtain his motion. Mars was then indicted a second time and again acquitted but not discharg'd; and, being a third time presented, was transferr'd to the supream Court and there tryed and convicted on ye same evidence on his two former tryals. This prosecution was carryed on to gratify some private pique of Mr Bickleys against Mr Regnier, a gentleman of his own profession, which appearing so partial, and the evidence being represented to me as very defective, and being wholly acquitted of ever having known any thing of the Conspiracy by the Negroe witnesses who were made use of in the tryals of all the criminals before the Justices (and without whose testimonies very few could have been punished), I thought fit to reprieve him till Her Majesties pleasure be known therin. In this supream court were likewise tryed one Husea belonging to Mrs Wenham, and one John belonging Mr. Vantilbourgh—and convicted; these two are prisoners taken in a Spanish prize this was and brought into this Port by a Privateer about six or seven years agoe; and by reason of their colour, which is swarthy, they were said to be slaves and as such were sold among many others of the same colour and country; these two I have likewise reprieved till Her Majesties pleasure be signified. Soon after my arrival in this government I received petitions from several of these Spanish Indians, as they are called here, representing to me that they were free men, subjects to the King of Spain but sold here as slaves; I secretely pittyed their condition but, haveing no other evidence of wt they asserted then their own words, I had it not in my power to releive them. I am informed that in the West Indies, where their laws against their slaves are most severe, that in case of a conspiracy in which many are engaged a few only are executed for an example. In this case 21 are executed, and six having done that Justice on themselves, more have suffered than we can find were active in this bloody affair—which are reasons for my repreiving these; and if your Lordships think them of sufficient weight, I beg you will procure Her Majesty's pleasure to be signifyed to me for their pardon, for they lye now in prison at their masters charge. I have likewise repreived one Tom, a Negroe belonging to mr Van Dam, and Coffee a Negroe belonging to Mr Walton; these two I have repreived at the instance of the Justices of the Court, who where of oppinion that the evidence against them was not sufficient to convict them.

April 1712

Lucy Terry
(1730–1821)

Although it was not published until after the author's death, Lucy Terry's "Bars Fight" was the first poem composed by an African-American. Kidnapped in Africa as a small child, Terry was bought when she was five by Ensign Ebenezer Wells of Deerfield, Massachusetts, and was baptized during the Great Awakening movement in New England. Her only extant poem, "Bars Fight" was written after an Indian ambush of two families in Deerfield on August 25, 1746. Recited or sung by the poet, it was passed down by oral historians until it was published in Josiah Gilbert Holland's *History of Western Massachusetts* (1855). Terry later married Abijah Prince, a former slave who bought her freedom, and gained a reputation as a speaker, arguing before the trustees of Williams College for the admission of one of her sons (her request was denied) and before the Supreme Court in a suit brought against a neighbor for infringing upon her land. Her poem recalls the popular captivity narrative genre of the colonial period, in which the writer recounts his or her experience in captivity among the Indians, and establishes early on the central role of African-American women in American literary history.

Bars Fight

August 'twas, the twenty-fifth,
Seventeen hundred forty-six,
The Indians did in ambush lay,
Some very valient men to slay,
The names of whom I'll not leave out:
Samuel Allen like a hero fout,
And though he was so brave and bold,
His face no more shall we behold;
Eleazer Hawks was killed outright,
Before he had time to fight,
Before he did the Indians see,
Was shot and killed immediately;
Oliver Amsden, he was slain,
Which caused his friends much grief and pain;
Simeon Amsden they found dead,
Not many rods off from his head;
Adonijah Gillet, we do hear,
Did lose his life, which was so dear;
John Saddler fled across the water,
And so escaped the dreadful slaughter;
Eunice Allen see the Indians comeing,
And hoped to save herself by running,
And had not her petticoats stopt her,
The awful creatures had not cotched her,
And tommyhawked her on the head,
And left her on the ground for dead;
Young Samuel Allen, oh! lack-a-day,
Was taken and carried to Canada.

1746

Jupiter Hammon
(1720?–1800)

Though Jupiter Hammon's broadside "An Evening Thought" marks the first publication of a poem by an African-American, little is known of its author's life. Hammon lived on rural Long Island, New York, as a domestic slave to the Lloyd family, who encouraged him to learn to read and write. This poem, published in 1761, reflects a preoccupation with Christian piety typical of the period in its content and hymnlike qualities. In it Hammon could draw upon his own experience to write, "Salvation now comes from the Lord,/He being thy captive slave," but he reconciles the contradictions of Christian ideals and enforced bondage by relying on salvation in the next world if not in this one; these contradictions will continue to be explored by many African-American writers after him. Hammon published several other poems in his lifetime and in 1778 acknowledged his distinguished contemporary with the publication of "An Address to Miss Phillis Wheatley, Ethiopian Poetess," using the term often applied to all Africans.

An Evening Thought:
Salvation by Christ with Penetential Cries

Salvation comes by Christ alone,
  The only Son of God;
Redemption now to every one,
  That loves his holy Word.

Dear Jesus, give thy Spirit now,
  Thy grace to every Nation,
That han't the Lord to whom we bow,
  The Author of Salvation.

Dear Jesus, unto Thee we cry,
  Give us the Preparation;
Turn not away thy tender Eye;
  We seek thy true Salvation.

Lord, hear our penetential Cry;
  Salvation from above;
It is the Lord that doth supply,
  With his Redeeming Love.

Dear Jesus, by thy precious Blood,
  The World Redemption have;
Salvation now comes from the Lord,
  He being thy captive slave.

Dear Jesus, let the Nations cry,
  And all the People say,
Salvation comes from Christ on high,
  Haste on Tribunal Day.

We cry as Sinners to the Lord,
  Salvation to obtain;
It is firmly fixed, his holy Word,
  Ye shall not cry in vain.

Lord, turn our dark benighted Souls;
  Give us a true Motion,
And let the Hearts of all the World,
  Make Christ their Salvation.

Lord, unto whom now shall we go,
  or seek a safe abode?

Thou hast the Word, Salvation Too:
  The only Son of God.

"Ho! every one that hunger hath,
  Or pineth after me,
Salvation be thy leading Staff,
  To set the Sinner free."

Dear Jesus, unto Thee we fly;
  Depart, depart from Sin,
Salvation doth at length supply,
  The glory of our King.

Come, ye Blessed of the Lord,
  Salvation greatly given;
O, turn your hearts, accept the Word,
  Your Souls are fit for Heaven.

Dear Jesus, we now turn to Thee,
  Salvation to obtain;
Our Hearts and Souls do meet again,
  To magnify thy Name.

Come, holy Spirit, Heavenly Dove,
  The Object of our Care;
Salvation doth increase our Love;
  Our Hearts hath felt thy fear.

Now Glory be to God on High,
  Salvation high and low;
And thus the Soul on Christ rely,
  To Heaven surely go.

Come, Blessed Jesus, Heavenly Dove,
  Accept Repentence here;
Salvation give, with tender Love;
  Let us with Angels share.

1761

African-Americans in the American Revolution

While African-Americans fought under Generals Edward Braddock and George Washington during the French and Indian War that ended in 1763, it was with the coming of the American Revolution that their role in this country's military conflicts began to define itself. As would be true in most American wars, the African-American soldier was called up only as a last resort, often not until dire circumstances required all available manpower. This hesitation stemmed both from suspicion regarding the individual's loyalty and from a reluctance to arm what was certainly a discontented class. As the historian Benjamin Quarles puts it, "A slave with a gun was an open invitation to trouble."

Antislavery activists, particularly Quakers, were quick to point out the similarity between slavery and what the colonists saw as their own repression under England, and slaves themselves began to petition for better treatment, if not their freedom. The debate caused the Continental Congress to halt the importation of slaves on December 1, 1775, and Thomas Jefferson drafted a plank into the Declaration of Independence that castigated the British king for "violating the most sacred rights of life and liberty in the persons of a distant people who never offended him, captivating and carrying them into slavery in another hemisphere, or to incur miserable death in their transportation thither." Due to protests from the Southern delegates, however, the clause was stricken, and Thomas Jefferson himself remained a slaveholder. (This contradiction is felt in the works of Phillis Wheatley and Benjamin Banneker that are included here.)

One of the first casualties of the deepening hostility between Great Britain and her colonies was Crispus Attucks. Thought to be of mixed African and Native American descent and with an imposing physical presence, Attucks had escaped from slavery in Framingham, Massachusetts, in 1750 and had made his way to Boston, where he was a seaman. In November 1768, two British regiments had been moved to Boston, causing much friction among the townspeople, and on the evening of March 5, 1770, an altercation arose between the troops and a young boy as more British troops and townspeople gathered. One of the soldiers was struck, and in the scuffle that followed, the troops fired upon the largely unarmed crowd, killing Attucks and two others instantly, and wounding eight others, two of whom died later. Defending the British officers in the trial that followed, John Adams argued that it was Crispus Attucks, who "appears to have undertaken to be the hero of the night."

African-Americans also participated in some of the most significant early confrontations. Prince Estabrook was one of the seven rebels killed by British Major John Pitcairn at the opening battle of the war at Lexington and Concord, and Pitcairn himself may have been killed at Bunker Hill by Peter Salem, from Framington, Massachusetts, who served with much commendation throughout the war. Others who fought at the early battles at Lexington and Concord and Bunker Hill included Salem Poor, Barzillai Lew, Alexander Ames, Titus Coburn, Prince Hall, and Lemuel Haynes. Black soldiers also fought at Monmouth, Saratoga, Princeton, Yorktown, and elsewhere.

As the war progressed, a gradual policy of excluding African-Americans from military service developed. But faced with the strategy of the British Governor of Virginia, Lord Dunmore, who promised freedom to slaves who joined the British cause, on December 31, 1775, Washington allowed the enlistment of free blacks and, after heavy losses at Valley Forge in 1778, of all blacks, slave or free. In early 1777 the Massachusetts militia made African-Americans eligible for service, as did Rhode Island in February of the following year. Of the Southern colonies, South Carolina and Georgia alone never legalized slave enlistments. Most of the black soldiers served in integrated units, but there were also predominantly black units in Massachusetts, Connecticut, and Rhode Island.

Nearly five thousand African-Americans fought on the side of the patriots throughout the Revolution. While some of their names are recorded, others are lost to history, as Quarles points out, known only by the depersonalizing "Negro Man" or "Negro by Name." Some individuals were manumitted after the war, and thousands of others had been liberated by joining the British forces, though their emigration with the departing British troops to Canada, the West Indies, and England after the war was the source of much diplomatic tension. (Unsatisfied with their reward, a group of twelve hundred men were granted permission by the Sierra Leone Company to settle in West Africa in 1792 in one of the earliest expressions of the colonization movement.) Others had taken advantage of the chaos to escape slavery in Canada and Spanish Florida, some launching guerrilla campaigns against their former masters.

But the war that was fought in the name of freedom had more lasting effect than on the lives of just those who had served in it. As the notion that "all men are created equal" became the abiding promise of the new nation, Vermont became the first state to abolish slavery in 1777; by 1780 Pennsylvania had enacted a law establishing a gradual abolition of the children of slaves; and within two decades all of the Northern states had begun the process of emancipation. Finally, in 1787, Congress legislated that slavery would not be introduced in the Northwest Territories. "In the Revolutionary War," writes Quarles, "the American Negro was a participant and a symbol. He was active on the battlefronts and behind the lines; in his expectations and in the gains he registered during the war, he personified the goal of that freedom in whose name the struggle was waged."

Petition of the Africans, Living in Boston

"We . . . rest our Cause on your Humanity and Justice. . . ."

PROVINCE OF THE MASSACHUSETTS-BAY.

To his Excellancy THOMAS HUTCHINSON, Esq;
Governor;
To the Honorable His Majesty's Council, and
To the Honorable House of REPRESENTATIVES in
General Court
assembled at BOSTON, the 6th Day of January,
1773.

The humble PETITION of many SLAVES, living in the Town of BOSTON, and other Towns in the Province, is this, namely,

That your Excellency and Honors, and the Honorable the Representatives would be pleased to take their unhappy State and Condition under your wise and just Consideration.

We desire to bless GOD, who loves Mankind, who sent his Son to die for their Salvation, and who is no Respector of Persons; that he hath lately put it into the Hearts of Multitudes on both Sides of the Water, to bear our Burthens, some of whom are Men of great Note and Influence; who have pleaded our Cause with Arguments which we hope will have their weight with this Honorable Court.

We presume not to dictate to your EXCELLENCY and Honors, being willing to rest our Cause on your Humanity and Justice; yet would beg leave to say a Word or two on the Subject.

Although some of the Negroes are vicious, (who doubtless may be punished and restrained by the same Laws which are in Force against other of the King's Subjects) there are many others of a quite different Character, and who if made free, would soon be able as well as willing to bear a Part in the Public Charges; many of them good natural Parts, are discreet, sober, honest, and industrious; and may it not be said of many, that they are virtuous and religious, although their Condition is in itself so unfriendly to Religion, and every moral Virtue except *Patience.* How many of that Number have there been, and now are in this Province, who have had every Day of their Lives imbittered with this most intolerable Reflection, That, let their Behaviour be what it will, neither they, nor their Children to all Generations, shall ever be able to do, or to possess and enjoy any Thing, no, not even *Life itself,* but in a Manner as the *Beasts that perish.*

We have no Property! We have no Wives! No Children! We have no City! No Country! But we have a Father in Heaven, and we are determined as far as his Grace shall enable us, and as far as our degraded contemptuous Life will admit, to keep all his Commandments: Especially will we be obedient to our Masters, so long as GOD in his sovereign Providence shall *suffer* us to be holden in Bondage.

It would be impudent, if not presumptuous in us, to suggest to your Excellency and Honors any Law or Laws proper to be made in relation to our unhappy State, which, although our greatest Unhappiness, is not our *Fault;* and this gives us great Encouragement to pray and hope for such Relief as is consistent with your Wisdom, Justice, and Goodness.

We think ourselves very happy that we may thus address the Great and General Court of this Province, which great and good Court is to us, the best judge, under GOD, of what is wise, just, and good.

We humbly beg leave to add but this one Thing more: We pray for such Relief only, which by no Possibility can ever be productive of the least Wrong or Injury to our Masters; but to us will be as Life from the dead.

Signed, FELIX

1773

The Declaration of Independence

In Congress, July 4, 1776

THE UNANIMOUS DECLARATION OF THE THIRTEEN UNITED STATES OF AMERICA

HEN IN THE COURSE OF HUMAN EVENTS, IT BECOMES necessary for one people to dissolve the political bands which have connected them with another, and to assume among the powers of the earth, the separate and equal station to which the laws of Nature and of Nature's God entitle them, a decent respect to the opinions of mankind requires that they should declare the cause which impels them to the separation.

We hold these truths to be self-evident, that all men are created equal, that they are endowed by their Creator with certain unalienable rights, that among these are life, liberty and the pursuit of happiness. That to secure these rights, governments are instituted among men, deriving their just powers from the consent of the governed,—That whenever any form of government becomes destructive of these ends, it is the right of the people to alter or to abolish it, and to institute new government, laying its foundation on such principles and organizing its powers in such form, as to them shall seem most likely to effect their safety and happiness. Prudence, indeed, will dictate that governments long established should not be changed for light and transient causes; and accordingly all experience hath shown, that mankind are more disposed to suffer, while evils are sufferable, than to right themselves by abolishing the forms to which they are accustomed. But when a long train of abuses and usurpations, pursuing invariably the same object evinces a design to reduce them under absolute despotism, it is their right, it is their duty, to throw off such government, and to provide new guards for their future security. —Such has been the patient sufferance of these Colonies; and such is now the necessity which constrains them to alter their former systems of government. The history of the present King of Great Britain is a history of repeated injuries and usurpations, all having in direct object the establishment of an absolute tyranny over these States. To prove this, let facts be submitted to a candid world.

He has refused his assent to laws, the most wholesome and necessary for the public good.

He has forbidden his Governors to pass laws of immediate and pressing importance, unless suspended in their operation till his assent should be obtained; and when so suspended, he has utterly neglected to attend to them.

He has refused to pass other laws for the accommodation of large districts of people, unless those people would relinquish the right of representation in the legislature, a right inestimable to them and formidable to tyrants only.

He has called together legislative bodies at places unusual, uncomfortable, and distant from the depository of their public records, for the sole purpose of fatiguing them into compliance with his measure.

He has dissolved Representative Houses repeatedly, for opposing with manly firmness his invasions on the rights of the people.

He has refused for a long time, after such dissolutions, to cause others to be elected; whereby the legislative powers, incapable of annihilation, having returned to the people at large for their exercise; the State remaining in the mean time exposed to all the dangers of invasion from without, and convulsions within.

He has endeavoured to prevent the population of these States; for that purpose obstructing the laws for naturalization of foreigners; refusing to pass others to encourage their migrations hither, and raising the conditions of new appropriations of lands.

He has obstructed the administration of justice, by refusing his assent to laws for establishing judiciary powers.

He has made judges dependent on his will alone, for the tenure of their offices, and the amount and payment of their salaries.

He has erected a multitude of new offices, and sent hither swarms of officers to harass our people, and eat out their substance.

He has kept among us, in times of peace, standing armies without the consent of our legislatures.

He has affected to render the military independent of and superior to the civil power.

He has combined with others to subject us to a jurisdiction foreign to our constitution, and unacknowledged by our laws; giving his assent to their acts of pretended legislation;

For quartering large bodies of armed troops among us;

For protecting them, by a mock trial, from punishment for any murders which they should commit on the inhabitants of these States;

For cutting off our trade with all parts of the world;

For imposing taxes on us without our consent;

For depriving us in many cases, of the benefits of trial by jury;

For transporting us beyond seas to be tried for pretended offenses;

For abolishing the free system of English laws in a neighbouring province, establishing therein an arbitrary government, and enlarging its boundaries so as to render it at once an example and fit instrument for introducing the same absolute rule into these colonies;

For taking away our charters, abolishing our most valuable laws, and altering fundamentally the forms of our governments;

For suspending our own legislatures, and declaring themselves invested with power to legislate for us in all cases whatsoever.

He has abdicated government here, by declaring us out of his protection and waging war against us.

He has plundered our seas, ravaged our coasts, burnt our towns, and destroyed the lives of our people.

He is at this time transporting large armies of foreign mercenaries to complete the works of death, desolation and tyranny, already begun with circumstances of cruelty and perfidy scarcely paralleled in the most barbarous ages, and totally unworthy the head of a civilized nation.

He has constrained our fellow citizens taken captive on the high seas to bear arms against their country, to become the executioners of their friends and brethren, or to fall themselves by their hands.

He has excited domestic insurrections amongst us, and has endeavoured to bring on the inhabitants of our frontiers, the merciless Indian savages, whose known rule of warfare is an undistinguished destruction of all ages, sexes and conditions.

In every state of these oppressions we have petitioned for redress in the most humble terms; Our repeated petitions have been answered only by repeated injury. A prince, whose character is thus marked by every act which may define a tyrant, is unfit to be the ruler of a free people.

Nor have we been wanting in attentions to our British brethren. We have warned them from time to time of attempts by their legislature to extend an unwarrantable jurisdiction over us. We have reminded them of the circumstances of our emigration and settlement here. We have appealed to their native justice and magnanimity, and we have conjured them by the ties of our common kindred to disavow these usurpations, which would inevitably interrupt our connections and correspondence. They too have been deaf to the voice of justice and of consanguinity. We must, therefore, acquiesce in the necessity which denounces our separation, and hold them, as we hold the rest of mankind, enemies in war, in peace friends.

WE, THEREFORE, the Representatives of the United States of America, in Generous Congress, Assembled, appealing to the Supreme Judge of the world for the rectitude of our intentions, do, in the name, and by authority of the good people of these Colonies, solemnly publish and declare, That these United Colonies are, and of right ought to be FREE AND INDEPENDENT STATES; that they are absolved from all allegiance to the British Crown, and that all political connection between them and the State of Great Britain, is and ought to be totally dissolved; and that as free and independent States, they have full power to levy war, conclude peace, contract alliances, establish commerce, and to do all other acts and things which independent States may of right do. And for the support of this Declaration, with a firm reliance on the protection of Divine Providence, we mutually pledge to each other our lives, our fortunes and our sacred honor.

Emancipation of Slaves for Military Service During the American Revolution

". . . it appears just and reasonable, that all persons . . . who have faithfully served . . . and have thereby of course contributed towards the establishment of American liberty and independence, should enjoy the blessings of freedom as a reward for their toils and labors."

AN ACT DIRECTING THE EMANCIPATION OF CERTAIN SLAVES who have served as Soldiers in this State, and for the Emancipation of the Slave Aberdeen.

I. Whereas it hath been represented to the present General Assembly, that during the course of the war, many persons in this State had caused their slaves to enlist in certain regiments or corps raised within the same, having tendered such slaves to the officers appointed to recruit forces within the States, as substitutes for free persons whose lot or duty it was to serve in such regiments or corps, at the same time representing to such recruiting officers that the slaves, so enlisted by their direction and concurrence, were freemen; and it appearing further to this Assembly, that on the expiration of the term of enlistment of such slaves, that the former owners have attempted again to force them to return to a state of servitude, contrary to the principles of justice, and to their own solemn promise;

II. And whereas it appears just and reasonable, that all persons enlisted as aforesaid, who have faithfully served agreeable to the terms of their enlistment, and have thereby of course contributed towards the establishment of American liberty and independence, should enjoy the blessings of freedom as a reward for their toils and labors;

Be it therefore enacted, That each and every slave who, by the appointment and direction of his owner, hath enlisted in any regiment or corps raised within this State, either on Continental or State establishment, and hath been received as a substitute for any free person whose duty or lot it was to serve in such regiment or corps, and hath served faithfully during the terms of such enlistment, or hath been discharged from such service by some officer duly authorized to grant such discharge, shall, from and after the passing of this act, be fully and completely emancipated, and shall be held and deemed free, in as full and ample a manner as if each and every of them were specially named in this act; and the Attorney-general for the Commonwealth is hereby required to commence an action, *in forma pauperis,* in behalf of any of the persons above described who shall, after the passing of this act, be detained in servitude by any person whatsoever; and if, upon such prosecution, it shall appear that the pauper is entitled to his freedom in consequence of this act, a jury shall be empanelled to assess the damages for his detention.

III. And whereas it has been represented to this General Assembly, that Aberdeen, a negro man slave, hath labored a number of years in the public service at the lead mines, and for his meritorious services is entitled to freedom; *Be it therefore enacted*, That the said slave Aberdeen shall be, and he is hereby, emancipated and declared free in as full and ample a manner as if he had been born free.

Hening's Statutes at Large of Virginia, 1783

Phillis Wheatley
(1753?–1784)

In 1773, with the publication of *Poems on Various Subjects, Religious and Moral,* Phillis Wheatley became the first African-American author to be published in book form. Wheatley had been kidnapped in Senegal as a child and was purchased by the Boston tailor John Wheatley in 1761. According to John Wheatley, "she, in sixteen months time from her arrival, attained the English language, to which she was an utter stranger before, to such a degree, as to read any, the most difficult parts of the Sacred Writings, to the great astonishment of all who heard her." Phillis began writing verse at age fourteen and in 1770 published her first poem on the death of the Reverend George Whitefield.

John Wheatley attempted to have Phillis's poems published in Boston in 1772, but publishers would not believe that she, a young female slave, had actually written them. Only after an oral examination by a group of eminent Bostonians, including Thomas Hutchinson, governor of Massachusetts, were skeptics satisfied. With an "Attestation" as to the poems' authenticity in hand, she accompanied Wheatley's son Nathaniel to England, where, with the sponsorship of the Countess of Huntingdon and the Earl of Dartmouth, her *Poems* were published. (Slavery had ended in England the year before her arrival, a circumstance that surely must have made an impression upon her.)

The thirty-nine poems in the volume, written in an iambic pentameter influenced by Alexander Pope, include elegies, hymns, occasional pieces, and poems on neoclassical and political subjects. Wheatley's "On being brought from AFRICA to AMERICA" gives a uniquely African-American stamp to the *felix culpa* poetic tradition—only by virtue of her removal from Africa, she argues, could she enjoy the benefits of a Christian baptism. While such religious sentiments appear in many poems in the volume, her apparent ability to reconcile slavery and Christian precepts is undermined in others in which she clearly compares the tyranny of the British—"the iron chain"—to bondage. Her sentiments are even plainer in the letter to the Native American missionary Samson Occom included here.

Wheatley was later freed (perhaps upon the death of Mrs. Susannah Wheatley in 1774 or of John Wheatley in 1778) and married John Peters, a freeman, in Boston. The marriage was unhappy and she had two children who died in infancy. She wrote at least eighty-seven poems and planned other volumes, but died in poverty on December 5, 1784, at the age of thirty-one. She was buried alongside her third child, who had died soon after her, in an unmarked grave.

Despite criticism that Wheatley's poetry is formally imitative and too accepting of Christian and colonial norms, her place in the African-American literary tradition is secure. That she wrote poetry at such a young age in a new language, under the restrictions of slavery, gaining an international reputation in an age when few white women were educated, is a remarkable achievement. Her impact on her contemporaries was enormous—Jupiter Hammon dedicated his "Address to Miss Phillis Wheatley, Ethiopian Poetess" to her—and it would be more than fifty years before another book of African-American poetry was published. It is from Phillis Wheatley, argues Henry Louis Gates, "that all subsequent black writers have evolved in a matrilinear line of descent, and that each, consciously or unconsciously, has extended and revised a canon whose foundation was the poetry of a black woman." Her voice, in a 1772 letter to her friend and fellow African slave Obour Tanner, urging her "no longer to be so excessively charm'd with fleeting vanities; but pressing forward to the fix'd mark for the prize," echoes uncannily in our century.

On Being Brought from AFRICA to AMERICA

'Twas mercy brought me from my *Pagan* land,
Taught my benighted soul to understand
That there's a God, that there's a *Saviour* too:
Once I redemption neither fought nor knew.
Some view our fable race with scornful eye,
"Their colour is a diabolic die."
Remember, *Christians, Negros,* black as *Cain,*
May be refin'd, and join th'angelic train.

1773

On Imagination

Thy various works, imperial queen, we see,
How bright their forms! how deck'd with pomp by thee!
Thy wond'rous acts in beauteous order stand,
And all attest how potent is thine hand.

From *Hellicon*'s refulgent heights attend,
Ye sacred choir, and my attempts befriend:
To tell her glories with a faithful tongue,
Ye blooming graces, triumph in my song.

Now here, now there, the roving *Fancy* flies,
Till some lov'd object strikes her wand'ring eyes,
Whose silken fetters all the sense bind,
And soft captivity involves the mind.

Imagination! who can sing thy force?
Or who describe the swiftness of thy course?
Soaring through air to find the bright abode,
Th'empyreal palace of the thund'ring God,
We on thy pinions can surpass the wind,
And leave the rolling universe behind:
From star to star the mental optics rove,
Measure the skies, and range the realms above.
There in one view we grasp the mighty whole,
Or with new worlds amaze th'unbounded soul.

Though *Winter* frowns to *Fancy*'s raptur'd eyes,
The fields may flourish, and gay scenes arise;
The frozen deeps may break their iron bands,
And bid their waters murmur o'er the sands.
Fair *Flora* may resume her fragrant reign,
And with her flow'ry riches deck the plain;
Sylvanus may diffuse his honours round,
And all the forest may with leaves be crown'd;
Show'rs may descend, and dews their gems disclose,
And nectar sparkle on the blooming rose.

Such is thy pow'r, nor are thine orders vain,
O thou the leader of the mental train:
In full perfection all thy works are wrought,
And thine the sceptre o'er the realms of thought.
Before thy throne the subject-passions bow,
Of subject-passions sov'reign ruler Thou;

At thy command joy rushes on the heart,
And through the glowing veins the spirits dart.

Fancy might now her silken pinions try
To rife from earth, and sweep th'expanse on high;
From *Tithon*'s bed now might *Aurora* rise,
Her cheeks all glowing with celestial dies,
While a pure stream of light o'erflows the skies.
The monarch of the day I might behold.
And all the mountains tipt with radiant gold,
But I reluctant leave the pleasing views,
Which *Fancy* dresses to delight the *Muse;*
Winter austere forbids me to aspire,
And northern tempests damp the rising fire;
They chill the tides of *Fancy*'s flowing sea,
Cease then, my song, cease the unequal lay.

1773

To the Right Honourable WILLIAM, Earl of DARTMOUTH, His Majesty's Principal Secretary of State for North America

"No longer shall thou dread the iron chain. . . ."

Hail, happy day, when, smiling like the morn,
Fair *Freedom* rose *New-England* to adorn:
The northern clime beneath her genial ray,
Dartmouth, congratulates thy blissful sway:
Elate with hope her race no longer mourns,
Each soul expands, each grateful bosom burns,
While in thine hand with pleasure we behold
The silken reins, and *Freedom*'s charms unfold.
Long lost to realms beneath the northern skies
She shines supreme, while hated *faction* dies:
Soon as appear'd the *Goddess* long desir'd,
Sick at the view, she languished and expir'd;
Thus from the splendors of the morning light
The owl in sadness seeks the caves of night.

No more *America*, in mournful strain
Of wrongs, and grievance unredress'd complain,
No longer shall thou dread the iron chain,
Which wanton *Tyranny* with lawless hand
Had made, and with it meant t'enslave the land.

Should you, my lord, while you peruse my song,
Wonder from whence my love of *Freedom* sprung,
Whence flow these wishes for the common good,
By feeling hearts alone best understood,
I, young in life, by seeming cruel fate
Was snatch'd from *Afric*'s fancy'd happy seat:
What pangs excruciating must molest,
What sorrows labour in my parent's breast?
Steel'd was that soul and by no misery mov'd
That from a father seiz'd his babe belov'd:
Such, such my case. And can I then but pray
Others may never feel tyrannic sway?

For favours past, great Sir, our thanks are due,
And thee we ask favours to renew,
Since in thy pow'r, as in thy will before,
To sooth the griefs, which thou did'st once deplore.
May heav'nly grace the sacred sanction give
To all thy works, and thou for ever live
Not only on the wings of fleeting *Fame*,
Though praise immortal crowns the patriot's name,
But to conduct to heav'ns refulgent fane,
May fiery coursers sweep th'ethereal plain,
And bear thee upwards to that blest abode,
Where, like the prophet, thou shalt find thy God.

1773

Letter to Samson Occom

". . . in every human Breast, God has implanted a Principle, which we call Love of Freedom. . . ."

Reverend and Honoured Sir

I have this Day your obliging kind Epistle, and am greatly satisfied with your Reasons representing the Negroes, and think highly reasonable what you offer in Vindication of their natural Rights: Those that invade them cannot be insensible that the divine Light is chasing away the thick Darkness which broods over the Land of Africa; and the Chaos which has reigned so long, is converting into beautiful Order, and reveals more and more clearly, the glorious Dispensation of civil and religious Liberty, which are so inseparably united, that there is little or no Enjoyment of one without the other: Otherwise, perhaps, the Israelites had been less solicitous for their Freedom from Egyptian Slavery; I do not say they would have been contented without it, by no Means, for in every human Breast, God has implanted a Principle, which we call Love of Freedom; it is impatient of Oppression, and pants for Deliverance; and by the Leave of our Modern Egyptians I will assert, that the same Principle lives in us. God grant Deliverance in his own way and Time, and get him honor upon all those whose Avárice impels them to countenance and help forward the Calamities of their Fellow Creatures. This I desire not for their Hurt, but to convince them of the strange Absurdity of their Conduct whose Words and Actions are so diametrically opposite. How well the Cry for Liberty, and the reverse Disposition for the Exercise of oppressive Power over others agree,—I humbly think it does not require the Penetration of a Philosopher to determine.

February 11, 1774

Benjamin Banneker
(1731–1806)

Naturalist, astronomer, inventor, and poet, Banneker was an early American scientific and mathematical genius. He was born free near Ellicott Mills in Maryland, the grandson of an Englishwoman, who had come to America as an indentured servant, and an African native. When in his twenties, he constructed a perfectly functioning wooden clock with a penknife, without ever having seen another one. Befriended by the wealthy Ellicott family, he devoted himself to the study of astronomy while earning his living as a farmer. From his calculations, which he described to George Ellicott as "the first attempt of the kind that ever was made in America by a person of my complexion," he developed an *Almanac,* first published in 1792. He sent the manuscript to fellow inventor and future president Thomas Jefferson, then secretary of state, with the letter included here, using the opportunity to engage in political protest as well. In 1791 Banneker was appointed by President George Washington to a three-member commission, headed by French civil engineer Pierre-Charles L'Enfant, to map out the city of Washington, still considered one of the finest examples of urban planning. Banneker continued to publish his *Almanac* annually until 1802, and also wrote a charming yet rigorous "Mathematical Problem in Verse" and "A Plan of Peace Office for the United States."

Letter to Thomas Jefferson

". . . how pitiable is it . . . that you should at the same time be found guilty of that most criminal act which you professedly detested in others with respect to yourselves."

Maryland, Baltimore County
Near Ellicotts' Lower Mills, August 19th, 1791

Thomas Jefferson, Secretary of State.

Sir:—I am fully sensible of the greatness of that freedom, which I take with you on the present occasion, a liberty which seemed to me scarcely allowable, when I reflected on that distinguished and dignified station in which you stand, and the almost general prejudice and prepossession which is so prevalent in the world against those of my complexion.

I suppose it is a truth too well attested to you, to need a proof here, that we are a race of beings who have long laboured under the abuse and censure of the world, that we have long been considered rather as brutish than human, and scarcely capable of mental endowments.

Sir, I hope I may safely admit, in consequence of that report which hath reached me, that you are a man far less inflexible in sentiments of this nature than many others, that you are measurably friendly and well disposed towards us, and that you are willing and ready to lend your aid and assistance to our relief, from those many distresses and numerous calamities, to which we are reduced.

Now, sir, if this is founded in truth, I apprehend you will readily embrace every opportunity to eradicate that train of absurd and false ideas and opinions, which so generally prevails with respect to us, and that your sentiments are concurrent with mine, which are that one universal Father hath given Being to us all, and that he hath not only made us all of one flesh, but that he hath also without partiality afforded us all the same sensations, and endued us all with the same faculties, and that however variable we may be in society or religion, however diversified in situation or colour, we are all of the same family, and stand in the same relation to him.

Sir, if these are sentiments of which you are fully persuaded, I hope you cannot but acknowledge, that it is the indispensable duty of those who maintain for themselves the rights of human nature, and who profess the obligations of christianity, to extend their power and influence to the relief of every part of the human race, from whatever burden or oppression they may unjustly labour under, and this I apprehend a full conviction of the truth and obligation of these principles should lead all to.

Sir, I have long been convinced that if your love for yourselves and for those inesteemable laws, which preserve to you the rights of human nature, was found on sincerity, you could not but be solicitous that every individual of whatever rank or distinction, might with you equally enjoy the blessings thereof, neither could you rest satisfied, short of the most active diffusion of your exertions in order to their promotions from any state of degradation to which the unjustifiable cruelty and barbarism of men have reduced them.

Sir, I freely and cheerfully acknowledge that I am of the African race, and in that colour which is natural to them of the deepest dye, and it is under a sense of the most profound gratitude to the Supreme Being of the universe that I now confess to you that I am not under that state of tyrannical thraldom and inhuman captivity to which too many of my brethren are doomed; but that I have abundantly tasted of the fruition of those blessings which proceed from that free and unequalled liberty with which you are favoured and which, I hope you will willingly allow you have received from the immediate hand of that Being, from whom proceedeth every good and perfect gift.

Sir, suffer me to recall to your mind that time in which the arms and tyranny of the British Crown were exerted with every powerful effort in order to reduce you to a State of Servitude, look back I entreat you on the variety of dangers to which you were exposed; reflect on that time in which every human aid appeared unavailable, and in which even hope and fortitude wore the aspect of inability to the conflict and you cannot but be led to a serious and grateful sense of your miraculous and providential preservation; you cannot but acknowledge that the present freedom and tranquility which you enjoy you have mercifully received and that it is the peculiar blessing of Heaven.

This sir, was a time in which you clearly saw into the injustice of a state of slavery and in which you had just apprehensions of the horrors of its condition, it was now, sir that your abhorence thereof was so excited, that you publickly held forth this true and valuable doctrine, which is worthy to be recorded and remembered in all succeeding ages. "We hold these truths to be self-evident, that all men are created equal, and that they are endowed by their creator with certain unalienable rights, that among these are life, liberty and the pursuit of happiness."

Here, sir, was a time in which your tender feelings for yourselves had engaged you thus to declare, you were then impressed with proper ideas of the great valuation of liberty and the free possession of those blessings to which you were entitled by nature; but, sir, how pitiable is it to reflect that although you were so fully convinced of the benevolence of the Father of mankind and of his equal and impartial distribution of those rights and privileges which he had conferred upon them, that you should at the same time counteract his mercies in detaining by fraud and violence so numerous a part of my brethren under groaning captivity and cruel oppression, that you should at the same time be found guilty of that most criminal act which you professedly detested in others with respect to yourselves.

Sir, I suppose that your knowledge of the situation of my brethren is too extensive to need a recital here; neither shall I presume to prescribe methods by which they may have been relieved, otherwise than by recommending to you and all others to wean yourselves from those narrow prejudices which you have imbibed with respect to them and as Job proposed to his friends, "put your souls in their souls stead," thus shall your hearts be enlarged with kindness and benevolence toward them, and thus shall you need neither the direction of myself or others, in what manner to proceed herein.

And now, sir, although my sympathy and affection for my brethren hath caused my enlargement thus far, I ardently hope that your candour and generosity will plead with you in my behalf when I make known to you that it was not originally my design; but that having taken up my pen in order to direct to you as a present, a copy of an almanac, which I have calculated for the succeeding year, I was unexpectedly and unavoidably led thereto.

This calculation, sir, is the production of my arduous study in this my advanced stage of life; for having long had unbounded desires to become acquainted with the secrets of nature, I have had to gratify my curiosity herein through my own assidous application to astronomical study, in which I need not to recount to you the many difficulties and disadvantages which I have had to encounter.

And although I had almost declined to make my calculation for the ensuing year, in consequence of that time which I had allotted therefor being taken up at the Federal Territory by the request of Mr. Andrew Ellicott, yet finding myself under several engagements to printers of this state, to whom I had communicated my design, on my return to my place of residence I industriously applied myself thereto which I hope I have accomplished with correctness and accuracy, a copy of which I have taken the liberty to direct to you and which I humbly request you will favorably receive. Although you may have the opportunity of perusing it after its publication yet I chose to send it to you in manuscript previous thereto that you might not only have an earlier inspection but that you might also view it in my own handwriting.

And now, sir, I shall conclude and subscribe myself, with the most profound respect, your most obedient humble servant,

B. BANNEKER

1791

Slave Revolts

GABRIEL'S REVOLT

As the site of the documented introduction of slavery in America, Virginia would also reap its bloodiest consequences. A gathering of nearly two hundred armed slaves who had murdered numerous inhabitants had been frustrated in 1722, but it was the revolt of slaves in southern Virginia in 1800, what Governor James Monroe described as "unquestionably the most serious and formidable conspiracy we have ever known of the kind," that came to national attention. Resisting a reputedly harsh slaveholder, Thomas Prosser, Gabriel organized a plot in which some eleven hundred slaves were to take Richmond, joined by as many as fifty thousand as the action progressed. Two of the men warned authorities of the plot, but as they lay in wait the night the insurrection was to begin, a torrential downpour let loose and no suspicious activity was reported. Nonetheless, Monroe became convinced of a general conspiracy and gave the order to "commit to prison without delay all the slaves in the county whose guilt they had good cause to suspect." Thirty-six slaves, including Gabriel, were executed. Additional plots were reported in Virginia in 1802, 1808, 1809, and 1816, many resulting in deaths and deportations after "confessions" were obtained.

THE VESEY CONSPIRACY

Like Virginia, South Carolina had long been plagued by slave plots, real and imaginary. On May 6, 1720, three whites were killed in a revolt, while in 1730 an extensive plot aimed at Charleston was put down by the militia. In the famous Stono rebellion on September 9, 1739, about twenty Angolans led by Cato (or Jeremy) seized arms from a warehouse, burned buildings, and killed numerous whites before they stopped in a field to celebrate their victory and were met by the militia. Though patrols were increased, the colony was left in "a state of constant fear and agitation" and enforced among the most restrictive measures of Southern states, leading to six uprisings from 1800 to 1821. Tensions heightened with an increase in the black population, and suspected plots in 1797 and 1816 resulted in several executions, tilling the ground for the most well known of revolts in Charleston.

On May 25, 1822, two slaves, William and Peter, struck up a conversation on the wharf, recorded here, in which William encouraged Peter to join in a plot led by Denmark Vesey to "shake off our bondage." A native of St. Thomas in the West Indies, Vesey had traveled as a sailor in his youth and had purchased his own freedom in 1800. Working as a carpenter in the city, for seven months he planned a well-organized uprising in which arms were to be seized, ships commandeered, and the conspirators to sail for the West Indies. Secrecy was maintained through an organization employing cabalistic words and numbers, and no household servants were to be included in the plot. After being apprised of the plot by William, Peter, a household servant, relayed the news to a freeman, who encouraged him to tell his master.

Two of the rebels, Peter Poyas and Mingo Harth, were arrested. The men withstood questioning and were released, but spies were sent out after them and 131 blacks and four whites were arrested. A tribunal was held and witnesses heard, including Rollo, a slave of the governor and a close associate of Vesey. At least thirty-five men, including Vesey, were executed. According to the report of Governor Thomas Bennett, "Having established the existence of a plot and the places of rendezvous, all that was deemed requisite for conviction was to prove an association with the ringleaders and an expression of their assent to the measure. On such, the sentence of death has been executed." All of the men went to their deaths in silence, and historians disagree widely on the extent of the conspiracy, some claiming as many as nine thousand were involved, while others argue that the "plot" was the loose talk of a handful of men. Nonetheless, laws were enacted seeking to limit the entrance of free blacks and slaves from the North and the West Indies.

Numerous other plots and uprisings were rumored throughout the states. Because it became a matter of faith to slaveholders that slaves not be taught to read and write, firsthand accounts are rare, but include the two letters that follow. The first was found on a street in Yorktown, Virginia, in August 1793. The second, written to one Cornell Lucas, in Halifax County, North Carolina, was picked up in March 1810; a second letter is said to have been found at the same time, but is now lost. These documents, together with reports of isolated events in Georgia, Florida, and Louisiana, entries in plantation journals, legislative history, and patrol records confirm that while the institution of slavery was maintained there would be no peace.

Testimony on Gabriel's Revolt

". . . while this class of people exists among us we can never count with certainty on its tranquil submission."

RICHMOND, DECEMBER 5th, 1800

SIRS,—An important incident has occurred since your last session, which I consider it my duty to submit fully and accurately in all its details to the wisdom of the General Assembly. On the 30th of August, about two in the afternoon, Mr. Moseby Shephard, a respectable citizen of this county, called and informed me he had just received advice from two slaves that the negroes in the neighbourhood of Thomas H. Prosser intended to rise that night, kill their masters, and proceed to Richmond where they would be joined by the negroes of the city; that they would then take possession of the arms, ammunition, and the town. He added he had long known these two slaves and had no doubt of the truth of the information they gave him, and that he communicated it to me that the proposed insurrection might be defeated if possible. This communication was very interesting, and the source from whence it derived calculated to inspire a belief it was true. The day was far advanced when I received it, so that if any provision was to be made to avert the danger not a moment was to be lost. I immediately called in the officers commanding the regiment of Militia & troop of Cavalry in town and made the best disposition for such an emergency the time would allow. A guard of a Captain and thirty men was placed at the Penitentiary where the publick arms were deposited, twenty at the Magazine, and fifteen at the Capitol, and the Horse was ordered to patrol the several routes leading to the city from Mr. Prosser's estate, and to apprize me without delay if anything like a movement of the negroes was seen, or other circumstance creating a suspicion such was contemplated. The close of the day was marked by one of the most extraordinary falls of rain ever known in our country. Every animal sought shelter from it. Nothing occurred in the night, of the kind suspected, to disturb the tranquility of the city, and in the morning the officer commanding the Horse reported he had seen but one circumstance unusual in the neighbourhood, which was that all the negroes he passed on the road in the intervals of the storm were going from the town, whereas it was their custom to visit it every Saturday night. This circumstance was not otherwise important thn as it was said the first rendezvous of the negroes was to be in the country. The same precautions were observed the next night against the threatened insurrection and the same report made the next day by the officers on duty, so that I was on the point of concluding there was no foundation for the alarm when I was informed by Major Mosby and other gentlemen of character from his neighborhood they were satisfied a project of insurrection, such as above described, did exist, and that the parties to it meant still to carry it into effect. These gentlemen stated facts and gave details which left no doubt in my mind of the existence of such a project. From this period the affair assumed a more important aspect. It did not seem probable the slaves in this city and neighbourhood would undertake so bold an enterprise without support from the slaves in other quarters of the State. It was more reasonable to presume an extensive combination had been formed among them for that purpose. Heretofore I had endeavoured to give the affair as little importance as the measures necessary for defence would permit. I had hoped it would even pass unnoticed by the community. But as soon as I was satisfied a conspiracy existed, it became my duty to estimate the crisis according to its magnitude and to take regular and systematic measures to avert the danger. In consequence I issued a summons to convene the Council at ten the next day, and in the interim advised the gentlemen who gave me the information to apprehend and commit to prison without delay all the slaves in the county whose guilt they had good cause to suspect. . . . In the evening of the same day about twenty of the conspirators were brought to town from Mr. Prosser's and the neighbouring estates, and as the jail could not contain them they were lodged in the Penitentiary. The chiefs were not to be found. Some of the arms which they had prepared for the occasion, formed of scythe blades, well calculated for execution, were likewise brought with them. By the information now received, as by former communications, it appeared that the inhabitants of that neighbourhood were in a particular degree exposed to danger; the conspiracy commenced with their slaves, and they were to be its first victims. . . . Every day now threw new light on this affair and increased the idea of its importance. . . . The trials had now commenced whereby the nature and extent of the conspiracy became better understood. It was satisfactorily proven that a general insurrection of the slaves was contemplated by those who took the lead in the affair. A species of organization had taken place among them. At a meeting held for the purpose, they had appointed a commander, to whom they gave the title of General, and had also appointed some other officers. They contemplated a force of cavalry as well as infantry, and had formed a plan of attack on the city which was to commence by setting fire to the lower end of the town where the houses consisted chiefly of wood, in expectation of drawing the people to that quarter while they assailed the Penitentiary, Magazine and Capitol, intending, after achieving these and getting possession of the arms, to meet the people unarmed on their return. The accounts of the number of those who were to commence the movement varied. Some made it considerable, others less so. It was distinctly seen that it embraced most of the slaves in this city and neighbourhood, and that the combination extended to several of the adjacent counties, Hanover, Caroline, Louisa, Chesterfield, and to the neighbourhood of the Point of Fork; and there was good cause to believe that the knowledge of such a project pervaded other parts, if not the whole State. At this time there was no reason to believe if such a project was ever conceived, that it was abandoned. Those who gave the earliest information and were best informed on the subject thought otherwise. It was understood that the leaders in the conspiracy, who had absconded, were concealed in the neighborhood. And as several of the parties to it were confined in the Jail condemned to suffer death, and many others in the Penitentiary likely to experience the same fate, it was probable sympathy for their associates might drive them to despair and prompt them to make a bolder effort for their relief. The opposite effect was expected from the measures pursued by the Government, but yet the result was uncertain. Other considerations presented themselves to view in weighing the part it was then incumbent on me to take. The number of slaves in this city and its neighbourhood, comprising those at work on the publick buildings, the canal, and the coal pits, was considerable. These might be assembled in a few hours, and could only be opposed by a respectable force, which force, if the city was surprised, could not be collected in a short time. The probability was if their first effort succeeded, we should see the town in flames, its inhabitants butchered, and a scene of horror extending through the country. This spectacle, it is true, would be momentary only, for as soon as a body of militia could be formed the insurrection would be suppressed. The superiority in point of numbers, in the knowledge and use of arms, and indeed every other species of knowledge which the whites have over the blacks in this Commonwealth, is so decisive that the latter could only sustain themselves for a moment in a rebellion against the former. Still it was a crisis to be avoided so far as prudent precautions could accomplish it. There was one other consideration which engaged the mind in the commencement of this affair from which it was not easy to withdraw it. It seemed strange that the slaves should embark in this novel and unexampled enterprise of their own accord. Their treatment has been more favorable since the revolution, and as the importation was prohibited among the first acts of our independence, their number has not increased in proportion with that of the whites. It was natural to suspect they were prompted to it by others who were invisible but whose agency might be powerful. And if this was the case it became proportionally more difficult to estimate the extent of the combination, and the consequent real importance of the crisis. On consideration of all these circumstances it was deemed necessary to call out such a force as might be fully adequate to the emergency—such an one as would likely to overawe and keep down the spirit of insurrection, or sufficient to suppress it in case it broke out. On that principle I called into service on the 9th the 19th and 24th regiments, and a detachment of fifty men additional from the 23rd; which detachment with the whole of the 19th regiment and one hundred men of the 23rd, were ordered to take post in this city. The residue of the 23rd were stationed in the town of Manchester. . . . It was paraded daily on the Capitol square, and trained as well that it might be prepared for action if occasion required as that our strength might be known to the conspirators. The effect which this measure produced was easily and soon perceived. It was evident that the collection and display of this force inspired the citizens with confidence, and depressed the spirits of the slaves. The former saw in it a security from the danger which menaced them; the latter a defeat of their nefarious projects. On the 12th of September, five, and on the fifteenth following, five others were executed. On those occasions the whole force in service in the city (infantry and horse) attended the execution. On the 27th Gabriel, one of the chiefs of the conspiracy, for whom a reward had been offered and who had been apprehended at Norfolk, was delivered up and committed to Jail. As these executions were carried into effect without any movement of the slaves, and their chief apprehended, it was fair to presume the danger of the crisis had passed. It became from that period the object of the Executive to diminish the force with a view to lessen the expense, which object was pursued with undeviating attention. . . . It belongs to the Legislature to weigh with profound attention this unpleasant incident in our history. What has happened may occur again at any time with more fatal consequences, unless suitable measures be taken to prevent it. Unhappily while this class of people exists among us we can never count with certainty on its tranquil submission. The fortunate issue of the late attempt should not lull us into repose. It ought rather to stimulate us to the adoption of a system, which, if it does not prevent the like in future, may secure the country from any calamitous consequences.

Testimony on the Vesey Conspiracy

". . . we are determined to shake off our bondage, and for this purpose we stand on a good foundation. . . ."

HE STATEMENT OF PETER, THE INFORMER:

On Saturday afternoon last (my master being out of town) I went to market; after finishing my business I strolled down the wharf below the fish market, from which I observed a small vessel in the stream with a singular flag; whilst looking at this object, a black man, (Mr. Paul's William) came up to me and remarking the subject which engaged my attention said, I have often seen a flag with the number 76 on it, but never with 96 before. After some trifling conversation on this point, he remarked with considerable earnestness to me. Do you know that something serious is about to take place? To which I replied no. Well, said he, there is, and many of us are determined to right ourselves! I asked him to explain himself—when he remarked, why, we are determined to shake off our bondage, and for this purpose we stand on a good foundation; many have joined, and if you will go with me, I will show you the man who has the list of names who will take yours down. I was so much astonished and horror struck at this information, that it was a moment or two before I could collect myself sufficient to tell him I would have nothing to do with this business, that I was satisfied with my condition, that I was grateful to my master for his kindness and wished no change. I left him instantly, lest, if this fellow afterwards got into trouble and I had been seen conversing with him in so public a place, I might be suspected and thrown into difficulty. I did not, however, remain easy under the burden of such a secret, and consequently determined to consult a free man of colour named —— and to ask his advice. On conferring with this friend, he urged me with great earnestness to communicate what had passed between Mr. Paul's man and myself to my master, and not lose a moment in so doing. I took his advice and, not waiting even for the return of my master to town, I mentioned it to my mistress and young master. On the arrival of my master, he examined me as to what had passed, and I stated to him what I have mentioned to yourselves.

The statement of Rolla, a conspirator:

I know Denmark Vesey. On one occasion he asked me what news, I told him none, he replied we are free but the white people here won't let us be so, and the only way is to rise up and fight the whites. I went to his house one night to learn where the meetings were held. I never conversed on this subject with Batteau or Ned—Vesey told me he was the leader in this plot. I never conversed either with Peter or Mingo. Vesey induced me to join; when I went to Vesey's house there was a meeting there, the room was full of people, but none of them white. That night at Vesey's we determined to have arms made, and each man put in 12½ cents toward that purpose. Though Vesey's room was full I did not know one individual there. At this meeting Vesey said we were to take the Guard-House and Magazine to get arms; that we ought to rise up and speak, and he *read to us from the Bible, how the Children of Israel were delivered out of Egypt from bondage.*

from "An Official Report of the Trials of Sundry Negroes, Charged with an Attempt to Raise an Insurrection in the State of South Carolina"

1822

Letter from a Slave Rebel

". . . don't be feared have a good heart, fight brave and we will get free. . . ."

Dear Friend—The great secret that has been so long in being with our own color has come nearly to a head tho some on our Town has told of it but in such a slight manner it is not believed, we have got about five hundred Guns aplenty of lead but not much powder, I hope you have made a good collection of powder and ball and will hold yourself in readiness to strike whenever called for and never be out of the way it will not be long before it will take place, and I am fully satisfied we shall be in full possission of the whole country in a few weeks, since I wrote you last I got a letter from our freind in Charleston he tells me has listed near six thousand men, there is a gentleman that says he will give us as much powder as we want, and when we begin he will help us all he can, the damn'd brutes patroles is going all night in Richmond but will soon cill them all, there an't many, we will appoint a night to begin with fire clubs and shot, we will kill all before us, it will begin in every town in one nite Keep ready to receive orders, when I hear from Charleston again I shall no and will rite to you, he that give you this is a good friend and don't let any body see it, rite me by the same hand he will give it to me out his hand and he will be up next week don't be feared have a good heart, fight brave and we will get free, i had like to get each. . . . but God was for me, and I got away, no more now but remain your friend—Secret Keeper Richmond to secret keeper Norfolk.

1793

Letter from a Slave Rebel in Georgia

". . . for freedom we want and will have, for we have served this cruel land long enuff. . . ."

Dear Sir—I received your letter to the fourteenth of June, 1809 with great freedom and joy to hear and understand what great proceedance you have made, and the resolution you have in proceeding on in business as we have undertook, and hope you will still continue in the same mind. We have spread the sense nearly over the continent in our part of the country, and have the day when we are to fall to work, and you must be sure not to fail on that day and that is the 22nd April, to begin about midnight, and do the work at home first, and then take the armes of them you slay first, and that will strengthen us more in armes—for freedom we want and will have, for we have served this cruel land long enuff, & be as secret convaing your nuse as possabel, and be sure to send it by some cearfull hand, and if it happens to be discovered, fail not in the day, for we are full abel to conquer by any means.—Sir, I am your Captain James, living in the state of Jorgy, in Green county—so no more at present, but remaining your sincer friend and captain until death.

1810

The Founding of the African-American Press

Though the role of William Lloyd Garrison's *Liberator* in shaping public opinion in the mid-nineteenth century is well known, the first black newspaper in America, *Freedom's Journal,* was founded four years earlier, in 1827, with the same avowed purpose. Published in the decades that followed were dozens of significant black papers whose pages recorded the events of the day as well as the dominant concerns of the African-American community. The journals admonished education and social "uplift"; recounted the treatment accorded freemen, including growing prejudice and kidnapping; debated abolition, colonization, and emigration to Canada and the West; published convention proceedings and resolutions; offered the opinions of black nations around the world; and provided an outlet for fiction and poetry. Even through such mundane information as the published notices of births, marriages, and deaths, and advertisements for black enterprises, these papers offer a significant window onto African-American history and intellectual life.

The weekly *Freedom's Journal* began publication on March 30, 1827, in New York City, its editors Rev. Samuel E. Cornish and John B. Russwurm arguing in their opening editorial, "We wish to plead our own cause. Too long have others spoken for us." David Walker contributed to its pages and acted as an agent for the paper in Boston, and it was sold by subscription as far away as Washington, D.C., Baltimore, and Haiti. In August of that year, the paper recorded an early women's perspective when it published an anonymous letter asking, "Will you allow a female to offer a few remarks upon a subject that you must allow to be all important. I don't know that in any of your papers, you have said sufficient upon the education of females." Cornish and Russwurm split soon after, however, over the debate on colonization to Africa, and Russwurm emigrated to Liberia in 1829, while Cornish revived the paper that year under the masthead *The Rights of All.*

The colonization debate† continued in other papers, such as the New York *Colored American,* which editorialized, "All such agitations introduced among us, with a view to our emigrating, ought to be frowned upon by us, and we ought to teach people that they may as well come here and agitate the emigration of the Jays, the Rings, the Adamses, the Otises, the

Hancocks, *et al,* as agitate our removal." The debate would resurface in the twentieth century in Marcus Garvey's *Negro World.*

Other notable early papers included Samuel Ringgold Ward's *Impartial Citizen,* published in Rochester, the *Baltimore Afro-American,* the Buffalo *American,* and the Pittsburgh *Courier.* While many of these journals were short-lived due to financial difficulties, others sprang up to replace them, ironically at a time when laws in the South sought to prevent slaves from learning to read and write. As the abolition crisis accelerated, papers such as Frederick Douglass's *North Star* (later *Frederick Douglass's Paper*) reflected the heightened rhetoric of the schism. The *North Star* also acted as a printer, issuing the Resolutions of the Women's Rights Convention at Seneca Falls in 1848.

After the Civil War, papers like T. Thomas Fortune's *New York Age* continued to advocate equal rights, a plea that became more muffled as the press was taken over by Booker T. Washington. *The Chicago Defender* and Ida Wells-Barnett's Memphis *Free Speech* denounced lynch law so unsparingly that Wells's newspaper office was ransacked in her absence and a price was put on her head. W. E. B. Du Bois's frank assessment of the situation that faced black soldiers during World War I in *The Crisis,* the official paper of the NAACP, brought a warning from the Justice Department, which, the First Amendment notwithstanding, viewed the paper as near treasonous. *The Messenger,* edited by A. Philip Randolph, ultimately the official organ of the Brotherhood of Sleeping Car Porters, which opposed the war, supported unionism, and advocated the meeting of force with force during the Red Summer of 1919[†] was viewed as even more dangerous and was investigated by the Justice Department's Palmer Commission. Photographs of lynch victims in the black press were tragically eloquent, and the battered body of Emmett Till on the front page of *The Chicago Defender* shocked the nation in 1955. In the mid-twentieth century, the *New York Amsterdam News,* for which W. E. B. Du Bois wrote the column "As the Crow Flies," was among the most prominent of black journals.

"Too long has the publick been deceived by misrepresentations, in things which concern us dearly," wrote Cornish and Russwurm in 1827, "though in the estimation of some mere trifles. . . . whatever concerns us as a people, will ever find a ready admission into the *Freedom's Journal.*" Because the African-American press has often uniquely provided a side of history not reflected in standard texts or the mainstream press, numerous articles from black journals appear throughout this volume.

Editorial from the First Edition of *Freedom's Journal*

"We wish to plead our own cause."

TO OUR PATRONS

IN PRESENTING OUR FIRST NUMBER TO OUR PATRONS, WE FEEL all the diffidence of persons entering upon a new and untried line of business. But a moment's reflection upon the noble objects, which we have in view by the publication of this Journal: the expediency of its appearance at this time, when so many schemes are in action concerning our people—encourage us to come boldly before an enlightented publick. For we believe, that a paper devoted to the dissemination of useful knowledge among our brethren, and to their moral and religious improvement, must meet with the cordial approbation of every friend to humanity.

The peculiarities of this Journal, renders it important that we should advertise to the world our motives by which we are actuated, and the objects which we contemplate.

We wish to plead our own cause. Too long have others spoken for us. Too long has the publick been deceived by misrepresentations, in things which concern us dearly, though in the estimation of some mere trifles; for though there are many in society who exercise towards us benevolent feelings; still (with sorrow we confess it) there are others who make it their business to enlarge upon the least trifle, which tends to the discredit of any person of colour; and pronounce anathemas and denounce our whole body for the misconduct of this guilty one. We are aware that there are many instances of vice among us, but we avow that it is because no one has taught its subjects to be virtuous; many instances of poverty, because no sufficient efforts accommodated to minds contracted by slavery, and deprived of early education have been made, to teach them how to husband their hard earnings, and to secure to themselves comfort.

Education being an object of the highest importance to the welfare of society, we shall endeavour to present just and adequate views of it, and to urge upon our brethren the necessity and expediency of training their children, while young, to habits of industry, and thus forming them for becoming useful members of society. It is surely time that we should awake from this lethargy of years, and make a concentrated effort for the education of our youth. We form a spoke in the human wheel and it is necessary that we should understand our pendence on the different parts, and theirs on us, in order to perform our part with propriety.

Though not desiring of dictating, we shall feel it our incumbent duty to dwell occasionally upon the general principles and rules of economy. The world has grown too enlightened, to estimate any man's character by his personal appearance. Though all men acknowledge the excellency of Franklin's maxims, yet comparatively few practise upon them. We may deplore when it is too late, the neglect of these self-evident truths, but it avails little to mourn. Ours will be the task of admonishing our brethren on these points.

The civil rights of a people being of the greatest value, it shall ever be our duty to vindicate our brethren, when oppressed; and to lay the case before the publick. We shall also urge upon our brethren, (who are qualified by the laws of the different states) the expediency of using their elective franchise; and of making an independent use of the same. We wish them not to become the tools of party.

And as much time is frequently lost, and wrong principles instilled, by the perusal of works of trivial importance, we shall consider it a part of our duty to recommend to our young readers, such authors as will not only enlarge their stock of useful knowledge, but such as will also serve to stimulate them to higher attainments in science.

We trust also, that through the columns of the FREEDOM'S JOURNAL, many practical pieces, having for their bases, the improvement of our brethren, will be presented to them, from the pens of many of our respected friends, who have kindly promised their assistance.

It is our earnest wish to make our Journal a medium of intercourse between our brethren in the different states of this great confederacy: that through its columns an expression of our sentiments, on many interesting subjects which concern us, may be offered to the publick: that plans which apparently are beneficial may be candidly discussed and properly weighed; if worth, receive our cordial approbation; if not, our marked disapprobation.

Useful knowledge of every kind, and everything that relates to Africa, shall find a ready admission into our columns; and as that vast continent becomes daily more known, we trust that many things will come to light, proving that the natives of it are neither so ignorant nor stupid as they have generally been supposed to be.

And while these important subjects shall occupy the columns of the FREEDOM'S JOURNAL, we would not be unmindful of our brethren who are still in the iron fetters of bondage. They are our kindred by all the times of nature; and though but little can be effected by us, still let our sympathies be poured forth, and our prayers in their behalf, ascend to Him who is able to succour them.

From the press and the pulpit we have suffered much by being incorrectly represented. Men whom we equally love and admire have not hesitated to represent us disadvantageously, without becoming personally acquainted with the true state of things, nor discerning between virtue and vice among us. The virtuous part of our people feel themselves sorely aggrieved under the existing state of things—they are not appreciated.

Our vices and our degradation are ever arrayed against us, but our virtues are passed by unnoticed. And what is still more lamentable, our friends, to whom we concede all the principles of humanity and religion, from these very causes seem to have fallen into the current of popular feeling and are imperceptibly floating on the stream—actually living in the practice of prejudice, while they abjure it in theory, and feel it not in their hearts. Is it not very desirable that such should know more of our actual condition; and of our efforts and feelings, that in forming or advocating plans for our amelioration, they may do it more understandingly? In the spirit of candor and humility we intend by a simple representation of facts to lay our case before the public, with a view to arrest the progress of prejudice, and to shield ourselves against the consequent evils. We wish to conciliate all and to irritate none, yet we must be firm and unwavering in our principles, and persevering in our efforts.

If ignorance, poverty and degradation have hitherto been our unhappy lot; has the Eternal decree gone forth, that our race alone are to remain in this state, while knowledge and civilization are shedding their enlivening rays over the rest of the human family? The recent travels of Denham and Clapperton in the interior of Africa, and the interesting narrative which they have published; the establishment of the republic of Hayti after years of sanguinary warfare; its subsequent progress in all the arts of civilization; and the advancement of liberal ideas in South America, where despotism has given place to free governments, and where many of our brethren now fill important civil and military stations, prove the contrary.

The interesting fact that there are FIVE HUNDRED THOUSAND free persons of colour, one half of whom might peruse, and the whole be benefitted by the publication of the Journal; that no publication, as yet, has been devoted exclusively to their improvement—that many selections from approved standard authors, which are within the reach of few, may occasionally be made—and more important still, that this large body of our citizens have no public channel—all serve to prove the real necessity, at present, for the appearance of the FREEDOM'S JOURNAL.

It shall ever be our desire so to conduct the editorial department of our paper as to give offence to none of our patrons; as nothing is farther from us than to make it the advocate of any partial views, either in politics or religion. What few days we can number, have been devoted to the improvement of our brethren; and it is our earnest wish that the remainder may be spent in the same delightful service.

In conclusion, whatever concerns us as a people, will ever find a ready admission into the FREEDOM'S JOURNAL, interwoven with all the principal news of the day.

And while every thing in our power shall be performed to support the character of our Journal, we would respectfully invite our numerous friends to assist by their communications, and our coloured brethren to strengthen our hands by their subscriptions, as our labour is one of common cause, and worthy of their consideration and support. And we most earnestly solicit the latter, that if at any time we should seem to be zealous, or too pointed in the inculcation of any important lesson, they will remember, that they are equally interested in the cause in which we are engaged, and attribute our zeal to the peculiarities of our situation; and our earnest engagedness in their well-being.

Freedom's Journal, New York, March 16, 1827

The Colonization Debate

Almost as soon as Africans were forcibly kidnapped and brought to America, freemen, slaves, abolitionists, and slaveholders began to discuss their return to Africa, often in the context of "civilizing" the dark continent and bringing Christianity to that benighted land. Articulating the peculiar sense of limbo that early African-Americans felt, in 1774 Phillis Wheatley declined the suggestion that she return to Africa as a missionary. "Upon my arrival," she wrote, "how like a Barbarian shou'd I look to the Natives." During the next two centuries, the debate over the "place" of African-Americans in the New World would rage.

As early as 1789, the Free African Societies of Rhode Island and Philadelphia had considered jointly sponsoring a colony in Africa. In 1811 Paul Cuffee, a successful shipowner with religious zeal, made a trip to Sierra Leone, returning a few years later with thirty-eight of his compatriots. But the organized impulse toward colonization began in earnest with the founding of the American Colonization Society in December 1816, attributing its plan to relocate free blacks in Africa to the poor treatment they received in America and a general incompatibility of the races. In 1822 the Society established a colony in Monravia, later called Liberia. The true motive of many of the white procolonizers was made transparent, however, by Henry Clay, who remarked that the scheme would "rid our own country of a useless and pernicious, if not dangerous portion of its population." In other words, free blacks represented a real problem to slaveholders.

Within a month, groups of freemen who met in Richmond and Philadelphia expressed their "deep abhorrence" of the plan. The Philadelphia meeting, which included James Forten and Bishop Richard Allen, resolved that "we will never separate ourselves voluntarily from the slave population in this country; they are our brethren by the ties of consanguinity, of suffering, and of wrong; and we feel that there is more virtue in suffering privations with them, than fancied advantages for a season." The debate was taken up almost immediately in John Russwurm's newly established *Freedom's Journal,* in which the two articles included here appeared. Russwurm and his colleague, Samuel E. Cornish, eventually clashed over the issue of colonization, and Russwurm left for Liberia in 1829. In his own fiery 1829 *Appeal,* David Walker argued, "Let no man of us budge one step . . . America is more ours than it is the whites' . . . The greatest riches in all America have arisen from our blood and tears—and will they drive us from our property and homes, which we have earned with our *blood?*"

Colonization emerged as one of the central issues of the convention movement† and was advocated by a number of prominent men throughout the nineteenth century. Martin Delany, whose *Condition, Elevation, and Destiny of the Colored People of the United States, Politically Considered*† was published in 1852, attended the largest convention favorable to the movement in August 1854 and traveled to Liberia in 1859, as did Alexander Crummell, who spent twenty years in Africa, and Henry Highland Garnet, who died there in 1882. Bishop Henry McNeal Turner established AME churches in Sierra Leone and Liberia, and after the ACS discontinued its activities in 1892, Turner launched his own International Immigration Society. By the end of the nineteenth century, almost twelve thousand African-Americans had relocated to Liberia; unfortunately, numerous fraudulent ventures sprang up to accommodate interest in emigration and many black Americans lost their savings and property. Other freemen were kidnapped and deported.

In the twentieth century, there would be a growing antipathy to the religious colonization of Africa and emigration in general. Alain Locke, the voice of *The New Negro,* wrote, "We now see that the missionary condescension of the past generations in their attitude toward Africa was a pious but sad mistake. In taking it, we have fallen into the snare of enemies and have given grievous offence to our brothers." Nonetheless, in the 1920s Marcus Garvey's Universal Negro Improvement Association—championing the motto "Africa for Africans"—became the most heavily subscribed colonization movement ever. Many other prominent African-Americans, including Richard Wright, Paul Robeson, and James Baldwin, while never denying their loyalties—and rights—as true Americans, exiled themselves to Europe to escape racial harassment.

In addition to the establishment of an émigré community in Africa, many African-Americans considered the foundation of a black nation closer to home. The Underground Railroad spirited escaped slaves north to Canada, where a large African-American community flourished. In 1879 the Exodusters† migrated to Kansas and other western territories to found black communities, and in the twentieth century, both the Black Panthers and Elijah Muhammad's Nation of Islam sought a grant of territory within the United States as reparation for centuries of oppression.

But despite the various waves of procolonization and nationalist sentiment, the great majority of African-Americans has steadfastly declared its intention to live freely in the land of its birth. "Our minds are made up," declared Frederick Douglass, "to live here if we can, or die here if we must; so every attempt to remove us, will be as it ought to be, labor lost. . . . We live here—have lived here—have a right to live here, and mean to live here."

The Argument For

". . . prejudices now in our part of the country, are so high, that it is often the remark of liberal men from the south, that their free people are treated better than we are. . . ."

E FEEL PROUD IN ANNOUNCING TO OUR DISTANT READERS, that many of our brethren in this city, who have lately taken this subject into consideration, have like ourselves, come out from the examination warm advocates of the Colony, and ready to embrace the first convenient opportunity to embark for the shores of Africa. This we may say looks like coming to the point—as if they had examined for themselves and satisfied of the practicability of the plan, are not afraid the world should know it.

The subject of Colonization is certainly important, as having a great bearing on that of slavery: for it must be evident that the universal emancipation so ardently desired by *us* & by all our friends can never take place unless some door is opened whereby the emancipated may be removed, as fast as they drop their galling chains, to some other land beside the free states; for it is a fact, that prejudices now in our part of the country, are so high, that it is often the remark of liberal men from the south, that their free people are treated better than we are, in the boasted free states of the north. If the free states have passed no law as yet forbidding the emigration of free persons of colour into their limits; it is no reason that they will not, as soon as they find themselves a little more burdened. We will suppose that a general law of emancipation should be promulgated in the state of Virginia, under the existing statutes which require every emancipated slave to leave the state, would not the other states, in order to shield themselves from the evils of having so many thousands of ignorant beings thrown upon them be obliged in self-defense to pass prohibitory laws? Much as we may deplore the evils of slavery—much as we *may* desire the freedom of the enslaved; who could reproach the free states for enacting such laws? so, that if no good whatever arose from the establishment of colonies, the fact that they remove all obstacles in the way of emancipation should gain for them the support and good wishes of every friend of humanity, & of every enlightened man of colour. It is true, that no such laws at present are in force to our knowledge, but who can foretell how soon before they may, without waiting for the period of a general emancipation in any of the slaveholding states.

Our wiseacres may talk as much as they please upon amalgamations, and our future standing in society, but it does not alter the case in the least; it does not improve our situation in the least; but it is calculated rather to stay the exertions of those who are really willing to make some efforts to improve their own present conditions. We are considered a distinct people, in the midst of the millions around us, and in the most favorable parts of the country; and it matters not from what cause this sentence has been passed upon us; the fiat has gone forth and should each of us live to the age of Methuselah, at the end of the thousand years, we should be exactly in our present situation: a proscribed race, however unjustly—a degraded people, deprived of all the rights of freemen and in the eyes of the community, a race who had no lot nor portion with them.

We hope none of our readers will from our remarks think that we approve in the least of the present prejudices in the way of the man of colour; far from it, we deplore them as much as any man; but they are not of our creating, and they are not in our power to remove. They at present exist against us—and from the length of their existence—from the degraded light in which we have ever been held—we are bold in saying, that it will never be in our power to remove or overcome them. So easily are these prejudices imbibed that we have often noticed the effects on young children who could hardly speak plainly, and were we a believer in dreams, charms, etc., we should believe they imbibed them with their mothers' milk.

Sensible then, as all are of the disadvantages under which we at present labour, can any consider it a mark of folly, for us to cast our eyes upon some other portion of the globe where all these inconveniences are removed—where the Man of Colour freed from the fetters and prejudice and degradation, under which he labours in this land, may walk forth in all the majesty of his creation—a new born creature—a Free Man! It was, we believe, the remark of Sir James Yeo, while on the African coast, that the natives whom he saw were a fine athletic race, walking fearlessly as if sensible of their important station as men, and quite different from the thousands of their brethren whom he had seen in the West Indies and the United States; and never was truer remark made, if we are to credit all other travellers on that Continent, who have likewise born testimony to the same fact.

While some of our friends have wondered at our change, others have been bold enough to call them in question and to accuse us of improper motive; of such, we ask, who has made half the sacrifice we have to oppose the Colonization society? who has labored half so much by night and by day for the same end? who has had to bear the brunt of the battle while those who led us into action were sitting quietly at home? who has suffered much for conscience sake? Let none consider these as vain boastings. We merely insert them to refresh the memories of those who are now loud in denouncing our change. . . .

John Russwurm
Freedom's Journal, March 14, 1829

The Argument Against

***"This land which we have watered with our* tears *and our* blood, *is now our* mother country. . . ."**

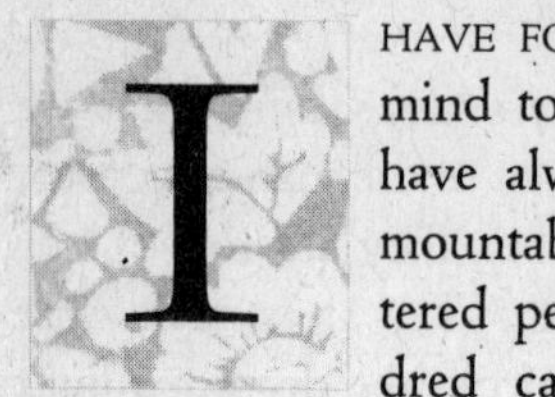

I HAVE FOR SEVERAL YEARS BEEN STRIVING TO RECONCILE MY mind to the colonization of Africans in Liberia, but there have always been, and there still remain great and unsurmountable objections against the scheme. We are an unlettered people, brought up in ignorance, not one in a hundred can read or write; not one in a thousand has a liberal education. Is there any fitness for such to be sent into a far country, among Heathens, to convert or civilize them; when they themselves are neither *civilized* nor *christianized?* See the great bulk of the poor ignorant Africans in this country; exposed to every temptation before them; all for the want of their morals being refined by education, and proper attendance paid unto them by their owners, or those who had the charge of them. It is said by the southern slaveholders, that the more ignorant they can bring up the Africans, the *better slaves* they make. It is enough for them to know the words, *"go* and *come."* Is there any *fitness* for such people to be colonized in a far country, to be their *own rulers?* Can we not discern the *project* of sending the free people of colour away from this country? Is it not for the *interest* of the slave holder, to select the free people of colour out of the different states and send them to Liberia? Will it not make their slaves uneasy to see free men of colour enjoying *liberty?* It is against the law in some of the southern states, that a person of colour should receive an education under a severe penalty. Colonizationists speak of America being first colonized, but is there any comparison between the two? America was colonized by as *wise, judicious,* and *educated* men as the world afforded. William Penn did not want for *learning, wisdom,* or *intelligence.* If all the people in Europe and America were as ignorant, and in the same situation as our brethren, what would become of the world; where would be the principle or piety that would govern the people? We were *stolen* from our mother country and brought *here.* We have *tilled* the ground and made fortunes for thousands, and still they are not weary of our services. *But they who stay to till the ground must be slaves.* Is there not land enough in America, or "corn enough in Egypt?" Why would they send us into a far country to die? See the thousands of foreigners emigrating to America every year: and if there be ground sufficient for them to cultivate, and bread for them to eat; why would they wish to send the first tillers of the land away? Africans have made fortunes for thousands, who are yet unwilling to part with their services, but the free must be sent away, and those who remain must be *slaves?* I have no doubt that there are many good men who do not see as I do and who are for sending us to Liberia, but they have not duly considered the subject—they are not men of colour. This land which we have watered with our *tears* and our *blood,* is now our *mother country* and we are well satisfied to stay where wisdom abounds and the gospel is free.

Bishop Richard Allen
Freedom's Journal, November 2, 1827

David Walker
(1785–1830)

The appearance in 1829 of David Walker's *Appeal,* one of the most powerful documents in American history, escalated a struggle for freedom that would culminate in civil war thirty years later. In his fiery plea, Walker passionately condemned the wretched condition of slavery, the denial of the means of education, the perversion of the Christian faith for economic ends, and recent attempts to colonize American blacks outside the borders of the United States, in all of these forcefully articulating the terms of national debate for the next three decades.

David Walker was born the son of a slave father and a free mother in Wilmington, North Carolina. He settled in Boston, where he owned a clothing store and was active in abolition activity, helping to circulate Samuel Cornish's journal, *The Rights of All,* and contributing to the recently established *Freedom's Journal* when his *Appeal* was printed in 1829.

His widely read work, written with a preamble and four "articles" that ironically echoed the Constitution, spoke to both a white and black audience. While Walker warranted that "we would not wish to see them destroyed notwithstanding," he spoke to slaveholders in apocalyptic terms of the destruction that was at hand unless they repented of a system based on avarice and lust for power. He appealed as well to blacks for unity and action, for he saw the future of slaves and free blacks irrevocably intertwined. While Northern blacks were nominally free, they were threatened with kidnapping and forced into the most menial professions. "Look into our freedom and happiness," Walker urged, "and see of what kind they are composed!! They are of the very lowest kind—they are the very *dregs!*" "Your full glory and happiness," he argued, "shall never be fully consummated, but with the *entire emancipation of your enslaved brethren all over the world.*"

Walker drew upon a number of sources to buttress his argument. He recalled ancient history and "the renown of that once mighty people of Africa or of Ham among whom learning originated" and the exploits of its glorious son, Hannibal, as well as the founding principles of the democratic republic embedded in her Declaration of Independence.† He invoked reason, the God of justice, and even sheer pragmatism, arguing that would it not be far better to "gain our affections now" through civil justice than "by the crushing arm of power"? But what finally distinguished Walker's appeal from previous abolitionist documents was its utter fearlessness. He refrained neither from advocating that the inevitable consequence of slavery was "the final overthrow of its government" nor from upbraiding a "death-like apathy" among blacks. Should the time be at hand, he urged his readers, "make sure work—do not trifle, for they will not trifle with you . . . if there is an *attempt* made by us, kill or be killed."

In its boldness and its power, Walker's document had a profound impact. It went into several editions and was widely circulated in the North and smuggled into the South, where weapons were distributed in anticipation of armed revolt, where it became illegal to teach slaves to read and write, and where possession of publications urging slave revolt was made a capital offense. A price was put on Walker's head, and on June 28, 1830, soon after the third edition of the book appeared, Walker was found dead near his shop, possibly poisoned. The controversy he unleashed, however, did not abate; a new Hannibal emerged in the messianic figure of Nat Turner[†] and the nation did indeed rise up, "one against another, to be split and divided, and to oppress each other . . . with sword in hand."

from *Walker's Appeal in Four Articles, together with a Preamble, to the Coloured Citizens of the World, but in Particular, and very Expressly, to Those of the United States of America*

"I believe there are some true-hearted sons of Africa, in this land of oppression, but pretended liberty!!!!!"

APPEAL, &C. PREAMBLE.

M*Y DEARLY BELOVED BRETHREN AND FELLOW CITIZENS.* Having travelled over a considerable portion of these United States, and having, in the course of my travels, taken the most accurate observations of things as they exist—the result of my observations has warranted the full and unshaken conviction, that we, (coloured people of these United States,) are the most degraded, wretched, and abject set of beings that ever lived since the world began; and I pray God that none like us ever may live again until time shall be no more. They tell us of the Israelites in Egypt, the Helots in Sparta, and of the Roman Slaves, which last were made up from almost every nation under heaven, whose sufferings under those ancient and heathen nations, were, in comparison with ours, under this enlightedned and Christian nation, no more than a cypher—or, in other words, those nations of antiquity, had but little more among them than the name and form of slavery; while wretchedness and endless miseries were reserved apparently in a phial, to be poured out upon our fathers, ourselves and our children, by *Christian* Americans!

These positions I shall endeavour, by the help of the Lord, to demonstrate in the course of this APPEAL, to the satisfaction of the most incredulous mind—and may God Almighty, who is the Father of our Lord Jesus Christ, open your hearts to understand and believe the truth.

The *causes,* my brethren, which produce our wretchedness and miseries, are so very numerous and aggravating, that I believe the pen only of a Josephus or a Plutarch, can well enumerate and explain them. Upon subjects, then, of such incomprehensible magnitude, so impenetrable, and so notorious, I shall be obliged to omit a large class of, and content myself with giving you an exposition of a few of those, which do indeed rage to such an alarming pitch, that they cannot but be a perpetual source of terror and dismay to every reflecting mind.

I am fully aware, in making this appeal to my much afflicted and suffering brethren, that I shall not only be assailed by those whose greatest earthly desires are, to keep us in abject ignorance and wretchedness, and who are of the firm conviction that Heaven has designed us and our children to be slaves and *beasts of burden* to them and their children. I say, I do not only expect to be held up to the public as an ignorant impudent and restless disturber of the public peace, by such avaricious creatures, as well as a mover of insubordination—and perhaps put in prison or to death, for giving a superficial exposition of our miseries, and exposing tyrants. But I am persuaded, that many of my brethren, particularly those who are ignorantly in league with slave-holders or tyrants, who acquire their daily bread by the blood and sweat of their more ignorant brethren—and not a few of those too, who are too ignorant to see an inch beyond their noses, will rise up and call me cursed—Yea, the jealous ones among us will perhaps use more abject subtlety, by affirming that this work is not worth perusing, that we are well situated, that there is no use in trying to better our condition, for we cannot. I will ask one question here.—Can our condition be any worse?—Can it be more mean and abject? If there are any changes will they not be for the better, though they may appear for the worst at first? Can they get us any lower? Where can they get us? They are afraid to treat us worse, for they know well, the day they do it they are gone. But against all accusations which may or can be preferred against me, I appeal to Heaven for my motive in writing—who knows that my object is, if possible, to awaken in the breasts of my afflicted, degraded and slumbering brethren, a spirit of inquiry and investigation respecting our miseries and wretchedness in this REPUBLICAN LAND OF LIBERTY!!!!!!

The sources from which our miseries are derived, and on which I shall comment, I shall not combine in one, but shall put them under distinct heads and expose them in their turn; in doing which, keeping truth on my side and not departing from the strictest rules of morality, I shall endeavour to penetrate, search out, and lay them open for your inspection. If you cannot or will not profit by them, I shall have done *my* duty to you, my country and my God.

And as the inhuman system of *slavery,* is the *source* from which most of our miseries proceed, I shall begin with that *curse to nations,* which has spread terror and devastation through so many nations of antiquity, and which is raging to such a pitch at present day in Spain and in Portugal. It had one tug in England, in France, and in the United States of America; yet the inhabitants therof, do not learn wisdom, and erase it entirely from their dwellings and from all with whom they have to do. The fact is, the labour of slaves comes too cheap to the avaricious usurpers, and is (as they think) of such great utility to the country where it exists, that those who are actuated by sordid avarice only, overlook the evils, which will as sure as the Lord lives, follow after the good. In fact, they are so happy to keep in ignorance and degradation, and to receive the homage and the labour of the slaves, they forget that God rules in the armies of heaven and among the inhabitants of the earth, having his ears continually open to the cries, tears and groans of his oppressed people; and being a just and holy Being will at one day appear fully in behalf of the oppressed, and arrest the progress of the avaricious oppressors; for although the destruction of the oppressors God may not effect by the oppressed, yet the Lord our God will bring other destructions upon them—for not unfrequently will he cause them to rise up one against another, to be split and divided, and to oppress each other, and sometimes to open hostilities with sword in hand.

Some may ask, what is the matter with this united and happy people?—Some say it is the curse of political usurpers, tyrants, oppressors, &c. But has not the Lord an oppressed and suffering people among them? Does the Lord condescend to hear their cries and see their tears in consequence of oppression? Will he let the oppressors rest comfortably and happy always? Will he not cause the very children of the oppressors to rise up against them, and oft times put them to death? "God works in many ways his wonders to perform."

I will not here speak of the destructions which the Lord brought upon Egypt, in consequence of the oppression and consequent groans of the oppressed—of the hundreds and thousands of Egyptians whom God hurled into the Red Sea for afflicting his people in their land—of the Lord's suffering people in Sparta or Lacedemon, the land of the truly famous Lycurgus—nor have I time to comment upon the cause which produced the fierceness with which Sylla usurped the title, and absolutely acted as dictator of the Roman people—the conspiracy of Cataline—the conspiracy against, and murder of Caesar in the Senate house—the spirit with which Marc Antony made himself master of the commonwealth—his associating Octavios and Lipidus with himself in power—their dividing the provinces of Rome among themselves—their attack and defeat, on the plains of Phillippi, of the last defenders of their liberty, (Brutus and Cassius)—the tyranny of Tiberius, and from him to the final overthrow of Constantinople by the Turkish Sultan, Mahomed II. A.D. 1453.

I say, I shall not take up time to speak for the *causes* which produced so much wretchedness and massacre among those heathen nations, for I am aware that you know too well, that God is just, as well as merciful!—I shall call your attention a few moments to that *Christian* nation, the Spaniards—while I shall leave almost unnoticed, that avaricious and cruel people, the Portuguese, among whom all true hearted Christians and lovers of Jesus Christ, must evidently see the judgments of God displayed. To show the judgments of God upon the Spaniards, I shall occupy but a little time, leaving a plenty of room for the candid and unprejudiced to reflect.

All persons who are acquainted with history, and particularly the Bible, who are not blinded by the God of this world, and are not actuated solely by avarice—who are able to lay aside prejudice long enough to view candidly and impartially, things as they were, are, and probably will be—who are willing to admit that God made man to serve Him *alone,* and that man should have no other Lord or Lords but Himself—that God Almighty is the *sole proprietor* or *master* of the WHOLE human family, and will not on any consideration admit of a colleague, being unwilling to divide his glory with another—and who can dispense with prejudice long enough to admit that we are *men,* notwithstanding our *improminent noses* and *woolly heads,* and believe that we feel for our fathers, mothers, wives and children, as well as the whites do their theirs.—I say, all who are permitted to see and believe these things, can easily recognize the judgments of God among the Spaniards. Though others may lay the cause of the fierceness with which they cut each other's throats, to some other circumstances, yet they who believe that God is a God of justice, will believe that SLAVERY *is the principal cause.*

While the Spaniards are running about upon the field of battle cutting each other's throats, has not the Lord an afflicted and suffering people in the midst of them, whose cries and groans in consequence of oppression are continually pouring into the ears of the God of justice? Would they not cease to cut each other's throats, if they could? But how can they? The very support which they draw from government to aid them in perpetrating such enormities, does it not arise in a great degree from the wretched victims of oppression among them? And yet they are calling for PEACE!—PEACE!! Will any peace be given unto them? Their destruction may indeed be procrastinated a while, but can it continue long, while they are oppressing the Lord's people? Has He not the hearts of all men in His hand? Will he suffer one part of his creatures to go on oppressing another like brutes always, with impunity? And yet, those avaricious wretches are calling for PEACE!!!! I declare, it does appear to me, as though some nations think God is asleep, or that he made the Africans for nothing else but to dig their mines and work their farms, or they cannot believe history, sacred or profane.

I ask every man who has a heart, and is blessed, with the privilege of believing—Is not God a God of justice to *all* his creatures? Do you say he is? Then if he gives peace and tranquillity to tyrants, and permits them to keep our fathers, our mothers, ourselves and our children in eternal ignorance and degradation, that ever a people were afflicted with since the world began—I say, if God gives you peace and tranquillity, and suffers you thus to go on afflicting us, and our children, who have never given you the least provocation—would he be to us *a God of justice?* If you will allow that we are MEN, who feel for each other, does not the blood of our fathers and of us their children, cry aloud to the Lord of Sabaoth against you, for the cruelties and murders with which you have, and do continue to afflict us. But it is time for me to close my remarks on the suburbs, just to enter more fully into the interior of this system of cruelty and oppression.

[*FROM* ARTICLE II]
OUR WRETCHEDNESS IN CONSEQUENCE OF IGNORANCE.

Ignorance, my brethren, is a mist, low down into the very dark and almost impenetrable abyss in which, our fathers for many centuries have been plunged. The Christians and enlightend of Europe, and some of Asia, seeing the ignorance and consequent degradation of our fathers, instead of trying to enlighten them, by teaching them that religion and light with which God had blessed them, they have plunged them into wretchedness ten thousand times more intolerable, than if they had left them entirely to the Lord, and to add to their miseries, deep down into which they have plunged them tell them, that they are an *inferior* and *distinct race* of beings, which they will be glad enough to recall and swallow by and by. Fortune and misfortune, two inseparable companions, lay rolled up in the wheel of events, which have from the creation of the world, and will continue to take place among men until God shall dash worlds together.

When we take a retrospective view of the arts and sciences—the wise legislators—the Pyramids, and other magnificent buildings—the turning of the channel of the river Nile, by the sons of Africa or of Ham, among whom learning originated, and was carried thence into Greece, where it was improved upon and refined. Thence among the Romans, and all over the then enlightened parts of the world, and it has been enlightening the dark and benighted minds of men from then, down to this day. I say, when I view retrospectively, the renown of that once mighty people, the children of our great progenitor I am indeed cheered. Yea further, when I view that mighty son of Africa, HANNIBAL, one of the greatest generals of antiquity, who defeated and cut off so many thousands of the white Romans or murderers, and who carried his victorious arms, to the very gate of Rome, and I give it as my candid opinion, that had Carthage been well united and had given him good support, he would have carried that cruel and barbarous city by storm. But they were dis-united, as the coloured people are now, in the United States of America, the reason our natural enemies are enabled to keep their feet on our throats.

Beloved brethren—here let me tell you, and believe it, that the Lord our God, as true as he sits on his throne in heaven, and as true as our Saviour died to redeem the world, will give you a Hannibal, and when the Lord shall have raised him up, and given him to you for your possession, O my suffering brethren! remember the divisions and consequent sufferings of *Carthage* and of *Hayti.* Read the history particularly of Hayti, and see how they were butchered by the whites, and do you take warning. The person whom God shall give you, give him your support and let him go his length, and behold in him the salvation of your God. God will indeed, deliver you through him from your deplorable and wretched condition under the Christians of America. I charge you this day before my God to lay no obstacle in his way, but let him go.

The whites want slaves and want us for their slaves, but some of them will curse the day they ever saw us. As true as the sun ever shone in its meridian splendor, my colour will root some of them out of the very face of the earth. They shall have enough of making slaves of, and butchering, and murdering us in the maner which they have. No doubt some may say that I write with a bad spirit, and that I being a black, wish these things to occur. Whether I write with a bad or a good spirit, I say if these things do not occur in their proper time, it is because of the world in which we live does not exist, and we are deceived with regard to its existence—It is immaterial however to me, who believe or who refuse—though I should like to see the whites repent peradventure God may have mercy on them, some however, have gone so far that their cup must be filled. . . .

[I]f you can only get courage into the blacks, I do declare it, that one good black man can put to death six white men; and I give it as a fact, let twelve black men get well armed for battle, and they will kill and put to flight fifty white.—The reason is the blacks, once you get them started, they glory in death. The whites have had us under them for more than three centuries, murdering, and treating us like brutes; and, as Mr. [Thomas] Jefferson wisely said, they have never *found us out*–they do not know, indeed, that there is an unconquerable disposition in the breasts of the blacks, which, when it is fully awakened and put in motion, will be subdued, only with the destruction of the animal existence. Get the blacks started, and if you do not have a gang of tigers and lions to deal with, I am a deceiver of the blacks and of the whites. . . . If you commence, make sure work—do not trifle, for they will not trifle with you—they want us for their slaves, and think nothing of murdering us in order to subject us to that wretched condition—therefore, if there is an *attempt* made by us, kill or be killed. Now, I ask you, had you not rather be killed than to be a slave to a tyrant, who takes the life of your mother, wife, and dear little children? Look upon your mother, wife and children, and answer God Almighty! and believe this, that it is no more harm for you to kill a man, who is trying to kill you, than it is for you to take a drink of water when thirsty; in fact, the man who will stand still and let another murder him, is worse than an infidel, and, if he has common sense, ought not to be pitied. . . .

Oh! coloured people of these United States, I ask you, in the name of that God who made us, have we, in consequence of oppression, nearly lost the spirit of man, and, in no very trifling degree, adopted that of brutes? Do you answer, no?—I ask you, then, what set of men can you point me to, in all the world, who are so abjectly employed by their oppressors, as we are by our *natural enemies?*

[*FROM* ARTICLE IV] OUR WRETCHEDNESS IN CONSEQUENCE OF THE COLONIZING PLAN.

. . . I have several times called the white Americans our *natural enemies.*—I shall here define my meaning of the phrase. Shem, Ham and Japheth, together with their father Noah and wives, I believe were not natural enemies to each other. When the ark rested after the flood upon Mount Arrarat, in Asia, they (eight) were all the people which could be found alive in all the earth—in fact if Scriptures be true, (which I believe they are) there were no other living men in all the earth, notwithstanding some ignorant creatures hesitate not to tell us that we, (the blacks) are the seed of Cain the murderer of his brother Abel.

But where or of whom those ignorant and avaricious wretches could have got their information, I am unable to declare. Did they receive it from the Bible? I have searched the Bible as well as they, if I am not as well learned as they are, and have never seen a verse which testifies whether we are the seed of Cain or of Abel. Yet those men tell us that we are the seed of Cain, and that God put a dark stain upon us, that we might be known as their slaves!!! Now, I ask those avaricious and ignorant wretches, who act more like the seed of Cain, by murdering the whites or the blacks? How many vessel loads of human beings have the blacks thrown into the seas? How many thousand souls have the blacks murdered in cold blood, to make them work in wretchedness and ignorance, to support them and their families?*

However, let us be the seed of *Cain, Harry, Dick,* or *Tom!!!* God will show the whites what we are, yet. I say, from the beginning, I do not think that we were natural enemies to each other. By the whites having made us so wretched, by subjecting us to slavery, and having murdered so many millions of us, in order to make us work for them, and out of devilishness—and they taking our wives, whom we love as we do ourselves—our mothers, who bore the pains of death to give us birth—our fathers and dear little children, and ourselves, and strip and beat us one before the other—chain, hand-cuff, and drag us about like rattle-snakes—shoot us down like wild bears, before each other's faces, to make us submissive to, and work to support them and their families. They (the whites) know well, if we are *men*—and there is a secret

* How many millions souls of the human family have the blacks beat nearly to death, to keep them from learning to read the Word of God, and from writing. And telling lies about them, by holding them up to the world as a tribe of TALKING APES, void of INTELLECT!!! *incapable* of LEARNING, &c.

monitor in their hearts which tells them we are—they know, I say, if we *are* men, and see them treating us in the manner they do, that there cn be nothing in our hearts but death alone, for them, notwithstanding we may appear cheerful, when we see them murdering our dear mothers and wives, because we cannot help ourselves.

Man, in all ages and all nations of the earth, is the same. Man is a peculiar creature—he is the image of his God, though he may be subjected to the most wretched condition upon earth, yet the spirit and feeling which constitute the creature, man, can never be entirely erased from his breast, because God who made him after his own image, planted it in his heart; he cannot get rid of it. The whites knowing this, they do not know what to do; they know they have done us so much injury, they are afraid that we, being men, and not brutes, will retaliate, and woe will be to them; therefore the dreadful fear, together with an avaricious spirit, and the natural love in them, to be called masters, (which term will yet honour them with to their sorrow) bring them to the resolve that they will keep us in ignorance and wretchedness, as long as they possibly can,* and make the best of their time, while it lasts. Consequently they, themselves, (and not us) render themselves our natural enemies by treating us so cruel.

They keep us miserable now, and call us their property, but some of them will have enough of us by and by—their stomachs shall run over with us; they want us for their slaves, and shall have us to their fil. (We are all in the world together!!—I said above, because we cannot help ourselves, (viz. we cannot help the whites murdering our mothers and our wives) but this statement is incorrect—for we can help ourslves; for, if we lay aside abject servility, and be determined to act like men, and not brutes—the murderers among the whites would be afraid to show their cruel heads. But O, my God! in sorrow I must say it, that my colour, all over the world have a mean, servile spirit. They yield in a moment to the whites, let them be right or wrong—the reason they are able to keep their feet on our throats. Oh! my coloured brethren, all over the world, when shall we arise from this death-like apathy?—And be men!! You will notice, if ever we become men, (I mean *respectable* men, such as other people are,) we must exert ourselves to the full. . . .

I acknowledge that there are some deceitful and hypocritical wretches

* And still hold us up with indignity as being incapable of acquiring knowledge!!!! See the inconsistency of the assertions of those wretches—they beat us inhumanely, sometimes almost to death, for attempting to inform ourselves, by reading the *Word* of our Maker, and at the same time tell us that we are beings *void of intellect!!!* How admirably their practices agree with their professions in this case. Let me cry shame upon you Americans, for such outrages upon human nature!!! If it were possible for the whites always to keep us ignorant and miserable, and make us work to enrich them and their children, and insult our feelings by representing us as *talking Apes,* what would they do? But glory, honour and praise to Heaven's King, that the sons and daughters of Africa, will, in spite of all the opposition of their enemies, stand forth in all the dignity and glory that is granted by the Lord to his creature man.

among us, who will tell us one thing while they mean another, and thus they go on aiding our enemies to oppress themselves and us. But I declare this day before my Lord and Master, that I believe there are some true-hearted sons of Africa, in this land of oppression, but pretended *liberty!!!!!*—who do in reality feel for their suffering brethren, who are held in bondage by tyrants. Some of the advocates of this cunningly devised plot of Satan represent us to be the greatest set of cut-throats in the world, as though God wants us to take his work out of his hand before he is ready. Does not vengeance belong to the Lord? Is he not able to repay the Americans for their cruelties, with which they have afflicted Africa's sons and daughters, without our interference, unless we are ordered?

It is surprising to think that the Americans, having the Bible in their hands, do not believe it. Are not the hearts of all men in the hands of the God of battles? And does he not suffer some, in consequence of cruelties, to go on until they are irrecoverably lost? Now, what can be more aggravating, than for the Americans, after having treated us so bad, to hold us up to the world as such great throat-cutters? It appears to me as though they are resolved to assail us with every species of affliction that their ingenuity can invent. See the African Repository and Colonial Journal, from its commencement to the present day—see how we are through the medium of that periodical, abused and held up by the Americans, as the greatest nuisance to society, and throat-cutters in the world. But the Lord sees their actions.

Americans! notwithstanding you have and do continue to treat us more cruel than any heathen nation ever did a people it had subjected to the same condition that you have us. Now let us reason—I mean you of the United States, whom I believe God designs to save from destruction, if you will hear. For I declare to you, whether you believe it or not, that there are some on the continent of America, who will never be able to repent. God will surely destroy them, to show you his disapprobation of the murders they and you have inflicted on us. I say, let us reason; had you not better take our body, while you have it in your power, and while we are yet ignorant and wretched, not knowing but a little, give us education, and teach us the pure religion of our Lord and Master, which is calculated to make the lion lay down in peace with the lamb, and which millions of you have beaten us nearly to death for trying to obtain since we have been among you, and thus at once, gain our affection while we are ignorant? Remember Americans, that we must and shall be free and enlightened as you are, will you wait until we shall, under God, obtain our liberty by the crushing arm of power? Will it not be dreadful for you? I speak Americans for your good. We must and shall be free I say, in spite of you. You may do your best to keep us in wretchedness and misery, to enrich you and your children, but God will deliver us from under you. And wo, wo, will be to you if we have to obtain our freedom by fighting. Throw away your fears and prejudices then, and enlighten us and treat us like men, and we will like you more than we do now hate you,* and tell us now no more about colonization, for America is as much our country, as it is yours.—

Treat us like men, and there is no danger but we will all live in peace and happiness together. For we are not like you, hard hearted, unmerciful, and unforgiving. What a happy country this will be, if the whites will listen. What nation under heaven, will be able to do any thing with us, unless God gives us up into his hand? But Americans, I declare to you, while you keep us and our children in bondage, and treat us like brutes, to make us support you and your families, we cannot be your friends. You do not look for it, do you? Treat us then like men, and we will be your friends. And there is not a doubt in my mind, but that the whole of the past will be sunk into oblivion, and we yet, under God, will become a united and happy people. The whites may say it is impossible, but remember that nothing is impossible with God. . . .

If any are anxious to ascertain who I am, know the world, that I am one of the oppressed, degraded and wretched sons of Africa, rendered so by the avaricious and unmerciful among the whites.—If any wish to plunge me into the wretched incapacity of a slave, or murder me for the truth, know ye, that I am in the hand of God, and at your disposal. I count my life not dear unto me, but I am ready to be offered at any moment. For what is the use of living, when in fact I am dead. But remember, Americans, that as miserable, wretched, degraded and abject as you have made us in preceding, and in this generation, to support you and your families, that some of you, (whites) on the continent of America, will yet curse the day that you ever were born. You want slaves, and want us for your slaves!!! My colour will yet, root some of you out of the very face of the earth!!!!!! . . . The Americans may be as vigilant as they please, but they cannot be vigilant enough for the Lord, neither can they hide themselves, where he will not find and bring them out.

1829

* You are not astonished at my saying we hate you, for if we are men, we cannot but hate you, while you are treating us like dogs.

Nat Turner
(1800–1831)

The most notorious slave revolt in American history broke out in Southampton County, Virginia, on August 21, 1831. As the growing band of rebels went from house to house during the next forty-eight hours, sparing "neither age nor sex," about sixty whites were killed, while in its aftermath, more than 120 blacks, most of whom had played no role in the revolt, died.

Turner was born into slavery on the farm of Benjamin Turner in Southampton County on October 2, 1800. His father had escaped from slavery, and Turner was raised by his mother and grandmother, who encouraged his strong visionary streak, his feeling that he was "intended for some great purpose." He displayed a natural precosity and ascetic temperament, but most startling were his messianic religious visions, in which he saw black and white spirits engaged in conflict. Turner was later sold to Putnam Moore, and upon Moore's death, his widow married Joseph Travis in 1830.

Turner plotted the revolt for six months, informing four others of his plan. On the day it was to begin, the rebels gathered in the woods for a barbecue, remaining there eleven hours before beginning their raid at the Travis farm. As the revolt progressed, slaves from the victimized households joined the swiftly moving party in the work of death. The band was finally stopped on its way to Jerusalem, the county seat, for ammunition and support. Thirteen slaves and three free blacks were hanged immediately. Hiding out in the woods, Turner was not captured until two months later, on October 30, less than five miles from where the raid had begun.

Turner made his famous "confession" to Thomas R. Gray, his assigned counsel, who published the account in Baltimore in 1831. Hostile to the rebel, Gray made no argument in his client's defense, nor were any witnesses called. Turner was hanged on November 11, 1831. His corpse was skinned and his flesh was used for grease.

Turner's revolt resulted in harsh measures throughout the South.

Many innocent blacks were killed, greater control was exerted over slaves, and new statutes were imposed to limit the movement and even to evict free blacks. At the same time, the bloodshed galvanized blacks and abolitionists and heightened the tension between the free North and the slave-holding South.

from *The Confessions of Nat Turner*

"I am here loaded with chains, and willing to suffer the fate that awaits me."

SIR,—YOU HAVE ASKED ME TO GIVE A HISTORY OF THE motives which induced me to undertake the late insurrection, as you call it—To do so I must go back to the days of my infancy, and even before I was born. I was thirty-one years of age the second of October last, and born the property of Benjamin Turner, of this county. In my childhood a circumstance occurred which made an indelible impression on my mind, and laid the groundwork of that enthusiasm which has terminated so fatally to many, both white and black, and for which I am about to atone at the gallows. It is here necessary to relate this circumstance. Trifling as it may seem, it was the commencement of that belief which has grown with time, and even now, sir, in this dungeon, helpless and forsaken as I am, I cannot divest myself of. Being at play with other children, when three or four years old, I was telling them something, which my mother, overhearing, said it had happened before I was born. I stuck to my story, however, and related some things which went, in her opinion, to confirm it. Others being called on, were greatly astonished, knowing that these things had happened, and caused them to say, in my hearing, I surely would be a prophet, as the Lord had shown me things that had happened before my birth. And my mother and grandmother strengthened me in this my first impression, saying, in my presence, I was intended for some great purpose, which they had always thought from certain marks on my head and breast.

My grandmother, who was very religious, and to whom I was much attached—my master, who belonged to the church, and other religious persons who visited the house, and whom I often saw at prayers, noticing the singularity of my manners, I suppose, and my uncommon intelligence for a child, remarked I had too much sense to be raised, and, if I was, I would never be of any service to any one as a slave. To a mind like mine, restless, inquisitive, and observant of everything that was passing, it is easy to suppose that religion was the subject to which it would be directed; and, although this subject principally occupied my thoughts, there was nothing that I saw or heard of to which my attention was not directed. The manner in which I learned to read and write, not only had great influence on my own mind, as I acquired it with the most perfect ease,—so much so, that I have no recollection whatever of learning the alphabet—but, to the astonishment of the family, one day, when a book was shown me, to keep me from crying, I began spelling the names of different objects. This was a source of wonder to all in the neighborhood, particularly the blacks—and this learning was constantly improved at all opportunities. When I got large enough to go to work, while employed, I was reflecting on many things that would present themselves to my imagination, and whenever an opportunity occurred of looking at a book, when the school-children were getting their lessons, I would find many things that the fertility of my own imagination had depicted to me before. All my time, not devoted to my master's service, was spent either in prayer, or in making experiments in casting different things in moulds made of earth, in attempting to make paper, gunpowder, and many other experiments, that, although I could not perfect, yet convinced me of its practicability if I had the means.*

I was not addicted to stealing in my youth, nor have ever been; yet such was the confidence of the Negroes in the neighborhood, even at this early period of my life, in my superior judgment, that they would often carry me with them when they were going on any roguery, to plan for them. Growing up among them with this confidence in my superior judgment, and when this, in their opinions, was perfected by Divine inspiration, from the circumstances already alluded to in my infancy, and which belief was ever afterwards zealously inculcated by the austerity of my life and manners, which became the subject of remark by white and black; having soon discovered to be great, I must appear so, and therefore studiously avoided mixing in society, and wrapped myself in mystery, devoting my time to fasting and prayer.

By this time, having arrived to man's estate, and hearing the Scriptures commented on at meetings, I was struck with that particular passage which says, "Seek ye the kingdom of heaven, and all things shall be added unto you." I reflected much on this passage, and prayed daily for light on this subject. As I was praying one day at my plough, the Spirit spoke to me, saying, "Seek ye the kingdom of heaven, and all things shall be added unto you."

Question. What do you mean by the Spirit?

Answer. The Spirit that spoke to the prophets in former days,—and I was greatly astonished, and for two years prayed continually, whenever my duty would permit; and then again I had the same revelation, which fully confirmed me in the impression that I was ordained for some great purpose in the hands of the Almighty. Several years rolled round, in which many events occurred to strengthen me in this my belief. At this time I reverted in my mind to the remarks made of me in my childhood, and the things that had been shown me; and as it had been said of me in my childhood, by those by whom I had been taught to pray, both white and black, and in whom I had the greatest confidence, that I had too much sense to be raised, and if I

* When questioned as to the manner of manufacturing those different articles, he was found well informed on the subject.

was I would never be of any use to any one as a slave; now, finding I had arrived at man's estate, and was a slave, and these revelations being made known to me, I began to direct my attention to this great object, to fulfil the purpose for which, by this time, I felt assured I was intended. Knowing the influence I had obtained over the minds of my fellow-servants—(not by the means of conjuring and such-like tricks—for to them I always spoke of such things with contempt), but by the communion of the Spirit, whose revelations I often communicated to them, and they believed and said my wisdom came from God,—I now began to prepare them for my purpose, by telling them something was about to happen that would terminate in fulfilling the great promise that had been made to me.

About this time I was placed under an overseer, from whom I ran away, and after remaining in the woods thirty days, I returned, to the astonishment of the Negroes on the plantation, who thought I had made my escape to some other part of the country, as my father had done before. But the reason of my return was, that the Spirit appeared to me and said I had my wishes directed to the things of this world, and not to the kingdom of heaven, and that I should return to the service of my earthly master—"For he who knoweth his Master's will, and doeth it not, shall be beaten with many stripes, and thus have I chastened you." And the Negroes found fault, and murmured against me, saying that if they had my sense they would not serve any master in the world. And about this time I had a vision—and I saw white spirits and black spirits engaged in battle, and the sun was darkened—the thunder rolled in the heavens, and blood flowed in streams—and I heard a voice saying, "Such is your luck, such you are called to see; and let it come rough or smooth, you must surely bear it."

I now withdrew myself as much as my situation would permit from the intercourse of my fellow-servants, for the avowed purpose of serving the Spirit more fully; and it appeared to me, and reminded me of the things it had already shown me, and that it would then reveal to me the knowledge of the elements, the revolution of the planets, the operation of tides, and changes of the seasons. After this revelation in the year 1825, and the knowledge of the elements being made known to me, I sought more than ever to obtain true holiness before the great day of judgment should appear, and then I began to receive the true knowledge of faith. And from the first steps of righteousness until the last, was I made perfect; and the Holy Ghost was with me, and said, "Behold me as I stand in the heavens." And I looked and saw the forms of men in different attitudes; and there were lights in the sky, to which the children of darkness gave other names than what they really were; for they were the lights of the Saviour's hands, stretched forth from east to west, even as they were extended on the cross on Calvary for the redemption of sinners. And I wondered greatly at these miracles, and prayed to be informed of a certainty of the meaning thereof; and shortly afterwards, while laboring in the field, I discovered drops of blood on the corn, as though it were dew from heaven; and I communicated it to many, both white and black, in the neighborhood—and I then found on the leaves in the woods hieroglyphic characters and numbers, with the forms of men in different attitudes, portrayed in blood, and representing the figures I had seen before in the heavens. And now the Holy Ghost had revealed itself to me, and made plain the miracles it had shown me; for as the blood of Christ had been shed on this earth, and had ascended to heaven for the salvation of sinners, and was now returning to earth again in the form of dew,—and as the leaves on the trees bore the impression of the figures I had seen in the heavens,—it was plain to me that the Saviour was about to lay down the yoke he had borne for the sins of men, and the great day of judgment was at hand.

About this time I told these things to a white man (Etheldred T. Brantley), on whom it had a wonderful effect; and he ceased from his wickedness, and was attacked immediately with a cutaneous eruption, and blood oozed from the pores of his skin, and after praying and fasting nine days he was healed. And the Spirit appeared to me again, and said, as the Saviour had been baptized, so should we be also; and when the white people would not let us be baptized by the church, we went down into the water together, in the sight of many who reviled us, and were baptized by the Spirit. After this I rejoiced greatly, and gave thanks to God. And on the 12th of May, 1828, I heard a loud noise in the heavens, and the Spirit instantly appeared to me and said the Serpent was loosened, and Christ had laid down the yoke he had borne for the sins of men, and that I should take it on and fight against the Serpent, for the time was fast approaching when the first should be last and the last should be first.

Ques. Do you not find yourself mistaken now?

Ans. Was not Christ crucified? And by signs in the heavens that it would make known to me when I should commence the great work, and until the first sign appeared I should conceal it from the knowledge of men; and on the appearance of the sign (the eclipse of the sun, last February), I should arise and prepare myself, and slay my enemies with their own weapons. And immediately on the sign appearing in the heavens, the seal was removed from my lips, and I communicated the great work laid out for me to do, to four in whom I had the greatest confidence (Henry, Hark, Nelson, and Sam). It was intended by us to have begun the work of death on the 4th of July last. Many were the plans formed and rejected by us, and it affected my mind to such a degree that I fell sick, and the time passed without our coming to any determination how to commence—still forming new schemes and rejecting them, when the sign appeared again, which determined me not to wait longer.

Since the commencement of 1830 I had been living with Mr. Joseph

Travis, who was to me a kind master, and placed the greatest confidence in me; in fact, I had no cause to complain of his treatment to me. On Saturday evening, the 20th of August, it was agreed between Henry, Hark, and myself, to prepare a dinner the next day for the men we expected, and then to concert a plan, as we had not yet determined on any. Hark, on the following morning, brought a pig, and Henry brandy; and being joined by Sam, Nelson, Will, and Jack, they prepared in the woods a dinner, where, about three o'clock, I joined them.

Q. Why were you so backward in joining them?

A. The same reason that has caused me not to mix with them years before, I saluted them on coming up, and asked Will how came he there. He answered, his life was worth no more than others, and his liberty as dear to him. I asked him if he thought to obtain it. He said he would, or lose his life. This was enough to put him in full confidence. Jack, I knew, was only a tool in the hands of Hark. It was quickly agreed we should commence at home (Mr. J. Travis') on that night; and until we had armed and equipped ourselves, and gathered sufficient force, neither age nor sex was to be spared—which was invariably adhered to. We remained at the feast until about two hours in the night, when we went to the house and found Austin. They all went to the cider press and drank, except myself.

On returning to the house, Hark went to the door with an axe, for the purpose of breaking it open, as we knew we were strong enough to murder the family, if they were awaked by the noise; but reflecting that it might create an alarm in the neighborhood, we determined to enter the house secretly, and murder them whilst sleeping. Hark got a ladder and set it against the chimney, on which I ascended, and hoisting a window, entered and came down stairs, unbarred the door, and removed the guns from their places. It was then observed that I must spill the first blood. On which, armed with a hatchet, and accompanied by Will, I entered my master's chamber, it being dark, I could not give a death blow, the hatchet glanced from his head. He sprang from the bed and called his wife. It was his last word. Will laid him dead, with a blow of his axe, and Mrs. Travis shared the same fate, as she lay in bed. The murder of this family, five in number, was the work of a moment, not one of them awoke; there was a little infant sleeping in a cradle, that was forgotten, until we had left the house and gone some distance, when Henry and Will returned and killed it; we got here, four guns that would shoot, and several old muskets, with a pound or two of powder.

We remained some time at the barn, where we paraded. I formed them in a line as soldiers, and after carrying them through all the manoeuvers I was master of marched them off to Mr. Salathiel Francis', about six hundred yards distant. Sam and Will went to the door and knocked. Mr. Francis asked who was there. Sam replied it was him, and he had a letter for him, on which he got up and came to the door. They immediately seized him, and dragging him out a little from the door, he was dispatched by repeated blows on the head; there was no other white person in the family.

We started from there for Mrs. Reese's, maintaining the most perfect silence on our march, where finding the door unlocked, we entered, and murdered Mrs. Reese in her bed, while sleeping. Her son awoke, but it was only to sleep the sleep of death, he had only time to say who is that, and he was no more. From Mrs. Reese's we went to Mrs. Turner's, a mile distant, which we reached about sunrise, on Monday morning. Henry, Austin, and Sam, went to the still, where, finding Mr. Peebles, Austin shot him, and the rest of the family discovered us, and shut the door. Vain hope! Will, with one stroke of his axe, opened it, and we entered and found Mrs. Turner and Mrs. Newsome in the middle of a room, almost frightened to death. Will immediately killed Mrs. Turner, with one blow of his axe. I took Mrs. Newsome by the hand, and with the sword I had when I was apprehended, I struck her several blows over the head, but not being able to kill her, as the sword was dull. Will turning around and discovering it, despatched her also.

A general destruction of property and search for money and ammunition, always succeeded the murders. By this time my company amounted to fifteen, and nine men mounted, who started for Mrs. Whitehead's, (the other six were to go through a by way to Mr. Bryant's, and rejoin us at Mrs. Whitehead's). As we approached the house we discovered Mr. Richard Whitehead standing in the cotton patch, near the lance fence. We called him over into the lane, and Will, the executioner, was near at hand, with his fatal axe, to send him to an untimely grave. As we pushed on to the house, I discovered some one run round the garden, and thinking it was some of the white family, I pursued them, but finding it was a servant girl belonging to the house, I returned to commence the work of death, but they whom I left, had not been idle. All the family were already murdered, but Mrs. Whitehead and her daughter Margaret. As I came round to the door I saw Will pulling Mrs. Whitehead out of the house, and at the step he nearly severed her head from her body, with his broad axe. Miss Margaret, when I discovered her, had concealed herself in the corner, formed by the projection of cellar cap from the house. On my approach she fled, but was soon overtaken, and after repeated blows with a sword, I killed her by a blow on the head, with a fence rail. By this time, the six who had gone by Mr. Bryant's, rejoined us, and informed me they had done the work of death assigned them.

We again divided, part going to Mr. Richard Porter's, and from thence to Nathaniel Francis', the others to Mr. Howell Harris', and Mr. T. Doyle's. On my reaching Mr. Porter's, he had escaped with his family. I understood there, that the alarm had already spread, and I immediately returned to bring up those sent to Mr. Doyle's, and Mr. Howell Harris'; the party I left going on to Mr. Francis', having told them I would join them in that neighborhood. I met these sent to Mr. Doyle's and Mr. Harris' returning, having met Mr. Doyle on the road and killed him; and learning from some who joined them, pursued the course taken by the party gone on before. But knowing they would complete the work of death and pillage, at Mr. Francis' before I could get there, I went to Mr. Peter Edwards', expecting to find them there, but they had been here also. I then went to Mr. John T. Barrow's, they had been here and murdered him. I pursued on their track to Capt. Newit Harris', where I found the greater part mounted, and ready to start. The men now amounting to about forty, shouted and hurraed as I rode up, some were in the yard, loading their guns, others drinking. They said Captain Harris and his family had escaped, the property in the house they destroyed, robbing him of money and other valuables. I ordered them to mount and march instantly, this was about nine or ten o'clock, Monday morning. I proceeded to Mr. Levi Waller's two or three miles distant.

I took my station in the rear, and, as it was my object to carry terror and devastation wherever we went, I placed fifteen or twenty of the best armed and most to be relied on in front, who generally approached the houses as fast as their horses could run. This was for two purposes—to prevent their escape, and strike terror to the inhabitants; on this account I never got to the houses, after leaving Mrs. Whitehead's, until the murders were committed, except in one case. I sometimes got in sight in time to see the work of death completed; viewed the mangled bodies as they lay, in silent satisfaction, and immediately started in quest of other victims. Having murdered Mrs. Waller and ten children, we started from Mr. William Williams', —having killed him and two little boys that were there; while engaged in this, Mrs. Williams fled and got some distance from the house, but she was pursued, overtaken, and compelled to get up behind one of the company, who brought her back, and, after showing her the mangled body of her lifeless husband, she was told to get down and lay by his side, where she was shot dead.

I then started for Mr. Jacob Williams, where the family were murdered. Here we found a young man named Drury, who had come on business with Mr. Williams. He was pursued, overtaken and shot. Mrs. Vaughan was the next place we visited—and after murdering the family here, I determined on starting for Jerusalem. Our number amounted now to fifty or sixty, all mounted and armed with guns, axes, swords and clubs. On reaching Mr. James W. Parker's gate, immediately on the road leading to Jerusalem, and about three miles distant, it was proposed to me to call there, but I objected, as I knew he was gone to Jerusalem, and my object was to reach there as soon as possible. But some of the men having relations at Mr. Parker's it was agreed that they might call and get his people. I remained at the gate on the road, with seven or eight; the others going across the field to the house, about half a mile off. After waiting some time for them, I became impatient, and started to the house for them, and on our return we were met by a party of white men, who had pursued our blood-stained track, and who had fired on those at the gate, and dispersed them, which I knew nothing of, not having been at that time rejoined by any of them.

Immediately on discovering the whites, I ordered my men to halt and form, as they appeared to be alarmed. The white men, eighteen in number, approached us in about one hundred yards, when one of them fired, (this was against the positive orders of Captain Alexander P. Peete, who commanded, and who had directed the men to reserve their fire until within thirty paces). And I discovered about half of them retreating, I then ordered my men to fire and rush on them; the few remaining stood their ground until we approached within fifty yards, when they fired and retreated. We pursued and overtook some of them who we thought we left dead; (they were not killed) after pursuing them about two hundred yards, and rising a little hill, I discovered they were met by another party, and had halted, and were reloading their guns, (this was a small party from Jerusalem who knew the negroes were in the field, and had just tied their horses to await their return to the road, knowing that Mr. Parker and family were in Jerusalem, but knew nothing of the party that had gone in with Captain Peete; on hearing the firing they immediately rushed to the spot and arrived just in time to arrest the progress of these barbarous villains, and save the lives of their friends and fellow citizens). Thinking that those who retreated first, and the party who fired on us at fifty or sixty yards distant, had all fallen back to meet others with ammunition. As I saw them reloading their guns, and more coming up than I saw at first, and several of my bravest men being wounded, the others became panic-struck and squandered over the field.

The white men pursued and fired on us several times. Hark had his horse shot under him, and I caught another for him as it was running by me; five or six of my men were wounded, but none left on the field. Finding myself defeated here, I instantly determined to go through a private way, and cross the Nottoway River at the Cypress Bridge, three miles below Jerusalem, and attack that place in the rear, as I expected they would look for me on the other road, and I had a great desire to get there to procure arms and ammunition. After going a short distance in this private way, accompanied by about twenty men, I overtook two of them, who told me the others were dispersed in every direction.

After trying in vain to collect a sufficient force to proceed to Jerusalem, I determined to return, as I was sure they would make back to their old neighborhood, where they would rejoin me, make new recruits, and come down again. On my way back, I called at Mrs. Thomas's, Mrs. Spencer's, and several other places, the white families having fled, we found no more victims to gratify our thirst for blood, we stopped at Maj. Ridley's quarter for the night, and being joined by four of his men, with the recruits made since my defeat, we mustered now about forty strong. After placing out sentinels, I laid down to sleep, but was quickly roused by a great racket; starting up, I found some mounted, and others in great confusion; one of the sentinels having given the alarm that we were about to be attacked, I ordered some to ride round and reconnoitre, and on their return the others being more alarmed, not knowing who they were, fled in different ways, so that I was reduced to about twenty again.

With this I determined to attempt to recruit, and proceed on to rally in the neighborhood, I had left. Dr. Blunt's was the nearest house, which we reached just before day. On riding up the yard, Hark fired a gun. We expected Dr. Blunt and his family were at Maj. Ridley's, as I knew there was a company of men there. The gun was fired to ascertain if any of the family were at home; we were immediately fired upon and retreated, leaving several of my men. I do not know what became of them, as I never saw them afterwards. Pursuing our course back and coming in sight of Captain Harris', where we had been the day before, we discovered a party of white men at the house, on which all deserted me but two, (Jacob and Nat), we concealed ourselves in the woods until near night, when I sent them in search of Henry, Sam, Nelson, and Hark, and directed them to rally all they could, at the place we had had our dinner the Sunday before, where they would find me, and I accordingly returned there as soon as it was dark and remained until Wednesday evening, when discovering white men riding around the place as though they were looking for some one, and none of my men joining me, I concluded Jacob and Nat had been taken, and compelled to betray me.

On this, I gave up all hope for the present; and on Thursday night, after having supplied myself with provisions from Mr. Travis', I scratched a hole under a pile of fence-rails in a field, where I concealed myself for six weeks, never leaving my hiding-place but for a few minutes in the dead of the night to get water, which was very near. Thinking by this time I could venture out, I began to go about in the night, and eavesdrop the houses in the neighborhood; pursuing this course for about a fortnight, and gathering little or no intelligence, afraid of speaking to any human being, and returning every morning to my cave before the dawn of day. I know not how long I might have led this life, if accident had not betrayed me. A dog in the neighborhood passing by my hiding-place one night while I was out, was attracted by some meat I had in my cave, and crawled in and stole it, and was coming out just as I returned. A few nights after, two Negroes having started to go hunting with the same dog, and passed that way, the dog came again to the place, and having just gone out to walk about, discovered me and barked; on which, thinking myself discovered, I spoke to them to beg concealment. On making myself known, they fled from me. Knowing then they would betray me, I immediately left my hiding-place, and was pursued almost incessantly, until I was taken, a fortnight afterwards, by Mr. Benjamin Phipps, in a little hole I had dug out with my sword, for the purpose of concealment, under the top of a fallen tree.

On Mr. Phipps' discovering the place of my concealment, he cocked his gun and aimed at me, I requested him not to shoot and I would give up, upon which he demanded my sword, I delivered it to him, and he brought me to prison. During the time I was pursued, I had many hair-breadth escapes, which your time will not permit you to relate. I am here loaded with chains, and willing to suffer the fate that awaits me.

November 1, 1831

George Moses Horton
(1797–?1880)

Born a slave in Northampton County, North Carolina, Horton nonetheless enjoyed some mobility and traveled in his twenties to Raleigh, and then Chapel Hill, where he worked as a janitor and wrote and sold love poems to students at the university. In 1829 his collection *The Hope of Liberty* appeared, the first book of poems by an African-American to be published since Phillis Wheatley's volume more than fifty years earlier. The book contained a number of poems regarding slavery, including the one here, as well as poems on lighter themes and occasional verse. The volume was reprinted as *Poems by a Slave* in Philadelphia in 1827, and was published in an edition together with poems by Phillis Wheatley in Boston in 1838. Horton's second volume, *The Poetical Works of George M. Horton, The Colored Bard of North Carolina,* was issued in 1845, and he contributed poems to William Lloyd Garrison's *The Liberator* and Frederick Douglass's *North Star.* Though Horton's poetry often employed a rigid hymnlike form, it lacked the somber religious tone of the works of Phillis Wheatley and Jupiter Hammon.

Horton hoped to earn enough money by the sale of his poetry to purchase his freedom and immigrate to Liberia. Though unsuccessful, he was freed by the Union Army in 1865, the same year that his final book of poetry, *Naked Genius,* was published. He traveled North after the war, but was unable to further his career as a poet and died in obscurity in, varying sources record, 1880 or 1883.

The Slave's Complaint

Am I sadly cast aside,
On misfortune's rugged tide?
Will the world my pains deride
    Forever?

Must I dwell in Slavery's night,
And all pleasure take its flight,
Far beyond my feeble sight,
    Forever?

Worst of all, must hope grow dim,
And withold her cheering beam?
Rather let me sleep and dream
    Forever!

Something still my heart surveys,
Groping through this dreary maze;
Is it Hope?—then burn and blaze
    Forever!

Leave me not a wretch confined,
Altogether lame and blind—
Unto gross despair consigned,
    Forever!

Heaven! in whom can I confide?
Canst thou not for all provide?
Condescend to be my guide
    Forever:

And when this transient life shall end,
Oh, may some kind, eternal friend,
Bid me from servitude ascend,
    Forever!

1829

The Amistad Case

In the summer of 1839, a "mysterious long black schooner" was seen off the coast of Montauk, Long Island, drifting aimlessly, its sails in tatters. On August 26 a U.S. frigate approached the vessel, and its commander boarded the *Amistad.* The ship's two Spanish owners claimed that the slaves on board had murdered their captain and commandeered the vessel. But while the *Amistad*'s papers claimed that it was a cargo ship and that the Africans were the property of the Spaniards, the men appeared to know no English or European language, which seemed strange unless they had been recently uprooted from Africa. This observation was not insignificant, since the international slave trade had been abolished in 1808. Three days later, José Montez and Pedro Ruiz brought charges of murder and piracy against the Africans and filed a bill of salvage to recover the ship. They were freed, the Africans jailed. Since no one could either speak to or comprehend the African men, their story remained unheard.

Much legal maneuvering ensued in the months that followed. After the ship's owners applied to the Spanish consul, President Martin Van Buren and the secretary of state indicated that whether or not the ship's papers were legitimate was none of their affair; they expressed their desire to see the case resolved in the Spaniards' favor. The press actively debated whether the imprisoned men were cutthroats or martyrs.

Local abolitionists followed the case closely. As no one had yet been able to communicate with the men, sympathizers solicited a professor at Yale who had some knowledge of African languages; he met with the prisoners and learned from them how to count in their tongue. He then traveled to the seaport in New York, where he walked up and down the docks counting until two seamen approached him. One of them, who had himself been kidnapped from Africa and sold into slavery, met with the prisoners. At last they were able to recount their harrowing tale.

The men recalled that they had been stolen from their home in Mendi, near Sierra Leone. They had been enchained and suffered the privations of the Middle Passage to Havana, where they were sold at auction. On June 28, 1839, fifty-three slaves were boarded onto the *Amistad* and sailed for Puerto Príncipe. Once under way, the cook had told the Africans that they were to be eaten. Sengbe (called Cinquez in the Spanish court documents) managed to free himself from his chains using a nail, and he liberated the others. They killed the captain and cook, and the two crew members fled, leaving Ruiz and Montez. Ten of the Africans also died.

Sengbe ordered the Spaniards to turn the ship toward Africa; during the day they would sail toward the sun in the east, but at night the Spaniards would adjust their course for Havana. During the next two months, the *Amistad* passed several ships, but was not acknowledged, and a party of the Africans had gone ashore on Long Island, causing quite a stir. They were captured soon after by the frigate. Once their account was published in the press, the more liberal papers argued, "Cinquez is no pirate, no murderer, no felon. His homicide is justifiable. Had a white man done it it would have been glorious. It would have immortalized him."

The case of the *Amistad* captives was finally heard in district court in Hartford, Connecticut, on January 13, 1840. Despite political pressure, the court found that the men were freeborn Africans who had been transported illegally. The district attorney appealed the verdict, and the opinion was upheld by the higher court three months later. The case was then appealed to the Supreme Court. The elder statesman John Quincy Adams, who had not appeared before the Court in more than thirty years, agreed to argue the case. In his newfound English, the youngest captive wrote to him, "Dear Friend Mr. Adams, I want to write a letter to you because you love Mendi people. . . . All we want is make us free." The Supreme Court's verdict, handed down on March 9, 1841, follows.

The liberators of the *Amistad* set sail for Africa on November 27, 1841, aboard the *Gentleman.* Robert Hayden's epic, "Middle Passage"[†] is based upon this famous case.

United States Appellants v. the Libellants and Claimants of the Schooner Amistad

". . . there does not seem to us to be any ground for doubt, that these negroes ought to be deemed free. . . ."

R. JUSTICE STORY, DELIVERED THE OPINION OF THE COURT.

This is the case of an appeal from the decree of the circuit court of the district of Connecticut, sitting in admiralty. The leading facts, as they appear upon the transcript of the proceedings, are as follows: On the 27th of June 1839, the schooner "L'Amistad," being the property of Spanish subjects, cleared out from the port of Havana, in the island of Cuba, for Puerto Principe, in the same island. On board of the schooner were the master, Ramon Ferrer, and Jose Ruiz and Pedro Montez, all Spanish subjects. The former had with him a negro boy, named Antonio, claimed to be his slave. Jose Ruiz had with him forty-nine negroes, claimed by him as his slaves, and stated to be his property, in a certain pass or document, signed by the governor-general of Cuba. Pedro Montez had with him four other negroes, also claimed by him as his slaves, and stated to be his property, in a similar pass or document, also signed by the governor-general of Cuba.

On the voyage, and before the arrival of the vessel at her port of destination, the negroes rose, killed the master, and took possession of her. On the 26th of August, the vessel was discovered by Lieutenant Gedney, of the United States brig "Washington," at anchor on the high seas, at the distance of half a mile from the shore of Long Island. A part of the negroes were then on shore, at Culloden Point, Long Island, who were seized by Lieutenant Gedney, and brought on board. The vessel, with the negroes and other persons on board, was brought by Lieutenant Gedney into the district of Connecticut, and there libelled for salvage in the district court of the United States. A libel for salvage was also filed by Henry Green and Pelatiah Fordham, of Sag Harbor, Long Island. On the 18th of September, Ruiz and Montez filed claims and libels, in which they asserted their ownership of the negroes as their slaves, and of certain parts of the cargo, and prayed that the same might be "delivered to them, or to the representatives of her Catholic Majesty, as might be most proper." On the 19th of September, the attorney of the United States for the district of Connecticut filed an information or libel, setting forth, that the Spanish minister had officially presented to the proper department of the government of the United States, a claim for the restoration of the vessel, cargo, and slaves, as the property of Spanish subjects, which had arrived within the jurisdictional limits of the United States, and were taken possession of by the said public armed brig of the

United States, under such circumstances as made it the duty of the United States to cause the same to be restored to the true proprietors, pursuant to the treaty between the United States and Spain; and praying the court, on its being made legally to appear that the claim of the Spanish minister was well founded, to make such order for the disposal of the vessel, cargo and slaves, as would best enable the United States to comply with their treaty stipulations. But if it should appear, that the negroes were persons transported from Africa, in violation of the laws of the United States, and brought within the United States, contrary to the same laws; he then prayed the court to make such order for their removal to the coast of Africa, pursuant to the laws of the United States, as it should deem fit. . . .

On the 7th of January 1840, the negroes, Cinque and others, with the exception of Antonio, by their counsel, filed an answer, denying that they were slaves, or the property of Ruiz and Montez, or that the court could, under the constitution or laws of the United States, or under any treaty, exercise any jurisdiction over their persons, by reason of the premises; and praying that they might be dismissed. They specially set forth and insisted in this answer, that they were native-born Africans; born free, and still, of right, ought to be free and not slaves; that they were, on or about the 15th of April 1839, unlawfully kidnapped, and forcibly and wrongfully carried on board a certain vessel, on the coast of Africa, which was unlawfully engaged in the slave-trade, and were unlawfully transported in the same vessel to the island of Cuba, for the purpose of being there unlawfully sold as slaves; that Ruiz and Montez, well knowing the premises, made a pretended purchase of them; that afterwards, on or about the 28th of June 1839, Ruiz and Montez, confederating with Ferrer (master of the Amistad), caused them, without law or right, to be placed on board of the Amistad, to be transported to some place unknown to them, and there to be enslaved for life; that, on the voyage, they rose on the master, and took possession of the vessel, intending to return therewith to their native country, or to seek an asylum in some free state; and the vessel arrived, about the 26th of August 1839, off Montauk Point, near Long Island; a part of them were sent on shore, and were seized by Lieutenant Gedney, and carried on board; and all of them were afterwards brought by him into the district of Connecticut. . . .

No question has been here made, as to the proprietary interests in the vessel and cargo. It is admitted, that they belong to Spanish subjects, and that they ought to be restored. The only point on this head is, whether the restitution ought to be upon the payment of salvage, or not? The main controversy is, whether these negroes are the property of Ruiz and Montez, and ought to be delivered up; and to this, accordingly, we shall first direct our attention.

It has been argued on behalf of the United States, that the court are bound to deliver them up, according to the treaty of 1795, with Spain, which has in this particular been continued in full force, by the treaty of 1819, ratified in 1821. The sixth article of that treaty seems to have had, principally in view, cases where the property of the subjects of either state had been taken possession of within the territorial jurisdiction of the other, during war. The eighth article provides for cases where the shipping of the inhabitants of either state are forced, through stress of weather, pursuit of pirates or enemies, or any other urgent necessity, to seek shelter in the ports of the other. There may well be some doubt entertained, whether the present case, in its actual circumstances, falls within the purview of this article. But it does not seem necessary, for reasons hereafter stated, absolutely to decide it. The ninth article provides, "that all ships and merchandize, of what nature soever, which shall be rescued out of the hands of any pirates or robbers, on the high seas, shall be brought into some port of either state, and shall be delivered to the custody of the officers of that port, in order to be taken care of and restored, entire, to the true proprietor, as soon as due and sufficient proof shall be made concerning the property thereof." This is the article on which the main reliance is placed on behalf of the United States, for the restitution of these negroes. To bring the case within the article, it is essential to establish: 1st, That these negroes, under all the circumstances, fall within the description of merchandize, in the sense of the treaty. 2d, That there has been a rescue of them on the high seas, out of the hands of the pirates and robbers; which, in the present case, can only be, by showing that they themselves are pirates and robbers: and 3d, That Ruiz and Montez, the asserted proprietors, are the true proprietors, and have established their title by competent proof.

If these negroes were, at the time, lawfully held as slaves, under the laws of Spain, and recognised by those laws as property, capable of being lawfully bought and sold; we see no reason why they may not justly be deemed, within the intent of the treaty, to be included under the denomination of merchandize, and as such ought to be restored to the claimants; for upon that point the laws of Spain would seem to furnish the proper rule of interpretation. But admitting this, it is clear, in our opinion, that neither of the other essential facts and requisites has been established in proof; and the *onus probandi* of both lies upon the claimants to give rise to the *casus foederis*. It is plain, beyond controversy, if we examine the evidence, that these negroes never were the lawful slaves of Ruiz or Montez, or of any other Spanish subjects. They are natives of Africa, and were kidnapped there, and were unlawfully transported to Cuba, in violation of the laws and treaties of Spain, and the most solemn edicts and declarations of that government. By those laws and treaties, and edicts, the African slave-trade is utterly abolished; the dealing in that trade is deemed a heinous crime; and the negroes thereby introduced into the dominions of Spain, are declared to be free. Ruiz and Montez are proved to have made the pretended purchase of these negroes, with a full knowledge of all the circumstances. And so cogent and irresistible is the evidence in this respect, that the district-attorney has admitted in open court, upon the record, that these negroes were native Africans, and recently imported into Cuba, as alleged in their answers to the libels in the case. The supposed proprietary interest of Ruiz and Montez is completely displaced, if we are at liberty to look at the evidence, or the admissions of the district-attorney.

If then, these negroes are not slaves, but are kidnapped Africans, who, by the laws of Spain itself, are entitled to their freedom, and were kidnapped and illegally carried to Cuba, and illegally detained and restrained on board the Amistad; there is no pretence to say, that they are pirates or robbers. We may lament the dreadful acts by which they asserted their liberty, and took possession of the Amistad, and endeavored to regain their native country; but they cannot be deemed pirates or robbers, in the sense of the law of nations, or the treaty with Spain, or the laws of Spain itself; at least, so far as those laws have been brought to our knowledge. Nor do the libels of Ruiz or Montez assert them to be such. . . .

It is also a most important consideration, in the present case, which ought not to be lost sight of, that, supposing these African negroes not to be slaves, but kidnapped, and free negroes, the treaty with Spain cannot be obligatory upon them; and the United States are bound to respect their rights as much as those of Spanish subjects. The conflict of rights between the parties, under such circumstances, becomes positive and inevitable, and must be decided upon the eternal principles of justice and international law. If the contest were about any goods on board of this ship, to which American citizens asserted a title, which was denied by the Spanish claimants, there could be no doubt of the right of such American citizens to litigate their claims before any competent American tribunal, notwithstanding the treaty with Spain. *A fortiori*, the doctrine must apply, where human life and human liberty are in issue, and constitute the very essence of the controversy. The treaty with Spain never could have intended to take away the equal rights of all foreigners, who should contest their claims before any of our courts, to equal justice; or to deprive such foreigners of the protection given them by other treaties, or by the general law of nations. Upon the merits of the case, then, there does not seem to us to be any ground for doubt, that these negroes ought to be deemed free; and that the Spanish treaty interposes no obstacle to the just assertion of their rights. . . .

1841

The Convention Movement, 1830–1864

"On the fifteenth day of September, 1830," began an article in the October 1859 number of the *Anglo-African,* "there was held at Bethel Church, in the city of Philadelphia, the first Convention of the colored people of these United States. . . . If the times of 1830 were eventful, there were among our people, as well as among other peoples, men equal to the occasion. We had giants in those days!" Indeed, the convention movement of the mid-1800s provided a highly visible platform for such significant figures as Richard Allen, Hezekiah Grice, James Cornish, Austin Steward, Martin R. Delany, Henry Highland Garnet, and the great orator Frederick Douglass.

The convention movement began in Philadelphia when a few dozen freemen from Pennsylvania, New York, Connecticut, Rhode Island, Maryland, Delaware, and Virginia joined to consider "the enactment of laws in several States of the Union . . . abridging the liberties and privileges of the Free People of Color. . . . a course altogether incompatible with the principles of civil and religious liberty." After a "chaste and appropriate prayer by the venerable Bishop Allen," the group elected officers, devised a constitution, composed an address to the public, and formed "The American Society of Free Persons of Color."

The movement quickly spread, so that in 1859 the *Anglo-African* would contend that "at the present day . . . colored conventions are almost as frequent as churchmeetings." Eleven more national conventions were held from 1831 to 1864, four in Philadelphia, with others held in Buffalo, Troy, Rochester, Syracuse, and Cleveland; numerous state conventions were held from Maine to California. The gatherings shared in the zeal for temperance, education, and social improvement prevalent in a generally reform-minded America, while addressing as well the special concerns of the freeman.

There was the obvious problem of slavery in the South to be considered, for while slaves remained in bondage, the Northern freeman often found himself facing conditions not far removed. Before the Civil War, only five Northern states had unrestricted suffrage and free blacks were in danger of being kidnapped and sold to the South. In addition, growing prejudice, caused in part by increased job competition from new European immigrants and the migration of laborers from the South, accomplished what the laws might restrict. Such prejudice was rife even among abolitionists.

At the same time, by 1830 African-Americans were impatient to speak for themselves. The number of freemen had greatly increased, through manumissions and legal emancipation, from about 60,000 in 1790 to nearly 320,000 by 1830, when emancipation took place in New York. Within black communities educated orators and churchmen had honed their debating skills, the black press, launched by *Freedom's Journal* in 1827, was growing in influence, and David Walker's incendiary *Appeal*† had recently been published. Through debates on the assembly floor, adopted resolutions, public addresses, and petitions to state legislatures and to Congress, convention men sought to make their voices heard.

From the start, the conventions grappled with the widely debated question of emigration. The convention of 1830 saw as one of its primary goals the "location of a settlement in the province of Upper Canada," while at the same time rebuffing the efforts of the American Colonization Society which sought to remove American blacks to Africa as missionaries. The convention resolved: "However great the debt which these United States may owe to injured Africa, and however unjustly her sons have been made to bleed, and her daughters to drink of the cup of affliction, still we who have been born and nurtured on this soil, we, whose habits, manners, and customs are the same in common with other Americans, can never . . . be the bearers of the redress offered by that Society to that much afflicted country." The convention of 1848 would condemn the goals of the Society, some of whose members sought to press their cause by force, as a plot "clothed with the livery of heaven to serve the devil in." Nonetheless, throughout the next three decades the convention movement would lose men like Hezekiah Grice, who spent twenty-five years in Haiti, and Alexander Crummell, John Russwurm, Henry Highland Garnet, and Martin R. Delany, who immigrated to Africa. But their numbers were few compared to the majority who, like Frederick Douglass, demanded their full rights as Americans.

The goals of the conventions shifted over time. The early gatherings were attended by numerous whites, while those of the 1840s and later were more independent. Previously all-male, the 1848 convention pronounced that as "we fully believe in the equality of the sexes. . . . we hereby invite females hereafter to take part in our deliberations," and Frances E. W. Harper was invited to speak at the National Convention of Colored Men in Syracuse in 1864.

The tone of the conventions changed as well. While the delegates in 1830 emphasized moral reform, sought the ballot, and strove to "pursue all legal means for the speedy elevation of ourselves and brethren to the scale and standing of men," later conventions became more militant.

Henry Highland Garnet's "Call to Rebellion"† was delivered, though not endorsed, at the 1843 National Convention of Colored Citizens in Buffalo, New York, while the Colored National Convention of 1848 in Cleveland, representing perhaps the high point of the movement and whose address is reprinted here, pledged "to use all justifiable means for [the] speedy and immediate overthrow" of slavery. "Whereas, we find ourselves far behind the military tactics of the civilized world," its resolutions continued, "this Convention recommend[s] to the Colored Freemen of North America to use every means in their power to obtain that science, so as to enable them to measure arms with assailants *without* and invaders within." In fact, the convention movement dissolved as the nation took up arms in civil war, fulfilling Frederick Douglass's famous exhortation that "Action! not criticism, [was] the plain duty of this hour."

An Address to the Colored People of the United States, from the Colored National Convention of 1848

". . . our own country shakes with the agitation of our rights."

ELLOW COUNTRYMEN:—

Under a solemn sense of duty, inspired by our relation to you as fellow sufferers under the multiplied and grievous wrongs to which we, as a people, are universally subjected,—we, a portion of your brethren, assembled in National Convention, at Cleveland, Ohio, take the liberty to address you on the subject of our mutual improvement and social elevation.

The condition of our variety of the human family, has long been cheerless, if not hopeless, in this country. The doctrine perseveringly proclaimed in high places in church and state, that it is impossible for colored men to rise from ignorance and debasement, to intelligence and respectability in this country, has made a deep impression upon the public mind generally, and is not without its effect upon us. Under this gloomy doctrine, many of us have sunk under the pall of despondency, and are making no effort to relieve ourselves, and have no heart to assist others. It is from this despond that we would deliver you. It is from this slumber we would rouse you. The present, is a period of activity and hope. The heavens above us are bright, and much of the darkness that overshadowed us has passed away. We can deal in the language of brilliant encouragement, and speak of success with certainty. That our condition has been gradually improving, is evident to all, and that we shall yet stand on a common platform with our fellow-countrymen, in respect to political and social rights, is certain. The spirit of the age—the voice of inspiration—the deep longings of the human soul—the conflict of right with wrong—the upward tendency of the oppressed throughout the world, abound with evidence, complete and ample, of the final triumph of right over wrong, of freedom over slavery, and equality over caste. To doubt this, is to forget the past, and blind our eyes to the present, as well as to deny and oppose the great law of progress, written out by the hand of God on the human soul.

Great changes for the better have taken place and are still taking place. The last ten years have witnessed a mighty change in the estimate in which we as a people are regarded, both in this and other lands. England has given liberty to nearly one million, and France has emancipated three hundred thousand of our brethren, and our own country shakes with the agitation of our rights. Ten or twelve years ago, an educated colored man was regarded as a curiosity, and the thought of a colored man as an author, editor, lawyer or doctor, had scarce been conceived.—Such, thank Heaven, is no longer the case. There are now those among us, whom we are not ashamed to regard as gentlemen and scholars, and who are acknowledged to be such, by many of the most learned and respectable in our land. Mountains of prejudice have been removed, and truth and light are dispelling the error and darkness of ages. The time was, when we trembled in the presence of a white man, and dared not assert, or even ask for our rights, but would be guided, directed, and governed, in any way we were demanded, without ever stopping to inquire whether we were right or wrong. We were not only slaves, but our ignorance made us willing slaves. Many of us uttered complaints against the faithful abolitionists, for the broad assertion of our rights; thought they went too far, and were only making our condition worse. This sentiment has nearly ceased to reign in the dark abodes of our hearts; we begin to see our wrongs as clearly, and comprehend our rights as fully, and as well as our white countrymen. This is a sign of progress; and evidence which cannot be gainsaid. It would be easy to present in this connection, a glowing comparison of our past with our present condition, showing that while the former was dark and dreary, the present is full of light and hope. It would be easy to draw a picture of our present achievements, and erect upon it a glorious future.

But, fellow-countrymen, it is not so much our purpose to cheer you by the progress we have already made, as it is to stimulate you to still higher attainments. We have done much, but there is much more to be done. While we have undoubtedly great cause to thank God, and take courage for the hopeful changes which have taken place in our condition, we are not without cause to mourn over the sad condition which we yet occupy. We are yet the most oppressed people in the world. In the Southern States of this Union, we are held as slaves. All over that wide region our paths are marked with blood. Our backs are yet scarred by the lash, and our souls are yet dark under the pall of slavery. Our sisters are sold for purposes of pollution, and our brethren are sold in the market, with beasts of burden. Shut up in the prison-house of bondage—denied all rights, and deprived of all privileges, we are blotted from the page of human existence, and placed beyond the limits of human regard. DEATH, moral DEATH, has palsied our souls in that quarter, and we are a murdered people.

In the Northern states, we are not slaves to individuals, no personal slaves, yet in many respects we are the slaves of the community. We are, however, far enough removed from the actual condition of the slave to make us largely responsible for their continued enslavement, or their speedy deliverance from chains. For in the proportion which we shall rise in the scale of human improvement, in that proportion do we augment the probabilities of a speedy emancipation of our enslaved fellow-countrymen. It is more than a mere figure of speech to say, that we are as a people, chained together. We are one people—one in general complexion, one in a common degradation, one in popular estimation.—As one rises, all must rise, and as one falls all must fall. Having now, our feet on the rock of freedom, we must drag our brethren from the slimy depths of slavery, ignorance, and ruin. Every one of us should be ashamed to consider himself free, while his brother is a slave. The wrongs of our brethren, should be our constant theme. There should be no time too precious, no calling too holy, no place too sacred, to make room for this cause. We should not only feel it to be the cause of humanity, but the cause of christianity, and fit work for men and angels. We ask you to devote yourselves to this cause, as one of the first, and most successful means of self improvement. In the careful study of it, you will learn your own rights, and comprehend your own responsibilities, and scan through the vista of coming time, your high, and God-appointed destiny. Many of the brightest and best of our number, have become such by their devotion to this cause, and the society of white abolitionists. The latter have been willing to make themselves of no reputation for our sake, and in return, let us show ourselves worthy of their zeal and devotion. Attend Anti-slavery meetings, show that you are interested in the subject, that you hate slavery, and love those who are laboring for its overthrow. Act with white Abolition societies wherever you can, and where you cannot, get up societies among yourselves, but without exclusiveness. It will be a long time before we gain all our rights; and although it may seem to conflict with our views of human brotherhood, we shall undoubtedly for many years be compelled to have institutions of a complexional character, in order to attain this very idea of human brotherhood. We would, however, advise our brethren to occupy memberships and stations among white persons, and in white institutions, just so fast as our rights are secured to us.

Never refuse to act with a white society or institution because it is white, or a black one, because it is black; but act with all men without distinction of color. By so acting, we shall find many opportunities for removing prejudices and establishing the rights of all men.—We say, avail yourselves of *white* institutions, not because they are white, but because they afford a more convenient means of improvement. But we pass from these suggestions, to others which may be deemed more important. In the Convention that now addresses you, there has been much said on the subject of labor, and especially those departments of it, with which we as a class have been long identified. You will see by the resolutions there adopted on that subject, that the Convention regarded those employments, though right in themselves, as being, nevertheless, degrading to us as a class, and therefore, counsel you to abandon them as speedily as possible, and to seek what are called the more respectable employments. While the Convention do not inculcate the doctrine that any kind of needful toil is in itself dishonorable, or that colored persons are to be exempt from what are called menial employments, they do mean to say that such employments have been so long and universally filled by colored men, as to become a badge of degradation, in that it has established the conviction that colored men are only fit for such employments. We therefore advise you, by all means, to cease from such employments, as far as practicable, by pressing into others. Try to get your sons into mechanical trades; press them into the blacksmith's shop, the machine shop, the joiner's shop, the wheelright's shop, the cooper's shop, and the tailor's shop.

Every blow of the sledge-hammer, wielded by a sable arm, is a powerful blow in support of our cause. Every colored mechanic, is by virtue of circumstances, an elevator of his race. Every house built by black men, is a strong tower against the allied hosts of prejudice. It is impossible for us to attach too much importance to this aspect of the subject. Trades are important. Wherever a man may be thrown by misfortune, if he has in his hands a useful trade, he is useful to his fellow-man, and will be esteemed accordingly; and of all men in the world who need trades, we are the most needy.

Understand this, that independence is an essential condition of respectability. To be dependent, is to be degraded. Men may indeed pity us, but they cannot respect us. We do not mean that we can become entirely independent of all men; that would be absurd and impossible, in the social state. But we mean that we must become equally independent with other members of the community. That other members of the community shall be as dependent upon us, as we upon them. That such is not now the case, is too plain to need an argument. The houses we live in are built by white men—the clothes we wear are made by white tailors—the hats on our heads are made by white hatters, and the shoes on our feet are made by white shoe-makers, and the food that we eat, is raised and cultivated by white men. Now it is impossible that we should ever be respected as a people, while we are so universally and completely dependent upon white men for the necessaries of life. We must make white persons as dependent upon us, as we are upon them.—This cannot be done while we are found only in two or three kinds of employments, and those employments have their foundation chiefly, if not entirely, in the pride and indolence of the white people. Sterner necessities, will bring higher respect.

The fact is, we must not merely make the white man dependent upon us to shave him, but to feed him; not merely dependent upon us to black his boots, but to make them. A man is only in a small degree dependent on us, when he only needs his boots blacked, or his carpet-bag carried; as a little less pride, and a little more industry on his part, may enable him to dispense with our services entirely. As wise men it becomes us to look forward to a state of things, which appears inevitable.—The time will come, when those menial employments will afford less means of living than they now do. What shall a large class of our fellow-countrymen do, when white men find it economical to black their own boots, and shave themselves? What will they do when white men learn to wait on themselves? We warn you brethren, to seek other and more enduring vocations.

Let us entreat you to turn your attention to agriculture. Go to farming. Be tillers of the soil. On this point we could say much, but the time and space will not permit. Our cities are overrun with menial laborers, while the country is eloquently pleading for the hand of industry to till her soil, and reap the reward of honest labor. We beg and intreat you, to save your money —live economically—dispense with finery, and the gaities which have rendered us proverbial, and save your money. Not for the senseless purpose of being better off than your neighbor, but that you may be able to educate your children, and render your share to the common stock of prosperity and happiness around you. It is plain that the equality which we aim to accomplish, can only be achieved by us, when we can do for others, just what others can do for us. We should therefore, press into all the trades, professions and callings into which honorable white men press.

We would in this connection, direct your attention to the means by which we have been oppressed and degraded. Chief among those means, we may mention the press. This engine has brought to the aid of prejudice, a thousand stings. Wit, ridicule, false philosophy, and an impure theology, with a flood of low black-guardism, come through this channel into the public mind; constantly feeding and keeping alive against us, the bitterest hate. The pulpit too, has been arrayed against us. Men with sanctimonious face, have talked of our being descendants of Ham—that we are under a curse, and to try to improve our condition, is virtually to counteract the purposes of God!

It is easy to see that the means which have been used to destroy us, must be used to save us. The press must be used in our behalf: aye! we must use it ourselves; we must take and read newspapers; we must read books, improve our minds, and put to silence and to shame, our opposers.

Dear Brethren, we have extended these remarks beyond the length which we had allotted to ourselves, and must now close, though we have but hinted at the subject. Trusting that our words may fall like good seed upon good ground; and hoping that we may all be found in the path of improvement and progress.

We are your friends and servants,
(Signed by the Committee, in behalf
of the convention) FREDERICK DOUGLASS,
H. BIBB, W.L. DAY
D.H. JENKINS, A.H. FRANCIS.

September 6, 1848

Henry Highland Garnet
(1815–1882)

Like Frederick Douglass, Henry Highland Garnet had been born in slavery on the eastern shore of Maryland but escaped with his family to the free state of New York at the age of nine. He attended the New African Free School in New York and later, briefly, the Noyes Academy in Canaan, New Hampshire, where a violent protest by local citizens to the enrollment of Garnet and three other black youths shut down the school. He studied for the ministry at the Oneida Theological Institute near Utica, New York, and became the pastor of the predominantly white Presbyterian Church in Troy, New York.

Garnet delivered the address included here in August 1843 at the National Negro Convention held in Buffalo, New York, attended by over seventy delegates, including Frederick Douglass and William Wells Brown, from a dozen states. The great-grandson of a Mandingo chieftain who extolled his listeners to "think of the undying glory that hangs around the ancient name of Africa," Garnet urged the slaves to "use every means, both moral, intellectual, and physical that promises success," arguing that "however much you and all of us may desire it, there is not much hope of redemption without the shedding of blood."

By boldly proposing in such a forum the necessity of armed revolt, the speech, which became known as Garnet's "Call to Rebellion," caused an immediate controversy. As the author wrote in a preface to its publication in 1843 (in an edition with David Walker's *Appeal*): "The document elicited more discussion than any other paper that was ever brought before that, or any other deliberative body of colored persons, and their friends." Opposed by Douglass, the speech failed by one vote to be adopted by the convention, which still advocated "moral suasion" over political, or even military, action, but it gained national attention. Garnet became one of the country's most prominent abolitionists, lecturing in England and Scotland and contributing to William Lloyd Garrison's *Liberator* and *Douglass' Monthly,* and he was the first African-American clergyman to preach a sermon to Congress, delivering his Memorial Discourse in the Hall of the House of Representatives† on February 12, 1865.

An Address to the Slaves of the United States of America

". . . rather die freemen, than live to be slaves."

BRETHREN AND FELLOW CITIZENS:— YOUR BRETHREN OF THE North, East, and West have been accustomed to meet together in National Conventions, to sympathize with each other, and to weep over your unhappy condition. In these meetings we have addressed all classes of the free, but we have never until this time, sent a word of consolation and advice to you. We have been contented in sitting still and mourning over your sorrows, earnestly hoping that before this day your sacred liberty would have been restored. But, we have hoped in vain. Years have rolled on, and tens of thousands have been borne on streams of blood and tears, to the shores of eternity. While you have been oppressed, we have also been partakers with you; nor can we be free while you are enslaved. We, therefore, write to you as being bound with you.

Many of you are bound to us, not only by the ties of a common humanity, but we are connected by the more tender relations of parents, wives, husbands, children, brothers, and sisters, and friends. As such we most affectionately address you.

Slavery has fixed a deep gulf between you and us, and while it shuts out from you the relief and consolation which your friends would willingly render, it affects and persecutes you with a fierceness which we might not expect to see in the fiends of hell. But still the Almighty Father of mercies has left to us a glimmering ray of hope, which shines out like a lone star in a cloudy sky. Mankind are becoming wiser, and better—the oppressor's power is fading, and you, every day, are becoming better informed, and more numerous. Your grievances, brethren, are many. We shall not attempt, in this short address, to present to the world all the dark catalogue of this nation's sins, which have been committed upon an innocent people. Nor is it indeed necessary, for you feel them from day to day, and all the civilized world look upon them with amazement.

Two hundred and twenty-seven years ago, the first of our injured race were brought to the shores of America. They came not with glad spirits to select their homes in the New World. They came not with their own consent, to find an unmolested enjoyment of the blessings of this fruitful soil. The first dealings they had with men calling themselves Christians, exhibited to them the worst features of corrupt and sordid hearts; and convinced them that no cruelty is too great, no villainy and no robbery too abhorrent for even enlightened men to perform, when influenced by avarice and lust.

Neither did they come flying upon the wings of Liberty, to a land of freedom. But they came with broken hearts, from their beloved native land, and were doomed to unrequited toil and deep degradation. Nor did the evil of their bondage end at their emancipation by death. Succeeding generations inherited their chains, and millions have come from eternity into time, and have returned again to the world of spirits, cursed and ruined by American slavery.

The propagators of the system, or their immediate ancestors, very soon discovered its growing evil, and its tremendous wickedness, and secret promises were made to destroy it. The gross inconsistency of a people holding slaves, who had themselves "ferried o'er the wave" for freedom's sake, was too apparent to be entirely overlooked. The voice of Freedom cried, "Emancipate your slaves." Humanity supplicated with tears for the deliverance of the children of Africa. Wisdom urged her solemn plea. The bleeding captive plead his innocence, and pointed to Christianity who stood weeping at the cross. Jehovah frowned upon the nefarious institution, and thunderbolts, red with vengeance, struggled to leap forth to blast the guilty wretches who maintained it. But all was in vain. Slavery had stretched its dark wings of death over the land, the Church stood silently by—the priests prophesied falsely, and the people loved to have it so. Its throne is established, and now it reigns triumphant.

Nearly three millions of your fellow-citizens are prohibited by law and public opinion, (which in this country is stronger than law,) from reading the Book of Life. Your intellect has been destroyed as much as possible, and every ray of light they have attempted to shut out from your minds. The oppressors themselves have become involved in the ruin. They have become weak, sensual, and rapacious—they have cursed you—they have cursed themselves—they have cursed the earth which they have trod.

The colonists threw the blame upon England. They said that the mother country entailed the evil upon them, and that they would rid themselves of it if they could. The world thought they were sincere, and the philanthropic pitied them. But time soon tested their sincerity.

In a few years the colonists grew strong, and severed themselves from the British Government. Their independence was declared, and they took their station among the sovereign powers of the earth. The declaration was a glorious document. Sages admired it, and the patriotic of every nation reverenced the God-like sentiments which it contained. When the power of Government returned to their hands, did they emancipate the slaves? No; they rather added new links to our chains. Were they ignorant of the principles of Liberty? Certainly they were not. The sentiments of their revolutionary orators fell in burning eloquence upon their hearts, and with one voice they cried, LIBERTY OR DEATH. Oh what a sentence was that! It ran from soul to soul like electric fire, and nerved the arm of thousands to fight in the holy cause of Freedom. Among the diversity of opinions that are entertained in regard to physical resistance, there are but a few found to gainsay that stern declaration. We are among those who do not.

SLAVERY! How much misery is comprehended in that single word? What mind is there that does not shrink from its direful effects? Unless the image of God be obliterated from the soul, all men cherish the love of Liberty. The nice discerning political economist does not regard the sacred right more than the untutored African who roams in the wilds of Congo. Nor has the one more right to the full enjoyment of his freedom than the other. In every man's mind the good seeds of liberty are planted, and he who brings his fellow down so low, as to make him contented with a condition of slavery, commits the highest crime against God and man. Brethren, your oppressors aim to do this. They endeavor to make you as much like brutes as possible. When they have blinded the eyes of your mind—when they have embittered the sweet waters of life—then, and not till then, has American slavery done its perfect work.

TO SUCH DEGRADATION IT IS SINFUL IN THE EXTREME FOR YOU TO MAKE VOLUNTARY SUBMISSION. The divine commandments you are in duty bound to reverence and obey. If you do not obey them, you will surely meet with the displeasure of the Almighty. He requires you to love him supremely, and your neighbor as yourself—to keep the Sabbath day holy—to search the Scriptures—and bring up your children with respect for his laws, and to worship no other God but him. But slavery sets all these at nought, and hurls defiance in the face of Jehovah. The forlorn condition in which you are placed, does not destroy your moral obligation to God. You are not certain of heaven, because you suffer yourselves to remain in a state of slavery, where you cannot obey the commandments of the Sovereign of the universe. If the ignorance of slavery is a passport to heaven, then it is a blessing, and no curse, and you should rather desire its perpetuity than its abolition. God will not receive slavery, nor ignorance, nor any other state of mind, for love and obedience to him. Your condition does not absolve you from your moral obligation. The diabolical injustice by which your liberties are cloven down, NEITHER GOD, NOR ANGELS, OR JUST MEN, COMMAND YOU TO SUFFER FOR A SINGLE MOMENT. THEREFORE IT IS YOUR SOLEMN AND IMPERATIVE DUTY TO USE EVERY MEANS, BOTH MORAL, INTELLECTUAL, AND PHYSICAL THAT PROMISES SUCCESS. If a band of heathen men should attempt to enslave a race of Christians, and to place their children under the influence of some false religion, surely Heaven would frown upon the men who would not resist such aggression, even to death. If, on the other hand, a band of Christians should attempt to enslave a race of heathen men, and to entail slavery upon them, and to keep them in heathenism in the midst of Christianity, the God of heaven would smile upon every effort which the injured might make to disenthral themselves.

Brethren, it is as wrong for your lordly oppressors to keep you in slavery as it was for the man thief to steal our ancestors from the coast of Africa. You should therefore now use the same manner of resistance, as would have been just in our ancestors when the bloody foot-prints of the first remorseless soul-thief was placed upon the shores of our fatherland. The humblest peasant is as free in the sight of God as the proudest monarch that ever swayed a sceptre. Liberty is a spirit sent out from God, and like its great Author, is no respecter of persons.

Brethren, the time has come when you must act for yourselves. It is an old and true saying that, "if hereditary bondmen would be free, they must themselves strike the blow." You can plead your own cause, and do the work of emancipation better than any others. The nations of the world are moving in the great cause of universal freedom, and some of them at least will, ere long, do you justice. The combined powers of Europe have placed their broad seal of disapprobation upon the African slave-trade. But in the slave-holding parts of the United States, the trade is as brisk as ever. They buy and sell you as though you were brute beasts. The North has done much—her opinion of slavery in the abstract is known. But in regard to the South, we adopt the opinion of the *New York Evangelist*—We have advanced so far, that the cause apparently waits for a more effectual door to be thrown open than has been yet. We are about to point out that more effectual door. Look around you, and behold the bosoms of your loving wives heaving with untold agonies! Hear the cries of your poor children! Remember the stripes your fathers bore. Think of the torture and disgrace of your noble mothers. Think of your wretched sisters, loving virtue and purity, as they are driven into concubinage and are exposed to the unbridled lusts of incarnate devils. Think of the undying glory that hangs around the ancient name of Africa—and forget not that you are native born American citizens, and as such, you are justly entitled to all the rights that are granted to the freest. Think how many tears you have poured out upon the soil which you have cultivated with unrequited toil and enriched with your blood; and then go to your lordly enslavers and tell them plainly, that you *are determined to be free*. Appeal to their sense of justice, and tell them that they have no more right to oppress you, than you have to enslave them. Entreat them to remove the grievous burdens which they have imposed upon you, and to remunerate you for your labor. Promise them renewed diligence in the cultivation of the soil, if they will render to you an equivalent for your services. Point them to the increase of happiness and prosperity in the British West Indies since the Act of Emancipation. Tell them in language which they cannot misunderstand, of the exceeding sinfulness of slavery, and of a future judgment, and of the righteous retributions of an indignant God. Inform them that all you desire is FREEDOM, and that nothing else will suffice. Do this, and for ever after cease to toil for the heartless tyrants, who give you no other reward but stripes and abuse. If they then commence the work of death, they, and not you, will be responsible for the consequences. You had better all die—*die immediately*, than live slaves and entail your wretchedness upon your posterity. If you would be free in this generation, here is your only hope. However much you and all of us may desire it, there is not much hope of redemption without the shedding of blood. If you must bleed, let it all come at once—rather *die freemen, than live to be slaves*. It is impossible like the children of Israel, to make a grand exodus from the land of bondage. The Pharaohs are on both sides of the blood-red waters! You cannot move *en masse*, to the dominions of the British Queen—nor can you pass through Florida and overrun Texas, and at last find peace in Mexico. The propagators of American slavery are spending their blood and treasure, that they may plant the black flag in the heart of Mexico and riot in the halls of the Montezumas. In the language of the Rev. Robert Hall, when addressing the volunteers of Bristol, who were rushing forth to repel the invasion of Napoleon, who threatened to lay waste the fair homes of England, "Religion is too much interested in your behalf, not to shed over you her most gracious influences."

You will not be compelled to spend much time in order to become inured to hardships. From the first moment that you breathed the air of heaven, you have been accustomed to nothing else but hardships. The heroes of the American Revolution were never put upon harder fare than a peck of corn and a few herrings per week. You have not become enervated by the luxuries of life. Your sternest energies have been beaten out upon the anvil of severe trial. Slavery has done this, to make you subservient, to its own purposes; but it has done more than this, it has prepared you for any emergency. If you receive good treatment, it is what you could hardly expect; if you meet with pain, sorrow, and even death, these are the common lot of slaves.

Fellow men! Patient sufferers! behold your dearest rights crushed to the earth! See your sons murdered, and your wives, mothers and sisters doomed to prostitution. In the name of the merciful God, and by all that life is worth, let it no longer be a debatable question whether it is better to choose *Liberty or death*.

In 1822, Denmark Veazie, of South Carolina, formed a plan for the liberation of his fellow men. In the whole history of human efforts to overthrow slavery, a more complicated and tremendous plan was never formed. He was betrayed by the treachery of his own people, and died a martyr to freedom. Many a brave hero fell, but history, faithful to her high trust, will transcribe his name on the same monument with Moses, Hampden, Tell, Bruce and Wallace, Toussaint L'Ouverture, Lafayette and Washington. That tremendous movement shook the whole empire of slavery. The guilty soul-thieves were overwhelmed with fear. It is a matter of fact, that at that time, and in consequence of the threatened revolution, the slave States talked strongly of emancipation. But they blew but one blast of the trumpet of freedom and then laid it aside. As these men became quiet, the slaveholders ceased to talk about emancipation; and now behold your condition today! Angels sigh over it, and humanity has long since exhausted her tears in weeping on your account!

The patriotic Nathaniel Turner followed Denmark Veazie. He was goaded to desperation by wrong and injustice. By despotism, his name has been recorded on the list of infamy, and future generations will remember him among the noble and brave.

Next arose the immortal Joseph Cinque, the hero of the *Amistad*. He was a native African, and by the help of God he emancipated a whole shipload of his fellow men on the high seas. And he now sings of liberty on the sunny hills of Africa and beneath his native palm-trees, where he hears the lion roar and feels himself as free as that king of the forest.

Next arose Madison Washington that bright star of freedom, and took his station in the constellation of true heroism. He was a slave on board the brig *Creole*, of Richmond, bound to New Orleans, that great slave mart, with a hundred and four others. Nineteen struck for liberty or death. But one life was taken, and the whole were emancipated, and the vessel was carried into Nassau, New Providence.

Noble men! Those who have fallen in freedom's conflict, their memories will be cherished by the true-hearted and the God-fearing in all future generations; those who are living, their names are surrounded by a halo of glory.

Brethren, arise, arise! Strike for your lives and liberties. Now is the day and the hour. Let every slave throughout the land do this, and the days of slavery are numbered. You cannot be more oppressed than you have been—you cannot suffer greater cruelties than you have already. *Rather die freemen than live to be slaves.* Remember that you are FOUR MILLIONS!

It is in your power so to torment the God-cursed slaveholders that they will be glad to let you go free. If the scale was turned, and black men were the masters and white men the slaves, every destructive agent and element would be employed to lay the oppressor low. Danger and death would hang over their heads day and night. Yes, the tyrants would meet with plagues more terrible than those of Pharaoh. But you are a patient people. You act as though, you were made for the special use of these devils. You act as though your daughters were born to pamper the lusts of your masters and overseers. And worse than all, you tamely submit while your lords tear your wives from your embraces and defile them before your eyes. In the name of God, we ask you, are you men? Where is the blood of your fathers? Has it all run out of your veins? Awake, awake; millions of voices are calling you! Your dead fathers speak to you from their graves. Heaven, as with a voice of thunder, calls on you to arise from the dust.

Let your motto be resistance! *resistance!* RESISTANCE! No oppressed people have ever secured their liberty without resistance. What kind of resistance you had better make, you must decide by the circumstances that surround you, and according to the suggestion of expediency. Brethren, adieu! Trust in the living God. Labor for the peace of the human race, and remember that you are FOUR MILLIONS.

August 21, 1843

Martin Delany
(1812–1885)

Martin Delany's seminal work *The Condition, Elevation, and Destiny of the Colored People of the United States, Politically Considered,* excerpted here, was the most significant theoretical work on race written before the Civil War. The grandson of an African chieftain, Delany was born free in Charles Town, West Virginia (then Virginia), and was educated in Pittsburgh, Pennsylvania, and in New York at the African Free School and the Oneida Institute. In Pittsburgh he first encountered the abolition movement and the Underground Railroad and after publishing his own journal, *The Mystery,* in 1847 he became coeditor of Frederick Douglass's *North Star.* In 1850 he attended Harvard Medical School, where he encountered extreme prejudice in the protests of his fellow students to his very presence. In 1843 Delany married a woman from a prominent black Pittsburgh family (they eventually had seven children, each of whom was named for a famous black figure), and as he practiced medicine in Chicago, Philadelphia, and elsewhere he lectured against slavery and became active in the emigration movement.

His major work on the prospects of African-Americans in the United States was published in 1852, and in 1854 he attended the National Emigration Convention of Colored Men, which issued the resolutions included here, one of the strongest expressions of black pride in the nineteenth century. Delany's views were sometimes in opposition to those of Frederick Douglass and others who vehemently opposed emigration, arguing that it was motivated by slaveholders who simply wished to get rid of free blacks who might agitate for abolition and allowed this nation to avoid grappling with the issue of the role of African-Americans in a country they had built with their own lives. In 1859 Delany's *Blake, or the Huts of America,* originally serialized in the *Anglo-African,* became only the second novel, after Harriet Wilson's *Our Nig,*† published by an African-American.

That same year Delany visited Liberia and secured a land agreement for American émigrés in Yorubaland (Nigeria). His emigration efforts were interrupted, however, by the Civil War and he actively recruited troops in Massachusetts, Connecticut, and Rhode Island, including the famed Massachusetts 54th. In December 1865 he wrote to War Secretary Edwin M. Stanton, arguing that given "the authority to recruit colored troops in any of the southern or seceded States, we will be ready and able to raise a regiment, or brigade, if required. . . . with the belief sir, that this is one of the measures in which the claims of the black man may be officially recognized, without seemingly infringing upon those of other citizens." He was commissioned by President Lincoln as a major in the Union Army and also acted as a surgeon.

After the war, Delany remained in South Carolina, where he worked for the Freedman's Bureau and entered local politics. As Reconstruction progressed, however, he became cynical about Northern politicians and eventually supported reactive Southern Democratic candidates. In the late 1870s he began to reconsider emigration, before his death in Xenia, Ohio, on January 24, 1885.

from *The Condition, Elevation, and Destiny of the Colored People of the United States, Politically Considered*

"Go or stay—of course each is free to do as he pleases—one thing is certain; our Elevation is the work of our own hands."

CHAPTER II: COMPARATIVE CONDITION OF THE COLORED PEOPLE OF THE UNITED STATES

HE UNITED STATES, UNTRUE TO HER TRUST AND UNFAITHFUL to her professed principles of republican equality, has also pursued a policy of political degradation to a large portion of her native born countrymen, and that class is the Colored People. Denied an equality not only of political, but of natural rights, in common with the rest of our fellow citizens, there is no species of degradation to which we are not subject.

Reduced to abject slavery is not enough, the very thought of which should awaken every sensibility of our common nature; but those of their descendants who are freemen even in the non-slaveholding States, occupy the very same position politically, religiously, civilly and socially, (with but few exceptions,) as the bondman occupies in the slave States.

In those States, the bondman is disfranchised, and for the most part so are we. He is denied all civil, religious, and social privileges, except such as he gets by mere sufferance, and so are we. They have no part nor lot in the government of the country, neither have we. They are ruled and governed without representation, existing as mere nonentities among the citizens, and excrescences on the body politic—a mere dreg in community, and so are we. Where then is our political superiority to the enslaved? none, neither are we superior in any other relation to society, except that we are defacto masters of ourselves and joint rulers of our own domestic household, while the bondman's self is claimed by another, and his relation to his family denied him. What the unfortunate classes are in Europe, such are we in the United States, which is folly to deny, insanity not to understand, blindness not to see, and surely now full time that our eyes were opened to these startling truths, which for ages have stared us full in the face.

It is time that we had become politicians, we mean, to understand the political economy and domestic policy of nations; that we had become as well as moral theorists, also the practical demonstrators of equal rights and self-government. Except we do, it is idle to talk about rights, it is mere chattering for the sake of being seen and heard—like the slave, saying something because his so called "master" said it, and saying just what he told him to say. Have we not now sufficient intelligence among us to understand our true position, to realise our actual condition, and determine for ourselves what is best to be done? If we have not now, we never shall have, and should at once cease prating about our equality, capacity, and all that. . . .

CHAPTER XXIII: THINGS AS THEY ARE

And if thou boast TRUTH to utter,
SPEAK, and leave the rest to God.

In presenting this work, we have but a single object in view, and that is, to inform the minds of the colored people at large, upon many things pertaining to their elevation, that but few among us are acquainted with. Unfortunately for us, as a body, we have been taught to believe, that we must have some person to think for us, instead of thinking for ourselves. So accustomed are we to submission and this kind of training, that it is with difficulty, even among the most intelligent of the colored people, an audience may be elicited for any purpose whatever, if the expounder is to be a colored person; and the introduction of any subject is treated with indifference, if not contempt, when the originator is a colored person. Indeed, the most ordinary white person, is almost revered, while the most qualified colored person is totally neglected. Nothing from them is appreciated.

We have been standing comparatively still for years, following in the footsteps of our friends, believing that what they promise us can be accomplished, just because they say so, although our own knowledge should long since, have satisfied us to the contrary. Because even were it possible, with the present hate and jealousy that the whites have towards us in this country, for us to gain equality of rights with them; we never could have an equality of the exercise and enjoyment of those rights—because, the great odds of numbers are against us. We might indeed, as some at present, have the right of the elective franchise—nay, it is not the elective franchise, because the *elective franchise* makes the enfranchised, *eligible* to any position attainable; but we may exercise the right of *voting* only, which to us, is but poor satisfaction; and we by no means care to cherish the privilege of voting somebody into office, to help to make laws to degrade us.

In religion—because they are both *translators* and *commentators,* we must believe nothing, however absurd, but what our oppressors tell us. In Politics, nothing but such as they promulge; in Anti-Slavery, nothing but what our white brethren and friends say we must; in the mode and manner of our elevation, we must do nothing, but that which may be laid down to be done by our white brethren from some quarter or other; and now, even on the subject of emigration, there are some colored people to be found, so lost to their own interest and self-respect, as to be gulled by slave owners and colonizationists, who are led to believe there is no other place in which they can become elevated, but Liberia, a government of American slave-holders, as we have shown—simply, because white men have told them so.

Upon the possibility, means, mode and manner, of our Elevation in the United States—Our Original Rights and Claims as Citizens—Our Determination not to be Driven from our Native Country—the Difficulties in the Way of our Elevation—Our Position in Relation to our Anti-Slavery Brethren—the Wicked Design and Injurious Tendency of the American Colonization Society—Objections to Liberia—Objections to Canada—Preferences to South America, &c., &c., all of which we have treated without reserve; expressing our mind freely, and with candor, as we are determined that as far as we can at present do so, the minds of our readers shall be enlightened. The custom of concealing information upon vital and important subjects, in which the interest of the people is involved, we do not agree with, nor favor in the least; we have therefore, laid this cursory treatise before our readers, with the hope that it may prove instrumental in directing the attention of our people in the right way, that leads to their Elevation. Go or stay —of course each is free to do as he pleases—one thing is certain; our Elevation is the work of our own hands. And Mexico, Central America, the West Indies, and South America, all present now, opportunities for the individual enterprise of our young men, who prefer to remain in the United States, in preference to going where they can enjoy real freedom, and equality of rights. Freedom of Religion, as well as of politics, being tolerated in all of these places.

Let our young men and women, prepare themselves for usefulness and business; that the men may enter into merchandise, trading, and other things of importance; the young women may become teachers of various kinds, and otherwise fill places of usefulness. Parents must turn their attention more to the education of their children. We mean, to educate them for useful practical business purposes. Educate them for the Store and the Counting House —to do every-day practical business. Consult the children's propensities, and direct their education according to their inclinations. It may be, that there is too great a desire on the part of parents, to give their children a professional education, before the body of the people, are ready for it. A people must be a business people, and have more to depend upon than mere help in people's houses and Hotels, before they are either able to support, or capable of properly appreciating the services of professional men among them. This has been one of our great mistakes—we have gone in advance of ourselves. We have commenced at the superstructure of the building, instead of the foundation—at the top instead of the bottom. We should first be mechanics and common tradesmen, and professions as a matter of course would grow out of the wealth made thereby. Young men and women, must now prepare for usefulness—the day of our Elevation is at hand—all the world now gazes at us—and Central and South America, and the West Indies, bid us come and be men and women, protected, secure, beloved and Free.

The branches of Education most desirable for the preparation of youth, for practical useful every-day life, are Arithmetic and good Penmanship, in order to be Accountants; and a good rudimental knowledge of Geography—which has ever been neglected, and under estimated—and of Political Economy; which without the knowledge of the first, no people can ever become adventurous—nor of the second, never will be an enterprising people. Geography, teaches a knowledge of the world, and Political Economy, a knowledge of the wealth of nations; or how to make money. These are not abstruse sciences, or learning not easily acquired or understood; but simply, common School Primer learning, that every body may get. And, although it is the very Key to prosperity and success in common life, but few know any thing about it. Unfortunately for our people, so soon as their children learn to read a Chapter in the New Testament, and scribble a miserable hand, they are pronounced to have "Learning enough;" and taken away from School, no use to themselves, nor community. This is apparent in our Public Meetings, and Official Church Meetings; of the great number of men present, there are but few capable of filling a Secretaryship. Some of the large cities may be an exception to this. Of the multitudes of Merchants, and Business men throughout this country, Europe, and the world, few are qualified, beyond the branches here laid down by us as necessary for business. What did John Jacob Astor, Stephen Girard, or do the millionaires and the greater part of the merchant princes, and mariners, know about Latin and Greek, and the Classics? Precious few of them know any thing. In proof of this, in 1841, during the Administration of President Tyler, when the mutiny was detected on board of the American Man of War Brig Somers, the names of the Mutineers, were recorded by young S—a Midshipman in Greek. Captain Alexander Slidell McKenzie, Commanding, was unable to read them; and in his despatches to the Government, in justification of his policy in executing the criminals, said that he "discovered some curious characters which he was unable to read," &c.; showing thereby, that that high functionary, did not understand even the Greek Alphabet, which was only necessary, to have been able to read proper names written in Greek.

What we most need then, is a good business practical Education; because, the Classical and Professional education of so many of our young men, before their parents are able to support them, and community ready to patronize them, only serves to lull their energy, and cripple the otherwise, praiseworthy efforts they would make in life. A Classical education, is only suited to the wealthy, or those who have a prospect of gaining a livelihood by it. The writer does not wish to be understood, as underrating a Classical and Professional education; this is not his intention; he fully appreciates them, having had some such advantages himself; but he desires to give a proper guide, and put a check to the extravagant idea that is fast obtaining, among our people especially, that a Classical, or as it is termed, a "finished education," is necessary to prepare one for usefulness in life. Let us have an education, that shall practically develope our thinking faculties and manhood; and then, and not until then, shall we be able to vie with our oppressors, go where we may. We as heretofore, have been on the extreme; either no qualification at all, or a Collegiate education. We jumped too far; taking a leap from the deepest abyss to the highest summit; rising from the ridiculous to the sublime; without medium or intermission.

Let our young women have an education; let their minds be well informed; well stored with useful information and practical proficiency, rather than the light superficial acquirements, popularly and fashionably called accomplishments. We desire accomplishments, but they must be *useful.*

Our females must be qualified, because they are to be the mothers of our children. As mothers are the first nurses and instructors of children; from them children consequently, get their first impressions, which being always the most lasting, should be the most correct. Raise the mothers above the level of degradation, and the offspring is elevated with them. In a word, instead of our young men, transcribing in their blank books, recipes for *Cooking;* we desire to see them making the transfer of *Invoices of Merchandise.* Come to our aid then; the *morning* of our *Redemption* from degradation, adorns the horizon.

In our selection of individuals, it will be observed, that we have confined ourself entirely to those who occupy or have occupied positions among the whites, consequently having a more general bearing as useful contributors to society at large. While we do not pretend to give all such worthy cases, we gave such as we possessed information of, and desire it to be understood, that a large number of our most intelligent and worthy men and women, have not been named, because from their more private position in community, it was foreign to the object and design of this work. If we have said aught to offend, "take the will for the deed," and be assured, that it was given with the purest of motives, and best intention, from a true hearted man and brother; deeply lamenting the sad fate of his race in this country, and sincerely desiring the elevation of man, and submitted to the serious consideration of all, who favor the promotion of the cause of God and humanity.

1852

Declaration of the Principles of the National Emigration Convention

"That we shall ever cherish our identity of origin, and race, as preferable, in our estimation, to any other people."

HEREAS, FOR YEARS THE COLORED PEOPLE OF THE UNITED States have been looking, hoping and waiting in expectation of realizing the blessings of Civil Liberty; and Whereas, during this long, tedious and anxious period, they have been depending upon their white fellow-countrymen to effect for them this desirable end but instead of which they have met with disappointment, discouragement and degradation; and Whereas, no people can ever attain to the elevated position of freemen, who are totally or partially ignorant of the constituent elements of Political Liberty; and

Whereas, in the multitude of Conventions heretofore held by our fathers and contemporaries among the colored people of the United States, no such principles as a basis have ever been adduced or demonstrated to us as a guide for action; and

Whereas, no people can maintain their freedom without an interested motive and a union of sentiment, as a rule of action and nucleus to hold them together; and

Whereas, all of the Conventions heretofore held by the whites in this country, of whatever political pretensions—whether Democrat, Whig, or Free Democracy—all have thrown themselves upon the declaration: "To sustain the Constitution as our forefathers *understood* it, and the *Union as they formed it;*" all of which plainly and boldly imply, unrestricted liberty to the whites, and the right to hold the blacks in slavery and degradation.

Therefore, as the Declaration of Sentiments and Platform of the Convention, be it—

Resolved,

1.—That we acknowledge the natural equality of the Human Race.

2.—That man is by nature free, and cannot be enslaved, except by injustice and oppression.

3.—That the right to breathe the Air and *use* the Soil on which the Creator has placed us, is co-inherent with the birth of man, and coeval with his existence; consequently, whatever interferes with this sacred inheritance, is the joint ally of Slavery, and at war against the just decree of Heaven. Hence, man cannot be independent without *possessing* the land on which he resides.

4.—That whatever interferes with the natural rights of man, should meet from him with adequate resistance.

5.—That, under no circumstances, let the consequences be as they may, will we ever submit to enslavement, let the power that attempts it, emanate from whatever source it will.

6.—That no people can have political liberty without the sovereign right to exercise a freeman's will.

7.—That no individual is politically *free* who is deprived of the right of self representation.

8.—That to be a freeman *necessarily* implies the right of the elective franchise. . . .

10.—That the elective franchise necessarily implies *eligibility to every position* attainable; the indisputable right of being chosen or elected as the representative of another, and otherwise than this the term is the sheerest imposition and delusion.

11.—That a people who are *liable*, under any pretext or circumstances whatever, to enslavement by the laws of a country, cannot be free in that country, because the rights of a freeman necessarily are sacred and inviolable.

12.—That, as men and equals, we demand every political right, privilege and position to which the whites are eligible in the United States, and we will either attain to these, or accept of nothing.

13.—That, as colored people, in whatever part of the country we may be located, we will accept of no political rights nor privileges but such as shall be impartial in their provisions; nor will we acknowledge these, except extended alike to each and every colored person in such State or territory.

14.—That the political distinctions in many of the States, made by the whites, and accepted of by the colored people, comprise, in many instances, our greatest social curses, and tend more than any thing else to divide our interests and make us indifferent to each others' welfare.

15.—That we pledge our integrity to use all honorable means, to unite us, as one people, on this continent.

16.—That we have no confidence in any political party nor politician —by whatever name they may be styled, or whatever their pretensions—who acknowledges the right of man to hold property in his fellow man—whether this right be admitted as a "necessary" part of the National Compact, the provisions of the Missouri Compromise, the detestably insulting and degrading Fugitive Slave Act, or the more recent contemptible Nebraska-Kansas Bill.

17.—That the Act of Congress of 1850, known as the Fugitive Bill, we declare to be a general law, tending to the virtual enslavement of every colored person in the United States; and consequently we abhor its existence, dispute its authority, refuse submission to its provisions and hold it in a state of the most contemptuous abrogation.

18.—That, as a people, we will never be satisfied nor contented until we occupy a position where we are acknowledged a necessary *constituent* in the *ruling element* of the country in which we live.

19.—That no oppressed people have ever obtained their rights by voluntary acts of generosity on the part of their oppressors.

20.—That it is futile hope on our part to expect such results through the agency of moral goodness on the part of our white American oppressors.

21.—That all great achievements by the Anglo-Saxon race have been accomplished through the agency of self-interest.

22.—That the liberty of a people is always insecure who have not absolute control of their own political destiny.

23.—That if we desire liberty, it can only be obtained at the price which others have paid for it.

24.—That we are willing to pay that price, *let the cost be what it may.*

25.—That according to the present social system of civilized society, the equality of persons is only recognized by their equality of attainments,—as with individuals, so is it with classes and communities;—therefore, we impress on the colored races throughout this Continent and the world, the necessity of having their children and themselves properly qualified in *every* respectable vocation pertaining to the Industrial and Wealth accumulating occupations; of arts, science, trades and professions; of agriculture, commerce and manufactures, so as to equal in *position* the leading characters and nations of the earth, without which we cannot, at best, but occupy a position of subserviency.

26.—That the potency and respectability of a nation or people, depends entirely upon the position of their women, therefore, it is essential to our elevation that the female portion of our children be instructed in all the arts and sciences pertaining to the highest civilization.

27.—That we will forever discountenance all invidious distinctions among us.

28.—That no people, as such, can ever attain to greatness who lose their identity, as they must rise entirely upon their own native merits.

29.—That we shall ever cherish our identity of origin and race, as preferable, in our estimation, to any other people.

30.—That the relative terms Negro, African, Black, Colored and Mulatto, when applied to us, shall ever be held with the same respect and pride; and synonymous with the terms, Caucasion, White, Anglo-Saxon and European, when applied to that class of people.

31.—That, as a people determined to be free, we individually pledge ourselves to support and sustain, on all occasions, by every justifiable effort, as far as possible, the declarations set forth in this bill of sentiments.

1854

The Case of Dred Scott

In one of the most infamous findings in its history, on March 6, 1857, the Supreme Court stated an opinion in *Dred Scott* v. *John F. A. Sandford* (19 Howard 393) that African-Americans were "so far inferior that they had no rights which a white man was bound to respect," providing legal sanction to the already practical abrogation of the rights of both freemen and slaves.

The complicated case originated in the late 1830s when Dr. John Emerson, an army surgeon, left his home in Missouri to spend several years in Illinois and the Louisiana Purchase Territory (now Minnesota), taking with him his slave Dred Scott. While Illinois was a free state under the Northwest Ordinance of 1787, according to the terms of the Missouri Compromise of 1820 Missouri was a slave state and the Louisiana Territory was free.

Emerson died shortly after he and Dred Scott returned to Missouri, and in 1847 Scott sued Emerson's wife for his freedom. Though the Circuit Court of St. Louis County decided in Scott's favor, the Missouri Supreme Court reversed the decision, ruling that Scott's residence in free territory did not make him free. Scott was then sold to Emerson's brother, John F. A. Sanford (misidentified in court documents as Sandford) of New York, apparently for the purpose of bringing a case in federal court, which, according to the Constitution, had the power to decide cases between citizens of different states.

The case came before the Supreme Court in 1856, but Chief Justice Roger B. Taney ordered it reargued the following year to avoid rendering a decision during a presidential election year. The argument of Scott's lawyer, Montgomery Blair, centered on the fundamental issue of whether or not Scott was a "citizen" whose rights were therefore protected by the Constitution.

The outcome of the trial clearly illuminated the deep divisions in the country surrounding the issue of slavery; each judge wrote a separate opinion. The prevailing opinion, however, was that of Chief Justice Taney, who argued that Scott neither gained his freedom by traveling into free territory nor could be considered a citizen either of the state of Missouri or under federal law. Taney further contended that slavery could not be banned in the territories and thus the Missouri Compromise was itself unconstitutional. Six other justices concurred in the opinion that Scott could not be a citizen, while antislavery justices John McLean of Ohio and Benjamin R. Curtis of Massachusetts dissented, arguing that Scott became free when he traveled into free territory. Though the decision was based on the conclusion that Scott remained a slave, in its far-reaching language it impinged on the rights of citizenship of freemen as well.

The reaction to the verdict was swift and clamorous. While the decision led some opponents to increase their emigration efforts, others loudly condemned it. In a meeting in Philadelphia in April 1857, two leading abolitionists, Robert Purvis and Charles Remond, resolved that "the only duty the colored man owes to a Constitution under which he is declared to be an inferior and degraded being . . . is to denounce and repudiate it."

The Dred Scott decision brought the nation a step closer to war, and was nullified only in its aftermath by the Thirteenth† and Fourteenth† Amendments.

Dred Scott's Petition for Freedom

Dred Scott vs. Alex. Sandford, Saml. Russell, and Irene Emerson	To the Honorable, the Circuit Court within and for the County of St. Louis.

Your petitioner, Dred Scott, a man of color, respectfully represents that sometime in the year 1835 your petitioner was purchased as a slave by one John Emerson, since deceased, who afterwards, to-wit; about the year 1836 or 1837, conveyed your petitioner from the State of Missouri to Fort Snelling, a fort then occupied by the troops of the United States and under the jurisdiction of the United States, situated in the territory ceded by France to the United States under the name of Louisiana, lying north of 36 degrees and 30′ North latitude, now included in the State of Missouri, and resided and continued to reside at Fort Snelling upwards of one year, and held your petitioner in slavery at such Fort during all that time in violation of the Act of Congress of 1806 and 1820, entitled An Act to Authorize the People of Missouri Territory to form a Constitution and State Government, and for the admission of such State into the Union on an equal footing with the original states, and to Prohibit Slavery in Certain Territories.

Your petitioner avers that said Emerson has since departed this life, leaving his widow and an infant child whose name is unknown to your petitioner; and that one Alexander Sandford administered upon the estate of said Emerson and that our petitioner is now unlawfully held in slavery by said Sandford and by said administrator and said Irene Emerson claims your petitioner as part of the estate of said Emerson and by one Samuel Russell.

Your petitioner therefore prays your Honorable Court to grant him leave to sue as a poor person, in order to establish his right to freedom, and that the necessary orders may be made in the premises.

Dred Scott

State of Missouri
County of St. Louis } ss.

This day personally came before me, the undersigned, a Justice of the Peace, Dred Scott, the person whose name is affixed to the foregoing petition, and made oath that the facts set forth in the above petition are true to the best of his knowledge and belief, that he is entitled to his freedom. Witness my hand this 1st day of July, 1847.

his
Dred X Scott
mark

Sworn to and subscribed before me this 1st day of July, 1847.

Peter W. Jonstone
Justice of the Peace.

ROBERT PURVIS

Reaction to the Dred Scott Decision

"We owe no allegiance to a country which grinds us under its iron hoof and treats us like dogs."

HEREAS, THE SUPREME COURT OF THE UNITED STATES HAS decided in the case of Dred Scott, that *people of African descent are not and cannot be citizens of the United States, and cannot sue in any of the United States courts;* and whereas, the Court in rendering its decision has declared that "this unfortunate class have, with the civilized and enlightened portion of the world, for more than a century, been regarded as being of an inferior order, and unfit associates for the white race, either socially or politically, having no rights which white men are bound to respect;" and whereas, this Supreme Court is the constitutionally approved tribunal to determine all such questions; therefore,

Resolved, That this atrocious decision furnishes final confirmation of the already well known fact that under the Constitution and Government of the United States, the colored people are nothing, and can be nothing but an alien, disfranchised and degraded class.

Resolved, That to attempt, as some do, to prove that there is no support given to Slavery in the Constitution and essential structure of the American Government, is to argue against palpable facts; and that while it may suit white men who do not feel the iron heel, to please themselves with such theories, it ill becomes the man of color whose daily experience refutes the absurdity, to indulge in any such idle phantasies.

Resolved, That to persist in supporting a Government which holds and exercises the power, as distinctly set forth by a tribunal from which there is no appeal, to trample a class under foot as an inferior and degraded race, is on the part of the colored man at once the height of folly and the depth of pusillanimity.

Resolved, That no allegiance is due from any man, or any class of men, to a Government founded and administered in iniquity, and that the only duty the colored man owes to a Constitution under which he is declared to be an inferior and degraded being, having no rights which white men are bound to respect, is to denounce and repudiate it, and to do what he can by all proper means to bring it into contempt.

Mr. Purvis's speech in support of these resolutions was brief but earnest. He scouted the idea of colored people taking comfort from the pretence that this decision of the Supreme Court was unconstitutional. The Supreme Court, he said, was the appointed tribunal, and what it said was constitutional, constitutional to all *practical* intents and purposes. There was nothing new in this decision; it was in perfect keeping with the treatment of the colored people by the American Government from the beginning to this day. Mr. Purvis was asked by one of the audience if he had not been acknowledged and treated as an American citizen. He said he had been, and that by the Cabinet of General Jackson. He stated that, intending to embark on a voyage to Europe, he applied to the Secretary of State for a passport, and an informal ticket of leave sort of paper was sent to him in return.

He showed this to Mr. Robert Vaux, father of the present Mayor, who was so indignant that he wrote to Washington on the subject, and as a result, a formal passport, giving him the protection of the Government, as a citizen of the United States, was sent to him. But, said Mr. Purvis, I was indebted for this not to the American Constitution or to the spirit of the American Government, but to the generous impulses of General Andrew Jackson, who had on more occasions than one in the then late war publicly tendered his gratitude to colored citizens for their brave assistance in the defence of the country.

Mr. Purvis was followed by C. L. Remond, of Salem, Mass., who, in reply to the same interrogation, stated that his father, being an immigrant from the West Indies, was formally naturalized as a citizen of the United States, but, like Mr. Purvis, he considered this no proof that the Supreme Court was not vested with power to declare that people of African descent could not be citizens of the United States. Mr. Remond then offered the following resolutions, with a view, as he said, of making the expression contained in those of Mr. Purvis more complete:—

Resolved, That though many of our fathers and some of us have, in time past, exercised the right of American citizenship; this was when a better spirit pervaded the land, and when the patriotic services of colored men in the defence of the country were fresh in the minds of the people; but that the power to oppress us lurked all the time in the Constitution only waiting to be developed; and that now when it suits the slave oligarchy to assert that power, we are made to feel its grinding weight.

Resolved, That what little remains to us of political rights in individual States, we hold, as we conceive, only by sufferance; and that when it suits the purposes of the slave power to do so, they will command their obedient dough-faced allies at the North to take these rights away from us, and leave us no more room under the State Government, than we have under the Federal.

Resolved, That we rejoice that slave holding despotism lays its ruthless hand not only on the humble black man, but on the proud Northern white man; and our hope is, that when our white fellow slaves in these so called free States see that they are alike subject with us to the slave oligarchy, the difference in our servitude being only in degree, they will make common cause with us, and that throwing off the yoke and striking for the impartial liberty, they will join with us in our efforts to recover the long lost boon of freedom.

Mr. Remond spoke at length and with much fervor. He considered that for colored people, after this, to persist in claiming citizenship under the United States Constitution would be mean-spirited and craven. We owe no allegiance to a country which grinds us under its iron hoof and treats us like dogs. The time has gone by for colored people to talk of patriotism: He used to be proud that the first blood shed in the American Revolution (that of Attucks, who fell in Boston) was that of a colored man. He used to be proud that his grandfather, on his mother's side, fought for liberty in the Revolutionary war. But that time has passed by. The liberty purchased by the Revolutionary men was used to enslave and degrade the colored man, and, as a colored man, he loathed and abhorred the government that could perpetrate such outrages. He repudiated, he denounced the American Union in strong terms. People might talk to him of "patience." He had no patience to submit quietly to chains and oppression. Let others bare their backs to the lash, and meekly and submissively wear their chains. That was not his idea of duty, of manhood, or of self-respect.

Mr. Remond made many remarks on other subjects, as did also Mr. Purvis, who again took the floor. When the resolutions came to be put, some opposition was made, and a rambling and somewhat personal debate ensued; the end of which was, that the question was taken on the resolutions as a whole, and the chair pronounced them carried.

The Liberator, April 10, 1857

Frederick Douglass
(1817–1895)

In the abolitionist struggle of the nineteenth century, it is perhaps accurate to say that the role of the Great Emancipator belonged not to President Abraham Lincoln, but to the great orator and race leader Frederick Douglass. In influential speeches, essays, and autobiographical writings that addressed every important issue of his time—from abolition, colonization, and Reconstruction to Jim Crow, lynching, and women's rights—Douglass spoke with remarkable vigor, eloquence, and passion.

Douglass was born Frederick Augustus Washington Bailey on the eastern shore of Maryland, the son of a slave mother and, it is believed, her white master. That he never knew with certainty his father's identity and the date of his birth epitomized the depersonalization of American slavery. Raised largely by his grandmother, Douglass saw little of his mother before her death when he was seven, and the severe beating of an aunt left a remarkable impression on him as a boy. Sent to live in Baltimore with his master's brother, he was at first encouraged to learn to read and write by his master's wife, but had to continue his self-education secretly when her husband objected that "learning would spoil the best nigger in the world." Given over to a famed "Negro-breaker," he then experienced what he called the "turning-point in my career as a slave." When the man attempted to beat him, Douglass fought back violently, and from that point onward the beatings stopped. "I now resolved," he wrote later, "that, however long I might remain a slave in form, the day had passed forever when I could be a slave in fact. I did not hesitate to let it be known of me, that the white man who expected to succeed in whipping me, must also succeed in killing me." When he returned to Baltimore, he learned the trade of a caulker and his services were hired out, allowing him to come into contact with the free black community in the city and providing him with the opportunity to escape.

In 1938 he fled to New York and continued North. In 1841 he joined the Massachusetts Anti-Slavery Society and was soon recognized as an imposing physical presence and an orator of unusual skill, who relied on both emotional appeal and rational argument. Describing Douglass's appearance at an antislavery convention in Nantucket in August of 1841, the abolitionist William Lloyd Garrison recalled "I shall never forget his first speech at the convention—the extraordinary emotion it excited in my own mind—the powerful impression it created upon a crowded auditory . . . As soon as he had taken his seat, filled with hope and admiration, I rose, and declared that *Patrick Henry,* of revolutionary fame, never made a speech more eloquent in the cause of liberty, than the one we had just listened to from the lips of that hunted fugitive." William Wells Brown said, simply, "White men and black men had talked against slavery, but none had ever spoken like Frederick Douglass." Douglass lectured for the Society for the next four years and at its urging penned his autobiography.

The *Narrative of the Life of Frederick Douglass: An American Slave,* published in Boston in 1845, enjoyed an immediate success and has come to represent perhaps the fullest expression of its literary type. Recounting both the author's years in captivity and his thrilling escape, his account was offered with endorsements by Garrison and Wendell Phillips attesting to the character of its author and the truth of a tale that represented the condition of an entire class of enslaved persons. "In reading your life," Phillips wrote, "no one can say that we have unfairly picked out some rare specimens of cruelty. We know that the bitter drops, which even you have drained from the cup, are no incidental aggravations, no individual ills, but such as must mingle always and necessarily in the lot of every slave." Douglass's account was unusual, however, in its forthright avoidance of a shielding pseudonym, its power, and its literary grace, marked particularly by the emphatic chiasmus—"You have seen how a man was made a slave; you shall see how a slave was made a man"—used in its pages. Moving beyond the details of his own life, Douglass delivered a biting critique of society, pointing out that even in Maryland, where slavery wore "its fairest features," it was an abomination; that race prejudice raged in the North; and that with fugitive slave laws that threatened to enslave a man under the barest of pretexts, even nonslaves in the North were left only "half-free."

After the publication of his *Narrative* made the fugitive Douglass's whereabouts known, he began a celebrated two-year lecture tour of England, during which he expanded on the themes of race prejudice, the hypocrisy of the Christian clergy, and the inherent racism of the American Constitution, which constituted a slave as "three-fifths" of a human being. Returning to America "for the sake of my brethren," Douglass at first subscribed to the Garrisonian brand of "moral suasion" (it had been largely through his influence that the National Negro Convention of 1843 failed to endorse Henry Highland Garnet's "Call to Rebellion"[†]), but later came to believe that slavery would only be thrown over violently—"Power concedes nothing without a demand," he argued. "It never did and it never will." And although he thought John Brown's raid on Harpers Ferry unwise, he later viewed it as a pivotal event that made "wars, votes, and compromises" obsolete. In 1852 Douglass delivered the oration, "What, to the Slave, is Your Fourth of July?" included here, to the Rochester Antislavery Sewing Society, citing a powerful litany of sham freedoms. In 1857 he condemned the "hell-black" decision in the Dred Scott case and predicted that, if the verdict held, "the lightning, whirlwind, and earthquake may come." Beginning to explore the possibility of immigration to Haiti, his plans were abandoned as the Civil War began and he urged Lincoln to frame the national conflict in abolitionist terms. Once African-Americans were accepted into the ranks of the Union Army, he recruited black troops and urged all "Men of Color to Arms!"† As the war neared an end, he insisted (in a speech delivered to the thirty-second annual convention of the American Anti-Slavery Society† in Boston) that continued vigilance was needed to secure the full rights of citizenship for African-Americans, and he argued strenuously in support of the Fourteenth and Fifteenth Amendments† and women's rights.

Douglass expanded on the story of his life in two later volumes, *My Bondage and My Freedom* (1855) and *The Life and Times of Frederick Douglass* (1881), and was for two decades a prolific journalist (editing in succession the *North Star, Frederick Douglass' Paper,* and *Douglass' Monthly*). In the 1860s he held several minor political posts; he edited the *New National Era* from 1870 to 1873; and from 1889 to 1891 he served as minister to Haiti. He died in Washington on February 20, 1895.

from *Narrative of the Life of Frederick Douglass*

"For my part, I should prefer death to hopeless bondage. . . ."

CHAPTER I

I WAS BORN IN TUCKAHOE, NEAR HILLSBOROUGH, AND ABOUT twelve miles from Easton, in Talbot county, Maryland. I have no accurate knowledge of my age, never having seen any authentic record containing it. By far the larger part of the slaves know as little of their ages as horses know of theirs, and it is the wish of most masters within my knowledge to keep their slaves thus ignorant. I do not remember to have ever met a slave who could tell of his birthday. They seldom come nearer to it than planting-time, harvest-time, cherry-time, spring-time, or fall-time. A want of information concerning my own was a source of unhappiness to me even during childhood. The white children could tell their ages. I could not tell why I ought to be deprived of the same privilege. I was not allowed to make any inquiries of my master concerning it. He deemed all such inquiries on the part of a slave improper and impertinent, and evidence of a restless spirit. The nearest estimate I can give makes me now between twenty-seven and twenty-eight years of age. I come to this, from hearing my master say, some time during 1835, I was about seventeen years old.

My mother was named Harriet Bailey. She was the daughter of Isaac and Betsey Bailey, both colored, and quite dark. My mother was of a darker complexion than either my grandmother or grandfather.

My father was a white man. He was admitted to be such by all I ever heard speak of my parentage. The opinion was also whispered that my master was my father; but of the correctness of this opinion, I know nothing; the means of knowing was withheld from me. My mother and I were separated when I was but an infant—before I knew her as my mother. It is a common custom, in the part of Maryland from which I ran away, to part children from their mothers at a very early age. Frequently, before the child has reached its twelfth month, its mother is taken from it, and hired out on some farm a considerable distance off, and the child is placed under the care of an old woman, too old for field labor. For what this separation is done, I do not know, unless it be to hinder the development of the child's affection toward its mother, and to blunt and destroy the natural affection of the mother for the child. This is the inevitable result.

I never saw my mother to know her as such, more than four or five times in my life; and each of these times was very short in duration, and at night. She was hired by a Mr. Stewart, who lived about twelve miles from my home. She made her journeys to see me in the night, travelling the whole distance on foot, after the performance of her day's work. She was a field hand, and a whipping is the penalty of not being in the field at sunrise, unless a slave has special permission from his or her master to the contrary—a permission which they seldom get, and one that gives to him that gives it the proud name of being a kind master. I do not recollect of ever seeing my mother by the light of day. She was with me in the night. She would lie down with me, and get me to sleep, but long before I waked she was gone. Very little communication ever took place between us. Death soon ended what little we could have while she lived, and with it her hardships and suffering. She died when I was about seven years old, on one of my master's farms, near Lee's Mill. I was not allowed to be present during her illness, at her death, or burial. She was gone long before I knew any thing about it. Never having enjoyed, to any considerable extent, her soothing presence, her tender and watchful care, I received the tidings of her death with much the same emotions I should have probably felt at the death of a stranger.

Called thus suddenly away, she left me without the slightest intimation of who my father was. The whisper that my master was my father, may or may not be true; and, true or false, it is of but little consequence to my purpose whilst the fact remains, in all its glaring odiousness, that slaveholders have ordained, and by law established, that the children of slave women shall in all cases follow the condition of their mothers; and this is done too obviously to administer to their own lusts, and make a gratification of their wicked desires profitable as well as pleasurable; for by this cunning arrangement, the slaveholder, in cases not a few, sustains to his slaves the double relation of master and father.

I know of such cases; and it is worthy of remark that such slaves invariably suffer greater hardships, and have more to contend with, than others. They are, in the first place, a constant offence to their mistress. She is ever disposed to find fault with them; they can seldom do any thing to please her; she is never better pleased than when she sees them under the lash, especially when she suspects her husband of showing to his mulatto children favors which he withholds from his black slaves. The master is frequently compelled to sell this class of his slaves, out of deference to the feelings of his white wife; and, cruel as the deed may strike any one to be, for a man to sell his own children to human flesh-mongers, it is often the dictate of humanity for him to do so; for, unless he does this, he must not only whip them himself, but must stand by and see one white son tie up his brother, of but few shades darker complexion than himself, and ply the gory lash to his naked back; and if he lisp one word of disapproval, it is set down to his parental partiality, and only makes a bad matter worse, both for himself and the slave whom he would protect and defend.

Every year brings with it multitudes of this class of slaves. It was doubtless in consequence of a knowledge of this fact, that one great statesman of the south predicted the downfall of slavery by the inevitable laws of population. Whether this prophecy is ever fulfilled or not, it is nevertheless plain that a very different-looking class of people are springing up at the south, and are now held in slavery, from those originally brought to this country from Africa; and if their increase will do no other good, it will do away the force of the argument, that God cursed Ham, and therefore American slavery is right. If the lineal descendants of Ham are alone to be scripturally enslaved, it is certain that slavery at the south must soon become unscriptural; for thousands are ushered into the world, annually, who, like myself, owe their existence to white fathers, and those fathers most frequently their own masters.

I have two masters. My first master's name was Anthony. I do not remember his first name. He was generally called Captain Anthony—a title which, I presume, he acquired by sailing a craft on the Chesapeake Bay. He was not considered a rich slaveholder. He owned two or three farms, and about thirty slaves. His farms and slaves were under the care of an overseer. The overseer's name was Plummer. Mr. Plummer was a miserable drunkard, a profane swearer, and a savage monster. He always went armed with a cowskin and a heavy cudgel. I have known him to cut and slash the women's heads so horribly, that even master would be enraged at his cruelty, and would threaten to whip him if he did not mind himself. Master, however, was not a humane slaveholder. It required extraordinary barbarity on the part of an overseer to affect him. He was a cruel man, hardened by a long life of slaveholding. He would at times seem to take great pleasure in whipping a slave. I have often been awakened at the dawn of day by the most heart-rending shrieks of an own aunt of mine, whom he used to tie up to a joist, and whip upon her naked back till she was literally covered with blood. No words, no tears, no prayers, from his gory victim, seemed to move his iron heart from its bloody purpose. The louder she screamed, the harder he whipped; and where the blood ran fastest, there he whipped longest. He would whip her to make her scream, and whip her to make her hush; and not until overcome by fatigue, would he cease to swing the blood-clotted cowskin. I remember the first time I ever witnessed this horrible exhibition. I was quite a child, but I well remember it. I never shall forget it whilst I remember any thing. It was the first of a long series of such outrages, of which I was doomed to be a witness and a participant. It struck me with awful force. It was the blood-stained gate, the entrance to the hell of slavery, through which I was about to pass. It was a most terrible spectacle. I wish I could commit to paper the feelings with which I beheld it. . . .

CHAPTER II

My master's family consisted of two sons, Andrew and Richard; one daugher, Lucretia, and her husband, Captain Thomas Auld. They lived in one house, upon the home plantation of Colonel Edward Lloyd. My master was Colonel Lloyd's clerk and superintendent. He was what might be called the overseer of the overseers. I spent two years of childhood on this plantation in my old master's family. It was here that I witnessed the bloody transaction recorded in the first chapter; and as I received my first impressions of slavery on this plantation, I will give some description of it, and of slavery as it there existed. The plantation is about twelve miles north of Easton, in Talbot county, and is situated on the border of Miles River. The principal products raised upon it were tobacco, corn, and wheat. These were raised in great abundance; so that, with the products of this and the other farms belonging to him, he was able to keep in almost constant employment a large sloop, in carrying them to market at Baltimore. This sloop was named Sally Lloyd, in honor of one of the colonel's daughters. My master's son-in-law, Captain Auld, was master of the vessel; she was otherwise manned by the colonel's own slaves. Their names were Peter, Isaac, Rich, and Jake. These were esteemed very highly by the other slaves, and looked upon as the privileged ones of the plantation; for it was no small affair, in the eyes of the slaves, to be allowed to see Baltimore.

Colonel Lloyd kept from three to four hundred slaves on his home plantation, and owned a large number more on the neighboring farms belonging to him. The names of the farms nearest to the home plantation were Wye Town and New Design. "Wye Town" was under the overseership of a man named Noah Willis. New Design was under the overseership of a Mr. Townsend. The overseers of these, and all the rest of the farms, numbering over twenty, received advice and direction from the managers of the home plantation. This was the great business place. It was the seat of government for the whole twenty farms. All disputes among the overseers were settled here. If a slave was convicted of any high misdemeanor, became unmanageable, or evinced a determination to run away, he was brought immediately here, severely whipped, put on board the sloop, carried to Baltimore, and sold to Austin Woolfolk, or some other slave-trader, as a warning to the slaves remaining.

Here, too, the slaves of all the other farms received their monthly allowance of food, and their yearly clothing. The men and women slaves received, as their monthly allowance of food, eight pounds of pork, or its equivalent in fish, and one bushel of corn meal. Their yearly clothing consisted of two coarse linen shirts, one pair of linen trousers, like the shirts, one jacket, one pair of trousers for winter, made of coarse negro cloth, one pair of stockings, and one pair of shoes; the whole of which could not have cost more than seven dollars. The allowance of the slave children was given to their mothers, or the old women having the care of them. The children unable to work in the field had neither shoes, stockings, jackets, nor trousers, given to them; their clothing consisted of two coarse linen shirts per year. When these failed them, they went naked until the next allowance-day. Children from seven to ten years old, of both sexes, almost naked, might be seen at all seasons of the year.

There were no beds given the slaves, unless one coarse blanket be considered such, and none but the men and women had these. This, however, is not considered a very great privation. They find less difficulty from the want of beds, than from the want of time to sleep; for when their day's work in the field is done, the most of them having their washing, mending, and cooking to do, and having few or none of the ordinary facilities for doing either of these, very many of their sleeping hours are consumed in preparing for the field the coming day; and when this is done, old and young, male and female, married and single, drop down side by side, on one common bed,—the cold, damp floor,—each covering himself or herself with their miserable blankets; and here they sleep till they are summoned to the field by the driver's horn. At the sound of this, all must rise, and be off to the field. There must be no halting; every one must be at his or her post; and woe betides them who hear not this morning summons to the field; for if they are not awakened by the sense of hearing, they are by the sense of feeling; no age nor sex finds any favor. Mr. Severe, the overseer, used to stand by the door of the quarter, armed with a large hickory stick and heavy cowskin, ready to whip any one who was so unfortunate as not to hear, or, from any other cause, was prevented from being ready to start for the field at the sound of the horn.

Mr. Severe was rightly named: he was a cruel man. I have seen him whip a woman, causing the blood to run half an hour at the time; and this, too, in the midst of her crying children, pleading for their mother's release. He seemed to take pleasure in manifesting his fiendish barbarity. Added to this cruelty, he was a profane swearer. It was enough to chill the blood and stiffen the hair of an ordinary man to hear him talk. Scarce a sentence escaped him but that was commenced or concluded by some horrid oath. The field was the place to witness his cruelty and profanity. His presence made it both the field of blood and of blasphemy. From the rising till the going down of the sun, he was cursing, raving, cutting, and slashing among the slaves of the field, in the most frightful manner. His career was short. He died very soon after I went to Colonel Lloyd's; and he died as he lived, uttering, with his dying groans, bitter curses and horrid oaths. His death was regarded by the slaves as the result of a merciful providence. . . .

The slaves selected to go to the Great House Farm, for the monthly allowance for themselves and their fellow-slaves, were peculiarly enthusiastic. While on their way, they would make the dense old woods, for miles around, reverberate with their wild songs, revealing at once the highest joy and the deepest sadness. They would compose and sing as they went along, consulting neither time nor tune. The thought that came up, came out—if not in the word, in the sound;—and as frequently in the one as in the other. They would sometimes sing the most pathetic sentiment in the most rapturous tone, and the most rapturous sentiment in the most pathetic tone. Into all of their songs they would manage to weave something of the Great House Farm. Especially would they do this, when leaving home. They would then sing most exultingly the following words:—

"I am going away to the Great House Farm!
O, yea! O, yea! O!"

This they would sing, as a chorus, to words which to many would seem unmeaning jargon, but which, nevertheless, were full of meaning to themselves. I have sometimes thought that the mere hearing of those songs would do more to impress some minds with the horrible character of slavery, than the reading of whole volumes of philosophy on the subject could do.

I did not, when a slave, understand the deep meaning of those rude and apparently incoherent songs. I was myself within the circle; so that I neither saw nor heard as those without might see and hear. They told a tale of woe which was then altogether beyond my feeble comprehension; they were tones loud, long, and deep; they breathed the prayer and complaint of souls boiling over with the bitterest anguish. Every tone was a testimony against slavery, and a prayer to God for deliverance from chains. The hearing of those wild notes always depressed my spirit, and filled me with ineffable sadness. I have frequently found myself in tears while hearing them. The mere recurrence to those songs, even now, afflicts me; and while I am writing these lines, an expression of feeling has already found its way down my cheek. To those songs I trace my first glimmering conception of the dehumanizing character of slavery. I can never get rid of that conception. Those songs still follow me, to deepen my hatred of slavery, and quicken my sympathies for my brethren in bonds. If any one wishes to be impressed with the soul-killing effects of slavery, let him go to Colonel Lloyd's plantation, and, on allowance-day, place himself in the deep pine woods, and there let him, in silence, analyze the sounds that shall pass through the chambers of his soul,—and if he is not thus impressed, it will only be because "there is no flesh in his obdurate heart."

I have often been utterly astonished, since I came to the north, to find persons who could speak of the singing, among slaves, as evidence of their contentment and happiness. It is impossible to conceive of a greater mistake. Slaves sing most when they are most unhappy. The songs of the slave represent the sorrows of his heart; and he is relieved by them, only as an aching heart is relieved by its tears. At least, such is my experience. I have often sung to drown my sorrow, but seldom to express my happiness. Crying for joy, and singing for joy, were alike uncommon to me while in the jaws of slavery. The singing of a man cast away upon a desolate island might be as appropriately considered as evidence of contentment and happiness, as the singing of a slave; the songs of the one and of the other are prompted by the same emotion.

CHAPTER VI

My new mistress proved to be all she appeared when I first met her at the door,—a woman of the kindest heart and finest feelings. She had never had a slave under her control previously to myself, and prior to her marriage she had been dependent upon her own industry for a living. She was by trade a weaver; and by constant application to her business, she had been in a good degree preserved from the blighting and dehumanizing effects of slavery. I was utterly astonished at her goodness. I scarcely knew how to behave towards her. She was entirely unlike any other white woman I had ever seen. I could not approach her as I was accustomed to approach other white ladies. My early instruction was all out of place. The crouching servility, usually so acceptable a quality in a slave, did not answer when manifested toward her. Her favor was not gained by it; she seemed to be disturbed by it. She did not deem it impudent or unmannerly for a slave to look her in the face. The meanest slave was put fully at ease in her presence, and none left without feeling better for having seen her. Her face was made of heavenly smiles, and her voice of tranquil music.

But, alas! this kind heart had but a short time to remain such. The fatal poison of irresponsible power was already in her hands, and soon commenced its infernal work. That cheerful eye, under the influence of slavery, soon became red with rage; that voice, made all of sweet accord, changed to one of harsh and horrid discord; and that angelic face gave place to that of a demon.

Very soon after I went to live with Mr. and Mrs. Auld, she very kindly commenced to teach me the A, B, C. After I had learned this, she assisted me in learning to spell words of three or four letters. Just at this point of my progress, Mr. Auld found out what was going on, and at once forbade Mrs. Auld to instruct me further, telling her, among other things, that it was unlawful, as well as unsafe, to teach a slave to read. To use his own words, further, he said, "If you give a nigger an inch, he will take an ell. A nigger should know nothing but to obey his master—to do as he is told to do. Learning would *spoil* the best nigger in the world. Now," said he, "if you teach that nigger (speaking of myself) how to read, there would be no keeping him. It would forever unfit him to be a slave. He would at once become unmanageable, and of no value to his master. As to himself, it could do him no good, but a great deal of harm. It would make him discontented and unhappy." These words sank deep into my heart, stirred up sentiments within that lay slumbering, and called into existence an entirely new train of thought. It was a new and special revelation, explaining dark and mysterious things, with which my youthful understanding had struggled, but struggled in vain. I now understood what had been to me a most perplexing difficulty —to whit, the white man's power to enslave the black man. It was a grand achievement, and I prized it highly. From that moment, I understood the pathway from slavery to freedom. It was just what I wanted, and I got it at a time when I the least expected it. Whilst I was saddened by the thought of losing the aid of my kind mistress, I was gladdened by the invaluable instruction which, by the merest accident, I had gained from my master. Though conscious of the difficulty of learning without a teacher, I set out with high hope, and a fixed purpose, at whatever cost of trouble, to learn how to read. The very decided manner with which he spoke, and strove to impress his wife with the consequences of giving me instruction, served to convince me that he was deeply sensible of the truths he was uttering. It gave me the best assurance that I might rely with the utmost confidence on the results which, he said, would flow from teaching me to read. What he most dreaded, that I most desired. What he most loved, that I most hated. That which to him was a great evil, to be carefully shunned, was to me a great good, to be diligently sought; and the argument which he so warmly urged, against my learning to read, only served to inspire me with a desire and determination to learn. In learning to read, I owe almost as much to the bitter opposition of my master, as to the kindly aid of my mistress. I acknowledge the benefit of both. . . .

CHAPTER X

. . . At the close of the year 1834, Mr. Freeland again hired me of my master, for the year 1835. But, by this time, I began to want to live *upon free land* as well as *with Freeland;* and I was no longer content, therefore, to live with him or any other slaveholder. I began, with the commencement of the year, to prepare myself for a final struggle, which should decide my fate one way or the other. My tendency was upward. I was fast approaching manhood, and year after year had passed, and I was still a slave. These thoughts roused me—I must do something. I therefore resolved that 1835 should not pass without witnessing an attempt, on my part, to secure my liberty. But I was not willing to cherish this determination alone. My fellow-slaves were dear to me. I was anxious to have them participate with me in this, my life-giving determination. I therefore, though with great prudence, commenced early to ascertain their views and feelings in regard to their condition, and to imbue their minds with thoughts of freedom. I bent myself to devising ways and means for our escape, and meanwhile strove, on all fitting occasions, to impress them with the gross fraud and inhumanity of slavery. I went first to Henry, next to John, then to the others. I found, in them all, warm hearts and noble spirits. They were ready to hear, and ready to act when a feasible plan should be proposed. This was what I wanted. I talked to them of our want of manhood, if we submitted to our enslavement without at least one noble effort to be free. We met often, and consulted frequently, and told our hopes and fears, recounted the difficulties, real and imagined, which we should be called on to meet. At times we were almost disposed to give up, and try to content ourselves with our wretched lot; at others, we were firm and unbending in our determination to go. Whenever we suggested any plan, there was shrinking—the odds were fearful. Our path was beset with the greatest obstacles; and if we succeeded in gaining the end of it, our right to be free was yet questionable—we were yet liable to be returned to bondage. We could see no spot, this side of the ocean, where we could be free. We knew nothing about Canada. Our knowledge of the north did not extend farther than New York; and to go there, and be forever harassed with the frightful liability of being returned to slavery—with the certainty of being treated tenfold worse than before—the thought was truly a horrible one, and one which it was not easy to overcome. The case sometimes stood thus: At every gate through which we were to pass, we saw a watchman—at every ferry a guard—on every bridge a sentinel—and in every wood a patrol. We were hemmed in upon every side. Here were the difficulties, real or imagined —the good to be sought, and the evil to be shunned. On the one hand, there stood slavery, a stern reality, glaring frightfully upon us,—its robes already crimsoned with the blood of millions, and even now feasting itself greedily upon our own flesh. On the other hand, away back in the dim distance, under the flickering light of the north star, behind some craggy hill or snow-covered mountain, stood a doubtful freedom—half frozen—beckoning us to come and share its hospitality. This in itself was sometimes enough to stagger us; but when we permitted ourselves to survey the road, we were frequently appalled. Upon either side we saw grim death, assuming the most horrid shapes. Now it was starvation, causing us to eat our own flesh;—now we were contending with the waves, and were drowned;—now we were overtaken, and torn to pieces by the fangs of the terrible bloodhound. We were stung by scorpions, chased by wild beasts, bitten by snakes, and finally, after having nearly reached the desired spot,—after swimming rivers, encountering wild beasts, sleeping in the woods, suffering hunger and nakedness,—we were overtaken by our pursuers, and, in our resistance, we were shot dead upon the spot! I say, this picture sometimes appalled us, and made us

> "rather bear those ills we had,
> Than fly to others, that we knew not of."

In coming to a fixed determination to run away, we did more than Patrick Henry, when he resolved upon liberty or death. With us it was a doubtful liberty at most, and almost certain death if we failed. For my part, I should prefer death to hopeless bondage. . . .

1845

Letter to Thomas Auld

"I am your fellow man, but not your slave."

THOMAS AULD:

SIR—The long and intimate, though by no means friendly relation which unhappily subsisted between you and myself, leads me to hope that you will easily account for the great liberty which I now take in addressing you in this open and public manner. The same fact may possibly remove any disagreeable surprise which you may experience on again finding your name coupled with mine, in any other way than in an advertisement, accurately describing my person, and offering a large sum for my arrest. In thus dragging you again before the public, I am aware that I shall subject myself to no inconsiderable amount of censure. I shall probably be charged with an unwarrantable, if not a wanton and reckless disregard of the rights and properties of private life. There are those North as well as South who entertain a much higher respect for rights which are merely conventional, than they do for rights which are personal and essential. Not a few there are in our country, who, while they have no scruples against robbing the laborer of the hard earned results of his patient industry, will be shocked by the extremely indelicate manner of bringing your name before the public. Believing this to be the case, and wishing to meet every reasonable or plausible objection to my conduct, I will frankly state the ground upon which I justify myself in this instance, as well as on former occasions when I have thought proper to mention your name in public. All will agree that a man guilty of theft, robbery, or murder, has forfeited the right to concealment and private life; that the community have a right to subject such persons to the most complete exposure. However much they may desire retirement, and aim to conceal themselves and their movements from the popular gaze, the public have a right to ferret them out, and bring their conduct before the proper tribunals of the country for investigation. Sir, you will undoubtedly make the proper application of these generally admitted principles, and will easily see the light in which you are regarded by me, I will not therefore manifest ill temper, by calling you hard names. I know you to be a man of some intelligence, and readily determine the precise estimate which I entertain of your character. I may therefore indulge in language which may seem to others indirect and ambiguous, and yet be quite well understood by yourself.

I have selected this day on which to address you, because it is the anniversary of my emancipation; and knowing of no better why, I am led to this as the best mode of celebrating that truly important event. Just ten years ago this beautiful September morning, yon bright sun beheld me a slave—a poor, degraded chattel—trembling at the sound of your voice, lamenting that I was a man, and wishing myself a brute. The hopes which I had treasured up for weeks of a safe and successful escape from your grasp, were powerfully confronted at this last hour by dark clouds of doubt and fear, making my person shake and my bosom to heave with the heavy contest between hope and fear. I have no words to describe to you the deep agony of soul which I experienced on that never to be forgotten morning—(for I left by daylight.) I was making a leap in the dark. The probabilities, so far as I could by reason determine them, were stoutly against the undertaking. The preliminaries and precautions I had adopted previously, all worked badly. I was like one going to war without weapons—the chances of defeat to one of victory. One in whom I had confided, and one who had promised me assistance, appalled by fear at the trial hour, deserted me, thus leaving the responsibility of success or failure solely with myself. You, sir, can never know my feelings. As I look back to them, I can scarcely realize that I have passed through a scene so trying. Trying however as they were, and gloomy as was the prospect, thanks be to the Most High, who is ever the God of the oppressed, at the moment which was to determine my whole early career. His grace was sufficient, my mind was made up. I embraced the golden opportunity, took the morning tide at the flood, and a free man, young, active and strong, is the result.

I have often thought I should like to explain to you the grounds upon which I have justified myself in running away from you. I am almost ashamed to do so now, for by this time you may have discovered them yourself. I will, however, glance at them. When yet but a child about six years old, I imbibed the determination to run away. The very first mental effort that I now remember on my part, was an attempt to solve the mystery, Why am I a slave? and with this question my youthful mind was troubled for many days, pressing upon me more heavily at times than others. When I saw the slave-driver whip a slave woman, cut the blood out of her neck, and heard her piteous cries, I went away into the corner of the fence, wept and pondered over the mystery. I had, through some medium, I know not what, got some idea of God, the Creator of all mankind, the black and the white, and that he had made the blacks to serve the whites as slaves. How he could do this and be *good*, I could not tell. I was not satisfied with this theory, which made God responsible for slavery, for it pained me greatly, and I have wept over it long and often. At one time, your first wife, Mrs. Lucretia, heard me singing and saw me shedding tears, and asked of me the matter, but I was afraid to tell her. I was puzzled with this question, till one night, while sitting in the kitchen, I heard some of the old slaves talking of their parents having been stolen from Africa by white men, and were sold here as slaves. The whole mystery was solved at once. Very soon after this my aunt Jinny and uncle Noah ran away, and the great noise made about it by your father-in-law, made me for the first time acquainted with the fact, that there were free States as well as slave States. From that time, I resolved that I would some day run away. The morality of the act, I dispose as follows: I am myself; you are yourself; we are two distinct persons, equal persons. What you are, I am. You are a man, and so am I. God created both, and made us separate beings.

I am not by nature bound to you, or you to me. Nature does not make your existence depend upon me, or mine to depend upon yours. I cannot walk upon your legs, or you upon mine. I cannot breathe for you, or you for me; I must breathe for myself, and you for yourself. We are distinct persons, and are each equally provided with faculties necessary to our individual existence. In leaving you, I took nothing but what belonged to me, and in no way lessened your means for obtaining an *honest* living. Your faculties remained yours, and mine became useful to their rightful owner. I therefore see no wrong in any part of the transaction. It is true, I went off secretly, but that was more your fault than mine. Had I let you into the secret, you would have defeated the enterprise entirely; but for this, I should have been really glad to have made you acquainted with my intentions to leave.

You may perhaps want to know how I like my present condition. I am free to say, I greatly prefer it to that which I occupied in Maryland. I am, however, by no means prejudiced against the State as such. Its geography, climate, fertility and products, are such as to make it a very desirable abode for any man; and but for the existence of slavery there, it is not impossible that I might again take up my abode in that State. It is not that I love Maryland less, but freedom more. You will be surprised to learn that people at the North labor under the strange delusion that if the slaves were emancipated at the South, they would flock to the North. So far from this being the case, in that event, you would see many old and familiar faces back again to the South. The fact is, there are few here who would not return to the South in the event of emancipation. We want to live in the land of our birth, and to lay our bones by the side of our fathers'; and nothing short of an intense love of personal freedom keeps us from the South. For the sake of this, most of us would live on a crust of bread and a cup of cold water.

Since I left you, I have had a rich experience. I have occupied stations which I never dreamed of when a slave. Three out of the ten years since I left you, I spent as a common laborer on the wharves of New Bedford, Massachusetts. It was there I earned my first free dollar. It was mine. I could spend it as I pleased. I could buy hams or herring with it, without asking any odds of any body. That was a precious dollar to me. You remember when I used to make seven or eight, or even nine dollars a week in Baltimore, you would take every cent of it from me every Saturday night, saying that I belonged to you, and my earnings also. I never liked this conduct on your part—to say the best, I thought it a little mean. I would not have served you so. But let that pass. I was a little awkward about counting money in New England fashion when I first landed in New Bedford. I like to have betrayed myself several times. I caught myself saying phip, for fourpence; and at one time a man actually charged me with being a runaway, whereupon I was silly enough to become one by running away from him, for I was greatly afraid he might adopt measures to get me again into slavery, a condition I then dreaded more than death.

I soon, however, learned to count money, as well as to make it, and got on swimmingly. I married soon after leaving you: in fact, I was engaged to be married before I left you; and instead of finding my companion a burden, she was truly a helpmeet. She went to live at service, and I to work on the wharf, and though we toiled hard the first winter, we never lived more happily. After remaining in New Bedford for three years, I met with Wm. Lloyd Garrison, a person of whom you have *possibly* heard, as he is pretty generally known among slaveholders. He put it into my head that I might make myself serviceable to the cause of the slave by devoting a portion of my time to telling my own sorrows, and those of other slaves which had come under my observation. This was the commencement of a higher state of existence than any to which I had ever aspired. I was thrown into society the most pure, enlightened and benevolent that the country affords. Among these I have never forgotten you, but have invariably made you the topic of conversation —thus giving you all the notoriety I could do. I need not tell you that the opinion formed of you in these circles, is far from being favorable. They have little respect for your honesty, and less for your religion.

But I was going on to relate to you something of my interesting experience. I had not long enjoyed the excellent society to which I have referred, before the light of its excellence exerted a beneficial influence on my mind and heart. Much of my early dislike of white persons was removed, and their manners, habits and customs, so entirely unlike what I had been used to in the kitchen-quarters on the plantations of the South, fairly charmed me, and gave me a strong disrelish for the coarse and degrading customs of my former condition. I therefore made an effort so to improve my mind and deportment, as to be somewhat fitted to the station to which I seemed almost providentially called. The transition from degradation to respectability was indeed great, and to get from one to the other without carrying some marks of one's former condition, is truly a difficult matter. I would not have you think that I am now entirely clear of all plantation peculiarities, but my friends here, while they entertain the strongest dislike to them, regard me with that charity to which my past life somewhat entitles me, so that my condition in this respect is exceedingly pleasant. So far as my domestic affairs are concerned, I can boast of as comfortable a dwelling as your own. I have an industrious and neat companion, and four dear children—the oldest a girl of nine years, and three fine boys, the oldest eight, the next six, and the youngest four years old. The three oldest are now going regularly to school—two can read and write, and the other can spell with tolerable correctness words of two syllables: Dear fellows! they are all in comfortable beds, and are sound asleep, perfectly secure under my own roof. There are no slaveholders here to rend my heart by snatching them from my arms, or blast a mother's dearest hopes by tearing them from her bosom. These dear children are ours—not to work up into rice, sugar and tobacco, but to watch over, regard, and protect, and to rear them up in the nurture and admonition of the gospel—to train them up in the paths of wisdom and virtue, and, as far as we can to make them useful to the world and to themselves. Oh! sir, a slaveholder never appears to me so completely an agent of hell, as when I think of and look upon my dear children. It is then that my feelings rise above my control. I meant to have said more with respect to my own prosperity and happiness, but thoughts and feelings which this recital has quickened unfits me to proceed further in that direction. The grim horrors of slavery rise in all their ghastly terror before me, the wails of millions pierce my heart, and chill my blood. I remember the chain, the gag, the bloody whip, the death-like gloom overshadowing the broken spirit of the fettered bondman, the appalling liability of his being torn away from wife and children, and sold like a beast in the market. Say not that this is a picture of fancy. You well know that I wear stripes on my back inflicted by your direction; and that you, while we were brothers in the same church, caused this right hand, with which I am now penning this letter, to be closely tied to my left, and my person dragged at the pistol's mouth, fifteen miles, from the Bay side to Easton to be sold like a beast in the market, for the alleged crime of intending to escape from your possession. All this and more you remember, and know to be perfectly true, not only of yourself, but of nearly all of the slaveholders around you.

At this moment, you are probably the guilty holder of at least three of my own dear sisters, and my only brother in bondage. These you regard as your property. They are recorded on your ledger, or perhaps have been sold to human flesh mongers, with a view to filling your own ever-hungry purse. Sir, I desire to know how and where these dear sisters are. Have you sold them? or are they still in your possession? What has become of them? are they living or dead? And my dear old grand-mother, whom you turned out like an old horse, to die in the woods—is she still alive? Write and let me know all about them. If my grandmother be still alive, she is of no service to you, for by this time she must be nearly eighty years old—too old to be cared for by one to whom she has ceased to be of service, send her to me at Rochester, or bring her to Philadelphia, and it shall be the crowning happiness of my life to take care of her in her old age. Oh! she was to me a mother, and a father, so far as hard toil for my comfort could make her such. Send me my grandmother! that I may watch over and take care of her in her old age. And my sisters, let me know all about them. I would write to them, without disturbing you in any way, but that, through your unrighteous conduct, they have been entirely deprived of the power to read and write. You have kept them in utter ignorance, and have therefore robbed them of the sweet enjoyments of writing or receiving letters from absent friends and relatives. Your wickedness and cruelty committed in this respect on your fellow-creatures, are greater than all the stripes you have laid upon my back, or theirs. It is an outrage upon the soul—a war upon the immortal spirit, and one for which you must give account at the bar of our common Father and Creator.

The responsibility which you have assumed in this regard is truly awful—and how you could stagger under it these many years is marvellous. Your mind must have become darkened, your heart hardened, your conscience seared and petrified, or you would have long since thrown off the accursed load and sought relief at the hands of a sin-forgiving God. How, let me ask, would you look upon me, were I some dark night in company with a band of hardened villains, to enter the precincts of your elegant dwelling and seize the person of your own lovely daughter Amanda, and carry her off from your family, friends and all the loved ones of her youth—make her my slave—compel her to work, and I take her wages—place her names on my ledger as property—disregard her personal rights—fetter the powers of her immortal soul by denying her the rights and privilege of learning to read and write—feed her coarsely—clothe her scantily, and whip her on the naked back occasionally; more and still more horrible, leave her unprotected—a degraded victim to the brutal lust of fiendish overseers, who would pollute, blight, and blast her fair soul—rob her of all dignity—destroy her virtue, and annihilate all in her person the graces that adorn the character of virtuous womanhood? I ask how would you regard me, if such were my conduct? Oh! the vocabulary of the damned would not afford a word sufficiently infernal, to express your idea of my God-provoking wickedness. Yet sir, your treatment of my beloved sisters is in all essential points, precisely like the case I have now supposed. Damning as would be such a deed on my part, it would be no more so than that which you have committed against me and my sisters.

I will now bring this letter to a close, you shall hear from me again unless you let me hear from you. I intend to make use of you as a weapon with which to assail the system of slavery—as a means of concentrating public attention on the system, and deepening their horror of trafficking in the souls and bodies of men. I shall make use of you as a means of exposing the character of the American church and clergy—and as a means of bringing this guilty nation with yourself to repentance. In doing this I entertain no malice towards you personally. There is no roof under which you would be more safe than mine, and there is nothing in my house which you might need for your comfort, which I would not readily grant. Indeed, I should esteem it a privilege, to set you an example as to how mankind ought to treat each other.

I am your fellow man, but not your slave.

FREDERICK DOUGLASS

The Liberator, September 22, 1848

What to the Slave Is the Fourth of July?

"For it is not light that is needed but fire. . . ."

ELLOW CITIZENS: PARDON ME, AND ALLOW ME TO ASK WHY AM I called upon to speak here today? What have I or those I represent to do with your national independence? Are the great principles of political freedom and of natural justice, embodied in that Declaration of Independence, extended to us? And am I, therefore, called upon to bring our humble offering to the national altar, and to confess the benefits, and express devout gratitude for the blessings resulting from your independence to us?

Would to God, both for your sakes and ours, that an affirmative answer could be truthfully returned to these questions. Then would my task be light, and my burden easy and delightful. For who is there so cold that a nation's sympathy could not warm him? Who so obdurate and dead to the claims of gratitude, that would not thankfully acknowledge such priceless benefits? Who so stolid and selfish that would not give his voice to swell the halleluiahs of a nation's jubilee, when the chains of servitude had been torn from his limbs? I am not that man. In a case like that, the dumb might eloquently speak, and the "lame man leap like a hare."

But such is not the state of the case. I say it with a sad sense of disparity between us. I am not included within the pale of this glorious anniversary! Your high independence only reveals the immeasurable distance between us. The blessings in which you this day rejoice are not enjoyed in common. The rich inheritance of justice, liberty, prosperity, and independence bequeathed by your fathers is shared by you, not by me. The sunlight that brought life and healing to you has brought stripes and death to me. This Fourth of July is *yours*, not *mine*. *You* may rejoice, *I* must mourn. To drag a man in fetters into the grand illuminated temple of liberty, and call upon him to join you in joyous anthems, were inhuman mockery and sacrilegious irony. Do you mean, citizens, to mock me, by asking me to speak today? If so, there is a parallel to your conduct. And let me warn you, that it is dangerous to copy the example of a nation whose crimes, towering up to heaven, were thrown down by the breath of the Almighty, burying that nation in irrecoverable ruin. I can today take up the lament of a peeled and woe-smitten people.

"By the rivers of Babylon, there we sat down. Yes! We wept when we remembered Zion. We hanged our harps upon the willows in the midst thereof. For there they that carried us away captive, required of us a song; and they who wasted us, required of us mirth, saying, Sing us one of the songs of Zion. How can we sing the Lord's song in a strange land? If I forget thee, O Jerusalem, let my right hand forget her cunning. If I do not remember thee, let my tongue cleave to the roof of my mouth."

Fellow citizens, above your national, tumultuous joy, I hear the mournful wail of millions, whose chains, heavy and grievous yesterday, are today rendered more intolerable by the jubilant shouts that reach them. If I do forget, if I do not remember those bleeding children of sorrow this day, "may my right hand forget her cunning, and may my tongue cleave to the roof of my mouth!" To forget them, to pass lightly over their wrongs, and to chime in with the popular themes, would be treason most scandalous and shocking, and would make me a reproach before God and the world. My subject, then, fellow citizens, is "American Slavery." I shall see this day and its popular characteristics from the slave's point of view. Standing here, identified with the American bondman, making his wrongs mine, I do not hesitate to declare, with all my soul, that the character and conduct of this nation never looked blacker to me than on this Fourth of July. Whether we turn to the declarations of the past, or to the professions of the present, the conduct of the nation seems equally hideous and revolting. America is false to the past, false to the present, and solemnly binds herself to be false to the future. Standing with God and the crushed and bleeding slave on this occasion, I will in the name of humanity, which is outraged, in the name of liberty, which is fettered, in the name of the Constitution and the Bible, which are disregarded and trampled upon, dare to call in question and to denounce, with all the emphasis I can command everything that serves to perpetuate slavery—the great sin and shame of America! "I will not equivocate; I will not excuse"; I will use the severest language I can command, and yet not one word shall escape me that any man, whose judgment is not blinded by prejudice, or who is not at heart a slave-holder, shall not confess to be right and just.

But I fancy I hear some of my audience say it is just in this circumstance that you and your brother Abolitionists fail to make a favorable impression on the public mind. Would you argue more and denounce less, would you persuade more and rebuke less, your cause would be much more likely to succeed. But, I submit, where all is plain there is nothing to be argued. What point in the anti-slavery creed would you have me argue? On what branch of the subject do the people of this country need light? Must I undertake to prove that the slave is a man? That point is conceded already. Nobody doubts it. The slave-holders themselves acknowledge it in the enactment of laws for their government. They acknowledge it when they punish disobedience on the part of the slave. There are seventy-two crimes in the State of Virginia, which, if committed by a black man (no matter how ignorant he be), subject him to the punishment of death; while only two of these same crimes will subject a white man to like punishment. What is this but the acknowledgment that the slave is a moral, intellectual, and responsible being? The manhood of the slave is conceded. It is admitted in the fact that Southern statute-books are covered with enactments, forbidding, under severe fines and penalties, the teaching of the slave to read and write. When you can point to any such laws in reference to the beasts of the fields, then I may consent to argue the manhood of the slave. When the dogs in your streets, when the fowls of the air, when the cattle on your hills, when the fish of the sea, and the reptiles that crawl, shall be unable to distinguish the slave from a brute, then I will argue with you that the slave is a man!

For the present it is enough to affirm the equal manhood of the Negro race. Is it not astonishing that, while we are plowing, planting, and reaping, using all kinds of mechanical tools, erecting houses, constructing bridges, building ships, working in metals of brass, iron, copper, silver, and gold; that while we are reading, writing, and cyphering, acting as clerks, merchants, and secretaries, having among us lawyers, doctors, ministers, poets, authors, editors, orators, and teachers; that while we are engaged in all the enterprises common to other men—digging gold in California, capturing the whale in the Pacific, feeding sheep and cattle on the hillside, living, moving, acting, thinking, planning, living in families as husbands, wives, and children, and above all, confessing and worshipping the Christian God, and looking hopefully for life and immortality beyond the grave—we are called upon to prove that we are men?

Would you have me argue that man is entitled to liberty? That he is the rightful owner of his own body? You have already declared it. Must I argue the wrongfulness of slavery? Is that a question for republicans? Is it to be settled by the rules of logic and argumentation, as a matter beset with great difficulty, involving a doubtful application of the principle of justice, hard to understand? How should I look today in the presence of Americans, dividing and subdividing a discourse, to show that men have a natural right to freedom, speaking of it relatively and positively, negatively and affirmatively? To do so would be to make myself ridiculous, and to offer an insult to your understanding. There is not a man beneath the canopy of heaven who does not know that slavery is wrong *for him.*

What! Am I to argue that it is wrong to make men brutes, to rob them of their liberty, to work them without wages, to keep them ignorant of their relations to their fellow men, to beat them with sticks, to flay their flesh with the last, to load their limbs with irons, to hunt them with dogs, to sell their flesh, to starve them into obedience and submission to their masters? Must I argue that a system thus marked with blood and stained with pollution is wrong? No; I will not. I have better employment for my time and strength than such arguments would imply.

What, then, remains to be argued? Is it that slavery is not divine; that God did not establish it; that our doctors of divinity are mistaken? There is blasphemy in the thought. That which is inhuman cannot be divine. Who can reason on such a proposition? They that can, may; I cannot. The time for such argument is past.

At a time like this, scorching irony, not convincing argument, is needed. Oh! had I the ability, and could I reach the nation's ear, I would today pour out a fiery stream of biting ridicule, blasting reproach, withering sarcasm, and stern rebuke. For it is not light that is needed but fire; it is not the gentle shower, but thunder. We need the storm, the whirlwind, and the earthquake. The feeling of the nation must be quickened; the conscience of the nation must be roused; the propriety of the nation must be startled; the hypocrisy of the nation must be exposed; and its crimes against God and man must be denounced.

What to the American slave is your Fourth of July? I answer, a day that reveals to him more than all other days of the year, the gross injustice and cruelty to which he is the constant victim. To him your celebration is a sham; your boasted liberty an unholy license; your national greatness, swelling vanity; your sounds of rejoicing are empty and heartless; your denunciation of tyrants, brass-fronted impudence; your shouts of liberty and equality, hollow mockery; your prayers and hymns, your sermons and thanksgivings, with all your religious parade and solemnity, are to him mere bombast, fraud, deception, impiety, and hypocrisy—a thin veil to cover up crimes which would disgrace a nation of savages. There is not a nation of the earth guilty of practices more shocking and bloody than are the people of these United States at this very hour.

Go where you may, search where you will, roam through all the monarchies and despotisms of the Old World, travel through South America, search out every abuse and when you have found the last, lay your facts by the side of the every-day practices of this nation, and you will say with me that, for revolting barbarity and shameless hypocrisy, America reigns without a rival.

July 1852

Harriet Jacobs (1813–1897)

In Harriet Jacobs's *Incidents in the Life of a Slave Girl,* published in 1861, is found an account of the brutal life and thrilling escape of a female slave to rival any of those written by the prominent men of her age. Deeply rooted in a woman's experience, *Incidents in the Life of a Slave Girl* relates in unsparing detail the objectification of the female slave while at the same time portraying the extraordinarily moving bonds of family between three generations of African-American women.

Though the work is autobiographical, the author uses the pseudonym Linda Brent. Born into slavery, Linda at first is treated with some compassion and taught to read and write, but her more benevolent mistress dies when she is twelve, and she and her brother fall into the hands of her mistress's sister and the sister's husband, Dr. Flint. From the time she is fifteen, Linda is pursued sexually by the doctor, "whose restless, craving, vicious nature roved about day and night," while suffering at the same time the jealous wrath of his wife. Learning that she would like to marry a freeman, Flint proposes that she marry one of his own slaves. "Don't you suppose, sir, that a slave can have some preference about marrying?" she retorts. "Do you suppose that all men are alike to her?"

To challenge Flint's power over her, she enters into a relationship with a seemingly beneficent white man, Mr. Sands, who fathers her two children. She takes great pains in her account to explain how she could choose to take an action that might offend her readers: "It seems less degrading to give one's self, than to submit to compulsion," she writes. "There is something akin to freedom in having a lover who has no control over you, except that which he gains by kindness and attachment."

When Dr. Flint persists in his affronts, she decides to flee, hoping that Flint will sell her children to their father. When her escape is thwarted, she spends the next seven years of her life hiding in a crawl space—nine feet long, seven feet wide, and three feet at its greatest height—"dreaming strange dreams of the dead and the living." From this "dungeon" in a shed abutting her grandmother's house she can observe her children and others pass in the street, and she writes numerous letters to Dr. Flint, which are carried away and mailed from Boston, leading him North several times to find her. In her seven years of confinement, she shows herself to the outside world but once—to implore the father of her children to buy their freedom.

At last, in 1842, she escapes by boat to Philadelphia then New York, only to discover in the North that "every where I found the same manifestations of that cruel prejudice." While her status is further compromised with the passage of the Fugitive Slave Law of 1850, giving slaveholders greater authority to reclaim escaped slaves in the North, she nonetheless eludes her pursuers. Several years later she is reunited with her children, and her freedom is purchased by her employer. (Jacobs's own children, Joseph and Louisa Matilda, were fathered by a young white man, Samuel Tredwell Sawyer, before she was nineteen.)

Incidents in the Life of a Slave Girl is centered throughout on the strong connections among the women portrayed in its pages. While in her preface Jacobs states her purpose—"I do earnestly desire to arouse the women of the North to a realizing sense of the condition of two millions of women at the South"—in her text it is the spirit of her grandmother, "the faithful old friend of my whole life," invoked on its first and last pages, that makes endurance possible. A freed woman, her grandmother sees her own children and grandchildren separated and suffering, but sustains for them a determined constancy, an unshakable bond of kinship. "Stand by your own children," she advises Linda, "and suffer with them till death."

Jacobs's account was prepared for publication by the abolitionist Lydia Maria Child and was accompanied by testimonials typically used to corroborate such a work, but Jacobs's use of a pseudonym seemingly cast doubt on the veracity of her tale. Recently, however, the scholar Jean Fagan Yellin has definitely established the authenticity of the work, and the pseudonym may instead demonstrate an ambivalence about the uses of fiction and autobiography seen in *Clotel,*† *Our Nig,*† and other narratives of the period. While the pseudonym might serve a practical purpose in protecting those left behind in slavery, or those who aided in an escape, as it does itself stand for something else, another name, so too does this account bear truth about the experiences of countless enslaved women. "Reader it is not to awaken sympathy for myself that I am telling you truthfully what I suffered," Jacobs writes, "I do it to kindle a flame of compassion in your hearts for my sisters who are still in bondage."

After her own escape, Jacobs traveled to Europe with her employer, remarking on the relative lack of race prejudice there, and worked for abolition before the Civil War, when she moved to Washington, D.C., to work as a nurse to black troops. She remained there until her death in 1897.

from *Incidents in the Life of a Slave Girl*

"I would rather drudge out my life on a cotton plantation, till the grave opened to give me rest, than to live with an unprincipled master and a jealous mistress."

THE JEALOUS MISTRESS

I WOULD TEN THOUSAND TIMES RATHER THAT MY CHILDREN should be the half-starved paupers of Ireland than to be the most pampered among the slaves of America. I would rather drudge out my life on a cotton plantation, till the grave opened to give me rest, than to live with an unprincipled master and a jealous mistress. The felon's home in a penitentiary is preferable. He may repent, and turn from the error of his ways, and so find peace; but it is not so with a favorite slave. She is not allowed to have any pride of character. It is deemed a crime in her to wish to be virtuous.

Mrs. Flint possessed the key to her husband's character before I was born. She might have used this knowledge to counsel and to screen the young and the innocent among her slaves; but for them she had no sympathy. They were the objects of her constant suspicion and malevolence. She watched her husband with unceasing vigilance; but he was well practised in means to evade it. What he could not find opportunity to say in words he manifested in signs. He invented more than were ever thought of in a deaf and dumb asylum. I let them pass, as if I did not understand what he meant; and many were the curses and threats bestowed on my for my stupidity. One day he caught me teaching myself to write. He frowned, as if he was not well pleased; but I suppose he came to the conclusion that such an accomplishment might help to advance his favorite scheme. Before long, notes were often slipped into my hand. I would return them, saying "I can't read them, sir." "Can't you?" he replied; "then I must read them to you." He always finished the reading by asking, "Do you understand?" Sometimes he would complain of the heat of the tea room, and order his supper to be placed on a small table in the piazza. He would seat himself there with a well-satisfied smile, and tell me to stand by and brush away the flies. He would eat very slowly, pausing between the mouthfuls. These intervals were employed in describing the happiness I was so foolishly throwing away, and in threatening me with the penalty that finally awaited my stubborn disobedience. He boasted much of the forbearance he had exercised towards me, and reminded me that there was a limit to his patience. When I succeeded in avoiding opportunities for him to talk to me at home, I was ordered to come to his office, to do some errand. When there, I was obliged to stand and listen to such language as he saw fit to address to me. Sometimes I so openly expressed my contempt for him that he would become violently enraged, and I wondered why he did not strike me. Circumstanced as he was, he probably thought it was better policy to be forbearing. But the state of things grew worse and worse daily. In desperation I told him that I must and would apply to my grandmother for protection. He threatened me with death, and worse than death, if I made any complaint to her. Strange to say, I did not despair. I was naturally of a buoyant disposition, and always I had a hope of somehow getting out of his clutches. Like many a poor simple slave before me, I trusted that some threads of joy would yet be woven into my dark destiny.

I had entered my sixteenth year, and every day it became more apparent that my presence was intolerable to Mrs. Flint. Angry words frequently passed between her and her husband. He had never punished me himself, and he would not allow any body else to punish me. In that respect, she was never satisfied; but, in her angry moods, no terms were too vile for her to bestow upon me. Yet I, whom she detested so bitterly, had far more pity for her than he had, whose duty it was to make her life happy. I never wronged her, or wished to wrong her; and one word of kindness from her would have brought me to her feet.

After repeated quarrels between the doctor and his wife, he announced his intention to take his youngest daughter, then four years old, to sleep in his apartment. It was necessary that a servant should sleep in the same room, to be on hand if the child stirred. I was selected for that office, and informed for what purpose that arrangement had been made. By managing to keep within sight of people, as much as possible, during the day time, I had hitherto succeeded in eluding my master, though a razor was often held to my throat to force me to change this line of policy. At night I slept by the side of my great aunt, where I felt safe. He was too prudent to come into her room. She was an old woman, and had been in the family many years. Moreover, as a married man, and a professional man, he deemed it necessary to save appearances in some degree. But he resolved to remove the obstacle in the way of his scheme; and he thought he had planned it so that he should evade suspicion. He was well aware how much I prized my refuge by the side of my old aunt, and he determined to dispossess me of it. The first night the doctor had the little child in his room alone. The next morning, I was ordered to take my station as nurse the following night. A kind Providence interposed in my favor. During the day Mrs. Flint heard of his new arrangement and a storm followed. I rejoiced to hear it rage.

After a while my mistress sent for me to come to her room. Her first question was, "Did you know you were to sleep in the doctor's room?"

"Yes, ma'am."

"Who told you?"

"My master."

"Will you answer truly all the questions I ask?"

"Yes, ma'am."

"Tell me, then, as you hope to be forgiven, are you innocent of what I have accused you?"

"I am."

She handed me a Bible, and said, "Lay your hand on your heart, kiss this holy book, and swear before God that you tell me the truth."

I took the oath she required, and I did it with a clear conscience.

"You have taken God's holy word to testify your innocence," she said. "If you have deceived me, beware! Now take this stool, sit down, look me directly in the face, and tell me all that has passed between your master and you."

I did as she ordered. As I went on with my account her color changed frequently, she wept, and sometimes groaned. She spoke in tones so sad, that I was touched by her grief. The tears came to my eyes; but I was soon convinced that her emotions arose from anger and wounded pride. She felt that her marriage vows were desecrated, her dignity insulted; but she had no compassion for the poor victim of her husband's perfidy. She pitied herself as a martyr; but she was incapable of feeling for the condition of shame and misery in which her unfortunate, helpless slave was placed.

Yet perhaps she had some touch of feeling for me; for when the conference was ended, she spoke kindly, and promised to protect me. I should have been much comforted by this assurance if I could have had confidence in it; but my experiences in slavery had filled me with distrust. She was not a very refined woman, and had not much control over her passions. I was an object of her jealousy, and consequently, of her hatred; and I knew I could not expect kindness or confidence from her under the circumstances in which I was placed. I could not blame her. Slaveholders' wives feel as other women would under similar circumstances. The fire of her temper kindled from small sparks, and now the flame became so intense that the doctor was obliged to give up his intended arrangement.

I knew I had ignited the torch, and I expected to suffer for it afterwards; but I felt too thankful to my mistress for the timely aid she rendered me to care much about that. She now took me to sleep in a room adjoining her own. There I was an object of her especial care, though not of her especial comfort, for she spent many a sleepless night to watch over me. Sometimes I woke up, and found her bending over me. At other times she whispered in my ear, as though it was her husband who was speaking to me, and listened to hear what I would answer. If she startled me, on such occasions, she would glide stealthily away; and the next morning she would tell me I had been talking in my sleep, and ask who I was talking to. At last, I began to be fearful for my life. It had been often threatened; and you can imagine, better than I can describe, what an unpleasant sensation it must produce to wake up in the dead of the night and find a jealous woman bending over you. Terrible as this experience was, I had fears that it would give place to one more terrible.

My mistress grew weary of her vigils; they did not prove satisfactory. She changed her tactics. She now tried the trick of accusing my master of crime, in my presence, and gave my name as the author of the accusation. To my utter astonishment, he replied, "I don't believe it; but if she did acknowledge it, you tortured her into exposing me." Tortured into exposing him! Truly, Satan had no difficulty in distinguishing the color of his soul! I understood his object in making this false representation. It was to show me that I gained nothing by seeking the protection of my mistress; that the power was still all in his own hands. I pitied Mrs. Flint. She was a second wife, many years the junior of her husband; and the hoary-headed miscreant was enough to try the patience of a wiser and better woman. She was completely foiled, and knew not how to proceed. She would gladly have had me flogged for my supposed false oath; but, as I have already stated, the doctor never allowed any one to whip me. The old sinner was politic. The application of the lash might have led to remarks that would have exposed him in the eyes of his children and grandchildren. How often did I rejoice that I lived in a town where all the inhabitants knew each other! If I had been on a remote plantation, or lost among the multitude of a crowded city, I should not be a living woman at this day.

The secrets of slavery are concealed like those of the Inquisition. My master was, to my knowledge, the father of eleven slaves. But did the mothers dare to tell who was the father of their children? Did the other slaves dare to allude to it, except in whispers among themselves? No, indeed! They knew too well the terrible consequences.

My grandmother could not avoid seeing things which excited her suspicions. She was uneasy about me, and tried various ways to buy me; but the never-changing answer was always repeated: "Linda does not belong to *me*. She is my daughter's property, and I have no legal right to sell her." The conscientious man! He was too scrupulous to *sell* me; but he had no scruples whatever about committing a much greater wrong against the helpless young girl placed under his guardianship, as his daughter's property. Sometimes my persecutor would ask me whether I would like to be sold, I told him I would rather be sold to any body than to lead such a life as I did. On such occasions he would assume the air of a very injured individual, and reproach me for my ingratitude. "Did I not take you into the house, and make you the companion of my own children?" he would say. "Have I ever treated you like a negro? I have never allowed you to be punished, not even to please your mistress. And this is the recompense I get, you ungrateful girl!" I answered that he had reasons of his own for screening me from punishment, and that the course he pursued made my mistress hate me and persecute me. If I wept, he would say, "Poor child! Don't cry! don't cry! I will make peace for you with your mistress. Only let me arrange matters in my own way. Poor, foolish girl! you don't know what is for your own good. I would cherish you. I would make a lady of you. Now go, and think of all I have promised you."

I did think of it.

Reader, I draw no imaginary pictures of southern homes. I am telling you the plain truth. Yet when victims make their escape from this wild beast of Slavery, northerners consent to act the part of bloodhounds, and hunt the poor fugitive back into his den, "full of dead men's bones, and all uncleanness." Nay, more, they are not only willing, but proud, to give their daughters in marriage to slaveholders. The poor girls have romantic notions of a sunny clime, and of the flowering vines that all the year round shade a happy home. To what disappointments are they destined! The young wife soon learns that the husband in whose hands she has placed her happiness pays no regard to his marriage vows. Children of every shade of complexion play with her own fair babies, and too well she knows that they are born unto him of his own household. Jealousy and hatred enter the flowery home, and it is ravaged of its loveliness.

Southern women often marry a man knowing that he is the father of many little slaves. They do not trouble themselves about it. They regard such children as property, as marketable as the pigs on the plantation; and it is seldom that they do not make them aware of this by passing them into the slave-trader's hands as soon as possible, and thus getting them out of their sight. I am glad to say there are some honorable exceptions.

I have myself known two southern wives who exhorted their husbands to free those slaves towards whom they stood in a "parental relation": and their request was granted. These husbands blushed before the superior nobleness of their wives' natures. Though they had only counselled them to do that which it was their duty to do, it commanded their respect, and rendered their conduct more exemplary. Concealment was at an end, and confidence took the place of distrust.

Though this bad institution deadens the moral sense, even in white women, to a fearful extent, it is not altogether extinct. I have heard southern ladies say of Mr. Such a one, "He not only thinks it no disgrace to be the father of those little niggers, but he is not ashamed to call himself their master. I declare, such things ought not to be tolerated in any decent society."

1861

William Wells Brown
(1815–1884)

Antislavery lecturer, novelist, playwright, and author, William Wells Brown was one of the most prominent African-American men of his day. He was born in Lexington, Kentucky, the son of a slave mother and a slaveholder. A few years later, the household moved to Missouri and William was hired out to an innkeeper and later a river trader. After several attempts, William escaped on New Year's Day 1834 and fled to Canada, and, aided along the way by a Quaker, Wells Brown, he took the man's name as his own. His account of his escape, the *Narrative of William W. Brown, Fugitive Slave, Written by Himself,* was published in Boston by the Anti-Slavery Society in 1847, followed the next year by his song-poems *The Anti-Slavery Harp.* In 1849 Brown was invited to the Paris Peace Congress by Victor Hugo, and after the passage of the Fugitive Slave Law in 1850, he remained in England for five years. While in Europe, Brown met such notable figures as Alexis de Tocqueville, Charles Dickens, and Alfred Lord Tennyson, and he published *Three Years in Europe* (1852) and the earliest version of his novel, *Clotel; or, The President's Daughter: A Narrative of Slave Life in the United States* (1853). (*Clotel* is considered the first novel written by an African-American author, though Harriet Wilson's *Our Nig,*† printed in 1859, is the first such work originally published in the United States.)

Partly autobiographical, partly fictitious, and partly allegorical, *Clotel* is the episodic and melodramatic story of three generations of African-American women, the mistress of Thomas Jefferson and her descendants. While several themes run through the novel—the hypocrisy of a Christianity that perverts its teaching to its own ends; the complicity of all of society in the brutal social compact between slaves and masters; and the "prejudice [that] followed the coloured man into every place that he might enter," even in the free North—it takes as its central theme the corrupting influence of slavery on the family, demonstrated by the lustful tendencies of slaveholders and the practice of selling one's own children.

By using Thomas Jefferson as the slaveholding figure whose presence is ever felt behind the novel, Brown does not merely acknowledge the historical fact that this most famous of American statesmen held slaves, but that their story is part of the national drama as well. Citing the selective nature of the Founding Father's ardor for individual freedom, Brown notes:

> The same man, speaking of the probability that the slaves might some day attempt to gain their liberties by a revolution, said:
>
> "I tremble for my country, when I recollect that God is just, and that His justice cannot sleep for ever. The Almighty has no attribute that can take sides with us in such a struggle."
>
> But, sad to say, Jefferson is not the only American statesman who has spoken high-sounding words in favour of freedom, and then left his own children to die slaves.

For further emphasis, a passage from the Declaration of Independence[†] appears on the book's title page. (In the first American edition of the book, retitled *Clotelle; A Tale of the Southern States* [1864], a senator stands in for the president. The original version of the novel was not published in the United States until 1969.)

Like Harriet Wilson's *Our Nig, Clotel* belies its claim to be an imaginative work. In several places in the novel the author admonishes "This, reader, is no fiction," and the story is stocked with autobiographical elements and touched by the events of current history, including Nat Turner's rebellion, the colonization debate, and the increasing international isolation of the United States on the practice of slavery. Indeed, one wonders why Wells was drawn to fiction, rather than the more overtly political essays and pamphlets. He may have been influenced by the enormous popularity of Harriet Beecher Stowe's *Uncle Tom's Cabin,* published in 1852; or perhaps the newer form freed Brown's fictional characters from the specificity of a single time and place, using his "unvarnished narrative of one doomed by the laws of the Southern States" to tell "not only its own story of grief, but speak of a thousand wrongs and woes beside, which never see the light."

William Wells Brown was the author of more than sixteen volumes, including the first drama written by an African-American, *The Escape or a Leap for Freedom* (1858); *The Black Man: His Antecedents, His Genius, and His Achievements* (1863); a very early work of black history, *The Negro in the American Rebellion, His Heroism and His Fidelity* (1867); *The Rising Son: or the Antecedents and Advancement of the Colored Race* (1874); and *My Southern Home* (1880). He died in Chelsea, Massachusetts, in 1884.

from *Clotel; or, The President's Daughter: A Narrative of Slave Life in the United States*

"Society does not frown upon the man who sits with his mulatto child upon his knee, whilst its mother stands a slave behind his chair."

CHAPTER I
THE NEGRO SALE

"Why stand she near the auction stand,
That girl so young and fair?
What brings her to this dismal place,
Why stand she weeping there?"

WITH THE GROWING POPULATION OF SLAVES IN THE SOUTHERN States of America, there is a fearful increase of half whites, most of whose fathers are slaveowners, and their mothers slaves. Society does not frown upon the man who sits with his mulatto child upon his knee, whilst its mother stands a slave behind his chair. The late Henry Clay, some years since, predicted that the abolition of Negro slavery would be brought about by the amalgamation of the races. John Randolph, a distinguished slave-holder of Virginia, and a prominent statesman, said in a speech in the legislature of his native state, that "the blood of the first American statesmen coursed through the veins of the slave of the South." In all the cities and towns of the slave states, the real Negro, or clear black, does not amount to more than one in every four of the slave population. This fact is, of itself, the best evidence of the degraded and immoral condition of the relation of master and slave in the United States of America.

In all the slave states, the law says:—"Slaves shall be deemed, sold [held], taken, reputed, and adjudged in law to be chattels personal in the hands of their owners and possessors, and their executor, administrators and assigns, to all intents, constructions, and purposes whatsoever. A slave is one who is in the power of a master to whom he belongs. The master may sell him, dispose of his person, his industry, and his labour. He can do nothing, possess nothing, nor acquire anything, but what must belong to his master. The slave is entirely subject to the will of his master, who may correct and chastise him, though not with unusual rigour, or see as to maim and mutilate him, or expose him to the danger of loss of life, or to cause his death. The slave, to remain a slave, must be sensible that there is no appeal from his master." Where the slave is placed by law entirely under the control of the man who claims him, body and soul, as property, what else could be expected than the most depraved social condition? The marriage relation, the oldest and most sacred institution given to man by his Creator, is unknown and unrecognised in the slave laws of the United States. Would that we could say, that the moral and religious teaching in the slave states were better than the laws; but, alas! we cannot. A few years since, some slaveholders became a little uneasy in their minds about the rightfulness of permitting slaves to take to themselves husbands and wives, while they still had others living, and applied to their religious teachers for advice; and the following will show how this grave and important subject was treated:—

> "Is a servant, whose husband or wife has been sold by his or her master into a distant country, to be permitted to marry again?"

The query was referred to a committee, who made the following report; which, after discussion, was adopted:—

> "That in view of the circumstances in which servants in this country are placed, the committee are unanimous in the opinion, that it is better to permit servants thus circumstance to take another husband or wife."

Such was the answer from a committee of the "Shiloh Baptist Association;" and instead of receiving light, those who asked the question were plunged into deeper darkness!

A similar question was put to the "Savannah River Association," and the answer, as the following will show, did not materially differ from the one we have already given:—

> "Whether, in a case of involuntary separation, of such a character as to preclude all prospect of future intercourse, the parties ought to be allowed to marry again."

Answer—

> "That such separation among persons situated as our slaves are, is civilly a separation by death; and they believe that, in the sight of God, it would be so viewed. To forbid second marriages in such cases would be to expose the parties, not only to stronger hardships and strong temptation, but to church-censure for acting in obedience to their master, who cannot be expected to acquiesce in a regulation at variance with justice to the slaves, and to the spirit of that command which regulates marriage among Christians. The slaves are not free agents; and

> a dissolution by death is not more entirely without their consent, and beyond their control, than by such separation."

Although marriage, as the above indicates, is a matter which the slaveholders do not think is of any importance, or of any binding force with their slaves; yet it would be doing that degraded class an injustice, not to acknowledge that many of them do regard it as a sacred obligation, and show a willingness to obey the commands of God on this subject. Marriage is, indeed, the first and most important institution of human existence—the foundation of all civilisation and culture—the root of church and state. It is the most intimate covenant of heart formed among mankind; and for many reasons the only relation in which they feel the true sentiments of humanity. It gives scope for every human virtue, since each of these is developed from the love and confidence which here predominate. It unites all which ennobles and beautifies life,—sympathy, kindness of will and deed, gratitude, devotion, and every delicate, intimate feeling. As the only asylum for true education, it is the first and last sanctuary of human culture. As husband and wife, through each other become conscious of complete humanity, and every human feeling, and every human virtue; so children, at their first awakening in the fond covenant of love between parents, both of whom are tenderly concerned for the same object, find an image of complete humanity leagued in free love. The spirit of love which prevails between them acts with creative power upon the young mind, and awakens every germ of goodness within it. This invisible and incalculable, influence of parental life acts more upon the child than all the efforts of education, whether by means of instruction, precept, or exhortation. If this be a true picture of the vast influence for good of the institution of marriage, what must be the moral degradation of that people to whom marriage is denied? Not content with depriving them of all the higher and holier enjoyments of this relation, by degrading and darkening their souls, the slaveholder denies to his victim even that slight alleviation of his misery, which would result from the marriage relation being protected by law and public opinion. Such is the influence of slavery in the United States, that the ministers of religion, even in the so-called free states, are the mere echoes, instead of the correctors, of public sentiment.

We have thought it advisable to show that the present system of chattel slavery in America undermines the entire social condition of man, so as to prepare the reader for the following narrative of slave life, in that otherwise happy and prosperous country.

In all the large towns in the Southern States, there is a class of slaves who are permitted to hire their time of their owners, and for which they pay a high price. These are mulatto women, or quadroons, as they are familiarly known, and are distinguished for their fascinating beauty. The handsomest usually pays the highest price for her time. Many of these women are the favourites of persons who furnish them with the means of paying their owners, and not a few are dressed in the most extravagant manner. Reader, when you take into consideration the fact, that amongst the slave population no safeguard is thrown around virtue, and no inducement held out to slave women to be chaste, you will not be surprised when we tell you that immorality and vice pervade the cities of the Southern States in a manner unknown in the cities and towns of the Northern States. Indeed most of the slave women have no higher aspiration than that of becoming the finely-dressed mistress of some white man. And at Negro balls and parties, this class of women usually cut the greatest figure.

At the close of the year—the following advertisement appeared in a newspaper published in Richmond, the capital of the state of Virginia:—"Notice: Thirty-eight Negroes will be offered for sale on Monday, November 10th, at twelve o'clock, being the entire stock of the late John Graves, Esq. The Negroes are in good condition, some of them very prime; among them are several mechanics, able-bodied field hands, ploughboys, and women with children at the breast, and some of them very prolific in their generating qualities, affording a rare opportunity to any one who wishes to raise a strong and healthy lot of servants for their own use. Also several mulatto girls of rare personal qualities: two of them very superior. Any gentleman or lady wishing to purchase, can take any of the above slaves on trial for a week, for which no charge will be made." Amongst the above slaves to be sold were Currer and her two daughters, Clotel and Althesa; the latter were the girls spoken of in the advertisement as "very superior." Currer was a bright mulatto, and of prepossessing appearance, though then nearly forty years of age. She had hired her time for more than twenty years, during which time she had lived in Richmond. In her younger days Currer had been the housekeeper of a young slaveholder; but of later years had been a laundress or washerwoman, and was considered to be a woman of great taste in getting up linen. The gentleman for whom she had kept house was Thomas Jefferson, by whom she had two daughters. Jefferson being called to Washington to fill a government appointment, Currer was left behind, and thus took herself to the business of washing, by which means she paid her master, Mr. Graves, and supported herself and two children. At the time of the decease of her master, Currer's daughters, Clotel and Althesa, were aged respectively sixteen and fourteen years, and both, like most of their sex in America, were well grown. Currer early resolved to bring her daughters up as ladies, as she termed it, and therefore imposed little or no work upon them. As her daughters grew older, Currer had to pay a stipulated price for them; yet her notoriety as a laundress of the first class enabled her to put an extra price upon her charges, and thus she and her daughters lived in comparative luxury. To bring up Clotel and Althesa to attract attention, and especially at balls and parties, was the great aim of Currer. Although the term "Negro ball" is applied to most of these gatherings, yet a majority of the attendants are often whites. Nearly all the Negro parties in the cities and towns of the

Southern States are made up of quadroon and mulatto girls, and white men. These are democratic gatherings, where gentlemen, shopkeepers, and their clerks, all appear upon terms of perfect equality. And there is a degree of gentility and decorum in these companies that is not surpassed by similar gatherings of white people in the Slave States. It was at one of these parties that Horatio Green, the son of a wealthy gentleman of Richmond, was first introduce to Clotel. The young man had just returned from college, and was in his twenty-second year. Clotel was sixteen, and was admitted by all to be the most beautiful girl, coloured or white, in the city. So attentive was the young man to the quadroon during the evening that it was noticed by all, and became a matter of general conversation; while Currer appeared delighted beyond measure at her daughter's conquest. From that evening, young Green became the favourite visitor at Currer's house. He soon promised to purchase Clotel, as speedily as it could be effected, and make her mistress of her own dwelling; and Currer looked forward with pride to the time when she should see her daughter emancipated and free. It was a beautiful moonlight night in August, when all who reside in tropical climes are eagerly gasping for a breath of fresh air, that Horatio Green was seated in the small garden behind Currer's cottage, with the object of his affections by his side. And it was here that Horatio drew from his pocket the newspaper, wet from the press, and read the advertisement for the sale of the slaves to which we have alluded; Currer and her two daughters being of the number. At the close of the evening's visit, and as the young man was leaving, he said to the girl, "You shall soon be free and your own mistress."

As might have been expected, the day of sale brought an unusual large number together to compete for the property to be sold. Farmers who make a business of raising slaves for the market were there; slave-traders and speculators were also numerously represented; and in the midst of this throng was one who felt a deeper interest in the result of the sale than any other of the bystanders; this was young Green. True to his promise, he was there with a blank bank check in his pocket, awaiting with impatience to enter the list as bidder for the beautiful slave. The less valuable slaves were first placed upon the auction block, one after another, and sold to the highest bidder. Husbands and wives were separated with a degree of indifference that is unknown in any other relation of life, except that of slavery. Brothers and sisters were torn from each other; and mothers saw their children leave them for the last time on this earth.

It was late in the day, when the greatest number of persons were thought to be present, that Currer and her daughters were brought forward to the place of sale. Currer was first ordered to ascend the auction stand, which she did with a trembling step. The slave mother was sold to a trader. Althesa, the youngest, and who was scarcely less beautiful than her sister, was sold to the same trader for one thousand dollars. Clotel was the last, and, as was expected, commanded a higher price than any that had been offered for sale that day. The appearance of Clotel on the auction block created a deep sensation amongst the crowd. There she stood, with a complexion as white as most of those who were waiting with a wish to become her purchasers; her features as finely defined as any of her sex of pure Anglo-Saxon; her long black wavy hair done up in the neatest manner; her form tall and graceful, and her whole appearance indicating one superior to her position. The auctioneer commenced by saying that "Miss Clotel had been reserved for the last, because she was the most valuable. How much, gentlemen? Real Albino, fit for a fancy girl for any one. She enjoys good health, and has a sweet temper. How much do you say?"

"Five hundred dollars."

"Only five hundred for such a girl as this? Gentlemen, she is worth a deal more than that sum; you certainly don't know the value of the article you are bidding upon. Here, gentlemen, I hold in my hand a paper certifying that she has a good moral character."

"Seven hundred."

"Ah; gentlemen, that is something like. This paper also states that she is very intelligent."

"Eight hundred."

"She is a devoted Christian, and perfectly trustworthy."

"Nine hundred."

"Nine fifty."

"Ten."

"Eleven."

"Twelve hundred." Here the sale came to a dead stand. The auctioneer stopped, looked around, and began in a rough manner to relate some anecdotes relative to the sale of slaves, which, he said, had come under his own observation. At this juncture the scene was indeed strange. Laughing, joking, swearing, smoking, spitting, and talking kept up a continual hum and noise amongst the crowd; while the slave-girl stood with tears in her eyes, at one time looking towards her mother and sister, and at another towards the young man whom she hoped would become her purchaser.

"The chastity of this girl is pure; she has never been from under her mother's care; she is a virtuous creature."

"Thirteen."

"Fourteen."

"Fifteen."

"Fifteen hundred dollars," cried the auctioneer, and the maiden was struck for that sum. This was a Southern auction, at which the bones, muscles, sinews, blood, and nerves of a young lady of sixteen were sold for five hundred dollars; her moral character for two hundred; her improved intellect for one hundred; her Christianity for three hundred; and her chastity and virtue for four hundred dollars more. And this, too, in a city thronged with churches, whose tall spires look like so many signals pointing to heaven, and whose ministers preach that slavery is a God-ordained institution!

What words can tell the inhumanity, the atrocity, and the immorality of that doctrine which, from exalted office, commends such a crime to the favour of enlightened and Christian people? What indignation from all the world is not due to the government and people who put forth all their strength and power to keep in existence such an institution? Nature abhors it; the age repels it; and Christianity need all her meekness to forgive it.

Clotel was sold for fifteen hundred dollars, but her purchaser was Horatio Green. Thus closed a Negro sale, at which two daughters of Thomas Jefferson, the writer of the Declaration of American Independence, and one of the presidents of the great republic, were disposed of to the highest bidder!

"O God! My every heart-string cries,
Dost thou these scenes behold
In this our boasted Christian land,
And must the truth be told?

"Blush, Christian, blush! for e'en the dark,
Untutored heathen see
Thy inconsistency; and, lo!
They scorn thy God, and thee!"

1853

Harriet E. Wilson
(1807?–?1870)

Harriet Wilson's novel *Our Nig; or Sketches from the Life of a free Black, in a Two-Story White House, North, Showing that Slavery's Shadows Fall Even There,* printed in 1859, is considered the first novel published by an African-American in the United States. (William Wells Brown's *Clotel; or, The President's Daughter*† appeared six years earlier in London, but was not published in Boston until 1864.) What little is known about its author's life has been gleaned from several letters of support appended to the work, and recent diligent scholarship.

According to Henry Louis Gates, who has pieced together details of the author's life, Harriet E. Adams was probably born in Fredericksburg, Virginia, in 1807 or 1808. She married Thomas Wilson in 1851 in New Hampshire and gave birth to a son, George Mason, in 1852. The boy's father seems to have deserted the family before the child was born, and Wilson gave him up to foster care while she attempted to have her book published to raise funds, appealing directly to her readers in the book's preface: "Deserted by kindred, disabled by failing health, I am forced to some experiment which shall aid me in maintaining myself and child without extinguishing this feeble life."

Like other sentimental women's novels of the period, *Our Nig* is full of melodramatic scenes as it recounts the life of its heroine, Alfrado, a young mulatto referred to contemptuously as "Our Nig," abandoned by her impoverished white mother on the doorstep of an extended Northern family. While Mr. Bellmont is "a kind, humane man," Mrs. Bellmont is "self-willed, haughty, undisciplined, arbitrary and severe," and the novel is full of physical beatings and psychological cruelty, though in several instances Frado asserts herself with surprising boldness. The young girl eventually outlasts her period of servitude and, broken in health, makes various attempts at self-support. At the novel's end, she marries, has a child, and is abandoned before she comes into possession of "a valuable recipe, from which she might herself manufacture a useful article for her maintainance."

As did William Wells Brown in *Clotel,* Wilson displays here an ambivalence toward her novel as a work of "fiction." Though the work is credited to the pseudonymous "Our Nig" on the title page and the author refers throughout the book to her heroine in the third person, she nonetheless alludes to "my own life" in her preface, and the initial chapters of the book are curiously entitled "Mag Smith, My Mother," "My Father's Death," and "A New Home for Me." The heroine's frail health and desertion by a rambling husband mirror incidents from the author's own life, and the book incorporates elements of traditional autobiographical narratives, such as a preoccupation with learning to read, so that the book finally melds both conventions of the classic African-American literary genre and the more modern form of the novel.

Besides the place it holds in the chronology and development of African-American literature, *Our Nig* is perhaps chiefly of interest for its portrayal of the dissimulation of Northern attitudes toward free blacks. For while slavery did not exist in the North, prejudice clearly did. The author states in her preface, "My mistress was wholly imbued with *southern* principles," and even upon gaining her independence Frado remains "watched by kidnappers, maltreated by professed abolitionists who did n't want slaves at the South, nor niggers in their own houses, North." In the chapter included here, as Frado's favorite, James, lies near death, Frado herself feels weak and overburdened by her chores, hoping that "her misery would soon close" as well. But in the aura of Christian piety that surrounds James's death, and the attempts of Frado to find religion, lies the crux of Christian hypocrisy—"it was all for white people."

Sadly, Wilson's novel does not appear to have secured her future. The son whom she sought to support with the book's income died at the age of eight, six months after its publication, and the work seems to have remained obscure until its recent rediscovery in this century.

from Our Nig

"She did not feel responsible for her spiritual culture, and hardly believed she had a soul."

CHAPTER VIII.
VISITOR AND DEPARTURE.

"Other cares engross me, and my tired soul with emulative haste, Looks to its God."

THE BROTHER ASSOCIATED WITH JAMES IN BUSINESS, IN Baltimore, was sent for to confer with one who might never be able to see him there.

James began to speak of life as closing; of heaven, as of a place in immediate prospect; of aspirations, which waited for fruition in glory. His brother, Lewis by name, was an especial favorite of sister Mary; more like her, in disposition and preferences than James or Jack.

He arrived as soon as possible after the request, and saw with regret the sure indications of fatality in his sick brother, and listened to his admonitions —admonitions to a Christian life—with tears, and uttered some promises of attention to the subject so dear to the heart of James.

How gladly he would have extended healing aid. But, alas! it was not in his power; so, after listening to his wishes and arrangements for his family and business, he decided to return home.

Anxious for company home, he persuaded his father and mother to permit Mary to attend him. She was not at all needed in the sick room; she did not choose to be useful in the kitchen, and then she was fully determined to go.

So all the trunks were assembled and crammed with the best selections from the wardrobe of herself and mother, where the last-mentioned articles could be appropriated.

"Nig was never so helpful before," Mary remarked, and wondered what had induced such a change in place of former sullenness.

Nig was looking further than the present, and congratulating herself upon some days of peace, for Mary never lost opportunity of informing her mother of Nig's delinquencies, were she otherwise ignorant.

Was it strange if she were officious, with such relief in prospect?

The parting from the sick brother was tearful and sad. James prayed in their presence for their renewal in holiness; and urged their immediate attention to eternal realities, and gained a promise that Susan and Charlie should share their kindest regards.

No sooner were they on their way, than Nig slyly crept round to Aunt Abby's room, and tip-toeing and twisting herself into all shapes, she exclaimed,—

"She's gone, Aunt Abby, she's gone, fairly gone;" and jumped up and down, till Aunt Abby feared she would attract the notice of her mistress by such demonstrations.

"Well, she's gone, gone, Aunt Abby. I hope she'll never come back again."

"No! no! Frado, that's wrong! you would be wishing her dead; that won't do."

"Well, I'll bet she'll never come back again; somehow, I feel as though she wouldn't."

"She is James's sister," remonstrated Aunt Abby.

"So is our cross sheep just as much, that I ducked in the river; I'd like to try my hand at curing *her* too."

"But you forget what our good minister told us last week, about doing good to those that hate us."

"Didn't I do good, Aunt Abby, when I washed and ironed and packed her old duds to get rid of her, and helped her pack her trunks, and run here and there for her?"

"Well, well, Frado; you must go finish your work, or your mistress will be after you, and remind you severely of Miss Mary, and some others beside."

Nig went as she was told, and her clear voice was heard as she went, singing in joyous notes the relief she felt at the removal of one of her tormentors.

Day by day the quiet of the sick man's room was increased. He was helpless and nervous; and often wished change of position, thereby hoping to gain momentary relief. The calls upon Frado were consequently more frequent, her nights less tranquil. Her health was impaired by lifting the sick man, and by drudgery in the kitchen. Her ill health she endeavored to conceal from James, fearing he might have less repose if there should be a change of attendants; and Mrs. Bellmont, she well knew, would have no sympathy for her. She was at last so much reduced as to be unable to stand erect for any great length of time. She would *sit* at the table to wash her dishes; if she heard the well-known step of her mistress, she would rise till she returned to her room, and then sink down for further rest. Of course she was longer than usual in completing the services assigned her. This was a subject of complaint to Mrs. Bellmont; and Frado endeavored to throw off all appearance of sickness in her presence.

But it was increasing upon her, and she could no longer hide her indisposition. Her mistress entered one day, and finding her seated, commanded her to go to work. "I am sick," replied Frado, rising and walking slowly to her unfinished task, "and cannot stand long, I feel so bad."

Angry that she should venture a reply to her command, she suddenly inflicted a blow which lay the tottering girl prostrate on the floor. Excited by so much indulgence of a dangerous passion, she seemed left to understand malice; and snatching a towel, stuffed the mouth of the sufferer, and beat her cruelly.

Frado hoped she would end her misery by whipping her to death. She bore it with the hope of a martyr, that her misery would soon close. Though her mouth was muffled, and the sounds much stifled, there was a sensible commotion, which James' quick ear detected.

"Call Frado to come here," he said faintly, "I have not seen her to-day."

Susan retired with the request to the kitchen, where it was evident some brutal scene had just been enacted.

Mrs. Bellmont replied that she had "some work to do just now; when that was done, she might come."

Susan's appearance confirmed her husband's fears, and he requested his father, who sat by the bedside, to go for her. This was a messenger, as James well knew, who could not be denied; and the girl entered the room, sobbing and faint with anguish.

James called her to him, and inquired the cause of her sorrow. She was afraid to expose the cruel author of her misery, lest she should provide new attacks. But after much entreaty, she told him all, much which had escaped his watchful ear. Poor James shut his eyes in silence, as if pained to forgetfulness by the recital. Then turning to Susan, he asked her to take Charlie, and walk out; "she needed the fresh air," he said. "And say to mother I wish Frado to sit by me till you return. I think you are fading, from staying so long in this sick room." Mr. B. also left, and Frado was thus left alone with her friend. Aunt Abby came in to make her daily visit, and seeing the sick countenance of the attendant, took her home with her to administer some cordial. She soon returned, however, and James kept her with him the rest of the day; and a comfortable night's repose following, she was enabled to continue, as usual, her labors. James insisted on her attending religious meetings in the vicinity with Aunt Abby.

Frado, under the instructions of Aunt Abby and the minister, became a believer in a future existence—one of happiness or misery. Her doubt was, *is* there a heaven for the black? She knew there was one for James, and Aunt Abby, and all good white people; but was there any for blacks? She had listened attentively to all the minister said, and all Aunt Abby had told her; but then it was all for white people.

As James approached that blessed world, she felt a strong desire to follow, and be with one who was such a dear, kind friend to her.

While she was exercised with these desires and aspirations, she attended an evening meeting with Aunt Abby, and the good man urged all, young or old, to accept the offers of mercy, to receive a compassionate Jesus as their

Saviour. "Come to Christ," he urged, "all, young or old, white or black, bond or free, come all to Christ for pardon; repent, believe."

This was the message she longed to hear; it seemed to be spoken for. But he had told them to repent; "what was that?" she asked. She knew she was unfit for any heaven, made for whites or blacks. She would gladly repent, or do anything which would admit her to share the abode of James.

Her anxiety increased; her countenance bore marks of solicitude unseen before; and though she said nothing of her inward contest, they all observed a change.

James and Aunt Abby hoped it was the springing of good seed sown by the Spirit of God. Her tearful attention at the last meeting encouraged his aunt to hope that her mind was awakened, her conscience aroused. Aunt Abby noticed that she was particularly engaged in reading the Bible; and this strengthened her conviction that a heavenly Messenger was striving with her. The neighbors dropped in to inquire after the sick, and also if Frado was "*serious?*" They noticed she seemed very thoughtful and tearful at the meetings. Mrs. Redd was very inquisitive; but Mrs. Bellmont saw no appearance of change for the better. She did not feel responsible for her spiritual culture, and hardly believed she had a soul.

Nig was in truth suffering much; her feelings were very intense on any subject, when once aroused. She read her Bible carefully, and as often as an opportunity presented, which was when entirely secluded in her own apartment, or by Aunt Abby's side, who kindly directed her to Christ, and instructed her in the way of salvation.

Mrs. Bellmont found her one day quietly reading her Bible. Amazed and half crediting the reports of officious neighbors, she felt it was time to interfere. Here she was, reading and shedding tears over the Bible. She ordered her to put up the book, and go to work, and not be snivelling about the house, or stop to read again.

But there was one little spot seldom penetrated by her mistress' watchful eye: this was her room, uninviting and comfortless; but to herself a safe retreat. Here she would listen to the pleading of a Saviour, and try to penetrate the veil of doubt and sin which clouded her soul, and long to cast off the fetters of sin, and rise to the communion of saints.

Mrs. Bellmont, as we before said, did not trouble herself about the future destiny of her servant. If she did what she desired for *her* benefit, it was all the responsibility she acknowledged. But she seemed to have great aversion to the notice Nig would attract should she become pious. How could she meet this case? She resolved to make her complaint to John. Strange, when she was always foiled in this direction, she should resort to him. It was time something was done; she had begun to read the Bible openly.

The night of this discovery, as they were retiring, Mrs. Bellmont introduced the conversation, by saying:

"I want your attention to what I am going to say. I have let Nig go out to evening meetings a few times, and, if you will believe it, I found her reading the Bible to-day, just as though she expected to turn pious nigger, and preach to white folks. So now you see what good comes of sending her to school. If she should get converted she would have to go to meeting: at least, as long as James lives. I wish he had not such queer notions about her. It seems to trouble him to know he must die and leave her. He says if he should get well he would take her home with him, or educate her here. Oh, how awful! What can the child mean? So careful, too, of her! He says we shall ruin her health making her work so hard, and sleep in such a place. O, John! do you think he is in his right mind?"

"Yes, yes; she is slender."

"Yes, *yes!*" she repeated sarcastically, "you know these niggers are just like black snakes; you *can't* kill them. If she wasn't tough she would have been killed long ago. There was never one of my girls could do half the work."

"Did they ever try?" interposed her husband. "I think she can do more than all of them together."

"What a man!" said she, peevishly. "But I want to know what is going to be done with her about getting pious?"

"Let her do just as she has a mind to. If it is a comfort to her, let her enjoy the privilege of being good. I see no objection."

"I should think *you* were crazy, sure. Don't you know that every night she will want to go toting off to meeting? and Sundays, too? and you know we have a great deal of company Sundays, and she can't be spared."

"I thought you Christians held to going to church," remarked Mr. B.

"Yes, but who ever thought of having a nigger go, except to drive others there? Why, according to you and James, we should very soon have her in the parlor, as smart as our own girls. It's of no use talking to you or James. If you should go on as you would like, it would not be six months before she would be leaving me; and that won't do. Just think how much profit she was to us last summer. We had no work hired out; she did the work of two girls—"

"And got the whippings for two with it!" remarked Mr. Bellmont.

"I'll beat the money out of her, if I can't get her worth any other way," retorted Mrs. B. sharply. While this scene was passing, Frado was trying to utter the prayer of the publican, "God be merciful to me a sinner."

1859

Sojourner Truth
(c. 1797–1883)

A nearly mythical figure, Sojourner Truth was a strong proponent of equal rights for both African-Americans and women, never compromising her struggle for one to gain the other. Born into slavery in Ulster County, New York, she was named Isabella Baumfree by her Dutch master, who called her Bell, and spoke only Dutch until the age of ten. While still a young girl she was sold numerous times and witnessed the sale of several of her brothers and sisters. She was married to a fellow slave, Thomas, with whom she had five children and lost a five-year-old son to slave traders. She managed to escape with a baby and contracted her services to another man, before being freed in 1827, the same year that slavery ended in New York. She then sued for the freedom of her son, who had been illegally sold South, won her case, and was reunited with the boy.

Working as a domestic in New York City, she became involved in evangelical religious activity and had a vision after which she renamed herself. "When I left the house of bondage I left everything behind," she claimed. "I wa'n't goin' to keep nothin' of Egypt on me, an' so I went to the Lord an' asked him to give me a new name. And the Lord gave me Sojourner because I was to travel up an' down the land showin' the people their sins an' bein' a sign unto them. Afterward I told the Lord I wanted another name 'cause everybody else had two names; and the Lord gave me Truth, because I was to declare the truth to the people."

Sojourner left New York on foot in 1843 to preach and spent that autumn in Northampton, Massachusetts, on a farm owned by a relative of William Lloyd Garrison. There she met Frederick Douglass and the abolitionist Oliver Gilbert, who in 1884 wrote her life story, *Narrative of Sojourner Truth,* which she sold at her lectures as a means of support. During the Civil War, Sojourner Truth worked on behalf of the Union cause and gathered supplies and visited soldiers, singing spirituals and songs of her own composition. In 1864 she traveled to Washington, D.C., where she helped integrate the streetcars and was received by President Abraham Lincoln. After the war, she worked for freemen's relief and argued for the resettlement of freemen in the West.

As a lecturer, Sojourner Truth traveled to camp meetings, revivals, and conventions in twenty-one states and Washington between 1843 and 1878. She attended the First National Women's Rights Convention in Worcester, Massachusetts, in 1850, where she was the only black woman, and spoke the address included here the next year. Because she never learned to read or write, her speeches, characterized by their directness, common sense, use of homey metaphor, and biblical allusion, are known only by news accounts, several recorded in *History of Woman Suffrage* by Elizabeth Cady, Susan B. Anthony, and Matilda Joslyn Gage.

At a time when many suffragists felt that unpopular support of abolition would jeopardize their cause, and when few women even dared to "speak in meeting" for their own rights, Sojourner Truth's appearance onstage was often met initially with hisses and jeers. In her address to the Fourth National Women's Rights Convention in 1853 she chastised, "Sons and daughters ought to behave themselves before their mothers, but they do not. I can see them a-laughin' and pointin' at their mothers up here on the stage. They hiss when an aged woman comes forth. If they'd been brought up proper they'd have known better than hissing like snakes and geese." But she relied on the force of her physical presence, her experience in slavery, and her moral authority to refute common arguments for man's primacy on the grounds of superior intellect, the "manhood" of Christ, and the "sin of our first mother." Like Phillis Wheatley, Benjamin Banneker, and other African-American writers of the colonial period who saw a parallel between their own condition and that of the colonists chafing under the restrictions of the British, Sojourner exposed the utter hypocrisy of one group arguing for its own rights while denying them to another. "I wanted to tell you a mite about Woman's Rights," she warned, "and so I came out and said so. I am sittin' among you to watch; and every once and awhile I will come out and tell you what time of night it is."

Sojourner Truth died at her home in Battle Creek, Michigan, on November 26, 1883.

Address to the Ohio Women's Rights Convention

"And ain't I a woman?"

WELL, CHILDREN, WHERE THERE IS SO MUCH RACKET THERE must be somethin' out o'kilter. I think that 'twixt the Negroes of the North and the South and the women at the North, all talkin' 'bout rights, the white men will be in a fix pretty soon. But what's all this here talkin' 'bout?

That man over there say that women needs to be helped into carriages, and lifted over ditches, and to have the best place everywhere. Nobody ever helps me into carriages, or over mud-puddles, or give me any best place! And ain't I a woman? Look at me? Look at my arm! I have ploughed, and planted, and gathered into barns, and no man could head me! And ain't I a woman? I could work as much and eat as much as a man—when I could get it—and bear the lash as well! And ain't I a woman? I have borne thirteen children, and seen 'em mos' all sold off to slavery, and when I cried out with my mother's grief, none but Jesus heard me! And ain't I a woman?

Then they talk about this thing in the head; what's this they call it? ["Intellect," whispered some one near.] That's it honey. What's that got to do with women's rights or Negro's rights? If my cup won't hold but a pint and yours holds a quart, wouldn't you be mean not to let me have my little half measure full?

Then that little man in black there, he says women can't have as much rights as men, 'cause Christ wasn't a woman! Where did your Christ come from? Where did your Christ come from? From God and a woman! Man had nothin' to do with Him.

If the first woman God ever made was strong enough to turn the world upside down all alone, these women together ought to be able to turn it back, and get it right side up again? And now they is asking to do it, they better let 'em. 'Bliged to you for hearin' me, and now ole Sojourner hasn't got nothin' more to say.

Akron, Ohio, May 29, 1851

Address to the First Annual Meeting of the American Equal Rights Association

MY FRIENDS, I AM REJOICED THAT YOU ARE GLAD, BUT I DON'T know how you will feel when I get through. I come from another field—the country of the slave. They have got their liberty—so much good luck to have slavery partly destroyed; not entirely. I want it root and branch destroyed. Then we will all be free indeed. I feel that if I have to answer for the deeds done in my body just as much as a man, I have a right to have just as much as a man. There is a great stir about colored men gettin' their rights, but not a word about the colored women; and if colored men get their rights, and not colored women theirs, you see the colored men will be masters over the women, and it will be just as bad as it was before. So I am for keeping the thing going while things are stirring; because if we wait till it is still, it will take a great while to get it going again. White women are a great deal smarter, and know more than colored women, while colored women do not know scarcely anything. They go out washing, which is about as high as a colored woman gets, and their men go about idle, strutting up and down; and when the women come home, they ask for their money and take it all, and then scold because there is no food. I want you to consider on that, chil'n. I call you chil'n; you are somebody's chil'n, and I am old enough to be mother of all that is here. I want women to have their rights. In the courts women have no right, no voice; nobody speaks for them. I wish woman to have her voice there among the pettifoggers. If it is not a fit place for women, it is unfit for men to be there.

I am above eighty years old; it is about time for me to be going. I have been forty years a slave and forty years free, and would be here forty years more to have equal rights for all. I suppose I am kept here because something remains for me to do; I suppose I am yet to help to break the chain. I have done a great deal of work; as much as a man, but did not get so much pay. I used to work in the field and bind grain, keeping up with the cradler; but men doing no more, go twice as much pay; so with the German women. They work in the field and do as much work, but do not get the pay. We do as much, we eat as much, we want as much. I suppose I am about the only colored woman that goes about to speak for the rights of the colored women. I want to keep the thing stirring, now that the ice is cracked. What we want is a little money. You men know that you get as much again as women when you write, or for what you do. When we get our rights we shall not have to come to you for money, for then we shall have money enough in our own pockets; and may be you will ask us for money. But help us now until we get it. It is a good consolation to know that when we have got this battle once fought we shall not be coming to you any more. You have been having our rights so long, that you think, like a slave-holder, that you own us. I know that it is hard for one who has held the rein for so long to give up; it cuts like a knife. It will feel all the better when it closes up again. I have been in Washington about three years, seeing about these colored people. Now colored men have the right to vote. There ought to be equal rights now more than ever, since colored people have got their freedom. . . .

I am glad to see that men are getting their rights, but I want women to get theirs, and while the water is stirring I will step into the pool. Now that there is a great stir about colored men's getting their rights is the time for women to step in and have theirs. I am sometimes told that "Women ain't fit to vote. Why, don't you know that a woman had seven devils in her: and do you suppose a woman is fit to rule the nation?" Seven devils ain't no account; a man had a legion in him. The devils didn't know where to go; and so they asked that they might go into the swine. They thought that was as good a place as they came out from. They didn't ask to go into the sheep—no, into the hog; that was the selfish beast; and man is so selfish that he has got women's rights and his own too, and yet he won't give women their rights. He keeps them all to himself. . . .

I have lived on through all that has taken place these forty years in the anti-slavery cause, and I have plead with all the force I had that the day might come that the colored people might own their soul and body. Well, the day has come, although it came through blood. It makes no difference how it came—it did come. I am sorry it came in that way. We are now trying for liberty that requires no blood—that women shall have their rights—not rights from you. Give them what belongs to them; they ask it kindly too. I ask it kindly. Now, I want it done very quick. It can be done in a few years. How good it would be. I would like to go up to the polls myself. I own a little house in Battle Creek, Michigan. Well, every year I got a tax to pay. Taxes, you see, be taxes. Well, a road tax sounds large. . . . There was women there that had a house as well as I. They taxed them to build a road, and they went on the road and worked. It took'em a good while to get a stump up. Now, that shows that women can work. If they can dig up stumps they can vote. It is easier to vote than dig stumps. It doesn't seem hard work to vote, though I have seen some men that had a hard time of it . . . I don't want to take up your time, but I calculate to live. Now, if you want me to get out of the world, you had better get the women votin' soon. I shan't go till I can do that.

New York, May 9, 1867

Harriet Tubman
(c.1820–1913)

If Sojourner Truth was a highly visible symbol of abolition on the speaking platform, Harriet Tubman was a powerful underground force of liberation. After escaping from slavery herself, she became the most active "conductor" on the Underground Railroad, returning to the South nineteen times and helping at least three hundred slaves escape through the North to Canada.

Born on the eastern shore of Maryland (the estimated date of her birth ranges from 1815 to 1823), she was one of eleven children of Harriet and Benjamin Ross. When she was a girl, her master threw a heavy weight at her, causing a permanent injury and a lifelong tendency to fits of somnolence. She was hired out at various times as a child's nurse and laborer. When she was twenty-five, after seeing several of her siblings sold away, she determined to escape slavery and took off in the night, leaving behind her husband, parents, and siblings. Steeled by an unshakable faith, she returned to the South, leading not only her family but hundreds of others north to Canada, where they could escape the reach of the Fugitive Slave Law (1793), which left no escaped slave free of the threat of the professional slave chasers who would return them to the South. It is said that no slave she helped liberate was ever recaptured, and, she averred, she "nebber waited for no one." At one point, the bounty on her head reached $40,000. In Canada, she met the abolitionist John Brown and she was befriended by the abolitionists William H. Seward, Gerrit Smith, Wendell Phillips, William Lloyd Garrison, and Frederick Douglass.

During the Civil War, Tubman served for three years as a nurse, scout, and spy for the Union cause, especially in Florida and the Carolinas under the command of Colonels Thomas Wentworth Higginson and James Montgomery. With Montgomery she traveled on her most famous mission up the Combahee River, liberating 756 slaves. For her service, she was repaid only with a supply of twenty days' rations, and she supported herself by selling her own baked goods and root beer. After the war, she returned to her small plot in Auburn, New York, where she ran a Home for Aged and Indigent Negroes. She fought for many years to receive a pension, finally awarded a small sum to support the Home, where her own parents lived until past the age of one hundred.

Though Tubman herself could neither read nor write, in 1869 Sarah H. Bradford published *Scenes in the Life of Harriet Tubman,* which Tubman sold to support herself financially. Bradford republished the book in 1886 as *Harriet Tubman: The Moses of Her People*—in an expanded edition with additional testimonials—to provide funds for Tubman's Home. Though the book by Mrs. Bradford is full of condescending pronouncements and exaggerated dialect, it remains a useful source of information about Tubman. Included here from that volume are an account of Harriett's escape to freedom, a published biographical sketch, and several passes and letters appended to the narrative.

When she was in her seventies, Tubman spoke at the first meeting of the National Association of Colored Women in Washington, D.C., in 1896. She died in 1913.

from *Harriet Tubman: The Moses of Her People*

HAT WAS TO BECOME OF THE SLAVES ON THIS PLANTATION now that the master was dead? Were they all to be scattered and sent to different parts of the country? Harriet had many brothers and sisters, all of whom with the exception of the two, who had gone South with the chain-gang, were living on this plantation, or were hired out to planters not far away. The word passed through the cabins that another owner was coming in, and that none of the slaves were to be sold out of the State. This assurance satisfied the others, but it did not satisfy Harriet. Already the inward monitor was whispering to her, "Arise, flee for your life!" and in the visions of the night she saw the horsemen coming, and heard the shrieks of women and children, as they were being torn from each other, and hurried off no one knew whither.

And beckoning hands were ever motioning her to come, and she seemed to see a line dividing the land of slavery from the land of freedom, and on the other side of that line she saw lovely white ladies waiting to welcome her, and to care for her. Already in her mind her people were the Israelites in the land of Egypt, while far away to the north *somewhere,* was the land of Canaan; but had she as yet any prevision that *she* was to be the Moses who was to be their leader, through clouds of darkness and fear, and fires of tribulation to that promised land? This she never said.

One day there were scared faces seen in the negro quarter, and hurried whispers passed from one to another. No one knew how it had come out, but some one had heard that Harriet and two of her brothers were very soon, perhaps to-day, perhaps to-morrow, to be sent far South with a gang, bought up for plantation work. Harriet was about twenty or twenty-five years old at the time, and the constantly recurring idea of escape at *sometime,* took sudden form that day, and with her usual promptitude of action she was ready to start at once.

She held a hurried consultation with her brothers, in which she so wrought upon their fears, that they expressed themselves as willing to start with her that very night, for that far North, where, could they reach it in safety, freedom awaited them. But she must first give some intimation of her purpose to the friends she was to leave behind, so that even if not understood at the time, it might be remembered afterward as her intended farewell. Slaves must not be seen talking together, and so it came about that their communication was often made by singing, and the words of their familiar hymns, telling of the heavenly journey, and the land of Canaan, while they did not attract the attention of the masters, conveyed to their brethren and sisters in bondage something more than met the ear. And so she sang, accompanying the words, when for a moment unwatched, with a meaning look to one and another:

> "When dat ar ole chariot comes,
> I'm gwine to lebe you,
> I'm boun' for de promised land,
> Frien's, I'm gwine to lebe you."

Again, as she passed the doors of the different cabins, she lifted up her well-known voice; and many a dusky face appeared at door or window with a wondering or scared expression; and thus she continued:

> "I'm sorry, frien's, to lebe you,
> Farewell! oh, farewell!
> On de oder side of Jordan,
> For I'm boun' for de promised land."

The brothers started with her, but the way was strange, the north was far away, and all unknown, the master would pursue and recapture them, and they broke away from her, and bidding her goodbye, they hastened back to the known horrors of slavery, and the dread of that which was worse.

Harriet was now left alone, but after watching the retreating forms of her brothers, she turned her face toward the north, and fixing her eyes on the guiding star, and committing her way unto the Lord, she started again upon her long, lonely journey. Her farewell song was long remembered in the cabins, and the old mother sat and wept for her lost child. No intimation had been given her of Harriet's intention, for the old woman was of a most impulsive disposition, and her cries and lamentations would have made known to all within hearing Harriet's intended escape. And so, with only the North Star for her guide, our heroine started on the way to liberty. "For," said she, "I had reasoned dis out in my mind; there was one of two things I had a *right* to, liberty, or death; if I could not have one, I would have de oder; for no man should take me alive; I should fight for my liberty as long as my strength lasted, and when de time came for me to go, de Lord would let dem take me."

And so without money, and without friends, she started on through unknown regions; walking by night, hiding by day, but always conscious of an invisible pillar of cloud by day, and of fire by night, under the guidance of which she journeyed or rested. Without knowing whom to trust, or how near the pursuers might be, she carefully felt her way, and by her native cunning, or by God given wisdom, she managed to apply to the right people for food, and sometimes for shelter; though often her bed was only the cold ground, and her watchers the stars of night.

After many long and weary days of travel, she found that she had passed the magic line, which then divided the land of bondage from the land of freedom. But where were the lovely white ladies whom in her visions she had seen, who, with arms outstretched, welcomed her to their hearts and homes. All these visions proved deceitful: she was more alone than ever; but she had crossed the line; no one could take her now, and she would never call any man "Master" more.

"I looked at my hands," she said, "to see if I was de same person now I was free. Dere was such a glory ober eberything, de sun came like gold trou de trees, and ober de fields, and I felt like I was in heaven." But then came the bitter drop in the cup of joy. She was alone, and her kindred were in slavery, and not one of them had the courage to dare what she had dared. Unless she made the effort to liberate them she would never see them more, or even know their fate.

"I knew of a man," she said, "who was sent to the State Prison for twenty-five years. All these years he was always thinking of his home, and counting by years, months, and days, the time till he should be free, and see his family and friends once more. The years roll on, the time of imprisonment is over, the man is free. He leaves the prison gates, he makes his way to his old home, but his old home is not there. The house in which he had dwelt in his childhood had been torn down, and a new one had been put up in its place; his family were gone, their very name forgotten, there was no one to take him by the hand to welcome him back to life."

"So it was wid me," said Harriet, "I had crossed de line of which I had so long been dreaming. I was free; but dere was no one to welcome me to de land of freedom, I was a stranger in a strange land, and my home after all was down in de old cabin quarter, wid de ole folks, and my brudders and sisters. But to dis solemn resolution I came; I was free, and dey should be free also; I would make a home for dem in de North, and de Lord helping me, I would bring dem all dere. Oh, how I prayed den, lying all alone on de cold, damp ground; 'Oh, dear Lord,' I said, 'I haint got no friend but *you.* Come to my help, Lord, for I'm in trouble!' "

It would be impossible here to give a detailed account of the journeys and labors of this intrepid woman for the redemption of her kindred and friends, during the years that followed. Those years were spent in work, almost by night and day, with the one object of the rescue of her people from slavery. All her wages were laid away with this sole purpose, and as soon as a sufficient amount was secured, she disappeared from her Northern home, and as suddenly and mysteriously she appeared some dark night at the door of one of the cabins on a plantation, where a trembling band of fugitives, forewarned as to time and place, were anxiously awaiting their deliverer. Then she piloted them North, traveling by night, hiding by day, scaling the mountains, fording the rivers, threading the forests, lying concealed as the pursuers passed them. She, carrying the babies, drugged with paregoric, in a basket on her arm. So she went *nineteen* times, and so she brought away over three hundred pieces of living and breathing "property," with God given souls.

The way was so toilsome over the rugged mountain passes, that often the *men* who followed her would give out, and foot-sore, and bleeding, they would drop on the ground, groaning that they could not take another step. They would lie there and die, or if strength came back, they would return on their steps, and seek their old homes again. Then the revolver carried by this bold and daring pioneer, would come out, while pointing it at their heads she would say, "Dead niggers tell no tales; you go on or die!" And by this heroic treatment she compelled them to drag their weary limbs along on their northward journey.

The following account of the subject of this memoir is cut from the *Boston Commonwealth* of 1863, kindly sent the writer by Mr. Sanborn: . . .

"Araminta Ross, now known by her married name of Tubman, with her sounding Christian name changed to Harriet, is the grand-daughter of a slave imported from Africa, and has not a drop of white blood in her veins. Her parents were Benjamin Ross and Harriet Greene, both slaves, but married and faithful to each other. They still live in old age and poverty, but free, on a little property at Auburn, N.Y., which their daughter purchased for them from Mr. Seward, the Secretary of State. She was born, as near as she can remember, in 1820 or in 1821, in Dorchester County, on the Eastern shore of Maryland, and not far from the town of Cambridge. She had ten brothers and sisters, of whom three are now living, all at the North, and all rescued from slavery by Harriet, before the War. She went back just as the South was preparing to secede, to bring away a fourth, but before she could reach her, she was dead. Three years before, she had brought away her old father and mother, at great risk to herself.

"When Harriet was six years old, she was taken from her mother and carried ten miles to live with James Cook, whose wife was a weaver, to learn the trade of weaving. While still a mere child, Cook set her to watching his musk-rat traps, which compelled her to wade through the water. It happened that she was once sent when she was ill with the measles, and, taking cold from wading in the water in this condition, she grew very sick, and her mother persuaded her master to take her away from Cook's until she could get well.

"Another attempt was made to teach her weaving, but she would not learn, for she hated her mistress, and she did not want to live at home, as she would have done as a weaver, for it was the custom then to weave the cloth for the family, or a part of it, in the house.

"Soon after she entered her teens she was hired out as a field hand, and it was while thus employed that she received a wound, which nearly proved fatal, from the effects of which she still suffers. In the fall of the year, the slaves there work in the evening, cleaning up wheat, husking corn, etc. On this occasion, one of the slaves of a farmer named Barrett, left his work, and went to the village store in the evening. The overseer followed him, and so did Harriet. When the slave was found, the overseer swore he should be whipped, and called on Harriet, among others, to help tie him. She refused, and as the man ran away, she placed herself in the door to stop pursuit. The overseer caught up a two-pound weight from the counter and threw it at the fugitive, but it fell short and struck Harriet a stunning blow on the head. It was long before she recovered from this, and it has left her subject to a sort of stupor or lethargy at times; coming upon her in the midst of conversation, or whatever she may be doing, and throwing her into a deep slumber, from which she will presently rouse herself, and go on with her conversation or work.

"After this she lived for five or six years with John Stewart, where at first she worked in the house, but afterward 'hired her time,' and Dr. Thompson, son of her master's guardian, 'stood for her,' that is, was her surety for the payment of what she owed. She employed the time thus hired in the rudest labors,—drove oxen, carted, plowed, and did all the work of a man,—sometimes earning money enough in a year, beyond what she paid her master, 'to buy a pair of steers,' worth forty dollars. The amount exacted of a woman for her time was fifty or sixty dollars—of a man, one hundred to one hundred and fifty dollars. Frequently Harriet worked for her father, who was a timber inspector, and superintended the cutting and hauling of great quantities of timber for the Baltimore ship-yards. Stewart, his temporary master, was a builder, and for the work of Ross used to receive as much as five dollars a day sometimes, he being a superior workman. While engaged with her father, she would cut wood, haul logs, etc. Her usual 'stint' was half a cord of wood in a day.

"Harriet was married somewhere about 1844, to a free colored man named John Tubman, but she had no children. For the last two years of slavery she lived with Dr. Thompson, before mentioned, her own master not being yet of age, and Dr. T.'s father being his guardian, as well as the owner of her own father. In 1849 the young man died, and the slaves were to be sold, though previously set free by an old will. Harriet resolved not to be sold, and so, with no knowledge of the North—having only heard of Pennsylvania and New Jersey—she walked away one night alone. She found a friend in a white lady, who knew her story and helped her on her way. After many adventures, she reached Philadelphia, where she found work and earned a small stock of money. With this money in her purse, she traveled back to Maryland for her husband, but she found him married to another woman, and no longer caring to live with her. This, however, was not until two years after her escape, for she does not seem to have reached her old home in the first two expeditions. In December, 1850, she had visited Baltimore and brought away her sister and two children, who had come up from

Cambridge in a boat, under charge of her sister's husband, a free black. A few months after she had brought away her brother and two other men, but it was not till the fall of 1851, that she found her husband and learned of his infidelity. She did not give way to rage or grief, but collected a party of fugitives and brought them safely to Philadelphia. In December of the same year, she returned, and led out a party of eleven, among them her brother and his wife. With these she journeyed to Canada, and there spent the winter, for this was after the enforcement of Mason's Fugitive Slave Bill in Philadelphia and Boston, and there was not safety except 'under the paw of the British Lion' [in Canada] she quaintly said. But the winter was terribly severe for these poor runaways. They earned their bread by chopping wood in the snows of a Canadian forest; they were frost-bitten, hungry, and naked. Harriet was their good angel. She kept house for her brother, and the poor creatures boarded with her. She worked for them, begged for them, prayed for them, with the strange familiarity of communion with God which seems natural to these people, and carried them by the help of God through the hard winter.

"In the spring she returned to the States, and as usual earned money by working in hotels and families as a cook. From Cape May, in the fall of 1852, she went back once more to Maryland, and brought away nine more fugitives.

"Up to this time she had expended chiefly her own money in these expeditions—money which she had earned by hard work in the drudgery of the kitchen. Never did any one more exactly fulfill the sense of George Herbert—

> " 'A servant with this clause
> Makes drudgery divine.'

"But it was not possible for such virtues long to remain hidden from the keen eye of the Abolitionists. She became known to Thomas Garrett, the large-hearted Quaker of Wilmington, who has aided the escape of three thousand fugitives; she found warm friends in Philadelphia and New York, and wherever she went. These gave her money, which she never spent for her own use, but laid up for the help of her people, and especially for her journeys back to the 'land of Egypt,' as she called her old home. By reason of her frequent visits there, always carrying away some of the oppressed, she got among her people the name of 'Moses,' which it seems she still retains.

"Between 1852 and 1857, she made but two of these journeys, in consequence partly of the increased vigilance of the slave-holders, who had suffered so much by the loss of their property. A great reward was offered for her capture and she several times was on the point of being taken, but always escaped by her quick wit, or by 'warnings' from Heaven—for it is time to notice one singular trait in her character. She is the most shrewd and practical person in the world, yet she is a firm believer in omens, dreams, and warnings. She declares that before her escape from slavery, she used to dream of flying over fields and towns, and rivers and mountains, looking down upon them 'like a bird,' and reaching at last a great fence, or sometimes a river, over which she would try to fly, 'but it 'peared like I wouldn't hab de strength, and jes as I was sinkin' down dere would be ladies all drest in white ober dere, and dey would put out dere arms and pull me 'cross.' There is nothing strange in this, perhaps, but she declares that when she came North she remembered these very places as those she had seen in her dreams, and many of the ladies who befriended her were those she had been helped by in her vision.

"Then she says she always knows when there is danger near her—she does not know how, exactly, but ' 'pears like my heart go flutter, flutter, and den dey may say "Peace, Peace," as much as dey likes, *I know it's gwine to be war!'* She is very firm on this point, and ascribes to this her great impunity, in spite of the lethargy before mentioned, which would seem likely to throw her into the hands of her enemies. She says she inherited this power, that her father could always predict the weather, and that he foretold the Mexican war.

"In 1857 she made her most venturesome journey, for she brought with her to the North her old parents, who were no longer able to walk such distances as she must go by night. Consequently she must hire a wagon for them, and it required all her ingenuity to get them through Maryland and Delaware safe. She accomplished it, however, and by the aid of her friends she brought them safe to Canada, where they spent the winter. Her account of their sufferings there—of her mother's complaining and her own philosophy about it—is a lesson of trust in Providence better than many sermons. But she decided to bring them to a more comfortable place, and so she negotiated with Mr. Seward—then in the Senate—for a little patch of ground. To the credit of the Secretary of State it should be said, that he sold her the property on very favorable terms, and gave her some time for payment. To this house she removed her parents, and set herself to work to pay for the purchase. In was on this errand that she first visited Boston—we believe in the winter of 1858–59. She brought a few letters from her friends in New York, but she could herself neither read nor write, and she was obliged to trust to her wits that they were delivered to the right persons. One of them, as it happened, was to the present writer, who received it by another hand, and called to see her at her boarding-house. It was curious to see the caution with which she received her visitor until she felt assured that there was no mistake. One of her means of security was to carry with her the daguerreotypes of her friends, and show them to each new person. If they recognized the likeness, then it was all right.

"Pains were taken to secure her the attention to which her great services of humanity entitled her, and she left New England with a handsome sum of money toward the payment of her debt to Mr. Seward. Before she left, however, she had several interviews with Captain Brown, then in Boston. He is supposed to have communicated his plans to her, and to have been aided by her in obtaining recruits and money among her people. At any rate, he always spoke of her with the greatest respect, and declared that 'General Tubman,' as he styled her, was better officer than most whom he had seen, and could command an army as successfully as she had led her small parties of fugitives.

"Her own veneration for Captain Brown has always been profound, and since his murder, has taken the form of a religion. She has often risked her own life for her people, and she thought nothing of that; but that a white man, and a man so noble and strong, should so take upon himself the burden of a despised race, she could not understand, and she took refuge from her perplexity in the mysteries of her fervid religion.

"Again, she laid great stress on a dream which she had just before she met Captain Brown in Canada. She thought she was in 'a wilderness sort of place, all full of rocks, and bushes,' when she saw a serpent raise its head among the rocks, and as it did so, it became the head of an old man with a long white beard, gazing at her, 'wishful like, jes as ef he war gwine to speak to me,' and then two other heads rose up beside him, younger than he,—and as she stood looking at them, and wondering what they could want with her, a great crowd of men rushed in and struck down the younger heads, and then the head of the old man, still looking at her so 'wishful.' This dream she had again and again, and could not interpret it; but when she met Captain Brown, shortly after, behold, he was the very image of the head she had seen. But still she could not make out what her dream signified, till the news came to her of the tragedy of Harper's Ferry, and then she knew the two other heads were his two sons. She was in New York at that time, and on the day of the affair at Harper's Ferry she felt her usual warning that something was wrong—she could not tell what. Finally she told her hostess that it must be Captain Brown who was in trouble, and that they should soon hear bad news from him. The next day's newspaper brought tidings of what had happened.

"Her last visit to Maryland was made after this, in December, 1860; and in spite of the agitated condition of the country, and the greater watchfulness of the slave-holders, she brought away seven fugitives, one of them an infant, which must be drugged with opium to keep it from crying on the way, and so revealing the hiding-place of the party."

ST. HELENA ISLAND, S.C., *July* 6, 1863.
HEADQUARTERS COLORED BRIGADE.

BRIG.-GEN. GILMORE, Commanding Department of the South—

GENERAL: I wish to commend to your attention, Mrs. Harriet Tubman, a most remarkable woman, and invaluable as a scout. I have been acquainted with her character and actions for several years.

I am, General, your most ob't servant,

JAMES MONTGOMERY,
Col. Com. Brigade.

HEADQUARTERS DEPARTMENT OF THE SOUTH,
HILTON HEAD, PORT ROYAL, S.C., *Feb.* 19, 1863.

Pass the bearer, Harriet Tubman, to Beaufort and back to this place, and wherever she wishes to go; and give her free passage at all times, on all Government transports. Harriet was sent to me from Boston by Governor Andrew, of Massachusetts, and is a valuable woman. She has permission, as a servant of the Government, to purchase such provisions from the Commissary as she may need.

D. HUNTER,
Maj.-Gen. Com.

BEAUFORT, *Aug.* 28, 1862.

Will Capt. Warfield please let "Moses" have a little Bourbon whiskey for medicinal purposes.

HENRY K. DURANT,
Act. Ass. Surgeon.

ATLANTA, GA., *March* 21, 1868.

MY DEAR MADAME: I have just received your letter informing me that Hon. Wm. Seward, Secretary of State, would present a petition to Congress for a pension to Harriet Tubman, for services rendered in the Union Army during the late war. I can bear witness to the value of her services in South Carolina and Florida. She was employed in the hospitals and as a spy. She made many a raid inside the enemy's lines, displaying remarkable courage, zeal, and fidelity. She was employed by General Hunter, and I think by Generals Stevens and Sherman, and is as deserving of a pension from the Government for her services as any other of its faithful servants.

I am very truly yours,
RUFUS SAXTON,
Bvt. Brig.-Gen., U.S.A.

Frances Ellen Watkins Harper
(1825–1911)

A lifelong activist and reformer, Frances Ellen Watkins was born free in Baltimore, in the slave state of Maryland. Orphaned at three, she began to support herself by the time she was thirteen and from 1850 spent several years teaching in Ohio and Pennsylvania, where she was impressed by the activity of abolitionists and the Underground Railroad. She became a lecturer for the Anti-Slavery Society in Maine in 1854 and was soon speaking throughout New England, Ohio, New York, and Pennsylvania, earning a reputation as an effective platform orator and punctuating her lectures with her own rather inspirational verse. The first of her ten volumes of poetry, *Poems on Miscellaneous Subjects,* with an introduction by William Lloyd Garrison, was published in 1854. (A volume *Forest Leaves* had been privately printed around 1854.) She married Fenton Harper in Cincinnati in 1860, and they had a daughter before his death in 1864.

Like Mary Church Terrell, Harper became involved in the women's club movement, speaking out on the subjects of temperance, morality, education, and women's rights. She founded the National Association of Colored Women and was a delegate to the Women's Rights Convention in 1866. She was one of the few women ever to address the National Convention of Colored Men (in 1864), and she attended the Equal Rights Association Convention in 1869, where in a fractious debate she sided with Frederick Douglass and others who supported the Fifteenth Amendment,[†] despite its lack of enfranchisement of women.

In her work, Harper displayed a particular sensitivity to the concerns of women, as seen in one of her best known poems, "The Slave Mother," while "A Double Standard" exposes the hypocrisy of a society that accorded different treatment to "fallen women" and the men who hastened their falls. And in her letter to John Brown, she expresses her concern for his widow, with whom she stayed in Philadelphia for two weeks while awaiting his execution. Her other volumes include a work prompted by the death of Lincoln and emancipation, *Moses, A Story of the Nile* (1869);

Sketches of Southern Life (1893); *Idylls of the Bible* (1901); and the novel *Iola LeRoy* (1892). She is also credited with the first short story by an African-American, "The Two Offers," published in 1859.

Harper lived the last forty years of her life in Philadelphia, where she died on February 22, 1911.

Bury Me in a Free Land

Make me a grave where'er you will,
In a lowly plain, or a lofty hill;
Make it among earth's humblest graves,
But not in a land where men are slaves.

I could not rest if around my grave
I heard the steps of a trembling slave;
His shadow above my silent tomb
Would make it a place of fearful gloom.

I could not rest if I heard the tread
Of a coffle gang to the shambles led,
And the mother's shriek of wild despair
Rise like a curse on the trembling air.

I could not sleep if I saw the lash
Drinking her blood at each fearful gash,
And I saw her babes torn from her breast,
Like trembling doves from their parent nest.

I'd shudder and start if I heard the bay
Of bloodhounds seizing their human prey,
And I heard the captive plead in vain
As they bound afresh his galling chain.

If I saw young girls from their mothers' arms
Bartered and sold for their youthful charms,
My eye would flash with a mournful flame,
My death-paled cheek grow red with shame.

I would sleep, dear friends, where bloated might
Can rob no man of his dearest right;
My rest shall be calm in any grave
Where none can call his brother a slave.

I ask no monument, proud and high,
To arrest the gaze of the passers-by;
All that my yearning spirit craves,
Is bury me not in a land of slaves.

1854

The Slave Mother

Heard you that shriek: It rose
   So wildly on the air,
It seem'd as if a burden'd heart
   Was breaking in despair.

Saw you those hands so sadly clasped—
   The bowed and feeble head—
The shuddering of that fragile form—
   That look of grief and dread?

Saw you the sad, imploring eye?
   Its every glance was pain,
As if a storm of agony
   Were sweeping through the brain.

She is a mother pale with fear,
   Her boy clings to her side,
And in her kyrtle vainly tries
   His trembling form to hide.

He is not hers, although she bore
   For him a mother's pains;
He is not hers, although her blood
   Is coursing through his veins!

He is not hers, for cruel hands
   May rudely tear apart
The only wreath of household love
   That binds her breaking heart.

His love has been a joyous light
   That o'er her pathway smiled,
A fountain gushing ever new,
   Amid life's desert wild.

His lightest word has been a tone
   Of music round her heart,
Their lives a streamlet blent in one—
   Oh, Father! must they part?

They tear him from her circling arms,
   Her last and fond embrace:—
Oh! never more may her sad eyes
   Gaze on his mournful face.

No, marvel, then, those bitter shrieks
  Disturb the listening air;
She is a mother, and her heart
  Is breaking in despair.

1854

A Double Standard

Do you blame me that I loved him?
  If when standing all alone
I cried for bread a careless world
  Press to my lips a stone.

Do you blame me that I loved him
  That my heart beat glad and free,
When he told me in the sweetest tones
  He loved but only me?

Can you blame me that I did not see
  Beneath his burning kiss
The serpent's wiles, nor even hear
  The deadly adder hiss?

Can you blame me that my heart grew cold
  That the tempted, tempter turned;
When he was feted and caressed
  And I was coldly spurned?

Would you blame him, when you draw from me
  Your dainty robes aside,
If he with gilded baits should claim
  Your fairest as his bride?

Would you blame the world if it should press
  On him a civic crown;
And see me struggling in the depth
  Then harshly press me down?

Crime has no sex and yet to-day
  I wear the brand of shame;
Whilst he amid the gay and proud
  Still bears an honored name.

Can you blame me if I've learned to think
  Your hate of vice a sham,
When you so coldly crushed me down
  And then excused the man?

Would you blame me if to-morrow
  The coroner should say,
A wretched girl, outcast, forlorn,
  Has thrown her life away?

Yes, blame me for my downward course,
  But oh! remember well,
Within your homes you press the hand
  That led me down to hell.

I'm glad God's ways are not our ways,
  He does not see as man;
Within His love I know there's room
  For those whom others ban.

I think before His great white throne,
  His throne of spotless light,
That whited sepulchres shall wear
  The hue of endless night.

That I who fell, and he who sinned,
  Shall reap as we have sown;
That each the burden of his loss
  Must bear and bear alone.

No golden weights can turn the scale
  Of justice in His sight;
And what is wrong in woman's life
  In man's cannot be right.

John Brown's Raid at Harpers Ferry

On October 16, 1859, the militant abolitionist John Brown advanced with a group of twenty-one men on the federal arsenal in Harpers Ferry, Virginia. The men were quickly overcome by federal troops led by Colonel Robert E. Lee, while Brown was wounded and captured. Though the attempt to take the arsenal and provoke a general uprising had ended in defeat, not since Nat Turner's revolt in 1831 did a group of armed abolitionists arouse such deeply divided public opinion.

John Brown (1800–1859) was born in Torrington, Connecticut, and moved as a boy to Ohio. While pursuing numerous unsuccessful businesses, Brown moved his large family (eventually numbering twenty children) from Ohio to Massachusetts, Pennsylvania, and New York. Having already helped a number of slaves escape, in 1855 Brown joined several of his sons in Kansas, where, under the provisions of the Kansas-Nebraska Act of 1854, a struggle was being waged between Free-Soilers and proslavery elements to determine whether the territory would join the Union as slave or free.

After the town of Lawrence, Kansas, was attacked by proslavery activists in 1856, Brown, with four of his sons and others, massacred five suspected proslavery settlers outside their homes along Pottawatomie Creek. Claiming to have been carrying out the will of God, Brown and his sons soon gathered a band of equally fervent followers, leading a raid in Missouri which liberated eleven slaves and fleeing to Canada. Brown received funds for his cause from supporters like the abolitionists Thomas Wentworth Higginson and Gerrit Smith, and in Canada he met Harriet Tubman, who is supposed to have advised him on his Virginia campaign.

As the national crisis escalated, Brown planned to promote an insurrection in Virginia and establish a stronghold through which slaves could pass on their escape route to the North. In 1859 he rented a farm near Harpers Ferry, in what is now West Virginia, and gathered his army of men, including five African-Americans, Shields Green, Dangerfield Newby, Sherrard Lewis Leary, John A. Copeland, and Osborne P. Anderson. The men were to be joined in the assault on the arsenal by additional slaves and freemen, but once the action began, little support materialized. Ten men were killed in the struggle, five escaped (including Anderson, who published his account *A Voice from Harper's Ferry* two years later), and the rest were captured.

Brown was tried, convicted of treason, and sentenced to death. In refuting his sentence in court, he argued, "I believe that to have interfered as I have done, in behalf of His despised poor, I did no wrong, but right." Brown was hanged on December 2, 1859. The fate of his comrades was equally certain. "The five black men who followed John Brown like the heroes of the German myth," wrote Thomas Hamilton in *The Weekly Anglo-African,* which covered the proceedings extensively, "knew that for them there was no recrossing of the dark river." Copeland and Green were hanged on December 16; Copeland's letter to his family on the eve of his death is included here.

Brown's cause generated much support in both the white and black communities. Henry Highland Garnet eulogized Brown at his congregation in New York City, while Frederick Douglass wrote that though he had not pledged to join the assault at Harpers Ferry, as rumored, "The tools to those that can use them. Let every man work for the abolition of slavery in his own way." John Brown's ghost, he argued, would "haunt the bedchambers of all the born and unborn slaveholders of Virginia through all their generations." A supportive letter to Brown from Frances Ellen Watkins (Harper), who stayed with Brown's wife at the home of William Still in Philadelphia while Brown awaited his execution, is included here.

The leader of the doomed plot came to be seen in messianic terms. "In all ages and in every department of effort for the true advancement of mankind," stated *The Weekly Anglo-African* (November 5, 1859), "have been found men in advance of the masses. . . . Misunderstood, hated, denounced, traduced, and often deprived of life, though invariably in the right, they find few bold enough to espouse their cause and fewer still willing to become co-laborers with them. It was so in the days of Christ; and it was so before; and it has been so ever since. . . . Talk as we will—call him fanatic, madman, traitor, our word for it—Brown could not help it. It was his mission. He was impelled by an unseen hand—a hand notwithstanding, points the destinies of nations."

Brown's raid on Harpers Ferry, his trial, his death, and its aftermath did much to signal a shift in the struggle against slavery from moral suasion to militant resistance—an evolution that recalled the bold words of David Walker and Henry Highland Garnett—bringing the divided country even closer to war. "John Brown has struck his blow against the living iniquity of our land," wrote the *Anglo-African* (December 10, 1859). "Whether that blow will be as deep and lasting, as it has been sudden and powerful, time alone can tell."

Letter from John A. Copeland

". . . we shall meet in heaven, where we shall not be parted by the demands of the cruel and unjust monster Slavery."

Dear Father, Mother, Brothers Henry, William and
Freddy and Sisters Sarah and Mary:

The last Sabbath with me on earth has passed away. The last Monday, Tuesday, Wednesday and Thursday that I shall ever see on this earth, have now passed by. God's glorious sun, which he has placed in the heavens to illuminate this earth—whose warm rays make man's home on earth pleasant—whose refulgent beams are watched for by the poor invalid, to enter and make as it were a heaven of the room in which he is confined—I have seen declining behind the western mountains for the last time. Last night, for the last time, I beheld the soft bright moon as it rose, casting its mellow light into my felon's cell, dissipating the darkness, and filling it with that soft pleasant light which causes such thrills of joy to all those in like circumstances with myself. This morning, for the last time, I beheld the glorious sun of yesterday rising in the far-off East, away off in the country where our Lord Jesus Christ first proclaimed salvation to man; and now, as he rises higher and his bright light takes the place of the pale, soft moonlight, I will take my pen, for the last time, to write you who are bound to me by those strong ties, (yea, the strongest that God ever instituted,) the ties of blood and relationship. *I am well, both in body and in mind.* And now, dear ones, if it were not that I knew your hearts will be filled with sorrow at my fate, I could pass from this earth without a regret. Why should you sorrow? Why should your hearts be wracked with grief? Have I not everything to gain, and nothing to lose by the change? I fully believe that not only myself, but also all three of my poor comrades who are to ascend the same scaffold—(a scaffold already made sacred to the cause of freedom by the death of that great champion of human freedom—Captain John Brown) are *prepared* to meet our God.

I am only leaving a world filled with sorrow and woe, to enter one in which there is but one lasting day of happiness and bliss. I feel that God, in his mercy, has spoken peace to my soul, and that all my numerous sins are forgiven.

Dear parents, brothers and sisters, it is true that I am now in a few hours to start on a journey from which no traveler returns. Yes, long before this reaches you, I shall, as I sincerely hope, have met our brother and sister who have for years been worshiping God around his throne—singing praises to him and thanking him that he gave his Son to die that they might have eternal life. I pray daily and hourly that I may be fitted to have my home with them, and that you, one and all, may prepare your souls to meet your God, that so, in the end, though we meet no more on earth, we shall meet in heaven, where we shall not be parted by the demands of the cruel and unjust monster Slavery.

But think not that I am complaining, for I feel reconciled to meet my fate. *I pray God that his will be done, not mine.*

Let me tell you that it is not the mere fact of having to meet death, which I should regret, (if I should express regret I mean,) but that such an unjust institution should exist as the one which demands my life, and not my life only, but the lives of those to whom my life bears but the relative value of zero to the infinite. I beg of you, one and all, that you will not grieve about me; but that you will thank God that he spared me to make my peace with him.

And now, dear ones, attach no blame to any one for my coming here, for not any person but myself is to blame.

I have no antipathy against any one. I have freed my mind of all hard feelings against every living being, and I ask all who have any thing against me to do the same.

And now, dear Parents, Brothers and Sisters, I must bid you to serve your God, and meet me in heaven.

I must with a very few words close my correspondence with those who are the most near and dear to me: but I hope, in the end, we may again commune never more to cease.

Dear ones, he who writes this will, in a few hours, be in this world no longer. Yes, these fingers which hold the pen with which this is written will, before today's sun has reached his meridian, have laid it aside forever, and this poor soul have taken its light to meet its God.

And now, dear ones, I must bid you that last, long, sad farewell. Good by, Father, Mother, Henry, William and Freddy, Sarah and Mary! Serve your God and meet me in heaven.

Your Son and Brother to eternity,
JOHN A. COPELAND
December 16, 1859

Letter to John Brown from Frances Harper

Dear Friend: Although the Hands of Slavery throw a barrier between you and me, and it may not be my privilege to see you in your prison-house, Virginia has no bolts or bars through which I dread to send you my sympathy. In the name of the young girl sold from the warm clasp of a mother's arms to the clutches of a libertine or a profligate,—in the name of the slave mother, her heart rocked to and fro by the agony of her mournful separations,—I thank you, that you have been brave enough to reach out your hands to the crushed and blighted of my race. You have rocked the bloody Bastille; and I hope that from your sad fate great good may arise to the cause of freedom. Already from your prison has come a shout of triumph against the giant sin of our country. The hemlock is distilled with victory when it is pressed to the lips of Socrates. The Cross becomes a glorious ensign when Calvary's page-browed sufferer yields up his life upon it. And, if Universal Freedom is ever to be the dominant power of the land, your bodies may be only her first stepping stones to dominion. I would prefer to see Slavery go down peaceably by men breaking off their sins by righteousness and their iniquities by showing justice and mercy to the poor; but we cannot tell what the future may bring forth. God writes national judgments upon national sins; and what may be slumbering in the storehouse of divine justice we do not know.

We may earnestly hope that your fate will not be a vain lesson, that it will intensify our hatred of Slavery and love of Freedom, and that your martyr grave will be a sacred altar upon which men will record their vows of undying hatred to that system which tramples on man and bids defiance to God. I have written to your dear wife, and sent her a few dollars, and I pledge myself to you that I will continue to assist her. May the ever-blessed God shield you and your fellow-prisoners in the darkest hour. Send my sympathy to your fellow-prisoners; tell them to be of good courage; to seek a refuge in the Eternal God, and lean upon His everlasting arms for a sure support. If any of them, like you, have a wife or children that I can help, let them send me word.

Yours in the cause of freedom.
Kendallville, Indiana, November 25, 1859

from *Echoes of Harper's Ferry,* Boston, 1860

On John Brown's Raid

*". . . choose ye which method of emancipation you prefer—
Nat Turner's, or John Brown's."*

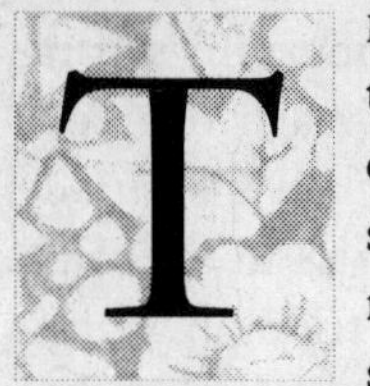

THERE ARE TWO REASONS WHY WE PRESENT OUR READERS WITH the "Confessions of Nat Turner." First, to place upon record this most remarkable episode in the history of human slavery, which proves to the philosophic observer that in the midst of this most perfectly contrived and apparently secure system of slavery, humanity will out, and engender from its bosom, forces that will contend against oppression, however unsuccessfully; and secondly, that the two methods of Nat Turner and of John Brown may be compared. The one is the mode in which the slave seeks freedom for his fellow, and the other mode in which the white man seeks to set the slave free. There are many points of similarity between these two men: they were both idealists; both governed by their views of the teachings of the Bible; both had harbored for years the purpose to which they gave up their lives; both felt themselves swayed as by some divine, or at least, spiritual impulse; the one seeking in the air, the earth, and the heavens for signs which came at last; and the other, obeying impulses which he believed to have been fore-ordained from the eternal past; both cool, calm, and heroic in prison and in the prospect of inevitable death; both confess with child-like frankness and simplicity the object they had in view—the pure and simple emancipation of their fellow men, both win from the judges who sentenced them, expressions of deep sympathy—and here the parallel ceases. Nat Turner's terrible logic could only see the enfranchisement of one race, compassed by the extirpation of the other; and he followed his gory syllogism with rude exactitude. John Brown, believing that the freedom of the enthralled could only be effected by placing them on an equality with the enslavers, and unable in the very effort at emancipation to tyrannize himself, is moved with compassion for tyrants, as well as slaves, and seeks to extirpate this formidable cancer, without spilling one drop of christian blood.

These two narratives present a fearful choice to the slaveholders, nay, to this great nation—which of the two modes of emancipation shall take place? The method of Nat Turner, or the method of John Brown?

Emancipation must take place, and soon. There can be no long delay in the choice of methods. If John Brown's be not soon adopted by the free North, then Nat Turner's will be by the enslaved South.

Had the order of the events been reversed—had Nat Turner been in John Brown's place at the head of these twenty-one men, governed by his inexorable logic and cool daring, the soil of Virginia and Maryland and the far South would by this time be drenched in the blood and the wild and sanguinary course of these men, no earthly power could stay.

The course which the South is now frantically pursuing will engender in its bosom and nurse into maturity a hundred Nat Turners, whom Virginia is infinitely less able to resist in 1860, than she was in 1831.

So, people of the South, people of the North! Men and brethren, choose ye which method of emancipation you prefer—Nat Turner's, or John Brown's.

The Weekly Anglo-African, New York, December 31, 1859

Emancipation Proclamation

Although President Abraham Lincoln was personally opposed to slavery—he had expressed a desire early in his political career to put it "in the course of ultimate extinction"—he felt bound by constitutional law and a desire to save the Union to uphold it in those states (several of which were supporting the Union cause) that had elected it. As a possible solution to the continually vexing problem of racial conflict, he had been a proponent of colonization, saying to a group of black leaders in August 1862, "I think your race suffer very greatly, many of them by living among us, while ours suffer from your presence." He suggested Central America as a possible site of relocation. As the Civil War progressed, however, under both political pressure and military expediency, he began to consider the possibility of abolishing the peculiar institution.

The effort to dismantle slavery proceeded by degrees. In August 1861, Congress declared that slaves held by rebel forces, like other species of "property," were contrabands of war. The next year, it forbade army officers to return fugitive slaves to their masters, and in mid-July, as the war was going badly, Congress passed an act that liberated contrabands and allowed their service in the military. Despite these changes, with the president's failure to position the federal government solidly behind emancipation, "hard war" abolitionists were growing impatient, while others observed more pragmatically that the deprivation of the rebel forces of their slaves would seriously weaken them economically and at the same time fund a new source of manpower for the North.

Lincoln began to formulate an emancipation policy in the summer of 1862, but was advised to delay its announcement until morale improved with a Union victory. After the qualified Union success at the Battle of Antietam, on September 22 Lincoln issued a preliminary proclamation stating that it was his intention that, on January 1, 1863, all slaves in rebel states would be freed. On January 1, the president issued his final proclamation, citing his position as "Commander-in-Chief," and describing it as "a practical measure" and "an act of justice, warranted by the Constitution, upon military necessity." Because the proclamation only applied to slaves in rebel-held areas—hence the lengthy list of localities in the document—the ability of the Union to enforce the law in those states was dubious, while one million people outside those areas—in Maryland, Kentucky, Missouri, and Tennessee, for example—remained enslaved. The very awkwardness of phrasing in the document—"that ALL PERSONS HELD AS SLAVES within said designated States and parts of States ARE, AND HENCEFORWARD SHALL BE FREE!"—in what might have been an edict of extreme clarity and force, belies the nature of the compromise that Lincoln made.

Nonetheless, a chink had been made in the armor of slavery. While many slaves had emancipated themselves at this point—as they had for centuries—the effect of the president's dictum was significant. As the historian John Hope Franklin observes, "Once the power of the government was enlisted on the side of freedom in one place, it could not successfully be restrained from supporting freedom in some other place. It was too fine a distinction to make. Not even the slaveholders in the excepted areas could make it. They knew, therefore, that the Emancipation Proclamation was the beginning of the end of slavery for them."

As the "Year of Jubilee" approached, numerous freedom watch-night observances were held; a description of these observances and the reaction to word of emancipation can be found in the accounts of Frederick Douglass, Booker T. Washington, and Thomas Wentworth Higginson,[†] among others. The symbolic importance of the event to future generations is reflected in James Weldon Johnson's "Fifty Years," James Baldwin's open letter to his nephew one hundred years later in *The Fire Next Time,* and Martin Luther King's "Letter from Birmingham City Jail."[†]

The emancipation of slavery throughout the United States was made law by the Thirteenth Amendment,[†] ratified December 18, 1865.

The Emancipation Proclamation

". . . I do order and declare that ALL PERSONS HELD AS SLAVES within said designated States and parts of States ARE, AND HENCEFORWARD SHALL BE FREE! . . ."

WHEREAS, ON THE TWENTY-SECOND DAY OF SEPTEMBER, IN THE year of our Lord one thousand eight hundred and sixty-two, a Proclamation was issued by the President of the United States, containing among other things the following, to wit:

"That on the First Day of January, in the Year of our Lord One Thousand Eight Hundred and Sixty-three, all persons held as Slaves within any State, or designated part of a State, the people whereof shall there be in rebellion against the United States, shall be then thenceforth and FOREVER FREE, and the Executive Government of the United States, including the Military and Naval authority thereof, will recognize and maintain the freedom of such persons, and will do no act or acts to repress such persons, or any of them, in any effort they make for their actual freedom.

"That the Executive will, on the first day of January aforesaid, by Proclamation, designate the States and parts of States, if any, in which the people therein respectively shall then be in Rebellion against the United States, and the fact that any State, or the people thereof, shall on that day be in good faith represented in the Congress of the United States by Members chosen thereto at elections wherein a majority of the qualified voters of such State shall have participated, shall, in the absence of strong countervailing testimony, be deemed conclusive evidence that such State and the people thereof are not then in Rebellion against the United States."

Now, therefore, I, Abraham Lincoln, President of the United States, by virtue of the power vested in me as Commander-in-Chief of the Army and Navy of the United States, in time of actual armed rebellion against the authority and Government of the United States, and as a fit and necessary war measure for suppressing said Rebellion, do, on this first day of January, in the year of our Lord one thousand eight hundred and sixty-three, and in accordance with my purpose so to do, publicly proclaim for the full period of one hundred days from the date of the first above-mentioned order, and designate, as the States and parts of States wherein the people thereof, respectively, are this day in rebellion against the United States, the following, to wit: Arkansas, Texas, Louisiana—except the Parishes of St. Bernard, Palquemines, Jefferson, St. John, St. Charles, St. James, Ascension, Assumption, Terre Bonne, Lafourch, St. Mary, St. Martin and Orleans, including the City of New Orleans—Mississippi, Alabama, Florida, Georgia, South Carolina, North Carolina, and Virginia—except the forty-eight counties designated as West Virginia, and also the counties of Berkley, Accomac, Northampton, Elizabeth City, York, Princess Ann, and Norfolk, including the cities of Norfolk and Portsmouth—and which excepted parts are, for the present, left precisely as if this Proclamation were not issued.

And by virtue of the power and for the purpose aforesaid, I do order and declare that ALL PERSONS HELD AS SLAVES within said designated States and parts of States ARE, AND HENCEFORWARD SHALL BE FREE! and that the Executive Government of the United States, including the Military and Naval Authorities thereof, will recognize and maintain the freedom of said persons.

And I hereby enjoin upon the people so declared to be free, to abstain from all violence, unless in necessary self-defense; and I recommend to them that in all cases, when allowed, they labor faithfully for reasonable wages.

And I further declare and make known, that such persons, of suitable condition, will be received into the armed service of the United States, to garrison forts, positions, stations, and other places, and to man vessels of all sorts in said service.

And, upon this, sincerely believed to be an act of justice, warranted by the Constitution, upon military necessity, I invoke the considerate judgment of mankind and the gracious favor of Almighty God.

January 1, 1863

The New York Draft Riots

On March 3, 1863, at the height of the Civil War, Congress passed a conscription act mandating military service for all men between the ages of twenty and forty-five. On July 13, 1863, resentment against this act led to the worst riot in the history of the city of New York, which had been the site of numerous bloody revolts since colonial times. When the riot broke out, the city was in the midst of a labor dispute in which thousands of longshoremen were on strike and black strikebreakers had been brought in to replace them under police protection. The violence that ignited was led largely by poor working-class Irish who resented both the competition from black workers and the obligation to fight a war they viewed as not of their making for which African-Americans were somehow to blame.

The violence lasted for four days. After destroying the draft office, the mob turned indiscriminately upon African-American citizens, many of whom were beaten and lynched. Some sought refuge in police stations and eventually hundreds were housed at the arsenal. In one of the worst excesses of the riot, a mob stormed the Colored Orphan's Asylum on Fifth Avenue, setting the building on fire as the children fled through a back door. Early reports after the disturbance claimed more than a thousand were killed, though casualties were probably somewhat more than a hundred. Many hundreds more were injured, saw their property destroyed, or were forced to flee for their lives, some to New Jersey and Long Island.

The brutality of the riots drew a sympathetic response from more law-abiding citizens, and within months of the violence the 20th United States Colored Infantry, a regiment of black troops raised by the Union League Club of New York, paraded down Broadway, applauded by a crowd numbering in the thousands.

An Eyewitness Account

"Strange to say the military were nowhere to be seen. . . ."

New York, July 13th, 1863

Dear Doctor—

. . . We have had great riots in New York to-day & they are still in progress. They were reported to us at the Assay office about noon, but I thought they were exaggerated. Fresh accounts came in every half hour, & some of our Treasury officers (occupying the same building with us) were alarmed. I had made arrangements for visiting Eliza, at Snedens, this afternoon, but just as I was starting Mr. Mason came in & said that he saw a mob stop two 3rd. Avenue cars to take out some Negroes & maltreat them. This decided me to return home, so as to protect my colored servants. I could go neither by the 3rd nor 6th Avenues, as the cars had stopped. Taking the 4th Ave. I found the street full of people, & when I reached the terminus (now 34th St.) I found the whole road way & sidewalks filled with rough fellows (& some equally rough women) who were tearing up rails, cutting down telegraph poles, & setting fire to buildings. I walked quietly along through the midst of them, without being molested. In 49 st. they were numerous, & made, as I was passing near the College, an attack upon one of a row of new houses in our street. The rioters were induced to go away by one or two Catholic priests, who made pacific speeches to them. I found Jane & Maggie a little alarmed, but not frightened. The mob had been in the College Grounds, & came to our house—wishing to know if a republican lived there, & what the College building was used for. They were going to burn Pres. King's house, as he was rich, & a decided republican. They barely desisted when addressed by the Catholic priests. The furious bareheaded & coatless men assembled under our windows & shouted aloud for Jef. Davis! We have some of the most valuable articles of small bulk, all packed & ready for removal at a moment's warning. All the family will remain the whole night with our clothes on, for there is no telling when they may return. Towards evening the mob, furious as demons, went yelling over to the Colored-Orphan Asylum in 5th Avenue a little below where we live—& rolling a barrel of kerosine in it, the whole structure was soon in a blaze, & is now a smoking ruin. What has become of the 300 poor innocent orphans I could not learn. They must have had some warning of what the rioters intended; & I trust the children were removed in time to escape a cruel death. Before this fire was extinguished, or rather burned out, for the wicked wretches who caused it would not permit the engines to be used, the northern sky was brilliantly illuminated, probably by the burning of the Aged Colored-woman's Home in 65th St.—or the Harlem R. Road Bridge—both of which places were threatened by the rioters. Just before dusk I took a walk a short distance down 5th Avenue, & seeing a group of rowdies in the grounds of Dr. Ward's large & superb mansion, I found they had gone there with the intention of setting fire to the building, which is filled with costly works of art! The family were all out, entreating the scamps to desist, as "they were all Brackenridge democrats & opposed to the *draft!*" They finally went off, but may return before morning. I conversed with one of the ringleaders who told me they would burn the whole city before they got through. He said they were to take Wall St. in hand tomorrow! We will be ready for them at the Assay Office & Treasury. Strange to say the military were nowhere to be seen at my latest investigation. There may be bloody times tomorrow.

Wednesday, July 15. You doubtless learn from the newspapers that our city is still in the power of a brutal mob. We were not molested on Monday night, & I slept well, partly undressed. We are all quite calm & are chiefly concerned about our servants. Yesterday there were cars only on the lower part of the 4th Avenue.—all the others in the city, & the omnibuses were withdrawn. I was obliged to walk up from Wall St. in the heat of the day. On reaching home I found that we had been warned that all the College buildings were to be destroyed at night. Jane & Maggie had some of their most valuable articles packed, but we did not know where to send them. A friend took our basket of silver to her house. I looked about to see what few articles I could put in a small travelling bag, but it was very difficult to make a selection. There were so many (to me) precious little souvenirs that it grieved me to think they would probably be destroyed. Then it *did* go hard with me to feel pretty well assured that the Herbarium & Botanical Books were to be given up! Yet we had a reprieve. Just as we were expecting the mob to come howling along, a person came in with a confidential message from a Catholic priest, that Gov. Seymour had taken the responsibility of stopping the draft, & the chief rioters were to be informed of this measure. So we made up our minds to take a good sleep. I was, however, mortified to find that the mob had, at least temporarily, triumphed. But we shall still have to finish the business with saltpetre.

This morning I was obliged to ride down to the office in a hired coach. A friend who rode with me had seen a poor Negro hung an hour or two before. The man had, in a frenzy, shot an Irish fireman, and they immediately strung up the unhappy African. At our office there had been no disturbance in the night. Indeed the people there were "spoiling for a fight." They had a battery of about 25 rifle barrels, carrying 3 balls each, & mounted on a guncarriage. It could be loaded & fired with rapidity. We had also 10-inches shells, to be lighted & thrown out of the windows. Likewise quantities of SO3, with arrangements for projecting it on the mob. Walking home we found that a large number of soldiers—infantry, artillery & cavalry are moving about, & bodies of armed citizens. The worst mobs are on the 1st & 2nd & 7th Avenues. Many have been killed there. They are very hostile to the Negroes, & scarcely one of them is to be seen. A person who called at our house this afternoon saw three of them hanging together. The Central Park has been a kind of refuge to them. Hundreds were there to-day, with no protection in a very severe shower. The Station Houses of the police are crowded with them.

Walking out on 5th Avenue near 48th st. a man who lives there told me that a few minutes before, in broad sunlight, three ruffians seized the horses of a gentlemen's carriage & demanded money. By whipping up, they barely escaped. Immediately afterwards they stopped another carriage, turned the persons out of it, & then got in themselves, shouting & brandishing their clubs. So that concessions have not yet quieted the mob, & the soldiers cannot be every where. Reenforcements will doubtless arrive, & we shall have law & order. Thieves are going about in gangs, calling at houses, & demanding money—threatening the torch if denied. They have been across the street this afternoon, & I saw them myself. Perhaps they will give us a call: but we are all going to bed in a few minutes.

This evening there was a great light north of us—& I found, on looking with a spyglass, that it was from the burning a fine bridge over the Harlem valley—used by one of the railroads. There was some cannon-firing in the 1st Avenue, with what result I don't know.

The city looks very strangely. Nothing in Broadway but a few coaches. Most of the stores closed, but the side walks are full of people—& not a few ladies are out. It is half past 10 o'clock, & I must go to bed. . . .

Ever yours—
JOHN TORREY

Henry Highland Garnet

Garnet, who as a militant figure in the convention movement of the mid-1800s had urged millions of African-Americans in his 1843 "Call to Rebellion"† to "die freemen rather than live to be slaves," had maintained his political advocacy throughout the Civil War. His Shiloh Presbyterian Church in New York was a gathering place for black activists, especially after the Draft Riots in 1863. With the support of white abolitionists, Garnet became the first African-American to deliver a sermon in Congress, and he made the following address on Sunday, February 12, 1865, calling upon the legislature to propose a constitutional amendment to abolish slavery. Though such action would be effected by the Thirteenth Amendment, ratified in 1865, Garnet became disillusioned by the imperfect work of Reconstruction and increasingly supported the emigration of black Americans to Africa. At the age of sixty-five, he was appointed the U.S. ambassador to Liberia, where he died soon after, on February 12, 1882.

A Memorial Discourse Delivered in the Hall of the House of Representatives

"The destroying angel has gone forth through this land to execute the fearful penalties of God's broken law."

MATTHEW XXIII. 4: FOR THEY BIND HEAVY BURDENS, AND grievous to be borne, and lay them on men's shoulders, but they themselves will not move them with one of their fingers.

In this chapter, of which my text is a sentence, the Lord Jesus addressed his disciples, and the multitude that hung spell-bound upon the words that fell from his lips. He admonished them to beware of the religion of the Scribes and the Pharisees, which was distinguished for great professions while it succeeded in urging them to do but a little, or nothing that accorded with the law of righteousness.

In theory they were right; but their practices were inconsistent and wrong. They were learned in the law of Moses, and in the traditions of their fathers, but the principles of righteousness failed to affect their hearts. They knew their duty, but did it not. The demands which they made upon others proved that they themselves knew what things men ought to do. In condemning others they pronounced themselves guilty. They demanded that others should be just, merciful, pure, peaceable, and righteous. But they were unjust, impure, unmerciful—they hated and wronged a portion of their fellow-men, and waged continual war against the government of God.

On other men's shoulders they bound heavy and grievous burdens of duties and obligations. The people groaned beneath the loads which were imposed upon them, and in bitterness of spirit cried out, and filled the land with lamentations. But with their eyes closed, and their hearts hardened, they heeded not, neither did they care. They regarded it to be but little less than intolerable insult to be asked to bear a small portion of the shoulders of their fellow-men. With loud voice, and proud and defiant mien, they said these burdens are for them, and not for us. Behold how patiently they bear them. Their shoulders are broad, and adapted to the condition to which we have doomed them. But as for us, it is irksome, even to adjust their burdens, though we see them stagger beneath them.

Such was their conduct in the Church and in the State. We have modern Scribes and Pharisees, who are faithful to their prototypes of ancient times.

With sincere respect and reverence for the instruction, and the warning given by our Lord, and in humble dependence upon him for his assistance, I shall speak this morning of the Scribes and Pharisees of our times who rule the State. In discharging this duty, I shall keep my eyes upon the picture which is painted so faithfully and life-like by the hand of the Saviour.

Allow me to describe them. They are intelligent and well-informed, and can never say, either before an earthly tribunal or at the bar of God, *"We knew not of ourselves what was right."* They are acquainted with the principles of the law of nations. They are proficient in the knowledge of Constitutional law. They are teachers of common law, and frame and execute statute law. They acknowledge that there is a just and impartial God, and are not altogether unacquainted with the law of Christian love and kindness. They claim for themselves the broadest freedom. Boastfully they tell us that they have received from the court of heaven the MAGNA CHARTA of human rights that was handed down through the clouds, and amid the lightnings of Sinai, and given again by the Son of God on the Mount of Beatitudes, while the glory of the Father shone around him. They tell us that from the Declaration of Independence and the Constitution they have obtained a guaranty of their political freedom, and from the Bible they derive their claim to all the blessings of religious liberty. With just pride they tell us that they are descended from the Pilgrims, who threw themselves upon the bosom of the treacherous sea, and braved storms and tempests, that they might find in a strange land, and among savages, free homes, where they might build their altars that should blaze with acceptable sacrifice unto God. Yes! they boast that their fathers heroically turned away from the precious light of Eastern civilization, and taking their lamps with oil in their vessels, joyfully went forth to illuminate this land, that then dwelt in the darkness of the valley of the shadow of death. With hearts strengthened by faith they spread out their standard to the winds of heaven, near Plymouth rock; and whether it was stiffened in the sleet and frosts of winter, or floated on the breeze of summer, it ever bore the motto, *"Freedom to worship God."*

But others, their fellow-men, equal before the Almighty, and made by him of the same blood, and glowing with immortality, they doom to lifelong servitude and chains. Yes, they stand in the most sacred places on earth, and beneath the gaze of the piercing eye of Jehovah, the universal Father of all men, and declare, *"that the best possible condition of the negro is slavery."**

> Thus man devotes his brother and destroys;
> And more than all, and most to be deplored,
> As human nature's broadest, foulest blot,
> Chains him, and tasks him, and exacts his sweat
> With stripes, that Mercy with bleeding heart,
> Weeps to see inflicted on a beast.

* Speech of Fernando Wood, of New York, in Congress, 1864.

In the name of the TRIUNE GOD I denounce the sentiment as unrighteous beyond measure, and the holy and just of the whole earth say in regard to it, Anathema-marantha.

What is slavery? Too well do I know what it is. I will present to you a bird's-eye view of it; and it shall be no fancy picture, but one that is sketched by painful experience. I was born among the cherished institutions of slavery. My earliest recollections of parents, friends, and the home of my childhood are clouded with its wrongs. The first sight that met my eyes was a Christian mother enslaved by professed Christians, but, thank God, now a saint in heaven. The first sounds that startled my ear, and sent a shudder through my soul, were the cracking of the whip, and the clanking of chains. These sad memories mar the beauties of my native shores, and darken all the slave-land, which, but for the reign of despotism, had been a paradise. But those shores are fairer now. The mists have left my native valleys, and the clouds have rolled away from the hills, and Maryland, the unhonored grave of my fathers, is now the free home of their liberated and happier children.

Let us view this demon, which the people have worshipped as a God. Come forth, though grim monster, that thou mayest be critically examined! There he stands. Behold him, one and all. Its work is to chattelize man; to hold property in human beings. Great God! I would as soon attempt to enslave GABRIEL or MICHAEL as to enslave a man made in the image of God, and for whom Christ died. Slavery is snatching man from the high place to which he was lifted by the hand of God, and dragging him down to the level of the brute creation, where he is made to be the companion of the horse and the fellow of the ox.

It tears the crown of glory from his head, and as far as possible obliterates the image of God that is in him. Slavery prey upon man, and man only. A brute cannot be made a slave. Why? Because a brute has no reason, faith, nor an undying spirit, nor conscience. It does not look forward to the future with joy or fear, nor reflect upon the past with satisfaction or regret. But who in this vast assembly, who in all this broad land, will say that the poorest and most unhappy brother in chains and servitude has not every one of these high endowments? Who denies it? Is there one? If so, let him speak. There is not one; no, not one.

But slavery attempts to make a man a brute. It treats him as a beast. Its terrible work is not finished until the ruined victim of its lusts, and pride, and avarice, and hatred, is reduced so low that with tearful eyes and feeble voice he faintly cries, *"I am happy and contented—I love this condition."*

Proud Nimrod first the bloody chase began,
A mighty hunter he; his prey was man.

The caged lion may cease to roar, and try no longer the strength of the bars of his prison, and lie with his head between his mighty paws and snuff the polluted air as though he heeded not. But is he contented? Does he not instinctively long for the freedom of the forest and the plain? Yes, he is a lion still. Our poor and forlorn brother whom thou has labelled *"slave,"* is also a man. He may be unfortunate, weak, helpless, and despised, and hated, nevertheless he is a man. His God and thine has stamped on his forehead his title to his inalienable rights in characters that can be read by every intelligent being. Pitiless storms of outrage may have beaten upon his defenceless head, and he may have descended through ages of oppression, yet he is a man. God made him such, and his brother cannot unmake him. Woe, woe to him who attempts to commit the accursed crime.

Slavery commenced its dreadful work in kidnapping unoffending men in a foreign and distant land, and in piracy on the seas. The plunderers were not the followers of Mahomet, nor the devotees of Hindooism, nor benighted pagans, nor idolaters, but people called Christians, and thus the ruthless traders in the souls and bodies of men fastened upon Christianity a crime and stain at the sight of which it shudders and shrieks.

It is guilty of the most heinous iniquities ever perpetrated upon helpless women and innocent children. Go to the shores of the land of my forefathers, poor bleeding Africa, which, although she has been bereaved, and robbed for centuries, is nevertheless beloved by all her worthy descendants wherever dispersed. Behold a single scene that there meets your eyes. Turn not away neither from shame, pity, nor indifference, but look and see the beginning of this cherished and petted institution. Behold a hundred youthful mothers seated on the ground, dropping their tears upon the hot sands, and filling the air with their lamentations.

Why do they weep? Ah, Lord God, thou knowest! Their babes have been torn from their bosoms and cast upon the plains to die of hunger, or to be devoured by hyenas or jackals. The little innocents would die on the "Middle Passage," or suffocate between the decks of the floating slavepen, freighted and packed with unparalleled human woe, and the slavers in mercy have cast them out to perish on their native shores. Such is the beginning, and no less wicked is the end of that system which the Scribes and Pharisees in the Church and the State pronounce to be just, humane, benevolent and Christian. If such are the deeds of mercy wrought by angels, then tell me what works of iniquity there remain for devils to do?

This commerce in human beings has been carried on until three hundred thousand have been dragged from their native land in a single year. While this foreign trade has been pursued, who can calculate the enormities and extent of the domestic traffic which has flourished in every slave State, while the whole country has been open to the hunters of men.

It is the highly concentrated essence of all conceivable wickedness. Theft, robbery, pollution, unbridled passion, incest, cruelty, cold-blooded murder, blasphemy, and defiance of the laws of God. It teaches children to disregard parental authority. It tears down the marriage altar, and tramples its sacred ashes under its feet. It creates and nourishes polygamy. It feeds and pampers its hateful handmaid, prejudice.

It has divided our national councils. It has engendered deadly strife between brethren. It has wasted the treasure of the Commonwealth, and the lives of thousands of brave men, and driven troops of helpless women and children into yawning tombs. It has caused the bloodiest civil war recorded in the book of time. It has shorn this nation of its locks of strength that was rising as a young lion in the Western world. It has offered us as a sacrifice to the jealousy and cupidity of tyrants, despots, and adventurers of foreign countries. It has opened a door through which a usurper, a perjured, but powerful prince, might stealthily enter and build an empire on the golden borders of our southwestern frontier, and which is but a stepping-stone to further and unlimited conquests on this continent. It has desolated the fairest portions of our land, "until the world long since driven back by the march of civilization returns after the lapse of a hundred years and howls amidst its ruins."

It seals up the Bible, and mutilates its sacred truths, and flies into the face of the Almighty, and impiously asks, *"Who art thou that I should obey thee?"* Such are the outlines of this fearful national sin; and yet the condition to which it reduces man, it is affirmed, is the best that can possibly be devised for him.

When inconsistencies similar in character, and no more glaring, passed beneath the eye of the Son of God, no wonder he broke forth in language of vehement denunciation. Ye Scribes, Pharisees, and hypocrites? Ye blind guides! Ye compass sea and land to make one proselyte, and when he is made ye make him twofold more the child of hell than yourselves. Ye are like unto whited sepulchres, which indeed appear beautiful without, but within are full of dead men's bones, and all uncleanness!

Let us here take up the golden rule, and adopt the self-application mode of reasoning to those who hold these erroneous views. Come, gird up thy loins and answer like a man, if thou canst. Is slavery, as it is seen in its origin, continuance, and end the best possible condition for thee? Oh, no! Wilt thou bear that burden on thy shoulders, which thou wouldest lay upon thy fellow-man? No. Wilt thou bear a part of it, or remove a little of its weight with one of thy fingers? The sharp and indignant answer is no, no! Then how, and when, and where, shall we apply to thee the golden rule, which says, *"Therefore all things that ye would that others should do to you, do ye even so unto them, for this is the law and the prophets."*

Let us have the testimony of the wise and great of ancient and modern times:

Sages who wrote and warriors who bled.

PLATO declared that "Slavery is a system of complete injustice."

SOCRATES wrote that "Slavery is a system of outrage and robbery."

CYRUS said "To fight in order not to be a slave is noble."

If Cyrus had lived in our land a few years ago he would have been arrested for using incendiary language, and for inciting servile insurrection, and the royal fanatic would have been hanged on a gallows higher than Haman. But every man is fanatical when his soul is warmed by the generous fires of liberty. Is it then truly noble to fight in order not to be a slave? The Chief Magistrate of the nation, and our rulers, and all truly patriotic men think so; and so think legions of black men, who for a season were scorned and rejected, but who came quickly and cheerfully when they were at last invited, bearing a heavy burden of proscriptions upon their shoulders, and having faith in God, and in their generous fellow-countrymen, they went forth to fight a double battle. The foes of their country were before them, while the enemies of freedom and of their race surrounded them.

AUGUSTINE, CONSTANTINE, IGNATIUS, POLYCARP, MAXIMUS, and the most illustrious lights of the ancient church denounced the sin of slaveholding.

THOMAS JEFFERSON said at a period of his life, when his judgment was matured, and his experience was ripe, "There is preparing, I hope, under the auspices of heaven, a way for a total emancipation."

The sainted WASHINGTON said, near the close of his mortal career, and when the light of eternity was beaming upon him, "It is among my first wishes to see some plan adopted by which slavery in this country shall be abolished by law. I know of but one way by which this can be done, and that is by legislative action, and so far as my vote can go, it shall not be wanting."

The other day, when the light of Liberty streamed through this marble pile, and the hearts of the noble band of patriotic statesmen leaped for joy, and this our national capital shook from foundation to dome with the shouts of a ransomed people, then methinks the spirits of Washington, Jefferson, the Jays, the Adamses, and Franklin, and Lafayette, and Giddings, and Lovejoy, and those of all the mighty, and glorious dead, remembered by history, because they were faithful to truth, justice, and liberty, were hovering over the august assembly. Though unseen by mortal eyes, doubtless they joined the angelic choir, and said, Amen.

POPE LEO X, testifies, "That not only does the Christian religion, but nature herself, cry out against a state of slavery."

PATRICK HENRY said, "We should transmit to posterity our abhorrence of slavery." So also thought the Thirty-Eighth Congress.

LAFAYETTE proclaimed these words: "Slavery is a dark spot on the face of the nation." God be praised, that stain will soon be wiped out.

JONATHAN EDWARDS declared "that to hold a man in slavery is to be every day guilty of robbing, or of man stealing."

REV. DR. WILLIAM ELLERY CHANNING, in a *Letter on the Annexation of Texas* in 1837, writes as follows:

"The evil of slavery speaks for itself. To state is to condemn the institution. The choice which every freeman makes of death for his child and for every thing he loved in preference to slavery, shows what it is. The single consideration that by slavery one human being is placed powerless and defenceless in the hands of another to be driven to whatever labor that other may impose, to suffer whatever punishment he may inflict, to live as his tool, the instrument of his pleasure, this is all that is needed to satisfy such as know the human heart and its unfitness for irresponsible power, that of all conditions slavery is the most hostile to the dignity, self-respect, improvement, rights, and happiness of human beings. . . . Every principle of our government and religion condemns slavery. The spirit of our age condemns it. The decree of the civilized world has gone out against it. . . . Is there an age in which a free and Christian people shall deliberately resolve to extend and perpetuate the evil? In so going we cut ourselves off from the communion of nations; we sink below the civilization of our age; we invite the scorn, indignation, and abhorrence of the world."

MOSES, the greatest of all lawgivers and legislators, said, while his face was yet radiant with the light of Sinai: "Whoso stealeth a man, and selleth him, or if he be found in his hand, he shall surely be put to death." The destroying angel has gone forth through this land to execute the fearful penalties of God's broken law.

The Representatives of the nation have bowed with reverence to the Divine edict, and laid the axe at the root of the tree, and thus saved succeeding generations from the guilt of oppression, and from the wrath of God.

Statesmen, Jurists, and Philosophers, most renowned for learning, and most profound in every department of science and literature, have testified against slavery. While oratory has brought its costliest, golden treasures, and laid them on the altar of God and of freedom, it has aimed its fiercest lightning and loudest thunder at the strongholds of tyranny, injustice, and despotism.

From the days of Balak to those of Isaiah and Jeremiah, up to the times of Paul, and through every age of the Christian Church, the sons of thunder have denounced the abominable thing. The heroes who stood in the shining ranks of the hosts of the friends of human progress, from Cicero to Chatham, and Burke, Sharp, Wilberforce, and Thomas Clarkson, and Curran, assaulted the citadel of despotism. The orators and statesmen of our own land, whether they belong to the past, or to the present age, will live and shine in the annals of history, in proportion as they have dedicated their genius and talents to the defence of Justice and man's God-given rights.

All the poets who live in sacred and profane history have charmed the world with their most enchanting strains, when they have tuned their lyres to the praise of Liberty. When the Muses can no longer decorate her altars with their garlands, then they hang their harps upon the willows and weep.

From Moses to Terence and Homer, from thence to Milton and Cowper, Thomson and Thomas Campbell, and on to the days of our own bards, our Bryants, Longfellows, Whittiers, Morrises, and Bokers, all have presented their best gifts to the interests and rights of man.

Every good principle, and every great and noble power, have been made the subjects of the inspired verse, and the songs of poets. But who of them has attempted to immortalize slavery? You will search in vain the annals of the world to find an instance. Should any attempt the sacrilegious work, his genius would fall to the earth as if smitten by the lightning of heaven. Should he lift his hand to write a line in its praise, or defence, the ink would freeze on the point of his pen.

Could we array in one line, representatives of all the families of men, beginning with those lowest in the scale of being, and should we put to them the question, Is it right and desirable that you should be reduced to the condition of slaves, to be registered with chattels, to have your persons, and your lives, and the products of your labor, subjected to the will and the interests of others? Is it right and just that the persons of your wives and children should be at the disposal of others, and be yielded to them for the purpose of pampering their lusts and greed of gain? Is it right to lay heavy burdens on other men's shoulders which you would not remove with one of your fingers? From the rude savage and barbarian the negative response would come, increasing in power and significance as it rolled up the line. And when those should reply, whose minds and hearts are illuminated with the highest civilization and with the spirit of Christianity, the answer deep-toned and prolonged would thunder forth, no, no!

With all the moral attributes of God on our side, cheered as we are by the voices of universal human nature,—in view of the best interests of the present and future generations—animated with the noble desire to furnish the nations of the earth with a worthy example, let the verdict of death which has been brought in against slavery, by the THIRTY-EIGHTH CONGRESS, be affirmed and executed by the people. Yes, perish now, and perish forever!

Down let the shrine of Moloch sink
  And leave no traces where it stood;
No longer let its idol drink,
  His daily cup of human blood.
But rear another altar there,
  To truth, and love, and mercy given,
And freedom's gift and freedom's prayer,
  Shall call an answer down from heaven.

It is often asked when and where will the demands of the reformers of this and coming ages end? It is a fair question, and I will answer.

When all unjust and heavy burdens shall be removed from every man in the land. When all invidious and proscriptive distinctions shall be blotted out from our laws, whether they be constitutional, statutes, or municipal laws. When emancipation shall be followed by enfranchisement, and all men holding allegiance to the government shall enjoy every right of American citizenship. When our brave and gallant soldiers shall have justice done unto them. When the men who endure the sufferings and perils of the battle-field in the defence of their country, and in order to keep our rulers in their places, shall enjoy the well-earned privilege of voting for them. When in the army and navy, and in every legitimate and honorable occupation, promotion shall smile upon merit without the slightest regard to the complexion of a man's face. When there shall be no more class-legislation, and no more trouble concerning the black man and his rights, than there is in regard to other American citizens. When, in every respect, he shall be equal before the law, and shall be left to make his own way in the social walks of life.

We ask, and only ask, that when our poor frail barks are launched on life's ocean—

> Bound on a voyage of awful length
> And dangers little known,

that, in common with others, we may be furnished with rudder, helm, and sails, and charts, and compass. Give us good pilots to conduct us to the open seas; lift no false lights along the dangerous coasts, and if it shall please God to send us propitious winds, or fearful gales, we shall survive or perish as our energies or neglect shall determine. We ask no special favors, but we plead for justice. While we scorn unmanly dependence; in the name of God, the universal Father, we demand the right to live, and labor, and to enjoy the fruits of our toil. The good work which God has assigned for the ages to come, will be finished, when our national literature shall be so purified as to reflect a faithful and a just light upon the character and social habits of our race, and the brush, and pencil, and chisel, and Lyre of Art, shall refuse to lend their aid to scoff at the afflictions of the poor, or to caricature, or ridicule a long-suffering people. When caste and prejudice in Christian churches shall be utterly destroyed, and shall be regarded as totally unworthy of Christians, and at variance with the principles of the gospel. When the blessings of the Christian religion, and of sound, religious education, shall be freely offered to all, then, and not till then, shall the effectual labors of God's people and God's instruments cease.

If slavery has been destroyed merely from *necessity,* let every class be enfranchised at the dictation of *justice.* Then we shall have a Constitution that shall be reverenced by all; rulers who shall be honored, and revered, and a Union that shall be sincerely loved by a brave and patriotic people, and which can never be severed.

Great sacrifices have been made by the people; yet, greater still are demanded ere atonement can be made for our national sins. Eternal justice holds heavy mortgages against us, and will require the payment of the last farthing. We have involved ourselves in the sin of unrighteous gain, stimulated by luxury, and pride, and the love of power and oppression; and prosperity, and peace can be purchased only by blood, and with tears of repentance. We have paid some of the fearful installments, but there are other heavy obligations to be met.

The great day of the nation's judgment has come, and who shall be able to stand? Even we, whose ancestors have suffered the afflictions which are inseparable from a condition of slavery, for the period of two centuries and a half, now pity our land and weep with those who weep.

Upon the toil and complete destruction of this accursed sin depends the safety and perpetuity of our Republic and its excellent institutions.

Let slavery die. It has had a long and fair trial. God himself has pleaded against it. The enlightened nations of the earth have condemned it. Its death warrant is signed by God and man. Do not commute its sentence. Give it no respite, but let it be ignominiously executed.

Honorable Senators and Representatives! illustrious rulers of this great nation! I cannot refrain this day from invoking upon you, in God's name, the blessings of millions who were ready to perish, but to whom a new and better life has been opened by your humanity, justice, and patriotism. You have said, "Let the Constitution of the country be so amended that slavery and involuntary servitude shall no longer exist in the United States, except in punishment for crime." Surely, an act so sublime could not escape Divine notice; and doubtless the deed has been recorded in the archives of heaven. Volumes may be appropriated to your praise and renown in the history of the world. Genius and art may perpetuate the glorious act on canvas and in marble, but certain and more lasting monuments in commemoration of your decision are already erected in the hearts and memories of a grateful people.

The nation has begun its exodus from worse than Egyptian bondage; and I beseech you that you say to the people, *"that they go forward."* With the assurance of God's favor in all things done in obedience to his righteous will, and guided by day and by night by the pillars of cloud and fire, let us not pause until we have reached the other and safe side of the stormy and crimson sea. Let freemen and patriots mete out complete and equal justice to all men, and thus prove to mankind the superiority of our Democratic, Republican Government.

Favored men, and honored of God as his instruments, speedily finish the work which he has given you to do. *Emancipate, Enfranchise, Educate, and give the blessings of the gospel to every American citizen.*

Hear ye not how, from all high points of Time,—
From peak to peak adown the mighty chain
That links the ages—echoing sublime
A Voice Almighty—leaps one grand refrain,

Wakening the generations with a shout,
And trumpet-call of thunder—Come ye out!

Out from old forms and dead idolatries;
  From fading myths and superstitious dreams;
From Pharisaic rituals and lies,
  And all the bondage of the life that seems!
Out—on the pilgrim path, of heroes trod,
Over earth's wastes, to reach forth after God!

The Lord hath bowed his heaven, and come down!
  Now, in this latter century of time,
Once more his tent is pitched on Sinai's crown!
  Once more in clouds must Faith to meet him climb!
Once more his thunder crashes on our doubt
And fear and sin—"My people! come ye out!"

From false ambitions and base luxuries;
  From puny aims and indolent self-ends;
From cant of faith, and shams of liberties,
  And mist of ill that Truth's pure day-beam bends:
Out, from all darkness of the Egypt-land,
Into my sun-blaze on the desert sand!

. . .

Show us our Aaron, with his rod in flower!
  Our Miriam, with her timbrel-soul in tune!
And call some Joshua, in the Spirit's power,
  To poise our sun of strength at point of noon!
God of our fathers! over sand and sea,
Still keep our struggling footsteps close to thee!

Then before us a path of prosperity will open, and upon us will descend the mercies and favors of God. Then shall the people of other countries, who are standing tip-toe on the shores of every ocean, earnestly looking to see the end of this amazing conflict, behold a Republic that is sufficiently strong to outlive the ruin and desolation of civil war, having the magnanimity to do justice to the poorest and weakest of her citizens. Thus shall we give to the world the form of a model Republic, founded on the principles of justice and humanity, and Christianity, in which the burdens of war and the blessings of peace are equally borne and enjoyed by all.

February 12, 1865

African-Americans in the Civil War

As was true in the American Revolution, early in the armed conflict between the North and the South, free African-Americans in Boston, New York, and Philadelphia came forward to volunteer for military service. Though their offers were rebuffed as the Union Army sought to recruit 75,000 white volunteers, hundreds of slaves nonetheless defected to Union lines, offering their services in the Union Army. While at first these fugitives were returned to their masters, they were soon deemed "contrabands" of war—confiscated property—and by mid-1861, Lincoln issued orders to his commanders that the escaped slaves not be returned.

It was not long before African-Americans took a more active role. In May 1862 Robert Smalls, who would later serve in Congress, commandeered a Confederate gunboat in Charleston harbor and became a hero. In March, General David Hunter, a white abolitionist, raised the 1st South Carolina Volunteers; former U.S. senator Jim Lane recruited the 1st Kansas Colored Volunteers; and in New Orleans, General Ben Butler declared martial law, emancipated the slaves (without authorization from the president), and commissioned the 1st Louisiana Native Guards, called the *Chasseurs d'Afrique.* "We come of a fighting race," vouched the leader of the Native Guards to his commanding officer. "Pardon me, General, but the only cowardly blood we have got in our veins is the white blood." In July 1862 Congress wrote into law what had been established in fact and authorized the employment of "persons of African descent" in the Union Army. Lincoln's Emancipation Proclamation,[†] issued January 1, 1863, cleared away the remaining obstacles to the enlistment of black men, not merely as laborers, but as soldiers.

The two most celebrated black units during the war were the Massachusetts 54th, led by Robert Gould Shaw, and the 1st South Carolina Volunteers under Thomas Wentworth Higginson. In Massachusetts, black troops were raised with the promise of "the same wages, the same rations, the same equipment, the same protection, the same treatment, and the same bounty secured to white soldiers." Now that the enlistment of black troops had become federal policy, in the editorial included here, Frederick Douglass resoundingly urged "Men of Color to Arms." Under Shaw, the Massachusetts 54th marched on Fort Wagner, South Carolina, in July

1863, and in the bloody and futile battle, more than fifteen hundred black soldiers were killed next to their commander, but their bravery under fire had been tragically demonstrated.

In South Carolina, Higginson, an abolitionist, essayist, and former Unitarian minister who had participated in the Underground Railroad, traveled to Kansas as a Free-Soil gunrunner, and backed John Brown's raid on Harpers Ferry, now held the strategic position at Beaufort in the Sea Islands off the coast of South Carolina. His troops played a critical part in the naval blockade of the South, and in the public debate over the use of black soldiers. In his diary, *Army Life in a Black Regiment,* from which the following excerpts are taken, Higginson claims that "this particular regiment was watched with microscopic scrutiny by friends and foes. I felt sometimes as if we were a plant trying to take root, but constantly pulled up to see if we were growing." Higginson's eight hundred men made several forays upriver and participated in a raid on Jacksonville, Florida. Of their successes, he wrote, "There were more than a hundred men in the ranks, who had voluntarily met more dangers in their escape from slavery than any of my young captains had incurred in their lives."

Despite their demonstrated bravery, black soldiers faced numerous obstacles. As Higginson's letter to the *New York Times* that follows attests, black troops also waged a constant struggle for pay, being given almost half of what white troops earned. Many black troops refused all pay rather than accept reduced wages. Before the pressing need for their assistance was made clear, some Union officers stated that if black troops rose up in the rebel South, they would turn to fighting *them* instead of the enemy. The animosity the sight of black troops unleashed in the Confederate Army led to the brutal massacre of three hundred black troops (as well as women and children) at Fort Pillow, Tennessee, on April 12, 1864, where Confederate troops under the command of Major General Nathan Bedford Forrest went beyond performance of duty to a display of wanton savagery later condemned by the Congressional Committee on the Conduct of the War. At the bloody battle of the Crater near Petersburg, Virginia, black troops found themselves fired upon by both Confederate forces and Union troops who at best showed little regard for the lives of their comrades and at worst intentionally vented their race hostility. Black troops sometimes returned what they got, however, and charging under the black flag and fired by the cry "Remember Fort Pillow," they often gave no quarter to Confederate soldiers.

For its part, as the tide of war turned, the South began to consider utilizing the available black manpower. While it was initially suggested that blacks would defend their "homeland" out of a sense of fidelity, the depth of their loyalty must soon have become apparent and official policy never sanctioned the use of black troops. Nonetheless, some individuals, usually freemen, served in various regiments as soldiers and laborers, and by the end of the war General Lee was advocating the use of black troops who would thereby win their freedom.

About 185,000 African-Americans served as soldiers on the Union side throughout the war, nearly half raised in the South, while another 200,000 blacks supported the troops as mechanics, stevedores, cooks, and laborers. Black troops participated in significant battles at Port Hudson, Milliken's Bend, Chaffin's Farm, New Market, Charleston, Little Rock, Memphis, Nashville, Richmond, Vicksburg, and Appomattox Court House among others, as well as during the famed naval confrontation between the *Merrimac* and the *Monitor.* More than 37,000 men lost their lives in the war, and at least twenty black soldiers and sailors won the Congressional Medal of Honor. In addition, blacks served as spies and scouts—none more useful than Harriet Tubman—and engaged in sabotage. The gains black soldiers achieved were more than merely strategical. As one of Higginson's men, Thomas Long, argued, "If we hand't become sojers, all might have gone back as it was before. . . . suppose you kept your freedom witout enlisting in dis army; your chilen might have grown up free and been well cultivated so as to be equal to any business, but it would have been always flung in dere faces—'Your fader never fought for he own freedom'—and what could dey answer? Neber can say that to dis African Race any more." "It was their demeanor under arms," wrote Higginson, "that shamed the nation into recognizing them as men."

Men of Color, to Arms!

"Action! Action! not criticism, is the plain duty of this hour."

WHEN FIRST THE REBEL CANNON SHATTERED THE WALLS OF Sumter and drove away its starving garrison, I predicted that the war then and there inaugurated would not be fought out entirely by white men. Every month's experience during these weary years has confirmed that opinion. A war undertaken and brazenly carried on for the perpetual enslavement of colored men, calls logically and loudly for colored men to help suppress it. Only a moderate share of sagacity was needed to see that the arm of the slave was the best defense against the arm of the slaveholder. Hence with every reverse to the national arms, with every exulting shout of victory raised by the slaveholding rebels, I have implored the imperiled nation to unchain against her foes, her powerful black hand.

Slowly and reluctantly that appeal is beginning to be heeded. Stop not now to complain that it was not heeded sooner. That it should not, may or may not have been best. This is not the time to discuss that question. Leave it to the future. When the war is over, the country is saved, peace is established, and the black man's rights are secured, as they will be, history with an impartial hand will dispose of that and sundry other questions. Action! Action! not criticism, is the plain duty of this hour. Words are now useful only as they stimulate to blows. The office of speech now is only to point out when, where, and how to strike to the best advantage.

There is no time to delay. The tide is at its flood that leads on to fortune. From East to West, from North to South, the sky is written all over, "Now or Never." "Liberty won by white men would lose half its luster." "Who would be free themselves must strike the blow." "Better even die free, than to live slaves." This is the sentiment of every brave colored man amongst us.

There are weak and cowardly men in all nations. We have them amongst us. They tell you this is the "white man's war"; that you will be no "better off after than before the war"; that the getting of you into the army is to "sacrifice you on the first opportunity." Believe them not; cowards themselves, they do not wish to have their cowardice shamed by your brave example. Leave them to their timidity, or to whatever motive may hold them back.

I have not thought lightly of the words I am now addressing you. The counsel I give comes of close observation of the great struggle now in progress, and of the deep conviction that this is your hour and mine. In good earnest then, and after the best deliberation, I now for the first time during this war feel at liberty to call and counsel you to arms.

By every consideration which binds you to your enslaved fellow-countrymen, and the peace and welfare of your country; by every aspiration which you cherish for the freedom and equality of yourselves and your children; by all the ties of blood and identity which make us one with the brave black men now fighting our battles in Louisiana and in South Carolina, I urge you to fly to arms, and smite with death the power that would bury the government and your liberty in the same hopeless grave.

I wish I could tell you that the State of New York calls you to this high honor. For the moment her constituted authorities are silent on the subject. They will speak by and by, and doubtless on the right side; but we are not compelled to wait for her. We can get at the throat of treason and slavery through the State of Massachusetts. She was the first in the War of Independence; first to break the chains of her slaves; first to make the black man equal before the law; first to admit colored children to her common schools, and she was first to answer with her blood the alarm cry of the nation, when its capital was menaced by rebels. You know her patriotic governor, and you know Charles Sumner. I need not add more.

Massachusetts now welcomes you to arms as soldiers. She has but a small colored population from which to recruit. She has full leave of the general government to send one regiment to the war, and she has undertaken to do it. Go quickly and help fill up the first colored regiment from the North. I am authorized to assure you that you will receive the same wages, the same rations, the same equipments, the same protection, the same treatment, and the same bounty, secured to the white soldiers. You will be led by able and skillful officers, men who will take especial pride in your efficiency and your valor, and see that your rights and feelings are respected by other soldiers. I have assured myself on these points, and can speak with authority.

More than twenty years of unswerving devotion to our common cause may give me some humble claim to be trusted at this momentous crisis. I will not argue. To do so implies hesitation and doubt, and you do not hesitate. You do not doubt. The day dawns; the morning star is bright upon the horizon! The iron gate of our prison stands half open. One gallant rush from the North will fling it wide open, while four millions of our brothers and sisters shall march out into liberty. The chance is now given you to end in a day the bondage of centuries, and to rise in one bound from social degradation to the plane of common equality with all other varieties of men.

Remember Denmark Vesey of Charleston; remember Nathaniel Turner of Southampton; remember Shields Green and Copeland, who followed noble John Brown, and fell as glorious martyrs for the cause of the slave. Remember that in a contest with oppression, the Almighty has no attribute which can take sides with oppressors.

The case is before you. This is our golden opportunity. Let us accept it, and forever wipe out the dark reproaches unsparingly hurled against us by our enemies. Let us win for ourselves the gratitude of our country, and the best blessings of our posterity through all time. The nucleus of this first regiment is now in camp at Readville, a short distance from Boston. I will undertake to forward to Boston all persons adjudged fit to be mustered into the regiment, who shall apply to me any time within the next two weeks.

Frederick Douglass, March 2, 1863

Camp Diary

". . . the life of the whole day was in those unknown people's song."

January 1, 1863 (evening).

. . . The services began at half past eleven o'clock, with prayer by our chaplain, Mr. Fowler, who is always, on such occasions, simple, reverential, and impressive. Then the President's Proclamation was read by Dr. W. H. Brisbane, a thing infinitely appropriate, a South Carolinian addressing South Carolinians; for he was reared among these very islands, and here long since emancipated his own slaves. Then the colors were presented to us by the Rev. Mr. French, a chaplain who brought them from the donors in New York. All this was according to the programme. Then followed an incident so simple, so touching, so utterly unexpected and startling, that I can scarcely believe it on recalling, though it gave the keynote to the whole day. The very moment the speaker had ceased, and just as I took and waved the flag, which now for the first time meant anything to these poor people, there suddenly arose, close beside the platform, a strong male voice (but rather cracked and elderly), into which two women's voices instantly blended, singing, as if by an impulse that could no more be repressed than the morning note of the song-sparrow.—

"My Country, 'tis of thee,
Sweet land of liberty,
Of thee I sing!"

People looked at each other, and then at us on the platform, to see whence came this interruption, not set down in the bills. Firmly and irrepressibly the quavering voices sang on, verse after verse; others of the colored people joined in; some whites on the platform began, but I motioned them to silence. I never saw anything so electric; it made all other words cheap; it seemed the choked voice of a race at last unloosed. Nothing could be more wonderfully unconscious; art could not have dreamed of a tribute to the day of jubilee that should be so affecting; history will not believe it; and when I came to speak of it, after it was ended, tears were everywhere. If you could have heard how quaint and innocent it was! Old Tiff and his children might have sung it; and close before me was a little slave-boy, almost white, who seemed to belong to the party, and even he must join in. Just think of it! —the first day they had ever had a country, the first flag they had ever seen which promised anything to their people, and here, while mere spectators stood in silence, waiting for my stupid words, these simple souls burst out in their lay, as if they were by their own hearths at home! When they stopped, there was nothing to do for it but to speak, and I went on; but the life of the whole day was in those unknown people's song.

January 14.

. . . Of one thing I am sure, that their best qualities will be wasted by merely keeping them for garrison duty. They seem peculiarly fitted for offensive operations, and especially for partisan warfare; they have so much dash and such abundant resources, combined with such an Indian-like knowledge of the country and its ways. These traits have been often illustrated in expeditions sent after deserters. For instance, I despatched one of my best lieutenants and my best sergeant with a squad of men to search a certain plantation, where there were two separate negro villages. They went by night, and the force was divided. The lieutenant took one set of huts, the sergeant the other. Before the lieutenant had reached his first house, every man in the village was in the woods, innocent and guilty alike. But the sergeant's mode of operation was thus described by a corporal from a white regiment who happened to be in one of the negro houses. He said that not a sound was heard until suddenly a red leg appeared in the open doorway, and a voice outside said, "Rally." Going to the door, he observed a similar pair of red legs before every hut, and not a person was allowed to go out, until the quarters had been thoroughly searched, and the three deserters found. This was managed by Sergeant Prince Rivers, our color-sergeant, who is provost-sergeant also, and has entire charge of the prisoners and of the daily policing of the camp. He is a man of distinguished appearance, and in old times was the crack coachman of Beaufort, in which capacity he once drove Beauregard from this plantation to Charleston, I believe. They tell me that he was once allowed to present a petition to the Governor of South Carolina in behalf of slaves, for the redress of certain grievances; and that a placard, offering two thousand dollars for his recapture, is still to be seen by the wayside between here and Charleston. He was a sergeant in the old "Hunter Regiment," and was taken by General Hunter to New York last spring, where the *chevrons* on his arm brought a mob upon him in Broadway, whom he kept off till the police interfered. There is not a white officer in this regiment who has more administrative ability, or more absolute authority over the men; they do not love him, but his mere presence has controlling power over them. He writes well enough to prepare for me a daily report of his duties in the camp; if his education reached a higher point, I see no reason why he should not command the Army of the Potomac. He is jet-black, or rather, I should say, *wine-black;* his complexion, like that of others of my darkest men, having a sort of rich, clear depth, without a trace of sootiness, and to my eye very handsome. His features are tolerably regular, and full of command, and his figure superior to that of any of our white officers,—being six feet high, perfectly proportioned, and of apparently inexhaustible strength and activity. His gait is like a panther's; I never saw such a tread. No anti-slavery novel has described a man of such marked ability. He makes Toussaint perfectly intelligible; and if there should ever be a black monarchy in South Carolina, he will be its king.

The Struggle for Pay

"Cannot even the fact of their being in arms for the nation, liable to die any day in its defence, secure them ordinary justice?"

HEADQUARTERS FIRST SOUTH CAROLINA VOLUNTEERS,

BEAUFORT, S.C.,
Sunday, February 14, 1864.

To the Editor of the New York Times:

May I venture to call your attention to the great and cruel injustice which is impending over the brave men of this regiment?

They have been in military service for over a year, having volunteered, every man, without a cent of bounty, on the written pledge of the War Department that they should receive the same pay and rations with white soldiers.

This pledge is contained in the written instructions of Brigadier-General Saxton, Military Governor, dated August 25, 1862. Mr. Solicitor Whiting, having examined those instructions, admits to me that "the faith of the Government was thereby pledged to every officer and soldier under that call."

Surely, if this fact were understood, every man in the nation would see that the Government is degraded by using for a year the services of the brave soldiers, and then repudiating the contract under which they were enlisted. This is what will be done, should Mr. Wilson's bill, legalizing the back pay of the army, be defeated.

We presume too much on the supposed ignorance of these men. I have never yet found a man in my regiment so stupid as not to know when he was cheated. If fraud proceeds from Government itself, so much the worse, for this strikes at the foundation of all rectitude, all honor, all obligation.

Mr. Senator Fessenden said, in the debate on Mr. Wilson's bill, January 4, that the Government was not bound, by the unauthorized promises of irresponsible recruiting officers. But is the Government itself an irresponsible recruiting officer? and if men have volunteered in good faith on the written assurances of the Secretary of War, is not Congress bound, in all decency, either to fulfill those pledges or to disband the regiments?

Mr. Senator Doolittle argued in the same debate that white soldiers should receive higher pay than black ones, because the families of the latter were often supported by Government. What an astounding statement of fact is this! In the white regiment in which I was formerly an officer (the Massachusetts Fifty-First) nine tenths of the soldiers' families, in addition to the pay and bounties, drew regularly their "State aid." Among my black soldiers, with half-pay and no bounty, not a family receives any aid. Is there to be no limit, no end to the injustice we heap upon this unfortunate people? Cannot even the fact of their being in arms for the nation, liable to die any day in its defence, secure them ordinary justice? Is the nation so poor, and so utterly demoralized by its pauperism, that after it has had the lives of these men, it must turn round to filch six dollars of the monthly pay which the Secretary of War promised to their widows? It is even so, if the excuses of Mr. Fessenden and Mr. Doolittle are to be accepted by Congress and by the people.

Very respectfully, your obedient servant,

T. W. HIGGINSON,
Colonel commanding 1st S.C. Volunteers

Farewell Address to the Troops

". . . amidst the terrible prejudices that then surrounded us, has grown an army of a hundred and forty thousand black soldiers, whose valor and heroism has won for your race a name which will live as long as the undying pages of history shall endure. . . ."

HEADQUARTERS 33D UNITED STATES COLORED TROOPS, LATE 1ST SOUTH CAROLINA VOLUNTEERS,

MORRIS ISLAND, S.C.
February 9, 1866.

GENERAL ORDERS, NO.1.

COMRADES,—The hour is at hand when we must separate forever, and nothing can ever take from us the pride we feel, when we look back upon the history of the First South Carolina Volunteers,—the first black regiment that ever bore arms in defence of freedom on the continent of America.

On the ninth day of May, 1862, at which time there were nearly four millions of your race in a bondage sanctioned by the laws of the land, and protected by our flag,—on that day, in the face of floods of prejudice, that wellnigh deluged every avenue to manhood and true liberty, you came forth to do battle for your country and your kindred. For long and weary months without pay, or even the privilege of being recognized as soldiers, you labored on, only to be disbanded and sent to your homes, without even a hope of reward. And when our country, necessitated by the deadly struggle with armed traitors, finally granted you the opportunity *again* to come forth in defence of the nation's life, the alacrity with which you responded to the call gave abundant evidence of your readiness to strike a manly blow for the liberty of your race. And from that little band of hopeful, trusting, and brave men, who gathered at Camp Saxton, on Port Royal Island, in the fall of 1862, amidst the terrible prejudices that then surrounded us, has grown an army of a hundred and forty thousand black soldiers, whose valor and heroism has won for your race a name which will live as long as the undying pages of history shall endure; and by whose efforts, united with those of the white man, armed rebellion has been conquered, the millions of bondmen have been emancipated, and the fundamental law of the land has been so altered as to remove forever the possibility of human slavery being re-established within the borders of redeemed America. The flag of our fathers, restored to its rightful significance, now floats over every foot of our territory, from Maine to California, and beholds only freemen! The prejudices which formerly existed against you are wellnigh rooted out.

Soldiers, you have done your duty, and acquitted yourselves like men, who, actuated by such ennobling motives, could not fail; and as the result of your fidelity and obedience, you have won your freedom. And O, how great the reward!

It seems fitting to me that the last hours of our existence as a regiment should be passed amidst the unmarked graves of your comrades,—at Fort Wagner. Near you rest the bones of Colonel Shaw, buried by an enemy's hand, in the same grave with his black soldiers, who fell at his side; where, in future, your children's children will come on pilgrimages to do homage to the ashes of those that fell in this glorious struggle.

The flag which was presented to us by the Rev. George B. Cheever and his congregation, of New York City, on the first of January, 1863,—the day when Lincoln's immortal proclamation of freedom was given to the world,—and which you have borne so nobly through the war, is now to be rolled up forever, and deposited in our nation's capital. And while there it shall rest, with the battles in which you have participated inscribed upon its folds, it will be a source of pride to us all to remember that it has never been disgraced by a cowardly faltering in the hour of danger or polluted by a traitor's touch.

Now that you are to lay aside your arms, and return to the peaceful avocations of life, I adjure you, by the associations and history of the past, and the love you bear for your liberties, to harbor no feelings of hatred toward your former masters, but to seek in the paths of honesty, virtue, sobriety, and industry, and by a willing obedience to the laws of the land, to grow up to the full stature of American citizens. The church, the schoolhouse and the right forever to be free are now secured to you, and every prospect before you is full of hope and encouragement. The nation guarantees to you full protection and justice, and will require from you in return the respect for the laws and orderly deportment which will prove to every one your right to all the privileges of freemen.

To the officers of the regiment I would say, your toils are ended, your mission is fulfilled, and we separate forever. The fidelity, patience, and patriotism with which you have discharged your duties, to your men and to your country, entitle you to a far higher tribute than any words of thankfulness which I can give you from the bottom of my heart. You will find your reward in the proud conviction that the cause for which you have battled so nobly has been crowned with abundant success.

Officers and soldiers of the First South Carolina Volunteers, I bid you all farewell.

By order of Lt.-Col. C. T. TROWBRIDGE, commanding Regiment.

E. W. HYDE,
Lieutenant and Acting Adjutant.

Folk Culture and Literature

At the same time that eloquent black orators and writers were creating a body of work to express publicly the feelings and desires of their people, the mass of the black folk enjoyed a rich literature of their own, one that reflected both their African roots and the particular details of the African-American experience. Forbidden by slave masters first from speaking in their native tongues, and then from learning to read and write in English, folk literature was transmitted orally, like the tales of the African griot, or oral historians, employing a patois that was a blend of the old and the new languages; it had the added advantage that it was often incomprehensible to whites.

Though snatches of songs and poems appeared in the early narratives (Frederick Douglass included the following "Slave Song" in *My Bondage and My Freedom*), it was after the Civil War that the range of black folk culture became widely known. The first extensive written account of the black spirituals† appeared in Union Army Captain William Wentworth Higginson's account of *Army Life in a Black Regiment.* After the Civil War, William Allen, Charles Ware, and Lucy Garrison collected black folk lyrics in *Slave Songs of the United States* (1867), and in 1880 Joel Chandler Harris published *Uncle Remus: His Songs and Sayings.* The tales were so popular that a second volume, *Nights with Uncle Remus,* appeared in 1883. The new *Journal of American Folklore,* which began publishing in 1888, devoted much of its pages to black folk culture. Though the collectors, and much of the audience, of these early works were white, they remain a valuable source of information about the black folk tradition.

The expression of folk culture took many forms. Stories might be told to explain the origin of the world or of the white and black races. Other stories were "history remembered" or conveyed important cultural and familial norms. Some were told just to entertain and amuse, while tales of "haints" played upon universal fears or were warnings about bad behavior. In the African-American context, folk characters often subtly conveyed a people's longings to be free, to defend themselves, or to escape from those who exercised greater power. As Uncle Remus says of the animals in his tales, "In those days the creatures were obliged to look out for themselves, most especially those that didn't have horns or hooves. Br'er Rabbit now, didn't have any horns or hooves so he had to be his own lawyer."

The origin of songs like "Slave Song," "Promises of Freedom," and "Slave Marriage Ceremony Supplement" remain unknown. "Aphorisms" and "Proverbs" from *Uncle Remus* demonstrate wry asides on behavior, advice on "how to act," and the virtue of minding one's own business. "All God's Chillun Had Wings," influenced by magical African tales, is representative of the cruelties of slavery and ways to elude the Master, and is recounted by an elderly gentleman from the isolated Sea Islands off the coasts of Georgia and South Carolina (a milieu captured with stunning effect in Juliet Dash's recent film, *Daughters of the Dust*), where African culture survived most intact. Heroes and bad men like John Henry, Shine, and Stackalee were cultural outlaws whose tales inspired their listeners. The rhetorical jives of the Signifying Monkey, whose origins can be traced to animal tales in Africa, generally sought to "stir things up," and many meanings were encoded in his rhyming nonsense. There are literally hundreds of variations on these tales.

One particularly enduring and expressive form of black culture was the blues, which sprang up in the barrooms, train yards, street corners, and brothels of the Mississippi Delta. Unlike the spirituals, which were communal and religious, the blues were worldy laments, often for a long-gone lover, and drew upon other forms of popular music like work songs, love songs, and stomps. One of the first blues, *Joe Turner,* was sung all over the South with different lyrics. W. C. Handy, the Father of the Blues, took this art form and made it respectable. He played trumpet and piano with a variety of quartets in Birmingham, Alabama, and St. Louis, and toured from New York to California from 1896 to 1903. In 1926 he performed his music at Carnegie Hall and published the classic anthology, *Blues.* Performers like Robert Johnson, Bessie Smith (the Empress of the Blues), Alberta Hunter, Leadbelly, Ma Rainey, Jelly Roll Morton, and Blind Lemon Jefferson fixed blues in American culture, and their influence is still felt today.

Black folk culture, blues, and jazz would form a rich vein for numerous later African-American authors. Charles Chestnutt and Paul Laurence Dunbar incorporated dialect and folk elements into much of their work. Arna Bontemps and Langston Hughes collaborated on *The Book of Negro Folklore,* and blues rhythms infuse Hughes's verse. Zora Neale Hurston made several trips to the south to collect the folklore, which she called "lies," included in *Mules and Men,* while James Weldon Johnson captured the black preacher's sermon in "Go Down, Death" and other orations from *God's Trombones.* Much of the poetry of Sterling Brown flows with the rhythm of blues, ballads, and work songs, and Etheridge Knight and Larry Neal have both introduced their own versions of the legend of

Shine, and the plays of August Wilson acknowledge the blues heritage. Today, rap lyrics carry on the tradition of "doing the dozens" and the jive of the rhyming trickster. Remarking on the enduring influence of black folk culture, Henry Louis Gates has said, "Telling ourselves our own stories . . . has as much as any single factor been responsible for the survival of African-Americans and their culture. The stories that we tell ourselves and our children function to order our world, serving to create both a foundation upon which each of us constructs our sense of reality and a filter through which we process each event that confronts us every day. The values we cherish and wish to preserve, the behavior that we wish to censure, the fears and dread that we can barely confess in ordinary language, the aspirations and goals that we most dearly prize—all of these things are encoded in the stories that each culture invents and preserves for the next generation, stories that, in effect, we live by and *through.*"

Slave Song

We raise de wheat,
Dey gib us de corn.
We bake de bread,
Dey gib us de crust.
We sif de meal,
Dey gib us de huss.
We peel de meat,
Dey gib us de skin.
And dat's de way
Dey take us in;
We skim de pot,
Dey gib us de liquor,
And say dat's good enough for nigger.

from *My Bondage and My Freedom,*
1853, by Frederick Douglass

Promises of Freedom

My ole Mistiss promise me,
W'en she died, she'd set me free,
She lived so long dat 'er head got bal',
An' she give out'n de notion a-dyin' at all.

My ole Mistiss say to me:
"Sambo, I'se gwine ter set you free."
Dut w'en dat head git slick an' bal',
De Lawd couldn't a' killed 'er wid a big green maul.

My ole Mistiss never die,
Wid' er nose all hooked an' skin all dry.
But my ole Miss, she's somehow gone,
An' she lef' Uncle Sambo a-hillin' up co'n.

Ole Mosser lakwise promise me,
W'en he died, he'd set me free.
But ole Mosser go an' make his will
Fer to leave me a-plowin' ole Beck still.

Yes, my ole Mosser promise me;
But "his papers" didn't leave me free.
A dose of pizen he'ped 'm along.
May de Devil Preach 'is funer'l song.

Slave Marriage Ceremony Supplement

Dark an' stormy may come de wedder;
I jines dis he-male an' dis she-male togedder.
Let none, but Him dat makes de thunder,
Put dis he-male an' dis she-male asunder.
I darfore 'nounce you bofe de same.
Be good, go 'long, an' keep up yo' name.
De broomstick's jumped, de world's not wide.
She's now yo' own. Salute yo' bride!

Plantation Proverbs

Big 'possum clime little tree.
Dem w'at eats kin say grace.
Ole man Know-All died las' year.
Better de gravy dan no grease 'tall.
Lazy fokes' stummucks don't git tired.
Mole don't see w'at his naber doin'.
Don't rain eve'y time de pig squeal.
Crow en corn can't grow in de same fiel'.
Tattlin' 'oman can't make de bread rise.
Rails split 'fo' brekfus' 'll season de dinner.
Hog dunner w'ich part un' im'll season de turnip salad.
Mighty po' bee dat don't make mo' honey dan he want.
Kwishins on mule's foots done gone out er fashun.
Pigs dunno w'at a pen's fer.
Possum's tail good as a paw.
Dogs don't bite at de front gate.
Colt in de barley-patch kick high.
Jay-bird don't rob his own nes'.
Pullet can't roost too high for de owl.
De howlin' dog know w'at he sees.
Bline hoss don't fall w'en he follers de bit.
Don't fling away de empty wallet.
Settin' hens don't hanker arter fresh aigs.
Tater-vine growin' w'ile you sleep.
Hit take two birds fer to make a nes'.
Ef you bleedzd ter eat dirt, eat clean dirt.
Tarrypin walk fast 'nuff fer to go visitin'.
Empty smoke house makes de pullet holler.
W'en coon take water he fixin' fer ter fight.
Corn make mo' at de mill dan its does in de crib.
Good luck say: "Op'n yo' mouf en shet yo' eyes."
Rooster makes mo' racket dan de hin w'at lay de aig.
Meller mush-million hollers at you fum over de fence.
Rain-crow don't sing no chune, but youk'n 'pen' on 'im.
One-eyed mule can't be handled on de bline side.
Moon may shine, but a lightered knot's mighty handy.
Licker talks mighty loud w'en it git loose fum de jug.
De proudness un a man don't count w'en his head's cold.
Hongry rooster don't cackle w'en he fine a wum.
Youk'n hide de fier, but w'at you gwine do wid de smoke?

Ter-morrow may be de carridge-driver's day for ploughin'.
Hit's a mighty deaf field hand dat don't year de dinner ho'n.
Hit takes a bee fer ter git de sweetness out'n de hoar-houn' blossom.
You'd see mo'er de mink ef he know'd whar de yard dog sleeps.
Watch out w'en you'er gittin all you want. Fattenin' hogs ain't in luck.

from *Uncle Remus*

Aphorisms

It's hard to make clothes fit a miserable man.
De stopper get de longest rest in de empty jug.
De church bells sometimes do better work dan de sermon.
De price of your hat ain't de measure of your brain.
Ef your coat-tail catch a-fire, don't wait till you kin see de blaze 'fo' you put it out.
De graveyard is de cheapes' boardin'-house.
Dar's a fam'ly coolness 'twix' de mule an' de single-tree.
It pesters a man dreadful when he git mad an' don't know who to cuss.
Buyin' on credit is robbin' next year's crop.
Christmas without holiday is like a candle without a wick.
De crawfish in a hurry look like he tryin' to git dar yesterday.
Lean hound lead de pack when de rabbit in sight.
Little flakes make de deepest snow.
Knot in de plank will show through de whitewash.
Dirt show de quickest on de cleanest cotton.
De candy-pulling can call louder dan de log-rolling.
De right sort of religion heaps de half-bushel.
De stell hoe dat laughs at de iron one is like de man dat is shamed of his grand-daddy.
A mule can tote so much goodness in his face that he don't have none left for his hind legs.
De cow-bell can't keep a secret.
Ripe apples made de tree look taller.
Blind horse knows when de trough is empty.
De noise of de wheels don't measure de load in de wagon.
Last year's hot spell cools off mighty fast.
Little hole in your pocket is worse than a big one at de knee.
Appetite don't regulate de time of day.
He drinks so much whisky that he staggers in his sleep.
De rich git richer and de po' git children.
Persimmons ain't no good until dey're frost-bit.
Man who gits hurt working oughta show de scars.
Life is short and full of blisters.
If you want to see how much folks is goin' to miss you, just stick your finger in de pond den pull it out and look at de hole.
De quagmire don't hang out no sign.
One person can thread a needle better than two.
De point of de pin is de easiest end to find.
Muzzle on de yard dog unlocks de smokehouse.

It's hard for de best and smartest folks in de world to git along without a little touch of good luck.
De billy-goat gets in his hardest licks when he looks like he's going to back out of de fight.
In God we trust, all others cash.
He may mean good, but he do' so doggone po'.

A whistling woman and a crowing hen,
Don't never come to no good end.

from *Uncle Remus*

All God's Chillen Had Wings

NCE ALL AFRICANS COULD FLY LIKE BIRDS; BUT OWING TO their many transgressions, their wings were taken away. There remained, here and there, in the sea islands and out-of-the-way places in the low country, some who had been overlooked, and had retained the power of flight, though they looked like other men.

There was a cruel master on one of the sea islands who worked his people till they died. When they died he bought others to take their places. These also he killed with overwork in the burning summer sun, through the middle hours of the day, although this was against the law.

One day, when all the worn-out Negroes were dead of overwork, he bought, of a broker in the town, a company of native Africans just brought into the country, and put them at once to work in the cottonfield.

He drove them hard. They went to work at sunrise and did not stop until dark. They were driven with unsparing harshness all day long, men, women and children. There was no pause for rest during the unendurable heat of the midsummer noon, though trees were plenty and near. But through the hardest hours, when fair plantations gave their Negroes rest, this man's driver pushed the work along without a moment's stop for breath, until all grew weak with heat and thirst.

There was among them one young woman who had lately borne a child. It was her first; she had not fully recovered from bearing, and should not have been sent to the field until her strength had come back. She had her child with her, as the other women had, astraddle on her hip, or piggyback.

The baby cried. She spoke to quiet it. The driver could not understand her words. She took her breast with her hand and threw it over her shoulder that the child might suck and be content. Then she went back to chopping knot-grass; but being very weak, and sick with the great heat, she stumbled, slipped and fell.

The driver struck her with his lash until she rose and staggered on.

She spoke to an old man near her, the oldest man of them all, tall and strong, with a forked beard. He replied; but the driver could not understand what they said; their talk was strange to him.

She returned to work; but in a little while she fell again. Again the driver lashed her until she got to her feet. Again she spoke to the old man. But he said: "Not yet, daughter; not yet." So she went on working, though she was very ill.

Soon she stumbled and fell again. But when the driver came running with his lash to drive her on with her work, she turned to the old man and asked: "Is it time yet, daddy?" He answered: "Yes, daughter; the time has come. Go; and peace be with you!" . . . and stretched out his arms toward her . . . so.

With that she leaped straight up into the air and was gone like a bird, flying over field and wood.

The driver and overseer ran after her as far as the edge of the field; but she was gone, high over their heads, over the fence, and over the top of the woods, gone, with her baby astraddle of her hip, sucking at her breast.

Then the driver hurried the rest to make up for her loss; and the sun was very hot indeed. So hot that soon a man fell down. The overseer himself lashed him to his feet. As he got up from where he had fallen the old man called to him in an unknown tongue. My grandfather told me the words that he said; but it was a long time ago, and I have forgotten them. But when he had spoken, the man turned and laughed at the overseer, and leaped up into the air, and was gone, like a gull, flying over field and wood.

Soon another man fell. The driver lashed him. He turned to the old man. The old man cried out to him, and stretched out his arms as he had done for the other two; and he, like them, leaped up, and was gone through the air, flying like a bird over field and wood.

Then the overseer and the driver ran at the old man with lashes ready; and the master ran too, with a picket pulled from the fence, to beat the life out of the old man who had made those Negroes fly.

But the old man laughed in their faces, and said something loudly to all the Negroes in the field, the new Negroes and the old Negroes.

And as he spoke to them they all remembered what they had forgotten, and recalled the power which once had been theirs. Then all the Negroes, old and new, stood up together; the old man raised his hands; and they all leaped up into the air with a great shout; and in a moment were gone, flying, like a flock of crows, over the field, over the fence, and over the top of the wood; and behind them flew the old man.

The men went clapping their hands; and the women went singing; and those who had children gave them their breasts; and the children laughed and sucked as their mothers flew, and were not afraid.

The master, the overseer, and the driver looked after them as they flew, beyond the wood, beyond the river, miles on miles, until they passed beyond the last rim of the world and disappeared in the sky like a handful of leaves. They were never seen again.

Where they went I do not know; I never was told. Nor what it was that the old man said . . . that I have forgotten. But as he went over the last fence he made a sign in the master's face, and cried "Kuli-ba! Kuli-ba!" I don't know what that means.

But if I could only find the old wood sawyer, he could tell you more; for he was there at the time, and saw the Africans fly away with their women and children. He is an old, old man, over ninety years of age, and remembers a great many strange things.

Told by Caesar Grant of Johns' Island

John Henry

Some say he's from Georgia,
Some say he's from Alabam,
But it's wrote on the rock at the Big Ben Tunnel,
John Henry's a East Virginia Man,
John Henry's a East Virginia Man.

John Henry he could hammah,
He could whistle, he could sing,
He went to the mountain early in the mornin'
To hear his hammah ring,
To hear his hammah ring.

John Henry went to the section boss,
Says the section boss what kin you do?
Say I can line a track, I kin histe a jack,
I kin pick and shovel, too,
I kin pick and shovel, too.

John Henry went to the tunnel
And they put him in lead to drive,
The rock was so tall and John Henry so small
That he laid down his hammah and he cried,
That he laid down his hammah and he cried.

The steam drill was on the right han' side,
John Henry was on the left,
Says before I let this steam drill beat me down,
I'll hammah myself to death,
I'll hammah myself to death.

Oh the cap'n said to John Henry,
I bleeve this mountain's sinkin' in.
John Henry said to the cap'n, Oh my!
Tain't nothin' but my hammah suckin' wind,
Tain't nothin' but my hammah suckin' wind.

John Henry had a pretty liddle wife,
She come all dressed in blue.
And the last words she said to him,
John Henry I been true to you,
John Henry I been true to you.

John Henry was on the mountain
The mountain was so high,
He called to his pretty liddle wife,

Said Ah kin' almos' touch the sky,
Said Ah kin' almos' touch the sky.

All the women in the West
That heard of John Henry's death,
Stood in the rain, flagged the east bound train,
Goin' where John Henry dropped dead,
Goin' where John Henry dropped dead.

They took John Henry to the White House,
And buried him in the san',
And every locomotive come roarin' by,
Says there lays that steel drivin' man,
Says there lays that steel drivin' man.

The Signifying Monkey

The Monkey and the Lion
Got to talking one day.
Monkey looked down and said, Lion,
I hear you's king in every way.
But you know somebody
Who do not think that is true—
He told me he could whip
The living daylights out of you.
Lion said, Who?
Monkey said, Lion,
He talked about your mama
And talked about your grandma, too,
And I'm too polite to tell you
What he said about you.
Lion said, Who said what? Who?
Monkey in the tree,
Lion on the ground.
Monkey kept on signifying
But he didn't come down.
Monkey said, His name is Elephant—
He stone sure is not your friend.
Lion said, He don't need to be
Because today will be his end.
Lion took off through the jungle
Lickity-split,
Meaning to grab Elephant
And tear him bit to bit.
He come across Elephant copping a righteous nod
Under a fine cool shady tree.
Lion said, You big old no-good so-and-so,
It's either you or me.
Lion let out a solid roar
And bopped Elephant with his paw.
Elephant just took his trunk
And busted old Lion's jaw.
Lion let out another roar,
Reared up six feet tall.
Elephant just kicked him in the belly
And laughed to see him drop and fall.
Lion rolled over,
Copped Elephant by the throat.

Elephant just shook him loose
And butted him like a goat.
Then he tromped him and he stomped him
Till the Lion yelled, Oh, no!
And it was near-nigh sunset
When Elephant let Lion go.
The signifying Monkey
Was still setting in his tree
When he looked down and saw the Lion.
Said, Why, Lion, who can that there be?
Lion said, It's me.
Monkey rapped, Why, Lion,
You look more dead than alive!
Lion said, Monkey, I don't want
To hear your jive-end jive.
Monkey just kept signifying,
Lion, you for sure caught hell—
Mister Elephant's done whipped you
To a fare-thee-well!
Why, Lion, you look like to me
You been in the precinct station
And had the third-degree,
Else you look like
You been high on gage
And done got caught
In a monkey cage!
You ain't no king to me.
Facts, I don't think that you
Can even as much as roar—
And if you try I'm liable
To come down out of this tree and
Whip your tail some more.
The Monkey started laughing
And jumping up and down.
But he jumped so hard the limb broke
And he landed—*bam!*—on the ground.
When he went to run, his foot slipped
And he fell flat down.
Grr-rrr-rr-r! The Lion was on him
With his front feet and his hind.
Monkey hollered, Ow!
Lion said, You little flea-bag you!
Why, I'll eat you up alive.
I wouldn't a-been in this fix a-tall

Wasn't for your signifying jive.
Please, said Monkey, Mister Lion,
If you'll just let me go,
I got something to tell you, *please,*
I think you ought to know.
Lion let the Monkey loose
To see what his tale could be—
And Monkey jumped right back on up
Into his tree.
What I was gonna tell you, said Monkey,
Is you square old so-and-so,
If you fool with me I'll get
Elephant to whip your head some more.
Monkey, said the Lion,
Beat to his unbooted knees,
You and all your signifying children
Better stay up in them trees.
Which is why today
Monkey does his signifying
A-way-up out of the way.

Stackalee

It was in the year of eighteen hundred and sixty-one
In St. Louis on Market Street where Stackalee was born.
Everybody's talkin about Stackalee.
It was on one cold and frosty night
When Stackalee and Billy Lyons had one awful fight,
Stackalee got his gun. Boy, he got it fast!
He shot poor Billy through and through;
Bullet broke a lookin glass.
Lord, O Lord, O Lord!
Stackalee shot Billy once; his body fell to the floor.
He cried out, Oh, please, Stack, please don't shoot me no more.

The White Elephant Barrel House was wrecked that night;
Gutters full of beer and whiskey; it was an awful sight.
Jewelry and rings of the purest solid gold
Scattered over the dance and gamblin hall.
The can-can dancers they rushed for the door
When Billy cried, Oh, please, Stack, don't shoot me no more.
Have mercy, Billy groaned, Oh, please spare my life;

Stack says, God bless your children, damn your wife!
You stold my magic Stetson; I'm gonna steal your life.
But, says Billy, I always treated you like a man.
'Tain't nothin to that old Stetson but the greasy band.
He shot poor Billy once, he shot him twice,
And the third time Billy pleaded, please go tell my wife.
Yes, Stackalee, the gambler, everybody knowed his name;
Made his livin hollerin high, low, jack and the game.

Meantime the sergeant strapped on his big forty-five,
Says now we'll bring in this bad man, dead or alive.
And brass-buttoned policemen tall dressed in blue
Came down the sidewalk marchin two by two.
Sent for the wagon and it hurried and come
Loaded with pistols and a big gatlin gun.
At midnight on that stormy night there came an awful wail
Billy Lyons and a graveyard ghost outside the city jail.
Jailer, jailer, says Stack, I can't sleep,
For around my bedside poor Billy Lyons still creeps.
He comes in shape of a lion with a blue steel in his hand,
For he knows I'll stand and fight if he comes in shape of man.

Stackalee went to sleep that night by the city clock bell,
Dreaming the devil had come all the way up from hell.
Red devil was sayin, you better hunt your hole;
I've hurried here from hell just to get your soul.

Stackalee told him yes, maybe you're right,
But I'll give even you one hell of a fight.
When they got into the scuffle, I heard the devil shout,
Come and get this bad man before he puts my fire out.
The next time I seed the devil he was scramblin up the wall,
Yellin, come and get this bad man fore he mops up with us all.

II

Then here come Stack's woman runnin, says, daddy, I love you true;
See what beer, whiskey, and smokin hop has brought you to.
But before I'll let you lay in there, I'll put my life in pawn.
She hurried and got Stackalee out on a five thousand dollar bond.
Stackalee said, ain't but one thing that grieves my mind,
When they take me away, babe, I leave you behind.
But the woman he really loved was a voodoo queen
From Creole French market, way down in New Orleans.
He laid down at home that night, took a good night's rest,
Arrived in court at nine o'clock to hear the coroner's inquest.
Crowds jammed the sidewalk, far as you could see,
Tryin to get a good look at tough Stackalee.
Over the cold, dead body Stackalee he did bend,
Then he turned and faced those twelve jury men.
The judge says, Stackalee, I would spare your life,
But I know you're a bad man; I can see it in your red eyes.
The jury heard the witnesses, and they didn't say no more;
They crowded into the jury room, and the messenger closed the door.

The jury came to agreement, the clerk he wrote it down,
And everybody was whisperin, he's penitentiary bound.
When the jury walked out, Stackalee didn't budge,
They wrapped the verdic and passed it to the judge.
Judge looked over his glasses, says, Mr. Bad Man Stackalee,
The jury finds you guilty of murder in the first degree.
Now the trial's come to an end, how the folks gave cheers;
Bad Stackalee was sent down to Jefferson pen for seventy-five years.

Now late at night you can hear him in his cell,
Arguin with the devil to keep from goin to hell.

And the other convicts whisper, whatcha know about that?
Gonna burn in hell forever over an old Stetson hat!
Everybody's talkin bout Stackalee.
That bad man, Stackalee!

An old version, collected by Onah L. Spencer

Shine and the Titanic

It was 1912 when the awful news got around
That the great Titanic was sinking down.
Shine came running up on deck, told the Captain, "Please,
The water in the boiler room is up to my knees."

Captain said, "Take your black self on back down there!
I got a hundred-fifty pumps to keep the boiler room clear."
Shine went back in the hole, started shovelling coal,
Singing, "Lord, have mercy, Lord, on my soul!"

Just then half the ocean jumped across the boiler room deck.
Shine yelled to the Captain, "The water's 'round my neck!"
Captain said, "Go back! Neither fear nor doubt!
I got a hundred more pumps to keep the water out."

"Your words sound happy and your words sound true,
But this is one time, Cap, your words won't do.
I don't like chicken and I don't like ham—
And I don't believe your pumps is worth a damn!"

The old Titanic was beginning to sink.
Shine pulled off his clothes and jumped in the brink.
He said, "Little fish, big fish, and shark fishes, too,
Get out of my way because I'm coming through."

Captain on bridge hollered, "Shine, Shine, save poor me,
And I'll make you as rich as any man can be."
Shine said, "There's more gold on land than there is on sea."
And he swimmed on.

Jay Gould's millionary daughter came running up on deck
With her suitcase in her hand and her dress 'round her neck.
She cried, "Shine, Shine, save poor me!
I'll give you everything your eyes can see."
Shine said, "There's more on land than there is on sea."
And he swimmed on.

Big fat banker begging, "Shine, Shine, save poor me!
I'll give you a thousand shares of T and T."
Shine said, "More stocks on land than there is on sea."
And he swimmed on.

When all them white folks went to heaven,
Shine was in Sugar Ray's Bar drinking Seagrams Seven.

Easy Rider

Easy rider, see what you done done, Lawd, Lawd,
Made me love you, now yo sweet man done
   come,
Gonna love you, baby, right on to Kingdom
   come.

When you see me comin,
   Hist yo windas high, Lawd, Lawd,
When you see me comin,
   Hist yo windas high.
You know darn well
   I ain't gonna pass you by.

When you see me leavin,
   Hang yo haid an cry, Lawd, Lawd,
When you see me leavin,
   Hang yo haid an cry.
Gonna love you
   Til the day I die.

If I was a cap'n on some western train, Lawd, Lawd,
If I was a cap'n on some western train,
I'd keep on a-goin
   An never come back again.

If I was a catfish swimmin in the deep blue sea, Lawd, Lawd,
If I was a catfish swimmin in the deep blue sea,
I'd keep these putty wimmins from fussin over me.
I'm goin buy me a shotgun long as I am tall, Lawd, Lawd,
Gonna buy me a shotgun long as I am tall.
If you don't treat me right,
   You ain't goin ta hav no haid atall.

Joe Turner

They tell me that Joe Turner's come and gone,
Oh Lord!
They tell me that Joe Turner's come and gone,
Got my man and gone.
He come with forty links of chain,
Oh, Lord!
He come with forty links of chain,
Got my man and gone.

St. Louis Blues

I hate to see de ev'nin' sun go down,
Hate to see de ev'nin' sun go down,
'Cause ma baby, he done lef dis town.

Feelin' tomorrow lak ah feel today,
Feel tomorrow lak ah feel today,
I'll pack my trunk, make ma git away.

St. Louis woman, wid her diamon' rings,
Pulls dat man roun' by her apron strings.
'Twant for powder an' for store-bought hair,
De man ah love would not gone no where, no where.

Got de St. Louis Blues jes as blue as ah can be,
Dat man got a heart lak a rock cast in the sea,
Or else he wouldn't have gone so far from me.

Been to de Gypsy to get ma fortune tole,
To de Gypsy done got ma fortune tole,
'Cause I'm most wile 'bout ma Jelly Roll.

Gypsy done tole me, "Don't you wear no black."
Yes she done tole me, "Don't you wear no black,
Go to St. Louis, You can win him back."

Help me to Cairo, make St. Louis by ma self,
Git to Cairo, find ma ole friend Jeff.
Gwine to pin maself close to his side,
If ah flag his train, I sho' can ride.

I loves dat man lak a schoolboy loves his pie,
Lak a Kentucky Col'nel loves his mint an' rye,
I'll love ma baby till the day ah die.

You ought to see dat stovepipe brown of mine,
Lak he owns de Dimon Joseph line,
He'd make a cross-eyed 'oman go stone blin'.

Blacker than midnight, teeth lak flags of truce,
Blackest man in de whole St. Louis,
Blacker de berry, sweeter am de juice.

About a crap game, he knows a pow'ful lot,
But when worktime comes, he's on de dot.
Gwine to ask him for a cold ten spot,
What it takes to git it, he's cert'nly got.

A black-headed woman makes a freight train jump the track,
Said a black-headed gal makes a freight train jump the track,
But a long tall gal makes a preacher ball the Jack.

Lawd, a blond-headed woman makes a good man leave the town,
I said blonde-headed woman makes a good man leave the town,
But a red-headed woman makes a boy slap his papa down.

Oh ashes to ashes and dust to dust,
I said ashes to ashes and dust to dust,
If my blues don't get you my jazzing must.

W. C. Handy, 1914

Joe Turner Blues

You'll never miss the water till your well runs dry,
Till your well runs dry.
You'll never miss Joe Turner till he says "Good Bye."
Sweet Babe, I'm goin' to leave you, and the time ain't long.
No, the time ain't long.
If you don't b'lieve I'm leavin', count the days I'm gone.

You will be sorry, be sorry from your heart,
Sorry to your heart,
Some day when you and I must part.
And ev'ry time you hear a whistle blow,
Hear a steamboat blow,
You'll hate the day you lost your Joe.

I bought a bulldog for to watch you while you sleep,
Guard you while you sleep.
Spend all my money, now you call Joe Turner "Cheap."
You never 'preciate the little things I do,
Not one thing I do.
And that's the very reason why I'm leavin' you.

Sometimes I feel like nothin', somethin' throwed away,
Somethin' throwed away.
And then I get my guitar, play the blues all day.
Now if your heart beat like mine it's not made of steel,
No, tain't made of steel.
And when you learn I left you this is how you'll feel.

W. C. Handy, 1915

Beale Street Blues

I've seen the lights of gay Broadway,
Old Market Street down by the Frisco Bay
I've strolled the Prado,
I've gambled on the Bourse
The seven wonders of the world I've seen
And many are the places I have been
Take my advice folks and see Beale Street first.

You'll see pretty Browns in beautiful gowns,
You'll see tailor-mades and hand-me-downs,
You'll meet honest men and pickpockets skilled,
You'll find that bus'ness never closes till somebody gets killed.

You'll see Hog-Nose rest'rants and Chitlin' Cafes,
You'll see Jugs that tell of bygone days,
And places, once places, now just a sham,
You'll see Golden Balls enough to pave the New Jerusalem.

If Beale Street could talk, If Beale Street could talk,
Married men would have to take their beds and walk,
Except one or two, who never drink booze,
And the blind man on the corner who sings the Beale Street Blues.

I'd rather be here than any place I know,
I'd rather be here than any place I know,
It's goin' to take the Sargent
For to make me go,

Goin' to the river,
Maybe, bye and bye,
Goin' to the river,
And there's a reason why,
Because the river's wet,
And Beale Street's done gone dry.

W. C. Handy, 1916

Spirituals

In his *Book of American Negro Spirituals,* published in 1925, James Weldon Johnson wrote: "As the years go by and I understand more about this music and its origin the miracle of its production strikes me with increasing wonder. It would have been a notable achievement if the white people who settled this country, having a common language and heritage, seeking liberty in a new land, faced with the task of conquering untamed nature, and stirred with the hope of building an empire, had created a body of folk music comparable to the Negro Spirituals. But from whom did these songs spring—these songs unsurpassed among the folk songs of the world and, in the poignancy of their beauty, unequalled?" In *The Souls of Black Folk,* W. E. B. Du Bois extolled the "sorrow songs" of the "children of disappointment" as "the singular spiritual heritage of the nation and the greatest gift of the Negro people," while Paul Robeson, who brought them to the concert stage around the world in the twentieth century, spoke of the "healing comfort to be found in the illimitable sorrow of the spirituals."

Because they were devised and reworked orally, the exact origin of the spirituals is not known. But they had been sung for generations before they were recorded in *Army Life in a Black Regiment* (1869) by Thomas Wentworth Higginson, who commanded the 1st South Carolina Volunteers in the Civil War. He understood at once their importance to his men, as well as their beauty and their art. Of the lovely "I Know Moon-Rise" he wrote, "Never, it seems to me, since man first lived and suffered, was his infinite longing for peace uttered more plaintively."

The central role of the spirituals in the African-American heritage may be due to the appeal of a religion that spoke to the slaves' own status, as well as to their ability to use the received doctrine to forge a new art form in their own idiom. From Phillis Wheatley's poetry onward, despite the obvious conflict between Christian teachings and those who claimed to practice them, African-American texts emphasize the strength found in a doctrine that promised deliverance, even if in another life. And yet it was not the New Testament God of love, but the Old Testament God of vengeance that most captured the slaves' imagination.

Striking parallels could be found between their own situation and that of the "chosen people" held in bondage in Egypt and led out of captivity by Moses. The triumphs of Daniel and Joshua, the "valiant soldier," and martial imagery figure prominently in spirituals like "Heav'n Boun' Soldier," "Joshua Fit de Battle ob Jerico," "Ride On, Moses," "Singin' wid a Sword in Ma Han'," and others. Even when the New Testament was evoked, the image of Jesus as martyr rarely appears, but rather that of "King Jesus" riding onward as the "conquering king." "Images of the Apocalypse and the books of Moses," wrote Higginson, "constituted their Bible; all that lay between, even the narratives of the life of Jesus, they hardly cared to read or hear."

While the image of the Christian engaged in battle with the Devil was a familiar one, in the spirituals such battles could have a temporal as well as a spiritual meaning, particularly during the Civil War era when the coming of the Kingdom might be equated, literally, with freedom. Higginson noted that slaves had been jailed for singing spirituals in South Carolina. " 'We'll soon be free' was too dangerous an assertion," he wrote, "and though the chant was an old one, it was no doubt sung with redoubled emphasis during the new events." "De tink *dè Lord* mean for say *de Yankees,"* one soldier told Higginson, and the Potomac, rather than the Jordan, represented the "One More River to Cross."

The slaves not only chose their Christian texts carefully but infused them with African tradition as well. The repetitive choruses recall the communal African call and response, as did the ring shout, with the singers moving in a circle. Some spirituals contained allusions to African folktales, and the mighty Jordan, a staple in the songs, recalls the many rivers in Africa and concepts of the underworld. In some songs, "Mr. Devil" is portrayed as "a liar an' a conjurer too," and "The Devil's mad and I'm glad/He lost the soul he thought he had" recalls a triumph against a wily trickster, typical of many African tales.

After the war, the spirituals found widespread acclaim with both white and black audiences when the Jubilee Singers of Fisk University introduced them across the country from 1871 to 1875. In the twentieth century, they reached world audiences when sung by Roland Hayes, Paul Robeson, Marian Anderson, Jules Bledsoe, and more recently, Jessye Norman and Kathleen Battle, among others. And many of the spirituals found new meaning in the songs of the civil rights movement† of the 1960s.

In a modern reading, the perception of the role of the spirituals in African-American life has been debated. Countee Cullen wrote of their representative status, "Without in the least depreciating the beauty of Negro spirituals or the undeniable fact that Negro singers do them, as it were, to the manner born, we have always resented the natural inclination of most white people to demand spirituals the moment it is known that a Negro is about to sing. So often the request has seemed to savor of the feeling that we could do this and this alone." And of their troubling association with slavery and long-suffering Christian patience, Malcom X wrote in his *Autobiography,* "The white man has taught us to shout and sing and pray until we *die,* to wait until *death,* for some dreamy heaven-in-the-hereafter, when we're *dead,* while this white man has his milk and honey in the streets paved with golden dollars right here on *this* earth!" But the tragic and poignant beauty of the spirituals is irrefutable. "By these," wrote Higginson, the slaves "could sing themselves, as had their fathers before them, out of the contemplation of their own low estate, into the sublime scenery of the Apocalypse."

Go Down, Moses

Go down, Moses,
Way down in Egyptland
Tell old Pharaoh
To let my people go.

When Israel was in Egyptland
Let my people go
Oppressed so hard they could not stand
Let my people go.

Go down, Moses,
Way down in Egyptland
Tell old Pharaoh
"Let my people go."

"Thus saith the Lord," bold Moses said,
"Let my people go;
If not I'll smite your first-born dead
Let my people go.

No more shall they in bondage toil,
Let my people go;
Let them come out with Egypt's spoil,
Let my people go."

The Lord told Moses what to do
Let my people go;
To lead the children of Israel through,
Let my people go.

Go down Moses,
Way down in Egyptland,
Tell old Pharaoh,
"Let my people go!"

Who'll Be a Witness for My Lord?

My soul is a witness for my Lord,
My soul is a witness for my Lord,
My soul is a witness for my Lord,
My soul is a witness for my Lord.

You read in de Bible an' you understan',
Methuselah was de oldes' man,
He lived nine hundred an' sixty nine,
He died an' went to heaven, Lord, in a due time.

O, Methuselah was a witness for my Lord,
Methuselah was a witness for my Lord,
Methuselah was a witness for my Lord,
Methuselah was a witness for my Lord.

You read in de Bible an' you understan',
Samson was de strongest man;
Samson went out at-a one time,
An' he killed about a thousan' of de Philistine.

Delilah fooled Samson, dis-a we know,
For de Holy Bible tells us so,
She shaved off his head jus' as clean as yo' han',
An' his strength became de same as any natch'al man.

O, Samson was a witness for my Lord,
O, Samson was a witness for my Lord,
O, Samson was a witness for my Lord,
O, Samson was a witness for my Lord.

Now, Daniel was a Hebrew child,
He went to pray to his God awhile,
De king at once for Daniel did sen',
An' he put him right down in de lion's den;

God sent His angels de lions for to keep,
An' Daniel laid down an' went to sleep.
Now Daniel was a witness for my Lord,
Now Daniel was a witness for my Lord.

O, who'll be a witness for my Lord?
O, who'll be a witness for my Lord?
My soul is a witness for my Lord,
My soul is a witness for my Lord.

Joshua Fit de Battle ob Jerico

Joshua fit de battle ob Jerico,
Jerico, Jerico,
Joshua fit de battle ob Jerico,
And de walls come tumblin' down.

You may talk about yo' king ob Gideon,
You may talk about yo' man ob Saul,
Dere's none like good ole Joshua
At de battle ob Jerico.

Up to de walls ob Jerico.
He marched with spear in han'
"Go blow dem ram horns" Joshua cried,
"Kase de battle am in my han'."

Den de lam'ram sheep horns begin to blow,
Trumpets begin to soun',
Joshua commanded de chillen to shout,
An' de walls come tumblin' down.

Dat mornin' Joshua fit de battle ob Jerico,
Jerico, Jerico,
Joshua fit de battle ob Jerico,
An' de walls come tumblin' down.

I Got a Home in Dat Rock

I got a home in dat Rock,
Don't you see?
I got a home in dat Rock,
Don't you see?
Between de earth an' sky,
Thought I heard my Saviour cry,
You got a home in dat Rock,
Don't you see?

Poor man Laz'rus, poor as I,
Don't you see?
Poor man Laz'rus, poor as I,
Don't you see?
Poor man Laz'rus, poor as I,
When he died he found a home on high,
He had a home in dat Rock,
Don't you see?

Rich man Dives, he lived so well,
Don't you see?
Rich man Dives, he lived so well,
Don't you see?
Rich man Dives, he lived so well,
When he died he found a home in Hell,
He had no home in dat Rock,
Don't you see?

God gave Noah de Rainbow sign,
Don't you see?
God gave Noah de Rainbow sign,
Don't you see?
God gave Noah de Rainbow sign,
No more water but fire next time,
Better get a home in dat Rock,
Don't you see?

Roll Jordan, Roll

Roll Jordan, roll,
Roll Jordan, roll,
I wanter go to heav'n when I die,
To hear ol' Jordan roll.

O, bretheren,
Roll Jordan, roll,
Roll Jordan, roll,
I wanter go to heav'n when I die,
To hear ol' Jordan roll.

Oh, brothers you oughter been dere,
Yes my Lord a sittin' up in de kingdom,
To hear ol' Jordan roll,
Sing it ovah,

Oh, sinner you oughter been dere,
Yes my Lord a sittin' up in de kingdom,
To hear ol' Jordan roll.

O, Roll Jordan, roll,
Roll Jordan, roll,
I wanter go to heav'n when I die,
To hear ol' Jordan roll.

My Way's Cloudy

O, bretheren, my way, my way's cloudy, my way,
Go sen'a dem angels down,
O, bretheren, my way, my way's cloudy, my way,
Go sen'a dem angels down.

Dere's fire in de eas' an' fire in de wes',
Sen' dem angels down,
Dere's fire among dem Methodis',
Oh, sen'a dem angels down.

Old Satan is mad an' I'm so glad,
Sen' dem angels down,
He missed de soul he thought he had,
Oh, sen'a dem angels down.

O, bretheren, my way, my way's cloudy, my way,
Go sen'a dem angels down.
O, bretheren, my way's cloudy, my way,
Go sen'a dem angels down.

Steal Away to Jesus

Steal away, steal away, steal away to Jesus!
Steal away, steal away home,
I ain't got long to stay here.

Steal away, steal away, steal away to Jesus!
Steal away, steal away home,
I ain't got long to stay here.

My Lord, He calls me, He calls me by the thunder,
The trumpet sounds within-a my soul,
I ain't got long to stay here.

Steal away, steal away, steal away to Jesus!
Steal away, steal away home,
I ain't got long to stay here.

Steal away, steal away, steal away to Jesus!
Steal away, steal away home,
I ain't got long to stay here.

Green trees a-bending, po' sinner stand a-trembling,
The trumpet sounds within-a my soul,
I ain't got long to stay here,
Oh, Lord, I ain't got long to stay here.

I Know Moon-Rise

I know moon-rise, I know star-rise,
  Lay dis body down.
I walk in de moonlight, I walk in de starlight,
  To lay dis body down.
I'll walk in de graveyard, I'll walk through de graveyard,
  To lay dis body down.
I'll lie in de grave and stretch out my arms;
  Lay dis body down.
I go to de judgment in de evenin' of de day,
  When I lay dis body down;
And my soul and your soul will meet in de day
  When I lay dis body down.

Deep River

Deep river, my home is over Jordan,
Deep river, Lord; I want to cross over into camp ground.

O, don't you want to go to that gospel feast,
That promised land where all is peace?

Deep river, my home is over Jordan,
Deep river, Lord; I want to cross over into camp ground.

Down in the Valley

We'll run and never tire,
We'll run and never tire,
We'll run and never tire,
   Jesus set poor sinners free.
Way down in de valley,
   Who will rise and go with me?
You've heern talk of Jesus,
   Who set poor sinners free.

De lightnin' and de flashin'
De lightnin' and de flashin'
De lightnin' and de flashin'
   Jesus set poor sinners free.

I can't stand the fire.
I can't stand the fire.
I can't stand the fire.
   Jesus set poor sinners free.

De green trees a-flamin'.
De green trees a-flamin'.
De green trees a-flamin'.
   Jesus set poor sinners free.

Way down in de valley,
   Who will rise and go with me?
You've heern talk of Jesus,
   Who set poor sinners free.

Swing Low Sweet Chariot

Swing low sweet chariot,
Comin' for to carry me home,
Swing low sweet chariot,
Comin' for to carry me home,

O, swing low sweet chariot,
Comin' for to carry me home,
Swing low sweet chariot,
Comin' for to carry me home.

I look'd over Jordan, an' what did I see,
Comin' for to carry me home,
A band of angels comin' after me,
Comin' for to carry me home.
If you get-a dere befo' I do,
Tell all of my friends I'm comin' too,

O, swing low sweet chariot,
Comin' for to carry me home,
Swing low sweet chariot,
Comin' for to carry me home,
Comin' for to carry me home.

Ride In, Kind Saviour

Ride in, kind Saviour!
  No man can hinder me.
O, Jesus is a mighty man!
  No man can hinder me.
We're marching through Virginny fields.
  No man can hinder me.
O, Satan is a busy man,
  No man can hinder me.
And he has his sword and shield,
  No man can hinder me.
O, old Secesh done come and gone!
  No man can hinder me.

My Army Cross Over

My army cross over,
My army cross over,
O, Pharaoh's army drownded!
My army cross over.

We'll cross de mighty river,
   My army cross over.
We'll cross de river Jordan,
   My army cross over.
We'll cross de danger water,
   My army cross over.
We'll cross de mighty Myo,
   My army cross over.

My army cross over,
My army cross over,
O, Pharaoh's army drownded!
My army cross over.

Many Thousand Gone

No more peck o' corn for me,
No more, no more,
No more peck o' corn for me,
Many thousand gone.

No more driver's lash for me,
No more, no more,
No more driver's lash for me,
Many thousand gone.

No more pint o' salt for me,
No more, no more,
No more pint o' salt for me,
Many thousand gone.

No more hundred lash for me,
No more, no more,
No more hundred lash for me,
Many thousand gone.

No more mistress' call for me,
No more, no more,
No more mistress' call for me,
Many thousand gone.

We'll Soon Be Free

We'll soon be free,
We'll soon be free,
We'll soon be free,
   When de Lord will call us home.

My brudder, how long,
My brudder, how long,
My brudder, how long,
   'Fore we done sufferin' here?

It won't be long,
It won't be long,
It won't be long,
   'Fore de Lord will call us home.

We'll walk de miry road,
We'll walk de miry road,
We'll walk de miry road,
   Where pleasure never dies.

We'll walk de golden street,
We'll walk de golden street,
We'll walk de golden street,
   Where pleasure never dies.

My brudder, how long,
My brudder, how long,
My brudder, how long,
   'Fore we done sufferin' here?

We'll soon be free,
We'll soon be free,
We'll soon be free,
   When Jesus sets me free.

We'll fight for liberty,
We'll fight for liberty,
We'll fight for liberty,
   When de Lord will call us home.

I Thank God I'm Free at Las'

Free at las', free at las',
I thank God I'm free at las'.
Free at las', free at las',
I thank God I'm free at las'.

Way down yonder in de graveyard walk,
I thank God I'm free at las'.
Me an' my Jesus gwineter meet an' talk,
I thank God I'm free at las'.

On-a my knees when de light pass by,
I thank God I'm free at las'.
Thought my soul would arise and fly,
I thank God I'm free at las'.

Some o'dese mornin's bright and fair,
I thank God I'm free at las',
Gwineter meet my Jesus in de middle of de air,
I thank God I'm free at las'.

The Civil War Amendments

In the rapid span of five years, from 1865 to 1870, three significant amendments to the Constitution were ratified by a sufficient number of states to become law. Though the Emancipation Proclamation,† issued on January 1, 1863, had abolished slavery in the rebel-held states, it had denied many others the status of freemen. During the election of 1864, the Republican Party platform stated that while the Proclamation had "aimed a deathblow at this gigantic evil," the party called for its "complete extirpation from the soil of the Republic." On April 8, 1864, the Republican Senate passed the Thirteenth Amendment; the House on January 31, 1865. Three quarters of the states—including eight former Confederate states—ratified the amendment and it became law on December 18, 1865.

The Fourteenth Amendment was passed by the first Reconstruction Congress, and its ratification was made a condition of reinstatement of the Confederate states into the Union. Calling for "equal protection" under the law, its effects would be radical and long-standing. The abolitionist Wendell Phillips said of the amendment, "Slavery is dead. We have not only abolished slavery, but we have abolished the Negro. We have actually washed color out of the Constitution." The amendment, which was adopted in 1868, formed the basis for much of the great judicial battles, including *Brown* v. *Board of Education of Topeka,*† of the twentieth century.

The adoption of the Fifteenth Amendment, which granted universal male suffrage, regardless of "race, color, or previous condition of servitude," was the subject of greater controversy as it pitted former abolitionists against women's suffragists, white feminists against black women's groups. In the national debate over the political rights of the former slaves, many women felt that the right to vote was their due, recompense for the role that they had played in the abolitionist movement; others who were more patient believed that the amendment represented a first step on the path toward suffrage for women. And some women within the suffrage movement, in which prejudice had never been entirely expunged, argued that native white women should be given the vote before black citizens of either sex.

Many African-Americans, including Frances Harper, Sojourner Truth, and Frederick Douglass, argued against a "race first" policy, denying that the right of African-American men to vote needed to be firmly established before attempting the more radical goal of female suffrage. With her characteristic bluntness, Sojourner Truth contended that "if colored men get their rights, and not colored women theirs, you see the colored men will be masters over the women, and it will be just as bad as it was before . . . I am glad to see that men are getting their rights, but I want women to get theirs, and while the water is stirring I will step into the pool." Reiterating that without the right to vote women were in the hands of their "political masters," Douglass stated: "So far as respects its relation to woman, our Government is in its essence, a simple usurpation, a Government of force, and not of reason. We legislate for woman, and protect her, precisely as we legislate for and protect animals, asking the consent of neither. . . . By every fact and by every argument which man can wield in defence of his natural right to participate in government, the right of woman so to participate is equally defended and rendered unassailable." Women would wait until the Nineteenth Amendment was adopted in 1920 for the right of suffrage.

Initially the Civil War Amendments represented the most tangible political gains of the conflict for African-Americans. By the end of the century, however, their status appeared to weaken as some Southern states passed "Black Codes"† aimed at restricting the rights of citizenship and called for the repeal of the Fourteenth and Fifteenth Amendments. The 1896 Supreme Court decision in *Plessy* v. *Ferguson*† that "separate" sufficed for "equal," opened the floodgates to a torrent of race-based restrictions; while in 1900, only one Southern state used Jim Crow streetcars, by 1905 ten of them did. Well into the twentieth century Southern states would circumvent the Fifteenth Amendment by instituting poll taxes, literacy tests, property and registration requirements, and the "grandfather clause" that allowed an individual to vote only if his forebears enjoyed suffrage as of January 1, 1866, thereby eliminating many blacks from voting rolls. The poll tax would finally be outlawed by the Twenty-fourth Amendment, adopted in 1964, and other voting restrictions were abolished by the Federal Voting Rights Act of 1965.

The Thirteenth Amendment

ARTICLE XIII

ECTION 1. NEITHER SLAVERY NOR INVOLUNTARY SERVITUDE, except as a punishment for crime whereof the party shall have been duly convicted, shall exist within the United States, or any place subject to their jurisdiction.

SECTION 2. Congress shall have power to enforce this article by appropriate legislation.

1865

The Fourteenth Amendment

ARTICLE XIV

ECTION 1. ALL PERSONS BORN OR NATURALIZED IN THE United States, and subject to the jurisdiction thereof, are citizens of the United States and of the State wherein they reside. No State shall make or enforce any law which shall abridge the privileges or immunities of citizens of the United States; nor shall any State deprive any person of life, liberty, or property, without due process of law; nor deny to any person within its jurisdiction the equal protection of the laws.

SECTION 2. Representatives shall be apportioned among the several States according to their respective numbers, counting the whole number of persons in each State, excluding Indians not taxed. But when the right to vote at any election for the choice of electors for President and Vice-President of the United States, Representatives in Congress, the executive and judicial officers of a State, or the members of the legislature thereof, is denied to any of the male inhabitants of such State, being twenty-one years of age, and citizens of the United States, or in any way abridged, except for participation in rebellion, or other crime, the basis of representation therein shall be reduced in the proportion which the number of such male citizens shall bear to the whole number of male citizens twenty-one years of age in such State.

SECTION 3. No person shall be a Senator or Representative in Congress, or elector of President and Vice-President, or hold any office, civil or military, under the United States, or under any State, who, having previously taken an oath, as a member of Congress, or as an officer of the United States, or as a member of any State Legislature, or as an executive or judicial officer of any State, to support the Constitution of the United States, shall have engaged in insurrection or rebellion against the same, or given aid or comfort to the enemies thereof. But Congress may by a vote of two-thirds of each house, remove such disability.

SECTION 4. The validity of the public debt of the United States, authorized by law, including debts incurred for payment of pensions and bounties for services in suppressing insurrection or rebellion, shall not be questioned. But neither the United States nor any State shall assume or pay any debt or obligation incurred in aid of insurrection or rebellion against the United States, or any claim for the loss or emancipation of any slave; but all such debts, obligations and claims shall be held illegal and void.

SECTION 5. The Congress shall have power to enforce, by appropriate legislation, the provisions of this article.

1868

The Fifteenth Amendment

ARTICLE XV

SECTION 1. THE RIGHT OF CITIZENS OF THE UNITED STATES TO vote shall not be denied or abridged by the United States or by any State on account of race, color, or previous condition of servitude.

SECTION 2. The Congress shall have power to enforce this article by appropriate legislation.

1870

Reconstruction

Even before the Civil War ended with the surrender of General Lee's troops at Appomattox Court House, Northern politicians had begun to consider the terms under which the rebel states might rejoin the Union and what role freemen would play in the country's future. In March 1865 Congress passed legislation establishing the Freedman's Bureau. Organized under the War Department and headed by General O. O. Howard, it sought to provide assistance in securing food, clothing, land, education, and employment to newly freed slaves and others dislocated by war.

The act, however, was intended to continue for only one year after the war, and when Vice President Andrew Johnson took office after Lincoln's assassination in late April, he quickly issued a series of proclamations establishing state governments that in effect restored the old Southern elites to power, while rigid new Black Codes, like that of South Carolina included here, limited the economic and political rights of freemen, providing for apprenticeships that amounted to little more than indentured servitude, imposing restrictions on certain professions, and regulating "vagrancy and idleness." And since the federal government returned much of the confiscated rebel lands to their former owners, many freedmen were forced to work as laborers or sharecroppers, leaving them largely in debt. That continued vigilance was necessary to secure freemen's full participation in any rebirth of American democracy is made clear in Frederick Douglass's speech to the Anti-Slavery Association in Boston, which follows.

By December 1865, Radical Republicans like Thaddeus Stevens and Charles Sumner, displeased with the course of reconstruction in the South, called for a more aggressive federal policy. In 1866 Congress passed the nation's first Civil Rights Act, which sought to counter the Black Codes and secure "full and equal benefit of all laws and proceedings for the security of person and property, as is enjoyed by white citizens." Significantly, the law stipulated that in "all questions of law arising in any cause under the provisions of this act a final appeal may be taken to the Supreme Court of the United States," establishing the role of federal courts in the protection of civil rights that would be used so effectively during the 1950s and 1960s. The following year, over Johnson's veto,

Congress extended the power of the Freedman's Bureau for two more years in the first piece of legislation ever to become law without the president's support. Congress continued its work with the Reconstruction Act of 1867, which divided the South into five military districts whose commanders were to protect "rights of persons and property, to suppress insurrection, disorder, and violence, and to punish, or cause to be punished, all disturbers of the public peace." The bill also outlined the form of new state governments and legislated universal manhood suffrage. Partly because of Johnson's opposition to Radical Reconstruction, impeachment hearings were begun against him, and in the fall of 1868, Republican Ulysses S. Grant was elected president.

With newly established rights of citizenship, African-Americans now constituted the majority of the Republican Party in much of the South, and during the next decade sixteen black legislators would serve in Congress, more than six hundred in state legislatures, and many hundreds more in local governments. The most prominent congressional figures included John R. Lynch, who served as Speaker of the Mississippi legislature before being elected to the U.S. House, Representative Robert Smalls, who served the longest (1875–1887), Hiram R. Revels, who served in the Senate, and Blanche K. Bruce. Born a slave in Virginia, Bruce (1841–1898) spent several years as a fugitive, and after the war established a black school in Hannibal, Missouri, and studied briefly at Oberlin College. In 1869 he moved to Mississippi and became a Republican organizer, and held various local political positions before being elected to the Senate in 1874. Although initially rather moderate, as conditions worsened in the South, Bruce became more outspoken, and on March 31, 1876, he delivered the speech that follows in the Senate condemning the fraudulent congressional election in Mississippi in 1875.

Whatever gains the freemen achieved did not go uncontested. Elected black representatives to state legislatures and Congress were denied their seats, and Henry McNeal Turner, who would later become a strong supporter of emigration, delivered his withering speech to the Georgia House on September 3, 1868, after he was refused admission. Violence was also used to intimidate African-Americans, and in May 1866 almost fifty black citizens, most of them Union veterans, were massacred in Memphis. That same year, several Confederate veterans, led by General Nathan Bedford Forrest, who had led Southern troops in the massacre of black soldiers at Fort Pillow during the war, joined together in Pulaski, Tennessee, to form the Ku Klux Klan. Similar groups sprang up elsewhere in the South, and while some states organized militias to oppose them, in other areas they held local officials in thrall.

In April 1871 a congressional committee was appointed to investigate the complaints of KKK violence. As numerous individuals testified how they had been attacked in their homes, members of their families murdered, their land seized, and their right to vote challenged, one witness from Alabama reported that as he approached the ballot box, an observer told him that "he had a coffin already made for me, because he thought I was going to vote the radical ticket." When asked the number of people he knew to have been beaten, he responded, "Hundreds. I could not number them to you." Various state committees also presented their collective grievances to Congress. The petition from black citizens in Kentucky, included here, provides a detailed list of the activities of the Klan during the previous four years. Later that year, Congress passed the Ku Klux Klan Act, which made any attempt to prevent a citizen from enjoying "the equal protection of the laws" a "high crime," and any organized attempt to do so "a rebellion, against the government of the United States." To some extent, the legislation weakened the Klan movement, though it would reappear early in the twentieth century, overlaid with the romantic sense of the "lost cause" exemplified in Thomas Dixon's novel *The Clansman* (1905) and D. W. Griffith's *Birth of a Nation* (1915). In its final Reconstruction legislative act, Congress passed a second Civil Rights Act in March 1875, which sought to prohibit racial discrimination in "accommodations, advantages, facilities, and privileges of inns, public conveyances on land or water, theaters, and other places of public amusement."

But while a remarkable amount of significant legislation was passed within a very few years, the gains of Radical Reconstruction were not long-lasting. By 1873, the South had begun to suffer the effects of a severe depression in which the price of cotton dropped almost fifty percent in four years, Democrats regained control of the House of Representatives in the election of 1874, and during the presidential election of 1876 Republican president-elect Rutherford Hayes recognized several disputed Southern Democratic seats in Congress in return for validation of his election. By the time Reconstruction ended with the withdrawal of federal troops in 1877, the Southern states had begun to nullify, in both the letter and the spirit, the hard-won political gains of African-Americans, and in October 1883 the Supreme Court nullified the Civil Rights Act of 1875. The triumph of Jim Crow legislation and the epidemic of lynching that followed in the so-called nadir of African-American history would lead to the great migrations of Southern blacks first to the West in 1879 and then to the cities in the North in the early part of the twentieth century.

Freedman's Bureau

AN ACT TO ESTABLISH A BUREAU FOR THE RELIEF OF FREEDMEN AND REFUGEES

B*E IT ENACTED BY THE SENATE AND HOUSE OF REPRESENTatives of the United States of America in Congress assembled,* That there is hereby established in the War Department, to continue during the present war of rebellion, and for one year thereafter, a bureau of refugees, freedmen, and abandoned lands, to which shall be committed, as hereinafter provided, the supervision and management of all abandoned lands, and the control of all subjects relating to refugees and freedmen from rebel states, or from any district of country within the territory embraced in the operations of the army, under such rules and regulations as may be prescribed by the head of the bureau and approved by the President. The said bureau shall be under the management and control of a commissioner to be appointed by the President, by and with the advice and consent of the Senate, whose compensation shall be three thousand dollars per annum, and such number of clerks as may be assigned to him by the Secretary of War, not exceeding one chief clerk, two of the fourth class, two of the third class, and five of the first class. And the commissioner and all persons appointed under this act, shall, before entering upon their duties, take the oath of office prescribed in an act entitled "An act to prescribe an oath of office, and for other purposes," approved July second, eighteen hundred and sixty-two, and the commissioner and the chief clerk shall, before entering upon their duties, give bonds to the treasurer of the United States, the former in the sum of fifty thousand dollars, and the latter in the sum of ten thousand dollars, conditioned for the faithful discharge of their duties respectively, with securities to be approved as sufficient by the Attorney-General, which bonds shall be filed in the office of the first comptroller of the treasury, to be by him put in suit for the benefit of any injured party upon any breach of the conditions thereof.

SEC. 2. *And be it further enacted,* That the Secretary of War may direct such issues of provisions, clothing, and fuel, as he may deem needful for the immediate and temporary shelter and supply of destitute and suffering refugees and freedmen and their wives and children, under such rules and regulations as he may direct.

SEC. 3. *And be it further enacted,* That the President may, by and with the advice and consent of the Senate, appoint an assistant commissioner for each of the states declared to be in insurrection, not exceeding ten in number, who shall, under the direction of the commissioner, aid in the execution of the provisions of this act; and he shall give a bond to the Treasurer of the United States, in the sum of twenty thousand dollars, in the form and manner prescribed in the first section of this act. Each of said commissioners shall receive an annual salary of two thousand and five hundred dollars in full compensation for all his services. And any military officer may be detailed and assigned to duty under this act without increase of pay or allowances. The commissioner shall, before the commencement of each regular session of congress, make full report of his proceedings with exhibits of the state of his accounts to the President, who shall communicate the same to congress, and shall also make special reports whenever required to do so by the President or either house of congress; and the assistant commissioners shall make quarterly reports of their proceedings to the commissioner, and also such other special reports as from time to time may be required.

SEC. 4. *And be it further enacted,* That the commissioner, under the direction of the President, shall have authority to set apart, for the use of loyal refugees and freedmen, such tracts of land within the insurrectionary states as shall have been abandoned, or to which the United States shall have acquired title by confiscation or sale, or otherwise, and to every male citizen, whether refugee or freedman, as aforesaid, there shall be assigned not more than forty acres of such land, and the person to whom it was so assigned shall be protected in the use and enjoyment of the land for the term of three years at an annual rent not exceeding six per centum upon the value of such land, as it was appraised by the state authorities in the year eighteen hundred and sixty, for the purpose of taxation, and in case no such appraisal can be found, then the rental shall be based upon the estimated value of the land in said year, to be ascertained in such manner as the commissioner may by regulation prescribe. At the end of said term, or at any time during said term, the occupants of any parcels so assigned may purchase the land and receive such title thereto as the United States can convey, upon paying therefor the value of the land, as ascertained and fixed for the purpose of determining the annual rent aforesaid.

SEC. 5. *And be it further enacted,* That all acts and parts of acts inconsistent with the provisions of this act, are hereby repealed.

APPROVED, March 3, 1865.

South Carolina Black Code, December 21, 1865–
An act to establish and regulate the domestic relations of persons of color, and to amend the law in relation to paupers and vagrancy

"All persons of color who make contracts for service or labor, shall be known as servants, and those with whom they contract shall be known as masters."

Be it enacted by the Senate and House of Representatives, now met and sitting in General Assembly, and by the authority of the same, as follows:

HUSBAND AND WIFE

I. The relation of husband and wife amongst persons of color is established.

II. Those who now live as such, are declared to be husband and wife. . . .

VIII. One who is a pauper, or a charge to the public, shall not be competent to contract marriage. Marriage between a white person and a person of color, shall be illegal and void.

IX. The marriage of an apprentice shall not, without the consent of the master, be lawful. . . .

MASTER AND APPRENTICE

XV. A child over the age of two years, born of a colored parent, may be bound by the father, if he be living in the District, or in case of his death or absence from the District, by the mother, as an apprentice, to any respectable white or colored person, who is competent to make a contract—a male until he shall attain the age of twenty-one years and a female until she shall attain the age of eighteen years.

XVI. Illegitimate children, within the ages above specified, may be bound by the mother.

XVII. Colored children, between the ages mentioned, who have neither father nor mother living in the District in which they are found, or whose parents are paupers, or unable to afford to them maintenance, or whose parents are not teaching them habits of industry and honesty, or are persons of notoriously bad character, or are vagrants, or have been, either of them convicted of an infamous offense, may be bound as apprentices by the District Judge, or one of the Magistrates for the aforesaid term.

XVIII. Males of the age of twelve years, and females, of the age of ten years, shall sign the indenture of apprenticeship and be bound thereby.

XIX. When the apprentice is under these ages, and in all cases of compulsory apprenticeship, where the infant refuses assent, his signature shall not be necessary to the validity of the apprenticeship. . . .

XXII. The master or mistress shall teach the apprentice the business of husbandry, or some other useful trade or business, which shall be specified in the instrument of apprenticeship; shall furnish him wholesome food and suitable clothing; teach him habits of industry, honesty and morality; govern and treat him with humanity; and if there be a school within a convenient distance, in which colored children are taught, shall send him to school at least six weeks in every year of his apprenticeship, after he shall be of the age of ten years: *Provided,* That the teacher of such school shall have the license of the District Judge to establish the same.

XXIII. The master shall have authority to inflict moderate chastisement and impose reasonable restraint upon his apprentice, and to recapture him if he depart from his service.

XXIV. The master shall receive to his own use the profits of the labor of his apprentice. The relation of master and apprentice shall be dissolved by the death of the master, except where the apprentice is engaged in husbandry, and may be dissolved by the District Judge, when both parties consent, or it shall appear to be seriously detrimental to either party. In the excepted case it shall terminate at the end of the year in which the master died. . . .

CONTRACTS FOR SERVICE

XXXV. All persons of color who make contracts for service or labor, shall be known as servants, and those with whom they contract shall be known as masters.

XXXVI. Contracts between masters and servants, for one month or more, shall be in writing, be attested by one white witness, and be approved by the Judge of the District Court, or by a Magistrate. . . .

XLIII. For any neglect of the duty to make a contract as herein directed, or the evasion of that duty by the repeated employment of the same persons for periods less than one month, the party offending shall be guilty of a misdemeanor, and be liable on conviction to pay a sum not exceeding fifty dollars, and not less than five dollars, for each person so employed. No written contract shall be required, when the servant voluntarily receives no remuneration, except food and clothing. . . .

REGULATIONS OF LABOR ON FARMS

XLV. On farms or in out-door service, the hours of labor, except on Sunday, shall be from sun-rise to sun-set, with a reasonable interval for breakfast and dinner. Servants shall rise at the dawn in the morning, feed, water and care for the animals on the farm, do the usual and needful work about the premises, prepare their meals for the day, if required by the master, and begin the farm work or other work by sun-rise. The servant shall be careful of all the animals and property of his master, and especially of the animals and instruments used by him, shall protect the same from injury by other persons, and shall be answerable for all property lost, destroyed or injured by his negligence, dishonesty or bad faith.

XLVI. All lost time, not caused by the act of the master, and all losses occasioned by neglect of the duties hereinbefore prescribed, may be deducted from the wages of the servant; and food, nursing and other necessaries for the servant, while he is absent from work on account of sickness or other cause, may also be deducted from his wages. Servants shall be quiet and orderly in their quarters, at their work and on the premises; shall extinguish their lights and fires, and retire to rest at seasonable hours. Work at night, and out-door work in inclement weather, shall not be exacted unless in case of necessity. Servants shall not be kept at home on Sunday, unless to take care of the premises, or animals thereupon, or for work of daily necessity, or on unusual occasions; and in such cases only so many shall be kept at home as are necessary for these purposes. Sunday work shall be done by the servants in turn, except in cases of sickness or other disability, when it may be assigned to them out of their regular term. Absentees on Sunday shall return to their homes by sun-set. . . .

XLVIII. Visitors or other persons shall not be invited, or allowed by the servant, to come or remain upon the premises of the master, without his express permission.

XLIX. Servants shall not be absent from the premises without the permission of the master.

RIGHTS OF MASTER AS BETWEEN HIMSELF AND HIS SERVANT

L. When the servant shall depart from the service of the master without good cause, he shall forfeit the wages due to him. The servant shall obey all lawful orders of the master or his agent, and shall be honest, truthful, sober, civil, and diligent in his business. The master may moderately correct servants who have made contracts, and are under eighteen years of age. He shall not be liable to pay for any additional or extraordinary services or labor of his servant, the same being necessary, unless by his express agreement. . . .

RIGHTS OF SERVANT AS BETWEEN HIMSELF AND MASTER

LXI. The servant may depart from the master's service for an insufficient supply of wholesome food; for an unauthorized battery upon his own person, or one of his family, not committed in defence of the person, family, guests or agents of the master, nor to prevent a crime or aggravated misdemeanor; invasion by the master of the conjugal rights of the servant; or his failure to pay wages when due; and may recover wages due for services rendered to the time of his departure.

LXII. The contract for service shall not be terminated by the death of the master, without the assent of the servant. Wages due to white laborers and to white and colored servants, shall rank as rent does in case of the insufficiency of the master's property, to pay all debts and demands against him, but not more than one year's wages shall be so preferred. When wrongfully discharged from service, the servant may recover wages for the whole period of service according to the contract. If his wages have not been paid to the day of his discharge, he may regard his contract rescinded by the discharge, and recover wages up to that time. . . .

MECHANICS, ARTISANS AND SHOP-KEEPERS

LXXII. No person of color shall pursue or practice the art, trade or business of an artisan, mechanic or shop-keeper, or any other trade, employment or business (besides that of husbandry, or that of a servant under a contract for services or labor) on his own account and for his own benefit, or in partnership with a white person, or as agent or servant of any person, until he shall have obtained a license therefor from the Judge of the District Court, which license shall be good for one year only. This license the Judge may grant upon petition of the applicant, and upon being satisfied of his skill and fitness, and of his good moral character . . . : *Provided, however,* That upon complaint being made and proved to the District Judge of an abuse of such license, he shall revoke the same, and: *Provided, also,* That no person of color shall practice any mechanical art or trade, unless he shows that he has served an apprenticeship in such trade or art, or is now practicing such trade or art. . . .

VAGRANCY AND IDLENESS

XCV. These are public grievances, and must be punished as crimes.

XCVI. All persons who have not some fixed and known place of abode, and some lawful and reputable employment; those who have not some visible and known means of a fair, honest and reputable livelihood; all common prostitutes; those who are found wandering from place to place, vending, bartering, or peddling any articles or commodities, without a license from the District Judge, or other proper authorities; all common gamblers; persons who lead idle or disorderly lives, or keep or frequent disorderly or disreputable houses or places; those who, not having sufficient means of support, are able to work and do not work; those who, (whether or not they own lands, or are lessees or mechanics,) do not provide a reasonable and proper maintenance for themselves and families; those who are engaged in representing publicly or privately, for fee or reward, without license, any tragedy, interlude, comedy, farce, play, or other similar entertainment, exhibition of the circus, sleight of hand, wax work or the like; those who for private gain, without license, give any concert or musical entertainment of any description; fortune tellers; sturdy beggars; common drunkards; those who hunt game of any description, or fish on the land of others, or frequent the premises, contrary to the will of the occupants; shall be deemed vagrants, and be liable to the punishment hereinafter provided.

XCVII. Upon information, or oath, of another, or upon his own knowledge, the District Judge or a Magistrate shall issue a warrant for the arrest of any person of color known or believed to be a vagrant, within the meaning of this Act. The Magistrate may proceed to try, with the assistance of five freeholders, or call into his aid another Magistrate, and the two may proceed to try, with the assistance of three freeholders, as provided by the Act of 1787, concerning vagrants; or the Magistrate may commit the accused to be tried before the District Court. On conviction, the defendant shall be liable to imprisonment, and to hard labor, one or both, as shall be fixed by the verdict, not exceeding twelve months.

XCVIII. The defendant, if sentenced to hard labor after conviction, may, by order of the District Judge, or Magistrate, before whom he was convicted, be hired for such wages as can be obtained for his services, to any owner or lessee of a farm, for the term of labor to which he was sentenced, or be hired for the same labor on the streets, public roads, or public buildings. The person receiving such vagrant shall have all the rights and remedies for enforcing good conduct and diligence at labor that are herein provided in the case of master and servant.

Acts of the General Assembly of the State of South Carolina,
1864–1865

Frederick Douglass's Speech to the Thirty-second Annual Convention of the American Anti-Slavery Society

"You and I and all of us had better wait and see what new form this old monster will assume, in what new skin this old snake will come forth."

SEVERAL GENTLEMEN HAVE BEEN SO KIND AS TO REFER TO ME in the course of this discussion, and my friend, Mr. [Samuel J.] May, referred to me as being opposed to the disbandment of this Society at any time during the present year. Having been thus referred to, I wish to put myself properly before the meeting. Almost the first work the American Anti-Slavery Society asked me to do, after employing me as an agent more than twenty years ago, was to accompany Stephen S. Foster and Abby Kelley (now Mrs. Foster) into the State of Rhode Island, to wage a most unrelenting war against what was called the "Dorr Constitution," because that Constitution contained the odious word "white" in it. That was regarded as legitimate anti-slavery work at that time; and that work was most effectively performed amid mobs and all sorts of violence. We succeeded in defeating that Dorr Constitution, and secured the adoption of a Constitution in which the word "white" did not appear. We thought it was a grand *anti-slavery* triumph, and it was; it was a good *anti-slavery* work. When I came North, and went to Massachusetts, I found that the leading work of the Abolitionists was to put the State of Massachusetts in harmony with the platform of the American Anti-Slavery Society. They said charity began at home. They looked over their statute-book, and whenever they found the word "white," there they recognized slavery, and they made war upon it. The anti-slavery ladies made themselves of no reputation by going about with petitions, asking the Legislature to blot out the hated word "white" from the marriage law. That was good anti-slavery work twenty years ago; I do not see why it is not good anti-slavery work now. It was a part of anti-slavery work then; it is a part now, I think.

I do not wish to appear here in any fault-finding spirit, or as an impugner of the motives of those who believe that the time has come for this Society to disband. I am conscious of no suspicion of the purity and excellence of the motives that animate the President of this Society [William Lloyd Garrison], and other gentlemen who are in favor of its disbandment. I take this ground; whether this Constitutional Amendment [the thirteenth] is law or not, whether it has been ratified by a sufficient number of States to make it law or not, I hold that the work of Abolitionists is not done. Even if every State in the Union had ratified that Amendment, while the black man is confronted in the legislation of the South by the word "white," our work as Abolitionists, as I conceive it, is not done. I took the ground, last night, that the South, by unfriendly legislation, could make our liberty, under that provision, a delusion, a mockery, and a snare, and I hold that ground now. What advantage is a provision like this Amendment to the black man, if the Legislature of any State can to-morrow declare that no black man's testimony shall be received in a court of law? Where are we then? Any wretch may enter the house of a black man, and commit any violence he pleases; if he happens to do it only in the presence of black persons, he goes unwhipt of justice. (Hear, hear.) And don't tell me that those people down there have become so just and honest all at once that they will not pass laws denying to black men the right to testify against white men in the courts of law. Why, our Northern States have done it. Illinois, Indiana and Ohio have done it. Here, in the midst of institutions that have gone forth from old Plymouth Rock, the black man has been excluded from testifying in the courts of law; and if the Legislature of every Southern State to-morrow pass a law, declaring that no Negro shall testify in any courts of law, they will not violate that provision of the Constitution. Such laws exist now at the South, and they might exist under this provision of the Constitution, that there shall be neither slavery nor involuntary servitude in any State of the Union.

Then another point. I have thought, for the last fifteen years, that we had an anti-slavery Constitution—a Constitution intended to secure "the blessings of liberty to ourselves and our posterity." But we have had slavery all along. We had a Constitution that declared that the citizens of Massachusetts should enjoy all the rights and immunities of citizens in South Carolina—but what of it? Let Mr. Hoar go down to South Carolina, and point to that provision in the Constitution, and they would kick him out of the State.* There is something down in South Carolina higher than Constitutional provisions.

Slavery is not abolished until the black man has the ballot. While the Legislatures of the South retain the right to pass laws making any discrimination between black and white, slavery still lives there. (Applause.) As Edmund Quincy once said, "While the word 'white' is on the statute-book of Massachusetts, Massachusetts is a slave State. While a black man can be turned out of a car in Massachusetts, Massachusetts is a slave State. While a slave can be taken from old Massachusetts, Massachusetts is a slave State." That is what I heard Edmund Quincy say twenty-three or twenty-four years ago. I never forget such a thing. Now, while the black man can be denied a

* In November, 1844, Samuel Hoar, a former Congressman, was sent by Gov. Briggs of Massachusetts to Charleston. His mission was to test the validity of a South Carolina law providing for the jailing of all free Negro seamen entering the state's ports. Mr. Hoar was forced to flee Charleston under threat of physical injury.

vote, while the Legislatures of the South can take from him the right to keep and bear arms, as they can—they would not allow a Negro to walk with a cane where I came from, they would not allow five of them to assemble together—the work of the Abolitionists is not finished. Notwithstanding the provision in the Constitution of the United States, that the right to keep and bear arms shall not be abridged, the black man has never had the right either to keep or bear arms; and the Legislatures of the States will still have the power to forbid it, under this Amendment. They can carry on a system of unfriendly legislation, and will they not do it? Have they not got prejudice there to do it with? Think you, that because they are for the moment in the talons and beak of our glorious eagle, instead of the slave being there, as formerly, that they are converted? I hear of the loyalty at Wilmington, the loyalty at South Carolina—what is it worth?

Mr. MAY—Not a straw.

Mr. DOUGLASS—Not a straw. I thank my friend for admitting it. They are loyal while they see 200,000 sable soldiers, with glistening bayonets, walking in their midst. (Applause) But let the civil power of the South be restored, and the old prejudices and hostility to the Negro will revive. Aye, the very fact that the Negro has been used to defeat this rebellion and strike down the standards of the Confederacy will be a stimulus to all their hatred, to all their malice, and lead them to legislate with greater stringency towards this class than ever before. (Applause.) The American people are bound—bound by their sense of honor (I hope by their sense of honor, at least, by a just sense of honor), to extend the franchise to the Negro; and I was going to say, that the Abolitionists of the American Anti-Slavery Society were bound to "stand still, and see the salvation of God," until that work is done. (Applause.) Where shall the black man look for support, my friends, if the American Anti-Slavery Society fails him? (Hear, hear.) From whence shall we expect a certain sound from the trumpet of freedom, when the old pioneer, when this Society that has survived mobs, and martyrdom, and the combined efforts of priest-craft and state-craft to suppress it, shall all at once subside, on the mere intimation that the Constitution has been amended, so that neither slavery nor involuntary servitude shall hereafter be allowed in this land? What did the slaveholders of Richmond say to those who objected to arming the Negro, on the ground that it would make him a freeman? Why, they said, "The argument is absurd. We may make these Negroes fight for us; but while we retain the political power of the South, we can keep them in their subordinate positions." That was the argument; and they were right. They might have employed the Negro to fight for them, and while they retained in their hands power to exclude him from political rights, they could have reduced him to a condition similar to slavery. They would not call it slavery, but some other name. Slavery has been fruitful in giving itself names. It has been called "the peculiar institution," "the social system," and the "impediment," as it was called by the General Conference of the Methodist Episcopal Church. It has been called by a great many names, and it will call itself by yet another name; and you and I and all of us had better wait and see what new form this old monster will assume, in what new skin this old snake will come forth. (Loud Applause.)

The Liberator, May 10, 1865

Blanche K. Bruce's Speech to the United States Senate on the Mississippi Election

". . . differences of religion, nationality, or race can neither with safety nor propriety be permitted for a moment to enter into the party contests of the day."

THE CONDUCT OF THE LATE ELECTION IN MISSISSIPPI AFFECTED not merely the fortunes of the partisans—as the same were necessarily involved in the defeat or success of the respective parties to the contest—but put in question and jeopardy the sacred rights of the citizens; and the investigation contemplated in the pending resolution has for its object not the determination of the question whether the offices shall be held and the public affairs of the State be administered by democrats or republicans, but the higher and more important end, the protection in all their purity and significance of the political rights of the people and the free institutions of the country.

The evidence in hand and accessible will show beyond peradventure that in many parts of the State corrupt and violent influences were brought to bear upon the registrars of voters, thus materially affecting the character of the voting or poll lists; upon the inspectors of election, prejudicially and unfairly, thereby changing the number of votes cast; and finally threats and violence were practiced directly upon the masses of voters in such measures and strength as to produce grave apprehensions for personal safety and as to deter them from the exercise of their political franchises.

It will not accord with the laws of nature or history to brand colored people a race of cowards. On more than one historic field, beginning in 1776 and coming down to the centennial year of the Republic, they have attested in blood their courage as well as a love of liberty. I ask Senators to believe that no consideration of fear or personal danger has kept us quiet and forbearing under the provocations and wrongs that have so sorely tried our souls. But feeling kindly towards our white fellow-citizens, appreciating the good purposes and offices of the better classes, and, above all, abhorring war of races, we determined to wait until such time as an appeal to the good sense and justice of the American people could be made.

The sober American judgment must obtain in the South as elsewhere in the Republic, that the only distinctions upon which parties can be safely organized and in harmony with our institutions are differences of opinion relative to principles and policies of government, and that differences of religion, nationality, or race can neither with safety nor propriety be permitted for a moment to enter into the party contests of the day. The unanimity with which the colored voters act with a party is not referable to any race prejudice on their part. On the contrary, they invite the political co-operation of their white brethren, and vote as a unit because proscribed as such. They deprecate the establishment of the color line by the opposition, not only because the act is unwise, but because it isolates them from the white men of the South and forces them, in sheer self-protection, and against their inclination, to act seemingly upon the basis of a race prejudice that they neither respect nor entertain. They not only recognize the equality of citizenship and the right of every man to hold without proscription any position of honor and trust to which the confidence of the people may elevate him; but owing nothing to race, birth, or surroundings, they above all other classes, in the community, are interested to see prejudices drop out of both politics and the businesses of the country, and success in life proceed upon the integrity and merit of the man who seeks it. . . . But withal, as they progress in intelligence and appreciation of the dignity of their prerogatives as citizens, they as an evidence of growth begin to realize the significance of the proverb, "When thou doest well for thyself, men shall praise thee"; and are disposed to exact the same protection and concessions of rights that are conferred upon other citizens by the Constitution, and that too without humiliation involved in the enforced abandonment of their political convictions.

I have confidence, not only in my country and her institutions, but in the endurance, capacity and destiny of my people. We will, as opportunity offers and ability serves, seek our places, sometimes in the field of literary arts, science and the professions. More frequently mechanical pursuits will attract and elicit our efforts; more still of my people will find employment and livelihood as the cultivators of the soil. The bulk of this people—by surroundings, habits, adaptation, and choice will continue to find their homes in the South and constitute the masses of its yeomanry. We will there, probably of our own volition and more abundantly than in the past, produce the great staples that will contribute to the basis of foreign exchange, and in giving the nation a balance of trade and minister to the wants and comforts and build up the prosperity of the whole land. Whatever our ultimate position in the composite civilization of the Republic and whatever varying fortunes attend our career, we will not forget our instincts for freedom nor our love for country.

March 31, 1876

Henry M. Turner's Speech to the Georgia Legislature

"I shall neither fawn or cringe before any party, nor stoop to beg them for my rights."

MR. SPEAKER:

Before proceeding to argue this question upon its intrinsic merits, I wish the members of this House to understand the position that I take. I hold that I am a member of this body. Therefore, sir, I shall neither fawn or cringe before any party, nor stoop to beg them for my rights. Some of my colored fellow members, in the course of their remarks, took occasion to appeal to the sympathies of Members on the opposite side, and to eulogize their character for magnanimity. It reminds me very much, sir, of slaves begging under the lash. I am here to demand my rights, and to hurl thunderbolts at the men who would dare to cross the threshold of my manhood. There is an old aphorism which says, "Fight the Devil with fire," and if I should observe the rule in this instance, I wish gentlemen to understand that it is but fighting them with their own weapon.

The scene presented in this House, to-day, is one unparalleled in the history of the world. From this day, back to the day when God breathed the breath of life into Adam, no analogy for it can be found. Never, in the history of the world, has a man been arraigned before a body clothed with legislative, judicial or executive functions, charged with the offence of being of a darker hue than his fellowmen. I know that questions have been before the Courts of this country, and of other countries, involving topics not altogether dissimilar to that which is being discussed here to-day. But, sir, never in all the history of the great nations of this world—never before—has a man been arraigned, charged with an offence committed by the God of Heaven Himself. Cases may be found where men have been deprived of their rights for crimes and misdemeanors; but it has remained for the State of Georgia, in the very heart of the nineteenth century, to call a man before the bar, and there charge him with an act for which he is no more responsible than for the head which he carries upon his shoulders. The Anglo-Saxon race, sir, is a most surprising one. No man has ever been more deceived in that race than I have been for the last three weeks. I was not aware that there was in the character of that race so much cowardice, or so much pusillanimity. The treachery which has been exhibited in it by gentlemen belonging to that race has shaken my confidence in it more than anything that has come under my observation from the day of my birth.

What is the question at issue? Why, sir, this Assembly, to-day, is discussing and deliberating on a judgment; there is not a Cherubim that sits around God's eternal Throne, to-day, that would not tremble—even were an order issued by the Supreme God Himself—to come down here and sit in judgment on my manhood. Gentlemen may look at this question in whatever light they choose, and with just as much indifference as they may think proper to assume, but I tell you, sir, that this is a question which will not die to-day. This event shall be remembered by posterity for ages yet to come, and while the sun shall continue to climb the hills of heaven.

Whose Legislature is this? Is it a white man's Legislature, or is it a black man's Legislature? Who voted for a Constitutional Convention, in obedience to the mandate of the Congress of the United States? Who first rallied around the standard of Reconstruction? Who set the ball of loyalty rolling in the State of Georgia? And whose voice was heard on the hills and in the valleys of this State? It was the voice of the brawny-armed Negro, with the few humanitarian-hearted white men who came to our assistance. I claim the honor, sir, of having been the instrument of convincing hundreds—yea, thousands—of white men, that to reconstruct under the measures of the United States Congress was the safest and the best course for the interest of the State.

Let us look at some facts in connection with this matter. Did half the white men of Georgia vote for this Legislature? Did not the great bulk of them fight, with all their strength, the Constitution under which we are acting? And did they not fight against the organization of this Legislature? And further, sir, did they not vote against it? Yes, sir! And there are persons in this Legislature to-day, who are ready to spit their poison in my face, while they themselves opposed, with all their power, the ratification of this Constitution. They question my right to a seat in this body, to represent the people whose legal votes elected me. This objection, sir, is an unheard of monopoly of power. No analogy can be found for it, except it be the case of a man who should go into my house, take possession of my wife and children, and then tell me to walk out. I stand very much in the position of a criminal before your bar, because I dare to be the exponent of the views of those who sent me here. Or, in other words, we are told that if black men want to speak, they must speak through white trumpets; if black men want their sentiments expressed, they must be adulterated and sent through white messengers, who will quibble, and equivocate, and evade, as rapidly as the pendulum of a clock. If this be not done, then the black men have committed an outrage, and their Representatives must be denied the right to represent their constituents.

The great question, sir, is this: Am I a man? If I am such, I claim the rights of a man. Am I not a man because I happen to be of a darker hue than honorable gentlemen around me? . . .

But Mr. Speaker, I do not regard this movement as a thrust at me, it is a thrust at the Bible—a thrust at the God of the Universe, for making a man and not finishing him; it is simply calling the Great Jehovah a fool. Why, sir, though we are not white, we have accomplished much. We have pioneered civilization here; we have built up your country; we have worked in your fields, and garnered your harvests, for two hundred and fifty years! And what do we ask of you in return? Do we ask you for compensation for the sweat our fathers bore for you—for the tears you have caused, and the hearts you have broken, and the lives you have curtailed, and the blood you have spilled? Do we ask retaliation? We ask it not. We are willing to let the dead past bury its dead; but we ask you now for our RIGHTS. You have all the elements of superiority upon your side; you have our money and your own; you have our education and your own; and you have your land and our own, too. We, who number hundreds of thousands in Georgia, including our wives and families, with not a foot of land to call our own—strangers in the land of our birth; without money, without education, without aid, without a roof to cover us while we live, nor sufficient clay to cover us when we die! It is extraordinary that a race such as yours, professing gallantry, and chivalry, and education, and superiority, living in a land where ringing chimes call child and sire to the Church of God—a land where Bibles are read and Gospels truths are spoken, and where courts of justice are presumed to exist; it is extraordinary to say, that, with all these advantages on your side, you can make war upon the poor defenseless black man. . . .

You may expel us, gentlemen, but I firmly believe that you will someday repent it. The black man cannot protect a country, if the country doesn't protect him; and if, tomorrow, a war should arise, I would not raise a musket to defend a country where my manhood is denied. The fashionable way in Georgia when hard work is to be done, is, for the white man to sit at his ease, while the black man does the work; but, sir, I will say this much to the colored men of Georgia, as if I should be killed in this campaign, I may have no opportunity of telling them at any other time: Never lift a finger nor raise a hand in defense of Georgia, unless Georgia acknowledges that you are men, and invests you with the rights pertaining to manhood. Pay your taxes, however, obey all orders from your employers, take good counsel from friends, work faithfully, earn an honest living, and show, by your conduct, that you can be good citizens. . . .

You may expel us, gentlemen, by your votes, today; but, while you do it, remember that there is a just God in Heaven, whose All-Seeing Eye beholds alike the acts of the oppressor and the oppressed, and who, despite the machinations of the wicked, never fails to vindicate the cause of Justice, and the sanctity of His own handiwork.

September 3, 1868

Petition from Kentucky Citizens on Ku Klux Klan Violence

"We believe you are not familiar with the description of the Ku Klux Klan's riding nightly . . . spreading terror wherever they go."

TO THE SENATE AND HOUSE OF REPRESENTATIVES IN CONGRESS assembled: We the Colored Citizens of Frankfort and vicinity do this day memorialize your honorable bodies upon the condition of affairs now existing in this the state of Kentucky.

We would respectfully state that life, liberty and property are unprotected among the colored race of this state. Organized Bands of desperate and lawless men mainly composed of soldiers of the late Rebel Armies Armed disciplined and disguised and bound by Oath and secret obligations have by force terror and violence subverted all civil society among Colored people, thus utterly rendering insecure the safety of persons and property, overthrowing all those rights which are the primary basis and objects of the Government which are expressly guaranteed to us by the Constitution of the United States as amended; We believe you are not familiar with the description of the Ku Klux Klans riding nightly over the country going from County to County and in the County towns spreading terror wherever they go, by robbing whipping ravishing and killing our people without provocation, compelling Colored people to brake the ice and bathe in the Chilly waters of the Kentucky River.

The Legislature has adjourned they refused to enact any laws to suppress Ku Klux disorder. We regard them as now being licensed to continue their dark and bloody deeds under cover of the dark night. They refuse to allow us to testify in the state Courts where a white man is concerned. We find their deeds are perpetrated only upon Colored men and white Republicans. We also find that for our services to the Government and our race we have become the special object of hatred and persecution at the hands of the Democratic party. Our people are driven from their homes in great numbers having no redress only the U.S. Courts which is in many cases unable to reach them. We would state that we have been law abiding citizens, pay our tax and in many parts of the state our people have been driven from the poles, refused the right to vote. Many have been slaughtered while attempting to vote, we ask how long is this state of things to last.

We appeal to you as law abiding citizens to enact some laws that will protect us. And that will enable us to exercise the rights of citizens. We see that the senators from this state denies there being organized Bands of desperaders in the state, for information we lay before you an number of violent acts occured during his Administration. Although he Stevenson says half Dozen instances of violence did occur these are not more than one half the acts that have occured. They Democratic party has here a political organization composed only of Democrats not a single Republican can join them where many of these acts have been committed it has been proven that they were the men, don with Armies from the State Arsenal. We pray you will take some steps to remedy these evils.

Don by a Committee of Grievances appointed at a meeting of all the Colored Citizens of Frankfort & vicinity.

Mar. 25th, 1871

Henry Marrs, Teacher colored school
Henry Lynn, Livery stable keeper
N. N. Trumbo, Grocer
Samuel Damsey, B. Smith [Blacksmith]
B. T. Crampton, Barber

Committee

1. A mob visited Harrodsburg in Mercer County to take from jail a man name Robertson, Nov. 14, 1867.

2. Smith attacked and whipped by regulation in Zelun County Nov. 1867.

3. Colored school house burned by incendiaries in Breckinridge Dec. 24, 1867.

4. A Negro Jim Macklin taken from jail in Frankfort and hung by mob January 28, 1868.

5. Sam Davis hung by mob in Harrodsburg May 28, 1868.

6. Wm. Pierce hung by a mob in Christian July 12, 1868.

7. Geo. Roger hung by a mob in Bradsfordsville Martin County July 11, 1868.

8. Colored school Exhibition at Midway attacked by a mob July 31, 1868.

9. Seven person ordered to leave their homes at Standford, Ky. Aug. 7, 1868.

10. Silas Woodford age sixty badly beaten by disguised mob. Mary Smith Curtis and Margaret Mosby also badly beaten, near Keene Jessemine County Aug. 1868.

11. Cabe Fields shot—and killed by disguise men near Keene Jessamine County Aug. 3, 1868.

12. James Gaines expelled from Anderson by Ku Klux Aug. 1868.

13. James Parker killed by Ku Klux Pulaski, Aug. 1868.

14. Noah Blankenship whipped by a mob in Pulaski County Aug. 1868.

15. Negroes attacked robbed and driven from Summerville in Green County Aug. 21, 1868.

16. William Gibson and John Gibson hung by a mob in Washington County Aug. 1868.

17. F. H. Montford hung by an mob near Cogers landing in Jessamine County Aug. 28, 1868.

18. Wm. Glassgow killed by a mob in Warren County Sep. 5, 1868.

19. Negro hung by a mob Sep. 1868.

20. Two Negros beaten by Ku Klux in Anderson County Sept. 11, 1868.

21. Mob attacked house of Oliver Stone in Fayette County Sept. 11, 1868.

22. Mob attacked Cumins house in Pulaski County. Cumins his daughter and a man name Adams killed in the attack Sept. 18, 1868.

23. U.S. Marshall Meriwether attacked captured and beatened with death in Larue County by mob Sept. 1868.

24. Richardson house attacked in Conishville by mob and Crasban killed Sept. 28, 1868.

25. Mob attacks Negro cabin at hanging forks in Lincoln County. John Mosteran killed & Cash & Coffey killed Sept. 1869.

26. Terry Laws & James Ryan hung by mob at Nicholasville Oct. 26, 1868.

27. Attack on Negro cabin in Spencer County—a woman outraged Dec. 1868.

28. Two Negroes shot by Ku Klux at Sulphur Springs in Union County, Dec. 1868.

29. Negro shot at Morganfield Union County, Dec. 1868.

30. Mob visited Edwin Burris house in Mercer County, January, 1869.

31. William Parker whipped by Ku Klux in Lincoln County Jan. 20/69.

32. Mob attacked and fired into house of Jesse Davises in Lincoln County Jan. 20, 1868.

33. Spears taken from his room at Harrodsburg by disguise men Jan. 19, 1869.

34. Albert Bradford killed by disguise men in Scott County, Jan. 20, 1869.

35. Ku Klux whipped boy at Standford March 12, 1869.

36. Mob attacked Frank Bournes house in Jessamine County. Roberts killed March 1869.

37. Geo Bratcher hung by mob on sugar creek in Garrard County March 30, 1869.

38. John Penny hung by a mob at Nevada Mercer county May 29, 1869.

39. Ku Klux whipped Lucien Green in Lincoln county June 1869.

40. Miller whipped by Ku Klux in madison county July 2d, 1869.

41. Chas Henderson shot & his wife killed by mob on silver creek Madison county July 1869.

42. Mob decoy from Harrodsburg and hangs Geo Bolling July 17, 1869.

43. Disguise band visited home of I. C. Vanarsdall and T. J. Vanarsdall in Mercer county July 18/69.

44. Mob attack Ronsey's house in Casey county three men and one woman Killed July 1869.

45. James Crowders hung by mob near Lebanon Merion county Augt 9, 1869.

46. Mob tar and feather a citizen of Cynthiana in Harrison county Aug. 1869.

47. Mob whipped and bruised a Negro in Davis county Sept. 1869.

48. Ku Klux burn colored meeting-house in Carrol county Sept. 1869.

49. Ku Klux whipped a Negro at John Carmins's farm in Fayette county Sept. 1869.

50. Wiley Gevens killed by Ku Klux at Dixon Webster county Oct. 1869.

51. Geo Rose killed by Klu Klux near Kirkville in Madison county Oct. 18, 1869.

52. Ku Klux ordered Wallace Sinkhorn to leave his home near Parkville Boyle county Oct. 1869.

53. Man named Shepherd shot by mob near Parksville Oct. 1869.

54. Regulator killed Geo Tanhely in Lincoln county Nov. 2d, 1869.

55. Ku Klux attacked Frank Searcy house in madison county one man shot Nov. 1869.

56. Searcy hung by mob madison county at Richmond Nov. 4th, 1869.

57. Ku Klux killed Robt Mershon daughter shot Nov. 1869.

58. Mob whipped Pope Hall and Willett in Washington county Nov. 1869.

59. Regulators whipped Cooper in Palaski County Nov. 1869.

60. Ku Klux ruffians outraged Negroes in Hickman county Nov. 20, 1869.

61. Mob take two Negroes from jail Richmond Madison county one hung one whipped Dec. 12, 1869.

62. Two Negroes killed by mob while in civil custody near mayfield Graves county Dec. 1869.

63. Allen Cooper killed by Ku Klux in Adair county Dec. 24th, 1869.

64. Negroes whipped while on Scott's farm in Franklin county Dec. 1869.

65. Mob hung Chas Fields in Fayette county Jan. 20, 1870.

66. Mob take two men from Springfield jail and hung them Jan. 31, 1870.

67. Ku Klux whipped two Negros in Madison county Feb. 1870.

68. Simms hung by mob near Kingston Madison county Feb. 1870.

69. Mob hung up, then whipped Douglass Rodes near Kingston Madison County February 1870.

70. Mob takes Fielding Waller from jail at Winchester Feb. 19th, 1870.

71. R. L. Byrom hung by mob at Richmond Feb. 18th, 1870.

72. Perry hung by mob near Lancaster Garrard County April 5th, 70.

73. Negro hung by mob at Crab-orchard Lincoln county Apr. 6th, 1870.

74. Mob rescue prisoner from Summerset jail Apr. 5, 1870.

75. Mob attacked A. Owen's house in Lincoln county Hyatt killed and Saunders shot Apr. 1870.

76. Mob releases five prisoners from Federal Officers in Bullitt county Apr. 11th, 1870.

77. Sam Lambert shot & hung by mob in Mercer county Apr. 11th, 1870.

78. Mob attacks William Palmer house in Clark County William Hart killed Apr. 1870.

79. Three men hung by mob near Gloscow Warren county May 1870.

80. John Redman killed by Ku Klux in Adair county May 1870.

81. William Sheldon Pleasanton Parker Daniel Parker Willis Parker hung by mob in Laurel county May 14th, 1870.

82. Ku Klux visited Negro cabins at Deak's Mill Franklin county robbed and maltreated inmates May 14th, 1870.

83. Negro's school house burned by incendiaries in Christain county May 1870.

84. Negro hung by mob at Greenville Muhlenburgh county May 1870.

85. Colored school house on Glen creek in Woodford county burned by incendiaries June 4th, 1870.

86. Ku Klux visited Negro cabin robbing and maltreating inmates on Sand Riffle in Hay county June 10, 1870.

87. Mob attacked Jail in Whitley County two men shot June 1870.

88. Election riot at Harrodsburg four person killed Aug. 4, 1870.

89. Property burned by incendiaries in Woodford county Augt. 8, 1870.

90. Turpin & Parker killed by mob at Versailled Augt. 10, 1870.

91. Richard Brown's house attacked by Ku Klux, in Hay.

92. Simpson Grubbs killed by a band of men in Montgomery county Augt. 1870.

93. Jacob See rescued from Mt. Sterling jail by mob Sept. 1870.

94. Frank Timberlake hung by a mob at Flemingburg Fleming county Sept. 1870.

95. John Simes shot & his wife murdered by Ku Klux in Hay county Sept. 1870.

96. Oliver Williams hung by Ku Klux in Madison county Sept. 1870.

97. Ku Klux visited cabins of colored people robbed and maltreated inmates at Havey Mill Franklin county.

98. A mob abducted Hicks from Lancaster Oct. 1870.

99. Howard Gilbert shot by Ku Klux in Madison county Oct 9th, 1870.

100. Ku Klux drive colored people Bald-Knob Franklin county Oct. 1870.

101. Two Negroes shot on Harrison Blanton's farm near Frankfort Dec. 6th, 1870.

102. Two Negroes killed in Fayette county while in civil custody Dec. 18, 1870.

103. Howard Million murdered by Ku Klux in Fayette county Dec. 1870.

104. John Dickerson driven from his home in Hay county and his daughter ravished Dec. 12, 1870.

105. A Negro named George hung by a mob at Cynthiana Harrison county Dec. 1870.

106. Negro killed by Ku Klux near Ashland Fayette county January 7th, 1871.

107. A Negro named Hall whipped and shot near Shelbyville Shelby county Jan. 17, 1871.

108. Ku Klux visited Negro cabin at Stamping Ground in Scott county force (White) & Ku Klux killed two Negroes killed in self defence.

109. Negro killed by Ku Klux in Hay county January 14, 1871.

110. Negro church & school house in Scott county [burned?] Jan. 13, 1871.

111. Ku Klux maltreated Demar his two sons and Joseph Allen in Franklin Jan. 1871.

112. Dr Johnson whipped by Ku Klux in Magoffin county Dec. 1871.

113. Property burned by incendiaries in Fayette county Jan. 21, 1871.

114. Attack on mail agent—North Benson Jan. 26, 1871.

115. Winston Hawkins fence burned and notice over his door not come home any more April 2d, 1871.

116. Ku Klux to the number of two hundred in February came into Frankfort and rescued from jail one Scroggins that was in civil custody for shooting and killing one colored man named Steader Trumbo.

1871

The Exodusters

Throughout the nineteenth century, colonization movements had urged African-Americans to emigrate to Africa, Canada, and Haiti, and black settlers had been heading West since the Civil War. But new impetus was given to the trend when federal troops withdrew from the South in 1876, leaving freemen little protection under the "Black Codes" which had been effected in most Southern states. Forerunners of the rise of Jim Crow, from 1865 onward these statutes gave landlords almost absolute control over their tenants, allowing them to charge high rates for land use, forcing the laborer to pledge his crops in advance to buy overpriced supplies, and instituting laws for vagrancy and "insulting" behavior toward whites. Though Congress sought to neutralize these codes by passing the Civil Rights Act of 1866 over President Andrew Johnson's veto, the Supreme Court nullified the act in 1883, institutionalizing the segregation of the races in the South.

In 1868 one of the most significant westward migrants, Benjamin "Pap" Singleton, formed the Real Estate Association in Nashville, Tennessee, and in 1875 he led a group of settlers to Baxter Springs, Kansas. With the urging of land promoters, other "colonies" sprang up, and between 1875 and 1880 Singleton led nearly 7,500 settlers from Tennessee to Kansas. As the migration West took on the mythical dimension of the biblical Exodus out of Egypt, individuals banded together in "conferences" and immigrant aid societies; their sentiment is expressed by the resolution of the Committee on a Permanent Form of Organization in Nashville, Tennessee, that "the great current migration which has for the past few months taken so many of our people from their homes in the South, and which is still carrying hundreds to the free and fertile West, should be encouraged and kept in motion until those who remain are accorded every right and privilege guaranteed by the Constitution and laws" (*The People's Advocate,* Washington, D.C., May 17, 1879).

One of the most prosperous of the new communities was Nicodemus, in Graham County, northwest Kansas. First plotted on June 8, 1877, and eventually numbering between six hundred and seven hundred people in 1878, its citizens started a school, opened a post office ("a tea chest with a partition in it"), elected officials, and witnessed, the Nicodemus *Western*

Cyclone reports (April 27, 1887), "the first free-to-all fight in the town" between Rev. John Anderson and Deacon Joseph Jones "in an argument over scripture." Though Nicodemus suffered a decline in the mid-1880s, descendants of the original settlers continue to own much of the land there today.

The settlers found conditions in the new Promised Land harsh. Many were unable to buy land and worked as wage laborers while living in earthen "dugouts." Wrote one observer in the Baltimore *American Citizen* (April 26, 1879), "Some have asserted that the idea of a life of ease and triflingness has had much to do with prompting the people to join the great Exodus. Such talk to us seems the height of great nonsense. The people are leaving the South because they can't stay there without submitting to a slavery worse than that from which the war lifted them. They know that they will have to work for a living in Kansas, but the thought that they will get the living after they do work for and earn it is the great moving cause today that is propelling them forward." The exodus continued.

By 1880, nearly twenty thousand settlers had moved West. The loss of cheap labor alarmed businessmen in the Southern states, who attempted to restrict emigration; at the same time, tensions rose between more established workingmen in the new towns and the recent arrivals. In an effort to deter new migrations, *The Kansas Herald* was led to point out that "other western states hold out as great inducements as Kansas."

From 1883, smaller groups emigrated to Missouri, Colorado, Indian Territory (Oklahoma), Arkansas, Nebraska, Iowa, the Dakota territory, and Mexico, whose government had made a formal offer of land. While the movement had its critics, it also propelled African-Americans into the westward expansion that was one of the defining paradigms of the American experience. "Young man, if you are about to finish at Howard, Fisk, Wilberforce, or Hampton," the New York *Freeman* urged (May 15, 1886), "do not hang around Washington waiting for a chance to feed on government pop, or go to Boston to wait in a hotel, and thus sink what little manhood you had at first, but come this way—come to bear trial, come to work and wait, come to wait and win, come determined to be or die trying. You are wanted, come."

News Accounts from the Black Press

"Come West, friends, come west, and grow up with God's country."

—*The American Citizen*, Topeka, Kansas
March 22, 1889

To the Front
NICODEMUS LAND CO.

Officers

President—S. Garland
Secretary—Wm. H. Cotton
Vice President—J. T. Young
Corresp. Sec.—A. G. Tallman
Treasurer—D. Williamson

Locators

Z. T. Fletcher
J. T. Young

General Office, Nicodemus, Graham County, Kansas

CHEAP HOMES!
CHEAP LANDS!

Lands for the Millions
In the Solomon Valley in the
Vicinity of Nicodemus

The best lands in all Kansas, is in Graham county, in the Beautiful Solomon Valley—come and see for yourself.

Come one and all and settle in the garden of

THE NORTHWEST

Thousands of acres of Wild Lands, Improved Farms and Stock Ranches for sale in Graham and Rooks Counties.

If you want to get land cheap, call on us soon, as the land is

RAPIDLY INCREASING IN VALUE

If you want to get a home, cheap, come to us—we can make
YOU HAPPY

—*The Western Cyclone*, Nicodemus, Kansas, July 15, 1886

Many good people in the East have probably heard of a "Kansas dugout" and have thought of it as a sort of human habitation peculiar to partial civilization and frontier barbarity. This is by no means a fair conclusion. "Dugouts" are not simply holes in the ground. They are generally dug into a side hill. They have two or more sides, with windows and doors. The floor and the roof are of earth. They are warmer than most of the more pretentious dwellings. They are as comfortable as they are cheap, and in nearly every place they protect a happy and prosperous family. Though comparatively few in number at the present time, they are still foremost among the best devices for building a fortune from the ground up. "Despise not the day of small things" is the motto of those who would dwell in the dugouts.

—*The Kansas Herald*, Topeka, Kansas, February 6, 1880

What is to be the final destiny of the colored race of this country is a problem, the solving of which has long engaged the best attention of every thoughtful colored man and every friendly white man and is as yet unsolved. Almost every thinker has expressed his opinion upon the subject, and the opinions have been as various as the thinkers themselves. . . . I boldly assert that the only practical plan for ever settling the question is for the black men of this country to select one of the territories of this government and to gain by legal means possession of it, and then go into it, and settle it up and go to work and build towns, churches, and everything else necessary, and thus form a state of their own. In this way, and in this way only, can the Negroes make of themselves a happy and prosperous people. No thinking black man, who deserves the name of such, can doubt for a moment his ability to build up a powerful and prosperous State. We have the bone and the muscle to do the hard work, and we have among us the talent and the statesmanship to regulate the political machinery, and we have educated men to run the schools and colleges, the ministers to manage the churches, and the mechanical skill to run all business of that character, and capitalists to build railroads through our State will not be lacking. . . .

—*The Colored Visitor*, Logansport, Indiana, August 1, 1879

Charles W. Chesnutt
(1858–1932)

The writings of Charles W. Chesnutt represent a significant achievement in African-American letters, not only for Chesnutt's refinement of a novel literary form—the short story—but also because he became one of the first African-American writers, like Paul Laurence Dunbar, to gain a national audience.

Chesnutt was born in Cleveland, Ohio, on June 20, 1858, to free parents of mixed blood who had come North from Fayetteville, North Carolina, two years before his birth. His father served in the Union Army during the Civil War, and after the war ended, in 1866 he moved his family South. In addition to his formal schooling there, Charles studied German, French, and Greek, read both classic and modern literature, and served as a teacher and principal at a number of schools in North and South Carolina. In 1878 he married Susan Perry and five years later moved North to New York, where he worked briefly as a reporter for the *New York Mail and Express,* and then to Cleveland, where he became a court stenographer and passed the Ohio bar exam in 1887. But while Chesnutt used his legal career to support his family, his true desire was to become a writer.

Chesnutt had published numerous early writings and sketches in small journals and Sunday supplements when his story "The Goophered Grapevine" appeared in *The Atlantic Monthly* in August 1887. The piece was well received and the magazine published two more of his conjure stories. But it was not until a decade later that Chesnutt could interest the publishing house Houghton Mifflin, which owned the *Atlantic,* in a collection of his fiction. Intrigued by the conjure element in several of the tales, the publisher asked to see a few more in that vein, and the seven stories in *The Conjure Woman* were published in March 1899.

The stories in that volume introduce a transplanted Northern businessman and his wife who become the proprietors of an overgrown vineyard. Through an elaborate framing device, in each tale the wily "Uncle" Julius McAdoo, an ex-slave who lives on the property, is confronted with some business venture imagined by the planter. Taking his cue from the planter's intentions, Julius weaves a tale of magical events that took place on the property before the war, inevitably persuading the planter, largely through the agency of his more sensitive wife, to abandon his plans to Julius's own benefit. Though the stories employ familiar characters and regional dialect, they refute the more popular image of plantation life conveyed in the Uncle Remus tales of Joel Chandler Harris, exposing the economic greed and human cruelty of the slavery period—particularly its debilitating effect on the family—and limning complex psychological portraits rooted in a particular place and time.

The Conjure Woman enjoyed considerable success, and a few months later the publisher brought out *The Wife of His Youth and Other Stories of the Color Line.* Taken together, the two volumes demonstrate Chesnutt's ability to portray a wide range of African-American characters, from ex-slaves of limited economic means who inherit the whirlwind of Reconstruction in the South to the milieu of the striving sophisticates of the imaginary Groveland, Ohio, and the intricacies of the color line and black prejudice in the North. While dialect is a strong component in the first volume of stories, the portraits drawn in the Northern tales that make up much of *The Wife of His Youth*—including the title story that follows—are as finely limned as those found in the fiction of manners of Chesnutt's white contemporaries. As he abandoned the more "colorful" dialect stories and his tales took on a grimmer visage appropriate to the rising tide of racial violence in the South, Chesnutt's critical reception and commercial success waned (one is struck again with a comparison to Dunbar). By 1902, Chesnutt was forced to resume his career as a legal stenographer.

Chesnutt also wrote three novels: *The House Behind the Cedars* (1900), which is concerned with interracial relationships; *The Marrow of Tradition* (1901), based on the brutal riots in Wilmington, North Carolina, in 1898; and *The Colonel's Dream* (1905), about a white Southern aristocrat who is driven from the South because of his liberal views on the race question. He is the author as well of six unpublished novels, numerous speeches, essays, and reviews, and a brief biography of Frederick Douglass. Critics remain divided over whether the stories or novels represent Chesnutt's best work; Henry Louis Gates has called *The Marrow of Tradition* "certainly the most sophisticated rendering of life in the historical period of the post-Reconstruction South that we have," while others argue that it is in his stories that Chesnutt's wit, sense of irony, and elegance achieve their greatest effect.

Po' Sandy

ON THE NORTHEAST CORNER OF MY VINEYARD IN CENTRAL North Carolina, and fronting on the Lumberton plank-road, there stood a small frame house, of the simplest construction. It was built of pine lumber, and contained but one room, to which one window gave light and one door admission. Its weather-beaten sides revealed a virgin innocence of paint. Against one end of the house, and occupying half its width, there stood a huge brick chimney: the crumbling mortar had left large cracks between the bricks; the bricks themselves had begun to scale off in large flakes, leaving the chimney sprinkled with unsightly blotches. These evidences of decay were but partially concealed by a creeping vine, which extended its slender branches hither and thither in an ambitious but futile attempt to cover the whole chimney. The wooden shutter, which had once protected the unglazed window, had fallen from its hinges, and lay rotting in the rank grass and jimson-weeds beneath. This building, I learned when I bought the place, had been used as a schoolhouse for several years prior to the breaking out of the war, since which time it had remained unoccupied, save when some stray cow or vagrant hog had sought shelter within its walls from the chill rains and nipping winds of winter.

One day my wife requested me to build her a new kitchen. The house erected by us, when we first came to live upon the vineyard, contained a very conveniently arranged kitchen; but for some occult reason my wife wanted a kitchen in the back yard, apart from the dwelling-house, after the usual Southern fashion. Of course I had to build it.

To save expense, I decided to tear down the old schoolhouse, and use the lumber, which was in a good state of preservation, in the construction of the new kitchen. Before demolishing the old house, however, I made an estimate of the amount of material contained in it, and found that I would have to buy several hundred feet of lumber additional, in order to build the new kitchen according to my wife's plan.

One morning old Julius McAdoo, our colored coachman, harnessed the gray mare to the rockaway, and drove my wife and me over to the sawmill from which I meant to order the new lumber. We drove down the long lane which led from our house to the plank-road; following the plank-road for about a mile, we turned into a road running through the forest and across the swamp to the sawmill beyond. Our carriage jolted over the half-rotted corduroy road which traversed the swamp, and then climbed the long hill leading to the sawmill. When we reached the mill, the foreman had gone over to a neighboring farmhouse, probably to smoke or gossip, and we were compelled to await his return before we could transact our business. We remained seated in the carriage, a few rods from the mill, and watched the leisurely movements of the mill-hands. We had not waited long before a huge pine log was placed in position, the machinery of the mill was set in motion, and the circular saw began to eat its way through the log, with a loud whir which resounded throughout the vicinity of the mill. The sound rose and fell in a sort of rhythmic cadence, which, heard from where we sat, was not unpleasing, and not loud enough to prevent conversation. When the saw started on its second journey through the log, Julius observed, in a lugubrious tone, and with a perceptible shudder:—

"Ugh! but dat des do cuddle my blood!"

"What's the matter, Uncle Julius?" inquired my wife, who is of a very sympathetic turn of mind. "Does the noise affect your nerves?"

"No, Mis' Annie," replied the old man, with emotion, "I ain' narvous; but dat saw, a-cuttin' en grindin' thoo dat stick er timber, en moanin', en groanin', en sweekin', kyars my 'memb'ance back ter ole times, en 'min's me er po' Sandy." The pathetic intonation with which he lengthened out the "po' Sandy" touched a responsive chord in our own hearts.

"And who was poor Sandy?" asked my wife, who takes a deep interest in the stories of plantation life which she hears from the lips of the older colored people. Some of these stories are quaintly humorous; others wildly extravagant, revealing the Oriental cast of the negro's imagination; while others, poured freely into the sympathetic ear of a Northern-bred woman, disclose many a tragic incident of the darker side of slavery.

"Sandy," said Julius, in reply to my wife's question, "was a nigger w'at useter b'long ter ole Mars Marrabo McSwayne. Mars Marrabo's place wuz on de yuther side'n de swamp, right nex' ter yo' place. Sandy wuz a monst'us good nigger, en could do so many things erbout a plantation, en alluz 'ten' ter his wuk so well, dat w'en Mars Marrabo's chilluns growed up en married off, dey all un 'em wanted dey daddy fer ter gin 'em Sandy fer a weddin' present. But Mars Marrabo knowed de res' would n' be satisfied ef he gin Sandy ter a'er one un 'em; so w'en dey wuz all done married, he fix it by 'lowin' one er his chilluns ter take Sandy fer a mont' er so, en den ernudder fer a mont' er so, en so on dat erway tel dey had all had 'im de same lenk er time; en den dey would all take him roun' ag'in, 'cep'n' oncet in a w'ile w'en Mars Marrabo would len' 'im ter some er his yuther kinfolks 'roun' de country, w'en dey wuz short er han's; tel bimeby it got so Sandy did n' hardly knowed whar he wuz gwine ter stay fum one week's een' ter de yuther.

"One time w'en Sandy wuz lent out ez yushal, a spekilater come erlong wid a lot er niggers, en Mars Marrabo swap' Sandy's wife off fer a noo 'oman. W'en Sandy come back, Mars Marrabo gin 'im a dollar, en 'lowed he wuz monst'us sorry fer ter break up de fambly, but de spekilater had gin 'im big boot, en times wuz hard en money skase, en so he wuz bleedst ter make de trade. Sandy tuk on some 'bout losin' his wife, but he soon seed dey want no use cryin' ober split merlasses; en bein' ez he lacked de looks er de noo 'oman, he tuk up wid her atter she'd be'n on de plantation a mont' er so.

"Sandy en his noo wife got on mighty well tergedder, en de niggers all 'mence' ter talk about how lovin' dey wuz. W'en Tenie wuz tuk sick oncet, Sandy useter set up all night wid 'er, en den go ter wuk in de mawnin' des lack he had his reg'lar sleep; en Tenie would 'a' done anythin' in de worl' for her Sandy.

"Sandy en Tenie had n' be'n libbin' tergedder fer mo' d'n two mont's befo' Mars Marrabo's old uncle, w'at libbed down in Robeson County, sent up ter fin' out ef Mars Marrabo could n' len' 'im er hire 'im a good han' fer a mont' er so. Sandy's marster wuz one er dese yer easy-gwine folks w'at wanter please eve'ybody, en he says yas, he could len' 'im Sandy. En Mars Marrabo tol' Sandy fer ter git ready ter go down ter Robeson nex' day, fer ter stay a mont' er so.

"It wuz monst'us hard on Sandy fer ter take 'im 'way fum Tenie. It wuz so fur down ter Robeson dat he did n' hab no chance er comin' back ter see her tel de time wuz up; he would n' 'a' mine comin' ten er fifteen mile at night ter see Tenie, but Mars Marrabo's uncle's plantation wuz mo' d'n forty mile off. Sandy wuz mighty sad en cas' down atter w'at Mars Marrabo tol' 'im, en he says ter Tenie, sezee:—

" 'I'm gittin' monst'us ti'ed er dish yer gwine roun' so much. Here I is lent ter Mars Jeems dis mont', en I got ter do so-en-so; en ter Mars Archie de nex' mont', en I got ter do so-en-so; den I got ter go ter Miss Jinnie's: en hit's Sandy dis en Sandy dat, en Sandy yer en Sandy dere, tel it 'pears ter me I ain' got no home, ner no marster, ner no mistiss, ner no nuffin. I can't eben keep a wife: my yuther ole 'oman wuz sol' away without my gittin' a chance fer ter tell her good-by; en now I got ter go off en leab you, Tenie, en I dunno whe'r I'm eber gwine ter see you ag'in er no. I wisht I wuz a tree, er a stump, er a rock, er sump'n w'at could stay on de plantation fer a w'ile.'

"Atter Sandy got thoo talkin', Tenie did n' say naer word, but des sot dere by de fier, studyin' en studyin'. Bimeby she up'n' says:—

" 'Sandy, is I eber tol' you I wuz a cunjuh 'oman?'

"Co'se Sandy had n' nebber dremp' er nuffin lack dat, en he made a great 'miration w'en he hear w'at Tenie say. Bimeby Tenie went on:—

" 'I ain' goophered nobody, ner done no cunjuh wuk, fer fifteen year er mo'; en w'en I got religion I made up my mine I would n' wuk no mo' goopher. But dey is some things I doan b'lieve it's no sin fer ter do; en ef you doan wanter be sent roun' fum pillar ter pos', en ef you doan wanter go down ter Robeson, I kin fix things so you won't haf ter. Ef you'll des say de word, I kin turn you ter w'ateber you wanter be, en you kin stay right whar you wanter, ez long ez you mineter.'

"Sandy say he doan keer; he's willin' fer ter do anythin' fer ter stay close ter Tenie. Den Tenie ax 'im ef he doan wanter be turnt inter a rabbit.

"Sandy say, 'No, de dogs mought git atter me.'

" 'Shill I turn you ter a wolf?' sez Tenie.

" 'No, eve'ybody skeered er a wolf, en I doan want nobody ter be skeered er me.'

" 'Shill I turn you ter a mawkin'-bird?'

" 'No, a hawk mought ketch me. I wanter be turnt inter sump'n w'at 'll stay in one place.'

" 'I kin turn you ter a tree,' sez Tenie. 'You won't hab no mouf ner years, but I kin turn you back oncet in a w'ile, so you kin git sump'n ter eat, en hear w'at's gwine on.'

"Well, Sandy say dat 'll do. En so Tenie tuk 'im down by de aidge er de swamp, not fur fum de quarters, en turnt 'im inter a big pine-tree, en sot 'im out 'mongs' some yuther trees. En de nex' mawnin', ez some er de fiel' han's wuz gwine long dere, dey seed a tree w'at dey did n' 'member er habbin' seed befo'; it wuz monst'us quare, en dey wuz bleedst ter 'low dat dey had n' 'membered right, er e'se one er de saplin's had be'n growin' monst'us fas'.

"W'en Mars Marrabo 'skiver' dat Sandy wuz gone, he 'lowed Sandy had runned away. He got de dogs out, but de las' place dey could track Sandy ter wuz de foot er dat pine-tree. En dere de dogs stood en barked, en bayed, en pawed at de tree, en tried ter climb up on it; en w'en dey wuz tuk roun' thoo de swamp ter look fer de scent, dey broke loose en made fer dat tree ag'in. It wuz de beatenis' thing de w'ite folks eber hearn of, en Mars Marrabo 'lowed dat Sandy must 'a' clim' up on de tree en jump' off on a mule er sump'n, en rid fur ernuff fer ter spile de scent. Mars Marrabo wanted ter 'cuse some er de yuther niggers er heppin' Sandy off, but dey all 'nied it ter de las'; en eve'ybody knowed Tenie sot too much sto' by Sandy fer ter he'p 'im run away whar she could n' nebber see 'im no mo'.

"W'en Sandy had be'n gone long ernuff fer folks ter think he done got clean away, Tenie useter go down ter de woods at night en turn 'im back, en den dey 'd slip up ter de cabin en set by de fire en talk. But dey ha' ter be monst'us keerful, er e'se somebody would 'a' seed 'em, en dat would 'a' spile' de whole thing; so Tenie alluz turnt Sandy back in de mawnin' early, befo' anybody wuz a-stirrin'.

"But Sandy did n' git erlong widout his trials en tribberlations. One day a woodpecker come erlong en 'mence' ter peck at de tree; en de nex' time Sandy wuz turnt back he had a little roun' hole in his arm, des lack a sharp stick be'n stuck in it. Atter dat Tenie sot a sparrer-hawk fer ter watch de tree; en w'en de woodpecker come erlong nex' mawnin' fer ter finish his nes', he got gobble' up mos'fo' he stuck his bill in de bark.

"Nudder time, Mars Marrabo sent a nigger out in de woods fer ter chop tuppentime boxes. De man chop a box in dish yer tree, en hack' de bark up two er th'ee feet, fer ter let de tuppentime run. De nex' time Sandy wuz turnt back he had a big skyar on his lef' leg, des lack it be'n skunt; en it tuk Tenie nigh 'bout all night fer ter fix a mixtry ter kyo it up. Atter dat,

Tenie sot a hawnet fer ter watch de tree; en w'en de nigger come back ag'in fer ter cut ernudder box on de yuther side'n de tree, de hawnet stung 'im so hard dat de ax slip en cut his foot nigh 'bout off.

"W'en Tenie see so many things happenin' ter de tree, she 'cluded she'd ha' ter turn Sandy ter sump'n e'se; en atter studyin' de matter ober, en talkin' wid Sandy one ebenin', she made up her mine fer ter fix up a goopher mixtry w'at would turn herse'f en Sandy ter foxes, er sump'n, so dey could run away en go some'rs whar dey could be free en lib lack w'ite folks.

"But dey ain' no tellin' w'at 's gwine ter happen in dis worl'. Tenie had got de night sot fer her en Sandy ter run away, w'en dat ve'y day one er Mars Marrabo's sons rid up ter de big house in his buggy, en say his wife wuz monst'us sick, en he want his mammy ter len' 'im a 'oman fer ter nuss his wife. Tenie's mistiss say sen' Tenie; she wuz a good nuss. Young mars wuz in a tarrible hurry fer ter git back home. Tenie wuz washin' at de big house dat day, en her mistiss say she should go right 'long wid her young marster. Tenie tried ter make some 'scuse fer ter git away en hide 'tel night, w'en she would have eve'ything fix' up fer her en Sandy; she say she wanter go ter her cabin fer ter git her bonnet. Her mistiss say it doan matter 'bout de bonnet; her head-hankcher wuz good ernuff. Den Tenie say she wanter git her bes' frock; her mistiss say no, she doan need no mo' frock, en w'en dat one got dirty she could git a clean one whar she wuz gwine. So Tenie had ter git in de buggy en go 'long wid young Mars Dunkin ter his plantation, w'ich wuz mo' d'n twenty mile away; en dey wa'n't no chance er her seein' Sandy no mo' 'tel she come back home. De po' gal felt monst'us bad 'bout de way things wuz gwine on, en she knowed Sandy mus' be a wond'rin' why she did n' come en turn 'im back no mo'.

"W'iles Tenie wuz away nussin' young Mars Dunkin's wife, Mars Marrabo tuk a notion fer ter buil' 'im a noo kitchen; en bein' ez he had lots er timber on his place, he begun ter look 'roun' fer a tree ter hab de lumber sawed out'n. En I dunno how it come to be so, but he happen fer ter hit on de ve'y tree w'at Sandy wuz turnt inter. Tenie wuz gone, en dey wa'n't nobody ner nuffin fer ter watch de tree.

"De two men w'at cut de tree down say dey nebber had sech a time wid a tree befo': dey axes would glansh off, en did n' 'pear ter make no progress thoo de wood; en of all de creakin', en shakin', en wobblin' you eber see, dat tree done it w'en it commence' ter fall. It wuz de beatenis' thing!

"W'en dey got de tree all trim' up, dey chain it up ter a timber waggin, en start fer de sawmill. But dey had a hard time gittin' de log dere: fus' dey got stuck in de mud w'en dey wuz gwine crosst de swamp, en it wuz two er th'ee hours befo' dey could git out. W'en dey start' on ag'in, de chain kep' a-comin' loose, en dey had ter keep a-stoppin' en a-stoppin' fer ter hitch de log up ag'in. W'en dey commence' ter climb de hill ter de sawmill, de log broke loose, en roll down de hill en in 'mongs' de trees, en hit tuk nigh 'bout half a day mo' ter git it haul' up ter de sawmill.

"De nex' mawnin' atter de day de tree wuz haul' ter de sawmill, Tenie come home. W'en she got back ter her cabin, de fus' thing she done wuz ter run down ter de woods en see how Sandy wuz gittin' on. W'en she seed de stump standin' dere, wid de sap runnin' out'n it, en de limbs layin' scattered roun', she nigh 'bout went out'n her min'. She run ter her cabin, en got her goopher mixtry, en den follered de track er de timber waggin ter de sawmill. She knowed Sandy could n' lib mo' d'n a minute er so ef she turnt him back, fer he wuz all chop' up so he 'd 'a' be'n bleedst ter die. But she wanted ter turn 'im back long ernuff fer ter 'splain ter 'im dat she had n' went off a-purpose, en lef' 'im ter be chop' down en sawed up. She did n' want Sandy ter die wid no hard feelin's to'ds her.

"De han's at de sawmill had des got de big log on de kerridge, en wuz startin' up de saw, w'en dey seed a 'oman runnin' up de hill, all out er bref, cryin' en gwine on des lack she wuz plumb 'stracted. It wuz Tenie; she come right inter de mill, en th'owed herse'f on de log, right in front er de saw, a-hollerin' en cryin' ter her Sandy ter fergib her, en not ter think hard er her, fer it wa'n't no fault er hern. Den Tenie 'membered de tree did n' hab no years, en she wuz gittin' ready fer ter wuk her goopher mixtry so ez ter turn Sandy back, w'en de mill-hands kotch holt er her en tied her arms wid a rope, en fasten' her to one er de posts in de sawmill; en den dey started de saw up ag'in, en cut de log up inter bo'ds en scantlin's right befo' her eyes. But it wuz mighty hard wuk; fer of all de sweekin', en moanin', en groanin', dat log done it w'iles de saw wuz a-cuttin' thoo it. De saw wuz one er dese yer ole-timey, up-en-down saws, en hit tuk longer dem days ter saw a log 'en it do now. Dey greased de saw, but dat did n' stop de fuss; hit kep' right on, tel fin'ly dey got de log all sawed up.

"W'en de oberseah w'at run de sawmill come fum breakfas', de han's up en tell him 'bout de crazy 'oman—ez dey s'posed she wuz—w'at had come runnin' in de sawmill, a-hollerin' en gwine on, en tried ter th'ow herse'f befo' de saw. En de oberseah sent two er th'ee er de han's fer ter take Tenie back ter her marster's plantation.

"Tenie 'peared ter be out'n her min' fer a long time, en her marster ha' ter lock her up in de smoke-'ouse 'tel she got ober her spells. Mars Marrabo wuz monst'us mad, en hit would 'a' made yo' flesh crawl fer ter hear him cuss, 'caze he say de spekilater w'at he got Tenie fum had fooled 'im by wukkin' a crazy 'oman off on him. W'iles Tenie wuz lock up in de smoke-'ouse, Mars Marrabo tuk 'n' haul de lumber fum de sawmill, en put up his noo kitchen.

"W'en Tenie got quiet' down, so she could be 'lowed ter go 'roun' de plantation, she up'n' tole her marster all erbout Sandy en de pine-tree; en w'en Mars Marrabo hearn it, he 'lowed she wuz de wuss 'stracted nigger he eber hearn of. He did n' know w'at ter do wid Tenie: fus' he thought he'd put her in de po'-house; but fin'ly, seein' ez she did n' do no harm ter nobody ner nuffin, but des went 'roun' moanin', en groanin', en shakin' her head, he 'cluded ter let her stay on de plantation en nuss de little nigger chilluns w'en dey mammies wuz ter wuk in de cotton-fiel'.

"De noo kitchen Mars Marrabo buil' wuz n' much use, fer it had n' be'n put up long befo' de niggers 'mence' ter notice quare things erbout it. Dey could hear sump'n moanin' en groanin' 'bout de kitchen in de night-time, en w'en de win' would blow dey could hear sump'n a-hollerin' en sweekin' lack it wuz in great pain en sufferin'. En it got so atter a w'ile dat it wuz all Mars Marrabo's wife could do ter git a 'oman ter stay in de kitchen in de daytime long ernuff ter do de cookin'; en dey wa'n't naer nigger on de plantation w'at would n' rudder take forty dan ter go 'bout dat kitchen atter dark,—dat is, 'cep'n' Tenie; she did n' 'pear ter min' de ha'nts. She useter slip 'roun' at night, en set on de kitchen steps, en lean up agin de do'-jamb, en run on ter herse 'f wid some kine er foolishness w'at nobody could n' make out; fer Mars Marrabo had th'eaten' ter sen' her off'n de plantation ef she say anything ter any er de yuther niggers 'bout de pine-tree. But somehow er 'nudder de niggers foun' out all erbout it, en dey all knowed de kitchen wuz ha'nted by Sandy's sperrit. En bimeby hit got so Mars Marrabo's wife herse'f wuz skeered ter go out in de yard atter dark.

"W'en it come ter dat, Mars Marrabo tuk en to' de kitchen down, en use' de lumber fer ter buil' dat ole school'ouse w'at you er talkin' 'bout pullin' down. De school'ouse wuz n' use' 'cep'n' in de daytime, en on dark nights folks gwine 'long de road would hear quare soun's en see quare things. Po' ole Tenie useter go down dere at night, en wander 'roun' de school'ouse; en de niggers all 'lowed she went fer ter talk wid Sandy's sperrit. En one winter mawnin', w'en one er de boys went ter school early fer ter start de fire, w'at should he fin' but po' ole Tenie, layin' on de flo', stiff, en col', en dead. Dere did n' 'pear ter be nuffin pertickler de matter wid her,—she had des grieve' herse'f ter def fer her Sandy. Mars Marrabo did n' shed no tears. He thought Tenie wuz crazy, en dey wa'n't no tellin' w'at she mought do nex'; en dey ain' much room in dis worl' fer crazy w'ite folks, let 'lone a crazy nigger.

"Hit wa'n't long atter dat befo' Mars Marrabo sol' a piece er his track er lan' ter Mars Dugal' McAdoo,—*my* ole marster,—en dat's how de ole school'ouse happen to be on yo' place. W'en de wah broke out, de school stop', en de ole school'ouse be'n stannin' empty ever sence,—dat is, 'cep'n' fer de ha'nts. En folks sez dat de ole school'ouse, er any yuther house w'at got any er dat lumber in it w'at wuz sawed out'n de tree w'at Sandy wuz turnt inter, is gwine ter be ha'nted tel de las' piece er plank is rotted en crumble' inter dus'."

Annie had listened to this gruesome narrative with strained attention.

"What a system it was," she exclaimed, when Julius had finished, "under which such things were possible!"

"What things?" I asked, in amazement. "Are you seriously considering the possibility of a man's being turned into a tree?"

"Oh, no," she replied quickly, "not that;" and then she murmured absently, and with a dim look in her fine eyes, "Poor Tenie!"

We ordered the lumber, and returned home. That night, after we had gone to bed, and my wife had to all appearances been sound asleep for half an hour, she startled me out of an incipient doze by exclaiming suddenly,—

"John, I don't believe I want my new kitchen built out of the lumber in that old schoolhouse."

"You would n't for a moment allow yourself," I replied, with some asperity, "to be influenced by that absurdly impossible yarn which Julius was spinning to-day?"

"I know the story is absurd," she replied dreamily, "and I am not so silly as to believe it. But I don't think I should ever be able to take any pleasure in that kitchen if it were built out of that lumber. Besides, I think the kitchen would look better and last longer if the lumber were all new."

Of course she had her way. I bought the new lumber, though not without grumbling. A week or two later I was called away from home on business. On my return, after an absence of several days, my wife remarked to me,—

"John, there has been a split in the Sandy Run Colored Baptist Church, on the temperance question. About half the members have come out from the main body, and set up for themselves. Uncle Julius is one of the seceders, and he came to me yesterday and asked if they might not hold their meetings in the old schoolhouse for the present."

"I hope you did n't let the old rascal have it," I returned, with some warmth. I had just received a bill for the new lumber I had bought.

"Well," she replied, "I could n't refuse him the use of the house for so good a purpose."

"And I'll venture to say," I continued, "that you subscribed something toward the support of the new church?"

She did not attempt to deny it.

"What are they going to do about the ghost?" I asked, somewhat curious to know how Julius would get around this obstacle.

"Oh," replied Annie, "Uncle Julius says that ghosts never disturb religious worship, but that if Sandy's spirit *should* happen to stray into meeting by mistake, no doubt the preaching would do it good."

The Wife of His Youth

I

MR. RYDER WAS GOING TO GIVE A BALL. THERE WERE SEVERAL reasons why this was an opportune time for such an event.

Mr. Ryder might aptly be called the dean of the Blue Veins. The original Blue Veins were a little society of colored persons organized in a certain Northern city shortly after the war. Its purpose was to establish and maintain correct social standards among a people whose social condition presented almost unlimited room for improvement. By accident, combined perhaps with some natural affinity, the society consisted of individuals who were, generally speaking, more white than black. Some envious outsider made the suggestion that no one was eligible for membership who was not white enough to show blue veins. The suggestion was readily adopted by those who were not of the favored few, and since that time the society, though possessing a longer and more pretentious name, had been known far and wide as the "Blue Vein Society," and its members as the "Blue Veins."

The Blue Veins did not allow that any such requirement existed for admission to their circle, but, on the contrary, declared that character and culture were the only things considered; and that if most of their members were light-colored, it was because such persons, as a rule, had had better opportunities to qualify themselves for membership. Opinions differed, too, as to the usefulness of the society. There were those who had been known to assail it violently as a glaring example of the very prejudice from which the colored race had suffered most; and later, when such critics had succeeded in getting on the inside, they had been heard to maintain with zeal and earnestness that the society was a lifeboat, an anchor, a bulwark and a shield,—a pillar of cloud by day and of fire by night, to guide their people through the social wilderness. Another alleged prerequisite for Blue Vein membership was that of free birth; and while there was really no such requirement, it is doubtless true that very few of the members would have been unable to meet it if there had been. If there were one or two of the older members who had come up from the South and from slavery, their history presented enough romantic circumstances to rob their servile origin of its grosser aspects.

While there were no such tests of eligibility, it is true that the Blue Veins had their notions on these subjects, and that not all of them were equally liberal in regard to the things they collectively disclaimed. Mr. Ryder was one of the most conservative. Though he had not been among the founders of the society, but had come in some years later, his genius for social leadership was such that he had speedily become its recognized adviser and head, the custodian of its standards, and the preserver of its traditions.

He shaped its social policy, was active in providing for its entertainment, and when the interest fell off, as it sometimes did, he fanned the embers until they burst again into a cheerful flame.

There were still other reasons for his popularity. While he was not as white as some of the Blue Veins, his appearance was such as to confer distinction upon them. His features were of a refined type, his hair was almost straight; he was always neatly dressed; his manners were irreproachable, and his morals above suspicion. He had come to Groveland a young man, and obtaining employment in the office of a railroad company as messenger had in time worked himself up to the position of stationery clerk, having charge of the distribution of the office supplies for the whole company. Although the lack of early training had hindered the orderly development of a naturally fine mind, it had not prevented him from doing a great deal of reading or from forming decidedly literary tastes. Poetry was his passion. He could repeat whole pages of the great English poets; and if his pronunciation was sometimes faulty, his eye, his voice, his gestures, would respond to the changing sentiment with a precision that revealed a poetic soul and disarmed criticism. He was economical, and had saved money; he owned and occupied a very comfortable house on a respectable street. His residence was handsomely furnished, containing among other things a good library, especially rich in poetry, a piano, and some choice engravings. He generally shared his house with some young couple, who looked after his wants and were company for him; for Mr. Ryder was a single man. In the early days of his connection with the Blue Veins he had been regarded as quite a catch, and young ladies and their mothers had manoeuvred with much ingenuity to capture him. Not, however, until Mrs. Molly Dixon visited Groveland had any woman ever made him wish to change his condition to that of a married man.

Mrs. Dixon had come to Groveland from Washington in the spring, and before the summer was over she had won Mr. Ryder's heart. She possessed many attractive qualities. She was much younger than he; in fact, he was old enough to have been her father, though no one knew exactly how old he was. She was whiter than he, and better educated. She had moved in the best colored society of the country, at Washington, and had taught in the schools of that city. Such a superior person had been eagerly welcomed to the Blue Vein Society, and had taken a leading part in its activities. Mr. Ryder had at first been attracted by her charms of person, for she was very good looking and not over twenty-five; then by her refined manners and the vivacity of her wit. Her husband had been a government clerk, and at his death had left a considerable life insurance. She was visiting friends in Groveland, and, finding the town and the people to her liking, had prolonged her stay indefinitely. She had not seemed displeased at Mr. Ryder's attentions, but on the contrary had given him every proper encouragement; indeed, a younger and less cautious man would long since have spoken. But he had made up his mind, and had only to determine the time when he would ask her to be his wife. He decided to give a ball in her honor, and at some time during the evening of the ball to offer her his heart and hand. He had no special fears about the outcome, but, with a little touch of romance, he wanted the surroundings to be in harmony with his own feelings when he should have received the answer he expected.

Mr. Ryder resolved that this ball should mark an epoch in the social history of Groveland. He knew, of course,—no one could know better,— the entertainments that had taken place in past years, and what must be done to surpass them. His ball must be worthy of the lady in whose honor it was to be given, and must, by the quality of its guests, set an example for the future. He had observed of late a growing liberality, almost a laxity, in social matters, even among members of his own set, and had several times been forced to meet in a social way persons whose complexions and callings in life were hardly up to the standard which he considered proper for the society to maintain. He had a theory of his own.

"I have no race prejudice," he would say, "but we people of mixed blood are ground between the upper and the nether millstone. Our fate lies between absorption by the white race and extinction in the black. The one does n't want us yet, but may take us in time. The other would welcome us, but it would be for us a backward step. 'With malice towards none, with charity for all,' we must do the best we can for ourselves and those who are to follow us. Self-preservation is the first law of nature."

His ball would serve by its exclusiveness to counteract leveling tendencies, and his marriage with Mrs. Dixon would help to further the upward process of absorption he had been wishing and waiting for.

II

The ball was to take place on Friday night. The house had been put in order, the carpets covered with canvas, the halls and stairs decorated with palms and potted plants; and in the afternoon Mr. Ryder sat on his front porch, which the shade of a vine running up over a wire netting made a cool and pleasant lounging place. He expected to respond to the toast "The Ladies" at the supper, and from a volume of Tennyson—his favorite poet— was fortifying himself with apt quotations. The volume was open at "A Dream of Fair Women." His eyes fell on these lines, and he read them aloud to judge better of their effect:—

"At length I saw a lady within call,
  Stiller than chisell'd marble, standing there;
A daughter of the gods, divinely tall,
  And most divinely fair."

He marked the verse, and turning the page read the stanza beginning,—

"O sweet pale Margaret,
O rare pale Margaret."

He weighed the passage a moment, and decided that it would not do. Mrs. Dixon was the palest lady he expected at the ball, and she was of a rather ruddy complexion, and of lively disposition and buxom build. So he ran over the leaves until his eye rested on the description of Queen Guinevere:—

"She seem'd a part of joyous Spring:
A gown of grass-green silk she wore,
Buckled with golden clasps before;
A light-green tuft of plumes she bore
Closed in a golden ring.

. . .

"She look'd so lovely, as she sway'd
The rein with dainty finger-tips,
A man had given all other bliss,
And all his worldly worth for this,
To waste his whole heart in one kiss
Upon her perfect lips."

As Mr. Ryder murmured these words audibly, with an appreciative thrill, he heard the latch of his gate click, and a light footfall sounding on the steps. He turned his head, and saw a woman standing before his door.

She was a little woman, not five feet tall, and proportioned to her height. Although she stood erect, and looked around her with very bright and restless eyes, she seemed quite old; for her face was crossed and recrossed with a hundred wrinkles, and around the edges of her bonnet could be seen protruding here and there a tuft of short gray wool. She wore a blue calico gown of ancient cut, a little red shawl fastened around her shoulders with an old-fashioned brass brooch, and a large bonnet profusely ornamented with faded red and yellow artificial flowers. And she was very black, —so black that her toothless gums, revealed when she opened her mouth to speak, were not red, but blue. She looked like a bit of the old plantation life, summoned up from the past by the wave of a magician's wand, as the poet's fancy had called into being the gracious shapes of which Mr. Ryder had just been reading.

He rose from his chair and came over to where she stood.

"Good-afternoon, madam," he said.

"Good-evenin', suh," she answered, ducking suddenly with a quaint curtsy. Her voice was shrill and piping, but softened somewhat by age. "Is dis yere whar Mistuh Ryduh lib, suh?" she asked, looking around her doubtfully, and glancing into the open windows, through which some of the preparations for the evening were visible.

"Yes," he replied, with an air of kindly patronage, unconsciously flattered by her manner, "I am Mr. Ryder. Did you want to see me?"

"Yas, suh, ef I ain't 'sturbin' of you too much."

"Not at all. Have a seat over here behind the vine, where it is cool. What can I do for you?"

" 'Scuse me, suh," she continued, when she had sat down on the edge of a chair, " 'scuse me, suh, I's lookin for my husban'. I heerd you wuz a big man an' had libbed heah a long time, an' I 'lowed you would n't min' ef I'd come roun' an' ax you ef you'd ever heerd of a merlatter man by de name er Sam Taylor 'quirin' roun' in de chu'ches ermongs' de people fer his wife 'Liza Jane?"

Mr. Ryder seemed to think for a moment.

"There used to be many such cases right after the war," he said, "but it has been so long that I have forgotten them. There are very few now. But tell me your story, and it may refresh my memory."

She sat back farther in her chair so as to be more comfortable, and folded her withered hands in her lap.

"My name's 'Liza," she began, " 'Liza Jane. W'en I wuz young I us'ter b'long ter Marse Bob Smif, down in ole Missoura. I wuz bawn down dere. W'en I wuz a gal I wuz married ter a man named Jim. But Jim died, an' after dat I married a merlatter man named Sam Taylor. Sam wuz free-bawn, but his mammy and daddy died, an' de w'ite folks 'prenticed him ter my marster fer ter work fer 'im 'tel he wuz growed up. Sam worked in de fiel', an' I wuz de cook. One day Ma'y Ann, old miss's maid, came rushin' out ter de kitchen, an' says she, ' 'Liza Jane, ole marse gwine sell yo' Sam down de ribber.'

" 'Go way f'm yere,' says I; 'my husban's free!'

" 'Don' make no diff'ence. I heerd ole marse tell ole miss he wuz gwine take yo' Sam 'way wid 'im ter-morrow, fer he needed money, an' he knowed whar he could git a t'ousan' dollars for Sam an' no questions axed.'

"W'en Sam come home f'm de fiel' dat night, I tole him 'bout ole marse gwine steal 'im, an' Sam run erway. His time wuz mos' up, an' he swo' dat w'en he wuz twenty-one he would come back an' he'p me run erway, er else save up de money ter buy my freedom. An' I know he'd 'a' done it, fer he thought a heap er me, Sam did. But w'en he come back he did n' fin' me, fer I wuz n' dere. Ole marse had heerd dat I warned Sam, so he had me whip' an' sol' down de ribber.

"Den de wah broke out, an' w'en it wuz ober de cullud folks wuz scattered. I went back ter de ole home; but Sam wuz n' dere, an' I could n' l'arn nuffin' 'bout 'im. But I knowed he 'd be'n dere to look fer me an' had n' foun' me, an' had gone erway ter hunt fer me.

"I's be'n lookin' fer 'im eber sence," she added simply, as though twenty-five years were but a couple of weeks, "an' I knows he's be'n lookin' fer me. Fer he sot a heap er sto' by me, Sam did, an' I know he's be'n huntin' fer me all dese years,—'less'n he's be'n sick er sump'n, so he could n' work, er out'n his head, so he could n' 'member his promise. I went back down de ribber, fer I 'lowed he'd gone down dere lookin' fer me. I's be'n ter Noo Orleens, an' Atlanty, an' Charleston, an' Richmon'; an' w'en I'd be'n all ober de Souf I come ter de Norf. Fer I knows I'll fin' 'im some er dese days," she added softly, "er he 'll fin' me, an' den we 'll bofe be as happy in freedom as we wuz in de ole days befo' de wah." A smile stole over her withered countenance as she paused a moment, and her bright eyes softened into a faraway look.

This was the substance of the old woman's story. She had wandered a little here and there. Mr. Ryder was looking at her curiously when she finished.

"How have you lived all these years?" he asked.

"Cookin', suh. I's a good cook. Does you know anybody w'at needs a good cook, suh? I's stoppin' wid a cullud fam'ly roun' de corner yonder 'tel I kin git a place."

"Do you really expect to find your husband? He may be dead long ago."

She shook her head emphatically. "Oh no, he ain' dead. De signs an' de tokens tells me. I dremp three nights runnin' on'y dis las' week dat I foun' him."

"He may have married another woman. Your slave marriage would not have prevented him, for you never lived with him after the war, and without that your marriage does n't count."

"Would n' make no diff'ence wid Sam. He would n' marry no yuther 'ooman 'tel he foun' out 'bout me. I knows it," she added. "Sump'n 's be'n tellin' me all dese years dat I's gwine fin' Sam 'fo' I dies."

"Perhaps he's outgrown you, and climbed up in the world where he would n't care to have you find him."

"No, indeed, suh," she replied, "Sam ain' dat kin' er man. He wuz good ter me, Sam wuz, but he wuz n' much good ter nobody e'se, fer he wuz one er de triflin'es' han's on de plantation. I 'spec's ter haf ter suppo't 'im w'en I fin' 'im, fer he nebber would work 'less'n he had ter. But den he wuz free, an' he did n' git no pay fer his work, an' I don' blame 'im much. Mebbe he's done better sence he run erway, but I ain' 'spectin' much."

"You may have passed him on the street a hundred times during the twenty-five years, and not have known him; time works great changes."

She smiled incredulously. "I'd know 'im 'mongs' a hund'ed men. Fer dey wuz n' no yuther merlatter man like my man Sam, an' I could n' be mistook. I 's toted his picture roun' wid me twenty-five years."

"May I see it?" asked Mr. Ryder. "It might help me to remember whether I have seen the original."

As she drew a small parcel from her bosom he saw that it was fastened to a string that went around her neck. Removing several wrappers, she brought to light an old-fashioned daguerreotype in a black case. He looked long and intently at the portrait. It was faded with time, but the features were still distinct, and it was easy to see what manner of man it had represented.

He closed the case, and with a slow movement handed it back to her.

"I don't know of any man in town who goes by that name," he said, "nor have I heard of any one making such inquiries. But if you will leave me your address, I will give the matter some attention, and if I find out anything I will let you know."

She gave him the number of a house in the neighborhood, and went away, after thanking him warmly.

He wrote the address on the fly-leaf of the volume of Tennyson, and, when she had gone, rose to his feet and stood looking after her curiously. As she walked down the street with mincing step, he saw several persons whom she passed turn and look back at her with a smile of kindly amusement. When she had turned the corner, he went upstairs to his bedroom, and stood for a long time before the mirror of his dressing-case, gazing thoughtfully at the reflection of his own face.

III

At eight o'clock the ballroom was a blaze of light and the guests had begun to assemble; for there was a literary programme and some routine business of the society to be gone through with before the dancing. A black servant in evening dress waited at the door and directed the guests to the dressing-rooms.

The occasion was long memorable among the colored people of the city; not alone for the dress and display, but for the high average of intelligence and culture that distinguished the gathering as a whole. There were a number of school-teachers, several young doctors, three or four lawyers, some professional singers, an editor, a lieutenant in the United States army spending his furlough in the city, and others in various polite callings; these were colored, though most of them would not have attracted even a casual glance because of any marked difference from white people. Most of the ladies were in evening costume, and dress coats and dancing pumps were the rule among the men. A band of string music, stationed in an alcove behind a row of palms, played popular airs while the guests were gathering.

The dancing began at half past nine. At eleven o'clock supper was served. Mr. Ryder had left the ballroom some little time before the intermission, but reappeared at the supper-table. The spread was worthy of the occasion, and the guests did full justice to it. When the coffee had been served, the toast-master, Mr. Solomon Sadler, rapped for order. He made a brief introductory speech, complimenting host and guests, and then presented in their order the toasts of the evening. They were responded to with a very fair display of after-dinner wit.

"The last toast," said the toast-master, when he reached the end of the list, "is one which must appeal to us all. There is no one of us of the sterner sex who is not at some time dependent upon woman,—in infancy for protection, in manhood for companionship, in old age for care and comforting. Our good host has been trying to live alone, but the fair faces I see around me to-night prove that he too is largely dependent upon the gentler sex for most that makes life worth living,—the society and love of friends,—and rumor is at fault if he does not soon yield entire subjection to one of them. Mr. Ryder will now respond to the toast,—The Ladies."

There was a pensive look in Mr. Ryder's eyes as he took the floor and adjusted his eyeglasses. He began by speaking of woman as the gift of Heaven to man, and after some general observations on the relations of the sexes he said: "But perhaps the quality which most distinguishes woman is her fidelity and devotion to those she loves. History is full of examples, but has recorded none more striking than one which only to-day came under my notice."

He then related, simply but effectively, the story told by his visitor of the afternoon. He gave it in the same soft dialect, which came readily to his lips, while the company listened attentively and sympathetically. For the story had awakened a responsive thrill in many hearts. There were some present who had seen, and others who had heard their fathers and grandfathers tell, the wrongs and sufferings of this past generation, and all of them still felt, in their darker moments, the shadow hanging over them. Mr. Ryder went on:—

"Such devotion and confidence are rare even among women. There are many who would have searched a year, some who would have waited five years, a few who might have hoped ten years; but for twenty-five years this woman has retained her affection for and her faith in a man she has not seen or heard of in all that time.

"She came to me to-day in the hope that I might be able to help her find this long-lost husband. And when she was gone I gave my fancy rein, and imagined a case I will put to you.

"Suppose that this husband, soon after his escape, had learned that his wife had been sold away, and that such inquiries as he could make brought no information of her whereabouts. Suppose that he was young, and she much older than he; that he was light, and she was black; that their marriage was a slave marriage, and legally binding only if they chose to make it so after the war. Suppose, too, that he made his way to the North, as some of us have done, and there, where he had larger opportunities, had improved them, and had in the course of all these years grown to be as different from the ignorant boy who ran away from fear of slavery as the day is from the night. Suppose, even, that he had qualified himself, by industry, by thrift, and by study, to win the friendship and be considered worthy the society of such people as these I see around me to-night, gracing my board and filling my heart with gladness; for I am old enough to remember the day when such a gathering would not have been possible in this land. Suppose, too, that, as the years went by, this man's memory of the past grew more and more indistinct, until at last it was rarely, except in his dreams, that any image of his bygone period rose before his mind. And then suppose that accident should bring to his knowledge the fact that the wife of his youth, the wife he had left behind him, —not one who had walked by his side and kept pace with him in his upward struggle, but one upon whom advancing years and a laborious life had set their mark,—was alive and seeking him, but that he was absolutely safe from recognition or discovery, unless he chose to reveal himself. My friends, what would the man do? I will presume that he was one who loved honor, and tried to deal justly with all men. I will even carry the case further, and suppose that perhaps he had set his heart upon another, whom he had hoped to call his own. What would he do, or rather what ought he to do, in such a crisis of a lifetime?

"It seemed to me that he might hesitate, and I imagined that I was an old friend, a near friend, and that he had come to me for advice; and I argued the case with him. I tried to discuss it impartially. After we had looked upon the matter from every point of view, I said to him, in words that we all know:—

'This above all: to thine own self be true,
And it must follow, as the night the day,
Thou canst not then be false to any man.'

"Then, finally, I put the question to him, 'Shall you acknowledge her?'

"And now, ladies and gentlemen, friends and companions, I ask you, what should he have done?"

There was something in Mr. Ryder's voice that stirred the hearts of those who sat around him. It suggested more than mere sympathy with an imaginary situation; it seemed rather in the nature of a personal appeal. It was observed, too, that his look rested more especially upon Mrs. Dixon, with a mingled expression of renunciation and inquiry.

She had listened, with parted lips and streaming eyes. She was the first to speak: "He should have acknowledged her."

"Yes," they all echoed, "he should have acknowledged her."

"My friends and companions," responded Mr. Ryder, "I thank you, one and all. It is the answer I expected, for I knew your hearts."

He turned and walked toward the closed door of an adjoining room, while every eye followed him in wondering curiosity. He came back in a moment, leading by the hand his visitor of the afternoon, who stood startled and trembling at the sudden plunge into this scene of brilliant gayety. She was neatly dressed in gray, and wore the white cap of an elderly woman.

"Ladies and gentlemen," he said, "this is the woman, and I am the man, whose story I have told you. Permit me to introduce to you the wife of my youth."

Paul Laurence Dunbar

(1872–1906)

Born in Dayton, Ohio, the son of former slaves, Dunbar was the first African-American poet to gain a truly national audience. After his graduation from an otherwise all-white high school, Dunbar worked as an elevator operator, self-publishing his first book of poems, *Oak and Ivy,* in 1893. His second volume, *Majors and Minors,* was published in 1895 and was favorably reviewed by William Dean Howells in *Harper's Weekly.* But Howells's introduction to Dunbar's third volume, *Lyrics of Lowly Life,* in 1896—citing Dunbar's ability to "feel the Negro life aesthetically and express it lyrically"—and its publication by a prestigious New York press brought Dunbar to national attention. This volume was followed by *Lyrics of the Hearthside* (1899), *Lyrics of Love and Laughter* (1903), and *Lyrics of Sunshine and Shadow* (1905).

Dunbar's verse was free of the stolid religiosity that had characterized earlier American poetry, and though not the first to write in dialect, Dunbar became well known for the style through poems like "When de Co'n Pone's Hot," "A Negro Love Song," "The Party," and others that conjured up a "picturesque" view of black life, as did his volumes of short stories *Folks from Dixie* (1898), *In Old Plantation Days* (1903), and *The Heart of Happy Hollow* (1904). There is no mention in these works of the grinding rural poverty or of the rise in lynchings and Jim Crow statutes that had led many blacks North.

The popularity of the dialect poetry may actually have said more about its largely white audience than authentic black culture. (In fact, Dunbar first visited the South depicted in his work only after most of the dialect poems were written.) In his introduction to the poems Howells wrote, "They are really not dialect so much as personal attempts and failures for the written and spoken language. . . . He reveals in these a finely ironical perception of the Negro's limitations." Viewed through this prism, Dunbar's reassuring portraits of contented, accommodating figures allowed his readers to discount potential social conflict.

But there was another side to Dunbar's work decidedly not reflected in the dialect poems. Written in standard English, "The Colored

Soldiers," which praised the thousands of blacks who fought during the Civil War ("They were comrades then and brothers, /Are they more or less to-day?"), and "Harriet Beecher Stowe" acknowledged past injustice and praised black heroes. Other poems, like "Ere Sleep Comes Down to Soothe the Weary Eyes" and "A Song of Death," displayed a Romantic preoccupation with the fleetingness of life, made particular by Dunbar's awareness of his own fight against tuberculosis, which would kill him by age thirty-three.

Finally, Dunbar became embittered by the lack of acceptance for what he considered his finer work. In *The Book of American Negro Poetry* (1922), James Weldon Johnson wrote of Dunbar, a longstanding friend, "Often he said to me: 'I've got to write dialect poetry; it's the only way I can get them to listen to me.' " In poems like "Sympathy" and "We Wear the Mask," Dunbar expresses his frustration, felt most deeply in "The Poet," where he decries the popularity of his dialect verse, those cast in the "jingle of a broken tongue."

Dialect poetry became less popular after Dunbar. "The newer Negro poets show a tendency to discard dialect," wrote Johnson. "They are trying to break away from, not Negro dialect itself," he continued, ironically echoing Howells, "but the limitations on Negro dialect imposed by the fixing effects of long convention. . . . Negro dialect is at present a medium that is not capable of giving expression to the varied conditions of Negro life in America, and much less capable of giving the fullest interpretation of Negro character and psychology." Johnson predicted, accurately, that as long-held stereotypes associated with dialect dissipated with time, writers would find new use for black vernacular.

We Wear the Mask

We wear the mask that grins and lies,
It hides our cheeks and shades our eyes,—
This debt we pay to human guile;
With torn and bleeding hearts we smile,
And mouth with myriad subtleties.

Why should the world be overwise,
In counting all our tears and sighs?
Nay, let them only see us, while
We wear the mask.

We smile, but, O great Christ, our cries
To thee from tortured souls arise,
We sing, but oh the clay is vile
Beneath our feet, and long the mile;
But let the world dream otherwise,
We wear the mask.

Sympathy

I know what the caged bird feels, alas!
   When the sun is bright on the upland slopes;
When the wind stirs soft through the springing grass,
And the river flows like a stream of glass;
   When the first bird sings and the first bud opes,
And the faint perfume from its chalice steals—
I know what the caged bird feels!

I know why the caged bird beats his wing
   Till its blood is red on the cruel bars;
For he must fly back to his perch and cling
When he fain would be on the bough a-swing;
   And a pain still throbs in the old, old scars
And they pulse again with a keener sting—
I know why he beats his wing!

I know why the caged bird sings, ah me,
   When his wing is bruised and his bosom sore,—
When he beats his bars and would be free;
It is not a carol of joy or glee,
   But a prayer that he sends from his heart's deep core,
But a plea, that upward to Heaven, he flings—
I know why the caged bird sings!

A Negro Love Song

Seen my lady home las' night,
  Jump back, honey, jump back.
Hel' huh han' an' sque'z it tight,
  Jump back, honey, jump back.
Hyeahd huh sigh a little sigh,
Seen a light gleam f'om huh eye,
An' a smile go flittin' by—
  Jump back, honey, jump back.

Hyeahd de win' blow thoo de pine,
  Jump back, honey, jump back.
Mockin'-bird was singin' fine,
  Jump back, honey, jump back.
An' my hea't was beatin' so,
When I reached my lady's do',
Dat I could n't ba' to go—
  Jump back, honey, jump back.

Put my ahm aroun' huh wais',
  Jump back, honey, jump back.
Raised huh lips an' took a tase.
  Jump back, honey, jump back.
Love me, honey, love me true?
Love me well ez I love you?
An' she answe'd, "Cose I do"—
  Jump back, honey, jump back.

The Poet

He sang of life, serenely sweet,
With, now and then, a deeper note.
From some high peak, nigh yet remote,
He voiced the world's absorbing beat.

He sang of love when earth was young,
And Love, itself, was in his lays.
But ah, the world, it turned to praise
A jingle in a broken tongue.

Booker T. Washington (1856–1915)

Few African-Americans figures are now viewed with the mixture of admiration and contempt reserved for Booker T. Washington. Born into slavery, he became the most influential black in his day, shaping his Tuskegee Institute into a major institution, enjoying influence with the White House, dispensing political patronage, and writing a dozen books, including his immensely popular autobiography, *Up from Slavery.*

Born on a small Virginia farm, perhaps of a white father, Washington was freed with the coming of the Civil War at the age of nine. Moving with his family to West Virginia, he worked in the salt furnaces and coal mines as a child laborer. In 1872 he walked the five hundred miles to Hampton Institute, where he inculcated the school's norms of self-reliance and industry. After brief attempts to study law and for the ministry in Washington, D.C., he returned to teach at Hampton and then in 1881 founded Tuskegee Normal and Industrial Institute in Alabama.

Washington showed a remarkable ability to gain the support for the institution among varied groups, including conservative whites, wealthy patrons, and prosperous blacks. At Tuskegee, Washington stressed industrial, rather than academic, education, seizing upon it as a means of gaining economic independence from the sharecropper system. At the same time he sought to influence whites, he ruled among blacks with his "Tuskegee Machine" and the National Negro Business League, which he founded in 1900. He virtually controlled the black press, owning several newspapers himself, and was largely responsible for which individuals and institutions received political appointments and government funds.

The most famous articulation of Washington's methods was his Atlanta Exposition Address, delivered at a business convention on September 18, 1895, the same year that Frederick Douglass died. Dubbed the "Atlanta Compromise," this philosophy, which carved out a defined, and subordinate, "place" for blacks, found many critics, most notably W. E. B. Du Bois (see "Of Mr. Booker T. Washington and Others"[†]). Nonetheless, echoes of his self-reliant "mutual aid" philosophy may be seen in the later writings of Carter G. Woodson on education and contemporary emphasis on economic empowerment. Washington also, clandestinely, organized, funded, and directed lawyers who tested cases in the South of Jim Crow legal discrimination. Publicly, however, he maintained his accommodationist stance and remained opposed to Du Bois's NAACP and other groups that espoused equality of civil rights.

Washington's *Up from Slavery* reads today as a troublesome document. In it, he embodies many noble qualities and provides a damning portrait of slavery; yet the problem, for many readers, is in the author's willingness to dismiss the historical attitudes that made slavery a possibility. In the excerpt included here, Washington conveys the powerful desire to gain an education, an almost archetypal theme in African-American autobiography, sounded by dozens of writers before and since.

In 1900 the twice-widowed Washington married Margaret Murray, a dean at Tuskegee, who became active in the women's club movement. Washington's other books include *The Future of the American Negro* (1899), *Life of Frederick Douglass* (1907), and *My Larger Education, Being Chapters from My Experience* (1911). He died November 14, 1915, in Tuskegee, Alabama.

from *Up from Slavery*

"There was never a time in my youth, no matter how dark and discouraging the days might be, when one resolve did not continually remain with me, and that was a determination to secure an education at any cost."

BOYHOOD DAYS

AFTER THE COMING OF FREEDOM THERE WERE TWO POINTS upon which practically all the people on our place were agreed, and I find that this was generally true throughout the South: that they must change their names, and that they must leave the old plantation for at least a few days or weeks in order that they might really feel sure that they were free.

In some way a feeling got among the coloured people that it was far from proper for them to bear the surname of their former owners, and a great many of them took other surnames. This was one of the first signs of freedom. When they were slaves, a coloured person was simply called "John" or "Susan." There was seldom occasion for more than the use of the one name. If "John" or "Susan" belonged to a white man by the name of "Hatcher," sometimes he was called "John Hatcher," or as often "Hatcher's John." But there was a feeling that "John Hatcher" or "Hatcher's John" was not the proper title by which to denote a freeman; and so in many cases "John Hatcher" was changed to "John S. Lincoln" or "John S. Sherman," the initial "S" standing for no name, it being simply a part of what the coloured man proudly called his "entitles."

As I have stated, most of the coloured people left the old plantation for a short while at least, so as to be sure, it seemed, that they could leave and try their freedom on to see how it felt. After they had remained away for a time, many of the older slaves, especially, returned to their old homes and made some kind of contract with their former owners by which they remained on the estate.

My mother's husband, who was the stepfather of my brother John and myself, did not belong to the same owners as did my mother. In fact, he seldom came to our plantation. I remember seeing him there perhaps once a year, that being about Christmas time. In some way, during the war, by running away and following the Federal soldiers, it seems, he found his way into the new state of West Virginia. As soon as freedom was declared, he sent for my mother to come to the Kanawha Valley, in West Virginia. At that time a journey from Virginia over the mountains to West Virginia was rather a tedious and in some cases a painful undertaking. What little clothing and few household goods we had were placed in a cart, but the children walked the greater portion of the distance, which was several hundred miles.

I do not think any of us ever had been very far from the plantation, and the taking of a long journey into another state was quite an event. The parting from our former owners and the members of our own race on the plantation was a serious occasion. From the time of our parting till their death we kept up a correspondence with the older members of the family, and in later years we have kept in touch with those who were the younger members. We were several weeks making the trip, and most of the time we slept in the open air and did our cooking over a log fire out-of-doors. One night I recall that we camped near an abandoned log cabin, and my mother decided to build a fire in that for cooking, and afterward to make a "pallet" on the floor for our sleeping. Just as the fire had gotten well started a large black snake fully a yard and a half long dropped down the chimney and ran out on the floor. Of course we at once abandoned that cabin. Finally we reached our destination—a little town called Malden, which is about five miles from Charleston, the present capital of the state.

At that time salt-mining was the great industry in that part of West Virginia, and the little town of Malden was right in the midst of the salt-furnaces. My stepfather had already secured a job at a salt-furnace, and he had also secured a little cabin for us to live in. Our new house was no better than the one we had left on the old plantation in Virginia. In fact, in one respect it was worse. Notwithstanding the poor condition of our plantation cabin, we were at all times sure of pure air. Our new home was in the midst of a cluster of cabins crowded closely together, and as there were no sanitary regulations, the filth about the cabins was often intolerable. Some of our neighbours were coloured people, and some were the poorest and most ignorant and degraded white people. It was a motley mixture. Drinking, gambling, quarrels, fights, and shockingly immoral practices were frequent. All who lived in the little town were in one way or another connected with the salt business. Though I was a mere child, my stepfather put me and my brother at work in one of the furnaces. Often I began work as early as four o'clock in the morning.

The first thing I ever learned in the way of book knowledge was while working in this salt-furnace. Each salt-packer had his barrels marked with a certain number. The number allotted to my stepfather was "18." At the close of the day's work the boss of the packers would come around and put "18" on each of our barrels, and I soon learned to recognize that figure wherever I saw it, and after a while got to the point where I could make that figure, though I knew nothing about any other figures or letters.

From the time that I can remember having any thought about anything, I recall that I had an intense longing to learn to read. I determined, when quite a small child, that, if I accomplished nothing else in life, I would in some way get enough education to enable me to read common books and newspapers. Soon after we got settled in some manner in our new cabin in West Virginia, I induced my mother to get hold of a book for me. How or where she got it I do not know, but in some way she procured a copy of Webster's "blue-back" spelling-book, which contained the alphabet, followed by such meaningless words as "ab," "ba," "ca," "da." I began at once to devour the book, and I think that it was the first one I ever had in my hands. I had learned from somebody that the way to begin to read was to learn the alphabet, so I tried in all the ways I could think of to learn it,—all of course without a teacher, for I could find no one to teach me. At that time there was not a single member of my race anywhere near us who could read, and I was too timid to approach any of the white people. In some way, within a few weeks, I mastered the greater portion of the alphabet. In all my efforts to learn to read my mother shared fully my ambition, and sympathized with me and aided me in every way that she could. Though she was totally ignorant, so far as mere book knowledge was concerned, she had high ambitions for her children, and a large fund of good, hard, common sense which seemed to enable her to meet and master every situation. If I have done anything in life worth attention, I feel sure that I inherited the disposition from my mother.

In the midst of my struggles and longing for an education, a young coloured boy who had learned to read in the state of Ohio came to Malden. As soon as the coloured people found out that he could read, a newspaper was secured, and at the close of nearly every day's work this young man would be surrounded by a group of men and women who were anxious to hear him read the news contained in the papers. How I used to envy this man! He seemed to me to be the one young man in all the world who ought to be satisfied with his attainments.

About this time the question of having some kind of a school opened for the coloured children in the village began to be discussed by members of the race. As it would be the first school for Negro children that had ever been opened in that part of Virginia, it was, of course, to be a great event, and the discussion excited the widest interest. The most perplexing question was where to find a teacher. The young man from Ohio who had learned to read the papers was considered, but his age was against him. In the midst of the discussion about a teacher, another young coloured man from Ohio, who had been a soldier, in some way found his way into town. It was soon learned that he possessed considerable education, and he was engaged by the coloured people to teach their first school. As yet no free schools had been started for coloured people in that section, hence each family agreed to pay a certain amount per month, with the understanding that the teacher was to "board 'round"—that is, spend a day with each family. This was not bad for the teacher, for each family tried to provide the very best on the day the teacher was to be its guest. I recall that I looked forward with an anxious appetite to the "teacher's day" at our little cabin.

This experience of a whole race beginning to go to school for the first time, presents one of the most interesting studies that has ever occurred in connection with the development of any race. Few people who were not right in the midst of the scenes can form any exact idea of the intense desire which the people of my race showed for an education. As I have stated, it was a whole race trying to go to school. Few were too young, and one too old, to make the attempt to learn. As fast as any kind of teachers could be secured, not only were day-schools filled, but night-schools as well. The great ambition of the older people was to try to learn to read the Bible before they died. With this end in view, men and women who were fifty or seventy-five years old would often be found in the night-school. Sunday-schools were formed soon after freedom, but the principal book studied in the Sunday-school was the spelling-book. Day-school, night-school, Sunday-school, were always crowded, and often many had to be turned away for want of room.

The opening of the school in the Kanawha Valley, however, brought to me one of the keenest disappointments that I ever experienced. I had been working in a salt-furnace for several months, and my stepfather had discovered that I had a financial value, and so, when the school opened, he decided that he could not spare me from my work. This decision seemed to cloud my every ambition. The disappointment was made all the more severe by reason of the fact that my place of work was where I could see the happy children passing to and from school, mornings and afternoons. Despite this disappointment, however, I determined that I would learn something, anyway. I applied myself with greater earnestness than ever to the mastering of what was in the "blue-back" speller.

My mother sympathized with me in my disappointment, and sought to comfort me in all the ways she could, and to help me find a way to learn. After a while I succeeded in making arrangements with the teacher to give me some lessons at night, after the day's work was done. These night lessons were so welcome that I think I learned more at night than the other children did during the day. My own experiences in the night-school gave me faith in the night-school idea, with which, in after years, I had to do both at Hampton and Tuskegee. But my boyish heart was still set upon going to the day-school, and I let no opportunity slip to push my case. Finally I won, and was permitted to go to the school in the day for a few months, with the understanding that I was to rise early in the morning and work in the furnace till nine o'clock, and return immediately after school closed in the afternoon for at least two more hours of work.

The schoolhouse was some distance from the furnace, and as I had to work till nine o'clock, and the school opened at nine, I found myself in a difficulty. School would always be begun before I reached it, and sometimes my class had recited. To get around this difficulty I yielded to a temptation for which most people, I suppose, will condemn me; but since it is a fact, I might as well state it. I have great faith in the power and influence of facts. It is seldom that anything is permanently gained by holding back a fact. There was a large clock in a little office in the furnace. This clock, of course, all the hundred or more workmen depended upon to regulate their hours of beginning and ending the day's work. I got the idea that the way for me to reach school on time was to move the nine o'clock mark. This I found myself doing morning after morning, till the furnace "boss" discovered that something was wrong, and locked the clock in a case. I did not mean to inconvenience anybody. I simply meant to reach that schoolhouse on time.

When, however, I found myself at the school for the first time, I also found myself confronted with two other difficulties. In the first place, I found that all of the other children wore hats or caps on their heads, and I had neither hat nor cap. In fact, I did not remember that up to the time of going to school I had ever worn any kind of covering upon my head, nor do I recall that either I or anybody else had even thought anything about the need of covering for my head. But, of course, when I saw how all the other boys were dressed, I began to feel quite uncomfortable. As usual, I put the case before my mother, and she explained to me that she had no money with which to buy a "store hat," which was a rather new institution at that time among the members of my race and was considered quite the thing for young and old to own, but that she would find a way to help me out of the difficulty. She accordingly got two pieces of "homespun" (jeans) and sewed them together, and I was soon the proud possessor of my first cap.

The lesson my mother taught me in this has always remained with me, and I have tried as best I could to teach it to others. I have always felt proud, whenever I think of the incident, that my mother had strength of character enough not to be led into the temptation of seeming to be that which she was not—of trying to impress my schoolmates and others with the fact that she was able to buy me a "store hat" when she was not. I have always felt proud that she refused to go into debt for that which she did not have the money to pay for. Since that time I have owned many kinds of caps and hats, but never one of which I have felt so proud as of the cap made of the two pieces of cloth sewed together by my mother. I have noted the fact, but without satisfaction, I need not add, that several of the boys who began their careers with "store hats" and who were my schoolmates and used to join in the sport that was made of me because I had only a "homespun" cap, have ended their careers in the penitentiary, while others are not able now to buy any kind of hat.

My second difficulty was with regard to my name, or rather *a* name. From the time when I could remember anything, I had been called simply "Booker." Before going to school it had never occurred to me that it was needful or appropriate to have an additional name. When I heard the school-roll called, I noticed that all of the children had at least two names, and some of them indulged in what seemed to me the extravagance of having three. I was in deep perplexity, because I knew that the teacher would demand of me at least two names, and I had only one. By the time the occasion came for the enrolling of my name, an idea occurred to me which I thought would make me equal to the situation; and so, when the teacher asked me what my full name was, I calmly told him "Booker Washington," as if I had been called by that name all my life; and by that name I have since been known. Later in my life I found that my mother had given me the name of "Booker Taliaferro" soon after I was born, but in some way that part of my name seemed to disappear and for a long while was forgotten, but as soon as I found out about it I revived it, and made my full name "Booker Taliaferro Washington." I think there are not many men in our country who have had the privilege of naming themselves in the way that I have.

More than once I have tried to picture myself in the position of a boy or man with an honoured and distinguished ancestry which I could trace back through a period of hundreds of years, and who had not only inherited a name, but fortune and a proud family homestead; and yet I have sometimes had the feeling that if I had inherited these, and had been a member of a more popular race, I should have been inclined to yield to the temptation of depending upon my ancestry and my colour to do that for me which I should do for myself. Years ago I resolved that because I had no ancestry myself I would leave a record of which my children would be proud, and which might encourage them to still higher effort.

The world should not pass judgment upon the Negro, and especially the Negro youth, too quickly or too harshly. The Negro boy has obstacles, discouragements, and temptations to battle with that are little known to those not situated as he is. When a white boy undertakes a task, it is taken for granted that he will succeed. On the other hand, people are usually surprised if the Negro boy does not fail. In a word, the Negro youth starts out with the presumption against him.

The influence of ancestry, however, is important in helping forward any individual or race, if too much reliance is not placed upon it. Those who constantly direct attention to the Negro youth's moral weaknesses, and compare his advancement with that of white youths, do not consider the influence of the memories which cling about the old family homesteads. I have no idea, as I have stated elsewhere, who my grandmother was. I have, or have had, uncles and aunts and cousins, but I have no knowledge as to where most of them are. My case will illustrate that of hundreds of thousands of black people in every part of our country. The very fact that the white boy is conscious that, if he fails in life, he will disgrace the whole family record, extending back through many generations, is of tremendous value in helping him to resist temptations. The fact that the individual has behind and surrounding him proud family history and connection serves as a stimulus to help him to overcome obstacles when striving for success.

The time that I was permitted to attend school during the day was short, and my attendance was irregular. It was not long before I had to stop attending day-school altogether, and devote all of my time again to work. I resorted to the night-school again. In fact, the greater part of the education I secured in my boyhood was gathered through the night-school after my day's work was done. I had difficulty often in securing a satisfactory teacher. Sometimes, after I had secured some one to teach me at night, I would find, much to my disappointment, that the teacher knew but little more than I did. Often I would have to walk several miles at night in order to recite my night-school lessons. There was never a time in my youth, no matter how dark and discouraging the days might be, when one resolve did not continually remain with me, and that was a determination to secure an education at any cost.

Soon after we moved to West Virginia, my mother adopted into our family, notwithstanding our poverty, an orphan boy, to whom afterward we gave the name of James B. Washington. He has ever since remained a member of the family.

After I had worked in the salt-furnace for some time, work was secured for me in a coal-mine which was operated mainly for the purpose of securing fuel for the salt-furnace. Work in the coal-mine I always dreaded. One reason for this was that any one who worked in a coal-mine was always unclean, at least while at work, and it was a very hard job to get one's skin clean after the day's work was over. Then it was fully a mile from the opening of the coal-mine to the face of the coal, and all, of course, was in the blackest darkness. I do not believe that one ever experiences anywhere else such darkness as he does in a coal-mine. The mine was divided into a large number of different "rooms" or departments, and, as I never was able to learn the location of all these "rooms," I many times found myself lost in the mine. To add to the horror of being lost, sometimes my light would go out, and then, if I did not happen to have a match, I would wander about in the darkness until by chance I found some one to give me a light. The work was not only hard, but it was dangerous. There was always the danger of being blown to pieces by a premature explosion of powder, or of being crushed by falling slate. Accidents from one or the other of these causes were frequently occurring, and this kept me in constant fear. Many children of the tenderest years were compelled then, as is now true I fear, in most coal-mining districts, to spend a large part of their lives in these coal-mines, with little opportunity to get an education; and, what is worse, I have often noted that, as a rule, young boys who begin life in a coal-mine are often physically and mentally dwarfed. They soon lose ambition to do anything else than to continue as a coal-miner.

In those days, and later as a young man, I used to try to picture in my imagination the feelings and ambitions of a white boy with absolutely no limit placed upon his aspirations and activities. I used to envy the white boy who had no obstacles placed in the way of his becoming a Congressman, Governor, Bishop, or President by reason of the accident of his birth or race. I used to picture the way that I would act under such circumstances; how I would begin at the bottom and keep rising until I reached the highest round of success.

In later years, I confess that I do not envy the white boy as I once did. I have learned that success is to be measured not so much by the position that one has reached in life as by the obstacles which he has overcome while trying to succeed. Looked at from this standpoint, I almost reach the conclusion that often the Negro boy's birth and connection with an unpopular race is an advantage, so far as real life is concerned. With few exceptions, the Negro youth must work harder and must perform his tasks even better than a white youth in order to secure recognition. But out of the hard and unusual struggle through which he is compelled to pass, he gets a strength, a confidence, that one misses whose pathway is comparatively smooth by reason of birth and race.

From any point of view, I had rather be what I am, a member of the Negro race, than be able to claim membership with the most favoured of any other race. I have always been made sad when I have heard members of any race claiming rights and privileges, or certain badges of distinction, on the ground simply that they were members of this or that race, regardless of their own individual worth or attainments. I have been made to feel sad for such persons because I am conscious of the fact that mere connection with what is known as a superior race will not permanently carry an individual forward unless he has individual worth, and mere connection with what is regarded as an inferior race will not finally hold an individual back if he possesses intrinsic, individual merit. Every persecuted individual and race should get much consolation out of the great human law, which is universal and eternal, that merit, no matter under what skin found, is, in the long run, recognized and rewarded. This I have said here, not to call attention to myself as an individual, but to the race to which I am proud to belong.

1901

The Atlanta Exposition Address

"Cast down your bucket where you are. . . ."

NE-THIRD OF THE POPULATION OF THE SOUTH IS OF THE Negro race. No enterprise seeking the material, civil, or moral welfare of this section can disregard this element of our population and reach the highest success. I but convey to you, Mr. President and Directors, the sentiment of the masses of my race when I say that in no way have the value and manhood of the American Negro been more fittingly and generously recognized than by the managers of this magnificent Exposition at every stage of its progress. It is a recognition that will do more to cement the friendship of the two races than any occurrence since the dawn of freedom.

Not only this, but the opportunity here afforded will awaken among us a new era of industrial progress. Ignorant and inexperienced, it is not strange that in the first years of our new life we began at the top instead of at the bottom; that a seat in Congress or the State Legislature was more sought than real estate or industrial skill; that the political convention or stump speaking had more attractions than starting a dairy farm or truck garden.

A ship lost at sea for many days suddenly sighted a friendly vessel. From the mast of the unfortunate vessel was seen a signal: "Water, water, we die of thirst." The answer from the friendly vessel at once came back, "Cast down your bucket where you are." A second time the signal, "Water, water, send us water," ran up from the distressed vessel and was answered, "Cast down your bucket where you are." And a third and fourth signal for water was answered "Cast down your bucket where you are." The captain of the distressed vessel, at last heeding the injunction, cast down his bucket and it came up full of fresh, sparkling water from the mouth of the Amazon River.

To those of my race who depend on bettering their condition in a foreign land, or who underestimate the importance of cultivating friendly relations with the Southern white man who is their next-door neighbor, I would say: Cast down your bucket where you are; cast it down in making friends, in every manly way, of the people of all races by whom we are surrounded. Cast it down in agriculture, mechanics, in commerce, in domestic service, and in the professions. And in this connection it is well to bear in mind that whatever other sins the South may be called upon to bear, when it comes to business pure and simple, it is in the South that the Negro is given a man's chance in the commercial world, and in nothing is this Exposition more eloquent than in emphasizing this chance. Our greatest danger is that, in the great leap from slavery to freedom, we may overlook the fact that the masses of us are to live by the productions of our hands and fail to keep in mind that we shall prosper in the proportion as we learn to dignify and glorify common labor, and put brains and skill into the common occupations of life; shall prosper in proportion as we learn to draw the line between the superficial and the substantial, the ornamental gewgaws of life and the useful. No race can prosper till it learns that there is as much dignity in tilling a field as in writing a poem. It is at the bottom of life we must begin, and not at the top. Nor should we permit our grievances to overshadow our opportunities.

To those of the white race who look to the incoming of those of foreign birth and strange tongue and habits for the prosperity of the South, were I permitted I would repeat what I say to my own race, "Cast down your bucket where you are." Cast it down among the 8,000,000 Negroes whose habits you know, whose fidelity and love you have tested in days when to have proved treacherous meant the ruin of your firesides. Cast down your bucket among these people who have, without strikes and labor wars, tilled your fields, cleared your forests, builded your railroads and cities, and brought forth treasures from the bowels of the earth and helped make possible this magnificent representation of the progress of the South. Casting down your bucket among my people, helping and encouraging them as you are doing on these grounds, and, with education of head, hand and heart, you will find that they will buy your surplus land, make blossom the waste places in your fields, and run your factories.

While doing this, you can be sure in the future, as in the past, that you and your families will be surrounded by the most patient, faithful, law-abiding, and unresentful people that the world has seen. As we have proved our loyalty to you in the past, in nursing your children, watching by the sick-bed of your mothers and fathers, and often following them with tear-dimmed eyes to their graves, so in the future, in our humble way, we shall stand by you with a devotion that no foreigner can approach, ready to lay down our lives, if need be, in defense of yours; interlacing our industrial, commercial, civil, and religious life with yours in a way that shall make the interests of both races one. In all things that are purely social we can be as separate as the fingers, yet one as the hand in all things essential to mutual progress.

There is no defense or security for any of us except in the highest intelligence and development of all. If anywhere there are efforts tending to curtail the fullest growth of the Negro, let these efforts be turned into stimulating, encouraging and making him the most useful and intelligent citizen. Effort or means so invested will pay a thousand percent interest. These efforts will be twice blessed—"blessing him that gives and him that takes."

There is no escape, through law of man or God, from the inevitable:

> The laws of changeless justice bind
> Oppressor with oppressed,

And close as sin and suffering joined
We march to fate abreast.

Nearly sixteen million hands will aid you in pulling the load upward, or they will pull against you the load downward. We shall constitute one-third and more of the ignorance and crime of the South, or one-third its intelligence and progress; we shall contribute one-third to the business and industrial prosperity of the South, or we shall prove a veritable body of death, stagnating, depressing, retarding every effort to advance the body politic.

Gentlemen of the Exposition: As we present to you our humble effort at an exhibition of our progress, you must not expect over much. Starting thirty years ago with ownership here and there in a few quilts and pumpkins and chickens (gathered from miscellaneous sources), remember: the path that has led us from these to the invention and production of agricultural implements, buggies, steam engines, newspapers, books, statuary, carving, paintings, the management of drugstores and banks, has not been trodden without contact with thorns and thistles. While we take pride in what we exhibit as a result of our independent efforts, we do not for a moment forget that our part in this exhibition would fall far short of your expectations but for the constant help that has come to our educational life, not only from the Southern states, but especially from Northern philanthropists who have made their gifts a constant stream of blessing and encouragement.

The wisest among my race understand that the agitation of questions of social equality is the extremest folly, and that progress in the enjoyment of all the privileges that will come to us must be the result of severe and constant struggle rather than of artificial forcing. No race that has anything to contribute to the markets of the world is long in any degree ostracized. It is important and right that all privileges of the laws be ours, but it is vastly more important that we be prepared for the exercise of those privileges. The opportunity to earn a dollar in a factory just now is worth infinitely more than the opportunity to spend a dollar in an opera house.

In conclusion, may I repeat that nothing in thirty years has given us more hope and encouragement and drawn us so near to you of the white race as this opportunity offered by the Exposition; and here bending, as it were, over the altar that represents the results of the struggles of your race and mine, both starting practically empty-handed three decades ago, I pledge that, in your effort to work out the great and intricate problem which God has laid at the doors of the South, you shall have at all times the patient, sympathetic help of my race. Only let this be constantly in mind that, while from representations in these buildings of the product of field, of forest, of mine, of factory, letters and art, much good will come—yet by far above and beyond material benefits, will be that higher good, that let us pray God will come, in a blotting out of sectional differences and racial animosities and suspicions, in a determination to administer absolute justice, in a willing obedience among all classes to the mandates of law. This, coupled with material prosperity, will bring into our beloved South a new heaven and a new earth.

September 18, 1895

W. E. B. Du Bois
(1868–1963)

Throughout his long and influential life, W. E. B. Du Bois remained one of the most significant intellectual forces of his time. Of African, French, and Dutch ancestry, William Edward Burghardt Du Bois was born in Great Barrington, Massachusetts, of a family with deep roots in America's history (his maternal great-great-grandfather had been kidnapped from West Africa to Massachusetts and freed during the Revolutionary War). Du Bois's mother separated from his father soon after he was born and he spent much of his childhood in difficult circumstances but relatively untouched by color prejudice. While still in high school, Du Bois wrote articles for the *Springfield Republican* and the *New York Globe.* Though he had aspired to attend Harvard, after his mother's death in 1885, with the aid of local patrons, he attended Fisk University in Nashville, where he read classics and edited the school newspaper. It was in the South that he first confronted Jim Crow segregation and during two summers teaching in rural areas encountered the extreme privation of Southern blacks. In 1888 he was admitted to Harvard, where he studied philosophy with William James and George Santayana and from which he received his M.A. in history in 1891. He studied for a year in Berlin, and, barred from teaching at any of the white universities for which he was qualified, in 1894 he took a position as professor of classics at Wilberforce University in Ohio. The following year he earned his Ph.D. from Harvard, becoming the first African-American to be awarded a doctorate; his dissertation, "The Suppression of the African Slave Trade to the United States of America, 1638 to 1870," was published in 1896.

In 1896 Du Bois married Nina Gomer and left for the University of Pennsylvania, where he worked on *The Philadelphia Negro, a Sociological Study* (published in 1899) and helped found the American Negro Academy. The following year, he moved to Atlanta University, where he would teach for more than a decade, and his son, Burghardt Gomer Du Bois, was born. The boy died two years later. In 1900 his daughter, Nina Yolande (who would marry the celebrated young poet Countee Cullen in 1928, only to separate a year later), was born.

Though Du Bois had expressed a strong, albeit rather removed, interest in black life and culture, after seeing the aftermath of a lynching of a black man in Georgia firsthand in 1899, his focus became less academic as he argued, "One could not be a calm, cool, and detached scientist while Negroes were lynched, murdered, and starved." He began to write letters and petitions against the segregation of schools and travel accommodations, and in 1900 he attended the Paris Exposition and the Pan-African Congress in London, where he first articulated the statement that "the problem of the twentieth century is the problem of the color line." Already, Du Bois had begun to view African-American history in its world historical context. He became increasingly drawn to the views of William Monroe Trotter and others who rejected the policy of accommodation expressed in Booker T. Washington's Atlanta Compromise.†

In 1903 Du Bois published his most well known work, *The Souls of Black Folk.* In a series of eloquent, though highly stylized, essays, Du Bois analyzes emancipation and Reconstruction, the role of black colleges and the black Church, prejudice in the South—which he called "an armed camp for intimidating black folk"—and the genius of black music, especially the "sorrow songs" which he termed "the singular spiritual heritage of the nation and the greatest gift of the Negro people." In one of the most controversial essays in the book, "Of Booker T. Washington and Others," included here, he put the growing rift between Washington and his critics very much in the public's eye. Writing primarily for a white audience and the black intelligentsia, Du Bois employs the analogy of "the Veil of Race" to describe the distance between the races. "I have stepped within the veil," he writes, "raising it that you may view faintly its deeper recesses,—the meaning of its religion, the passion of its human sorrow, and the struggle of its greater souls." Immediately upon its publication, the book was a commercial and critical success and brought Du Bois a national audience. That same year, he published the essay "The Talented Tenth," which argued for the education of a black elite, in the anthology *The Negro Problem,* and the following year his "Credo" appeared in the New York *Independent.* His prose-poem, *A Litany of Atlanta,* was written after a white mob attacked blacks in Atlanta in September 1906.

In 1905 Du Bois and Trotter became the founding members of the Niagara Movement.† Though the organization dissolved within five years, in 1909 Du Bois joined a group of about fifty other prominent black and white men and women to form a National Negro Committee, reorganized in 1910 as the NAACP.† Based in New York, Du Bois became the director of publications and research for the organization and, during the course of the next twenty-four years, was editor of its influential journal, *The Crisis.* After investigating the East St. Louis riot in 1917, he participated in the silent parade down Fifth Avenue in protest. Growing dissatisfied with President Woodrow Wilson's do-nothing attitude toward lynching and the introduction of segregation into government jobs, he wrote in an open letter to the president, "You have now been President of the United States for six months and what is the result? It is not exaggeration to say that every enemy of the Negro race is greatly encouraged. . . . not a single act and not a single word of yours since election has given anyone reason to infer that you have the slightest interest in the colored people or desire to alleviate their intolerable position." As the nation edged toward war, however, in a highly controversial article in *The Crisis* he urged blacks to "close ranks" with whites in support of the Allied effort. As segregation in the military emerged as the official policy, Du Bois published "A Directive to French Troops"† that outlined the U.S. government's policy toward black servicemen, and after the war he wrote the scathing editorial "Returning Soldiers"† in which he vehemently condemned the lynching of black troops and demanded an earned share of the privileges of democracy.

After the war, Du Bois became involved in the struggle of African nations for independence from colonial rule. In 1919 he organized the Pan-African Congress in Paris and in December 1923 he made his first trip to Africa, traveling for a month in Liberia, Sierra Leone, Guinea, and Senegal. At this time, Marcus Garvey was successfully promoting his own "Back to Africa" movement, and Du Bois ultimately attacked Garvey's financial and political methods in *The Crisis.* In 1926 Du Bois spent two months in the Soviet Union and wrote favorably on the gains of the Bolshevik Revolution. Increasingly out of step with Walter White and the more conservative leadership of the NAACP, in June 1934 he broke with the organization and returned to Atlanta University, at age sixty-six, as chairman of the department of sociology, soon after publishing his major work, *Black Reconstruction in America* (1935) and the autobiographical essays in *Dusk of Dawn* (1940). In 1944 Du Bois became the first African-American elected to the prestigious National Institute of Arts and Letters and he traveled extensively in Europe on the eve of World War II. Forced to retire from Atlanta University in 1944, he resumed his work with the NAACP, but was dismissed four years later after publishing a highly critical article about the NAACP's alignment with the "colonial imperialism" of the current administration.

In the 1950s Du Bois became involved in the world pacifist movement, calling for a ban on nuclear weapons, and in 1951, as the head of the Peace Information Center, he was indicted for his relationship to a "foreign agent." In the climate of the times he was shunned by many associates, black and white, and his passport was denied. When the Supreme Court struck down the validity of the statute used to indict him in 1958, he embarked, at the age of ninety, on a world tour of Europe, Asia, and the Soviet Union and in 1961 traveled to Ghana, where he resumed work on a major study, *Encyclopedia Africana,* which he had begun many years earlier. Disillusioned with his native land, Du Bois joined the Communist Party and became a citizen of Ghana, where he died on August 27, 1963.

A prolific writer, Du Bois edited, in addition to *The Crisis,* the journals *Horizon, Phylon,* and for children, *The Brownies' Book,* and he was the author of nineteen books, including the novels *The Quest of the Silver Fleece* (1911), *Dark Princess* (1928), and the *Black Flame* trilogy (1957–1961); a historical pageant, *The Star of Ethiopia* (1913); two volumes on African-American history, *The Negro* (1915) and *The Gift of Black Folk: The Negroes in the Making of America* (1924); and *Darkwater* (1920), a collection of essays and poetry. He contributed an article on Africa to Alain Locke's seminal volume *The New Negro* (1925),† and he wrote dozens of essays for *The Atlantic Monthly, The Chicago Defender,* and *The People's Voice* in New York. The *Autobiography of W. E. B. Du Bois* was published posthumously in 1968.

from *The Souls of Black Folk*

"By every civilized and peaceful method we must strive for the rights which the world accords to men. . . ."

OF MR. BOOKER T. WASHINGTON AND OTHERS

EASILY THE MOST STRIKING THING IN THE HISTORY OF THE American Negro since 1876 is the ascendancy of Mr. Booker T. Washington. It began at the time when war memories and ideals were rapidly passing; a day of astonishing commercial development was dawning; a sense of doubt and hesitation overtook the freedmen's sons,—then it was that his leading began. Mr. Washington came, with a single definite programme, at the psychological moment when the nation was a little ashamed of having bestowed so much sentiment on Negroes, and was concentrating its energies on Dollars. His programme of industrial education, conciliation of the South, and submission and silence as to civil and political rights, was not wholly original; the Free Negroes from 1830 up to war-time had striven to build industrial schools, and the American Missionary Association had from the first taught various trades; and Price and others had sought a way of honorable alliance with the best of the Southerners. But Mr. Washington first indissolubly linked these things; he put enthusiasm, unlimited energy, and perfect faith into his programme, and changed it from a by-path into a veritable Way of Life. And the tale of the methods by which he did this is a fascinating study of human life.

It startled the nation to hear a Negro advocating such a programme after many decades of bitter complaint; it startled and won the applause of the South, it interested and won the admiration of the North; and after a confused murmur of protest, it silenced if it did not convert the Negroes themselves.

To gain sympathy and cooperation of the various elements comprising the white South was Mr. Washington's first task; and this, at the time Tuskegee was founded, seems, for a black man, well-nigh impossible. And yet ten years later it was done in the words spoken at Atlanta: "In all things purely social we can be as separate as the five fingers, and yet one as the hand in all things essential to mutual progress." This "Atlanta Compromise" is by all odds the most notable thing in Mr. Washington's career. The South interpreted it in different ways: the radicals received it as a complete surrender of the demand for civil and political equality; the conservatives, as a generously conceived working basis for mutual understanding. So both approved it, and to-day its author is certainly the most distinguished Southerner since Jefferson Davis, and the one with the largest personal following.

Next to this achievement comes Mr. Washington's work in gaining place and consideration in the North. Others less shrewd and tactful had formerly essayed to sit on these two stools and had fallen between them; but as Mr. Washington knew the heart of the South from birth and training, so by singular insight he intuitively grasped the spirit of the age which was dominating the North. And so thoroughly did he learn the speech and thought of triumphant commercialism, and the ideals of material prosperity, that the picture of a lone black boy poring over a French grammar amid the weeds and dirt of a neglected home soon seemed to him the acme of absurdities. One wonders what Socrates and St. Francis of Assisi would say to this.

And yet this very singleness of vision and thorough oneness with his age is a mark of the successful man. It is as though Nature must needs make men narrow in order to give them force. So Mr. Washington's cult has gained unquestioning followers, his work has wonderfully prospered, his friends are legion, and his enemies are confounded. To-day he stands as the one recognized spokesman of his ten million fellows, and one of the most notable figures in a nation of seventy millions. One hesitates, therefore, to criticise a life which, beginning with so little, has done so much. And yet the time is come when one may speak in all sincerity and utter courtesy of the mistakes and shortcomings of Mr. Washington's career, as well as of his triumphs, without being thought captious or envious, and without forgetting that it is easier to do ill than well in the world.

The criticism that has hitherto met Mr. Washington has not always been of this broad character. In the South especially has he had to walk warily to avoid the harshest judgments,—and naturally so, for he is dealing with the one subject of deepest sensitiveness to that section. Twice—once when at the Chicago celebration of the Spanish-American War he alluded to the color-prejudice that is "eating away the vitals of the South," and once when he dined with President Roosevelt—has the resulting Southern criticism been violent enough to threaten seriously his popularity. In the North the feeling has several times forced itself into words, that Mr. Washington's counsels of submission overlooked certain elements of true manhood, and that his educational programme was unnecessarily narrow. Usually, however, such criticism has not found open expression, although, too, the spiritual sons of the Abolitionist have not been prepared to acknowledge that the schools founded before Tuskegee, by men of broad ideals and self-sacrificing spirit, were wholly failures or worthy of ridicule. While, then, criticism has not failed to follow Mr. Washington, yet the prevailing public opinion of the land has been but too willing to deliver the solution of a wearisome problem into his hands, and say, "If that is all you and your race ask, take it."

Among his own people, however, Mr. Washington has encountered the strongest and most lasting opposition, amounting at times to bitterness, and even today continuing strong and insistent even though largely silenced in outward expression by the public opinion of the nation. Some of this opposition is, of course, mere envy; the disappointment of displaced demagogues and the spite of narrow minds. But aside from this, there is among educated and thoughtful colored men in all parts of the land a feeling of deep regret, sorrow, and apprehension at the wide currency and ascendancy which some of Mr. Washington's theories have gained. These same men admire his sincerity of purpose, and are willing to forgive much to honest endeavor which is doing something worth the doing. They cooperate with Mr. Washington as far as they conscientiously can; and, indeed, it is no ordinary tribute to this man's tact and power that, steering as he must between so many diverse interests and opinions, he so largely retains the respect of all.

But the hushing of the criticism of honest opponents is a dangerous thing. It leads some of the best of the critics to unfortunate silence and paralysis of effort, and others to burst into speech so passionately and intemperately as to lose listeners. Honest and earnest criticism from those whose interests are most nearly touched,—criticism of writers by readers, of government by those governed, of leaders by those led,—this is the soul of democracy and the safeguard of modern society. If the best of the American Negroes receive by outer pressure a leader whom they had not recognized before, manifestly there is here a certain palpable gain. Yet there is also irreparable loss,—a loss of that peculiarly valuable education which a group receives when by search and criticism it finds and commissions its own leaders. The way in which this is done is at once the most elementary and the nicest problem of social growth. History is but the record of such group-leadership; and yet how infinitely changeful is its type and character! And of all types and kinds, what can be more instructive than the leadership of a group within a group?—that curious double movement where real progress may be negative and actual advance be relative retrogression. All this is the social student's inspiration and despair.

Now in the past the American Negro has had instructive experience in the choosing of group leaders, founding thus a peculiar dynasty which in the light of present conditions is worth while studying. When sticks and stones and beasts form the sole environment of a people, their attitude is largely one of determined opposition to and conquest of natural forces. But when to earth and brute is added an environment of men and ideas, then the attitude of the imprisoned group may take three main forms,—a feeling of revolt and revenge; an attempt to adjust all thought and action to the will of the greater group; or, finally, a determined effort at self-realization and self-development despite environing opinion. The influence of all of these attitudes at various times can be traced in the history of the American Negro, and in the evolution of his successive leaders.

Before 1750, while the fire of African freedom still burned in the veins of the slaves, there was in all leadership or attempted leadership but the one motive of revolt and revenge,—typified in the terrible Maroons, the Danish blacks, and Cato of Stono, and veiling all the Americas in fear of insurrection. The liberalizing tendencies of the latter half of the eighteenth century brought, along with kindlier relations between black and white, thought of ultimate adjustment and assimilation. Such aspiration was especially voiced in the earnest songs of Phyllis, in the martyrdom of Attucks, the fighting of Salem and Poor, the intellectual accomplishments of Banneker and Derham, and the political demands of the Cuffes.

Stern financial and social stress after the war cooled much of the previous humanitarian ardor. The disappointment and impatience of the Negroes at the persistence of slavery and serfdom voiced itself in two movements. The slaves in the South, aroused undoubtedly by vague rumors of the Haytian revolt, made three fierce attempts at insurrection,—in 1800 under Gabriel in Virginia, in 1822 under Vesey in Carolina, and in 1831 again in Virginia under the terrible Nat Turner. In the Free States, on the other hand, a new and curious attempt at self-development was made. In Philadelphia and New York color-prescription led to a withdrawal of Negro communicants from white churches and the formation of a peculiar socio-religious institution among the Negroes known as the African Church,—an organization still living and controlling in its various branches over a million of men.

Walker's wild appeal against the trend of the times showed how the world was changing after the coming of the cotton-gin. By 1830 slavery seemed hopelessly fastened on the South, and the slaves thoroughly cowed into submission. The free Negroes of the North, inspired by the mulatto immigrants from the West Indies, began to change the basis of their demands; they recognized the slavery of slaves, but insisted that they themselves were freemen, and sought assimilation and amalgamation with the nation on the same terms with other men. Thus, Forten and Purvis of Philadelphia, Shad of Wilmington, Du Bois of New Haven, Barbadoes of Boston, and others, strove singly and together as men, they said, not as slaves; as "people of color," not as "Negroes." The trend of the times, however, refused them recognition save in individual and exceptional cases, considered them as one with all the despised blacks, and they soon found themselves striving to keep even the rights they formerly had of voting and working and moving as freemen. Schemes of migration and colonization arose among them; but these they refused to entertain, and they eventually turned to the Abolition movement as a final refuge.

Here, led by Remond, Nell, Wells-Brown, and Douglass, a new period of self-assertion and self-development dawned. To be sure, ultimate freedom and assimilation was the ideal before the leaders, but the assertion of the manhood rights of the Negro by himself was the main reliance, and John Brown's raid was the extreme of its logic. After the war and emancipation, the great form of Frederick Douglass, the greatest of American Negro leaders, still led the host. Self-assertion, especially in political lines, was the main programme, and behind Douglass came Elliot, Bruce, and Langston, and the Reconstruction politicians, and, less conspicuous but of greater social significance, Alexander Crummell and Bishop Daniel Payne.

Then came the Revolution of 1876, the suppression of the Negro votes, the changing and shifting of ideals, and the seeking of new lights in the great night. Douglass, in his old age, still bravely stood for the ideals of his early manhood,—ultimate assimilation *through* self-assertion, and on no other terms. For a time Price arose as a new leader, destined, it seemed, not to give up, but to re-state the old ideals in a form less repugnant to the white South. But he passed away in his prime. Then came the new leader. Nearly all the former ones had become leaders by the silent suffrage of their fellows, had sought to lead their own people alone, and were usually, save Douglass, little known outside their race. But Booker T. Washington arose as essentially the leader not of one race but of two,—a compromiser between the South, the North, and the Negro. Naturally the Negroes resented, at first bitterly, signs of compromise which surrendered their civil and political rights, even though this was to be exchanged for larger chances of economic development. The rich and dominating North, however, was not only weary of the race problem, but was investing largely in Southern enterprises, and welcomed any method of peaceful cooperation. Thus, by national opinion, the Negroes began to recognize Mr. Washington's leadership; and the voice of criticism was hushed.

Mr. Washington represents in Negro thought the old attitude of adjustment and submission; but adjustment at such a peculiar time as to make his programme unique. This is an age of unusual economic development, and Mr. Washington's programme naturally takes an economic cast, becoming a gospel of Work and Money to such an extent as apparently almost completely to overshadow the higher aims of life. Moreover, this is an age when the more advanced races are coming in closer contact with the less developed races, and the race-feeling is therefore intensified; and Mr. Washington's programme practically accepts the alleged inferiority of the Negro races. Again, in our own land, the reaction from the sentiment of war time has given impetus to race-prejudice against Negroes, and Mr. Washington withdraws many of the high demands of Negroes as men and American citizens. In other periods of intensified prejudice all the Negro's tendency to self-assertion has been called forth; at this period a policy of submission is advocated. In the history of nearly all other races and peoples the doctrine preached at such crises has been that manly self-respect is worth more than lands and houses, and that a people who voluntarily surrender such respect, or cease striving for it, are not worth civilizing.

In answer to this, it has been claimed that the Negro can survive only through submission. Mr. Washington distinctly asks that black people give up, at least for the present, three things,—

First, political power,
Second, insistence on civil rights,
Third, higher education of Negro youth,—

and concentrate all their energies on industrial education, and accumulation of wealth, and the conciliation of the South. This policy has been courageously and insistently advocated for over fifteen years, and has been triumphant for perhaps ten years. As a result of this tender of the palm-branch, what has been the return? In these years there have occurred:

1. The disfranchisement of the Negro.
2. The legal creation of a distinct status of civil inferiority for the Negro.
3. The steady withdrawal of aid from institutions for the higher training of the Negro.

These movements are not, to be sure, direct results of Mr. Washington's teachings; but his propaganda has, without a shadow of a doubt, helped their speedier accomplishment. The question then comes: Is it possible, and probable, that nine millions of men can make effective progress in economic lines if they are deprived of political rights, made a servile caste, and allowed only the most meagre chance for developing their exceptional men? If history and reason give any distinct answer to these questions, it is an emphatic *No.* And Mr. Washington thus faces the triple paradox of his career:

1. He is striving nobly to make Negro artisans business men and property-owners; but it is utterly impossible, under modern competitive methods, for workingmen and property-owners to defend their rights and exist without the right of suffrage.

2. He insists on thrift and self-respect, but at the same time counsels a silent submission to civic inferiority such as is bound to sap the manhood of any race in the long run.

3. He advocates common-school and industrial training, and depreciates institutions of higher learning; but neither the Negro common-schools, nor Tuskegee itself, could remain open a day were it not for teachers trained in Negro colleges, or trained by their graduates.

This triple paradox in Mr. Washington's position is the object of criticism by two classes of colored Americans. One class is spiritually descended from Toussaint the Savior, through Gabriel, Vesey, and Turner, and they represent the attitude of revolt and revenge; they hate the white South blindly and distrust the white race generally, and so far as they agree on definite action, think that the Negro's only hope lies in emigration beyond the borders of the United States. And yet, by the irony of fate, nothing has more effectually made this programme seem hopeless than the recent course of the United States toward weaker and darker peoples in the West Indies,

Hawaii, and the Philippines,—for where in the world may we go and be safe from lying and brute force?

The other class of Negroes who cannot agree with Mr. Washington has hitherto said little aloud. They deprecate the sight of scattered counsels, of internal disagreement; and especially they dislike making their just criticism of a useful and earnest man an excuse for a general discharge of venom from small-minded opponents. Nevertheless, the questions involved are so fundamental and serious that it is difficult to see how men like the Grimkes, Kelly Miller, J. W. E. Bowen, and other representatives of this group, can much longer be silent. Such men feel in conscience bound to ask of this nation three things:

1. The right to vote.
2. Civic equality.
3. The education of youth according to ability.

They acknowledge Mr. Washington's invaluable service in counselling patience and courtesy in such demands; they do not ask that ignorant black men vote when ignorant whites are debarred, or that any reasonable restrictions in the suffrage should not be applied; they know that the low social level of the mass of the race is responsible for much discrimination against it, but they also know, and the nation knows, that relentless color-prejudice is more often a cause than a result of the Negro's degradation; they seek the abatement of this relic of barbarism, and not its systematic encouragement and pampering by all agencies of social power from the Associated Press to the Church of Christ. They advocate, with Mr. Washington, a broad system of Negro common schools supplemented by thorough industrial training; but they are surprised that a man of Mr. Washington's insight cannot see that no such educational system ever has rested or can rest on any other basis than that of the well-equipped college and university, and they insist that there is a demand for a few such institutions throughout the South to train the best of the Negro youth as teachers, professional men, and leaders.

This group of men honor Mr. Washington for his attitude of conciliation toward the white South; they accept the "Atlanta Compromise" in its broadest interpretation; they recognize, with him, many signs of promise, many men of high purpose and fair judgment, in this section; they know that no easy task has been laid upon a region already tottering under heavy burdens. But, nevertheless, they insist that the way to truth and right lies in straightforward honesty, not in indiscriminate flattery; in praising those of the South who do well and criticising uncompromisingly those who do ill; in taking advantage of the opportunities at hand and urging their fellows to do the same, but at the same time in remembering that only a firm adherence to their higher ideals and aspirations will ever keep those ideals within the realm of possibility. They do not expect that the free right to vote, to enjoy civic rights, and to be educated, will come in a moment; they do not expect to see the bias and prejudices of years disappear at the blast of a trumpet; but they are absolutely certain that the way for a people to gain their reasonable rights is not by voluntarily throwing them away and insisting that they do not want them; that the way for a people to gain respect is not by continually belittling and ridiculing themselves; that, on the contrary, Negroes must insist continually, in season and out of season, that voting is necessary to modern manhood, that color discrimination is barbarism, and that black boys need education as well as white boys.

In failing thus to state plainly and unequivocally the legitimate demands of their people, even at the cost of opposing an honored leader, the thinking classes of American Negroes would shirk a heavy responsibility,—a responsibility to themselves, a responsibility to the struggling masses, a responsibility to the darker races of men whose future depends so largely on this American experiment, but especially a responsibility to this nation,—this common Fatherland. It is wrong to encourage a man or a people in evil-doing; it is wrong to aid and abet a national crime simply because it is unpopular not to do so. The growing spirit of kindliness and reconciliation between the North and South after the frightful difference of a generation ago ought to be a source of deep congratulation to all, and especially to those whose mistreatment caused the war; but if that reconciliation is to be marked by the industrial slavery and civic death of those same black men, with permanent legislation into a position of inferiority, then those black men, if they are really men, are called upon by every consideration of patriotism and loyalty to oppose such a course by all civilized methods, even though such opposition involves disagreement with Mr. Booker T. Washington. We have no right to sit silently by while the inevitable seeds are sown for a harvest of disaster to our children, black and white.

First, it is the duty of black men to judge the South discriminatingly. The present generation of Southerners are not responsible for the past, and they should not be blindly hated or blamed for it. Furthermore, to no class is the indiscriminate endorsement of the recent course of the South toward Negroes more nauseating than to the best thought of the South. The South is not "solid"; it is a land in the ferment of social change, wherein forces of all kinds are fighting for supremacy; and to praise the ill the South is today perpetrating is just as wrong as to condemn the good. Discriminating and broad-minded criticism is what the South needs,—needs it for the sake of her own white sons and daughters, and for the insurance of robust, healthy mental and moral development.

To-day even the attitude of the Southern whites toward the blacks is not, as so many assume, in all cases the same; the ignorant Southerner hates the Negro, the workingmen fear his competition, the money-makers wish to use him as a laborer, some of the educated see a menace in his upward development, while others—usually the sons of the masters—wish to help him to rise. National opinion has enabled this last class to maintain the Negro common schools, and to protect the Negro partially in property, life, and limb. Through the pressure of the money-makers, the Negro is in danger of being reduced to semi-slavery, especially in the country districts; the workingmen and those of the educated who fear the Negro, have united to disfranchise him, and some have urged his deportation; while the passions of the ignorant are easily aroused to lynch and abuse any black man. To praise this intricate whirl of thought and prejudice is nonsense; to inveigh indiscriminately against "the South" is unjust; but to use the same breath in praising Governor Aycock, exposing Senator Morgan, arguing with Mr. Thomas Nelson Page, and denouncing Senator Ben Tillman, is not only sane, but the imperative duty of thinking black men.

It would be unjust to Mr. Washington not to acknowledge that in several instances he has opposed movements in the South which were unjust to the Negro; he sent memorials to the Louisiana and Alabama constitutional conventions, he has spoken against lynching, and in other ways has openly or silently set his influence against sinister schemes and unfortunate happenings. Notwithstanding this, it is equally true to assert that on the whole the distinct impression left by Mr. Washington's propaganda is, first, that the South is justified in its present attitude toward the Negro because of the Negro's degradation; secondly, that the prime cause of the Negro's failure to rise more quickly is his wrong education in the past; and, thirdly, that his future rise depends primarily on his own efforts. Each of these propositions is a dangerous half-truth. The supplementary truths must never be lost sight of: first, slavery and race-prejudice are potent if not sufficient causes of the Negro's position; second, industrial and common-school training were necessarily slow in planting because they had to await the black teachers trained by higher institutions,—it being extremely doubtful if any essentially different development was possible, and certainly a Tuskegee was unthinkable before 1880; and, third, while it is a great truth to say that the Negro must strive and strive mightily to help himself, it is equally true that unless his striving be not simply seconded, but rather aroused and encouraged, by the initiative of the richer and wiser environing group, he cannot hope for great success.

In his failure to realize and impress this last point, Mr. Washington is especially to be criticised. His doctrine has tended to make the whites, North and South, shift the burden of the Negro problem to the Negro's shoulders and stand aside as critical and rather pessimistic spectators; when in fact the burden belongs to the nation, and the hands of none of us are clean if we bend not our energies to righting these great wrongs.

The South ought to be led, by candid and honest criticism, to assert her better self and do her full duty to the race she has cruelly wronged and is still wronging. The North—her co-partner in guilt—cannot salve her conscience by plastering it with gold. We cannot settle this problem by diplomacy and suaveness, by "policy" alone. If worse come to worst, can the moral fibre of this country survive the slow throttling and murder of nine millions of men?

The black men of America have a duty to perform, a duty stern and delicate,—a forward movement to oppose a part of the work of their greatest leader. So far as Mr. Washington preaches Thrift, Patience, and Industrial Training for the masses, we must hold up his hands and strive with him, rejoicing in his honors and glorying in the strength of this Joshua called of God and of man to lead the headless host. But so far as Mr. Washington apologizes for injustice, North or South, does not rightly value the privilege and duty of voting, belittles the emasculating effects of caste distinctions, and opposes the higher training and ambition of our brighter minds,—so far as he, the South, or the Nation, does this,—we must unceasingly and firmly oppose them. By every civilized and peaceful method we must strive for the rights which the world accords to men, clinging unwaveringly to those great words which the sons of the Fathers would fain forget: "We hold these truths to be self-evident: That all men are created equal; that they are endowed by their Creator with certain unalienable rights; that among these are life, liberty, and the pursuit of happiness."

1903

The Talented Tenth

"Education is that whole system of human training within and without the school house walls, which molds and develops men."

HE NEGRO RACE, LIKE ALL RACES, IS GOING TO BE SAVED BY its exceptional men. The problem of education, then, among Negroes must first of all deal with the Talented Tenth; it is the problem of developing the Best of this race that they may guide the Mass away from the contamination and death of the Worst, in their own and other races. Now the training of men is a difficult and intricate task. Its technique is a matter for educational experts, but its object is for the vision of seers. If we make money the object of man-training, we shall develop money-makers but not necessarily men; if we make technical skill the object of education, we may possess artisans but not, in nature, men. Men we shall have only as we make manhood the object of the work of the schools—intelligence, broad sympathy, knowledge of the world that was and is, and of the relation of men to it—this is the curriculum of that Higher Education which must underlie true life. On this foundation we may build bread winning, skill of hand and quickness of brain, with never a fear lest the child and man mistake the means of living for the object of life.

If this be true—and who can deny it—three tasks lay before me; first to show from the past that the Talented Tenth as they have risen among American Negroes have been worthy of leadership; secondly, to show how these men may be educated and developed; and thirdly, to show their relation to the Negro problem.

You misjudge us because you do not know us. From the very first it has been the educated and intelligent of the Negro people that have led and elevated the mass, and the sole obstacles that nullified and retarded their efforts were slavery and race prejudice; for what is slavery but the legalized survival of the unfit and the nullification of the work of natural internal leadership? Negro leadership, therefore, sought from the first to rid the race of this awful incubus that it might make way for natural selection and the survival of the fittest. In colonial days came Phillis Wheatley and Paul Cuffe striving against the bars of prejudice; and Benjamin Banneker, the almanac maker, voiced their longings when he said to Thomas Jefferson, "I freely and cheerfully acknowledge that I am of the African race, and in colour which is natural to them, of the deepest dye; and it is under a sense of the most profound gratitude to the Supreme Ruler of the Universe, that I now confess to you that I am not under that state of tyrannical thraldom and inhuman captivity to which too many of my brethren are doomed, but that I have abundantly tasted of the fruition of those blessings which proceed from that free and unequalled liberty with which you are favored, and which I hope you will willingly allow, you have mercifully received from the immediate hand of that Being from whom proceedeth every good and perfect gift.

"Suffer me to recall to your mind that time, in which the arms of the British crown were exerted with every powerful effort, in order to reduce you to a state of servitude; look back, I entreat you, on the variety of dangers to which you were exposed; reflect on that period in which every human aid appeared unavailable, and in which even hope and fortitude wore the aspect of inability to the conflict, and you cannot but be led to a serious and grateful sense of your miraculous and providential preservation, you cannot but acknowledge, that the present freedom and tranquility which you enjoy, you have mercifully received, and that a peculiar blessing of heaven.

"This, sir, was a time when you clearly saw into the injustice of a state of Slavery, and in which you had just apprehensions of the horrors of its condition. It was then that your abhorrence thereof was so excited, that you publicly held forth this true and invaluable doctrine, which is worthy to be recorded and remembered in all succeeding ages: 'We hold these truths to be self evident, that all men are created equal; that they are endowed with certain inalienable rights, and that among these are life, liberty and the pursuit of happiness.' "

Then came Dr. James Derham, who could tell even the learned Dr. Rush something of medicine, and Lemuel Haynes, to whom Middlebury College gave a honorary A.M. in 1804. These and others we may call the Revolutionary group of distinguished Negroes—they were persons of marked ability, leaders of a Talented Tenth, standing conspicuously among the best of their time. They strove by word and deed to save the color line from becoming the line between the bond and free, but all they could do was nullified by Eli Whitney and the Curse of Gold. So they passed into forgetfulness.

But their spirit did not wholly die; here and there in the early part of the century came other exceptional men. Some were natural sons of unnatural fathers and were given often a liberal training and thus a race of educated mulattoes sprang up to plead for black men's rights. There was Ira Aldridge, whom all Europe loved to honor; there was that Voice crying in the Wilderness, David Walker, and saying:

"I declare it does appear to me as though some nations think God is asleep, or that he made the Africans for nothing else but to dig their mines and work their farms, or they cannot believe history, sacred or profane. I ask every man who has a heart, and is blessed with the privilege of believing—Is not God a God of justice to all his creatures? Do you say he is? Then if he gives peace and tranquility to tyrants and permits them to keep our fathers, our mothers, ourselves and our children in eternal ignorance and wretchedness to support them and their families, would he be to us a God of Justice? I ask, O, ye Christians, who hold us and our children in the most abject ignorance and degradation that ever a people were afflicted with since the world began—I say if God gives you peace and tranquility, and suffers you thus to go on afflicting us, and our children, who have never given you the least provocation—would He be to us a God of Justice? If you will allow that we are men, who feel for each other, does not the blood of our fathers and of us, their children, cry aloud to the Lord of Sabaoth against you for the cruelties and murder with which you have and do continue to afflict us?"

This was the wild voice that first aroused Southern legislation in 1829 to the terrors of abolitionism.

In 1831 there met that first Negro convention in Philadelphia, at which the world gaped curiously but which bravely attacked the problems of race and slavery, crying out against persecution and declaring that "Laws as cruel in themselves as they were unconstitutional and unjust, have in many places been enacted against our poor, unfriended and unoffending brethren (without a shadow of provocation on our part), at whose bare recital the very savage draws himself up for fear of contagion—looks noble and prides himself because he bears not the name of Christian." Side by side this free Negro movement, and the movement for abolition, strove until they merged into one strong stream. Too little notice has been taken of the work which the Talented Tenth among Negroes took in the great abolition crusade. From the very day that a Philadelphia colored man became the first subscriber to Garrison's "Liberator," to the day when Negro soldiers made the Emancipation Proclamation possible, black leaders worked shoulder to shoulder with white men in a movement, the success of which would have been impossible without them. There was [Robert] Purvis and [Charles Lenox] Remond, [James] Pennington and Highland Garnett, Sojourner Truth and Alexander Crummell, and above all, Frederick Douglass—what would the abolition movement have been without them? They stood as living examples of the possibilities of the Negro race, their own hard experiences and well wrought culture said silently more than all the drawn periods of orators—they were the men who made American slavery impossible. As Maria Weston Chapman once said, from the school of anti-slavery agitation "a throng of authors, editors, lawyers, orators and accomplished gentlemen of color have taken their degree! It has equally implanted hopes and aspirations, noble thoughts, and sublime purposes, in the hearts of both races. It has prepared the white man for the freedom of the black man, and it has made the black man scorn the thought of enslavement, as does a white man, as far as its influence has extended. Strengthen that noble influence! Before its organization, the country only saw here and there in slavery some faithful Cudjoe or Dinah, whose strong natures blossomed even in bondage, like a fine plant beneath a heavy stone. Now, under the elevating and cherishing influence of the American Anti-Slavery Society, the colored race, like the white, furnished Corinthian capitals for the noblest temples."

Where were these black abolitionists trained? Some, like Frederick Douglass were self-trained, but yet trained liberally; others, like Alexander Crummell and [James] McCune Smith, graduated from famous foreign universities. Most of them rose up through the colored schools of New York and Philadelphia and Boston, taught by college-bred men like [John Brown] Russworm, of Dartmouth, and college-bred white men like [Elias] Neau and [Anthony] Benezet.

After emancipation came a new group of educated and gifted leaders: [John Mercer] Langston, [Blanche K.] Bruce and [Robert Brown] Elliott, [Richard Theodore] Greener, [Dr. Daniel Hale] Williams and [Daniel A.] Payne. Through political organization, historical and polemic writing and moral regeneration, these men strove to uplift their people. It is the fashion of to-day to sneer at them and to say that with freedom Negro leadership should have begun at the plow and not in the Senate—a foolish and mischievous lie; two hundred and fifty years that black serf toiled at the plow and yet that toiling was in vain till the Senate passed the war amendments; and two hundred and fifty years more the half-free serf of to-day may toil at his plow, but unless he have political rights and righteously guarded civic status, he will still remain the poverty-stricken and ignorant plaything of rascals, that he now is. This all sane men know even if they dare not say it.

And so we come to the present—a day of cowardice and vacillation, of strident wide-voiced wrong and faint hearted compromise; of double-faced dallying with Truth and Right. Who are to-day guiding the work of the Negro people? The "exceptions" of course. And yet so sure as this Talented Tenth is pointed out, the blind worshippers of the Average cry out in alarm: "They are exceptions, look here at death, disease and crime—these are the happy rule." Of course they are the rule, because a silly nation made them the rule: Because for three long centuries this people lynched Negroes who dared to be brave, raped black women who dared to be virtuous, crushed dark-hued youth who dared to be ambitious, and encouraged and made to flourish servility and lewdness and apathy. But not even this was able to crush all manhood and chastity and aspiration from black folk. A saving remnant continually survives and persists, continually aspires, continually shows itself in thrift and ability and character. Exceptional it is to be sure, but this is its chiefest promise; it shows the capability of Negro blood, the promise of black men. Do Americans ever stop to reflect that there are in this land a million men of Negro blood, well-educated, owners of homes, against the honor of whose womanhood no breath was ever raised, whose men occupy positions of trust and usefulness, and who, judged by any standard, have reached the full measure of the best type of modern European culture? Is it fair, is it decent, is it Christian to ignore these facts of the

Negro problem, to belittle such aspiration, to nullify such leadership and seek to crush these people back into the mass out of which by toil and travail, they and their fathers have raised themselves?

Can the masses of the Negro people be in any possible way more quickly raised than by the effort and example of this aristocracy of talent and character? Was there ever a nation on God's fair earth civilized from the bottom upward? Never; it is, ever was and ever will be from the top downward that culture filters. The Talented Tenth rises and pulls all that are worth the saving up to their vantage ground. This is the history of human progress; and the two historical mistakes which have hindered that progress were the thinking first that no more could ever rise save the few already risen; or second, that it would better the unrisen to pull the risen down.

How then shall the leaders of a struggling people be trained and the hands of the risen strengthened? There can be but one answer: The best and most capable of their youth must be schooled in the colleges and universities of the land. We will not quarrel as to just what the university of the Negro should teach or how it should teach it—I willingly admit that each soul and each race-soul needs its own peculiar curriculum. But this is true: A university is a human invention for the transmission of knowledge and culture from generation to generation, through the training of quick minds and pure hearts, and for this work no other human invention will suffice, not even trade and industrial schools.

All men cannot go to college but some men must; every isolated group or nation must have its yeast, must have for the talented few centers of training where men are not so mystified and befuddled by the hard and necessary toil of earning a living, as to have no aims higher than their bellies, and no God greater than Gold. This is true training, and thus in the beginning were the favored sons of the freedmen trained. Out of the colleges of the North came, after the blood of war, Ware, Cravath, Chase, Andrews, Bumstead and Spence to build the foundations of knowledge and civilization in the black South. Where ought they to have begun to build? At the bottom, of course, quibbles the mole with his eyes in the earth. Aye! truly at the bottom, at the very bottom; at the bottom of knowledge, down in the very depths of knowledge there where the roots of justice strike into the lowest soil of Truth. And so they did begin; they founded colleges, and up from the colleges shot normal schools, and out from the normal schools went teachers, and around the normal teachers clustered other teachers to teach the public schools; the college trained in Greek and Latin and mathematics, 2,000 men; and these men trained full 50,000 others in morals and manners, and they in turn taught thrift and the alphabet to nine millions of men, who to-day hold $300,000,000 of property. It was a miracle—the most wonderful peace-battle of the 19th century, and yet to-day men smile at it, and in fine superiority tell us that it was all a strange mistake; that a proper way to found a system of education is to gather the children and buy them spelling books and hoes; afterward men may look about for teachers, if haply they may find them; or again they would teach men Work, but as for Life—why, what has Work to do with Life, they ask vacantly.

Was the work of these college founders successful; did it stand the test of time? Did the college graduates, with all their fine theories of life, really live? Are they useful men helping to civilize and elevate their less fortunate fellows? Let us see. Omitting all institutions which have not actually graduated students from a college course, there are to-day in the United States thirty-four institutions giving something above high school training to Negroes and designed especially for this race.

Three of these were established in border States before the War; thirteen were planted by the Freedman's Bureau in the years 1864–1869; nine were established between 1870 and 1880 by various church bodies; five were established after 1881 by Negro churches, and four are state institutions supported by United States' agricultural funds. In most cases the college departments are small adjuncts to high and common school work. As a matter of fact six institutions—Atlanta, Fisk, Howard, Shaw, Wilberforce and Leland, are the important Negro colleges so far as actual work and number of students are concerned. In all these institutions, seven hundred and fifty Negro college students are enrolled. . . . In addition to these students in the South, Negroes have attended Northern colleges for many years. As early as 1826 one was graduated from Bowdoin College, and from that time till to-day nearly every year has seen elsewhere, other such graduates. They have, of course, met much color prejudice. Fifty years ago very few colleges would admit them at all. Even to-day no Negro has ever been admitted to Princeton, and at some other leading institutions they are rather endured than encouraged. Oberlin was the great pioneer in the work of blotting out the color line in colleges, and has more Negro graduates by far than any other Northern college. . . .

The most interesting question, and in many respects the crucial question, to be asked concerning college-bred Negroes, is: Do they earn a living? It has been intimated more than once that the higher training of Negroes has resulted in sending into the world of work, men who could find nothing to do suitable to their talents. Now and then there comes a rumor of a colored college man working at menial service, etc. Fortunately, returns as to occupations of college-bred Negroes, gathered by the Atlanta conference, are quite full—nearly sixty per cent. of the total number of graduates.

This enables us to reach fairly certain conclusions as to the occupations of all college-bred Negroes. Of 1,312 persons reported. . . . over half are teachers, a sixth are preachers, another sixth are students and professional men; over 6 per cent. are farmers, artisans and merchants, and 4 per cent. are in government services. . . .

These figures illustrate vividly the function of the college-bred Negro. He is, as he ought to be, the group leader, the man who sets the ideals of the community where he lives, directs its thoughts and heads its social movements. It need hardly be argued that the Negro people need social leadership more than most groups; that they have no traditions to fall back upon, no long established customs, no strong family ties, no well defined social classes. All these things must be slowly and painfully evolved. The preacher was, even before the war, the group leader of the Negroes, and the church their greatest social institution. Naturally this preacher was ignorant and often immoral, and the problem of replacing the older type by better educated men has been a difficult one. Both by direct work and by direct influence on other preachers, and on congregations, the college-bred preacher has an opportunity for reformatory work and moral inspiration, the value of which cannot be overestimated.

It has, however, been in the furnishing of teachers that the Negro college has found its peculiar function. Few persons realize how vast a work, how mighty a revolution has been thus accomplished. To furnish five millions and more of ignorant people with teachers of their own race and blood, in one generation, was not only a very difficult undertaking, but a very important one, in that, it placed before the eyes of almost every Negro child an attainable ideal. It brought the masses of the blacks in contact with modern civilization, made black men the leaders of their communities and trainers of the new generation. In this work college-bred Negroes were first teachers, and then teachers of teachers. And here it is that the broad culture of college work has been of peculiar value. Knowledge of life and its wider meaning, has been the point of the Negro's deepest ignorance, and the sending out of teachers whose training has not been simply for bread winning, but also for human culture, has been of inestimable value in the training of these men.

In earlier years the two occupations of preacher and teacher were practically the only ones open to the black college graduate. Of later years a larger diversity of life among his people, has opened new avenues of employment. Nor have these college men been paupers and spendthrifts; 557 college-bred Negroes owned in 1899, $1,342,862.50 worth of real estate, (assessed value) or $2,411 per family. The real value of the total accumulations of the whole group is perhaps about $10,000,000 or $5,000 a piece. Pitiful, is it not, beside the fortunes of oil kings and steel trusts, but after all is the fortune of the millionaire the only stamp of true and successful living? Alas! it is, with many, and there's the rub.

The problem of training the Negro is to-day immensely complicated by the fact that the whole question of the efficiency and appropriateness of our present systems of education, for any kind of child, is a matter of active debate, in which final settlement seems still afar off. Consequently it often happens that persons arguing for or against certain systems of education for Negroes, have these controversies in mind and miss the real question at issue. The main question, so far as the Southern Negro is concerned, is:

What under the present circumstance, must a system of education do in order to raise the Negro as quickly as possible in the scale of civilization? The answer to this question seems to me clear: It must strengthen the Negro's character, increase his knowledge and teach him to earn a living. Now it goes without saying, that it is hard to do all these things simultaneously or suddenly, and that at the same time it will not do to give all the attention to one and neglect the others; we could give black boys trades, but that alone will not civilize a race of ex-slaves; we might simply increase their knowledge of the world, but this would not necessarily make them wish to use this knowledge honestly; we might seek to strengthen character and purpose, but to what end if this people have nothing to eat or to wear? A system of education is not one thing, nor does it have a single definite object, nor is it a mere matter of schools. Education is that whole system of human training within and without the school house walls, which molds and develops men. If then we start out to train an ignorant and unskilled people with a heritage of bad habits, our system of training must set before itself two great aims—the one dealing with knowledge and character, the other part seeking to give the child the technical knowledge necessary for him to earn a living under the present circumstances. These objects are accomplished in part by the opening of the common schools on the one, and of the industrial schools on the other. But only in part, for there must also be trained those who are to teach these schools—men and women of knowledge and culture and technical skill who understand modern civilization, and have the training and aptitude to impart it to the children under them. There must be teachers, and teachers of teachers, and to attempt to establish any sort of a system of common and industrial school training, without *first* (and I say *first* advisedly) without *first* providing for the higher training of the very best teachers, is simply throwing your money to the winds. School houses do not teach themselves—piles of brick and mortar and machinery do not send out *men.* It is the trained living human soul, cultivated and strengthened by long study and thought, that breathes the real breath of life into boys and girls and makes them human, whether they be black or white, Greek, Russian or American. Nothing, in these latter days, has so dampened the faith of thinking Negroes in recent educational movements, as the fact that such movements have been accompanied by ridicule and denouncement and decrying of those very institutions of higher training which made the Negro public school possible, and make Negro industrial schools thinkable. It was Fisk, Atlanta, Howard and Straight, those colleges born of the faith and sacrifice of the abolitionists, that placed in the black schools of the South the 30,000 teachers and more, which some, who depreciate the work of these higher schools, are using to teach their own new experiments. If Hampton, Tuskegee and the hundred other industrial schools prove in the future to be as successful as they deserve to be, then their success in training black artisans for the South, will be due primarily to the white colleges of the

North and the black colleges of the South, which trained the teachers who to-day conduct these institutions. . . .

I would not deny, or for a moment seem to deny, the paramount necessity of teaching the Negro to work, and to work steadily and skillfully; or seem to depreciate in the slightest degree the important part industrial schools must play in the accomplishment of these ends, but I *do* say, and insist upon it, that it is industrialism drunk with its vision of success, to imagine that its own work can be accomplished without providing for the training of broadly cultured men and women to teach its own teachers, and to teach the teachers of the public schools.

But I have already said that human education is not simply a matter of schools; it is much more a matter of family and group life—the training of one's home, of one's daily companions, of one's social class. Now the black boy of the South moves in a black world—a world with its own leaders, its own thoughts, its own ideas. In this world he gets by far the larger part of his life training, and through the eyes of this dark world he peers into the veiled world beyond. Who guides and determines the education which he receives in his world? His teachers here are the group-leaders of the Negro people—the physicians and clergymen, the trained fathers and mothers, the influential and forceful men about him of all kinds; here it is, if at all, that the culture of the surrounding world trickles through and is handed by the graduates of the higher schools. Can such culture training of group leaders be neglected? Can we afford to ignore it? Do you think that if the leaders of thought among Negroes are not trained and educated thinkers, that they will have no leaders? On the contrary a hundred half-trained demagogues will still hold the places they so largely occupy now, and hundreds of vociferous busy-bodies will multiply. You have no choice; either you must help furnish this race from within its own ranks with thoughtful men of trained leadership, or you must suffer the evil consequences of a headless misguided rabble.

I am an earnest advocate of manual training and trade teaching for black boys, and for white boys, too. I believe that next to the founding of Negro colleges the most valuable addition to Negro education since the war, has been industrial training for black boys. Nevertheless, I insist that the object of all true education is not to make men carpenters, it is to make carpenters men; there are two means of making the carpenter a man, each equally important: the first is to give the group and community in which he works, liberally trained teachers and leaders to teach him and his family what life means; the second is to give him sufficient intelligence and technical skill to make him an efficient workman; the first object demands the Negro college and college-bred men—not a quantity of such colleges, but a few of excellent quality; not too many college-bred men, but enough to leaven the lump, to inspire the masses, to raise a good system of common schools, well-taught, conveniently located and properly equipped. . . .

What is the chief need for the building up of the Negro public school in the South? The Negro race in the South needs teachers to-day above all else. This is the concurrent testimony of all who know the situation. . . . [I]t is safe to say that the Negro has not one-tenth his quota in college studies. How baseless, therefore, is the charge of too much training! We need Negro teachers for the Negro common schools, and we need first-class normal schools and colleges to train them. This is the work of higher Negro education and it must be done.

Further than this, after being provided with group leaders of civilization, and a foundation of intelligence in the public schools, the carpenter, in order to be a man, needs technical skill. This calls for trade schools. Now trade schools are not nearly such simple things as people once thought. The original idea was that the "Industrial" school was to furnish education, practically free, to those willing to work for it; it was to "do" things—i.e.: become a center of productive industry, it was to be partially, if not wholly, self-supporting, and it was to teach trades. Admirable as were some of the ideas underlying this scheme, the whole thing simply would not work in practice; it was found that if you were to use time and material to teach trades thoroughly, you could not at the same time keep the industries on a commercial basis and make them pay. Many schools started out to do this on a large scale and went into virtual bankruptcy. . . .

[M]odern industry has taken great strides since the war, and the teaching of trades is no longer a simple matter. Machinery and long processes of work have greatly changed the work of the carpenter, the ironworker and the shoemaker. A really efficient workman must be today an intelligent man who has had good technical training in addition to thorough common school, and perhaps even higher training. To meet this situation the industrial schools began a further development; they established distinct Trade Schools for the thorough training of better class artisans, and at the same time they sought to preserve for the purpose of general education, such of the simpler processes of elementary trade learning, as were best suited therefor. In this differentiation of the Trade School and manual training, the best of the industrial schools simply followed the plain trend of the present educational epoch. . . .

Thus, again, in the manning of trade schools and manual training schools we are thrown back upon the higher training as its source and chief support. There was a time when any aged and wornout carpenter could teach in a trade school. But not so to-day. Indeed the demand for college-bred men by a school like Tuskegee, ought to make Mr. Booker T. Washington the firmest friend of higher training. Here he has as helpers the son of a Negro senator, trained in Greek and the humanities, and graduated at Harvard; the son of a Negro congressman and lawyer, trained in Latin and mathematics, and graduated at Oberlin; he has as his wife, a woman who read Virgil and Homer in the same class room with me; he has as college chaplain, a classical graduate of Atlanta University; as teacher of science, a graduate of Fisk; as teacher of history, a graduate of Smith,—indeed some thirty of his chief teachers are college graduates, and instead of studying French grammars in the midst of weeds, or buying pianos for dirty cabins, they are at Mr. Washington's right hand helping him in a noble work. And yet one of the effects of Mr. Washington's propaganda has been to throw doubt upon the expedience of such training for Negroes, as these persons have had.

Men of America, the problem is plain before you. Here is a race transplanted through the criminal foolishness of your fathers. Whether you like it or not the millions are here, and here they will remain. If you do not lift them up, they will pull you down. Education and work are the levers to uplift a people. Work alone will not do it unless inspired by the right ideals and guided by intelligence. Education must not simply teach work—it must teach Life. The Talented Tenth of the Negro race must be made leaders of thought and missionaries of culture among their people. No others can do this work and Negro colleges must train men for it. The Negro race, like all other races, is going to be saved by its exceptional men.

The Negro Problem, 1903

Ida Wells-Barnett (1862–1931)

A fearless "crusader for justice," Ida Wells-Barnett waged a constant battle against racial discrimination and the rule of the mob. Born into slavery on July 16, 1862, in Holly Springs, Mississippi, Ida Bell Wells was the oldest of eight children. In 1878 Ida lost both of her parents and a younger brother in a yellow-fever epidemic. Determined to keep her family together, at age sixteen Ida supported her surviving siblings by working as a schoolteacher nearby, and then in 1882 or 1883 she moved to Memphis, where she studied for the teacher's examination and attended Fisk University.

Wells's first public protest began in 1882 when, en route from Memphis to her school in Woodstock, Tennessee, she was ordered to ride in the separate smoking car of the train. She refused, returned to Memphis, and brought charges against the train company. She won her case, but the decision was reversed by the state supreme court, a defeat she recounted bitterly in her diary: "I have firmly believed all along that the law was on our side and would, when we appealed to it, give us justice. I feel shorn of that belief and utterly discouraged, and just now, if it were possible, would gather my race in my arms and fly away with them." She wrote about the case in 1887 in the Baptist weekly *Living Way* under the pen name "Iola," and went on to contribute articles to numerous other church and secular journals. In 1889 she bought an interest in the Memphis *Free Speech ana Headlight,* where her article citing the inequalities of the public-school system cost her her teaching job in 1891. But it was her bold denunciation of lynching that would launch her true career.

On March 9, 1892, three successful black businessmen, whom Ida knew personally, were lynched by a mob. In an editorial she rejected the claim that an affront to a white woman was the cause of the incident and denied that all relations between white women and black men were coercive: "Nobody in this section of the country believes the old thread bare lie that Negro men rape white women. If Southern white men are not careful, they will over-reach themselves and. . . . a conclusion will then be reached which will be very damaging to the moral reputation of their women." She argued, instead, that the lynching was caused by economic competition and racial hatred. When the editorial appeared, Wells was attending an AME Conference in Philadelphia; her office was ransacked and she was warned that her life would be in danger if she returned.

She continued to press her claims in T. Thomas Fortune's *New York Age,* and in the pamphlet *Southern Horrors: Lynch Law in All Its Phases,* embarking on her lifelong protest against lynching—writing, speaking, and organizing resistance. She made trips to Great Britain in 1893 and 1894, where her speeches spurred the organization of an Antilynching Committee, and described her travels in the column "Ida B. Wells Abroad" for the Chicago *Inter-Ocean.*

Wells's lecture on the topic of lynching to a group of prominent black women became a catalyst to the women's-club movement. She helped organize the Women's Era Club in Boston, with Mrs. Josephine St. Pierre Raffin as president, and an Ida B. Wells club was formed in Chicago. In 1893 Wells coauthored with Frederick Douglass and others a protest against the exclusion of African-Americans from the 1893 Chicago World's Fair: "The colored people of this great Republic," it stated, ". . . were among the earliest settlers of this continent, landing at Jamestown, Virginia, in 1619 in a slave ship, before the Puritans, who landed at Plymouth in 1620. They have contributed a large share to American prosperity and civilization. The labor of one-half of this country has always been, and is still being done by them."

In Chicago, Wells continued to write for the *Conservator,* owned by a prominent attorney, Ferdinand Lee Barnett, whom she married in 1895. The same year her comprehensive account of lynching, *A Red Record: Tabulated Statistics and Alleged Causes of Lynching in the United States,* from which the following chapter is taken, was published. Soon after the first of her four children was born in 1896, she attended the first convention of the National Association of Colored Women, but after the birth of her next child, she retired temporarily from public life.

In 1908 she resumed her activity, establishing the Negro Fellowship League and a settlement house in South Side Chicago. She continued her work with women's clubs and was a founding member of the NAACP. In 1913 she established the Alpha Suffrage Club, the first group of black women to work for the ballot, in a mayoralty election in 1914. She also investigated and reported on the race riots in Springfield, Illinois (1908), East St. Louis (1917), and Chicago (1919), primarily for *The Chicago Defender.*

Wells began writing her memoirs in 1928, but died of uremic poisoning March 25, 1931, before the book was completed. *Crusade for Justice: The Autobiography of Ida B. Wells,* edited by her daughter Alfreda M. Duster, was published in 1970.

from *A Red Record*

"Out of their own mouths shall the murderers be condemned. . . ."

THE CASE STATED

THE STUDENT OF AMERICAN SOCIOLOGY WILL FIND THE YEAR 1894 marked by a pronounced awakening of the public conscience to a system of anarchy and outlawry which had grown during a series of ten years to be so common, that scenes of unusual brutality failed to have any visible effect upon the humane sentiments of the people of our land.

Beginning with the emancipation of the Negro, the inevitable result of unbridled power exercised for two and a half centuries, by the white man over the Negro, began to show itself in acts of conscienceless outlawry. During the slave *regime,* the Southern white man owned the Negro body and soul. It was to his interest to dwarf the soul and preserve the body. Vested with unlimited power over his slave, to subject him to any and all kinds of physical punishment, the white man was still restrained from such punishment as tended to injure the slave by abating his physical powers and thereby reducing his financial worth. While slaves were scourged mercilessly, and in countless cases inhumanly treated in other respects, still the white owner rarely permitted his anger to go so far as to take a life, which would entail upon him a loss of several hundred dollars. The slave was rarely killed, he was too valuable; it was easier and quite as effective, for discipline or revenge, to sell him "Down South."

But Emancipation came and the vested interests of the white man in the Negro's body were lost. The white man had no right to scourge the emancipated Negro, still less has he a right to kill him. But the Southern white people had been educated so long in that school of practice, in which might makes right, that they disdained to draw strict lines of action in dealing with the Negro. In slave times the Negro was kept subservient and submissive by the frequency and severity of the scourging, but, with freedom, a new system of intimidation came in vogue; the Negro was not only whipped and scourged; he was killed.

Not all nor nearly all of the murders done by white men, during the past thirty years in the South, have come to light, but the statistics as gathered and preserved by white men, and which have not been questioned, show that during these years more than ten thousand Negroes have been killed in cold blood, without the formality of judicial trial and legal execution. And yet, as evidence of the absolute impunity with which the white man dare to kill a Negro, the same record shows that during all these years, and for all these murders only three white men have been tried, convicted, and executed. As no white man has been lynched for the murder of colored people, these three executions are the only instances of the death penalty being visited upon white men for murdering Negroes.

Naturally enough the commission of these crimes began to tell upon the public conscience, and the Southern white man, as a tribute to the nineteenth century civilization, was in a manner compelled to give excuses for his barbarism. His excuses have adapted themselves to the emergency, and are aptly outlined by that greatest of all Negroes, Frederick Douglass, in an article of recent date, in which he shows that there have been three distinct eras of southern barbarism, to account for which three distinct excuses have been made.

The first excuse given to the civilized world for the murder of unoffending Negroes was the necessity of the white men to repress and stamp out alleged "race riots." For years immediately succeeding the war there was an appalling slaughter of colored people, and the wires usually conveyed to northern people and the world the intelligence, first, that an insurrection was being planned by Negroes, which, a few hours later, would prove to have been vigorously resisted and wounded. It was always a remarkable feature in these insurrections and riots that only Negroes were killed during the rioting, and that all the white men escaped unharmed.

From 1865 to 1872, hundreds of colored men and women were mercilessly murdered and the almost invariable reason assigned was that they met their death by being alleged participants in an insurrection or riot. But this story at last wore itself out. No insurrection ever materialized; no Negro rioter was ever apprehended and proven guilty, and no dynamite ever recorded the black man's protest against oppression and wrong. It was too much to ask thoughtful people to believe this transparent story, and the southern white people at last made up their minds that some other excuse must be had.

Then came the second excuse, which had its birth during the turbulent times of reconstruction. By an amendment to the Constitution the Negro was given the right of franchise, and, theoretically at least, his ballot became his invaluable emblem of citizenship. In a government "of the people, for the people, and by the people," the Negro's vote became an important factor in all matters of state and national politics. But this did not last long. The southern white man would not consider that the Negro had any right which a white man was bound to respect, and the idea of a republican form of government in the southern states grew into general contempt. It was maintained that "This is a white man's government," and regardless of numbers, the white man should rule. "No Negro domination" became the new legend on the sanguinary banner of the sunny South, and under it rode the Ku Klux Klan, the Regulators, and the lawless mobs, which for any cause chose to murder one man or a dozen as suited their purpose best. It was a long, gory campaign; the blood chills and the heart almost loses faith in Christianity when one thinks of Yazoo, Hamburg, Edgefield, Copiah, and the countless massacres of defenceless Negroes, whose only crime was the attempt to exercise their right to vote.

But it was a bootless strife for colored people. The government which had made the Negro a citizen found itself unable to protect him. It gave him the right to vote, but denied him the protection which should have maintained that right. Scourged from his home; hunted through the swamps; hung by midnight raiders, and openly murdered in the light of day, the Negro clung to this right of franchise with a heroism which would have wrung admiration from the heart of savages. He believed that in that small white ballot there was a subtle something which stood for manhood as well as citizenship, and thousands of brave black men went to their graves, exemplifying the one by dying for the other.

The white man's victory soon became complete by fraud, violence, intimidation and murder. The franchise vouchsafed to the Negro grew to be a "barren ideality," and regardless of numbers, the colored people found themselves voiceless in the councils of those whose duty it was to rule. With no longer the fear of "Negro Domination" before their eyes, the white man's second excuse became valueless. With the Southern governments all subverted and the Negro actually eliminated from all participation in state and national elections, there could be no longer an excuse for killing Negroes to prevent "Negro Domination."

Brutality still continued; Negroes were whipped, scourged, exiled, shot and hung whenever and wherever it pleased the white man so to treat them, and as the civilized world with increasing persistency held the white people of the South to account for its outlawry, the murderers invented the third excuse—that Negroes had to be killed to avenge their assaults upon women. There could be framed no possible excuse more harmful to the Negro and more unanswerable if true in its sufficiency for the white man.

Humanity abhors the assailant of womanhood, and this charge upon the Negro at once placed him beyond the pale of human sympathy. With such unanimity, earnestness and apparent candor was this charge made and reiterated that the world has accepted the story that the Negro is the monster which the Southern white man has painted him. And today, the Christian world feels, that while lynching is a crime, and lawlessness and anarchy the certain precursors of a nation's fall, it can not by word or deed, extend sympathy or help to a race of outlaws, who might mistake their plea for justice and deem it an excuse for their continued wrongs.

The Negro has suffered much and is willing to suffer more. He recognizes that the wrongs of two centuries can not be righted in a day, and he tries to bear his burden with patience for to-day and be hopeful for to-morrow. But there comes a time when the veriest worm will turn, and the Negro feels to-day that after all the work he has done, all the sacrifices he has made, and all the suffering he has endured, if he did not, now, defend his name and manhood from this vile accusation, he would be unworthy even of the contempt of mankind. It is to this charge he now feels he must make answer.

If the Southern people in defense of their lawlessness, would tell the truth and admit that colored men and women are lynched for almost any offense from murder to a misdemeanor, there would not now be the necessity for this defense. But when they intentionally, maliciously and constantly belie the record and bolster up these falsehoods by the words of legislators, preachers, governors and bishops, then the Negro must give to the world his side of the awful story.

A word as to the charge itself. In considering the third reason assigned by the Southern white people for the butchery of blacks, the question must be asked, what the white man means when he charges the black man with rape. Does he mean the crime which the statutes of the civilized states describe as such? Not by any means. With the Southern white man, any *mesalliance* existing between a white woman and a colored man is a sufficient foundation for the charge of rape. The Southern white man says that it is impossible for a voluntary alliance to exist between a white woman and a colored man, and therefore, the fact of an alliance is a proof of force. In numerous instances where colored men have been lynched on the charge of rape, it was positively known at the time of lynching, and indisputably proven after the victim's death, that the relationship sustained between the man and woman was voluntary and clandestine, and that in no court of law could even the charge of assault have been successfully maintained.

It was the assertion of this fact, in the defense of her own race, that the writer herself became an exile; her property destroyed and her return to her home forbidden under penalty of death, for writing the following editorial which was printed in her paper, *The Free Speech*, in Memphis, Tenn., May 21, 1892.

"Eight Negroes lynched since last issue of the 'Free Speech' one at Little Rock, Ark., last Saturday morning where the citizens broke (?) into the penitentiary and got their man; three near Anniston, Ala., for killing a white man, and five on the same old racket—the new alarm about raping white women. The same programme of hanging, then shooting bullets into the lifeless bodies was carried out to the letter. Nobody in this section of the country believes the old thread bare lie that Negro men rape white women. If Southern white men are not careful, they will over-reach themselves and public sentiment will have a reaction; a conclusion will then be reached which will be very damaging to the moral reputation of their women."

But threats cannot suppress the truth, and while the Negro suffers the soul deformity, resultant from two and a half centuries of slavery, he is no more guilty of this vilest of all vile charges than the white man who would blacken his name.

During all the years of slavery, no such charge was ever made, not even during the dark days of the rebellion, when the white man, following the fortunes of war went to do battle for the maintenance of slavery. While the master was away fighting to forge the fetters upon the slave, he left his wife and children with no protectors save the Negroes themselves. And yet during those years of trust and peril, no Negro proved recreant to his trust and no white man returned to a home that had been despoiled.

Likewise during the period of alleged "insurrection," and alarming "race riots," it never occurred to the white man, that his wife and children were in danger of assault. Nor in the Reconstruction era, when the hue and cry was against "Negro Domination," was there ever a thought that the domination would ever contaminate a fireside or strike to death the virtue of womanhood. It must appear strange indeed, to every thoughtful and candid man, that more than a quarter of a century elapsed before the Negro began to show signs of such infamous degeneration.

In his remarkable apology for lynching, Bishop Haygood, of Georgia, says: "No race, not the most savage, tolerates the rape of woman, but it may be said without reflection upon any other people that the Southern people are now and always have been most sensitive concerning the honor of their women—their mothers, wives, sisters and daughters." It is not the purpose of this defense to say one word against the white women of the South. Such need not be said, but it is their misfortune that the chivalrous white men of that section, in order to escape the deserved execration of the civilized world, should shield themselves by their cowardly and infamously false excuse, and call into question that very honor about which their distinguished priestly apologist claims they are most sensitive. To justify their own barbarism they assume a chivalry which they do not possess. True chivalry respects all womanhood, and no one who reads the record, as it is written in the faces of the million mulattoes in the South, will for a minute conceive that the southern white man had a very chivalrous regard for the honor due the women of his own race or respect for the womanhood which circumstances placed in his power. That chivalry which is "most sensitive concerning the honor of women" can hope for but little respect from the civilized world, when it confines itself entirely to the women who happen to be white. Virtue knows no color line, and the chivalry which depends upon complexion of skin and texture of hair can command no honest respect.

When the emancipation came to the Negroes, there arose in the northern part of the United States an almost divine sentiment among the noblest, purest and best white women of the North, who felt called to a mission to educate and Christianize the millions of southern ex-slaves. From every nook and corner of the North, brave young white women answered that call and left their cultural homes, their happy associations and their lives of ease, and with heroic determination went to the South to carry light and truth to the benighted blacks. It was a heroism no less than that which calls for volunteers for India, Africa and the Isles of the sea. To educate their unfortunate charges; to teach them the Christian virtues and to inspire in them the moral sentiments manifest in their own lives, these young women braved dangers whose record reads more like fiction than fact. They became social outlaws in the South. The peculiar sensitiveness of the southern white man for women, never shed its protecting influence about them. No friendly word from their own race cheered them in their work; no hospitable doors gave them the companionship like that from which they had come. No chivalrous white man doffed his hat in honor or respect. They were "Nigger teachers"—unpardonable offenders in the social ethics of the South, and were insulted, persecuted and ostracised, not by Negroes, but by the white manhood which boasts of its chivalry toward women.

And yet these northern women worked on, year after year, unselfishly, with a heroism which amounted almost to martyrdom. Threading their way through dense forests, working in school house, in the cabin and in the church, thrown at all times and in all places among the unfortunate and lowly Negroes, whom they had come to find and to serve, these northern women, thousands and thousands of them have spent more than a quarter of a century in giving to the colored people their splendid lessons for home and heart and soul. Without protection, save that which innocence gives to every good woman, they went about their work, fearing no assault and suffering none. Their chivalrous protectors were hundreds of miles away in their northern homes, and yet they never feared any "great dark faced mobs," they dared night or day to "go beyond their own roof trees." They never complained of assaults, and no mob was ever called into existence to avenge crimes against them. Before the world adjudges the Negro a moral monster, a vicious assailant of womanhood and a menace to the sacred precincts of home, the colored people ask the consideration of the silent record of gratitude, respect, protection and devotion of the millions of the race in the South, to the thousands of northern white women who have served as teachers and missionaries since the war.

The Negro may not have known what chivalry was, but he knew enough to preserve inviolate the womanhood of the South which was entrusted to his hands during the war. The finer sensibilities of his soul may have been crushed out by years of slavery, but his heart was full of gratitude to the white women of the North, who blessed his home and inspired his soul in all these years of freedom. Faithful to his trust in both of these instances, he should now have the impartial ear of the civilized world, when he dares to speak for himself as against the infamy wherewith he stands charged.

It is his regret, that, in his own defense, he must disclose to the world that degree of dehumanizing brutality which fixes upon America the blot of a national crime. Whatever faults and failings other nations may have in their dealings with their own subjects or with other people, no other civilized nation stands condemned before the world with a series of crimes so peculiarly national. It becomes a painful duty of the Negro to reproduce a record which shows that a large portion of the American people avow anarchy, condone murder and defy the contempt of civilization.

These pages are written in no spirit of vindictiveness, for all who give the subject consideration must concede that far too serious is the condition of that civilized government in which the spirit of unrestrained outlawry constantly increases in violence, and casts its blight over a continually growing area of territory. We plead not for the colored people alone, but for all victims of the terrible injustice which puts men and women to death without form of law. During the year 1894, there were 132 persons executed in the United States by due form of law, while in the same year, 197 persons were put to death by mobs who gave the victims no opportunity to make a lawful defense. No comment need be made upon a condition of public sentiment responsible for such alarming results.

The purpose of the pages which follow shall be to give the record which has been made, not by colored men, but that which is the result of compilations made by white men, of reports sent over the civilized world by white men in the South. Out of their own mouths shall the murderers be condemned. For a number of years the Chicago Tribune, admittedly one of the leading journals of America, has made a specialty of the compilation of statistics touching upon lynching. The data compiled by that journal and published to the world January 1st, 1894, up to the present time has not been disputed. In order to be safe from the charge of exaggeration, the incidents hereinafter reported have been confined to those vouched for by the Tribune.

1895

Mary Church Terrell
(1865–1954)

In her long life, Mary Church Terrell played an important role as a civil and women's-rights activist, lecturer, and suffragist. She was born in Memphis, Tennessee, where her father, a former slave and reputed millionaire, had become extremely wealthy in land speculation. Like Anna Julia Cooper, Church attended Oberlin College, where she pursued the "Gentlemen's Course," then taught at Wilberforce University and studied in Europe for two years. She returned to teach at the High School for Colored Youth in Washington, D.C., where she married the principal, Robert H. Terrell, in 1892. A Harvard graduate, through the patronage of Booker T. Washington Terrell became a municipal judge, while Mary received an important appointment to the Board of Education, where she served for eleven years. From 1896 to 1901 Terrell served as the first president of the National Association of Colored Women (Mrs. Booker Washington served as its vice president) and traveled abroad to represent the NACW in 1911, delivering her speech in Berlin in German and French, as well as English.

The women's-club movement had sprung up in the late nineteenth century as the feminine counterpart to the men's convention movement of the mid-1800s. Founded in Washington, D.C., in 1896, by 1911 the National Association of Colored Women had more than 45,000 members, the majority of them teachers. The club held national conventions and had state affiliates, or "federations," with such names as the Phillis Wheatley Club (Chicago and New Orleans), the Home Club, the Kindergarten Association, and the Fresh Air and Empty Stocking Association (Baltimore).

While the black-women's clubs in some ways reflected those organizations popular among white women of the day as well, they were in fact more practical. They had to be—in 1910 more than half of the nearly four million black women in the United States over the age of ten worked outside the home, compared to less than 20 percent of white women. The educated and the illiterate black woman thus already had more in common than their white counterparts and the clubs represented more broadly based, immediately felt concerns. (A century before such demands would enter the public debate again, the NACW argued for child support and day care. Terrell herself had four children, three of whom died within days of birth.) And while Terrell's stated goal of descending "among the lowly, the illiterate and even the vicious," may seem elitist, it was born of the realization that no matter how "cultured" the black woman, she was judged by the actions of her less fortunate sisters, rather than the most esteemed.

For the most part, the clubs' activities were limited to temperance, religion, morality, health, education, and all things related to the cult of the home (Terrell's paean to "Domestic Science" is reminiscent of Washington's pragmatic goals). Their philanthropy extended to old folks, orphans and "fallen women," though Terrell took special exception (as did Frances Harper in "A Double Standard"† to the prevalent attitude that the licentiousness of men was excusable while its effect on women was not.

While club women often split on the subject, a member of the National American Suffrage Association, Terrell herself strongly endorsed women's right to vote. In a special edition of *The Crisis,* she wrote, "How can any one who is able to use reason, and who believes in dealing out justice to all God's creatures, think it is right to withhold from one-half the human race rights and privileges freely accorded to the other half, which is neither more deserving nor more capable of exercising them?"

Terrell was a charter member of the NAACP, and in her later years led numerous protests in the nation's capital against discrimination. Her protest against the exclusion practiced by the D.C. chapter of the National Association of University Women resulted in its expulsion from the national organization, and her successful struggle to integrate restaurants in Washington went to the Supreme Court. In *The Independent* she wrote, "surely nowhere in the world do oppression and persecution based solely on the color of the skin appear more hateful and hideous than in the capital of the United States, because the chasm between the principles upon which this Government was founded, in which it still professes to believe, and those which are daily practiced under the protection of the flag, yawn so wide and deep."

What Role Is the Educated Negro Woman to Play in the Uplifting of Her Race?

"Carefully and conscientiously we shall study the questions which affect the race most deeply and directly."

SHOULD ANY ONE ASK WHAT SPECIAL PHASE OF THE NEGRO'S development makes me most hopeful of his ultimate triumph over present obstacles, I should answer unhesitatingly, it is the magnificent work the women are doing to regenerate and uplift the race. Judge the future of colored women by the past since their emancipation, and neither they nor their friends have any cause for anxiety.

For years, either banding themselves into small companies or struggling alone, colored women have worked with might and main to improve the condition of their people. The necessity of systemizing their efforts and working on a larger scale became apparent not many years ago and they decided to unite their forces. Thus it happened that in the summer of 1896 the National Association of Colored Women was formed by the union of two large organizations, each of which has done much to show our women the advantage of concerted action. So tenderly has this daughter of the organized womanhood of the race been nurtured and so wisely ministered unto, that it has grown to be a child hale, hearty and strong, of which its fond mothers have every reason to be proud. Handicapped though its members have been, because they lacked both money and experience, their efforts have, for the most part, been crowned with success in the twenty-six States where it has been represented.

Kindergartens have been established by some of our organizations, from which encouraging reports have come. A sanitarium with a training school for nurses has been set on such a firm foundation by the Phyllis Wheatley Club of New Orleans, Louisiana, and has proved itself to be such a blessing to the entire community that the municipal government has voted it an annual appropriation of several hundred dollars. By the Tuskegee, Alabama, branch of the association the work of bringing the light of knowledge and the gospel of cleanliness to their poor benighted sisters on the plantations has been conducted with signal success. Their efforts have thus far been confined to four estates, comprising thousands of acres of land, on which live hundreds of colored people, yet in the darkness of ignorance and the grip of sin, miles away from churches and schools.

Plans for aiding the indigent, orphaned and aged have been projected and in some instances have been carried into successful execution. One club in Memphis, Tennessee, has purchased a large tract of land, on which it intends to erect an old folk's home, part of the money for which has already been raised. Splendid service has been rendered by the Illinois Federation of Colored Women's Clubs, through whose instrumentality schools have been visited, truant children looked after, parents and teachers urged to co-operate with each other, rescue and reform work engaged in, so as to reclaim unfortunate women and tempted girls, public institutions investigated, garments cut, made and distributed to the needy poor.

Questions affecting our legal status as a race are sometimes agitated by our women. In Tennessee and Louisiana colored women have several times petitioned the legislature of their respective States to repeal the obnoxious Jim Crow car laws. In every way possible we are calling attention to the barbarity of the convict lease system, of which Negroes and especially the female prisoners are the principal victims, with the hope that the conscience of the country may be touched and this stain on its escutcheon be forever wiped away. Against the one room cabin we have inaugurated a vigorous crusade. When families of eight or ten men, women and children are all huddled promiscuously together in a single apartment, a condition common among our poor all over the land, there is little hope of inculcating morality and modesty. And yet in spite of the fateful heritage of slavery, in spite of the manifold pitfalls and peculiar temptations to which our girls are subjected, and though the safeguards usually thrown around maidenly youth and innocence are in some sections entirely withheld from colored girls, statistics compiled by men not inclined to falsify in favor of my race show that immorality among colored women is not so great as among women in some foreign countries who are equally ignorant, poor and oppressed.

Believing that it is only through the home that a people can become really good and truly great the National Association has entered that sacred domain. Homes, more homes, better homes, purer homes is the text upon which sermons have been and will be preached. There has been a determined effort to have heart to heart talks with our women that we may strike at the root of evils, many of which lie at the fireside. If the women of the dominant race, with all the centuries of education, culture and refinement back of them, with all the wealth of opportunity ever present with them, feel the need of a mother's congress, that they may be enlightened upon the best methods of rearing their children and conducting their homes, how much more do our women, from whom shackles have but yesterday been stricken, need information on the same vital subjects. And so the association is working vigorously to establish mothers' congresses on a small scale, wherever our women can be reached.

From this brief and meager account of the work which has been and is still being accomplished by colored women through the medium of their clubs, it is easy to observe how earnest and effective have been their efforts to elevate their race. No people need ever despair whose women are fully aroused to the duties which rest upon them and are willing to shoulder responsibilities which they alone can successfully assume. The scope of our endeavors is constantly widening. Into the various channels of generosity and beneficence we are entering more and more every day.

Some of our women are now using their clubs to establish day nurseries, a charity of which there is an imperative need. Thousands of our wage-earning mothers with large families dependent almost entirely upon them for support are obliged to leave their children all day, entrusted to the care of small brothers and sisters, or some good-natured neighbor who promises much, but who does little. Some of these infants are locked alone in the room from the time the mother leaves in the morning, until she returns at night. Not long ago I read in a Southern newspaper that an infant thus locked alone in a room all day, while its mother went out to wash, had cried itself to death. When one reflects upon the slaughter of the innocents which is occurring with pitiless persistency every day and thinks of the multitudes who are maimed for life or are rendered imbecile because of the treatment received during their helpless infancy, it is evident that by establishing day nurseries colored women will render one of the greatest services possible to humanity and to the race.

Nothing lies nearer the heart of colored women than the children. We feel keenly the need of kindergartens and are putting forth earnest efforts to honey-comb this country with them from one extremity to the other. The more unfavorable the environments of children the more necessary is it that steps be taken to counteract baleful influences upon innocent victims. How imperative is it then that as colored women we inculcate correct principles and set good examples for our own youth whose little feet will have so many thorny paths of temptation, injustice and prejudice to tread. So keenly alive is the National Association to the necessity of rescuing our little ones whose evil nature alone is encouraged to develop and whose noble qualities are deadened and dwarfed by the very atmosphere which they breathe, that its officers are trying to raise money with which to send out a kindergarten organizer, whose duty it shall be to arouse the conscience of our women and to establish kindergartens wherever means therefor can be secured.

Through the children of to-day we believe we can build the foundation of the next generation upon such a rock of morality, intelligence and strength, that the floods of proscription, prejudice and persecution may descend upon it in torrents and yet it will not be moved. We hear a great deal about the race problem and how to solve it. The real solution of the race problem lies in the children, both so far as we who are oppressed and those who oppress us are concerned. Some of our women who have consecrated their lives to the elevation of their race feel that neither individuals nor organizations working toward this end should be entirely satisfied with their efforts unless some of their energy, money or brain is used in the name and for the sake of the children.

The National Association has chosen as its motto: Lifting as We

Climb. In order to live strictly up to this sentiment, its members have determined to come into the closest possible touch with the masses of our women, through whom the womanhood of our people is always judged. It is unfortunate, but it is true, that the dominant race in this country insists upon gauging the Negro's worth by his most illiterate and vicious representatives rather than by the more intelligent and worthy classes. Colored women of education and culture know that they cannot escape altogether the consequences of the acts of their most depraved sisters. They see that even if they were wicked enough to turn a deaf ear to the call of duty, both policy and self-preservation demand that they go down among the lowly, the illiterate and even the vicious, to whom they are bound by the ties of race and sex, and put forth every possible effort to reclaim them. By coming into close touch with the masses of our women it is possible to correct many of the evils which militate so seriously against us and inaugurate the reforms, without which, as a race, we cannot hope to succeed.

Through the clubs we are studying the labor question and are calling the attention of our women to the alarming rapidity with which the Negro is losing ground in the world of labor. If this movement to withhold employment from him continues to grow, the race will soon be confronted by a condition of things disastrous and serious, indeed. We are preaching in season and out that it is the duty of every wage-earning colored woman to become thoroughly proficient in whatever work she engages, so that she may render the best service of which she is capable, and thus do her part toward establishing a reputation for excellent workmanship among colored women.

Our clubs all over the country are being urged to establish schools of domestic science. It is believed that by founding schools in which colored girls could be trained to be skilled domestics, we should do more toward solving the labor question as it affects our women, than by using any other means it is in our power to employ. We intend to lay the Negro's side of the labor question clearly before our large-hearted, broad-minded sisters of the dominant race and appeal to them to throw their influence on the right side. We shall ask that they train their children to be broad and just enough to judge men and women by their intrinsic merit rather than by the adventitious circumstances of race and color or creed. Colored women are asking the white mothers of the land to teach their children that when they grow to be men and women, if they deliberately prevent their fellow creatures from earning an honest living by closing their doors of trade against them, the Father of all men will hold them responsible for the crimes which are the result of their injustice and for the human wrecks which the ruthless crushing of hope and ambition always makes.

Through our clubs colored women hope to improve the social atmosphere by showing the enormity of the double standard of morals, which teaches that we should turn the cold shoulder upon a fallen sister, but greet her destroyer with open arms and a gracious smile. The duty of setting a high moral standard and living up to it devolves upon colored women in a peculiar way. False accusations and malicious slanders are circulated against them constantly, both by the press and by the direct descendants of those who in years past were responsible for the moral degradation of their female slaves.

Carefully and conscientiously we shall study the questions which affect the race most deeply and directly. Against the convict lease system, the Jim Crow car laws, lynchings and all other barbarities which degrade us, we shall protest with such force of logic and intensity of soul that those who oppress us will either cease to disavow the inalienability and equality of human rights, or be ashamed to openly violate the very principles upon which this government was founded. By discharging our obligation to the children, by coming into the closest possible touch with the masses of our people, by studying the labor question as it affects the race, by establishing schools of domestic science, by setting a high moral standard and living up to it, by purifying the home, colored women will render their race a service whose value it is not in my power to estimate or express. The National Association is being cherished with such loyalty and zeal by our women that there is every reason to hope it will soon become the power for good, the tower of strength and the source of inspiration to which it is destined.

And so lifting as we climb, onward and upward we go, struggling and striving and hoping that the buds and blossoms of our desires will burst into glorious fruition ere long. With courage born of success achieved in the past, with a keen sense of responsibility which we must continue to assume we look forward to the future, large with promise and hope. Seeking no favors because of our color or patronage because of our needs, we knock at the bar of justice and ask for an equal chance.

from *Twentieth Century Negro Literature*, 1902

Anna Julia Cooper
(1858–1964)

If Ida Wells-Barnett and Mary Church Terrell were the street activists in the battle for women's and civil rights, then Anna Julia Cooper was their theorist, putting forth in *A Voice from the South* her provocative challenge, "Only the BLACK WOMAN can say where and when I enter, in the quiet, undisputed dignity of my womanhood, without violence and without suing or special patronage, then and there the whole *Negro race enters with me.*"

As African-American men had found their voice in the pulpit, politics, and the black press earlier in the century, Cooper, too, sought to plead her own cause. "Our Caucasian barristers," she wrote, "are not to blame if they cannot *quite* put themselves in the dark man's place, neither should the dark man be wholly expected, fully and adequately to reproduce the exact voice of the Black Woman." Like Sojourner Truth before her, she was wary of both black men who sought to secure rights only for themselves as well as white women who saw in the black woman's plight none of their own.

She was born Annie Julia Haywood in Raleigh, North Carolina, the child of a slave woman, Hannah Stanley Haywood, and her white master, George Washington Haywood. At the age of nine, she entered the highly selective St. Augustine Normal School, where she studied and tutored for fourteen years and first encountered the barriers female students faced in gaining an education. Denied admission to a Greek class reserved for theology students, and thus only for men, she pressed her case, eventually marrying the teacher George A. C. Cooper in 1877.

As was commonly the case, marriage precluded a career, but Cooper's husband died just two years later, and in 1881 she applied to Oberlin College, the first in the country to accept women. There she pursued the "Gentlemen's Course," receiving her B.A. in 1884. She taught briefly at Wilberforce University and at St. Augustine, before receiving her M.A. from Oberlin in 1887. She was soon recruited by the Washington Colored High School (later called the Dunbar School), the only black school in the nation's capital, and in 1902 became its principal.

When Cooper's students performed exceptionally well in a citywide reading competition and gained acceptances to the most prestigious colleges—including Harvard, Yale, Amherst, Dartmouth, Brown, Oberlin, and Radcliffe—rather than going to segregated schools or preparing for trades, she encountered racist and sexist sentiment that she had overstepped her role. She was faced with trumped-up charges of certain lapses in procedure and discipline by the D.C. Board of Education in 1905, which led to a very public and humiliating year-long debate in the press.

There may also have been some suspicion that she had an "inappropriate" relationship with a fellow teacher who boarded in her home. Cooper had taken in John Love, thirteen years her junior, and his sister when they were orphaned in their teens. Cooper and Love were both dismissed, and Cooper went to teach at Lincoln Institute in Jefferson City, Missouri, before a new superintendent at the M Street School (as it was then called) sought her return four years later.

Cooper began to study for a doctorate from Columbia in 1914 but had not started the required residency when she found herself with five young orphaned children, grandchildren of her brother-in-law, whom she adopted. She then began pursuing her advanced degree at the Sorbonne, studying in Paris in the summers, receiving her doctorate in 1925 when she was in her mid-sixties.

Cooper also played some role in the women's-club movement, organizing the Women's League in Washington, D.C., in 1894, which later merged with the National Association of Colored Women's Clubs. She attended the World Congress of Representative Women in 1893 and spoke at the Pan-African Conference in London, which W. E. B. Du Bois had helped to organize, in 1900. When Cooper retired from the Dunbar High School in 1930, she became involved in adult education. She died on February 27, 1964, at the age of 105, and was buried in Raleigh, North Carolina.

In her one full-length book, *A Voice from the South,* Cooper argued vigorously for woman's role as an intellectual equal. Her preoccupation with liberal education and her acceptance of woman's place within the hallowed circle of the home rather than on the barricades—"Woman, Mother, your responsibility is one that might make angels tremble!"—may remove her somewhat from the club women of her time who sought to respond to more basic needs like social welfare, day care, and elementary education for their children. Nonetheless, contends the scholar Mary Helen Washington, in taking on the double burden of race and sex hers was "the most precise, forceful, well-argued statement of black feminist thought to come out of the nineteenth century. Ironically Cooper and other black women intellectuals were very much like poor black women who were engaged in the most difficult and poorly rewarded physical labor. They did the work that no one else was willing to do."

from *A Voice in the South*

". . . there is a feminine as well as a masculine side to truth."

THE HIGHER EDUCATION OF WOMEN

N THE VERY FIRST YEAR OF OUR CENTURY, THE YEAR 1801, there appeared in Paris a book by Silvain Marechal, entitled "Shall Woman Learn the Alphabet." The book proposes a law prohibiting the alphabet to women, and quotes authorities weighty and various, to prove that the woman who knows the alphabet has already lost part of her womanliness. The author declares that woman can use the alphabet only as Moliere predicted they would, in spelling out the verb *amo;* that they have no occasion to peruse Ovid's *Ars Amoris,* since that is already the ground and limit of their intuitive furnishings; that Madame Guion would have been far more adorable had she remained a beautiful ignoramus as nature made her; that Ruth, Naomi, the Spartan woman, the Amazons, Penelope, Andromache, Lucretia, Joan of Arc, Petrarch's Laura, the daughters of Charlemagne, could not spell their names; while Sappho, Aspasia, Madame de Maintenon, and Madame de Stael could read altogether too well for their good; finally, that if women were once permitted to read Sophocles and work with logarithms, or to nibble at any side of the apple of knowledge, there would be an end forever to their sewing on buttons and embroidering slippers.

Please remember this book was published at the *beginning* of the Nineteenth Century. At the end of its first third, (in the year 1833) one solitary college in America decided to admit women within its sacred precincts, and organized what was called a "Ladies' Course" as well as the regular B.A. or Gentlemen's course.

It was felt to be an experiment—a rather dangerous experiment—and was adopted with fear and trembling by the good fathers, who looked as if they had been caught secretly mixing explosive compounds and were guiltily expecting every moment to see the foundations under them shaken and rent and their fair superstructure shattered into fragments.

But the girls came, and there was no upheaval. They performed their tasks modestly and intelligently. Once in a while one or two were found choosing the gentlemen's course. Still no collapse; and the dear, careful, scrupulous, frightened old professors were just getting their hearts out of their throats and preparing to draw one good free breath, when they found they would have to change the names of those courses; for there were as many ladies in the gentlemen's course as in the ladies', and a distinctively Ladies' Course, inferior in scope and aim to the regular classical course, did not and could not exist.

Other colleges gradually fell into line, and to-day there are one hundred and ninety-eight colleges for women, and two hundred and seven coeducational colleges and universities in the United States alone offering the degree of B.A. to women, and sending out yearly active, energetic, well-equipped, thoughtful women—women quick to see and eager to help the needs of this needy world—women who can think as well as feel, and who feel none the less because they think—women who are none the less tender and true for the parchment scroll they bear in their hands—women who have given a deeper, richer, nobler and grander meaning to the word "womanly" than any one-sided masculine definition could ever have suggested or inspired—women whom the world has long waited for in pain and anguish till there should be at last added to its forces and allowed to permeate its thought the complement of that masculine influence which has dominated it for fourteen centuries.

Since the idea of order and subordination succumbed to barbarian brawn and brutality in the fifth century, the civilized world had been like a child brought up by his father. It has needed the great mother heart to teach it to be pitiful, to love mercy, to succor the weak and care for the lowly. . . .

As individuals, we are constantly and inevitably, whether we are conscious of it or not, giving out our real selves into our several little worlds, inexorably adding our own true ray to the flood of starlight, quite independently of our professions and our masquerading; and so in the world of thought, the influence of thinking woman far transcends her feeble declamation and may seem at times even opposed to it.

A visitor in Oberlin once said to the lady principal, "Have you no rabble in Oberlin? How is it that I see no police here, and yet the streets are as quiet and orderly as if there were an officer of the law standing on every corner."

Mrs. Johnston replied, "Oh, yes; there are vicious persons in Oberlin just as in other towns—*but our girls are our police.*"

With from five to ten hundred pure-minded young women threading the streets of the village every evening unattended, vice must slink away, like frost before the rising sun: and yet I venture to say there was not one in a hundred of those girls who would not have run from a street brawl as she would from a mouse, and who would not have declared she could never stand the sight of blood and pistols.

There is, then, a real and special influence of woman. An influence subtle and often involuntary, an influence so intimately interwoven in, so intricately interpenetrated by the masculine influence of the time that it is often difficult to extricate the delicate meshes and analyze and identify the closely clinging fibers. And yet, without this influence—so long as woman sat with bandaged eyes and manacled hands, fast bound in the clamps of ignorance and inaction, the world of thought moved in its orbit like the revolutions of the moon; with one face (the man's face) always out, so that the spectator could not distinguish whether it was disc or sphere.

Now I claim that it is the prevalence of the Higher Education among women, the making it a common everyday affair for women to reason and think and express their thought, the training and stimulus which enable and encourage women to administer to the world the bread it needs as well as the sugar it cries for; in short it is the transmitting the potential forces of her soul into dynamic factors that has given symmetry and completeness to the world's agencies. So only could it be consummated that Mercy, the lesson she teaches, and Truth, the task man has set himself, should meet together: that righteousness, or *rightness,* man's ideal,—and *peace,* its necessary "other half," should kiss each other.

We must thank the general enlightenment and independence of woman (which we may now regard as a *fait accompli*) that both these forces are now at work in the world, and it is fair to demand from them for the twentieth century a higher type of civilization than any attained in the nineteenth. Religion, science, art, economics, have all needed the feminine flavor; and literature, the expression of what is permanent and best in all of these, may be gauged at any time to measure the strength of the feminine ingredient. You will not find theology consigning infants to lakes of unquenchable fire long after women have had a chance to grasp, master, and wield its dogmas. You will not find science annihilating personality from the government of the Universe and making of God an ungovernable, unintelligible, blind, often destructive physical force; you will not find jurisprudence formulating as an axiom the absurdity that man and wife are one, and that one the man—that the married woman may not hold or bequeath her own property save as subject to her husband's direction; you will not find political economists declaring that the only possible adjustment between laborers and capitalists is that of selfishness and rapacity—that each must get all he can and keep all that he gets, while the world cries *laissez faire* and the lawyers explain, "it is the beautiful working of the law of supply and demand;" in fine, you will not find the law of love shut out from the affairs of men after the feminine half of the world's truth is completed.

Nay, put your ear now close to the pulse of the time. What is the keynote of the literature of these days? What is the banner cry of all the activities of the last half decade? What is the dominant seventh which is to add richness and tone to the final cadences of this century and lead by a grand modulation into the triumphant harmonies of the next? Is it not compassion for the poor and unfortunate, and, as Bellamy has expressed it, "indignant outcry against the failure of the social machinery as it is, to ameliorate the miseries of men!" Even Christianity is being brought to the bar of humanity and tried by the standard of its ability to alleviate the world's suffering and lighten and brighten its woe. What else can be the meaning of Matthew

Arnold's saddening protest, "We cannot do without Christianity," cried he, "and we cannot endure it as it is."

When went there by an age, when so much time and thought, so much money and labor were given to God's poor and God's invalids, the lowly and unlovely, the sinning as well as the suffering—homes for inebriates and homes for lunatics, shelter for the aged and shelter for babes, hospitals for the sick, props and braces for the falling, reformatory prisons and prison reformatories, all show that a "mothering" influence from some source is leavening the nation.

Now please understand me. I do not ask you to admit that these benefactions and virtues are the exclusive possession of women, or even that women are their chief and only advocates. It may be a man who formulates and makes them vocal. It may be, and often is, a man who weeps over the wrongs and struggles for the amelioration; but that man has imbibed those impulses from a mother rather than from a father and is simply materializing and giving back to the world in tangible form the ideal love and tenderness, devotion and care that have cherished and nourished the helpless period of his own existence.

All I claim is that there is a feminine as well as a masculine side to truth; that these are related not as inferior and superior, not as better and worse, not as weaker and stronger, but as complements—complements in one necessary and symmetric whole. That as the man is more noble in reason, so the woman is more quick in sympathy. That as he is indefatigable in pursuit of abstract truth, so is she in caring for the interests by the way—striving tenderly and lovingly that not one of the least of these "little ones" should perish. That while we not unfrequently see women who reason, we say, with the coolness and precision of a man, and men as considerate of helplessness as a woman, still there is a general consensus of mankind that the one trait is essentially masculine and the other as peculiarly feminine. That both are needed to be worked into the training of children, in order that our boys may supplement their virility by tenderness and sensibility, and our girls may round out their gentleness by strength and self-reliance. That, as both are alike necessary in giving symmetry to the individual, so a nation or a race will degenerate into mere emotionalism on the one hand, or bullyism on the other, if dominated by either exclusively; lastly, and most emphatically, that the feminine factor can have its proper effect only through woman's development and education so that she may fitly and intelligently stamp her force on the forces of her day, and add her modicum to the riches of the world's thought. . . .

It is true then that the higher education for women—in fact, the highest that the world has ever witnessed—belongs to the past; but we must remember that it was possible, down to the middle of our own century, only to select few; and that the fashions and traditions of the times were before that all against it. There were not only no stimuli to encourage women to make the most of their powers and to welcome their development as a helpful agency in the progress of civilization, but their little aspirations, when they had any, were chilled and snubbed in embryo, and any attempt at thought was received as a monstrous usurpation of man's prerogative. . . .

We have seen how the pendulum has swung across our present century. The men of our time have asked with Emerson, "that woman only show us how she can best be served;" and woman has replied: the chance of the seedling and of the animalcule is all I ask—the chance for growth and self development, the permission to be true to the aspirations of my soul without incurring the blight of your censure and ridicule.

"Audetque viris concurrere virgo."

In soul-culture woman at last dares to contend with men, and we may cite Grant Allen (who certainly cannot be suspected of advocating the unsexing of woman) as an example of the broadening effect of this content on the ideas at least of the men of the day. He says in his *Plain Words on the Woman Question,* recently published:

"The position of woman was not [in the past] a position which could bear the test of nineteenth-century scrutiny. Their education was inadequate, their social status was humiliating, their political power was nil, their practical and personal grievances were innumerable; above all, their relations to the family—to their husbands, their children, their friends, their property—was simply insupportable."

And again, "As a body we 'Advanced men' are, I think, prepared to reconsider, and to reconsider fundamentally, without prejudice or misconception, the entire question of the relation between the sexes. We are ready to make any modifications in those relations which will satisfy the woman's just aspiration for personal independence, for intellectual and moral development, for physical culture, for political activity, and for a voice in the arrangement of her own affairs, both domestic and national."

Now this is magnanimous enough, surely; and quite a step from eighteenth century preaching, is it not? The higher education of Woman has certainly developed the men;—let us see what it has done for the women.

Matthew Arnold during his last visit to America in '82 or '83, lectured before a certain co-educational college in the West. After the lecture he remarked, with some surprise, to a lady professor, that the young women in his audience, he noticed, paid as close attention as the men, *all the way through.* This led, of course, to a spirited discussion of the higher education for women, during which he said to his enthusiastic interlocutor, eyeing her philosophically through his English eyeglass: "But—eh—don't you think it —eh—spoils their *chances,* you know!"

Now, as to the result to women, this is the most serious argument ever used against higher education. If it interferes with marriage, classical training has a grave objection to weigh and answer.

For I agree with Mr. Allen at least on this one point, that there must be marrying and giving in marriage even till the end of time.

I grant you that intellectual development, with the self-reliance and capacity for earning a livelihood which it gives, renders woman less dependent on the marriage relation for physical support (which, by the way, does not always accompany it). Neither is she compelled to look to sexual love as the one sensation capable of giving tone and relish, movement and vim to the life she leads. Her horizon is extended. Her sympathies are broadened and deepened and multiplied. She is on closer touch with nature. Not a bud that opens, not a dew drop, not a ray of light, not a cloud-burst or a thunderbolt, but adds to the expansiveness and zest of her soul. And if the sun of an absorbing passion be gone down, still 'tis night that brings the stars. She has remaining the mellow, less obtrusive, but none the less enchanting and inspiring light of friendship, and into its charmed circle she may gather the best the world has known. She can commune with Socrates about the *daimon* he knew and to which she too can bear witness; she can revel in the majesty of Dante, the sweetness of Virgil, the simplicity of Homer, the strength of Milton. She can listen to the pulsing heart throbs of passionate Sappho's encaged soul, as she beats her bruised wings against her prison bars and struggles to flutter out into Heaven's aether, and the fires of her own soul cry back as she listens. "Yes: Sappho, I know it all; I know it all." Here, at last, can be communion without suspicion; friendship without misunderstanding; love without jealousy.

We must admit then that Byron's picture, whether a thing of beauty or not, has faded from the canvas of to-day.

> "Man's love," he wrote, "is of man's life a thing apart,
> 'Tis woman's whole existence.
> Man may range the court, camp, church, the vessel and the mart,
> Sword, gown, gain, glory offer in exchange.
> Pride, fame, ambition, to fill up his heart—
> And few there are whom these cannot estrange.
> Men have all these resources, we *but one—*
> *To love again and be again undone."*

This may have been true when written. *It is not true to-day.* The old, subjective, stagnant, indolent and wretched life for woman has gone. She has as many resources as men, as many activities beckon her on. As large possibilities swell and inspire her heart.

Now, then, does it destroy or diminish her capacity for loving?

Her standards have undoubtedly gone up. The necessity of speculating in "chawnces" has probably shifted. The question is not now with the woman "How shall I so cramp, stunt, simplify and nullify myself as to make me eligible to the honor of being swallowed up into some little man?" but the problem, I trow, now rests with the man as to how he can so develop his God-given powers as to reach the ideal of a generation of women who demand the noblest, grandest and best achievements of which he is capable; and this surely is the only fair and natural adjustment of the chances. Nature never meant that the ideals and standards of the world should be dwarfing and minimizing ones, and the men should thank us for requiring of them the richest fruits which they can grow. If it makes them work, all the better for them. . . .

. . . Is the intellectual woman *desirable* in the matrimonial market?

This I cannot answer. I confess my ignorance. I am no judge of such things. I have been told that strong-minded women could be, when they thought it worth their while, quite endurable, and, judging from the number of female names I find in college catalogues among the alumnae with double patronymics, I surmise that quite a number of men are willing to put up with them.

Now I would that my task ended here. Having shown that a great want of the world in the past has been a feminine force; that that force can have its full effect only through the untrammelled development of woman; that such development, while it gives her to the world and to civilization, does not necessarily remove her from the home and fireside; finally, that while past centuries have witnessed sporadic instances of this higher growth, still it was reserved for the latter half of the nineteenth century to render it common and general enough to be effective; I might close with a glowing prediction of what the twentieth century may expect from this heritage of twin forces—the masculine battered and toil-worn veteran after centuries of warfare, but still strong, active, and vigorous, ready to help with his hard-won experience the young recruit rejoicing in her newly found freedom, who so confidently places her hand in his with mutual pledges to redeem the ages.

"And so the twain upon the skirts of Time,
Sit side by side, full-summed in all their powers,
Dispensing harvest, sowing the To-be,
Self-reverent each and reverencing each."

Fain would I follow them, but duty is nearer home. The high ground of generalities is alluring but my pen is devoted to a special cause: and with a view to further enlightenment on the achievements of the century for THE HIGHER EDUCATION OF COLORED WOMEN, I wrote a few days ago to the colleges which admit women and asked how many colored women had completed the B.A. course in each during its entire history. These are the figures returned: Fisk leads the way with twelve; Oberlin next with five; Wilberforce, four; Ann Arbor and Wellesley three each, Livingston two, Atlanta one, Howard, as yet, none.

I then asked the principal of the Washington High School how many out of a large number of female graduates from his school had chosen to go forward and take a collegiate course. He replied that but one had ever done so, and she was then in Cornell.*

Others ask questions too, sometimes, and I was asked a few years ago by a white friend, "How is it that the men of your race seem to outstrip the women in mental attainment?" "Oh," I said, "so far as it is true, the men, I suppose, from the life they lead, gain more by contact; and so far as it is only apparent, I think the women are more quiet. They don't feel called to mount a barrel and harangue by the hour every time they imagine they have produced an idea."

But I am sure there is another reason which I did not at that time see fit to give. The atmosphere, the standards, the requirements of our little world do not afford any special stimulus to female development.

It seems hardly a gracious thing to say, but it strikes me as true, that while our men seem thoroughly abreast of the times on almost every other subject, when they strike the woman question they drop generally in regard to gallantry and chivalry, but they actually do not seem sometimes to have outgrown that old contemporary of chivalry—the idea that women may stand on pedestals or live in doll houses, (if they happen to have them) but they must not furrow their brows with thought or attempt to help men tug at the great questions of the world. I fear the majority of colored men do not yet think it worth while that women aspire to higher education. Not many will subscribe to the "advanced" ideas of Grant Allen already quoted. The three R's, a little music and a good deal of dancing, a first rate dressmaker and a bottle of magnolia balm, are quite enough generally to render charming any woman possessed of tact and the capacity for worshipping masculinity.

My readers will pardon my illustrating my point and also giving a reason for the fear that is in me, by a little bit of personal experience. When a child I was put into a school near home that professed to be normal and collegiate, i.e. to prepare teachers for colored youth, furnish candidates for the ministry, and offer collegiate training for those who should be ready for it. Well, I found after a while that I had a good deal of time on my hands. I had devoured what was put before me, and, like Oliver Twist, was looking around to ask for more. I constantly felt (as I suppose many an ambitious girl has felt) a thumping from within unanswered by any beckoning from without. Class after class was organized for these ministerial candidates (many of them men who had been preaching before I was born). Into every one of these classes I was expected to go, with the sole intent, I thought at the time, of enabling the dear old principal, as he looked from the vacant countenances of his sleepy old class over to where I sat, to get off his solitary pun—his never-failing pleasantry, especially in hot weather —which

* Graduated from Scientific Course, June 1890, the first colored woman to graduate from Cornell.

was, as he called out "Any one!" to the effect that "*any* one" then meant "*Annie* one."

Finally a Greek class was to be formed. My inspiring preceptor informed me that Greek had never been taught in the school, but that he was going to form a class *for the candidates for the ministry,* and if I liked I might join it. I replied—humbly I hope, as became a female of the human species—that I would like very much to study Greek, and that I was thankful for the opportunity, and so it went on. A boy, however meager his equipment and shallow his pretensions, had only to declare a floating intention to study theology and he could get all the support, encouragement and stimulus he needed, be absolved from work and invested beforehand with the dignity of his far away office. While a self-supporting girl had to struggle on by teaching in the summer and working after school hours to keep up with her board bills, and actually to fight her way against positive discouragements to the higher education; till one such girl one day flared out and told the principal "the only mission opening before a girl in his school was to marry one of those candidates." He said he didn't know but it was. And when at last that same girl announced her desire and intention to go to college it was received with about the same incredulity and dismay as if a brass button on one of those candidate's coats had propounded a new method for squaring the circle or trisecting the arc.

Now this is not fancy. It is a simple unvarnished photograph, and what I believe was not in those days exceptional in colored schools, and I ask the men and women who are teachers and co-workers for the highest interests of the race, that they give the girls a chance! We might as well expect to grow trees from leaves as hope to build up a civilization or a manhood without taking into consideration our women and the home life made by them, which must be the root and ground of the whole matter. Let us insist then on special encouragement for the education of our women and special care in their training. Let our girls feel that we expected something more of them than that there is a race with special needs which they and only they can help; that the world needs and is already asking for their trained, efficient forces. Finally, if there is an ambitious girl with pluck and brain to take the higher education, encourage her to make the most of it. Let there be the same flourish of trumpets and clapping of hands as when a boy announces his determination to enter the lists; and then, as you know that she is physically the weaker of the two, don't stand from under and leave her to buffet the waves alone. Let her know that your heart is following her, that your hand, though she sees it not, is ready to support her. To be plain, I mean let money be raised and scholarships be founded in our colleges and universities for self-supporting, worthy young women, to offset and balance the aid that can always be found for boys who will take theology.

The earnest well trained Christian young woman, as a teacher, as a home-maker, as wife, mother, or silent influence even, is as potent a missionary agency among our people as is the theologian; and I claim that at the present stage of our development in the South she is even more important and necessary.

Let us then, here and now, recognize this force and resolve to make the most of it—not the boys less, but the girls more.

1892

Plessy v. Ferguson

The 1896 Supreme Court decision in *Plessy* v. *Ferguson* institutionalized segregation through the doctrine of "separate but equal" that would stand in American law for more than fifty years. The case originated in 1892 in Louisiana when Homer Adolph Plessy (who was nearly white in complexion) insisted "upon going into and remaining in a compartment of a coach of said train which had been assigned to white passengers." The act put Plessy in violation of an 1890 Louisiana law that provided for "equal but separate accommodations for the white and colored races" on public conveyances. The case was brought to criminal court in New Orleans, which upheld the law, and the case was appealed to the Supreme Court on the grounds that it violated the Thirteenth and Fourteenth Amendments. The plaintiff's brief in the case argued that the Louisiana statute "very clearly says to the railway, 'You go forward and enforce this system of assorting the citizens of the United States on the line of race, and we will see that you suffer no loss through prosecution in OUR courts.' "

On May 18, 1896, the Supreme Court ruled 7 to 1 against Plessy. In the decision, included here, the Court argued that though the Fourteenth Amendment may have been effected "to enforce the absolute equality of the two races before the law, but in the nature of things it could not have been intended to abolish distinctions based upon color." Justice John Marshall Harlan of Kentucky alone dissented, stating that "in my opinion, the judgment this day rendered will, in time, prove to be quite as pernicious as the decision made by this tribunal in the *Dred Scott* case."

The *Plessy* verdict confirmed the shifting mood of the country, reversing the finding in an earlier case that the "one pervading purpose" of the postwar amendments was the "freedom of the slave race, the security and firm establishment of that freedom, and the protection of the newly made freeman and citizen from the oppressions of those who had formerly exercised unlimited dominion over him." In the face of this new direction on the part of the judiciary, Walter Hines Page, the editor of *The Atlantic Monthly,* wrote, "The Supreme Court of the United States is in my opinion a dangerous place for a colored man to seek justice."

Ironically, the Court argued in its decision that the separation of the two races in public transportation was not unlike that which occurred in the school system, "the constitutionality of which does not seem to have been questioned." In fact, *Plessy* would finally be reversed in 1954 in the case of *Brown* v. *Board of Education of Topeka,* when the Court overturned the *Plessy* doctrine with the finding that "in the field of public education the doctrine of 'separate but equal' has no place."

Plessy v. Ferguson

"The destinies of the two races, in this country, are indissolubly linked together, and the interests of both require that the common government of all shall not permit the seeds of race hatred to be planted under the sanction of law. . . ."
—Justice Harlan, dissenting

MR. JUSTICE BROWN, AFTER STATING THE CASE, DELIVERED THE opinion of the court.

This case turns upon the constitutionality of an act of the General Assembly of the State of Louisiana, passed in 1890, providing for separate railway carriages for the white and colored races. Acts 1890, No. 111, p. 152. . . .

The information filed in the criminal District Court charged in substance that Plessy, being a passenger between two stations within the State of Louisiana, was assigned by officers of the company to the coach used for the race to which he belonged, but he insisted upon going into a coach used by the race to which he did not belong. Neither in the information nor plea was his particular race or color averred.

The petition for the writ of prohibition averred that petitioneer was seven eighths Caucasian and one eighth African blood; that the mixture of colored blood was not discernible in him, and that he was entitled to every right, privilege and immunity secured to citizens of the United States of the white race; and that, upon such theory, he took possession of a vacant seat in a coach where passengers of the white race were accommodated, and was ordered by the conductor to vacate said coach and take a seat in another assigned to persons of the colored race, and having refused to comply with such demand he was forcibly ejected with the aid of a police officer, and imprisoned in the parish jail to answer a charge of having violated the above act.

The constitutionality of this act is attacked upon the ground that it conflicts both with the Thirteenth Amendment of the Constitution, abolishing slavery, and the Fourteenth Amendment, which prohibits certain restrictive legislation on the part of the States. . . .

A statute which implies merely a legal distinction between the white and colored races—a distinction which is founded in the color of the two races, and which must always exist so long as white men are distinguished from the other race by color—has no tendency to destroy the legal equality of the two races, or reëstablish a state of involuntary servitude. Indeed, we do not understand that the Thirteenth Amendment is strenuously relied upon by the plaintiff in error in this connection. . . .

The object of the [Fourteenth] amendment was undoubtedly to enforce the absolute equality of the two races before the law, but in the nature of things it could not have been intended to abolish distinctions based upon color, or to enforce social, as distinguished from political equality, or a commingling of the two races upon terms unsatisfactory to either. Laws permitting, and even requiring, their separation in places where they are liable to be brought into contact do not necessarily imply the inferiority of either race to the other, and have been generally, if not universally, recognized as within the competency of the state legislatures in the exercise of their police power. The most common instance of this is connected with the establishment of separate schools for white and colored children, which has been held to be a valid exercise of the legislative power even by courts of States where the political rights of the colored race have been longest and most earnestly enforced. . . .

It is claimed by the plaintiff in error that, in any mixed community, the reputation of belonging to the dominant race, in this instance the white race, is *property*, in the same sense that a right of action, or of inheritance, is property. Conceding this to be so, for the purposes of this case, we are unable to see how this statute deprives him of, or in any way affects his right to, such property. If he be a white man and assigned to a colored coach, he may have his action for damages against the company for being deprived of his so called property. Upon the other hand, if he be a colored man and be so assigned, he has been deprived of no property, since he is not lawfully entitled to the reputation of being a white man.

In this connection, it is also suggested by the learned counsel for the plaintiff in error that the same argument that will justify the state legislature in requiring railways to provide separate accommodations for the two races will also authorize them to require separate cars to be provided for people whose hair is of a certain color, or who are aliens, or who belong to certain nationalities, or to enact laws requiring colored people to walk upon one side of the street, and white people upon the other, or requiring white men's houses to be painted white, and colored men's black, or their vehicles or business signs to be of different colors, upon the theory that one side of the street is as good as the other, or that a house or vehicle of one color is as good as one of another color. The reply to all this is that every exercise of the police power must be reasonable, and extend only to such laws as are enacted in good faith for the promotion for the public good, and not for the annoyance or oppression of a particular class. . . .

So far, then, as a conflict with the Fourteenth Amendment is concerned, the case reduces itself to the question whether the statute of Louisiana is a reasonable regulation, and with respect to this there must necessarily be a large discretion on the part of the legislature. In determining the question of reasonableness it is at liberty to act with reference to the established usages, customs and traditions of the people, and with a view to the promotion of their comfort, and the preservation of the public peace and good order. Gauged by this standard, we cannot say that a law which authorizes or even requires the separation of the two races in public conveyances is unreasonable, or more obnoxious to the Fourteenth Amendment than the acts of Congress requiring separate schools for colored children in the District of Columbia, the constitutionality of which does not seem to have been questioned, or the corresponding acts of state legislatures.

We consider the underlying fallacy of the plaintiff's argument to consist in the assumption that the enforced separation of the two races stamps the colored race with a badge of inferiority. If this be so, it is not by reason of anything found in the act, but solely because the colored race chooses to put that construction upon it. The argument necessarily assumes that if, as has been more than once the case, and is not unlikely to be so again, the colored race should become the dominant power in the state legislature, and should enact a law in precisely similar terms, it would thereby relegate the white race to an inferior position. We imagine that the white race, at least, would not acquiesce in this assumption. The argument also assumes that social prejudices may be overcome by legislation, and that equal rights cannot be secured to the negro except by an enforced commingling of the two races. We cannot accept this proposition. If the two races are to meet upon terms of social equality, it must be the result of natural affinities, a mutual appreciation of each other's merits and a voluntary consent of individuals. As was said by the Court of Appeals of New York in *People* v. *Gallagher*, 93 N.Y. 438, 448, "this end can neither be accomplished nor promoted by laws which conflict with the general sentiment of the community upon whom they are designed to operate. When the government, therefore, has secured to each of its citizens equal rights before the law and equal opportunities for improvement and progress, it has accomplished the end for which it was organized and performed all of the functions respecting social advantages with which it is endowed." Legislation is powerless to eradicate racial instincts or to abolish distinctions based upon physical differences, and the attempt to do so can only result in accentuating the difficulties of the present situation. If the civil and political rights of both races be equal one cannot be inferior to the other civilly or politically. If one race be inferior to the other socially, the Constitution of the United States cannot put them upon the same plane. . . .

Affirmed.

MR. JUSTICE HARLAN dissenting. . . .

The white race deems itself to be the dominant race in this country. And so it is, in prestige, in achievements, in education, in wealth and in power. So, I doubt not, it will continue to be for all time, if it remains true to its great heritage and holds fast to the principles of constitutional liberty. But in view of the Constitution, in the eye of the law, there is in this country no superior, dominant, ruling class of citizens. There is no caste here. Our

Constitution is color-blind, and neither knows nor tolerates classes among citizens. In respect of civil rights, all citizens are equal before the law. The humblest is the peer of the most powerful. The law regards man as man, and takes no account of his surroundings or of his color when his civil rights as guaranteed by the supreme law of the land are involved. It is, therefore, to be regretted that this high tribunal, the final expositor of the fundamental law of the land, has reached the conclusion that it is competent for a State to regulate the enjoyment by citizens of their civil rights solely upon the basis of race.

In my opinion, the judgment this day rendered will, in time, prove to be quite as pernicious as the decision made by this tribunal in the *Dred Scott case.* It was adjudged in that case that the descendants of Africans who were imported into this country and sold as slaves were not included nor intended to be included under the word "citizens" in the Constitution, and could not claim any of the rights and privileges which that instrument provided for and secured to citizens of the United States; that at the time of the adoption of the Constitution they were "considered as a subordinate and inferior class of beings, who had been subjugated by the dominant race, and, whether emancipated or not, yet remained subject to their authority, and had no rights or privileges but such as those who held the power and the government might choose to grant them." 19 How. 393, 404. The recent amendments of the Constitution, it was supposed, had eradicated these principles from our institutions. But it seems that we have yet, in some of the States, a dominant race —a superior class of citizens, which assumes to regulate the enjoyment of civil rights, common to all citizens, upon the basis of race. The present decision, it may well be apprehended, will not only stimulate aggressions, more or less brutal and irritating, upon the admitted rights of colored citizens, but will encourage the belief that it is possible, by means of state enactments, to defeat the beneficient purposes which the people of the United States had in view when they adopted the recent amendments of the Constitution, by one of which the blacks of this country were made citizens of the United States and of the States in which they respectively reside, and whose privileges and immunities, as citizens, the States are forbidden to abridge. Sixty millions of whites are in no danger from the presence here of eight millions of blacks. The destinies of the two races, in this country, are indissolubly linked together, and the interests of both require that the common government of all shall not permit the seeds of race hate to be planted under the sanction of law. What can more certainly arouse race hate, what more certainly create and perpetuate a feeling of distrust between these races, than state enactments, which, in fact, proceed on the ground that colored citizens are so inferior and degraded that they cannot be allowed to sit in public coaches occupied by white citizens? That, as all will admit, is the real meaning of such legislation as was enacted in Louisiana. . . .

I am of opinion that the statute of Louisiana is inconsistent with the personal liberty of citizens, white and black, in that State, and hostile to both the spirit and letter of the Constitution of the United States. If laws of like character should be enacted in the several States of the Union, the effect would be in the highest degree mischievous. Slavery, as an institution tolerated by law would, it is true, have disappeared from our country, but there would remain a power in the States, by sinister legislation, to interfere with the full enjoyment of the blessings of freedom; to regulate civil rights, common to all citizens, upon the basis of race; and to place in a condition of legal inferiority a large body of American citizens, now constituting a part of the political community called the People of the United States, for whom, and by whom through representatives, our government is administered. Such a system is inconsistent with the guarantee given by the Constitution to each State of a republican form of government, and may be stricken down by Congressional action, or by the courts in the discharge of their solemn duty to maintain the supreme law of the land, anything in the constitution or laws of any State to the contrary notwithstanding.

For the reasons stated, I am constrained to withhold my assent from the opinion and judgment of the majority.

1896

The Niagara Movement

A successor to the convention movement of the mid-1800s and precursor to the National Association for the Advancement of Colored People,† the first African-American political organization of the twentieth century was born of the search for a more aggressive approach to race relations during the nadir of African-American history that stretched from the end of Reconstruction to the New Negro movement of the next several decades. It was, too, a reaction to the enormous power wielded by Booker T. Washington, whose philosophy of accommodation had been best outlined in his "Atlanta Compromise"† speech in 1895.

The movement was given its impetus by W. E. B. Du Bois and William Monroe Trotter. The two men had first met at Harvard, and while Du Bois went on to teach at Atlanta University, Trotter founded the weekly newspaper, the *Guardian,* dedicated largely to vocal opposition to Washington's policies. When Trotter and his followers heckled Washington at a meeting of the Negro Business League in Boston, he was sentenced to thirty days in jail. Du Bois, who had himself publicly taken exception to Washington's program in his essay "Of Booker T. Washington and Others,"† quickly came to Trotter's defense. The two men sent out a call to like-minded individuals who "do their own thinking," and from July 11 to 13, 1905, twenty-nine men from fourteen states met on the Ontario side of Niagara Falls. Though they represented the very embodiment of Du Bois's "Talented Tenth"—teachers, ministers, lawyers, editors, and businessmen—they would not have been allowed to register at hotels on the other side of the falls in New York. The men drafted a list of demands, the "Declaration of Principles" that follows, that called for an end to legal, economic, educational, and social discrimination.

In the subsequent months, Du Bois did much to publicize the movement, continuing his attacks on Washington and the control of political patronage and philanthropic funds wielded by the Tuskegee Machine. In an article that appeared in the Atlanta journal *The Voice of the Negro* in September, Du Bois wrote, "There has been a determined effort in this country to stop the free expression of opinion among black men," and in an address to the members of the movement convened at Harpers Ferry the following year, the rhetoric was even more pointed: "We live to tell these dark brothers of ours—scattered in counsel, wavering and weak—that no bribe of money or notoriety, no promise of wealth or fame, is worth the surrender of a people's manhood or the loss of a man's self-respect. We refuse to surrender the leadership of this race to cowards and trucklers."

Local and college chapters of the movement were organized, and meetings were held during the next few years in Boston and Oberlin. Never numbering more than several dozen members, however, and without financial resources and a national platform, by 1910 the movement had stalled. It was only after the particularly dramatic outbreak of racial violence during the "Atlanta Massacre" in September 1906 and the riots in Springfield, Illinois, in August 1908 that national attention was drawn to the persistence of virulent racism. After those events, members of the Niagara Program were joined by white liberals like Jane Addams, John Dewey, William Dean Howells, and Oswald Garrison Villard, the grandson of abolitionist William Lloyd Garrison, to form the National Association for the Advancement of Colored People, in which W. E. B. Du Bois would play such a prominent role.

The Niagara Movement

"We pray that this nation . . . will return to the faith of the fathers, that all men were created free and equal, with certain unalienable rights. . . ."

PROGRESS: THE MEMBERS OF THE CONFERENCE, KNOWN AS THE Niagara Movement, assembled in annual meeting at Buffalo, July 11th, 12th and 13th, 1905, congratulate the Negro-Americans on certain undoubted evidences of progress in the last decade, particularly the increase of intelligence, the buying of property, the checking of crime, the uplift in home life, the advance in literature and art, and the demonstration of constructive and executive ability in the conduct of great religious, economic and educational institutions.

Suffrage: At the same time, we believe that this class of American citizens should protest emphatically and continually against the curtailment of their political rights. We believe in manhood suffrage; we believe that no man is so good, intelligent or wealthy as to be entrusted wholly with the welfare of his neighbor.

Civil Liberty: We believe also in protest against the curtailment of our civil rights. All American citizens have the right to equal treatment in places of public entertainment according to their behavior and deserts.

Economic Opportunity: We especially complain against the denial of equal opportunities to us in economic life; in the rural districts of the South this amounts to peonage and virtual slavery; all over the South it tends to crush labor and small business enterprises; and everywhere American prejudice, helped often by iniquitous laws, is making it more difficult for Negro-Americans to earn a decent living.

Education: Common school education should be free to all American children and compulsory. High school training should be adequately provided for all, and college training should be the monopoly of no class or race in any section of our common country. We believe that, in defense of our own institutions, the United States should aid common school education, particularly in the South, and we especially recommend concerted agitation to this end. We urge an increase in public high school facilities in the South, where the Negro-Americans are almost wholly without such provisions. We favor well-equipped trade and technical schools for the training of artisans, and the need of adequate and liberal endowment for a few institutions of higher education must be patent to sincere well-wishers of the race.

Courts: We demand upright judges in courts, juries selected without discrimination on account of color and the same measure of punishment and the same efforts at reformation for black as for white offenders. We need orphanages and farm schools for dependent children, juvenile reformatories for delinquents, and the abolition of the dehumanizing convict-lease system.

Public Opinion: We note with alarm the evident retrogression in this land of sound public opinion on the subject of manhood rights, republican government and human brotherhood, and we pray God that this nation will not degenerate into a mob of boasters and oppressors, but rather will return to the faith of the fathers, that all men were created free and equal, with certain unalienable rights.

Health: We plead for health—for an opportunity to live in decent houses and localities, for a chance to rear our children in physical and moral cleanliness.

Employers and Labor Unions: We hold up for public execration the conduct of two opposite classes of men: The practice among employers of importing ignorant Negro-American laborers in emergencies, and then affording them neither protection nor permanent employment; and the practice of labor unions in proscribing and boycotting and oppressing thousands of their fellow-toilers, simply because they are black. These methods have accentuated and will accentuate the war of labor and capital, and they are disgraceful to both sides.

Protest: We refuse to allow the impression to remain that the Negro-American assents to inferiority, is submissive under oppression and apologetic before insults. Through helplessness we may submit, but the voice of protest of ten million Americans must never cease to assail the ears of their fellows, so long as America is unjust.

Color-Line: Any discrimination based simply on race or color is barbarous, we care not how hallowed it be by custom, expediency or prejudice. Differences made on account of ignorance, immorality, or disease are legitimate methods of fighting evil, and against them we have no word of protest; but discriminations based simply and solely on physical peculiarities, place of birth, color of skin, are relics of that unreasoning human savagery of which the world is and ought to be thoroughly ashamed.

"Jim Crow" Cars: We protest against the "Jim Crow" car, since its effect is and must be to make us pay first-class fare for third-class accommodations, render us open to insults and discomfort and to crucify wantonly our manhood, womanhood and self-respect.

Soldiers: We regret that this nation has never seen fit adequately to reward the black soldiers who, in its five wars, have defended their country with their blood, and yet have been systematically denied the promotions which their abilities deserve. And we regard as unjust, the exclusion of black boys from the military and naval training schools.

War Amendments: We urge upon Congress the enactment of appropriate legislation for securing the proper enforcement of those articles of freedom, the thirteenth, fourteenth and fifteenth amendments of the Constitution of the United States.

Oppression: We repudiate the monstrous doctrine that the oppressor should be the sole authority as to the rights of the oppressed. The Negro race in America stolen, ravished and degraded, struggling up through difficulties and oppression, needs sympathy and receives criticism; needs help and is given hindrance, needs protection and is given mob-violence, needs justice and is given charity, needs leadership and is given cowardice and apology, needs bread and is given a stone. This nation will never stand justified before God until these things are changed.

The Church: Especially are we surprised and astonished at the recent attitude of the church of Christ—of an increase of a desire to bow to racial prejudice, to narrow the bounds of human brotherhood, and to segregate black men to some outer sanctuary. This is wrong, unchristian and disgraceful to the twentieth-century civilization.

Agitation: Of the above grievances we do not hesitate to complain, and to complain loudly and insistently. To ignore, overlook, or apologize for these wrongs is to prove ourselves unworthy of freedom. Persistent manly agitation is the way to liberty, and toward this goal the Niagara Movement has started and asks the cooperation of all men of all races.

Help: At the same time we want to acknowledge with deep thankfulness the help of our fellowmen from the Abolitionists down to those who today still stand for equal opportunity and who have given and still give of their wealth and of their poverty for our advancement.

Duties: And while we are demanding and ought to demand, and will continue to demand the rights enumerated above, God forbid that we should ever forget to urge corresponding duties upon our people:

The duty to vote.
The duty to respect the rights of others.
The duty to work.
The duty to obey the laws.
The duty to be clean and orderly.
The duty to send our children to school.
The duty to respect ourselves, even as we respect others.

This statement, complaint and prayer we submit to the American people, and Almighty God.

July 1905

The Founding of the NAACP

Founded in New York City in 1910, the National Association for the Advancement of Colored People grew out of the Niagara Movement† of 1905, and its early administrators represent some of the most distinguished African-American leaders of the twentieth century. While the Niagara Movement had clearly articulated aims, it never gained momentum and, after several years, its founders, W. E. B. Du Bois and William Monroe Trotter, joined forces with a number of leading white liberals, including Oswald Garrison Villard, John Dewey, Jane Addams, and Joel E. and Arthur Spingarn, to formulate an organization that would take a more active role in the determination of African-American affairs. Its General Committee soon included the Reverend Adam Clayton Powell, Charles W. Chesnutt, Ida Wells-Barnett, Clarence Darrow, Mary Church Terrell, and many other distinguished citizens.

Through a broadly based program that relied on organization, conferences, articles, debates, legislation, and challenges to existing legal and judicial statutes, the NAACP sought to secure for African-Americans voting rights, educational opportunity, fair treatment in the courts, protection against lynching, equal access to public accommodations, and opportunities in employment. It placed great emphasis on publicity and public education, and its influential journal, *The Crisis,* edited for twenty-four years by W. E. B. Du Bois, not only focused on political matters but also published the work of many talented literary writers like Claude McKay and Langston Hughes. The prolific writer James Weldon Johnson was highly active in the organization, becoming field secretary in the South in 1916 and executive secretary in 1920, and Walter White, who would make a career out of field investigations of lynchings, served as secretary from 1930 to 1955. The program of the NAACP and editorials from the first number of *The Crisis* follow.

Developing a strategy of using the legal system to gain redress of political grievances, the NAACP scored an early success in 1915 in a Supreme Court case that outlawed the "grandfather clause" that had restricted black suffrage. Several decades later, through the agency of the brilliant legal tacticians Charles Hamilton Houston and Thurgood Marshall, the NAACP became particularly effective in working through the courts to chip away at Jim Crow legislation and discrimination in education and employment. In 1950 it began its assault on the *Plessy* v. *Ferguson*† doctrine of "separate but equal" in a series of cases that culminated in its greatest legal triumph, the 1954 landmark decision in *Brown* v. *Board of Education of Topeka.*†

As the political climate heated up in the 1960s, some black civil rights leaders became impatient with the painstaking process of legal maneuvering and turned to more direct, mass action like the marches, sit-ins, and demonstrations employed by groups such as Martin Luther King's Southern Christian Leadership Council and the Student Non-Violent Coordinating Committee. Nonetheless, the NAACP joined those groups in the 1963 March on Washington, and the organization continues to be a prominent, albeit mainstream, civil rights advocacy group.

Principles of the NAACP

"To assure to every citizen of color the common rights of American citizenship . . ."

NATIONAL ASSOCIATION
for the
ADVANCEMENT OF COLORED PEOPLE
Organized, February 1910
Incorporated, May 1911

1. To abolish legal injustice against Negroes.
2. To stamp out race discriminations.
3. To prevent lynchings, burnings and torturings of black people.
4. To assure every citizen of color the common rights of American citizenship.
5. To compel equal accommodations in railroad travel, irrespective of color.
6. To secure for colored children an equal opportunity to public school education through a fair apportionment of public education funds.
7. To emancipate in fact, as well as in name, a race of nearly 12,000,000 American-born citizens.

The only means we can employ are education, organization, agitation, publicity—the force of an enlightened public opinion.

1911

The Crisis

". . . the editors believe that this is a critical time in the history of the advancement of men."

THE OBJECT OF THIS PUBLICATION IS TO SET FORTH THOSE facts and arguments which show the danger of race prejudice, particularly as manifested to-day toward colored people. It takes its name from the fact that the editors believe that this is a critical time in the history of the advancement of men. Catholicity and tolerance, reason and forbearance can to-day make the world-old dream of human brotherhood approach realization; while bigotry and prejudice, emphasized race consciousness and force can repeat the awful history of the contact of nations and groups in the past. We strive for this higher and broader vision of Peace and Good Will.

The policy of THE CRISIS will be simple and well defined:

It will first and foremost be a newspaper: it will record important happenings and movements in the world which bear on the great problem of inter-racial relations, and especially those which affect the Negro-American.

Secondly, it will be a review of opinion and literature, recording briefly books, articles, and important expressions of opinion in the white and colored press on the race problem.

Thirdly, it will publish a few short articles.

Finally, its editorial page will stand for the rights of men, irrespective of color or race, for the highest ideals of American democracy, and for reasonable but earnest and persistent attempt to gain these rights and realize these ideals. The magazine will be the organ of no clique or party and will avoid personal rancor of all sorts. In the absence of proof to the contrary it will assume honesty of purpose on the part of all men, North and South, white and black.

The Crisis, November 1910

Agitation

SOME GOOD FRIENDS OF THE CAUSE WE REPRESENT FEAR agitation. They say: "Do not agitate—do not make a noise; *work.*" They add, "Agitation is destructive or at best negative—what is wanted is positive constructive work."

Such honest critics mistake the function of agitation. A toothache is agitation. Is a toothache a good thing? No. Is it therefore useless? No. It is supremely useful, for it tells the body of decay, dyspepsia and death. Without it the body would suffer unknowingly. It would think: All is well, when lo! danger lurks.

The same is true of the Social Body. Agitation is a necessary evil to tell of the ills of the Suffering. Without it many a nation has been lulled to false security and preened itself with virtues it did not possess.

The function of this Association is to tell this nation the crying evil of race prejudice. It is a hard duty but a necessary one—a divine one. It is Pain; Pain is not good but Pain is necessary. Pain does not aggravate disease—Disease causes Pain. Agitation does not mean Aggravation—Aggravation calls for Agitation in order that Remedy may be found.

The Crisis, November 1910

Jack Johnson
(1878–1946)

When Jack Johnson defeated Tommy Burns in a fourteen-round fight in Sydney, Australia, on December 26, 1908, he became the first African-American to hold the world heavyweight title. It is perhaps hard now to remember the difficulty black fighters had opposing the color bar; Johnson had tried for two years to get Burns to consent to the fight. As Lawrence W. Levine recounts in *Black Culture and Black Consciousness,* when Johnson triumphed, the fight took on enormous significance.

Writing in the *New York World,* Jack London described the fight as a "massacre," "a mismatch between a pygmy and a colossus." He called for Jim Jeffries, the former champion, to come out of retirement to avenge the loss. Jeffries agreed, deferring to "that portion of the white race that has been looking to me to defend its athletic superiority." Jeffries became the Great White Hope, while African-Americans pinned their aspirations on Johnson to uphold their own honor. "The future welfare of his people forms a part of the stake," argued *The Chicago Defender.* Highly educated individuals like James Weldon Johnson and W. E. B. Du Bois might garner prestige in intellectual circles, but the outcome of the Jeffries-Johnson fight would become known to millions.

On July 4, 1910, Jeffries and Johnson squared off in Reno, Nevada. Baiting his opponent throughout the match, Johnson ended the fight in the fifteenth round when he nearly knocked Jeffries out of the ring. He later described the fight in incendiary language: "Hardly had a blow been struck," he claimed, "when I knew that I was Jeff's master." Hours after Johnson's victory, race riots erupted throughout the South, in New York, Massachusetts, Ohio, Missouri, the District of Columbia, and elsewhere. Some questioned, in the violent aftermath, if the price for Johnson's victory had been too high. "It is better," argued *The Chicago Defender,* "for us to succeed, though some die, than for us to fail, though all live."

As Johnson defended his title over the next decade, what was particularly galling to whites was that he did it with such self-confidence and attitude. Johnson tended to taunt his opponents in the ring; though he was often extremely witty, whites didn't find him so funny. Even worse, he lived fast and went through a series of white wives and mistresses.

The legend grew, as Johnson's prowess was celebrated in story and song. In one tall tale Levine records (which also appears in Richard Wright's *Lawd Today!*), Johnson was speeding through a small town in Georgia when he was stopped by the local sheriff. "Where you think you're going, boy, speeding like that? That'll cost you fifty dollars." When Johnson slipped him a hundred-dollar bill, the sheriff asked, "Don't you want your change?" "Keep it," Jack replied, " 'cause I'm coming back the same way I'm going!" It was even said that Johnson had been refused passage on the *Titanic;* when it sank on April 15, 1912, of course, more than a thousand rich white folks went to their deaths.

Johnson held his title until 1915, when he lost it against Jess Willard in a fight in Cuba that went twenty-six rounds. His notoriety lasted much longer, causing the sort of disapprobation in the white press to which Du Bois alludes in the article that follows. Johnson had accomplished what no other black man before him had, and his like would not be seen again until Joe Louis† recaptured the heavyweight title in 1937.

The Prize Fighter

"It comes down, then, after all to this unforgivable blackness."

BOXING IS AN ANCIENT SPORT. IT IS MENTIONED IN HOMER'S Iliad and Virgil's Aeneid and was a recognized branch of the celebrated Olympic games. During the middle age boxing went out of style among most nations, the preference being given to various sorts of encounters with weapons. In England it was revived in the Seventeenth Century, and fighting with bare fists became a national sport in the Eighteenth Century. Boxing gloves were invented late in that century, and in the beginning of the Nineteenth Century, John Jackson (note the prophecy!) became champion and teacher of Lord Byron and other great and titled personages.

Gradually the more brutal features of the sport were eliminated and the eighth Marquess of Queensberry drew up a set of rules in the sixties which have since prevailed.

There is still today some brutality connected with boxing, but as compared with football and boat racing it may be seriously questioned whether boxing deserves to be put in a separate class by reason of its cruelty. Certainly it is a highly civilized pastime as compared with the international game of war which produces so many "heroes" and national monuments.

Despite all this, boxing has fallen into disfavor—into very great disfavor. To see publications like the New York *Times* roll their eyes in shivery horror at the news from Paris (to which it is compelled to give a front page) makes one realize the depths to which we have fallen.

The cause is clear: Jack Johnson, successor of the Eighteenth Century John Jackson, has out-sparred an Irishman. He did it with little brutality, the utmost fairness and great good nature. He did not "knock" his opponent senseless. Apparently he did not even try. Neither he nor his race invented prize fighting or particularly like it. Why then this thrill of national disgust? Because Johnson is black. Of course, some pretend to object to Mr. Johnson's character. But we have yet to hear, in the case of white America, that marital troubles have disqualified prize fighters or ball players or even statesmen. It comes down, then, after all to this unforgivable blackness. Wherefore we conclude that at present prize fighting is very, very immoral, and that we must rely on football and war for pastime until Mr. Johnson retires or permits himself to be "knocked out."

The Crisis, August 1914

James Weldon Johnson
(1871–1938)

Poet, novelist, lyricist, essayist, critic and anthologist, Johnson remains one of the preeminent figures in African-American letters. He was born James Williams Johnson in Jacksonville, Florida, into a family with a deep appreciation of the arts. He attended the Stanton Public School for Blacks, where his mother taught, and later Atlanta University. He returned to Jacksonville in 1894 as a teacher and principal and began "reading law," becoming the first black lawyer to pass the Florida bar examination. With his brother John Rosamond Johnson (1873–1954), who had studied music and worked in the theater in Boston, he wrote "Lift Ev'ry Voice and Sing" for a Lincoln's birthday celebration in 1900. Sung by schoolchildren throughout the country, it became known as the "Negro National Anthem."

In 1901 Johnson went to New York, where he studied drama and literature at Columbia University from 1903 to 1906, and, together with his brother and Bob Cole, wrote a number of highly successful songs for black musicals. Proposed by Booker T. Washington (the source of most political patronage at the time) for the post, from 1906 to 1913 Johnson served as consul to Venezuela and Nicaragua, where he wrote the novel *The Autobiography of an Ex-Coloured Man,* which was published anonymously in 1912.

If the early narratives of the Middle Passage form the literary bridge between the Old World and the New, Johnson's novel represents a similar leap from African-American writing of the nineteenth century to the modern novel. Written as if it were as autobiography—the dominant African-American literary form up to that point—it is in fact an imaginative work of fiction, its unnamed protagonist a literary antecedent of Ralph Ellison's *Invisible Man.*† And while Johnson's fair-skinned hero, who passes for white, feels a "sort of dual personality" that is reminiscent of the dichotomy expressed by Dunbar in "We Wear the Mask"† or Du Bois's statement that a black man "ever feels his twoness—an American, a Negro," in his rootless migrations from the South, to New York, through Europe and back, and in his entrapment in the materialism of the twentieth century, he is as well a thoroughly modern hero.

Johnson returned to New York in 1914, where he became the editor of the *New York Age* and embarked upon a lengthy career with the NAACP, serving as field secretary from 1916 to 1920 and General Secretary from 1920 to 1930. At the same time, he published numerous volumes of poetry and prose, including *Fifty Years and Other Poems* (1917); *God's Trombones: Seven Negro Sermons in Verse* (1927); a survey of the African-American history and culture of New York, *Black Manhattan* (1930); *Saint Peter Relates an Incident* (1930). He also contributed the essay "The Making of Harlem" to the influential collection *The New Negro,* published in 1925. In 1930 Johnson became a professor of creative literature at Fisk University, publishing his autobiography, *Along This Way,* in 1933 and his last work, *Negro Americans, What Now?* in 1934.

In addition to his own creative works, as an anthologist and essayist, Johnson sought to establish a critical foundation for the recovery and study of African-American culture. In his two volumes of Negro spirituals (1925, 1926), he traced the history of what he called "America's only folk music and, up to this time, the finest distinctive artistic contribution she has to offer the world." And in his ground-breaking *Book of American Negro Poetry* (1922), he sought to establish a critical framework for the appreciation and discussion of African-American verse. In his preface, Johnson argues, "A people may become great through many means, but there is only one measure by which its greatness is recognized and acknowledged. The final measure of the greatness of all peoples is the amount and standard of the literature and art they have produced. . . . Because this is the first collection of its kind, I realized the absence of a starting-point and was led to provide one and to fill in with historical data what I felt to be a gap."

James Weldon Johnson and J. Rosamond Johnson

Lift Ev'ry Voice and Sing

Lift ev'ry voice and sing,
Till earth and heaven ring,
Ring with the harmonies of Liberty;
Let our rejoicing rise
High as the list'ning skies,
Let it resound loud as the rolling sea.
Sing a song full of the faith that the dark past
  has taught us
Sing a song full of the hope that the present has
  brought us
Facing the rising sun of our new day begun,
Let us march on till victory is won.

Stony the road we trod,
Bitter the chast'ning rod,
Felt in the days when hope unborn had died;
Yet with a steady beat,
Have not our weary feet
Come to the place for which our fathers sighed?
We have come over a way that with tears has
  been watered
We have come, treading our path thro' the
  blood of the slaughtered,
Out from the gloomy past, till now we stand at last
Where the white gleam of our bright star is cast.

God of our weary years,
God of our silent tears,
Thou who hast brought us thus far on the way;
Thou who hast by Thy might,
Led us into the light,
Keep us forever in the path, we pray.

Lest our feet stray from the places, our God,
  where we met Thee,
Lest our hearts, drunk with the wine of the
  world, we forget thee;
Shadowed beneath Thy hand, may we forever stand,
True to our God, true to our native land.

1900

from *The Autobiography of an Ex-Coloured Man*

"I felt that the psychic moment of my life had come, a moment which, if lost, could never be called back."

CHAPTER XI

I HAVE NOW REACHED THAT PART OF MY NARRATIVE WHERE I must be brief and touch only on important facts; therefore the reader must make up his mind to pardon skips and jumps and meager details.

When I reached New York, I was completely lost. I could not have felt more a stranger had I been suddenly dropped into Constantinople. I knew not where to turn or how to strike out. I was so oppressed by a feeling of loneliness that the temptation to visit my old home in Connecticut was well-nigh irresistible. I reasoned, however, that unless I found my old music teacher, I should be, after so many years of absence, as much of a stranger there as in New York; and, furthermore, that in view of the step which I had decided to take, such a visit would be injudicious. I remembered, too, that I had some property there in the shape of a piano and a few books, but decided that it would not be worth what it might cost me to take possession.

By reason of the fact that my living-expenses in the South had been very small, I still had nearly four hundred dollars of my capital left. In contemplation of this, my natural and acquired Bohemian tastes asserted themselves, and I decided to have a couple of weeks' good time before worrying seriously about the future. I went to Coney Island and the other resorts, took in the pre-season shows along Broadway, and ate at first-class restaurants; but I shunned the old Sixth Avenue district as though it were pest-infected. My few days of pleasure made appalling inroads upon what cash I had, and caused me to see that it required a good deal of money to live in New York as I wished to live and that I should have to find, very soon, some more or less profitable employment. I was sure that unknown, without friends or prestige, it would be useless to try to establish myself as a teacher of music; so I gave that means of earning a livelihood scarcely any consideration. And even had I considered it possible to secure pupils, as I then felt, I should have hesitated about taking up a work in which the chances for any considerable financial success are necessarily so small. I had made up my mind that since I was not going to be a Negro, I would avail myself of every possible opportunity to make a white man's success; and that, if it can be summed up in any one word, means "money."

I watched the "want" columns in the newspapers and answered a number of advertisements, but in each case found the positions were such as I could not fill or did not want. I also spent several dollars for "ads" which brought me no replies. In this way I came to know the hopes and disappointments of a large and pitiable class of humanity in this great city, the people who look for work through the newspapers. After some days of this sort of experience I concluded that the main difficulty with me was that I was not prepared for what I wanted to do. I then decided upon a course which, for an artist, showed an uncommon amount of practical sense and judgment. I made up my mind to enter a business college. I took a small room, ate at lunch counters, in order to economize, and pursued my studies with the zeal that I have always been able to put into any work upon which I set my heart. Yet, in spite of all my economy, when I had been at the school for several months, my funds gave out completely. I reached the point where I could not afford sufficient food for each day. In this plight I was glad to get, through one of the teachers, a job as an ordinary clerk in a downtown wholesale house. I did my work faithfully, and received a raise of salary before I expected it. I even managed to save a little money out of my modest earnings. In fact, I began then to contract the money fever, which later took strong possession of me. I kept my eyes open, watching for a chance to better my condition. It finally came in the form of a position with a house which was at the time establishing a South American department. My knowledge of Spanish was, of course, the principal cause of my good luck; and it did more for me: it placed me where the other clerks were practically put out of competition with me. I was not slow in taking advantage of the opportunity to make myself indispensable to the firm.

What an interesting and absorbing game is money-making! After each deposit at my savings-bank I used to sit and figure out, all over again, my principal and interest, and make calculations on what the increase would be in such and such a time. Out of this I derived a great deal of pleasure. I denied myself as much as possible in order to swell my savings. As much as I enjoyed smoking, I limited myself to an occasional cigar, and that was generally of a variety which in my old days at the "Club" was known as a "Henry Mud." Drinking I cut out altogether, but that was no great sacrifice.

The day on which I was able to figure up a thousand dollars marked an epoch in my life. And this was not because I had never before had money. In my gambling days and while I was with my millionaire I handled sums running high up into the hundreds; but they had come to me like fairy godmother's gifts, and at a time when my conception of money was that it was made only to spend. Here, on the other hand, was a thousand dollars which I had earned by days of honest and patient work, a thousand dollars which I had carefully watched grow from the first dollar; and I experienced, in owning them, a pride and satisfaction which to me was an entirely new sensation. As my capital went over the thousand-dollar mark, I was puzzled to know what to do with it, how to put it to the most advantageous use. I turned down first one scheme and then another, as though they had been devised for the sole purpose of gobbling up my money. I finally listened to a friend who advised me to put all I had in New York real estate; and under his guidance I took equity in a piece of property on which stood a rickety old tenement-house. I did not regret following this friend's advice, for in something like six months I disposed of my equity for more than double my investment. From that time on I devoted myself to the study of New York real estate and watched for opportunities to make similar investments. In spite of two or three speculations which did not turn out well, I have been remarkably successful. Today I am the owner and part-owner of several flat-houses. I have changed my place of employment four times since returning to New York, and each change has been a decided advancement. Concerning the position which I now hold I shall say nothing except that it pays extremely well.

As my outlook on the world grew brighter, I began to mingle in the social circles of the men with whom I came in contact; and gradually, by a process of elimination, I reached a grade of society of no small degree of culture. My appearance was always good and my ability to play on the piano, especially rag-time, which was then at the height of its vogue, made me a welcome guest. The anomaly of my social position often appealed strongly to my sense of humour. I frequently smiled inwardly at some remark not altogether complimentary to people of colour; and more than once I felt like declaiming: "I am a coloured man. Do I not disprove the theory that one drop of Negro blood renders a man unfit?" Many a night when I returned to my room after an enjoyable evening, I laughed heartily over what struck me as the capital joke I was playing.

Then I met her, and what I had regarded as a joke was gradually changed into the most serious question of my life. I first saw her at a musical which was given one evening at a house to which I was frequently invited. I did not notice her among the other guests before she came forward and sang two sad little songs. When she began, I was out in the hallway, where many of the men were gathered; but with the first few notes I crowded with others into the doorway to see who the singer was. When I saw the girl, the surprise which I had felt at the first sound of her voice was heightened; she was almost tall and quite slender, with lustrous yellow hair and eyes so blue as to appear almost black. She was as white as a lily, and she was dressed in white. Indeed, she seemed to me the most dazzlingly white thing I had ever seen. But it was not her delicate beauty which attracted me most; it was her voice, a voice which made one wonder how tones of such passionate colour could come from so fragile a body.

I determined that when the program was over, I would seek an introduction to her; but at the moment, instead of being the easy man of the world, I became again the bashful boy of fourteen, and my courage failed me. I contented myself with hovering as near her as politeness would permit; near enough to hear her voice, which in conversation was low, yet thrilling, like the deeper middle tones of a flute. I watched the men gather round her talking and laughing in an easy manner, and wondered how it was possible for them to do it. But destiny, my special destiny, was at work. I was standing near, talking with affected gaiety to several young ladies, who, however, must have remarked my preoccupation; for my second sense of hearing was alert to what was being said by the group of which the girl in white was the centre, when I heard her say: "I think his playing of Chopin is exquisite." And one of my friends in the group replied: "You haven't met him? Allow me—" Then turning to me, "Old man, when you have a moment I wish you to meet Miss—." I don't know what she said to me or what I said to her. I can remember that I tried to be clever, and experienced a growing conviction that I was making myself appear more and more idiotic. I am certain, too, that, in spite of my Italian-like complexion, I was as red as a beet.

Instead of taking the car, I walked home. I needed the air and exercise as a sort of sedative. I am not sure whether my troubled condition of mind was due to the fact that I had been struck by love or to the feeling that I had made a bad impression upon her.

As the weeks went by, and when I had met her several more times, I came to know that I was seriously in love; and then began for me days of worry, for I had more than the usual doubts and fears of a young man in love to contend with.

Up to this time I had assumed and played my role as a white man with a certain degree of nonchalance, a carelessness as to the outcome, which made the whole thing more amusing to me than serious; but now I ceased to regard "being a white man" as a sort of practical joke. My acting had called for mere external effects. Now I began to doubt my ability to play the part. I watched her to see if she was scrutinizing me, to see if she was looking for anything in me which made me differ from the other men she knew. In place of an old inward feeling of superiority over many of my friends I began to doubt myself. I began even to wonder if I really was like the men I associated with; if there was not, after all, an indefinable something which marked a difference.

But, in spite of my doubts and timidity, my affair progressed, and I finally felt sufficiently encouraged to decide to ask her to marry me. Then began the hardest struggle of my life, whether to ask her to marry me under false colours or to tell her the whole truth. My sense of what was exigent made me feel there was no necessity of saying anything; but my inborn sense of honour rebelled at even indirect deception in this case. But however much I moralized on the question, I found it more and more difficult to reach the point of confession. The dread that I might lose her took possession of me each time I sought to speak, and rendered it impossible for me to do so. That moral courage requires more than physical courage is no mere poetic fancy. I am sure I should have found it easier to take the place of a gladiator, no matter how fierce the Numidian lion, than to tell that slender girl that I had Negro blood in my veins. That fact which I had at times wished to cry out, I now wished to hide for ever.

During this time we were drawn together a great deal by the mutual bond of music. She loved to hear me play Chopin and was herself far from being a poor performer of his compositions. I think I carried her every new song that was published which I thought suitable to her voice, and played the accompaniment for her. Over these songs we were like two innocent children with new toys. She had never been anything but innocent; but my innocence was a transformation wrought by my love for her, love which melted away my cynicism and whitened my sullied soul and gave me back the wholesome dreams of my boyhood.

My artistic temperament also underwent an awakening. I spent many hours at my piano, playing over old and new composers. I also wrote several little pieces in a more or less Chopinesque style, which I dedicated to her. And so the weeks and months went by. Often words of love trembled on my lips, but I dared not utter them, because I knew they would have to be followed by other words which I had not the courage to frame. There might have been some other woman in my set whom I could have fallen in love with and asked to marry me without a word of explanation; but the more I knew the girl, the less could I find it in my heart to deceive her. And yet, in spite of the spectre that was constantly looming up before me, I could never have believed that life held such happiness as was contained in those dream days of love.

One Saturday afternoon, in early June, I was coming up Fifth Avenue, and at the corner of Twenty-third Street I met her. She had been shopping. We stopped to chat for a moment, and I suggested that we spend half an hour at the Eden Musée. We were standing leaning on the rail in front of a group of figures, more interested in what we had to say to each other than in the group, when my attention became fixed upon a man who stood at my side studying his catalogue. It took me only an instant to recognize in him my old friend "Shiny." My first impulse was to change my position at once. As quick as a flash I considered all the risks I might run in speaking to him, and most especially the delicate question of introducing him to her. I confess that in my embarrassment and confusion I felt small and mean. But before I could decide what to do, he looked round at me and, after an instant, quietly asked: "Pardon me; but isn't this—?" The nobler part in me responded to the sound of his voice and I took his hand in a hearty clasp. Whatever fears I had felt were quickly banished, for he seemed, at a glance, to divine my situation, and let drop no word that would have aroused suspicion as to the truth. With a slight misgiving I presented him to her and was again relieved of fear. She received the introduction in her usual gracious manner, and without the least hesitancy or embarrassment joined in the conversation. An amusing part about the introduction was that I was upon the point of introducing him as "Shiny," and stammered a second or two before I could recall his name. We chatted for some fifteen minutes. He was spending his vacation north, with the intention of doing four or six weeks' work in one of the summer schools; he was also going to take a bride back with him in the fall. He asked me about myself, but in so diplomatic a way that I found no difficulty in answering him. The polish of his language and the unpedantic manner in which he revealed his culture greatly impressed her; and after we had left the Musée she showed it by questioning me about him. I was surprised at the amount of interest a refined black man could arouse. Even after changes in the conversation she reverted several times to the subject of "Shiny." Whether it was more than mere curiosity I could not tell, but I was convinced that she herself knew very little about prejudice.

Just why it should have done so I do not know, but somehow the "Shiny" incident gave me encouragement and confidence to cast the die of my fate. I reasoned, however, that since I wanted to marry her only, and since it concerned her alone, I would divulge my secret to no one else, not even her parents.

One evening, a few days afterwards, at her home we were going over some new songs and compositions when she asked me, as she often did, to play the Thirteenth Nocturne. When I began, she drew a chair near to my right and sat leaning with her elbow on the end of the piano, her chin resting on her hand, and her eyes reflecting the emotions which the music awoke in her. An impulse which I could not control rushed over me, a wave of exultation, the music under my fingers sank almost to a whisper, and calling her for the first time by her Christian name, but without daring to look at her, I said: "I love you, I love you, I love you." My fingers were trembling so that I ceased playing. I felt her hand creep to mine, and when I looked at her, her eyes were glistening with tears. I understood, and could scarcely resist the longing to take her in my arms; but I remembered, remembered that which has been the sacrificial altar of so much happiness—Duty; and bending over her hand in mine, I said: "Yes, I love you; but there is something more, too, that I must tell you." Then I told her, in what words I do not know, the truth. I felt her hand grow cold, and when I looked up, she was gazing at me with a wild, fixed stare as though I was some object she had never seen. Under the strange light in her eyes I felt that I was growing black and thick-featured and crimp-haired. She appeared not to have comprehended what I had said. Her lips trembled and she attempted to say something to me, but the words stuck in her throat. Then, dropping her head on the piano, she began to weep with great sobs that shook her frail body. I tried to console her, and blurted out incoherent words of love, but this seemed to increase her distress, and when I left her, she was still weeping.

When I got into the street, I felt very much as I did the night after meeting my father and sister at the opera in Paris, even a similar desperate inclination to get drunk; but my self-control was stronger. This was the only time in my life that I ever felt absolute regret at being coloured, that I cursed the drops of African blood in my veins and wished that I were really white. When I reached my rooms, I sat and smoked several cigars while I tried to think out the significance of what had occurred. I reviewed the whole history of our acquaintance, recalled each smile she had given me, each word she had said to me that nourished my hope. I went over the scene we had just gone through, trying to draw from it what was in my favour and what was against me. I was rewarded by feeling confident that she loved me, but I could not estimate what was the effect upon her of my confession. At last, nervous and unhappy, I wrote her a letter, which I dropped into the mail-box before going to bed, in which I said:

> I understand, understand even better than you, and so I suffer even more than you. But why should either of us suffer for what neither of us is to blame for? If there is any blame, it belongs to me and I can only make the old, yet strongest plea that can be offered, I love you; and I know that my love, my great love, infinitely overbalances that blame and blots it out. What is it that stands in the way of our happiness? It is not what you feel or what I feel; it is not what you are or what I am. It is what others feel and are. But, oh! is that a fair price? In all the endeavours and struggles of life, in all our starving and longings, there is only one thing worth seeking, only one thing worth winning, and that is love. It is not always found; but when it is, there is nothing in all the world for which it can be profitably exchanged.

The second morning after, I received a note from her which stated briefly that she was going up into New Hampshire to spend the summer with relatives there. She made no reference to what had passed between us; nor did she say exactly when she would leave the city. The note contained no single word that gave me any clue to her feelings. I could gather hope only from the fact that she had written at all. On the same evening, with a degree of trepidation which rendered me almost frightened, I went to her house.

I met her mother, who told me that she had left for the country that very afternoon. Her mother treated me in her usual pleasant manner, which fact greatly reassured me; and I left the house with a vague sense of hope stirring in my breast, which sprang from the conviction that she had not yet divulged my secret. But that hope did not remain with me long. I waited one, two, three weeks, nervously examining my mail every day, looking for some word from her. All of the letters received by me seemed so insignificant, so worthless, because there was none from her. The slight buoyancy of spirit which I had felt gradually dissolved into gloomy heart-sickness. I became preoccupied; I lost appetite, lost sleep, and lost ambition. Several of my friends intimated to me that perhaps I was working too hard.

She stayed away the whole summer. I did not go to the house, but saw her father at various times, and he was as friendly as ever. Even after I knew that she was back in town, I did not go to see her. I determined to wait for some word or sign. I had finally taken refuge and comfort in my pride, pride which, I suppose, I came by naturally enough.

The first time I saw her after her return was one night at the theatre. She and her mother sat in company with a young man whom I knew slightly, not many seats away from me. Never did she appear more beautiful; and yet, it may have been my fancy, she seemed a trifle paler, and there was a suggestion of haggardness in her countenance. But that only heightened her beauty; the very delicacy of her charm melted down the strength of my pride. My situation made me feel weak and powerless, like a man trying with his bare hands to break the iron bars of his prison cell. When the performance was over, I hurried out and placed myself where, unobserved, I could see her as she passed out. The haughtiness of spirit in which I had sought relief was all gone, and I was willing and ready to undergo any humiliation.

Shortly afterward we met at a progressive card party, and during the evening we were thrown together at one of the tables as partners. This was really our first meeting since the eventful night at her house. Strangely enough, in spite of our mutual nervousness, we won every trick of the game, and one of our opponents jokingly quoted the old saw: "Lucky at cards, unlucky in love." Our eyes met and I am sure that in the momentary glance my whole soul went out to her in one great plea. She lowered her eyes and uttered a nervous little laugh. During the rest of the game I fully merited the unexpressed and expressed abuse of my various partners; for my eyes followed her wherever she was and I played whatever card my fingers happened to touch.

Later in the evening she went to the piano and began to play very softly, as to herself, the opening bars of the Thirteenth Nocturne. I felt that the psychic moment of my life had come, a moment which, if lost could never be called back; and, in as careless a manner as I could assume, I sauntered over to the piano and stood almost bending over her. She continued playing, but, in a voice that was almost a whisper, she called me by my Christian name and said: "I love you, I love you, I love you." I took her place at the piano and played the Nocturne in a manner that silenced the chatter of the company both in and out of the room, involuntarily closing it with the major triad.

We were married the following spring, and went to Europe for several months. It was a double joy for me to be in France again under such conditions.

First there came to us a little girl, with hair and eyes dark like mine, but who is growing to have ways like her mother. Two years later there came a boy, who has my temperament, but is fair like his mother, a little golden-headed god, with a face and head that would have delighted the heart of an old Italian master. And this boy, with his mother's eyes and features, occupies an inner sanctuary of my heart; for it was for him that she gave all; and that is the second sacred sorrow of my life.

The few years of our married life were supremely happy, and perhaps she was even happier than I; for after our marriage, in spite of all the wealth of her love which she lavished upon me, there came a new dread to haunt me, a dread which I cannot explain and which was unfounded, but one that never left me. I was in constant fear that she would discover in me some shortcoming which she would unconsciously attribute to my blood rather than to a failing of human nature. But no cloud ever came to mar our life together; her loss to me is irreparable. My children need a mother's care, but I shall never marry again. It is to my children that I have devoted my life. I no longer have the same fear for myself of my secret's being found out, for since my wife's death I have gradually dropped out of social life; but there is nothing I would not suffer to keep the brand from being placed on them.

It is difficult for me to analyze my feelings concerning my present position in the world. Sometimes it seems to me that I have never really been a Negro, that I have been only a privileged spectator of their inner life; at other times I feel that I have been a coward, a deserter, and I am possessed by a strange longing for my mother's people.

Several years ago I attended a great meeting in the interest of Hampton Institute at Carnegie Hall. The Hampton students sang old songs and awoke memories that left me sad. Among the speakers were R. C. Ogden, ex-Ambassador Choate, and Mark Twain; but the greatest interest of the audience was centered in Booker T. Washington, and not because he so much surpassed the others in eloquence, but because of what he represented with so much earnestness and faith. And it is this that all of that small but gallant band of coloured men who are publicly fighting the cause of their race have behind them. Even those who oppose them know that these men have the eternal principles of right on their side, and they will be victors even though they should go down in defeat. Beside them I feel small and selfish. I am an ordinarily successful white man who has made a little money. They are men who are making history and a race. I, too, might have taken part in a work so glorious.

My love for my children makes me glad that I am what I am and keeps me from desiring to be otherwise; and yet, when I sometimes open a little box in which I still keep my fast yellowing manuscripts, the only tangible remnants of a vanished dream, a dead ambition, a sacrificed talent, I cannot repress the thought that, after all, I have chosen the lesser part, that I have sold my birthright for a mess of pottage.

1912

O Black and Unknown Bards

"Those songs of sorrow, love and faith, and hope . . ."

O black and unknown bards of long ago,
How came your lips to touch the sacred fire?
How, in your darkness, did you come to know
The power and beauty of the minstrel's lyre?
Who first from midst his bond lifted his eyes?
Who first from out the still watch, lone and long,
Feeling the ancient faith of prophets rise
Within his dark-kept soul, burst into song?

Heart of what slave poured out such melody
As "Steal away to Jesus"? On its strains
His spirit must have nightly floated free,
Though still about his hands he felt his chains.
Who heard great "Jordan roll"? Whose starward eye
Saw chariot "swing low"? And who was he
That breathed that comforting, melodic sigh,
"Nobody knows de trouble I see"?

What merely living clod, what captive thing,
Could up toward God through all its darkness grope,
And find within its deadened heart to sing
Those songs of sorrow, love and faith, and hope?
How did it catch that subtle undertone,
That note in music heard not with the ears?
How sound the elusive reed so seldom blown,
Which stirs the soul or melts the heart to tears.

Not that great German master in his dream
Of harmonies that thundered amongst the stars
At the creation, ever heard a theme
Nobler than "Go down, Moses." Mark its bars
How like a mighty trumpet-call they stir
The blood. Such are the notes that men have sung
Going to valorous deeds; such tones there were
That helped make history when Time was young.

There is a wide, wide wonder in it all,
That from degraded rest and servile toil
The fiery spirit of the seer should call
These simple children of the sun and soil.
O black slave singers, gone, forgot, unfamed,

You—you alone, of all the long, long line
Of those who've sung untaught, unknown, unnamed,
Have stretched out upward, seeking the divine.

You sang not deeds of heros or of kings;
No chant of bloody war, no exulting paean
Of arms-won triumphs; but your humble strings
You touched in chord with music empyrean.
You sang far better than you knew; the songs
That for your listeners' hungry hearts sufficed
Still live,—but more than this to you belongs:
You sang a race from wood and stone to Christ.

1917

The Great Migration, 1910–1920

From 1916 to 1918, about a half million African-Americans moved from Southern to Northern states, accelerating the migration begun by runaway slaves following the North Star to freedom since the mid-1800s. In Chicago alone, the African-American population increased by almost 150 percent, from about 45,000 in 1910 to 110,000 in 1920, almost half due solely to migration; within a period of eighteen months in 1917–18, more than 50,000 migrants arrived in Chicago, some finding work there, others moving on to other Northern cities and towns.

The migrants came north for a variety of reasons. Low wages were certainly a factor. While workers in the South were paid from $.40 in the field to $1.75 a day in certain city jobs, workers in the North in 1916 received from $3.00 to $8.00 a day, often for shorter hours. One observer wrote, "The Negro farm hand gets for his compensation hardly more than the mule he plows; that is, his board and shelter. Some mules fare better than Negroes." Even this source of income dried up with the devastation of the cotton crop by the boll weevil in 1915 and 1916. At the same time, in the North, barriers to immigration during the war and the expanding wartime industry created a much greater demand for labor.

Schooling was equally poor in the South. In counties with more than a 75 percent black population, $22.22 was spent for education per white child, while $1.78 was spent for black children. Jim Crow statutes in the South resulted in isolated and inferior transportation and living facilities. While housing in the North was not much better, the greater integration of public schools made possible a higher level of instruction.

But there were more than economic incentives at work. Between 1885 and 1918, nearly three thousand African-Americans were lynched in the United States, more than 85 percent in the South. Mob law, as one paper noted, had furnished emigration agents with all the leverage they needed to encourage the exodus.

Pennsylvania was one of the early destinations on the route North. During the month of July 1916 a single railroad claimed to have drawn to Pennsylvania thirteen thousand Southerners, who wrote back of high wages and fair treatment. Word of mouth imbued the movement with near biblical significance. Songs and poems were written, such as "Flight Out of

Egypt," "Bound for the Promised Land," "Going into Canaan," "The Land of Hope," and others. Migrants swelled the main lines of transportation from Southeast to Northeast, others later followed the railway routes north from Mississippi, Arkansas, Alabama, Louisiana, and Texas to Chicago. While the Department of Labor initially provided transportation, that service ended with complaints from Southern businessmen that the supply of cheap labor was drying up. Groups of workers joined together in cooperative "clubs" to garner better travel rates, resulting in whole communities uprooting themselves and traveling North. The largest number of arrivals came with the "Great Drive" of May 1917.

The Chicago Defender, which ran news articles, poems, and letters about the movement, was instrumental in spreading the word. Because of its favorable report on conditions in the North, the paper was restricted and confiscated in some parts of the South. The *Defender* resoundingly refuted the claim advanced by desperate businessmen in the South that migrants would face a harsh climate in the North, citing instances of death by exposure even in the South: "If you can freeze to death in the North and be free, why freeze to death in the South and be a slave, where your mother, sister, and daughter are raped and burned at stake, where your father, brother, and son are treated with contempt and hung to a pole, riddled with bullets at the least mention that he does not like the way he has been treated?

"Come North, then, all of you folks, both good and bad. If you don't behave yourself up here, the jails will certainly make you wish you had. For the hard working man there is plenty of work—if you really want it. The *Defender* says come."

Tragically, not long after such portrayals of the North as a Promised Land, the disturbing reality of race hatred would explode in what E. Franklin Frazier termed "the cities of destruction," in a series of devastating riots during the Red Summer of 1919.†

Letters and Articles from *The Chicago Defender*

"There is a determination to leave and there is no hand save death to keep them from it."

LEAVING FOR THE EAST

UNTSVILLE, ALA., JAN. 19.—FIFTEEN FAMILIES, ALL MEMBERS of the Race, left here today for Pittsburgh, Pa., where they will take positions as butlers, and maids, getting sixty to seventy-five dollars per month, against fifteen and twenty paid here. Most of them claim that they have letters from their friends who went early and made good, saying that there was plenty of work, and this field of labor is short, owing to the vast amount of men having gone to Europe and not returned.

THEY'RE LEAVING MEMPHIS IN DROVES

Some are coming on the passenger,
Some are coming on the freight,
Others will be found walking,
For none have time to wait.

LEAVING FOR THE NORTH

Tampa, Fla. Jan. 19.—J. T. King, supposed to be a race leader, is using his wits to get on the good side of the white people by calling a meeting to urge our people not to migrate North. King has been termed a "good nigger" by his pernicious activity on the emigration question. Reports have been received here that 11 who have gone North are at work and pleased with the splendid conditions in the North. It is known here that in the North there is a scarcity of labor, mills and factories are open to them. People are not paying any attention to King and are packing and ready to travel North to the "promised land."

DETERMINED TO GO NORTH

Jackson, Miss., March 23.—Although the white police and sheriff and others are using every effort to intimidate the citizens from going North, even Dr. Redmond's speech was circulated around, this has not deterred our people from leaving. Many have walked miles to take the train for the North. There is a determination to leave and there is no hand save death to keep them from it.

Mobile, Ala., 4-26-17

Dear Sir Bro: I take great pane in droping you a few lines hopeing that this will find you enjoying the best of health as it leave me at this time present. Dear sir I seen in the Defender where you was helping us a long in securing a posission as brickmason plaster cementers stone masons. I am writing to you for advice about comeing north. I am a brickmason an I can do cement work an stone work. I written to a firm in Birmingham and they sent me a blank stateing $2.00 would get me a ticket an pay 10 per ct of my salary for the 1st month and $24.92c would be paid after I reach Detroit and went to work where they sent me to work. I had to stay there until I pay them the sum of $24.92c so I want to leave Mobile for there. if there nothing there for me to make a support for my self and family. My wife is seamstress. We want to get away the 15 or 20 of May so please give this matter your earnest consideration an let me her from you by return mail as my bro. in law want to get away to. He is a carpenter by trade. so please help us as we are in need of your help as we wanted to go to Detroit but if you says no we go where ever you sends us until we can get to Detroit. We expect to do whatever you says. There is nothing here for the colored man but a hard time wich these southern crackers gives us. We has not had any work to do in 4 wks. and every thing is high to the colored man so plese let me hear from you by return mail. Please do this for your brother.

New Orleans, La., May 2, 1917

Dear Sir: Please Sir will you kindly tell me what is meant by the Great Northern Drive to take place May the 15th on tuesday. It is a rumor all over town to be ready for the 15th of May to go in the drive. the Defender first spoke of the drive the 10th of February. My husband is in the north already preparing for our family but hearing that the excursion will be $6.00 from here north on the 15 and having a large family, I could profit by it if it is really true. Do please write me at once and say is there an excursion to leave the south. Nearly the whole of the south is getting ready for the drive or excursion it is termed. Please write at once. We are sick to get out of the solid south.

New Orleans, La., 5-20-17

Dear Sir: I am sure your time is precious, for being as you an editor of a newspaper such as the race has never owned and for which it must proudly boast of as being the peer in the pereoidical world. am confident that yours is a force of busy men. I also feel sure that you will spare a small amount of your time to give some needed information to one who wishes to relieve himselfe of the burden of the south. I indeed wish very much to come north anywhere in Ill. will do since I am away from the Lynchman's noose and torchman's fire. Myself and a friend wish to come but not without information regarding work and general surroundings. Now hon sir if for any reason you are not in position to furnish us with the information desired. please do the act of kindness of placing us in tuch with the organization who's business it is I am told to furnish said information. we are firemen machinist helpers practical painters and general laborers. And most of all, ministers of the gospel who are not afraid of labor for it put us where we are. Please let me hear from you.

Red Summer of 1919

The year after the Great War ended in November 1918, twenty-six riots exploded across the length and breadth of the country as several forces joined to signal a growing crisis in race relations in America. African-American soldiers were returning from a war in which they expected significant gains; instead, race violence and lynching escalated. The year 1919, marking three hundred years since Africans had come ashore in Jamestown, also had enormous symbolic significance; not enough had been gained in the intervening three centuries.

The riots of 1919 were only the climax of racial tension that had been festering for some time. On July 2, 1917, East St. Louis exploded in one of the worst riots in history, in which from forty to two hundred blacks were killed and six thousand more routed from their homes. Ida Wells-Barnett investigated the disturbance and found that though the community's black men, who because of labor trouble had been expecting violence, sought only to protect themselves, sixteen of them received sentences of at least fifteen years; the white participants received sentences from a few days to five years. "Many people wonder at the crime wave sweeping over our country," Wells wrote, "at the horrible murders committed by young bandits and the cold-blooded taking of life by the men and women of this generation with white skins. Strange they do not seem to realize that this is simply a reaping of the harvest which has been sown by those who administer justice as was done in the case of the East Saint Louis rioters." In protest, the NAACP led a silent march down Fifth Avenue in New York on July 28, 1917. As more than ten thousand people gathered, flanks of women and children, dressed in white, carried signs that read, "Mr. President, why not make America safe for democracy," and Claude McKay responded with "If We Must Die."

The next major confrontation took place in Houston, where a "Negro in military uniform," wrote the *Baltimore Afro-American,* was as exasperating as "the flaunting of a red flag in the face of an enraged bull." After a white mob attacked black soldiers stationed there, sixty-three of the soldiers were court-martialed; thirteen were executed in December, five more in September 1918.

In the early part of 1919, riots broke out in Charleston, Atlanta,

Norfolk, and Longview, Texas. After meeting with a delegation of African-American leaders in March, President Woodrow Wilson issued a statement that "great principles are won by hard fighting and they are attained by slow degrees. With thousands of your sons in the camps and in France out of this conflict you must expect nothing less than the enjoyment of full citizenship rights." The directive that had been issued to French troops during the war regarding their attitudes to African-American servicemen belies an entirely different race policy. As Du Bois put it in his study "Toward a History of the Black Man in the Great War," "a nation with a great disease set out to rescue civilization; it took the disease with it in virulent form." Though he had argued before the war—"Let us while this war lasts, forget our special grievances and close our ranks shoulder to shoulder with our white fellow citizens and the allied nations that are fighting for democracy"— the time for patience was long gone. His scathing editorial "Returning Soldiers" appeared in *The Crisis* in May.

It was the riots in Washington, D.C., and in Chicago in July that were most explosive. In Washington, blacks and whites clashed in the streets not far from the White House, while in Chicago, from July 27 to 30, riots broke out between whites and blacks at segregated beaches when a black youth drowned after he had been assaulted by white youths. The violence spread and six thousand National Guardsmen were called in to restore order, but not until nearly forty people were killed and more than five hundred injured.

More violence erupted in Elaine, Arkansas, in October. Wells wrote that "after scores of helpless Negroes were killed, scores more of them were herded into prison in Helena, Arkansas, where the mob tried to lynch them and where they were shocked by electricity, beaten, and tortured to make them confess they had a conspiracy to kill white folks. After the mockery of a trial, twelve of them were sentenced to be electrocuted!" Wells wrote articles and collected funds to be used for their defense, and black leaders issued appeals to President Woodrow Wilson and to Congress to make lynching a federal crime.

In a pattern that would be followed throughout the twentieth century, after the Chicago riot, a municipal commission was drawn up to investigate the sources of the violence. Their report, full of footnotes and statistics, located the causes of the outbreak in a doubling of the black population in Chicago, lack of housing, labor organization, and a newfound race solidarity earned in the war. But while the study, like the Kerner Commission report[†] in the 1960s and the one issued after the conflagration in Los Angeles in 1992, was long on statistics, it was short on solutions, and without the power to implement them.

A Directive to French Troops

"Recognize that American opinion is unanimous on the "color question," and does not admit of any discussion."

[To the] French Military Mission stationed with the American Army, August 7, 1918. Secret information concerning the Black American Troops.

It is important for French officers who have been called upon to exercise command over black American troops, or to live in close contact with them, to have an exact idea of the position occupied by Negroes in the United States. The information set forth in the following communication ought to be given to these officers and it is to their interest to have these matters known and widely disseminated. It will devolve likewise on the French Military Authorities, through the medium of the Civil Authorities, to give information on this subject to the French population residing in the cantonments occupied by American colored troops.

The American attitude upon the Negro question may seem a matter for discussion to many French minds. But we French are not in our province if we undertake to discuss what some call "prejudice." *[recognize that] American opinion is unanimous on the "color question," and does not admit of any discussion.*

The increasing number of Negroes in the United States (about 15,000,000) would create for the white race in the Republic a menace of degeneracy were it not that an impassable gulf has been made between them.

As this danger does not exist for the French race, *the French public has become accustomed to treating the Negro with familiarity and indulgence.*

This indulgence and this familiarity *[These] are matters of grievous concern to the Americans. They consider them an affront to their national policy.* They are afraid that contact with the French will inspire in black Americans aspirations to which to them (the whites) appear intolerable. *It is of the utmost importance that every effort be made to avoid profoundly estranging American opinion.*

Although a citizen of the United States, the black man is regarded by the white American as an inferior being with whom relations of business or service only are possible. The black is constantly being censured for his want of intelligence and discretion, his lack of civic and professional conscience, and for his tendency toward undue familiarity.

The vices of the Negro are a constant menace to the American who has to repress them sternly. For instance, the black American troops in France have, by themselves, given rise to as many complaints for attempted rape as all the rest of the army. And yet the (black American) soldiers sent us have been the choicest with respect to physique and morals, for the number disqualified at the time of mobilization was enormous.

CONCLUSION

1. We must prevent the rise of any pronounced degree of intimacy between French officers and black officers. We may be courteous and amiable with these last, but we cannot deal with them on the same plane as with the white American officers without deeply wounding the latter. We *must not eat with [the blacks]* them, *must not shake hands or seek to talk or meet with them outside of the requirements of military service.*

2. We must not commend too highly the black American troops, particularly in the presence of (white) Americans. It is all right to recognize their good qualities and their services, but only in moderate terms strictly in keeping with the truth.

3. Make a point of keeping the native cantonment population from "spoiling" the Negroes. (White) *Americans become greatly incensed at any public expression of intimacy between white women with black men.* They have recently uttered violent protests against a picture in the "Vie Pariesienne" entitled "The Child of the Desert" which shows a (white) woman in a "cabinet particulier" with a Negro. Familiarity on the part of white women with black men is furthermore a source of profound regret to our experienced colonials who see in it an overweening menace to the prestige of the white race.

Military authority cannot intervene directly in this question, but it can through the civil authorities exercise some influence on the population.

[Signed] LINARD

The Crisis, May 1919

Returning Soldiers

"Make way for Democracy!"

WE ARE RETURNING FROM WAR. *THE CRISIS* AND TENS OF THOUSANDS of black men were drafted into a great struggle. For bleeding France and what she means and has meant and will mean to us and humanity and against the threat of German race arrogance, we fought gladly and to the last drop of blood; for America and her highest ideals, we fought in far-off hope; for the dominant southern oligarchy entrenched in Washington, we fought in bitter resignation. For the America that represents and gloats in lynching, disfranchisement, caste, brutality and devilish insult—for this, in the hateful upturning and mixing of things, we were forced by vindictive fate to fight, also.

But to-day we return! We return from the slavery of uniform which the world's madness demanded us to don to the freedom of civil garb. We stand again to look America squarely in the face and call a spade a spade. We sing: This country of ours, despite all its better souls have done and dreamed, is yet a shameful land.

It *lynches.*

And lynching is barbarism of a degree of contemptible nastiness unparalleled in human history. Yet for fifty years we have lynched two Negroes a week, and we have kept this up right through the war.

It *disfranchises* its own citizens.

Disfranchisement is the deliberate theft and robbery of the only protection of poor against rich and black against white. The land that disfranchises its citizens and calls itself a democracy lies and knows it lies.

It encourages *ignorance.*

It has never really tried to educate the Negro. A dominant minority does not want Negroes educated. It wants servants, dogs, whores and monkeys. And when this land allows a reactionary group by its stolen political power to force as many black folk into these categories as it possibly can, it cries in contemptible hypocrisy: "They threaten us with degeneracy; they cannot be educated."

It *steals* from us.

It organizes industry to cheat us. It cheats us out of our land; it cheats us out of our labor. It confiscates our savings. It reduces our wages. It raises our rent. It steals our profit. It taxes us without representation. It keeps us consistently and universally poor, and then feeds us on charity and derides our poverty.

It *insults* us.

It has organized a nation-wide and latterly a world-wide propaganda of deliberate and continuous insult and defamation of black blood wherever found. It decrees that it shall not be possible in travel nor residence, work nor play, education nor instruction for a black man to exist without tacit or open acknowledgment of his inferiority to the dirtiest white dog. And it looks upon any attempt to question or even discuss this dogma as arrogance, unwarranted assumption and treason.

This is the country to which we Soldiers of Democracy return. This is the fatherland for which we fought! But it is *our* fatherland. It was right for us to fight. The faults of *our* country are *our* faults. Under similar circumstances, we would fight again. But by the God of Heaven, we are cowards and jackasses if now that that war is over, we do not marshal every ounce of our brain and brawn to fight a sterner, longer, more unbending battle against the forces of hell in our own land.

We *return.*

We *return from fighting.*

We *return fighting.*

Make way for Democracy! We saved it in France, and by the Great Jehovah, we will save it in the United States of America, or know the reason why.

The Crisis, May 1919

Three Hundred Years

"We commemorate this day, lest we forget. . . ."

THREE HUNDRED YEARS AGO THIS MONTH A "DUTCH MAN of Warre sold us twenty Negars." They were not slaves. They were stolen freemen. They were free in Africa; they were free by the laws of Virginia. By force and fraud they and their children were gradually reduced to a slavery, the legality of which was not fully recognized for nearly a century after 1619. From their loins and the bodies of their fellows of after-years have sprung—counting both "white" and "black"—fully twenty million souls. Those still visibly tinged with their blood are still enslaved—by compulsory ignorance, disfranchisement and public insult. In sack-cloth and ashes, then, we commemorate this day, lest we forget; lest a single drop of blood, a single moan of pain, a single bead of sweat, in all these three, long, endless centuries should drop into oblivion.

Why must we remember? Is this but a counsel of Vengeance and Hate? God forbid! We must remember because if once the world forgets evil, evil is reborn; because if the suffering of the American Negro is once forgotten, then there is no guerdon, down to the last pulse of time, that Devils will not again enslave and maim and murder and oppress the weak and unfortunate.

Behold, then, this month of mighty memories; celebrate it, Children of the Sun, in solemn song and silent march and grim thanksgiving. The Fourth Century dawns and through it, God guide our thrilling hands.

The Crisis, August 1919

Claude McKay
If We Must Die!

If we must die, let it not be like hogs
   Hunted and penned in an inglorious spot,
While round us bark the mad and hungry dogs,
   Making their mock at our accursed lot.
If we must die, let it not be like hogs
   So that our precious blood may not be shed
In vain; then even the monster we defy
   Shall be constrained to honor us, though dead!

Oh kinsman! We must meet the common foe;
   Though far outnumbered, let us still be brave,
And for their thousand blows deal one deathblow!
   What though before us lies the open grave?
Like men we'll face the murderous, cowardly pack,
   Pressed to the wall, dying, but—fighting back!

1919

Marcus Garvey
(1887–1940)

Arising out of the profound cynicism bred by the broken promises of the Great War, the wave of riots and lynchings, and the huge movement of mostly Southern rural blacks to urban areas, Marcus Garvey assembled in the 1920s the largest black mass organization in this nation's history. Garvey was born in Jamaica of ancestors who had taken part in one of the most successful of the slave revolts that had been widespread in the Caribbean from the seventeenth century. According to Garvey's wife, Garvey's mother sensed that her son would become a leader of his people, and though he was named Marcus Mosiah Garvey, he was called Mose. When he was fifteen, Garvey learned the printing trade, and at eighteen continued his profession in Kingston, where he became involved in a printers' union strike and worked on the first of many newspapers. He traveled over the next two years in Costa Rica, Guatemala, Panama, Nicaragua, Ecuador, Chile, and Peru, trying to organize West Indian laborers.

Sometime around 1912, Garvey went to England, where he worked on the docks in London, Cardiff, and Liverpool, and met Duse Mohammed Ali, an Egyptian scholar and pan-Africanist who impressed upon Garvey the link between present-day Africa and ancient Egyptian civilization and the current exploitation of Africa's resources by the European nations that had neatly divided her up. Garvey also studied law and philosophy and there first read Booker T. Washington's *Up from Slavery.* It was then, he writes, that "my doom—if I may so call it—of being a race leader dawned upon me . . . I asked 'Where is the black man's Government?' 'Where is his King and his kingdom?' 'Where is his President, his country, and his ambassador, his army, his navy, his men of big affairs?' I could not find them, and then I declared, 'I will help to make them.' " In a 1913 article he wrote that the scattered peoples of the West Indies would create "an Empire on which the sun shall shine as ceaselessly as it shines on the Empire of the North today."

In 1914 Garvey returned to Jamaica and founded the Universal Negro Improvement Association and African Communities League with the program of "uniting all the Negro peoples of the world into one great body to establish a country and Government absolutely their own." He corresponded with Booker T. Washington and established educational and industrial colleges modeled after Tuskegee Institute. In 1916 Garvey came to New York and the following year began a speaking tour. By 1919, there were branches of UNIA in thirty-six states and around the world, and Garvey had established his widely read journal, *Negro World,* and had launched the Black Star line to transport people and goods to and from Africa.

The high point of the early Garvey movement was the First International Convention of the Negro Peoples of the World held in New York City in August 1920, which issued the declaration that follows. The opening ceremony held in Madison Square Garden was attended by an estimated 20,000 to 25,000 persons spilling over into the streets. "The thousands who could not get in the auditorium," wrote Garvey's widow, "just stayed around the adjacent streets and discussed the day's happenings as something they never thought possible." The movement adopted an anthem and colors, and eventually the African Orthodox Church was established. "Now the Black man was searching for a new God as well as a new land," writes historian John Henrik Clark.

Garvey was not without his detractors, white and black. Du Bois, who was himself highly involved in pan-African efforts, sharply criticized Garvey publicly. Though Garvey was "an extraordinary leader of men," Du Bois wrote, "he also has very serious defects of temperament and training: he is dictatorial, domineering, inordinately vain and very suspicious. . . . His dreams of Negro industry, commerce and the ultimate freedom of Africa are feasible; but his methods are bombastic, wasteful, illogical and ineffective and almost illegal." Du Bois regretted, too, that Garvey had chosen to emphasize the "antagonism between blacks and mulattoes," of which of course Du Bois was one. "The whites are delighted at the prospect of a division of our solidifying phalanx."

In January 1922 Garvey and three Black Star officials were arrested for defrauding their shareholders. Garvey was convicted in 1923, and soon after he was transferred to Atlanta Prison in 1925, he issued an impassioned letter to his followers, arguing that he would be redeemed by history. "When I am dead," he wrote, "wrap the mantle of the Red, Black and Green around me, for in the new life I shall rise with God's grace and blessing to lead the millions up the heights of triumph with the colors that you well know. Look for me in the whirlwind of the storm, look for me all around you, for, with God's grace, I shall come and bring with me countless millions of black slaves who had died in America and the West Indies and the millions in Africa to aid you in the fight for Liberty, Freedom and Life."

Garvey's five-year sentence was commuted in 1927 and he was de-

ported to Jamaica. Though he tried to revive his movement, he had lost his important base of power in the United States, his interests were bankrupt, and the Depression had set in. He moved to London in 1935, where he died on June 10, 1940. Despite his failure, Garvey had made his name and organization, writes Clark, "household words in nearly every part of the world where Black people lived" and had demonstrated the profound and widespread discontent among the masses.

Declaration of the Rights of the Negro Peoples of the World

". . . we place on record our most solemn determination to reclaim the treasures and possessions of the vast continent of our forefathers."

PREAMBLE

BE IT RESOLVED. THAT THE NEGRO PEOPLE OF THE WORLD, through their chosen representatives in convention assembled in Liberty Hall, in the City of New York and United States of America, from August 1 to August 31, in the year of our Lord, one thousand nine hundred and twenty, protest against the wrongs and injustices they are suffering at the hands of their white brethren, and state what they deem their fair and just rights, as well as the treatment they propose to demand of all men in the future.

We complain:

I. That nowhere in the world, with few exceptions, are black men accorded equal treatment with white men, although in the same situation and circumstances, but on the contrary, are discriminated against and denied the common rights due to human beings for no other reason than their race and color.

We are not willingly accepted as guests in the public hotels and inns of the world for no other reason than our race and color.

II. In certain parts of the United States of America our race is denied the right of public trial accorded to other races when accused of crime, but are lynched and burned by mobs, and such brutal and inhuman treatment is even practised upon our women.

III. That European nations have parcelled out among them and taken possession of nearly all of the continent of Africa, and the natives are compelled to surrender their lands to aliens and are treated in most instances like slaves.

IV. In the southern portion of the United States of America, although citizens under the Federal Constitution, and in some states almost equal to the whites in population and are qualified land owners and taxpayers, we are, nevertheless, denied all voice in the making and administration of the laws and are taxed without representation by the state governments, and at the same time compelled to do military service in defense of the country.

V. On the public conveyances and common carriers in the Southern portion of the United States we are jim-crowed and compelled to accept separate and inferior accommodations, and made to pay the same fare charged for first-class accommodations, and our families are often humiliated and insulted by drunken white men who habitually pass through the jim-crow cars going to the smoking car.

VI. The physicians of our race are denied the right to attend their patients while in the public hospitals of the cities and states where they reside in certain parts of the United States.

Our children are forced to attend inferior separate schools for shorter terms than white children and the public school funds are unequally divided between the white and colored schools.

VII. We are discriminated against and denied an equal chance to earn wages for the support of our families, and in many instances are refused admission into labor unions, and nearly everywhere are paid smaller wages than white men.

VIII. In Civil Service and departmental offices we are everywhere discriminated against and made to feel that to be a black man in Europe, America, and the West Indies is equivalent to being an outcast and a leper among the races of men, no matter what the character and attainments of the black man may be.

IX. In the British and other West Indian Islands and colonies, Negroes are secretly and cunningly discriminated against, and denied those fuller rights of government to which white citizens are appointed, nominated and elected.

X. That our people in those parts are forced to work for lower wages than the average standard of white men and are kept in conditions repugnant to good civilized tastes and customs.

XI. That the many acts of injustice against members of our race before the courts of law in the respective islands and colonies are of such nature as to create disgust and disrespect for the white man's sense of justice.

XII. Against all such inhuman, unchristian and uncivilized treatment we here and now emphatically protest, and invoke the condemnation of all mankind.

In order to encourage our race all over the world and to stimulate it to a higher and grander destiny, we demand and insist on the following Declaration of Rights:

1. Be it known to all men that whereas, all men are created equal and entitled to the rights of life, liberty and the pursuit of happiness, and because of this we, the duly elected representatives of the Negro peoples of the world, invoking the aid of the just and Almighty God do declare all men,

women and children of our blood throughout the world free citizens, and do claim them as free citizens of Africa, the Motherland of all Negroes.

2. That we believe in the supreme authority of our race in all things racial; that all things are created and given to man as a common possession; that there should be an equitable distribution and apportionment of all such things, and in consideration of the fact that as a race we are now deprived of those things that are morally and legally ours, we believe it right that all such things should be acquired and held by whatsoever means possible.

3. That we believe the Negro, like any other race, should be governed by the ethics of civilization, and therefore, should not be deprived of any of those rights or privileges common to other human beings.

4. We declare that Negroes, wheresoever they form a community among themselves, should be given the right to elect their own representatives to represent them in legislatures, courts of law, or such institutions as may exercise control over the particular community.

5. We assert that the Negro is entitled to even-handed justice before all courts of law and equity in whatever country he may be found, and when this is denied him on account of his race or color such denial is an insult to the race as a whole and should be resented by the entire body of Negroes.

6. We declare it unfair and prejudicial to the rights of Negroes in communities where they exist in considerable numbers to be tried by a judge and jury composed entirely of an alien race, but in all such cases members of our race are entitled to representation on the jury.

7. We believe that any law or practice that tends to deprive any African of his land or the privileges of free citizenship within his country is unjust and immoral, and no native should respect any such law or practice.

8. We declare taxation without representation unjust and tyrannous, and there should be no obligation on the part of the Negro to obey the levy of a tax by any law-making body from which he is excluded and denied representation on account of his race and color.

9. We believe that any law especially directed against the Negro to his detriment and singling him out because of his race or color is unfair and immoral, and should not be respected.

10. We believe all men entitled to common human respect, and that our race should in no way tolerate any insults that may be interpreted to mean disrespect to our color.

11. We deprecate the use of the term "nigger" as applied to Negroes, and demand that the word "Negro" be written with a capital "N."

12. We believe that the Negro should adopt every means to protect himself against barbarous practices inflicted upon him because of color.

13. We believe in the freedom of Africa for the Negro people of the world, and by the principle of Europe for the Europeans and Asia for the Asiatics, we also demand Africa for the Africans at home and abroad.

14. We believe in the inherent right of the Negro to possess himself of

Africa, and that his possession of same shall not be regarded as an infringement on any claim or purchase made by any race or nation.

15. We strongly condemn the cupidity of those nations of the world who, by open aggression or secret schemes, have seized the territories and inexhaustible natural wealth of Africa, and we place on record our most solemn determination to reclaim the treasures and possession of the vast continent of our forefathers.

16. We believe all men should live in peace one with the other, but when races and nations provoke the ire of other races and nations by attempting to infringe upon their rights, war becomes inevitable, and the attempt in any way to free one's self or protect one's rights or heritage becomes justifiable.

17. Whereas, the lynching, by burning, hanging or any other means, of human beings is a barbarous practice, and a shame and disgrace to civilization, and we therefore declare any country guilty of such atrocities outside the pale of civilization.

18. We protest against the atrocious crime of whipping, flogging and overworking the native tribes of Africa and Negroes everywhere. These are methods that should be abolished, and all means should be taken to prevent a continuance of such brutal practices.

19. We protest against the atrocious practice of shaving the heads of Africans, especially of African women or individuals of Negro blood, when placed in prison as a punishment for crime by an alien race.

20. We protest against segregated districts, separate public conveyances, industrial discrimination, lynchings and limitations of political privileges of any Negro citizen in any part of the world on account of race, color or creed, and will exert our full influence and power against all such.

21. We protest against any punishment, inflicted upon a Negro with severity, as against lighter punishment inflicted upon another of an alien race for like offense, as an act of prejudice and injustice, and should be resented by the entire race.

22. We protest against the system of education in any country where Negroes are denied the same privileges and advantages as other races.

23. We declare it inhuman and unfair to boycott Negroes from industries and labor in any part of the world.

24. We believe in the doctrine of the freedom of the press, and we therefore emphatically protest against the suppression of Negro newspapers and periodicals in various parts of the world, and call upon Negroes everywhere to employ all available means to prevent such suppression.

25. We further demand free speech universally for all men.

26. We hereby protest against the publication of scandalous and inflammatory articles by an alien press tending to create racial strife and the exhibition of picture films showing the Negro as a cannibal.

27. We believe in the self-determination of all peoples.

28. We declare for the freedom of religious worship.

29. With the help of Almighty God, we declare ourselves the sworn protectors of the honor and virtue of our women and children, and pledge our lives for their protection and defense everywhere, and under all circumstances from wrongs and outrages.

30. We demand the right of unlimited and unprejudiced education for ourselves and our posterity forever.

31. We declare that the teaching in any school by alien teachers to our boys and girls, that the alien race is superior to the Negro race, is an insult to the Negro people of the world.

32. Where Negroes form a part of the citizenry of any country, and pass the civil service examination of such country, we declare them entitled to the same consideration as other citizens as to appointments in such civil service.

33. We vigorously protest against the increasingly unfair and unjust treatment accorded Negro travellers on land and sea by the agents and employees of railroad and steamship companies and insist that for equal fare we receive equal privileges with travellers of other races.

34. We declare it unjust for any country, state or nation to enact laws tending to hinder and obstruct the free immigration of Negroes on account of their race and color.

35. That the right of the Negro to travel unmolested throughout the world be not abridged by any person or persons, and all Negroes are called upon to give aid to fellow Negro when thus molested.

36. We declare that all Negroes are entitled to the same right to travel over the world as other men.

37. We hereby demand that the governments of the world recognize our leader and his representatives chosen by the race to look after the welfare of our people under such governments.

38. We demand complete control of our social institutions without interference by any alien race or races.

39. That the colors, Red, Black and Green, be the colors of the Negro race.

40. Resolved, that the anthem "Ethiopia, Thou Land of Our Fathers," etc., shall be the anthem of the Negro race.

THE UNIVERSAL ETHIOPIAN ANTHEM

(poem by Burrell and Ford)

Ethiopia, thou land of our fathers,
Thou land where the gods loved to be,
As storm cloud at night suddenly gathers
Our armies come rushing to thee.
We must in the fight be victorious
When swords are thrust outward to gleam;

For us will the vict'ry be glorious
When led by the red, black and green.

Chorus:
Advance, advance to victory,
Let Africa be free;
Advance to meet the foe
With the might
Of the red, the black and the green.

II

Ethiopia, the tyrant's falling,
Who smote thee upon thy knees,
And thy children are lustily calling
From over the distant seas.
Jehovah, the Great One has heard us,
Has noted our sighs and our tears,
With His spirit of Love He has stirred us
To be One through the coming years.

CHORUS: Advance, advance, etc.

III

O Jehovah, thou God of the Ages
Grant unto our sons that lead
The wisdom Thou gave to Thy sages
When Israel was sore in need.
Thy voice thro' the dim past has spoken,
Ethiopia shall stretch forth her hand,
By Thee shall all fetters be broken,
And Heav'n bless our dear fatherland.

CHORUS: Advance, advance, etc.

41. We believe that any limited liberty which deprives one of the complete rights and prerogatives of full citizenship is but a modified form of slavery.

42. We declare it an injustice to our people and a serious impediment to the health of the race to deny to competent licensed Negro physicians the right to practice in the public hospitals of the communities in which they reside for no other reason than their race and color.

43. We call upon the various governments of the world to accept and acknowledge Negro representatives who shall be sent to the said governments to represent the general welfare of the Negro peoples of the world.

44. We deplore and protest against the practice of confining juvenile prisoners in prisons with adults, and we recommend that such youthful prisons be taught gainful trades under humane supervision.

45. Be it further resolved, that we as a race of people declare the League of Nations null and void as far as the Negro is concerned, in that it seeks to deprive Negroes of their liberty.

46. We demand of all men to do unto us as we would do unto them, in the name of justice; and we cheerfully accord to all men all the rights we claim herein for ourselves.

47. We declare that no Negro shall engage himself in battle for an alien race without first obtaining the consent of the leader of the Negro people of the world, except in a matter of national self-defense.

48. We protest against the practice of drafting Negroes and sending them to war with alien forces without proper training, and demand in all cases that Negro soldiers be given the same training as the aliens.

49. We demand that instructions given Negro children in schools include the subject of "Negro History," to their benefit.

50. We demand a free and unfettered commercial intercourse with all the Negro people of the world.

51. We declare for the absolute freedom of the seas for all peoples.

52. We demand that our daily accredited representatives be given proper recognition in all leagues, conferences, conventions or courts of international arbitration wherever human rights are discussed.

53. We proclaim the 31st day of August of each year to be an international holiday to be observed by all Negroes.

54. We want all men to know we shall maintain and contend for the freedom and equality of every man, woman and child of our race, with our lives, our fortunes and our sacred honor.

These rights we believe to be justly ours and proper for the protection of the Negro race at large, and because of this belief, we, on behalf of the four hundred million Negroes of the world, do pledge herein the sacred blood of the race in defense, and we hereby subscribe our names as a guarantee of the truthfulness and faithfulness hereof in the presence of Almighty God, on the 13th day of August, in the year of our Lord one thousand nine hundred and twenty.

—Issued at the First International Convention of the Universal Negro Improvement Association, New York City, 1920

Alain Locke
(1886–1954)

The New Negro, a collection of fiction, essays, poetry, and art, edited by Alain Locke and published in 1925, is often considered the manifesto of the Harlem Renaissance, as it brought together some of the most important established African-American writers with those of a new generation. Locke clearly states his purpose in the book's foreword. "This volume aims to document the New Negro culturally and socially,—to register the transformations of the inner and outer life of the Negro in America that have so significantly taken place in the last few years. . . . There is a new race spirit that consciously and proudly sets itself apart. Justifiably then, we speak of the offerings of this book embodying these ripening forces as culled from the first fruits of the Negro Renaissance."

Locke had read widely in philosophy, the social sciences, and African-American intellectual life and culture. Born in Philadelphia, he received his undergraduate degree from Harvard in 1907. He was the first African-American Rhodes scholar and then studied in Paris and Berlin, before receiving his Ph.D. from Harvard in 1918. He would spend forty-one years associated with Howard University, whose faculty he joined in 1912, becoming head of its Department of Philosophy. He also taught at Fisk University, the New School for Social Research, City College of New York, and elsewhere. While Locke edited numerous volumes in his lifetime, including *Plays of Negro Life* (1927), *The Negro and His Music* (1936), and *Negro Art: Past and Present* (1936), he gained his greatest recognition as the editor of *The New Negro.*

The 1920s had seen an explosion of creative energy in African-American music and theater. "It was the musical revue, *Shuffle Along,* that gave a scintillating send-off to that Negro vogue in Manhattan," Langston Hughes writes in his autobiography. "Put down the 1920's for the rise of Roland Hayes, who packed Carnegie Hall, the rise of Paul

Robeson in New York and London," "the booming voice of Bessie Smith," "that grand comedienne of song, Ethel Waters." "Put down the 1920's for Louis Armstrong and Gladys Bentley and Josephine Baker."

Meant to take advantage of the spotlight now focused on black culture, *The New Negro* grew out of a special issue of *Survey Graphic* entitled "Harlem, Mecca of the New Negro," published March 1, 1925. The volume included pieces by established writers like W. E. B. Du Bois, James Weldon Johnson, William Stanley Braithwaite, and Claude McKay, and an impressive array of new talent, including Jean Toomer (whose *Cane* had been widely praised two years before), Countee Cullen, Langston Hughes, Rudolph Fisher, Jessie Fauset, and Zora Neale Hurston. Locke further edited and added to these pieces, bringing out the anthology *The New Negro* later that year, illustrated with striking Africanist drawings by Winold Reiss, Aaron Douglas, and Miguel Covarrubias (who had illustrated W. C. Handy's *Blues* anthology and would illustrate Zora Neale Hurston's *Mules and Men*), as well as photographs of African art from the Barnes collection and reproductions of title pages from major works in the collection of bibliophile Arthur A. Schomburg, who contributed the essay "The Negro Digs up His Past."

But underneath this impressive demonstration of talent and optimism, as critic Arnold Rampersad points out, a variety of disparate individuals were "made to conform to Locke's perception of a new breed of Negroes in a brave new world of Negro-ness." In his own account of "that period when the Negro was in vogue," Langston Hughes recalls, "All of us knew that the gay and sparkling life of the so-called Negro Renaissance of the '20s was not so gay and sparkling beneath the surface." Wishing to impress a largely white readership with the sophistication of the New Negro, Locke ignored much of popular culture, including the blues, which would become so important in the work of Hughes and later writers. Indeed, deep strains would eventually burden the relationships among Hughes, Cullen, Toomer, and Hurston.

The Harlem Renaissance was also circumscribed by aesthetic and cultural concerns, rather than political goals. Locke argues in his foreword that "liberal minds to-day cannot be asked to peer with sympathetic curiosity into the darkened Ghetto of a segregated race life," and as Rampersad points out, he ignored the social currents that had given rise to the mass-oriented philosophies of A. Philip Randolph, and especially Marcus Garvey, who had attracted the largest following that any race leader had known, and had ignominiously been sent to Atlanta Penitentiary in February 1925 for mail fraud. To Locke, as Rampersad puts it, "New Negroes did not go to jail." And though the Harlem Renaissance seemed to hold such promise, it was soon eclipsed by the social and economic conditions of the Great Depression, or as Langston Hughes recalls, "I was there. I had a swell time while it lasted. But I thought it wouldn't last long. For how long could a large and enthusiastic number of people be crazy about Negroes forever? But some Harlemites thought the millennium had come. . . . I don't know what made any Negroes think that—except that they were mostly intellectuals doing the thinking. The ordinary Negroes hadn't heard of the Negro Renaissance. And if they had, it hadn't raised their wages any."

The New Negro

IN THE LAST DECADE SOMETHING BEYOND THE WATCH AND guard of statistics has happened in the life of the American Negro, and the three norns who have traditionally presided over the Negro problem have a changeling in their laps. The Sociologist, the Philanthropist, the Race-leader are not unaware of the New Negro, but they are at a loss to account for him. He simply cannot be swathed in their formulae. For the younger generation is vibrant with a new psychology; the new spirit is awake in the masses, and under the very eyes of the professional observers is transforming what has been a perennial problem into the progressive phases of contemporary Negro life.

Could such a metamorphosis have taken place as suddenly as it has appeared to? The answer is no; not only because the New Negro is not here, but because the Old Negro had long become more of a myth than a man. The Old Negro, we must remember, was a creature of moral debate and historical controversy. His has been a stock figure perpetuated as an historical fiction partly in innocent sentimentalism, partly in deliberate reactionism. The Negro himself has contributed his share to this through a sort of protective social mimicry forced upon him by the adverse circumstances of dependence. So for generations in the mind of America, the Negro has been more of a formula than a human being—a something to be argued about, condemned or defended, to be "kept down," or "in his place," or "helped up," to be worried with or worried over, harassed or patronized, a social bogey or a social burden. The thinking Negro even has been induced to share this same general attitude, to focus his attention on controversial issues, to see himself in the distorted perspective of a social problem. His shadow, so to speak, has been more real to him than his personality. Through having had to appeal from the unjust stereotypes of his oppressors and traducers to those of his liberators, friends and benefactors he has had to subscribe to the traditional positions from which his case has been viewed. Little true social or self-understanding has or could come from such a situation.

But while the minds of most of us, black and white, have thus burrowed in the trenches of the Civil War and Reconstruction, the actual march of development has simply flanked these positions, necessitating a sudden reorientation of view. We have not been watching in the right direction; set North and South on a sectional axis, we have noticed the East till the sun has us blinking.

Recall how suddenly the Negro spirituals revealed themselves; suppressed for generations under the stereotypes of Wesleyan hymn harmony, secretive, half-ashamed, until the courage of being natural brought them out —and behold, there was folk-music. Similarly the mind of the Negro seems suddenly to have slipped from under the tyranny of social intimidation and to be shaking off the psychology of imitation and implied inferiority. By shedding the old chrysalis of the Negro problem we are achieving something like a spiritual emancipation. Until recently, lacking self-understanding, we have been almost as much of a problem to ourselves as we still are to others. But the decade that found us with a problem has left us with only a task. The multitude perhaps feels as yet only a strange belief and a new vague urge, but the thinking few know that in the reaction the vital inner grip of prejudice has been broken.

With this renewed self-respect and self-dependence, the life of the Negro community is bound to enter a new dynamic phase, the buoyancy from within compensating for whatever pressure there may be of conditions from without. The migrant masses, shifting from countryside to city, hurdle several generations of experience at a leap, but more important, the same thing happens spiritually in the life-attitudes and self-expression of the Young Negro, in his poetry, his art, his education and his new outlook, with the additional advantage, of course, of the poise and greater certainty of knowing what it is all about. From this comes the promise and warrant of a new leadership. As one of them has discerningly put it:

We have tomorrow
Bright before us
Like a flame.

Yesterday, a night-gone thing
A sun-down name.

And dawn today
Broad arch above the road we came.
We march!

This is what, even more than any "most creditable record of fifty years of freedom," requires that the Negro of to-day be seen through other than the dusty spectacles of past controversy. The day of "aunties," "uncles" and "mammies" is equally gone. Uncle Tom and Sambo have passed on, and even the "Colonel" and "George" play barnstorm rôles from which they escape with relief when the public spotlight is off. The popular melodrama has about played itself out, and it is time to scrap the fictions, garret the bogeys and settle down to a realistic facing of facts.

First we must observe some of the changes which since the traditional lines of opinion were drawn have rendered these quite obsolete. A main change has been, of course, that shifting of the Negro population which has made the Negro problem no longer exclusively or even predominantly Southern. Why should our minds remain sectionalized, when the problem itself no longer is? Then the trend of migration has not only been toward the

North and the Central Midwest, but city-ward and to the great centers of industry—the problems of adjustment are new, practical, local and not peculiarly racial. Rather they are an integral part of the large industrial and social problems of our present-day democracy. And finally, with the Negro rapidly in process of class differentiation, if it ever was warrantable to regard and treat the Negro *en masse* it is becoming with every day less possible, more unjust and more ridiculous.

In the very process of being transplanted, the Negro is being transformed.

The tide of Negro migration, northward and city-ward, is not to be fully explained as a blind flood started by the demands of war industry coupled with the shutting off of foreign migration, or by the pressure of poor crops coupled with increased social terrorism in certain sections of the South and Southwest. Neither labor demand, the boll-weevil nor the Ku Klux Klan is a basic factor, however contributory any or all of them may have been. The wash and rush of this human tide on the beach line of the northern city centers is to be explained primarily in terms of a new vision of opportunity, of social and economic freedom, of a spirit to seize, even in the face of an extortionate and heavy toll, a chance for the improvement of conditions. With each successive wave of it, the movement of the Negro becomes more and more a mass movement toward the larger and the more democratic chance—in the Negro's case a deliberate flight not only from countryside to city, but from medieval America to modern.

Take Harlem as an instance of this. Here in Manhattan is not merely the largest Negro community in the world, but the first concentration in history of so many diverse elements of Negro life. It has attracted the African, the West Indian, the Negro American; has brought together the Negro of the North and the Negro of the South; the man from the city and the man from the town and village; the peasant, the student, the business man, the professional man, artist, poet, musician, adventurer and worker, preacher and criminal, exploiter and social outcast. Each group has come with its own separate motives and for its own special ends, but their greatest experience has been the finding of one another. Proscription and prejudice have thrown these dissimilar elements into a common area of contact and interaction. Within this area, race sympathy and unity have determined a further fusing of sentiment and experience. So what began in terms of segregation becomes more and more, as its elements mix and react, the laboratory of a great race-welding. Hitherto, it must be admitted that American Negroes have been a race more in name than in fact, or to be exact, more in sentiment than in experience. The chief bond between them has been that of a common condition rather than a common consciousness; a problem in common rather than a life in common. In Harlem, Negro life is seizing upon its first chances for group expression and self-determination. It is—or promises at least to be—a race capital. That is why our comparison is taken with those nascent centers of folk-expression and self-determination which are playing a creative part in the world to-day. Without pretense to their political significance, Harlem has the same rôle to play for the New Negro as Dublin has had for the New Ireland or Prague for the New Czechoslovakia.

Harlem, I grant you, isn't typical—but it is significant, it is prophetic. No sane observer, however sympathetic to the new trend, would contend that the great masses are articulate as yet, but they stir, they move, they are more than physically restless. The challenge of the new intellectuals among them is clear enough—the "race radicals" and realists who have broken with the old epoch of philanthropic guidance, sentimental appeal and protest. But are we after all only reading into the stirrings of a sleeping giant the dreams of an agitator? The answer is in the migrating peasant. It is the "man farthest down" who is most active in getting up. One of the most characteristic symptoms of this is the professional man, himself migrating to recapture his constituency after a vain effort to maintain in some Southern corner what for years back seemed an established living and clientele. The clergyman following his errant flock, the physician or lawyer trailing his clients, supply the true clues. In a real sense it is the rank and file who are leading, the leaders who are following. A transformed and transforming psychology permeates the masses.

When the racial leaders of twenty years ago spoke of developing race-pride and stimulating race-consciousness, and of the desirability of race solidarity, they could not in any accurate degree have anticipated the abrupt feeling that has surged up and now pervades the awakened centers. Some of the recognized Negro leaders and a powerful section of white opinion identified with "race work" of the older order have indeed attempted to discount this feeling as a "passing phase," an attack of "race nerves" so to speak, an "aftermath of the war," and the like. It has not abated, however, if we are to gauge by the present tone and temper of the Negro press, or by the shift in popular support from the officially recognized and orthodox spokesmen to those of the independent, popular, and often radical type who are unmistakable symptoms of a new order. It is a social disservice to blunt the fact that the Negro of the Northern centers has reached a stage where tutelage, even of the most interested and well-intentioned sort, must give place to new relationships, where positive self-direction must be reckoned with in ever increasing measure. The American mind must reckon with a fundamentally changed Negro.

The Negro too, for his part, has idols of the tribe to smash. If on the one hand the white man has erred in making the Negro appear to be that which would excuse or extenuate his treatment of him, the Negro, in turn, has too often unnecessarily excused himself because of the way he has been treated. The intelligent Negro of to-day is resolved not to make discrimination an extenuation for his shortcomings in performance, individual or collective; he is trying to hold himself at par, neither inflated by sentimental allowances nor depreciated by current social discounts. For this he must know himself and be known for precisely what he is, and for that reason he welcomes the new scientific rather than the old sentimental interest. Sentimental interest in the Negro has ebbed. We used to lament this as the falling off of our friends; now we rejoice and pray to be delivered both from self-pity and condescension. The mind of each racial group has had a bitter weaning, apathy or hatred on one side matching disillusionment or resentment on the other; but they face each other to-day with the possibility at least of entirely new mutual attitudes.

It does not follow that if the Negro were better known, he would be better liked or better treated. But mutual understanding is basic for any subsequent co-operation and adjustment. The effort toward this will at least have the effect of remedying in large part what has been the most unsatisfactory feature of our present stage of race relationships in America, namely the fact that the more intelligent and representative elements of the two race groups have at so many points got quite out of vital touch with one another.

The fiction is that the life of the races is separate, and increasingly so. The fact is that they have touched too closely at the unfavorable and too lightly at the favorable levels.

While inter-racial councils have sprung up in the South, drawing on forward elements of both races, in the Northern cities manual laborers may brush elbows in their everyday work, but the community and business leaders have experienced no such interplay or far too little of it. These segments must achieve contact or the race situation in America becomes desperate. Fortunately this is happening. There is a growing realization that in social effort the co-operative basis must supplant long-distance philanthropy, and that the only safeguard for mass relations in the future must be provided in the carefully maintained contacts of the enlightened minorities of both race groups. In the intellectual realm a renewed and keen curiosity is replacing the recent apathy; the Negro is being carefully studied, not just talked about and discussed. In art and letters, instead of being wholly caricatured, he is being seriously portrayed and painted.

To all of this the New Negro is keenly responsive as an augury of a new democracy in American culture. He is contributing his share to the new social understanding. But the desire to be understood would never in itself have been sufficient to have opened so completely the protectively closed portals of the thinking Negro's mind. There is still too much possibility of being snubbed or patronized for that. It was rather the necessity for fuller, truer self-expression, the realization of the unwisdom of allowing social discrimination to segregate him mentally, and a counter-attitude to cramp and fetter his own living—and so the "spite-wall" that the intellectuals built over the "color line" has happily been taken down. Much of this reopening of intellectual contacts has centered in New York and has been richly fruitful not merely in the enlarging of personal experience, but in the definite enrichment of American art and letters and in the clarifying of our common vision of the social tasks ahead.

The particular significance in the re-establishment of contact between the more advanced and representative classes is that it promises to offset some of the unfavorable reactions of the past, or at least to re-surface race contacts somewhat for the future. Subtly the conditions that are molding a New Negro are molding a new American attitude.

However, this new phase of things is delicate; it will call for less charity but more justice; less help, but infinitely closer understanding. This is indeed a critical stage of race relationships because of the likelihood, if the new temper is not understood, of engendering sharp group antagonism and a second crop of more calculated prejudice. In some quarters, it has already done so. Having weaned the Negro, public opinion cannot continue to paternalize. The Negro to-day is inevitably moving forward under the control largely of his own objectives. What are these objectives? Those of his outer life are happily already well and finally formulated, for they are none other than the ideals of American institutions and democracy. Those of his inner life are yet in process of formation, for the new psychology at present is more of a consensus of feeling than of opinion, of attitude rather than of program. Still some points seem to have crystallized.

Up to the present one may adequately describe the Negro's "inner objectives" as an attempt to repair a damaged group psychology and reshape a warped social perspective. Their realization has required a new mentality for the American Negro. And as it matures we begin to see its effects; at first, negative, iconoclastic, and then positive and constructive. In this new group psychology we note the lapse of sentimental appeal, then the development of a more positive self-respect and self-reliance; the repudiation of social dependence, and then the gradual recovery from hyper-sensitiveness and "touchy" nerves, the repudiation of the double standard of judgement with its special philanthropic allowances and then the sturdier desire for objective and scientific appraisal; and finally the rise from social disillusionment to race pride, from the sense of social debt to the responsibilities of social contribution, and offsetting the necessary working and commonsense acceptance of restricted conditions, the belief in ultimate esteem and recognition. Therefore the Negro to-day wishes to be known for what he is, even in his faults and shortcomings, and scorns a craven and precarious survival at the price of seeming to be what he is not. He resents being spoken of as a social ward or minor, even by his own, and to being regarded a chronic patient for the sociological clinic, the sick man of American Democracy. For the same reasons, he himself is through with those social nostrums and panaceas, the so-called "solutions" of his "problem," with which he and the country have been so liberally dosed in the past. Religion, freedom, education, money—in turn, he has ardently hoped for and peculiarly trusted these things; he still believes in them, but not in blind trust that they alone will solve his life-problem.

Each generation, however, will have its creed, and that of the present is the belief in the efficacy of collective effort, in race co-operation. This deep feeling of race is at present the mainspring of Negro life. It seems to be the outcome of the reaction to proscription and prejudice; an attempt, fairly successful on the whole, to convert a defensive into an offensive position, a handicap into an incentive. It is radical in tone, but not in purpose and only the most stupid forms of opposition, misunderstanding or persecution could make it otherwise. Of course, the thinking Negro has shifted a little toward the left with the world-trend, and there is an increasing group who affiliate with radical and liberal movements. But fundamentally for the present the Negro is radical on race matters, conservative on others, in other words, a "forced radical," a social protestant rather than a genuine radical. Yet under further pressure and injustice iconoclastic thought and motives will inevitably increase. Harlem's quixotic radicalisms call for their ounce of democracy to-day lest to-morrow they be beyond cure.

The Negro mind reaches out as yet to nothing but American wants, American ideas. But this forced attempt to build his Americanism on race values is a unique social experiment, and its ultimate success is impossible except through the fullest sharing of American culture and institutions. There should be no delusion about this. American nerves in sections unstrung with race hysteria are often fed the opiate that the trend of Negro advance is wholly separatist, and that the effect of its operation will be to encyst the Negro as a benign foreign body in the body politic. This cannot be—even if it were desirable. The racialism of the Negro is no limitation or reservation with respect to American life; it is only a constructive effort to build the obstructions in the stream of his progress into an efficient dam of social energy and power. Democracy itself is obstructed and stagnated to the extent that any of its channels are closed. Indeed they cannot be selectively closed. So the choice is not between one way for the Negro and another way for the rest, but between American institutions frustrated on the one hand and American ideals progressively fulfilled and realized on the other.

There is, of course, a warrantably comfortable feeling in being on the right side of the country's professed ideals. We realize that we cannot be undone without America's undoing. It is within the gamut of this attitude that the thinking Negro faces America, but with variations of mood that are if anything more significant than the attitude itself. Sometimes we have it taken with the defiant ironic challenge of McKay:

> Mine is the future grinding down to-day
> Like a great landslip moving to the sea,
> Bearing its freight of debris far away

Where the green hungry waters restlessly
Heave mammoth pyramids, and break and roar
Their eerie challenge to the crumbling shore.

Sometimes, perhaps more frequently as yet, it is taken in the fervent and almost filial appeal and counsel of Weldon Johnson's:

O Southland, dear Southland!
Then why do you still cling
To an ideal age and a musty page,
To a dead and useless thing?

But between defiance and appeal, midway almost between cynicism and hope, the prevailing mind stands in the mood of the same author's *To America,* an attitude of sober query and stoical challenge:

How would you have us, as we are?
Or sinking 'neath the load we bear,
Our eyes fixed forward on a star,
Or gazing empty at despair?

Rising or falling? Men or things?
With dragging pace or footsteps fleet?
Strong, willing sinews in your wings,
Or tightening chains about your feet?

More and more, however, an intelligent realization of the great discrepancy between the American social creed and the American social practice forces upon the Negro the taking of the moral advantage that is his. Only the steadying and sobering effect of a truly characteristic gentleness of spirit prevents the rapid rise of a definite cynicism and counter-hate and a defiant superiority feeling. Human as this reaction would be, the majority still deprecate its advent, and would gladly see it forestalled by the speedy amelioration of its causes. We wish our race pride to be a healthier, more positive achievement than a feeling based upon a realization of the shortcomings of others. But all paths toward the attainment of a sound social attitude have been difficult; only a relatively few enlightened minds have been able as the phrase puts it "to rise above" prejudice. The ordinary man has had until recently only a hard choice between the alternatives of supine and humiliating submission and stimulating but hurtful counter-prejudice. Fortunately from some inner, desperate resourcefulness has recently sprung up the simple expedient of fighting prejudice by mental passive resistance, in other words by trying to ignore it. For the few, this manna may perhaps be effective, but the masses cannot thrive upon it.

Fortunately there are constructive channels opening out into which the balked social feelings of the American Negro can flow freely.

Without them there would be much more pressure and danger than there is. These compensating interests are racial but in a new and enlarged way. One is the consciousness of acting as the advance-guard of the African peoples in their contact with Twentieth Century civilization; the other, the sense of a mission of rehabilitating the race in world esteem from that loss of prestige for which the fate and conditions of slavery have so largely been responsible. Harlem, as we shall see, is the center of both these movements; she is the home of the Negro's "Zionism." The pulse of the Negro world has begun to beat in Harlem. A Negro newspaper carrying news material in English, French and Spanish gathered from all quarters of America, the West Indies and Africa has maintained itself in Harlem for over five years. Two important magazines, both edited from New York, maintain their news and circulation consistently on a cosmopolitan scale. Under American auspices and backing, three pan-African congresses have been held abroad for the discussion of common interests, colonial questions and the future co-operative development of Africa. In terms of the race question as a world problem, the Negro mind has leapt, so to speak, upon the parapets of prejudice and extended its cramped horizons. In so doing it has linked up with the growing group consciousness of the dark-peoples and is gradually learning their common interests. As one of our writers has recently put it: "It is imperative that we understand the white world in its relations to the non-white world." As with the Jew, persecution is making the Negro international.

As a world phenomenon this wider race consciousness is a different thing from the much asserted rising tide of color. Its inevitable causes are not of our making. The consequences are not necessarily damaging to the best interests of civilization. Whether it actually brings into being new Armadas of conflict or argosies of cultural exchange and enlightenment can only be decided by the attitude of the dominant races in an era of critical change. With the American Negro, his new internationalism is primarily an effort to recapture contact with the scattered peoples of African derivation. Garveyism may be a transient, if spectacular, phenomenon, but possible rôle of the American Negro in the future development of Africa is one of the most constructive and universally helpful missions that any modern people can lay claim to.

Constructive participation in such causes cannot help giving the Negro valuable group incentives, as well as increased prestige at home and abroad. Our greatest rehabilitation may possibly come through such channels, but for the present, more immediate hope rests in the revaluation by white and black alike of the Negro in terms of his artistic endowments and cultural contributions, past and prospective. It must be increasingly recognized that the Negro has already made very substantial contributions, not only in his folk-art, music especially, which has always found appreciation, but in larger, though humbler and less acknowledged ways. For generations the Negro has been the peasant matrix of that section of America which has most undervalued him, and here he has contributed not only materially in labor and in social patience, but spiritually as well. The South has unconsciously absorbed the gift of his folk-temperament. In less than half a generation it will be easier to recognize this, but the fact remains that a leaven of humor, sentiment, imagination and tropic nonchalance has gone into the making of the South from a humble, unacknowledged source. A second crop of the Negro's gifts promises still more largely. He now becomes a conscious contributor and lays aside the status of a beneficiary and ward for that of a collaborator and participant in American civilization. The great social gain in this is the releasing of our talented group from the arid fields of controversy and debate to the productive fields of creative expression. The especially cultural recognition they win should in turn prove the key to that revaluation of the Negro which must precede or accompany any considerable further betterment of race relationships. But whatever the general effect, the present generation will have added the motives of self-expression and spiritual development to the old and still unfinished task of making material headway and progress. No one who understandingly faces the situation with its substantial accomplishment or views the new scene with its still more abundant promise can be entirely without hope. And certainly, if in our lifetime the Negro should not be able to celebrate his full initiation into American democracy, he can at least, on the warrant of these things, celebrate the attainment of a significant and satisfying new phase of group development, and with it a spiritual Coming of Age.

1925

Claude McKay
(1889–1948)

Born in the rural village of Sunny Ville, Jamaica, in the British West Indies, Claude McKay spent much of his life as a wanderer, living for long periods in the United States, Europe, and North Africa. As a boy, McKay inherited an awareness of his African roots from his father, Thomas Francis McKay, who related to him the legends of his Ashanti ancestors. At the same time, he was introduced to the great works of Western literature by an English friend and an older brother, whose libraries included works by Dante, Milton, Goethe, Byron, Keats, Shelley, Baudelaire, Whitman, Schopenhauer, and others, all read by McKay by the time he was a teenager.

McKay was apprenticed as a carpenter when he was seventeen and two years later joined the Constabulary in Kingston. He had begun writing poetry and his works *Songs of Jamaica* and *Constab Ballads* were published in 1912. Many of these poems were imbued with the folk culture of the islands and were written in the Jamaican dialect. Though the life his poems depicted was a difficult one, McKay found beauty in the island landscape and its shared sense of community, and a nostalgic longing for the "sacred moments" of his youth is felt in later poems like "Flame-Heart" and "The Tropics in New York." His early poems earned McKay a reputation in Jamaica and he won a scholarship to study agriculture in the United States at Tuskegee Institute, which he attended briefly before moving on to Kansas State University.

Before receiving his degree, McKay left Kansas for New York in 1914. He quickly went through his savings and took work as a porter, longshoreman, and waiter in Pullman cars and hotels in New York and New England while he continued to write. In 1917 he gained widespread recognition with the sonnets "The Harlem Dancer" and "Invocation," published in the important literary magazine *The Seven Arts* under the pseudonym Eli Edwards. His work also appeared in *The Messenger, The Crisis,* and *The Liberator,* which published "If We Must Die" in July 1919, written by McKay in response to the racial violence that erupted across the country in the Red Summer† of that year. He contributed numerous poems, essays, and reviews to *The Liberator,* and later became an editor there.

In 1919 McKay traveled to London, where he met some of the leading British writers and critics, including George Bernard Shaw and I. A. Richards. McKay's *Constab Ballads* had been published in England and his volume *Spring in New Hampshire* followed in 1920 before McKay returned to New York. *Harlem Shadows,* which contained most of the poems from the British edition together with some new works, was published in the United States in 1922 to exceptional acclaim, and this major collection is often cited as one of the inaugural works of the Harlem Renaissance.

There is in McKay's poetry a seeming contradiction between his formal elegance and his often strong political statement. His expression of human transience, loss, and personal tragedy, expressed in such works as "Spring in New Hampshire," or the elegiac "My Mother," written upon his mother's death, like Countee Cullen's works, partake of the themes and rhythms of much lyrical poetry. In other poems like "If We Must Die" and "The Lynching," however, McKay belies the polished exterior of his art with the jagged truth of race hatred and violence. Calling McKay "the poet of rebellion," James Weldon Johnson wrote in his *Book of American Negro Poetry,* "This is masculine poetry, strong and direct, the sort of poetry that stirs the pulse, that quickens to action." Rather than undermining his subjects with his poetic discipline, McKay's artistry lent force and authority to his works.

After *Harlem Shadows* appeared, McKay embarked on a twelve-year voyage around the world, traveling to Russia, where his work was published in *Pravda* and he met the major political figures Trotsky and Bukharin, and to France. For much of the next decade, first in Paris, Marseilles, Nice, and Antibes, and then Spain and Morocco, McKay turned to prose and wrote the novels *Home to Harlem* (1928), *Banjo* (1929), and *Banana Bottom* (1933), and a collection of short stories, *Gingertown* (1932). When he returned to the United States in 1934, McKay's creative efforts waned, though an autobiography, *A Long Way from Home,* was published in 1937 and *Harlem: Negro Metropolis* in 1940. McKay's *Selected Poems* was published in 1953, five years after his death.

The Harlem Dancer

Applauding youths laughed with young prostitutes
And watched her perfect, half-clothed body sway;
Her voice was like the sound of blended flutes
Blown by black players upon a picnic day.
She sang and danced on gracefully and calm,
The light gauze hanging loose about her form;
To me she seemed a proudly-swaying palm
Grown lovelier for passing through a storm.
Upon her swarthy neck black shiny curls
Luxuriant fell; and tossing coins in praise,
The wine-flushed, bold-eyed boys, and even the girls,
Devoured her shape with eager, passionate gaze;
But looking at her falsely-smiling face,
I knew her self was not in that strange place.

Spring in New Hampshire

Too green the springing April grass,
  Too blue the silver-speckled sky,
For me to linger here, alas,
  While happy winds go laughing by,
Wasting the golden hours indoors,
Washing windows and scrubbing floors.

Too wonderful the April night,
  Too faintly sweet the first May flowers,
The stars too gloriously bright,
  For me to spend the evening hours,
When fields are fresh and streams are leaping,
Wearied, exhausted, dully sleeping.

The Lynching

His Spirit in smoke ascended to high heaven.
His father, by the cruelest way of pain,
Had bidden him to his bosom once again;
The awful sin remained still unforgiven.
All night a bright and solitary star
(Perchance the one that ever guided him,
Yet gave him up at last to Fate's wild whim)
Hung pitifully o'er the swinging char.
Day dawned, and soon the mixed crowds came to view
The ghastly body swaying in the sun.
The women thronged to look, but never a one
Showed sorrow in her eyes of steely blue.

And little lads, lynchers that were to be,
Danced round the dreadful thing in fiendish glee.

Tiger

The white man is a tiger at my throat,
Drinking my blood as my life ebbs away,
And muttering that his terrible striped coat
Is Freedom's and portends the Light of Day.
Oh white man, you may suck up all my blood
And throw my carcass into potter's field,
But never will I say with you that mud
Is bread for Negroes! Never will I yield.
Europe and Africa and Asia wait
The touted New Deal of the New World's hand!
New systems will be built on race and hate,
The Eagle and the Dollar will command,
Oh Lord! My body, and my heart too, break—
The tiger in his strength his thirst must slake!

The White City

I will not toy with it nor bend an inch.
Deep in the secret chambers of my heart
I muse my life-long hate, and without flinch
I bear it nobly as I live my part.
My being would be a skeleton, a shell,
If this dark Passion that fills my every mood,
And makes my heaven in the white world's hell,
Did not forever feed me vital blood.
I see the mighty city through a mist—
The strident trains that speed the goaded mass,
The poles and spires and towers vapor-kissed,
The fortressed port through which the great ships pass,
The tides, the wharves, the dens I contemplate,
Are sweet like wanton loves because I hate.

The Tropics in New York

Bananas ripe and green, and ginger-root,
  Cocoa in pods and alligator pears,
And tangerines and mangoes and grape fruit,
  Fit for the highest prize at parish fairs,
Set in the window, bringing memories
  Of fruit-trees laden by low-singing rills,
And dewy dawns, and mystical blue skies
  In benediction over nun-like hills.
My eyes grew dim, and I could no more gaze;
  A wave of longing through my body swept,
And hungry for the old, familiar ways,
  I turned aside and bowed my head and wept.

Langston Hughes
(1902–1967)

For more than forty years, Langston Hughes demonstrated a prodigious and protean talent, succeeding equally at poetry, fiction, autobiography, journalism, drama, essay, translation, and works for children, and maintaining throughout his long literary career a genuine and deep affection for the masses of his people. Born in Joplin, Missouri, he lived as a boy in Lawrence, Kansas, with his grandmother, whose husband had died in John Brown's raid on Harpers Ferry,[†] and who inspired him with tales of his self-reliant forebears. "Through my grandmother's stories, always life moved," he wrote in his autobiography, *The Big Sea,* "moved heroically toward an end. Nobody ever cried in my grandmother's stories. They worked, or schemed, or fought. But no crying. When my grandmother died, I didn't cry, either. Something about my grandmother's stories (without her having said so) taught me the uselessness of crying about anything."

He then moved with his mother through a number of cities in the Midwest, including Detroit, Topeka, and Cleveland. During this time, he recalled, "books began to happen to me," and he wrote his first poems while still in high school. He read furiously, and writes movingly of his discovery of the power of literature to affect people universally. "I will never forget the thrill of first understanding the French of de Maupassant . . . all of a sudden one night the beauty and the meaning of the words . . . came to me. I think it was de Maupassant who made me really want to be a writer and write stories about Negroes, so true that people in faraway lands would read them—even after I was dead."

After high school, Hughes spent two years in Mexico with his father, and then, because he "wanted to see Harlem, the greatest Negro city in the world," in 1921 he entered Columbia, which he left after a single unhappy year to begin a four-year journey around the world as a seaman. Symbolically throwing his books overboard as the journey began, he traveled to Africa, "My Africa, Motherland of the Negro peoples! And me a Negro! Africa! The real thing, to be touched and seen, not merely read about in a book." He had published his first major poem, "The Negro Speaks of

Rivers," in *The Crisis* that year, and he continued to write for that journal, *Opportunity,* and others while he traveled. In 1925, he returned and entered Lincoln University; during his years at Lincoln, he spent summers in New York, at the height of the Harlem Renaissance, that "period when the Negro was in vogue." He recalls in his autobiography, "I was there. I had a swell time while it lasted. But I thought it couldn't last long. . . . For how long could a large and enthusiastic number of people be crazy about Negroes forever?"

In 1926, he published his first volume of poems, *The Weary Blues,* rich in the inflections of black folk culture, blues, and jazz, and the following year *Fine Clothes to the Jew.* In his famous essay "The Negro Artist and the Racial Mountain," included here, he defends the culture of "the low-down folks, the so-called common element" as fertile ground for the artist. "Jazz to me is one of the inherent expressions of Negro life in America," he writes, "the eternal tom-tom beating in the Negro soul—the tom-tom of revolt against weariness in a white world, a world of subway trains, and work, work, work; the tom-tom of joy and laughter." He soon demonstrated the diversity of his talent with the publication of his novel *Not Without Laughter* in 1930, the collection of stories *The Ways of White Folks* in 1934, and the play *Mulatto,* which began a year-long run on Broadway in 1935.

During the thirties, Hughes, like Richard Wright and others, was attracted to socialism. Though he never joined the Communist Party, he wrote frequently for *New Masses* and traveled to the Soviet Union and Spain, but he abandoned the Left in the early forties. He made his home for the rest of his life in Harlem, the vivid backdrop of his long poem cycle, *Montage of a Dream Deferred,* from which "Harlem" is taken. For twenty years, he wrote a column based on the folk character Jesse B. Semple, or "Simple," a sort of black everyman whose observations combine mother wit, cynicism, naïveté, and insight. The popular pieces were eventually collected into five volumes, and many critics find them among Hughes's best work. Hughes collaborated with Zora Neale Hurston on the play *Mule Bone,* which resulted in their falling-out, and in 1947 he acted as lyricist in a collaboration with Kurt Weill and Elmer Rice in the avant-garde classic *Street Scenes.*

Hughes remained active until his death in 1967, and his later works include the stories in *Laughing to Keep from Crying* (1950), a second volume of autobiography, *I Wonder as I Wander* (1956), *Selected Poems* (1963), a second novel, *Tambourines to Glory* (1959), *Fight for Freedom: Story of the NAACP* (1962), the stories *Something in Common* and poems *Panther and the Lash,* both published in 1963, and a dozen books for children.

I, Too

I, too, sing America
I am the darker brother.
They send me to eat in the kitchen
When company comes,
But I laugh,
And eat well,
And grow strong.

Tomorrow,
I'll be at the table
When company comes
Nobody'll dare
Say to me,
"Eat in the kitchen,"
Then.

Besides,
They'll see how beautiful I am
And be ashamed—

I, too, am America.

The Negro Speaks of Rivers

I've known rivers:
I've known rivers ancient as the world and older than the flow of human blood in human veins.

My soul has grown deep like the rivers.

I bathed in the Euphrates when dawns were young.
I built my hut near the Congo and it lulled me to sleep.
I looked upon the Nile and raised the pyramids above it.
I heard the singing of the Mississippi when Abe Lincoln went down to New Orleans, and I've seen its muddy bosom turn all golden in the sunset.
I've known rivers:
Ancient, dusky rivers.

My soul has grown deep like the rivers.

The Negro Artist and the Racial Mountain

"An artist must be free to do what he does . . . but he must also never be afraid to do what he might choose."

NE OF THE MOST PROMISING OF YOUNG NEGRO POETS SAID TO me once, "I want to be a poet—not a Negro poet," meaning, I believe, "I want to write like a white poet"; meaning subconsciously, "I would like to be a white poet"; meaning behind that, "I would like to be white." And I was sorry the young man said that, for no great poet has ever been afraid of being himself. And I doubted then that, with his desire to run away spiritually from his race, this boy would ever be a great poet. But this is the mountain standing in the way of any true Negro art in America—this urge within the race toward whiteness, the desire to pour racial individuality into the mold of American standardization, and to be as little Negro and as much American as possible.

But let us look at the immediate background of this young poet. His family is of what I suppose one would call the Negro middle class: people who are by no means rich yet never uncomfortable nor hungry—smug, contented, respectable folk, members of the Baptist church. The father goes to work every morning. He is a chief steward at a large white club. The mother sometimes does fancy sewing or supervised parties for the rich families of the town. The children go to a mixed school. In the home they read white papers and magazines. And the mother often says "Don't be like niggers" when the children are bad. A frequent phrase from the father is, "Look how well a white man does things." And so the word white comes to be unconsciously a symbol of all the virtues. It holds for the children beauty, morality, and money. The whisper "I want to be white" runs silently through their minds. This young poet's home is, I believe, a fairly typical home of the colored middle class. One sees immediately how difficult it would be for an artist born in such a home to interest himself in interpreting the beauty of his own people. He is never taught to see that beauty. He is taught rather not to see it, or if he does to be ashamed of it when it is not according to Caucasian patterns.

For racial culture that home of a self-styled "high-class" Negro has nothing better to offer. Instead there will perhaps be more aping of things white than in a less cultured or less wealthy home. The father is perhaps a doctor, lawyer, landowner, or politician. The mother may be a social worker, or a teacher, or she may do nothing and have a maid. Father is often dark but he has usually married the lightest woman he could find. The family attend a fashionable church where few really colored faces are to be found. And they themselves draw a color line. In the North they go to white theaters and white movies. And in the South they have at least two cars and a house "like white folks." Nordic manners, Nordic faces, Nordic hair, Nordic art (if any), and an Episcopal heaven. A very high mountain indeed for the would-be racial artist to climb in order to discover himself and his people.

But then there are the low-down folks, the so-called common element, and they are the majority—may the Lord be praised? The people who have their nip of gin on Saturday nights and are not too important to themselves or the community, or too well read, or too learned to watch the lazy world go round. They live on Seventh Street in Washington or State Street in Chicago and they do not particularly care whether they are like white folks or anybody else. Their joy runs, bang! into ecstasy. Their religion soars to a shout. Work maybe a little today, rest a little tomorrow. Play awhile. Sing awhile. O, let's dance! These common people are not afraid of spirituals, as for a long time their more intellectual brethren were, and jazz is their child. They furnish a wealth of colorful, distinctive material for any artist because they still hold their own individuality in the face of American standardizations. And perhaps these common people will give to the world its truly great Negro artist, the one who is not afraid to be himself. Whereas the better-class Negro would tell the artist what to do, the people at least let him alone when he does appear. And they are not ashamed of him—if they know he exists at all. And they accept what beauty is their own without question.

Certainly there is, for the American Negro artist who can escape the restrictions the more advanced among his own group would put upon him, a great field of unused material ready for his art. Without going outside his race, and even among the better classes with their "white" culture and conscious American manners, but still Negro enough to be different, there is sufficient matter to furnish a black artist with a lifetime of creative work. And when he chooses to touch on the relations between Negroes and whites in this country with their innumerable overtones and undertones, surely, and especially for literature and drama, there is an inexhaustible supply of themes at hand. To these the Negro artist can give his racial individuality, his heritage of rhythm and warmth, and his incongruous humor that so often, as in the Blues, becomes ironic laughter mixed with tears. But let us look again at the mountain.

A prominent Negro clubwoman in Philadelphia paid eleven dollars to hear Raquel Meller sing Andalusian popular songs. But she told me a few weeks before she would not think of going to hear "that woman," Clara Smith, a great black artist, sing Negro folksongs. And many an upper-class Negro church, even now, would not dream of employing a spiritual in its services. The drab melodies in white folks' hymnbooks are much to be preferred. "We want to worship the Lord correctly and quietly. We don't believe in 'shouting.' Let's be dull like the Nordics," they say, in effect.

The road for the serious black artist, then, who would produce a racial art is most certainly rocky and the mountain is high. Until recently he received almost no encouragement for his work from either white or colored people. The fine novels of Chestnut got out of print with neither race noticing their passing. The quaint charm and humor of Dunbar's dialect verse brought to him, in his day, largely the same kind of encouragement one would give a side-show freak (A colored man writing poetry! How odd!) a clown (How amusing!).

The present vogue in things Negro, although it may do as much harm as good for the budding colored artist, has at least done this: it has brought him forcibly to the attention of his own people among whom for so long, unless the other race had noticed him beforehand, he was a prophet with little honor. I understand that Charles Gilpin acted for years in Negro theaters without any special acclaim from his own, but when Broadway gave him eight curtain calls, Negroes, too, began to beat a tin pan in his honor. I know a young colored writer, a manual worker by day, who had been writing well for the colored magazines for some years, but it was not until he recently broke into the white publications and his first book was accepted by a prominent New York publisher that the "best" Negroes in his city took the trouble to discover that he lived there. Then almost immediately they decided to give a grand dinner for him. But the society ladies were careful to whisper to his mother that perhaps she'd better not come. They were not sure she would have an evening gown.

The Negro artist works against an undertow of sharp criticism and misunderstanding from his own group and unintentional bribes from the whites. "O, be respectable, write about nice people, show how good we are," say the Negroes. "Be stereotyped, don't go too far, don't shatter our illusions about you, don't amuse us too seriously. We will pay you," say the whites. Both would have told Jean Toomer not to write *Cane*. The colored people did not praise it. The white people did not buy it. Most of the colored people who did read *Cane* hate it. They are afraid of it. Although the critics gave it good reviews, the public remained indifferent. Yet (excepting the work of Du Bois) *Cane* contains the finest prose written by a Negro in America. And like the singing of Robeson, it is truly racial.

But in spite of the Nordicized Negro intelligentsia and the desires of some white editors we have an honest American Negro literature already with us. Now I await the rise of the Negro theater. Our folk music, having achieved world-wide fame, offers itself to the genius of the great individual American Negro composer who is to come. And within the next decade I expect to see the work of a growing school of colored artists who paint and model the beauty of dark faces and create with new technique the expressions of their own soul-world. And the Negro dancers who will dance like flame and the singers who will continue our songs to all who listen—they will be with us in even greater numbers tomorrow.

Most of my own poems are racial in theme and treatment, derived from the life I know. In many of them I try to grasp and hold some of the meanings and rhythms of jazz. I am sincere as I know how to be in these poems and yet after every reading I answer questions like these from my own people: Do you think Negroes should always write about Negroes? I wish you wouldn't read some of your poems to white folks. How do you find anything interesting in a place like a cabaret? Why do you write about black people? You aren't black. What makes you do so many jazz poems?

But jazz to me is one of the inherent expressions of Negro life in America: the eternal tom-tom beating in the Negro soul—the tom-tom of revolt against weariness in a white world, a world of subway trains, and work, work, work; the tom-tom of joy and laughter, and pain swallowed in a smile. Yet the Philadelphia clubwoman is ashamed to say that her race created it and she does not like me to write about it. The old subconscious "white is best" runs through her mind. Years of study under white teachers, a lifetime of white books, pictures, and papers, and white manners, morals, and Puritan standards made her dislike the spirituals. And now she turns up her nose at jazz and all its manifestations—likewise almost everything else distinctly racial. She doesn't care for the Winold Reiss portraits of Negroes because they are "too Negro." She does not want a true picture of herself from anybody. She wants the artist to flatter her, to make the white world believe that all Negroes are as smug and as near white in soul as she wants to be. But, to my mind, it is the duty of the younger Negro artist, if he accepts any duties at all from outsiders, to change through the force of his art that old whispering "I want to be white," hidden in the aspirations of his people, to "Why should I want to be white? I am a Negro—and beautiful."

So I am ashamed for the black poet who says, "I want to be a poet, not a Negro poet," as though his own racial world were not as interesting as any other world. I am ashamed, too, for the colored artist who runs from the painting of Negro faces to the painting of sunsets after the manner of the academicians because he fears the strange unwhiteness of his own features. An artist must be free to choose what he does, certainly, but he must also never be afraid to do what he might choose.

Let the blare of Negro jazz bands and the bellowing voice of Bessie Smith singing Blues penetrate the closed ears of the colored near-intellectuals until they listen and perhaps understand. Let Paul Robeson singing "Water Boy," and Rudolph Fisher writing about the streets of Harlem, and Jean Toomer holding the heart of Georgia in his hands, and Aaron Douglas drawing strange black fantasies cause the smug Negro middle class to turn from their white, respectable, ordinary books and papers to catch a glimmer of their own beauty. We young Negro artists who create now intend to express our individual dark-skinned selves without fear or shame. If white people are pleased we are glad. If they are not, it doesn't matter. We know we are beautiful. And ugly too. The tom-tom cries and the tom-tom laughs. If colored people are pleased we are glad. If they are not, their displeasure doesn't matter either. We build our temples for tomorrow, strong as we know how, and we stand on top of the mountain, free within ourselves.

The Nation, June 23, 1926

Harlem

What happens to a dream deferred?
Does it dry up
like a raisin in the sun?
Or fester like a sore—
And then run?
Does it stink like rotten meat?
Or crust and sugar over—
like a syrupy sweet?

Maybe it just sags
like a heavy load.

Or does it explode?

Jean Toomer
(1894–1967)

The publication of *Cane* in 1923 by the twenty-eight-year-old Jean Toomer was one of the most heralded debuts in American letters. Critic William Stanley Braithwaite said of the widely praised volume: "*Cane* is a book of gold and bronze, of dusk and flame, of ecstasy and pain, and Jean Toomer is a bright morning star of a new day of the race in literature." But while Toomer would continue to write for the next three decades, *Cane,* now regarded as one of the masterworks of the Harlem Renaissance, would be his only commercially published volume.

Nathan Eugene Toomer was born December 26, 1894, the grandson of Pinckney B. S. Pinchback, who had been acting governor of Louisiana during Reconstruction. Toomer's father abandoned his mother before he was born, and he was raised in his legendary grandfather's household. He attended the prestigious Paul Lawrence Dunbar High School and in 1914 embarked on a four-year sojourn through a string of colleges, including the University of Wisconsin, the University of Chicago, New York University, and the City College of New York. Failing to stick to any program long enough to earn a degree, Toomer attempted a number of jobs in Chicago, Wisconsin, and New York.

By 1920 Toomer had become acquainted with a literary circle that included Edward Arlington Robinson, Hart Crane, and Waldo Frank, and had renamed himself "Jean" Toomer. He began writing profusely and his poems and stories appeared in *The Liberator, The Crisis, Opportunity,* and elsewhere. During this period he began what would be a lifelong spiritual inquiry and became interested in Christian Scripture, Eastern philosophy, music, and occultism.

In 1921 Toomer took a temporary position as superintendent of a black school in Sparta, Georgia, a landscape that became the setting for *Cane.* Before his journey South, Toomer had held his racial identity at a distance, but he was deeply impressed by his stay there: "A visit to Georgia last fall was the starting point of almost everything of worth that I have done," he later wrote of his four-month stay. "I heard folk-songs come from the lips of Negro peasants. I saw the rich dusk beauty that I had heard many false accents about, and of which til then, I was somewhat skeptical. And a deep part of my nature, a part that I had repressed, sprang suddenly to life and responded to them. Now I cannot conceive of myself as aloof and separated."

Written in an impressionistic, lyrical style, *Cane* contrasts the agrarian South with the concrete and asphalt of urban Washington and Chicago. In his innovative fusion of verse, prose-poems, and stories, Toomer conjures up a moonlit world redolent of cane- and cotton-fields, pine forests and cypress swamps. Yet even here racial and sexual violence intrude, Christian camp meetings vie with greegree and juju men, and the modern age confronts the past. Toomer wrote in his unpublished autobiography: "I realized with deep regret, that the spirituals, meeting ridicule, would be certain to die out. With Negroes also the trend was towards the small town and then towards the city—and industry and commerce and machines. The folk-spirit was walking in to die on the modern desert." *Cane* was a swan song, he believed. "It was a song of the end."

Toomer lived more than forty years after *Cane* was published, but while he continued to write prodigiously—poems, stories, essays, novels—he succeeded only in having a single collection of poems, *Essentials,* printed in 1931. In his later work Toomer moved away from the depiction of African-American life toward the portrayal of "universal man." As he wrote in the poem "Blue Meridian," "I am, we are, simply of the human race," a theme later echoed by Countee Cullen. Elsewhere he wrote, "I do not know whether colored blood flows through my veins," a sentiment that may have alienated other African-American writers; Toomer is an obvious omission from James Weldon Johnson's definitive *Book of American Negro Poetry* (1931).

In the 1920s Toomer came under the influence of George Gurdjieff, a Russian mystical philosopher whose program promised a wholeness of body, mind, and spirit through meditation and mental and physical discipline. In 1931 Toomer married a white writer, Margery Latimer, who died in childbirth a year later, and in 1934 he married Marjorie Content. Toomer continued to explore Eastern and Western spiritual beliefs until his death on March 30, 1967.

Cane remains today a work of enormous virtuosity. As the Toomer scholar Darwin Turner writes, "*Cane* was not Jean Toomer's total life; it was perhaps merely an interlude in his search for understanding. No matter what it may have been for him, *Cane* still sings to readers, not the swan song of an era that was dying, but the morning hymn of a Renaissance that was beginning."

from *Cane*

SONG OF THE SON

Pour O pour that parting soul in song;
O pour it in the sawdust glow of night,
Into the velvet pine-smoke air to-night,
And let the valley carry it along.
And let the valley carry it along.

O land and soil, red soil and sweet-gum tree,
So scant of grass, so profligate of pines,
Now just before an epoch's sun declines
Thy son, in time, I have returned to thee,
Thy son, I have in time returned to thee.

In time, for though the sun is setting on
A song-lit race of slaves, it has not set;
Though late, O soil, it is not too late yet
To catch thy plaintive soul, leaving, soon gone,
Leaving, to catch thy plaintive soul soon gone.

O Negro slaves, dark purple ripened plums,
Squeezed, and bursting in the pine-wood air,
Passing, before they stripped the old tree bare
One plum was saved for me, one seed becomes

An everlasting song, a singing tree,
Caroling softly souls of slavery,
What they were, and what they are to me,
Caroling softly souls of slavery.

1923

Karintha

Her skin is like dusk on the eastern horizon,
O cant you see it, O cant you see it,
Her skin is like dusk on the eastern horizon
. . . When the sun goes down.

Men had always wanted her, this Karintha, even as a child. Karintha carrying beauty, perfect as dusk when the sun goes down. Old men rode her hobby-horse upon their knees. Young men danced with her at frolics when they should have been dancing with their grown-up girls. God grant us youth, secretly prayed the old men. The young fellows counted the time to pass before she would be old enough to mate with them. This interest of the male, who wishes to ripen a growing thing too soon, could mean no good to her.

Karintha, at twelve, was a wild flash that told the other folks just what it was to live. At sunset, when there was no wind, and the pine-smoke from over by the sawmill hugged the earth, and you couldn't see more than a few feet in front, her sudden darting past you was a bit of vivid color, like a black bird that flashes in light. With the other children one could hear, some distance off, their feet flopping in the two-inch dust that sometimes makes a spiral in the road. At dusk, during the hush just after the sawmill had closed down, and before any of the women had started their supper-getting-ready songs, her voice, high-pitched, shrill, would put one's ears to itching. But no one ever thought to make her stop because of it. She stoned the cows, and beat her dog, and fought the other children . . . Even the preacher, who caught her at mischief, told himself that she was as innocently lovely as a November cotton flower. Already, rumors were out about her. Homes in Georgia are most often built on the two-room plan. In one, you cook and eat, in the other you sleep, and there love goes on. Karintha had seen or heard, perhaps she had felt her parents loving. One could but imitate one's parents, for to follow them was the way of God. She played "home" with a small boy who was not afraid to do her bidding. That started the whole thing. Old men could no longer ride her hobby-horse upon their knees. But young men counted faster.

Her skin is like dusk,
O cant you see it,
Her skin is like dusk,
When the sun goes down.

Karintha is a woman. She who carries beauty, perfect as dusk when the sun goes down. She has been married many times. Old men remind her that a few years back they rode her hobby-horse upon their knees. Karintha smiles, and indulges them, when she is in the mood for it. She has contempt for them. Karintha is a woman. Young men run stills to make her money. Young men go to the big cities and run on the road. Young men go away to college. They all want to bring her money. These are the young men who thought that all they had to do was to count time. But Karintha is a woman, and she has had a child. A child fell out of her womb onto a bed of pine-needles in the forest. Pine-needles are smooth and sweet. They are elastic to the feet of rabbits . . . A sawmill was nearby. Its pyramidal sawdust pile smouldered. It is a year before one completely burns. Meanwhile, the smoke curls up and hangs its odd wraiths about the trees, curls up, and spreads itself out over the valley . . . Weeks after Karintha returned home the smoke was so heavy you tasted it in water. Some one made a song:

Smoke is on the hills, Rise up.
Smoke is on the hills, O rise
And take my soul to Jesus.

Karintha is a woman. Men do not know that the soul of her was a growing thing ripened too soon. They will bring their money; they will die not having found it out . . . Karintha at twenty, carrying beauty, perfect as dusk when the sun goes down. Karintha . . .

Her skin is like dusk on the eastern horizon,
O cant you see it, O cant you see it,
Her skin is like dusk on the eastern horizon
. . . When the sun goes down.

Goes down . . .

1923

Countee Cullen
(1903–1946)

The publication in 1925 of Countee Cullen's first volume of poems, *Color,* made him, according to the critic Gerald Early, "the most celebrated and probably the most famous black writer in America," both the harbinger and the embodiment of the Renaissance proclaimed by Alain Locke in *The New Negro.* "He was, indeed," writes Early, "a boy wonder, a young handsome black Ariel ascending, a boyish, bronze-skinned titan who, in the early and mid-twenties, embodied many of the hopes, aspirations, and maturing expressive possibilities of his people."

The details of Cullen's early years are a bit unclear. Born either in Louisville, Kentucky, or, as he later claimed, New York City, he was adopted as a youth by the Reverend Dr. Frederick A. Cullen, a minister in the Salem Methodist Episcopal Church in Harlem and a social activist, with whom he remained close throughout his life. He attended mostly white schools in New York City, where he met his lifelong friend Harold Jackman, and was the editor of his high school paper. The top award in a citywide poetry contest brought him precocious attention. He attended New York University, where he was elected to Phi Beta Kappa, and, while he was still in school, his poem "The Shroud of Color" was published in H. L. Mencken's *American Mercury.* In his senior year, he published his career-making *Color,* a collection of lyric poems and sonnets that show their indebtedness to both the forms and subjects of Keats, Shelley, Wordsworth, and the Romantics. He did graduate work at Harvard, receiving his M.A. in 1926, and then joined the journal *Opportunity,* where he wrote the column "The Dark Tower." In 1927 Cullen published a second volume of poems, *Copper Sun,* and edited the anthology *Caroling Dusk,* and the following year he was awarded a Guggenheim Fellowship. Then, in April 1928, in one of the most celebrated social events of the Harlem Renaissance, he married the daughter of W. E. B. Du Bois, Nina Yolande, in a union that seemed to form a bridge between a literary giant of the previous generation with a scion of the new. The marriage lasted less than a year. Cullen spent two years in Paris, and upon his return took a job teaching French at Frederick Douglass, Jr., High School in New York, where he remained for the fifteen years until his death. His last major work, *The Black Christ, and Other Poems,* was published in 1929.

Despite Cullen's assertion in a 1924 interview, "If I am going to be a poet at all, I am going to be *poet* and not *Negro poet,*" perhaps no poet since Paul Laurence Dunbar struggled so publicly with the double-consciousness of belonging to both a black tradition and the dominant Anglo-American one. While employing the forms and often academic language of English verse, such poems as "The Shroud of Color," "Heritage," "A Brown Girl, Dead," "Black Magdalens," "Threnody for a Brown Girl," "A Negro Mother's Lullaby," "Black Majesty," and others clearly reflect a prodigious interest in racial matters. Yet for all the tension that Cullen sets up in his works between the "paganism" and "blackness" of Africa and Christianity (the ethos of the New World), he continually professed a distaste for some of the true expressions of black culture, or at least their appropriateness to literature. With no one would Cullen come more into conflict on this issue than Langston Hughes, whose works were infused with the rhythms of jazz and blues and whose love of the black masses seemed irrepressible, an argument delineated with particular emphasis in Hughes's "The Negro Artist and the Racial Mountain,"† published in *The Nation* in June 1926. Ironically, none of Cullen's later works excited the same attention as *Color* and *Copper Sun,* and many critics believe that Cullen's best poems, including those here, concern race. Of this conundrum the poet Owen Dodson remarked, "If you asked any Negro what he found in Cullen's poetry, he would say: all my dilemmas are written here."

In the thirties, Cullen entered a period marked perhaps not as much by a frequently cited lessening of production, as much as by a turning of his talent to new forms, including fiction, translation, drama, song lyrics, and children's literature. His only novel, the satirical look at the Harlem Renaissance *One Way to Heaven,* was published in 1932 (the same year as Wallace Thurman's own biting fictional portrait, *Infants of the Spring*); in 1935, he published *The Medea,* a translation of the Greek drama. In the forties, Cullen settled into a comfortable marriage to Ida Mae Roberson, published his children's volumes *The Lost Zoo* and *My Lives and How I Lost Them,* and collaborated with Arna Bontemps on *St. Louis Women,* a musical adaptation of Bontemps's novel, *God Sends Sunday.* On June 9, 1946, the bright and morning star of the Harlem Renaissance, who seemed, perhaps, to have a gift for arriving too soon, died at the age of forty-three.

Yet Do I Marvel

I doubt not God is good, well-meaning, kind,
And did He stoop to quibble could tell why
The little buried mole continues blind,
Why flesh that mirrors Him must some day die,
Make plain the reason tortured Tantalus
Is baited by the fickle fruit, declare
If merely brute caprice dooms Sisyphus
To struggle up a never-ending stair.
Inscrutable His ways are, and immune
To catechism by a mind too strewn
With petty care to slightly understand
What awful brain compels His awful hand.
Yet do I marvel at this curious thing:
To make a poet black, and bid him sing!

from *Color*, 1925

Heritage

For Harold Jackman

What is Africa to me:
Copper sun or scarlet sea,
Jungle star or jungle track,
Strong bronzed men, or regal black
Women from whose loins I sprang
When the birds of Eden sang?
One three centuries removed
From the scenes his fathers loved,
Spicy grove, cinnamon tree,
What is Africa to me?

So I lie, who all day long
Want no sound except the song
Sung by wild barbaric birds
Goading massive jungle herds,
Juggernauts of flesh that pass
Trampling tall defiant grass
Where young forest lovers lie,
Plighting troth beneath the sky.
So I lie, who always hear,
Though I cram against my ear
Both my thumbs, and keep them there,
Great drums throbbing through the air.
So I lie, whose fount of pride,
Dear distress, and joy allied,
Is my somber flesh and skin,
With the dark blood dammed within
Like great pulsing tides of wine
That, I fear, must burst the fine
Channels of the chafing net
Where they surge and foam and fret.

Africa? A book one thumbs
Listlessly, till slumber comes.
Unremembered are her bats
Circling through the night, her cats
Crouching in the river reeds.
Stalking gentle flesh that feeds
By the river brink; no more
Does that bugle-throated roar

Cry that monarch claws have leapt
From the scabbards where they slept.
Silver snakes that once a year
Doff the lovely coat you wear,
Seek no covert in your fear
Lest a mortal eye should see;
What's your nakedness to me?
Where no leprous flowers rear
Fierce corollas in the air;
Here no bodies sleek and wet,
Dripping mingled rain and sweat,
Tread the savage measures of
Jungle boys and girls in love.
What is last year's snow to me,
Last year's anything? The tree
Budding yearly must forget
How its past arose or set—
Bough and blossom, flower, fruit,
Even what shy bird with mute
Wonder at her travail there,
Meekly labored in its hair.
One three centuries removed
From the scenes his father loved,
Spicy grove, cinnamon tree,
What is Africa to me?

So I lie, who find no peace
Night or day, no slight release
From the unremittant beat
Made by cruel padded feet
Walking through my body's street.
Up and down they go, and back,
Treading out a jungle track.
So I lie, who never quite
Safely sleep from rain at night—
I can never rest at all
When the rain begins to fall;
Like a soul gone mad with pain
I must match its weird refrain;
Ever must I twist and squirm,
Writhing like a baited worm,
While its primal measures drip
Through my body, crying, "Strip!
Doff this new exuberance.

Come and dance the Lover's Dance!"
In an old remembered way
Rain works on me night and day.

Quaint, outlandish heathen gods
Black men fashion out of rods,
Clay, and brittle bits of stone,
In a likeness like their own,
My conversion came high-priced;
I belong to Jesus Christ,
Preacher of humility;
Heathen gods are naught to me.

Father, Son, and Holy Ghost,
So I make an idle boast:
Jesus of the twice-turned cheek,
Lamb of God, although I speak
With my mouth thus, in my heart
Do I play a double part.
Ever at Thy glowing altar
Must my heart grow sick and falter,
Wishing He I served were black,
Thinking then it would not lack
Precedent of pain to guide it,
Lest who would or might deride it;
Surely then this flesh would know
Yours had borne a kindred woe.
Lord, I fashion dark gods, too,
Daring even to give You
Dark despairing features where,
Crowned with dark rebellious hair,
Patience wavers just so much as
Mortal grief compels, while touches
Quick and hot, of anger, rise
To smitten cheek and weary eyes.
Lord, forgive me if my need
Sometimes shapes a human creed.

All day long and all night through,
One thing only must I do;
Quench my pride and cool my blood,
Lest I perish in the flood.
Lest a hidden ember set
Timber that I thought was wet
Burning like the dryest flax,

Melting like the merest wax,
Lest the grave restore its dead.
Not yet has my heart or head
In the least way realized
They and I are civilized.

from *Color*, 1925

From the Dark Tower

We shall not always plant while others reap
The golden increment of bursting fruit,
Not always countenance, abject and mute,
That lesser men should hold their brothers cheap;
Nor everlastingly while others sleep
Shall we beguile their limbs with mellow flute,
Not always bend to some more subtle brute;
We were not made eternally to weep.

The night whose sable breast relieves the stark,
White stars is no less lovely being dark,
And there are buds that cannot bloom at all
In light, but crumple, piteous, and fall;
So in the dark we hide the heart that bleeds,
And wait, and tend our agonizing seeds.

from *Copper Sun*, 1927

Zora Neale Hurston
(1891–1960)

The author of four novels, two collections of black folklore, an autobiography, and numerous stories and essays, Zora Neale Hurston was one of the most important and celebrated figures to emerge from the Harlem Renaissance. Born in the all-black town of Eatonville, Florida, Hurston was encouraged by her mother to "jump at de sun" and experienced a pride in black folk culture and self-sufficiency. As she says in her introduction to *Mules and Men,* "When I pitched headforemost into the world I landed in the crib of negroism." After her mother's early death, she lived with various relatives and began to support herself at the age of fourteen. Acting as a wardrobe girl and maid to a theater group, she traveled to Baltimore, where she attended Morgan Academy and then enrolled at Howard, briefly, and Barnard, where she studied with the anthropologist Franz Boas.

But despite the remarkable distance Hurston had traveled, she had not removed herself from her roots. "She was one of W. E. B. Du Bois's talented tenth," writes critic Arnold Rampersad, "without seeing herself, as members of the tenth often saw themselves, as victims caught tragically between two worlds, black and white. Instead, she draped folk culture about herself like a robe." In 1927 she returned to Eatonville in one of several trips she would make to Florida and the Caribbean investigating black folkways.

The story that follows, one of Hurston's earliest published works, appeared in an innovative journal planned by Hurston, Langston Hughes, Wallace Thurman, Gwendolyn Bennett, and three others in 1926. Illustrated by Aaron Douglas, the project represented the attempt by a younger generation to respond to Alain Locke's *New Negro.* As Hughes recalls, the magazine would be called *Fire!,* "the idea being that it would burn up a lot of the old, dead conventional Negro-white ideas of the past, *epater le bourgeois* into a realization of the existence of the younger Negro writers and artists." When it was published, he says, "None of the older Negro intellectuals would have anything to do with *Fire.*" The group distributed the magazine themselves, and ironically their inventory was destroyed by fire; both Thurman and Hughes spent the next few years paying off the printer.

Hurston's first novel, *Jonah's Gourd Vine,* appeared in 1934, and in rapid succession she published two collections of folklore, *Mules and Men* (1935) and *Tell My Horse* (1938), her most widely praised novel, *Their Eyes Were Watching God* (1937), *Moses, Man of the Mountain* (1939), and *Dust Tracks on a Road* (1942). But despite her success, Hurston was not without her critics. For five years early in her career, she worked under a contract to a white patron, Charlotte Osgood Mason. While Mason provided Hurston with an allowance (though one that required Hurston to press her for extra funds simply to buy a new pair of shoes), she demanded ownership of the writer's material and controlled its publication. For Mason's patronage, Hurston was attacked by some of her contemporaries. Langston Hughes wrote in his autobiography, "She was always getting scholarships and things from wealthy white people, some of whom simply paid her just to sit around and represent the Negro race for them," while Wallace Thurman satirized her in his novel of the Harlem Renaissance, *Infants of the Spring.* This same woman had also served at one time as a patron to Hughes, Alain Locke, and other young black writers, and the scholar Mary Helen Washington argues that these critics have simply missed the point. "Zora Hurston was fiercely determined," writes Washington, "to have a career no matter what or who had to be sacrificed."

As many prominent black intellectuals moved to the left in the forties and turned out literature of protest, Hurston fell out of step. She had written in a 1928 essay, "How It Feels to Be Colored Me," "I am not tragically colored. There is no great sorrow dammed up in my soul, nor lurking behind my eyes. . . . I do not belong to the sobbing school of Negrohood who hold that nature somehow has given them a lowdown dirty deal and whose feelings are hurt about it. . . . No, I do not weep at the world—I am too busy sharpening my oyster knife." Hurston was also criticized for her use of dialect (as would be Alice Walker after the publication of *The Color Purple*) and her iconoclastic political opinions.

Toward the end of her life, Hurston was devastated by a false charge of sexually molesting a child, and in poor health and with few financial resources, she worked in Florida as a librarian, substitute teacher, and maid. In January 1960 she died in the St. Lucie County Welfare Home. Renewed interest in Hurston followed the publication in 1975 of Alice Walker's essay, "In Search of Zora Neale Hurston," an account of Walker's pilgrimage South to find Hurston's unmarked grave. Today, all of Hurston's books, whose artistry utterly defeats her critics, have been returned to print.

Sweat

"Whatever goes over the Devil's back, is got to come under his belly. . . ."

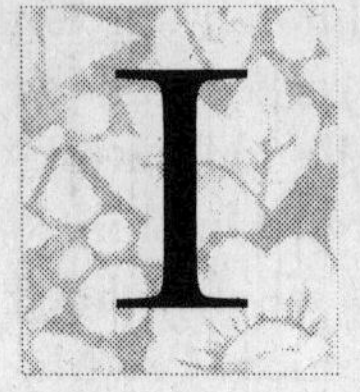

IT WAS ELEVEN O'CLOCK OF A SPRING NIGHT IN FLORIDA. IT was Sunday. Any other night, Delia Jones would have been in bed for two hours by this time. But she was a washwoman, and Monday morning meant a great deal to her. So she collected the soiled clothes on Saturday when she returned the clean things. Sunday night after church, she sorted them and put the white things to soak. It saved her almost a half day's start. A great hamper in the bedroom held the clothes that she brought home. It was so much neater than a number of bundles lying around.

She squatted in the kitchen floor beside the great pile of clothes, sorting them into small heaps according to color, and humming a song in a mournful key, but wondering through it all where Sykes, her husband, had gone with her horse and buckboard.

Just then something long, round, limp and black fell upon her shoulders and slithered to the floor beside her. A great terror took hold of her. It softened her knees and dried her mouth so that it was a full minute before she could cry out or move. Then she saw that it was the big bull whip her husband liked to carry when he drove.

She lifted her eyes to the door and saw him standing there bent over with laughter at her fright. She screamed at him.

"Sykes, what you throw dat whip on me like dat? You know it would skeer me—looks just like a snake, an' you knows how skeered Ah is of snakes."

"Course Ah knowed it! That's how come Ah done it." He slapped his leg with his hand and almost rolled on the ground in his mirth. "If you such a big fool dat you got to have a fit over a earth worm or a string, Ah don't keer how bad Ah skeer you."

"You aint got no business doing it. Gawd knows it's a sin. Some day Ah'm gointuh drop dead from some of yo' foolishness. 'Nother thing, where you been wid mah rig? Ah feeds dat pony. He aint fuh you to be drivin' wid no bull whip."

"You sho is one aggravatin' nigger woman!" he declared and stepped into the room. She resumed her work and did not answer him at once. "Ah done tole you time and again to keep them white folks' clothes outa dis house."

He picked up the whip and glared down at her. Delia went on with her work. She went out into the yard and returned with a galvanized tub and set it on the washbench. She saw that Sykes had kicked all of the clothes together again, and now stood in her way truculently, his whole manner hoping, *praying,* for an argument. But she walked calmly around him and commenced to re-sort the things.

"Next time, Ah'm gointer kick 'em outdoors," he threatened as he struck a match along the leg of his corduroy breeches.

Delia never looked up from her work, and her thin, stooped shoulders sagged further.

"Ah aint for no fuss t'night Sykes. Ah just come from taking sacrament at the church house."

He snorted scornfully. "Yeah, you just come from de church house on a Sunday night, but heah you is gone to work on them clothes. You ain't nothing but a hypocrite. One of them amen-corner Christians—sing, whoop, and shout, then come home and wash white folks clothes on the Sabbath."

He stepped roughly upon the whitest pile of things, kicking them helter-skelter as he crossed the room. His wife gave a little scream of dismay, and quickly gathered them together again.

"Sykes, you quit grindin' dirt into these clothes! How can Ah git through by Sat'day if Ah don't start on Sunday?"

"Ah don't keer if you never git through. Anyhow, Ah done promised Gawd and a couple of other men, Ah aint gointer have it in mah house. Don't gimme no lip neither, else Ah'll throw 'em out and put mah fist up side yo' head to boot."

Delia's habitual meekness seemd to slip from her shoulders like a blown scarf. She was on her feet; her poor little body, her bare knuckly hands bravely defying the strapping hulk before her.

"Looka heah, Sykes, you done gone too fur. Ah been married to you fur fifteen years, and Ah been takin' in washin' fur fifteen years. Sweat, sweat, sweat! Work and sweat, cry and sweat, pray and sweat!"

"What's that got to do with me?" he asked brutally.

"What's it got to do with you, Sykes? Mah tub of suds is filled yo' belly with vittles more times than yo' hands is filled it. Mah sweat is done paid for this house and Ah reckon Ah kin keep on sweatin' in it."

She seized the iron skillet from the stove and struck a defensive pose, which act surprised him greatly, coming from her. It cowed him and he did not strike her as he usually did.

"Naw you won't," she panted, "that ole snaggle-toothed black woman you runnin' with aint comin' heah to pile up on *mah* sweat and blood. You aint paid for nothin' on this place, and Ah'm gointer stay right heah till Ah'm toted out foot foremost."

"Well, you better quit gittin' me riled up, else they'll be totin' you out sooner than you expect. Ah'm so tired of you Ah don't know whut to do. Gawd! how Ah hates skinny wimmen!"

A little awed by this new Delia, he sidled out of the door and slammed the back gate after him. He did not say where he had gone, but she knew too well. She knew very well that he would not return until nearly daybreak also. Her work over, she went on to bed but not to sleep at once. Things had come to a pretty pass!

She lay awake, gazing upon the debris that cluttered their matrimonial trail. Not an image left standing along the way. Anything like flowers had long ago been drowned in the salty stream that had been pressed from her heart. Her tears, her sweat, her blood. She had brought love to the union and he had brought a longing after the flesh. Two months after the wedding, he had given her the first brutal beating. She had the memory of his numerous trips to Orlando with all of his wages when he had returned to her penniless, even before the first year had passed. She was young and soft then, but now she thought of her knotty, muscled limbs, her harsh knuckly hands, and drew herself up into an unhappy little ball in the middle of the big feather bed. Too late now to hope for love, even if it were not Bertha it would be someone else. This case differed from the others only in that she was bolder than the others. Too late for everything except her little home. She had built it for her old days, and planted one by one the trees and flowers there. It was lovely to her, lovely.

Somehow, before sleep came, she found herself saying aloud: "Oh well, whatever goes over the Devil's back, is got to come under his belly. Sometime or ruther, Sykes, like everybody else, is gointer reap his sowing." After that she was able to build a spiritual earthworks against her husband. His shells could no longer reach her. *Amen.* She went to sleep and slept until he announced his presence in bed by kicking her feet and rudely snatching the cover away.

"Gimme some kivah heah, an' git yo' damn foots over on yo' own side! Ah oughter mash you in yo' mouf fuh drawing dat skillet on me."

Delia went clear to the rail without answering him. A triumphant indifference to all that he was or did.

The week was as full of work for Delia as all other weeks, and Saturday found her behind her little pony, collecting and delivering clothes.

It was a hot, hot day near the end of July. The village men on Joe Clarke's porch even chewed cane listlessly. They did not hurl the cane-knots as usual. They let them dribble over the edge of the porch. Even conversation had collapsed under the heat.

"Heah come Delia Jones," Jim Merchant said, as the shaggy pony came 'round the bend of the road toward them. The rusty buckboard was heaped with baskets of crisp, clean laundry.

"Yep," Joe Lindsay agreed. "Hot or col', rain or shine, jes ez reg'lar ez de weeks roll roun' Delia carries 'em an' fetches 'em on Sat'day."

"She better if she wanter eat," said Moss. "Syke Jones aint wuth de shot an' powder hit would tek tuh kill 'em. Not to *huh* he aint."

"He sho' aint," Walter Thomas chimed in. "It's too bad, too, cause she wuz a right pritty lil trick when he got huh. Ah'd uh mah'ied huh mahseff if he hadnter beat me to it."

Delia nodded briefly at the men as she drove past.

"Too much knockin' will ruin *any* 'oman. He done beat huh 'nough tuh kill three women, let 'lone change they looks," said Elijah Mosely. "How Syke kin stommuck dat big black greasy Mogul he's layin' roun' wid, gits me. Ah swear dat eight-rock couldn't kiss a sardine can Ah done thowed out de back do' 'way las' yeah."

"Aw, she's fat, thass how come. He's allus been crazy 'bout fat women," put in Merchant. "He'd a' been tied up wid one long time ago if he could a' found one tuh have him. Did Ah tell yuh 'bout him come sidlin' roun' *mah* wife—bringin' her a basket uh pee-can outa his yard fuh a present? Yessir, mah wife! She tol' him tuh take 'em right straight back home, cause Delia works so hard ovah dat washtub she reckon everything on de place taste lak sweat an' soapsuds. Ah jus' wisht Ah'd a' caught 'em 'roun' dere! Ah'd a' made his hips ketch on fiah down dat shell road."

"Ah know he done it, too. Ah sees 'im grinnin' at every 'oman dat passes," Walter Thomas said. "But even so, he useter eat some mighty big hunks uh humble pie tuh git dat lil' 'oman he got. She wuz ez pritty ez a speckled pup! Dat wuz fifteen yeahs ago. He useter be so skeered uh losin' huh, she could make him do some parts of a husband's duty. Dey never wuz de same in de mind."

"There oughter be a law about him," said Lindsay. "He aint fit tuh carry guts tuh a bear."

Clarke spoke for the first time. "Taint no law on earth dat kin make a man be decent if it aint in 'im. There's plenty men dat takes a wife lak dey do a joint uh suger-cane. It's round, juicy an' sweet when dey gits it. But dey squeeze an' grind, squeeze an' grind an' wring tell dey wring every drop uh pleasure dat's in 'em out. When dey's satisfied dat dey is wrung dry, dey treats 'em jes lak dey do a cane-chew. Dey thows 'em away. Dey knows whut dey is doin' while dey is at it, an' hates theirselves fuh it but they keeps on hangin' after huh tell she's empty. Den dey hates huh fuh bein' a cane-chew an' in de way."

"We oughter take Syke an' dat stray 'oman uh his'n down in Lake Howell swamp an' lay on de rawhide till they cain't say 'Lawd a' mussy.' He allus wuz uh ovahbearin' niggah, but since dat white 'oman from up north done teached 'im how to run a automible, he done got too biggety to live—an' we oughter kill 'im," Old Man Anderson advised.

A grunt of approval went around the porch. But the heat was melting their civic virtue and Elijah Moseley began to bait Joe Clarke.

"Come on, Joe, git a melon outa dere an' slice it up for yo' customers. We'se all sufferin' wid de heat. De bear's done got *me*!"

"Thass right, Joe, a watermelons is jes' what Ah needs tuh cure de eppizudicks," Walter Thomas joined forces with Moseley. "Come on dere, Joe. We all is steady customers an' you aint set us up in a long time. Ah chooses dat long, bowlegged Floridy favorite."

"A god, an' be dough. You all gimme twenty cents and slice away," Clarke retorted. "Ah needs a col' slice m'self. Heah, everybody chip in. Ah'll lend y'll mah meat knife."

The money was quickly subscribed and the huge melon brought forth. At that moment, Sykes and Bertha arrived. A determined silence fell on the porch and the melon was put away again.

Merchant snapped down the blade of his jack-knife and moved toward the store door.

"Come on in, Joe, an' gimme a slab uh sow belly an' uh pound uh coffee—almost fughot 'twas Sat'day. Got to git on home." Most of the men left also.

Just then Delia drove past on her way home, as Sykes was ordering magnificently for Bertha. It pleased him for Delia to see.

"Git whutsoever yo' heart desires, Honey. Wait a minute, Joe. Give huh two botles uh strawberry soda-water, uh quart uh parched ground-peas, an' a block uh chewin' gum."

With all this they left the store, with Sykes reminding Bertha that this was his town and she could have it if she wanted it.

The men returned soon after they left, and held their watermelon feast.

"Where did Syke Jones git dat 'oman from nohow?" Lindsay asked.

"Ovah Apopka. Guess dey musta been cleanin' out de town when she lef'. She don't look lak a thing but a hunk uh liver wid hair on it."

"Well, she sho' kin squall," Dave Carter contributed. "When she gits ready tuh laff, she jes' opens huh mouf an' latches it back tuh de las' notch. No ole grandpa alligator down in Lake Bell ain't got nothin' on huh."

Bertha had been in town three months now. Sykes was still paying her room rent at Della Lewis'—the only house in town that would have taken her in. Sykes took her frequently to Winter Park to "stomps." He still assured her that he was the swellest man in the state.

"Sho' you kin have dat lil' ole house soon's Ah kin git dat 'oman out dere. Everything b'longs tuh me an' you sho' kin have it. Ah sho' 'bominates uh skinny 'oman. Lawdy, you sho' is got one portly shape on you! You kin git *anything* you wants. Dis is *mah* town an' you sho' kin have it."

Delia's work-worn knees crawled over the earth in Gethsemane and up the rocks of Calvary many, many times during these months. She avoided the villagers and meeting places in her efforts to be blind and deaf. But Bertha nullified this to a degree, by coming to Delia's house to call Sykes out to her at the gate.

Delia and Sykes fought all the time now with no peaceful interludes.

They slept and ate in silence. Two or three times Delia had attempted a timid friendliness, but she was repulsed each time. It was plain that the breaches must remain agape.

The sun had burned July to August. The heat streamed down like a million hot arrows, smiting all things living upon the earth. Grass withered, leaves browned, snakes went blind in shedding and men and dogs went mad. Dog days!

Delia came home one day and found Sykes there before her. She wondered, but started to go on into the house without speaking, even though he was standing in the kitchen door and she must either stoop under his arm or ask him to move. He made no room for her. She noticed a soap box beside the steps, but paid no particular attention to it, knowing that he must have brought it there. As she was stooping to pass under his outstretched arm, he suddenly pushed her backward, laughingly.

"Look in de box dere Delia, Ah done brun yuh somethin'!"

She nearly fell upon the box in her stumbling, and when she saw what it held, she all but fainted outright.

"Syke! Syke, mah Gawd! You take dat rattlesnake 'way from heah! You *gottuh.* Oh, Jesus, have mussy!"

"Ah ain't gut tuh do nuthin' ud de kin'—fact is Ah aint got tuh do nothin' but die. Taint no use uh you puttin' on airs makin' out lak you skeered uh dat snake—he's gointer stay right heah tell he die. He wouldn't bit me cause Ah knows how tuh handle 'im. Nohow he wouldn't risk breakin' out his fangs 'gin *yo'* skinny laigs."

"Naw, now Syke, don't keep dat thing 'roun' heah tuh skeer me tuh death. You knows Ah'm even feared uh earth worms. Thass de biggest snake Ah evah did see. Kill 'im Syke, please."

"Doan ast me tuh do nothin' fuh yuh. Goin' 'roun' tryin' tuh be so damn asterperious. Naw, Ah aint gonna kill it. Ah think uh damn sight mo' uh him dan you! Dat's a nice snake an' anybody doan lak 'im kin jes' hit de grit."

The village soon heard that Sykes had the snake, and came to see and ask questions.

"How de hen-fire did you ketch dat six-foot rattler, Syke?" Thomas asked.

"He's full uh frogs so he caint hardly move, thass how Ah eased up on 'm. But Ah'm a snake charmer an' knows how tuh handle 'em. Shux, dat aint nothin'. Ah could ketch one eve'y day if Ah so wanted tuh."

"What he needs is a heavy hick'ry club leaned real heavy on his head. Dat's de bes' way tuh charm a rattlesnake."

"Naw, Walt, y'll jes' don't understand dese diamon' backs lak Ah do," said Sykes in a superior tone of voice.

The village agreed with Walter, but the snake stayed on. His box remained by the kitchen door with its screen wire covering. Two or three days later it had digested its meal of frogs and literally came to life. It rattled at every movement in the kitchen or the yard. One day as Delia came down the kitchen steps she saw his chalky-white fangs curved like scimitars hung in the wire meshes. This time she did not run away with averted eyes as usual. She stood for a long time in the doorway in a red fury that grew bloodier for every second that she regarded the creature that was her torment.

That night she broached the subject as soon as Sykes sat down to the table.

"Syke, Ah wants you tuh take dat snake 'way fum heah. You done starved me an' Ah put up widcher, you done beat me an Ah took dat, but you done kilt all mah insides bringin' dat varmint heah."

Sykes poured out a saucer full of coffee and drank it deliberately before he answered her.

"A whole lot Ah keer 'bout how you feels inside uh out. Dat snake aint goin' no damn wheah till Ah gits ready fuh 'im tuh go. So fur as beatin' is concerned, yuh aint took near all dat you gointer take ef yuh stay 'roun' *me*."

Delia pushed back her plate and got up from the table. "Ah hates you, Sykes," she said calmly. "Ah hates you tuh de same degree dat Ah useter love yuh. Ah done took an' took till mah belly is full up tuh mah neck. Dat's de reason Ah got mah letter fum de church an' moved mah membership tuh Woodbridge—so Ah don't haftuh take no sacrament wid yuh. Ah don't wantuh see yuh 'roun' me atall. Lay 'roun' wid dat 'oman all yuh wants tuh, but gwan 'way fum me an' mah house. Ah hates yuh lak uh suck-egg dog."

Sykes almost let the huge wad of corn bread and collard greens he was chewing fall out of his mouth in amazement. He had a hard time whipping himself up to the proper fury to try to answer Delia.

"Well, Ah'm glad you does hate me. Ah'm sho' tiahed uh you hangin' ontuh me. Ah don't want yuh. Look at yuh stringey ole neck! Yo' rawbony laigs an' arms is enough tuh cut uh man tuh death. You looks jes' lak de devvul's doll-baby tuh *me*. You can't hate me no worse dan Ah hates you. Ah been hatin' *you* fuh years."

"Yo' ole black hide don't look lak nothin' tuh me, but uh passle uh wrinkled up rubber, wid yo' big ole yeahs flappin' on each side lak uh paih uh buzzard wings. Don't think Ah'm gointuh be run 'way fum mah house neither. Ah'm goin' tuh de white folks bout *you*, mah young man, de very nex' time you lay yo' han's on me. Mah cup is done run ovah." Delia said this with no signs of fear and Sykes departed from the house, threatening her, but made not the slightest move to carry out any of them.

That night he did not return at all, and the next day being Sunday, Delia was glad that she did not have to quarrel before she hitched up her pony and drove the four miles to Woodbridge.

She stayed to the night service—"love feast"—which was very warm and full of spirit. In the emotional winds her domestic trials were borne far and wide so that she sang as she drove homeward,

> *"Jurden water, black an' col'*
> *Chills de body, not de soul*
> *An' Ah wantah cross Jurden in uh calm time."*

She came from the barn to the kitchen door and stopped.

"Whut's de mattah, ol' satan, you aint kickin' up yo' racket?" She addressed the snake's box. Complete silence. She went on into the house with a new hope in its birth struggles. Perhaps her threat to go to the white folks had frightened Sykes! Perhaps he was sorry! Fifteen years of misery and suppression had brought Delia to the place where she would hope *anything* that looked towards a way over or through her wall of inhibitions.

She felt in the match safe behind the stove at once for a match. There was only one there.

"Dat niggah wouldn't fetch nothin' heah tuh save his rotten neck, but he kin run thew whut Ah brings quick enough. Now he done toted off nigh on tuh haff uh box uh matches. He done had dat 'oman heah in mah house, too."

Presently she brought in the tubs to put the white things to soak. This time she decided she need not bring the hamper out of the bedroom; she would go in there and do the sorting. She picked up the pot-bellied lamp and went in. The room was small and the hamper stood hard by the foot of the white iron bed. She could sit and reach through the bedposts—resting as she worked.

"Ah wantah cross Jurden in uh calm time." She was singing again. The mood of the "love feast" had returned. She threw back the lid of the basket almost gaily. Then, moved by both horror and terror, she sprang back toward the door. *There lay the snake in the basket!* He moved sluggishly at first, but even as she turned round and round, jumped up and down in an insanity of fear, he began to stir vigorously. She saw him pouring his awful beauty from the basket upon the bed, then she seized the lamp and ran as fast as she could to the kitchen. The wind from the open door blew out the light and the darkness added to her terror. She sped to the darkness of the yard, slamming the door after her before she thought to set down the lamp. She did not feel safe even on the ground, so she climbed up in the hay barn.

There for an hour or more she lay sprawled upon the hay a gibbering wreck.

Finally she grew quiet, and after that, coherent thought. With this, stalked through her a cold, bloody rage. Hours of this. A period of introspection, a space of retrospection, then a mixture of both. Out of this an awful calm.

"Well, Ah done de bes' Ah could. If things aint right, Gawd knows taint mah fault."

She went to sleep—a twitchy sleep—and woke up to a faint gray sky. There was a loud hollow sound below. She peered out, Sykes was at the wood-pile, demolishing a wire-covered box.

He hurried to the kitchen door, but hung outside there some minutes before he entered, and stood some minutes more inside before he closed it after him.

The gray in the sky was spreading. Delia descended without fear now, and crouched beneath the low bedroom window. The drawn shade shut out the dawn, shut in the night. But the thin walls held back no sound.

"Dat ol' scratch is woke up now!" She mused at the tremendous whirr inside, which every woodsman knows, is one of the sound illusions. The rattler is a ventriloquist. His whirr sounds to the right, to the left, straight ahead, behind, close under foot—everywhere but where it is. Woe to him who guesses wrong unless he is prepared to hold up his end of the argument! Sometimes he strikes without rattling at all.

Inside, Sykes heard nothing until he knocked a pot lid off the stove while trying to reach the match safe in the dark. He had emptied his pockets at Bertha's.

The snake seemed to wake up under the stove and Sykes made a quick leap into the bedroom. In spite of the gin he had had, his head was clearing now.

"Mah Gawd!" he chattered, "ef Ah could on'y strack uh light!"

The rattling ceased for a moment as he stood paralyzed. He waited. It seemed that the snake waited also.

"Oh, fuh de light! Ah thought he'd be too sick"—Sykes was muttering to himself when the whirr began again, closer, right underfoot this time. Long before this, Sykes' ability to think had been flattened down to primitive instinct and he leaped—onto the bed.

Outside Delia heard a cry that might have come from a maddened chimpanzee, a stricken gorilla. All the terror, all the horror, all the rage that man possibly could express, without a recognizable human sound.

A tremendous stir inside there, another series of animal screams, the intermittent whirr of the reptile. The shade torn violently down from the window, letting in the red dawn, a huge brown hand seizing the window stick, great dull blows upon the wooden floor punctuating the gibberish of sound long after the rattle of the snake had abruptly subsided. All this Delia could see and hear from her place beneath the window, and it made her ill. She crept over to the four-o'clocks and stretched herself on the cool earth to recover.

She lay there. "Delia, Delia!" She could hear Sykes calling in a most despairing tone as one who expected no answer. The sun crept on up, and he called. Delia could not move—her legs were gone flabby. She never moved, he called, and the sun kept rising.

"Mah Gawd!" She heard him moan, "Mah Gawd fum Heben!" She heard him stumbling about and got up from her flower-bed. The sun was growing warm. As she approached the door she heard him call out hopefully, "Delia, is dat you Ah heah?"

She saw him on his hands and knees as soon as she reached the door. He crept an inch or two toward her—all that he was able, and she saw his horribly swollen neck and his one open eye shining with hope. A surge of pity too strong to support bore her away from that eye that must, could not, fail to see the tubs. He would see the lamp. Orlando with its doctors was too far. She could scarcely reach the Chinaberry tree, where she waited in the growing heat while inside she knew the cold river was creeping up and up to extinguish that eye which must know by now that she knew.

from *Fire!*, November 1926

The Scottsboro Cases

The series of cases involving nine young African-American men convicted of a capital crime on scant evidence became an international cause during the 1930s and led to two significant Supreme Court rulings concerning fundamental constitutional rights.

The case originated in Scottsboro, Alabama, when nine young men between the ages of thirteen and twenty-one were arrested for the alleged rape of two white women, one of whom was an admitted prostitute, on a freight train they were all riding on March 25, 1931. After a trial that lasted less than two weeks, an all-white jury found eight of the men guilty and sentenced them to the electric chair; the ninth was sentenced to life imprisonment. The case drew the attention of the National Urban League and the NAACP, which, led by Charles Hamilton Houston, had been pursuing a strategy of securing in the courtroom the civil rights denied African-Americans by the political system, as well as the Communist-backed International Labor Defense.

On appeal, the Alabama Supreme Court set aside one of the convictions but upheld the rest, and appeals were filed with the Supreme Court. In *Powell* v. *Alabama* 278 U.S. 45 (1932), the Court found that the young, uneducated defendants had faced a hostile public with inadequate defense. The Court held that when defendants could neither employ counsel nor defend themselves, the court was obliged to assign appropriate, competent counsel. Though the right to counsel was guaranteed in federal court by the Sixth Amendment, *Powell* established the same right in state courts under the due-process clause of the Fourteenth Amendment.†

The case was remanded to the lower courts, and in March 1933 two of the defendants were given a second trial in a new venue, Morgan County, Alabama. Though the defense team led by prominent attorney Samuel Leibowitz produced witnesses who stated that they had "never known of a single instance where any negro sat on any grand or petit jury in the entire history of that county," the young men were again convicted and sentenced to death, to even more widespread protests. The case was appealed to the Supreme Court, which ruled on April 1, 1935, in *Norris* v. *Alabama* 294 U.S. 587 (1935) that the systematic exclusion of African-Americans from jury lists was a violation of the equal-protection clause of the Fourteenth Amendment.

The case was remanded once more to the lower courts, and under a compromise agreement, charges were dropped against four of the nine men; the others were retried and convicted in 1936 and 1937, receiving sentences ranging from twenty years to life. Though two men had been paroled earlier, the last of the convicted defendants was not released until 1950. In 1966 Judge James Edwin Horton claimed that confidential information not presented in the trial proved the defendants innocent.

Throughout the decade, numerous marches and demonstrations were staged to protest what was widely viewed as the manipulation and exploitation of both African-Americans and the working class.

Appeal of the Scottsboro Boys

"Us poor boys been sentenced to burn up on the electric chair for the reason we is workers—and the color of our skin is black. . . ."

FROM THE DEATH CELL HERE IN KILBY PRISON, EIGHT OF US Scottsboro boys is writing this to you.

We have been sentenced to die for something we ain't never done. Us poor boys been sentenced to burn up on the electric chair for the reason that we is workers—and the color of our skin is black. We like any one of you workers is none of us older than 20. Two of us is 14 and one is 13 years old.

What we guilty of? Nothing but being out of a job. Nothing but looking for work. Our kinfolk was starving for food. We wanted to help them out. So we hopped a freight—just like any one of you workers might a done—to go down to Mobile to hunt work. We was taken off the train by a mob and framed up on rape charges.

At the trial they give us in Scottsboro we could hear the crowds yelling, "Lynch the Niggers." We could see them toting those big shotguns. Call 'at a fair trial?

And while we lay here in jail, the boss-man make us watch 'em burning up other Negroes on the electric chair. "This is what you'll get," they say to us.

What for? We ain't done nothing to be in here at all. All we done was to look for a job. Anyone of you might have done the same thing—and got framed up on the same charge just like we did.

Only ones helped us down here been the International Labor Defense and the League of Struggle for Negro Rights. We don't put no faith in the National Association for the Advancement of Colored People. They give some of us boys eats to go against the other boys who talked for the I.L.D. But we wouldn't split. Nohow. We know our friends and our enemies.

Working class boys, we asks you to save us from being burnt on the electric chair. We's only poor working class boys whose skin is black. We shouldn't die for that.

We hear about working people holding meetings for us all over the world. We asks for more big meetings. It'll take a lot of big meetings to help the I.L.D. and the L.S.N.R. to save us from the boss-man down here.

Help us boys. We ain't done nothing wrong. We are only workers like you are. Only our skin is black.

Andy Wright, Olen Montgomery, Ozie Powell, Charlie Weems, Clarence Norris, Haywood Patterson, Eugene Williams, Willie Robertson.

April 1, 1932

The Negro Worker, May 1932

Joe Louis
(1914–1981)

In 1937 Joe Louis became the first African-American heavyweight boxing champion since Jack Johnson† held the title in 1905, and, like Johnson, this son of an Alabama sharecropper who had achieved international fame took on the outsized significance that pugilist champions have always held for the American public.

Louis neared his path to the top when he defeated Primo Carnera of Italy at Yankee Stadium on June 25, 1935. The fight took on symbolic overtones as the triumph of a black American somehow seemed to represent a victory over Italy, which was in the midst of a campaign of aggression against Ethiopia. In her autobiography, *I Know Why the Caged Bird Sings,* Maya Angelou describes how "all the Negroes around the world" listened to the Louis-Carnera fight on the radio and how Louis embodied the hopes of his race. Though at first the audience that had gathered in her grandmother's store was optimistic ("I ain't worried 'bout this fight. Joe's gonna whip that cracker like it's open season." "He's gone whip him till that white boy call him Momma."), as Louis faltered, the crowd agonized. "It was like our people falling," she writes. "It was another lynching, yet another Black man hanging on a tree. One more woman ambushed and raped. A Black boy whipped and maimed. It was hounds on the trail of a man running through slimy swamps. It was a white woman slapping her maid for being forgetful. . . . This might be the end of the world. If Joe lost we were back in slavery and beyond help." Richard Wright's account, included here, of the public celebration in the streets of Chicago after Louis knocked out Max Baer in 1935 similarly reveals the burden that Louis bore on his wide shoulders.

The next year, Louis suffered a defeat in a twelve-round fight with ex-champion Max Schmeling, but on June 22, 1937, he claimed the heavyweight title in a fight with James J. Braddock. In his *Autobiography,* Malcolm X recalls the reaction to Louis's achievement: "All the Negroes in Lansing, like Negroes everywhere, went wildly happy with the greatest celebration of race pride our generation had ever known." When Louis won a rematch with Schmeling in 1938, his victory signified the triumph of a black American over the representative of an increasingly bellicose Germany; seemingly fulfilling his destiny as avenger, Louis joined the army soon after. Louis's feats became the stuff of legend and folklore, blues songs and street boasts.

Louis defended his championship twenty-five times to hold the title for a record of nearly twelve years before he retired in 1949. Though he never managed to antagonize white audiences like Johnson had—he said of his fight against Braddock, "I didn't want to hurt him more than I had to"—it was his black followers who fully understood the significance of a white man bowed before a fighter proclaimed the strongest man in the world. As Malcolm X put it, "The ring was the only place a Negro could whip a white man and not be lynched." Plagued with debt and substance addiction in his later years, Louis nonetheless remained immensely popular. He died at the age of sixty-six on April 12, 1981, and was buried, as seems appropriate for this public figure, in Arlington National Cemetery.

Joe Louis Uncovers Dynamite

"Here's a fleeting glimpse of the heart of the Negro, the heart that beats and suffers and hopes—for freedom."

"WUN - TUH - THREEE - FOOO - FIIVE - SEEX - SEVEN - EIGHT - niine-thuun!"

Then:

"JOE LOUIS—THE WINNAH!"

On Chicago's South Side five minutes after these words were yelled and Joe Louis' hand was hoisted as victor in his four-round go with Max Baer, Negroes poured out of beer taverns, pool rooms, barber shops, rooming houses, and dingy flats and flooded the streets.

"LOUIS! LOUIS! LOUIS!" they yelled and threw their hats away. They snatched newspapers from the stands of astonished Greeks and tore them up, flinging the bits into the air. They wagged their heads. Lawd, they'd never seen or heard the like of it before. They shook the hands of strangers. They clapped one another on the back. It was like a revival. Really, there was a religious feeling in the air. Well, it wasn't exactly a religious feeling, but it was the *thing*, and you could feel it. It was a feeling of unity, of oneness.

Two hours after the fight the area between South Parkway and Prairie Avenue on 47th Street was jammed with no less than twenty-five thousand Negroes, joy-mad and moving so they didn't know where. Clasping hands they formed long writhing snake-lines and wove in and out of traffic. They seeped out of doorways, oozed from alleys, trickled out of tenements, and flowed down the street, a fluid mass of joy. White storekeepers hastily closed their doors against the tidal wave and stood peeping through plate glass with blanched faces.

Something had happened, all right. And it had happened so confoundingly sudden that the whites in the neighborhood were dumb with fear. They felt—you could see it in their faces—that *something* had ripped loose, exploded. Something which they had long feared and thought was dead. Or if not dead at least so safely buried under the pretense of good-will that they no longer had need to fear it. Where in the world did it come from? And what was worst of all, how far would it go? Say, what's got into these Negroes?

And the whites and the blacks began to *feel* themselves. The blacks began to remember all the little slights, and discriminations and insults they had suffered; and their hunger too and their misery. And the whites began to search their souls to see if they had been guilty of something, some time, somewhere, against which this wave of feeling was rising.

As the celebration wore on, the younger Negroes began to grow bold.

They jumped on the running boards of automobiles going east or west on 47th Street and demanded of the occupants:

"Who yuh fer—Baer or Louis?"

In the stress of the moment it seemed that the answer to the question marked out friend and foe.

A hesitating reply brought waves of scornful laughter. Baer, huh? That was funny. Now, hadn't Joe Louis just whipped Max Baer? Didn't think we had it in us, did you? Thought Joe Louis was scared, didn't you? Scared because Max talked loud and made boasts. We ain't scared either. We'll fight too when the time comes. We'll win, too.

A taxicab driver had his cab wrecked when he tried to put up a show of bravado.

Then they began stopping street cars. Like a cyclone sweeping through a forest, they went through them, shouting, stamping. Conductors gave up and backed away like children. Everybody had to join this celebration. Some of the people ran out of the cars and stood, pale and trembling, in the crowd. They felt it, too.

In the crush a pocketbook snapped open and money spilled on the street for eager black fingers.

"They stole it from us, anyhow," they said as they picked it up.

When an elderly Negro admonished them, a fist was shaken in his face. Uncle Toming, huh?

"What in hell yuh gotta do wid it?" they wanted to know.

Something had popped loose, all right. And it had come from deep down. Out of the darkness it had leaped from its coil. And nobody could have said just what it was, and nobody wanted to say. Blacks and whites were afraid. But it was a sweet fear, at least for the blacks. It was a mingling of fear and fulfillment. Something dreaded and yet wanted. A something had popped out of a dark hole, something with a hydra-like head, and it was darting forth its tongue.

You stand on the border-line, wondering what's beyond. Then you take one step and you feel a strange, sweet tingling. You take two steps and the feeling becomes keener. You want to feel some more. You break into a run. You know it's dangerous, but you're propelled in spite of yourself.

Four centuries of oppression, of frustrated hopes, of black bitterness, felt even in the bones of the bewildered young, were rising to the surface. Yes, unconsciously they had imputed to the brawny image of Joe Louis all the balked dreams of revenge, all the secretly visualized moments of retaliation. AND HE HAD WON! Good Gawd Almighty! Yes, Jesus, it could be done! Didn't Joe do it? You see, Joe was the consciously-felt symbol. He was the concentrated essence of black triumph over white. And it comes so seldom, so seldom. And what could be sweeter than long nourished hate vicariously gratified? From the symbol of Joe's strength they took strength, and in that moment all fear, all obstacles were wiped out, drowned. They stepped out of the mire of hesitation and irresolution and were free! Invincible! A merciless victor over a fallen foe! Yes, they had felt all that—for a moment. . . .

And then the cops came.

Not the carefully picked white cops who were used to batter the skulls of white workers and intellectuals who came to the South Side to march with the black workers to show their solidarity in the struggle against Mussolini's impending invasion of Ethiopia; oh, no, black cops, but trusted black cops and plenty tough. Cops who knew their business, how to handle delicate situations. They piled out of patrols, swinging clubs.

"Git back! Gawddammit, git back!"

But they were very careful, very careful. They didn't hit anybody. They, too, sensed *something*. And they didn't want to trifle with it. And there's no doubt but that they had been instructed not to. Better go easy here. No telling what might happen. They swung clubs, but pushed the crown back with their hands.

Finally, the street cars moved again. The taxis and automobiles could go through. The whites breathed easier. The blood came back to their cheeks.

The Negroes stood on the sidewalks, talking, wondering, looking, breathing hard. They had felt something, and it had been sweet—that feeling. They wanted some more of it, but they were afraid now. The spell was broken.

And about midnight down the street that feeling ebbed, seeping home —flowing back to the beer tavern, the pool room, the cafe, the barber shop, the dingy flat. Like a sullen river it ran back to its muddy channel, carrying a confused and sentimental memory on its surface, like water-soaked driftwood.

Say, Comrade, here's the wild river that's got to be harnessed and directed. Here's that *something,* that pent-up folk consciousness. Here's a fleeting glimpse of the heart of the Negro, the heart that beats and suffers and hopes—for freedom. Here's that fluid something that's like iron. Here's the real dynamite that Joe Louis uncovered!

from *New Masses,* October 8, 1935

Sterling Brown

(1901–)

If in his lengthy preface to *The Book of American Negro Poetry* (1922) the critic James Weldon Johnson expressed an uneasiness with the use of African-American dialect in verse, he argued nonetheless that Sterling Brown, who first came to prominence during the Harlem Renaissance, had composed an authentic voice from the raw material of African-American folk culture. "More than any other American poet," Johnson wrote, "He has made thematic use of the Negro folk epics and ballads. . . . He has, in fact, done the only thing that justifies the individual artist's taking material of this sort: he has worked it into original and genuine poetry."

Born on May 1, 1901, in Washington, D.C., Brown received his undergraduate education at Williams College, where he was elected to Phi Beta Kappa, and in 1923 he received his M.A. from Harvard. Despite such a highly academic background, Brown found a rich vein for his talents in African-American blues, work songs, sermons, and folktales and he brought blues singers like Ma Rainey, Bessie Smith, and Blind Lemon Jefferson to the attention of the Harlem literati. The poems in his *Southern Road,* published in 1932, are infused with the mythic spirit of Casey Jones, John Henry, and Stagolee, as well as a biting social protest ("They got the shotguns/They got the rope/We git the justice/in the end," as in *Old Lem*).

Brown served as literary editor of *Opportunity,* collaborated with James Weldon Johnson on the 1931 revised edition of *The Book of American Negro Poetry,* and from 1936 to 1939 was an editor with the Federal Writers' Project. His important critical works, *The Negro in American Fiction* and *Negro Poetry and Drama,* were published in 1937, and he edited the ground-breaking anthology *The Negro Caravan* in 1941 with Arthur Davis and Ulysses Lee. Brown has also been an influential teacher at Howard University, New York University, Vassar College, and elsewhere.

Strong Men

The strong men keep coming on.
—Sandburg

They dragged you from homeland,
They chained you in coffles,
They huddled you spoon-fashion in filthy hatches,
They sold you to give a few gentlemen ease.

They broke you in like oxen,
They scourged you,
They branded you,
They made your women breeders,
They swelled your numbers with bastards. . . .
They taught you the religion they disgraced.

You sang:
Keep a-inchin' along
Lak a po' inch worm . . .

You sang:
Bye and bye
I'm gonna lay down dis heaby load. . . .

You sang:
Walk togedder, chillen,
Dontcha git weary. . . .

The strong men keep a-comin' on
The strong men git stronger.

They point with pride to the roads you built for them,
They ride in comfort over the rails you laid for them.
They put hammers in your hands
And said—Drive so much before sundown.

You sang:
Ain't no hammah
In dis lan',
Strikes lak mine, bebby,
Strikes lak mine.

They cooped you in their kitchens,
They penned you in their factories,
They gave you the jobs that they were too good for,

They tried to guarantee happiness to themselves
By shunting dirt and misery to you.

You sang:
  Me an' muh baby gonna shine, shine
  Me an' muh baby gonna shine.
    The strong men keep a-comin' on
    The strong men git stronger. . . .

They bought off some of your leaders
You stumbled, as blind men will . . .
They coaxed you, unwontedly soft-voiced. . . .
You followed a way.
Then laughed as usual.

They heard the laugh and wondered;
Uncomfortable;
Unadmitting a deeper terror. . . .
    The strong men keep a-comin' on
    Gittin' stronger. . . .

What, from the slums
Where they have hemmed you,
What, from the tiny huts
They could not keep from you—
What reaches them
Making them ill at ease, fearful?
Today they shout prohibition at you
"Thou shalt not this"
"Thou shalt not that"
"Reserved for whites only"
You laugh.

One thing they cannot prohibit—
    The strong men . . . coming on
    The strong men gittin' stronger.
    Strong men. . . .
    Stronger. . . .

from *Southern Road,* 1932

Robert Hayden
(1913–1980)

A more academic poet than Sterling Brown, Robert Hayden produced a relatively small body of work, but one which is of enormous intelligence, integrity, and elegance. Born in Detroit in 1913, Hayden attended Wayne State and the University of Michigan. He taught briefly at Michigan, and then at Fisk University, where he remained for twenty-two years. His first volume of poetry, *Heart-Shape in the Dust* (1940) brought him some recognition, and was followed by *The Lion and the Archer* (with Myron O'Higgins) (1948) and *Figure of Time* (1955). But it was *Ballad of Remembrance,* published in London in 1962, and his *Selected Poems,* published in the United States in 1966, that yielded some of his finest work, including "Frederick Douglass" and "Middle Passage" included in this volume.

Though Hayden often used African-American figures and historical events in his work—his poem "Runagate Runagate" includes references to Harriet Tubman, spirituals, and abolitionist poetry, while "Middle Passage" recounts the revolt of slaves on the *Amistad*—Hayden resisted the tendency to see race as the defining quality of his work. Influenced by such modernists as T. S. Eliot and Gerard Manley Hopkins, like Countee Cullen before him Hayden opposed "a kind of literary ghetto," as he called it in his introduction to the anthology of African-American poetry *Kaleidoscope* (1967), and the role of poet as "a species of race-relations man, the leader of a cause, the voice of protest." In the late 1960s Hayden came under attack from more nationalist writers (one immediately juxtaposes his work with that of Amiri Baraka), but he rejected a narrower vision that sought separateness and militancy. As he writes in "Words in the Mourning Time" (1970):

> We must not be frightened nor cajoled
> into accepting evil as deliverance from evil.
> We must go on struggling to be human,

though monsters of abstractions
police and threaten us.

Hayden's later works include *Night-Blooming Cereus* (1972), *Angle of Ascent: New and Selected Poems* (1975), and *Collected Poems* (1985), published after his death, on February 25, 1980, as well as critical essays on music and drama.

Frederick Douglass

When it is finally ours, this freedom, this liberty, this beautiful
and terrible thing, needful to man as air,
usable as earth; when it belongs at last to all,
when it is truly instinct, brain matter, diastole, systole,
reflex action; when it is finally won; when it is more
than the gaudy mumbo jumbo of politicians:
this man, this Douglass, this former slave, this Negro
beaten to his knees, exiled, visioning a world
where none is lonely, none hunted, alien,
this man, superb in love and logic, this man
shall be remembered. O, not with statues' rhetoric,
not with legends and poems and wreaths of bronze alone,
but with the lives grown out of his life, the lives
fleshing his dream of the beautiful, needful thing.

Middle Passage

I

Jesús, Estrella, Esperanza, Mercy:

Sails flashing to the wind like weapons,
sharks following the moans the fever and the dying;
horror the corposant and compass rose.

Middle Passage:
voyage through death
to life upon these shores.
"10 April 1800—
Blacks rebellious. Crew uneasy. Our linguist says
their moaning is a prayer for death,
ours and their own. Some try to starve themselves.
Lost three this morning leaped with crazy laughter
to the waiting sharks, sang as they went under."

Desire, Adventure, Tartar, Ann:

Standing to America, bringing home
black gold, black ivory, black seed.

Deep in the festering hold thy father lies,
of his bones New England pews are made,
those are altar lights that were his eyes.

Jesus Savior Pilot Me
Over Life's Tempestuous Sea

We pray that thou wilt grant, O Lord,
safe passage to our vessels bringing
heathen souls unto Thy chastening.

Jesus Saviour

"8 bells. I cannot sleep, for I am sick
with fear, but writing eases fear a little
since still my eyes can see these words take shape
upon the page & so I write, as one
would turn to exorcism. 4 days scudding,
but now the sea is calm again. Misfortune
follows in our wake like sharks (our grinning
tutelary gods). Which one of us
has killed an albatross? A plague among
our blacks—Ophthalmia: blindness—& we

have jettisoned the blind to no avail.
It spreads, the terrifying sickness spreads.
Its claws have scratched sight from the Capt.'s eyes
& there is blindness in the fo'c'sle
& we must sail 3 weeks before we come
to port."

What port awaits us, Davy Jones'
or home? I've heard of slavers drifting, drifting,
playthings of wind and storm and chance, their crews
gone blind, the jungle hatred
crawling up on deck.

Thou Who Walked On Galilee

"Deponent further sayeth *The Bella J*
left the Guinea Coast
with cargo of five hundred blacks and odd
for the barracoons of Florida:

"That there was hardly room 'tween-decks for half
the sweltering cattle stowed spoon-fashion there;
that some went mad of thirst and tore their flesh
and sucked the blood:

"That Crew and Captain lusted with the comeliest
of the savage girls kept naked in the cabins;
that there was one they called The Guinea Rose
and they cast lots and fought to lie with her:

"That when the Bo's'n piped all hands, the flames
spreading from starboard already were beyond
control, the negroes howling and their chains
entangled with the flames:

"That the burning blacks could not be reached,
that the Crew abandoned ship,
leaving their shrieking negresses behind,
that the Captain perished drunken with the wenches:

"Further Deponent sayeth not."

Pilot Oh Pilot Me

II

Aye, lad, and I have seen those factories,
Gambia, Rio Pongo, Calabar;

have watched the artful mongos baiting traps
of war wherein the victor and the vanquished

Were caught as prizes for our barracoons.
Have seen the nigger kings whose vanity
and greed turned wild black hides of Fellatah,
Mandingo, Ibo, Kru to gold for us.

And there was one—King Anthracite we named him—
fetish face beneath French parasols
of brass and orange velvet, impudent mouth
whose cups were carven skulls of enemies:

He'd honor us with drum and feast and conjo
and palm-oil-glistening wenches deft in love,
and for tin crowns that shone with paste,
red calico and German-silver trinkets

Would have the drums talk war and send
his warriors to burn the sleeping villages
and kill the sick and old and lead the young
in coffles to our factories.

Twenty years a trader, twenty years,
for there was wealth aplenty to be harvested
from those black fields, and I'd be trading still
but for the fevers melting down my bones.

III

Shuttles in the rocking loom of history,
the dark ships move, the dark ships move,
their bright ironical names
like jests of kindness on a murderer's mouth;
plough through thrashing glister toward
fata morgana's lucent melting shore,
weave toward New World littorals that are
mirage and myth and actual shore.

Voyage through death,
voyage whose chartings
are unlove.

A charnel stench, effluvium of living death
spreads outward from the hold,

where the living and the dead, the horribly dying,
lie interlocked, lie foul with blood and excrement.

Deep in the festering hold thy father lies,
the corpse of mercy rots with him,
rats eat love's rotten gelid eyes.

But, oh, the living look at you
with human eyes whose suffering accuses you,
whose hatred reaches through the swill of dark
to strike you like a leper's claw.

You cannot stare that hatred down
or chain the fear that stalks the watches
and breathes on you its fetid scorching breath;
cannot kill the deep immortal human wish,
the timeless will.

"But for the storm that flung up barriers
of wind and wave, *The Amistad,* señores,
would have reached the port of Principe in two,
three days at most; but for the storm we should
have been prepared for what befell.
Swift as the puma's leap it came. There was
that interval of moonless calm filled only
with the water's and the rigging's usual sounds,
then sudden movement, blows and snarling cries
and they had fallen on us with machete
and marlinspike. It was as though the very
air, the night itself were striking us.
Exhausted by the rigors of the storm,
we were no match for them. Our men went down
before the murderous Africans. Our loyal
Celestino ran from below with gun
and lantern and I saw, before the cane-
knife's wounding flash, Cinquez,
that surly brute who calls himself a prince,
directing, urging on the ghastly work.
He hacked the poor mulatto down, and then
he turned on me. The decks were slippery
when daylight finally came. It sickens me
to think of what I saw, of how these apes
threw overboard the butchered bodies of
our men, true Christians all, like so much jetsam.
Enough, enough. The rest is quickly told:
Cinquez was forced to spare the two of us

you see to steer the ship to Africa,
and we like phantoms doomed to rove the sea
voyaged east by day and west by night,
deceiving them, hoping for rescue,
prisoners on our own vessel, till
at length we drifted to the shores of this
your land, America, where we were freed
from our unspeakable misery. Now we
demand, good sirs, the extradition of
Cinquez and his accomplices to La
Havana. And it distresses us to know
there are so many here who seem inclined
to justify the mutiny of these blacks.
We find it paradoxical indeed
that you whose wealth, whose tree of liberty
are rooted in the labor of your slaves
should suffer the august John Quincy Adams
to speak with so much passion of the right
of chattel slaves to kill their lawful masters
and with his Roman rhetoric weave a hero's
garland for Cinquez. I tell you that
we are determined to return to Cuba
with our slaves and there see justice done. Cinquez—
or let us say 'the Prince'—Cinquez shall die."

The deep immortal human wish,
the timeless will:

Cinquez its deathless primaveral image,
life that transfigures many lives.

Voyage through death
                    to life upon these shores.

Richard Wright
(1908–1960)

Working at various times in his life as a dishwasher, clerk, bellhop, delivery boy, street cleaner, and ditch digger, Richard Wright overcame circumstances in his early life faced by few writers of similar international stature. Born Richard Nathaniel Wright near Natchez, Mississippi, the son of a sharecropper and a schoolteacher and the grandson of slaves, he moved with his family to Memphis when he was five. His father soon left the family, and during the next thirteen years Wright would move more than twenty times, living for periods in an orphanage and with relatives in Mississippi and Arkansas as his mother's health deteriorated. He was forced to leave school for the first time at the age of ten to find work, and suffered extreme poverty and chronic hunger. After graduating, remarkably, from the ninth grade as his class valedictorian, in 1925 he moved to Memphis, where he found stability for the first time in his life, reading and writing on his own. In 1927 he left the South and moved to Chicago, where he worked in the post office and at other odd jobs throughout the Depression. He continued writing and read the works of Mencken, Dreiser, Conrad, Sinclair Lewis, Sherwood Anderson, O. Henry, and others. In the early thirties, he joined the literary John Reed Club and then the Communist Party, publishing poems in *New Masses, Anvil,* and *Left Front.* He began work on the novel *Cesspool,* about black life in Chicago (published posthumously in 1963 as *Lawd Today!*), and in 1935 his first piece of journalism, "Joe Louis Uncovers Dynamite,"† was published in *The New Masses.* He joined the Federal Writers' Project and met other Chicago writers, including Arna Bontemps, Margaret Walker, and the sociologist Horace Clayton. In 1937 Wright moved to New York, becoming the editor of the Communist *Daily Worker.* That year his essay, "The Ethics of Living Jim Crow—An Autobiographical Sketch," which is included here, appeared in a WPA anthology (and was later included in a second edition of *Uncle Tom's Children* and developed into his major autobiography). In New York, Wright met the twenty-three-year-old Ralph Ellison, who acted as best man at his wedding. In 1938, Wright's first book, *Uncle Tom's Children: Four Novellas,* depicting the world of violent race prejudice in the

South, was published to favorable reviews. Two years later, *Native Son,* his most important work of fiction, was published.

Documenting a world of limited possibilities in the tenements of Chicago, *Native Son* traces the story of Bigger ("bad nigger") Thomas, a young man played upon by forces of racism and poverty he can't control. He sees society as a "cold and distant world; a world of white secrets carefully guarded," and in the presence of whites he is made to feel "conscious of every square inch of skin on his black body." Motivated by primal instincts, he passes his days "trying to defeat or gratify powerful impulses in a world he feared." When he commits murder, at first accidentally, and then with intent, he experiences for the first time in his life a liberating potential. "He felt that he had his destiny in his grasp," Wright writes. "He was more alive than he could ever remember to have been." His means of escape are futile, however, and society's crushing weight falls around him again. Early in the book, Bigger glimpses another alternative of "solidarity with other black people"—"that one way to end fear and shame was to make all those black people act together." Though this option remains unfulfilled in the novel, Wright's own views that political mass action might end oppression infuse the work as Communist organizers take up Bigger's cause.

Wright elaborated further on the origins and significance of his novel in "How 'Bigger' Was Born," a talk delivered at Columbia University soon after *Native Son* was published. Viewing Bigger as a "meaningful and prophetic *symbol,*" he describes how he determined Bigger's fate as if in a "laboratory," creating scenes and incidents to illustrate "some abstract principle of Bigger's conduct." It is this creaking of ideological gears, as it were, that has caused some critics to fault the novel. Nonetheless, it was an immediate critical and commercial success, selling more than two hundred thousand copies in its first three weeks, and had a profound effect on the American public. With the previous *Uncle Tom's Children,* Wright felt that he had written a book that "even bankers' daughters could read and weep over and feel good about. I swore to myself that if I ever wrote another book, no one would weep over it; that it would be so hard and deep that they would have to face it without the consolation of tears." Despite its flaws, *Native Son* remains a landmark achievement.

After *Native Son,* Wright began work on the novel *The Man Who Lived Underground,* which would be the inspiration for Ellison's *Invisible Man,* and he started writing his autobiography, *American Hunger.* Responding to reservations expressed by the Book-of-the-Month Club about parts of the manuscript, Harper & Row published only the first half of the book as *Black Boy* in 1945, and it became an immediate bestseller. (The second half, picking up with Wright's life in Chicago, was published as *American Hunger* in 1977.) In the fall of 1944, Wright broke publicly with the Party with his essay, "I Tried to Be a Communist," published in the

Atlantic Monthly. At this time he also met twenty-year-old James Baldwin and helped him win an early literary award. The friendship between the two writers ended in 1951 with the publication in *Partisan Review* of Baldwin's essay, "Many Thousands Gone," which severely criticized the sociological overtones of *Native Son* at the expense, Baldwin argued, of art.

In 1947, wearying of the pervasiveness of racism in America, Wright moved to Paris, where his circle included Gertrude Stein, Claude Lévi-Strauss, Jean-Paul Sartre, Simone de Beauvoir, and the poets of negritude Leopold Senghor and Aime Césaire. Attracted to the writings of the existentialists (his own *Native Son* is concerned above all with man's ability to assume control of his life, to act), he started work on the novel, *The Outsider,* published in 1953. He began to study colonialism in Africa, Asia, and other parts of the Third World, and traveled widely in Africa. His later works include the novels *Savage Holiday* (1954) and *The Long Dream* (1959), the essays in *White Man, Listen!* (1957), and works on Africa, Asia, and Spain, none of which achieved the recognition and commercial success of his earlier works.

With insecure finances and declining health, alienated from many of his contemporaries and convinced that his political views had affected his literary career (the FBI had in fact kept files on him since 1942), Wright yet continued to work. On November 26, 1960, Langston Hughes visited him briefly in Paris. Wright died two days later and was cremated, together with a copy of what many critics think his finest work, the autobiographical *Black Boy,* perhaps symbolizing how deeply the incidents of his youth that it recalls remained with him throughout his life. With the posthumous publication of Wright's *Eight Men* (1961), James Baldwin observed, "Wright's unrelentingly bleak landscape was not merely that of the Deep South, or of Chicago, but that of the world, of the human heart."

The Ethics of Living Jim Crow
An Autobiographical Sketch

I

MY FIRST LESSON IN HOW TO LIVE AS A NEGRO CAME WHEN I was quite small. We were living in Arkansas. Our house stood behind the railroad tracks. Its skimpy yard was paved with black cinders. Nothing green ever grew in that yard. The only touch of green we could see was far away, beyond the tracks, over where the white folks lived. But cinders were good enough for me and I never missed the green growing things. And anyhow, cinders were fine weapons. You could always have a nice hot war with huge black cinders. All you had to do was crouch behind the brick pillars of a house with your hands full of gritty ammunition. And the first woolly black head you saw pop out from behind another row of pillars was your target. You tried your very best to knock it off. It was great fun.

I never fully realized the appalling disadvantages of a cinder environment till one day the gang to which I belonged found itself engaged in a war with the white boys who lived beyond the tracks. As usual we laid down our cinder barrage, thinking that this would wipe the white boys out. But they replied with a steady bombardment of broken bottles. We doubled our cinder barrage, but they hid behind trees, hedges, and the sloping embankments of their lawns. Having no such fortifications, we retreated to the brick pillars of our homes. During the retreat a broken milk bottle caught me behind the ear, opening a deep gash which bled profusely. The sight of blood pouring over my face completely demoralized our ranks. My fellow-combatants left me standing paralyzed in the center of the yard, and scurried for their homes. A kind neighbor saw me and rushed me to a doctor, who took three stitches in my neck.

I sat brooding on my front steps, nursing my wound and waiting for my mother to come from work. I felt that a grave injustice had been done me. It was all right to throw cinders. The greatest harm a cinder could do was leave a bruise. But broken bottles were dangerous; they left you cut, bleeding, and helpless.

When night fell, my mother came from the white folks' kitchen. I raced down the street to meet her. I could just feel in my bones that she would understand. I knew she would tell me exactly what to do next time. I grabbed her hand and babbled out the whole story. She examined my wound, then slapped me.

"How come yuh didn't hide?" she asked me. "How come yuh awways fightin'?"

I was outraged, and bawled. Between sobs I told her that I didn't have any trees or hedges to hide behind. There wasn't a thing I could have used as a trench. And you couldn't throw very far when you were hiding behind the brick pillars of a house. She grabbed a barrel stave, dragged me home, stripped me naked, and beat me till I had a fever of one hundred and two. She would smack my rump with the stave, and, while the skin was still smarting, impart to me gems of Jim Crow wisdom. I was never to throw cinders any more. I was never to fight any more wars. I was never, never, under any conditions, to fight *white* folks again. And they were absolutely right in clouting me with the broken milk bottle. Didn't I know she was working hard every day in the hot kitchens of the white folks to make money to take care of me? When was I ever going to learn to be a good boy? She couldn't be bothered with my fights. She finished by telling me that I ought to be thankful to God as long as I lived that they didn't kill me.

All that night I was delirious and could not sleep. Each time I closed my eyes I saw monstrous white faces suspended from the ceiling, leering at me.

From that time on, the charm of my cinder yard was gone. The green trees, the trimmed hedges, the cropped lawns grew very meaningful, became a symbol. Even today when I think of white folks, the hard, sharp outlines of white houses surrounded by trees, lawns, and hedges are present somewhere in the background of my mind. Through the years they grew into an overreaching symbol of fear.

It was a long time before I came in close contact with white folks again. We moved from Arkansas to Mississippi. Here we had the good fortune not to live behind the railroad tracks, or close to white neighborhoods. We lived in the very heart of the local Black Belt. There were black churches and black preachers; there were black schools and black teachers; black groceries and black clerks. In fact, everything was so solidly black that for a long time I did not even think of white folks, save in remote and vague terms. But this could not last forever. As one grows older one eats more. One's clothing costs more. When I finished grammar school I had to go to work. My mother could no longer feed and clothe me on her cooking job.

There is but one place where a black boy who knows no trade can get a job, and that's where the houses and faces are white, where the trees, lawns, and hedges are green. My first job was with an optical company in Jackson, Mississippi. The morning I applied I stood straight and neat before the boss, answering all his questions with sharp yessirs and nosirs. I was very careful to pronounce my *sirs* distinctly, in order that he might know that I was polite, that I knew where I was, and that I knew he was a *white* man. I wanted that job badly.

He looked me over as though he were examining a prize poodle. He questioned me closely about my schooling, being particularly insistent about how much mathematics I had had. He seemed very pleased when I told him I had had two years of algebra.

"Boy, how would you like to try to learn something around here?" he asked me.

"I'd like it fine, sir," I said, happy. I had visions of "working my way up." Even Negroes have those visions.

"All right," he said. "Come on."

I followed him to the small factory.

"Pease," he said to a white man of about thirty-five, "this is Richard. He's going to work for us."

Pease looked at me and nodded.

I was then taken to a white boy of about seventeen.

"Morrie, this is Richard, who's going to work for us."

"Whut yuh sayin' there, boy!" Morrie boomed at me.

"Fine!" I answered.

The boss instructed these two to help me, teach me, give me jobs to do, and let me learn what I could in my spare time.

My wages were five dollars a week.

I worked hard, trying to please. For the first month I got along O.K. Both Pease and Morrie seemed to like me. But one thing was missing. And I kept thinking about it. I was not learning anything and nobody was volunteering to help me. Thinking they had forgotten that I was to learn something about the mechanics of grinding lenses, I asked Morrie one day to tell me about the work. He grew red.

"Whut yuh tryin' t' do, nigger, git smart?" he asked.

"Naw; I ain' tryin' t' git smart," I said.

"Well, don't, if yuh know whut's good for yuh!"

I was puzzled. Maybe he just doesn't want to help me, I thought. I went to Pease.

"Say, are you crazy, you black bastard?" Pease asked me, his gray eyes growing hard.

I spoke out, reminding him that the boss had said I was to be given a chance to learn something.

"Nigger, you think you're *white*, don't you?"

"Naw, sir!"

"Well, you're acting mighty like it!"

"But, Mr. Pease, the boss said . . ."

Pease shook his fist in my face.

"This is a *white* man's work around here, and you better watch yourself!"

From then on they changed toward me. They said good-morning no more. When I was just a bit slow in performing some duty, I was called a lazy black son-of-a-bitch.

Once I thought of reporting all this to the boss. But the mere idea of what would happen to me if Pease and Morrie should learn that I had "snitched" stopped me. And after all, the boss was a white man, too. What was the use?

The climax came at noon one summer day. Pease called me to his workbench. To get to him I had to go between two narrow benches and stand with my back against a wall.

"Yes, sir," I said.

"Richard, I want to ask you something," Pease began pleasantly, not looking up from his work.

"Yes, sir," I said again.

Morrie came over, blocking the narrow passage between the benches. He folded his arms, staring at me solemnly.

I looked from one to the other, sensing that something was coming.

"Yes, sir," I said for the third time.

Pease looked up and spoke very slowly.

"Richard, *Mr.* Morrie here tells me you called me *Pease.*"

I stiffened. A void seemed to open up in me. I knew this was the showdown.

He meant that I had failed to call him *Mr.* Pease. I looked at Morrie. He was gripping a steel bar in his hands. I opened my mouth to speak, to protest, to assure Pease that I had never called him simply *Pease,* and that I had never had any intentions of doing so, when Morrie grabbed me by the collar, ramming my head against the wall.

"Now, be careful, nigger!" snarled Morrie, baring his teeth. "*I* heard yuh call 'im *Pease*! 'N' if yuh say yuh didn't, yuh're callin' me a *lie,* see?" He waved the steel bar threateningly.

If I had said: No, sir, Mr. Pease, I never called you *Pease,* I would have been automatically calling Morrie a liar. And if I had said: Yes, sir, Mr. Pease, I called you *Pease,* I would have been pleading guilty to having uttered the worst insult that a Negro can utter to a southern white man. I stood hesitating, trying to frame a neutral reply.

"Richard, I asked you a question!" said Pease. Anger was creeping into his voice.

"I don't remember calling you *Pease,* Mr. Pease," I said cautiously. "And if I did, I sure didn't mean . . ."

"You black son-of-a-bitch! You called me *Pease,* then!" he spat, slapping me till I bent sideways over a bench. Morrie was on top of me, demanding:

"Didn't yuh call 'im *Pease*? If yuh say yuh didn't, I'll rip yo' gut string loose with this bar, yuh black granny dodger! Yuh can't call a white man a lie 'n' git erway with it, you black son-of-a-bitch!"

I wilted. I begged them not to bother me. I knew what they wanted. They wanted me to leave.

"I'll leave," I promised. "I'll leave right *now.*"

They gave me a minute to get out of the factory. I was warned not to show up again, or tell the boss.

I went.

When I told the folks at home what had happened, they called me a fool. They told me that I must never again attempt to exceed my boundaries. When you are working for white folks, they said, you got to "stay in your place" if you want to keep working.

II

My Jim Crow education continued on my next job, which was portering in a clothing store. One morning, while polishing brass out front, the boss and his twenty-year-old son got out of their car and half dragged and half kicked a Negro woman into the store. A policeman standing at the corner looked on, twirling his nightstick. I watched out of the corner of my eye, never slackening the strokes of my chamois upon the brass. After a few minutes, I heard shrill screams coming from the rear of the store. Later the woman stumbled out, bleeding, crying, and holding her stomach. When she reached the end of the block, the policeman grabbed her and accused her of being drunk. Silently, I watched him throw her into a patrol wagon.

When I went to the rear of the store, the boss and his son were washing their hands at the sink. They were chuckling. The floor was bloody and strewn with wisps of hair and clothing. No doubt I must have appeared pretty shocked, for the boss slapped me reassuringly on the back.

"Boy, that's what we do to niggers when they don't want to pay their bills," he said, laughing.

His son looked at me and grinned.

"Here, hava cigarette," he said.

Not knowing what to do, I took it. He lit his and held the match for me. This was a gesture of kindness, indicating that even if they had beaten the poor old woman, they would not beat me if I knew enough to keep my mouth shut.

"Yes, sir," I said, and asked no questions.

After they had gone, I sat on the edge of a packing box and stared at the bloody floor till the cigarette went out.

That day at noon, while eating in a hamburger joint, I told my fellow Negro porters what had happened. No one seemed surprised. One fellow, after swallowing a huge bite, turned to me and asked:

"Huh! Is tha' all they did t' her?"

"Yeah. Wasn't tha' enough?" I asked.

"Shucks! Man, she's a lucky bitch!" he said, burying his lips deep into a juicy hamburger. "Hell, it's a wonder they didn't lay her when they got through."

III

I was learning fast, but not quite fast enough. One day, while I was delivering packages in the suburbs, my bicycle tire was punctured. I walked along the hot, dusty road, sweating and leading my bicycle by the handlebars.

A car slowed at my side.

"What's the matter, boy?" a white man called.

I told him my bicycle was broken and I was walking back to town.

"That's too bad," he said. "Hop on the running board."

He stopped the car. I clutched hard at my bicycle with one hand and clung to the side of the car with the other.

"All set?"

"Yes, sir," I answered. The car started.

It was full of young white men. They were drinking. I watched the flask pass from mouth to mouth.

"Wanna drink, boy?" one asked.

I laughed as the wind whipped my face. Instinctively obeying the freshly planted precepts of my mother, I said:

"Oh, no!"

The words were hardly out of my mouth before I felt something hard and cold smash me between the eyes. It was an empty whisky bottle. I saw stars, and fell backwards from the speeding car into the dust of the road, my feet becoming entangled in the steel spokes of my bicycle. The white men piled out and stood over me.

"Nigger, ain' yuh learned no better sense'n tha' yet?" asked the man who hit me. "Ain' yuh learned t' say *sir* t' a white man yet?"

Dazed, I pulled to my feet. My elbows and legs were bleeding. Fists doubled, the white man advanced, kicking my bicycle out of the way.

"Aw, leave the bastard alone. He's got enough," said one.

They stood looking at me. I rubbed my shins, trying to stop the flow of blood. No doubt they felt a sort of contemptuous pity, for one asked:

"Yuh wanna ride t' town now, nigger? Yuh reckon yuh know enough t' ride now?"

"I wanna walk," I said, simply.

Maybe it sounded funny. They laughed.

"Well, walk, yuh black son-of-a-bitch!"

When they left they comforted me with:

"Nigger, yuh sho better be damn glad it wuz us yuh talked t' tha' way. Yuh're a lucky bastard, 'cause if yuh'd said tha' t' somebody else, yuh might've been a dead nigger now."

IV

Negroes who have lived South know the dread of being caught alone upon the streets in white neighborhoods after the sun has set. In such a simple situation as this the plight of the Negro in America is graphically symbolized. While white strangers may be in these neighborhoods trying to get home, they can pass unmolested. But the color of a Negro's skin makes him easily recognizable, makes him suspect, converts him into a defenseless target.

Late one Saturday night I made some deliveries in a white neighborhood. I was pedaling my bicycle back to the store as fast as I could, when a police car, swerving toward me, jammed me into the curbing.

"Get down and put up your hands!" the policemen ordered.

I did. They climbed out of the car, guns drawn, faces set, and advanced slowly.

"Keep still!" they ordered.

I reached my hands higher. They searched my pockets and packages. They seemed dissatisfied when they could find nothing incriminating. Finally, one of them said:

"Boy, tell your boss not to send you out in white neighborhoods after sundown."

As usual, I said:

"Yes, sir."

V

My next job was as hall-boy in a hotel. Here my Jim Crow education broadened and deepened. When the bell-boys were busy, I was often called to assist them. As many of the rooms in the hotel were occupied by prostitutes, I was constantly called to carry them liquor and cigarettes. These women were nude most of the time. They did not bother about clothing, even for bell-boys. When you went into their rooms, you were supposed to take their nakedness for granted, as though it startled you no more than a blue vase or a red rug. Your presence awoke in them no sense of shame, for you were not regarded as human. If they were alone, you could steal sidelong glimpses at them. But if they were receiving men, not a flicker of your eyelids could show. I remember one incident vividly. A new woman, a huge, snowy-skinned blonde, took a room on my floor. I was sent to wait upon her. She was in bed with a thick-set man; both were nude and uncovered. She said she wanted some liquor and slid out of bed and waddled across the floor to get her money from a dresser drawer. I watched her.

"Nigger, what in hell you looking at?" the white man asked me, raising himself upon his elbows.

"Nothing," I answered, looking miles deep into the blank wall of the room.

"Keep your eyes where they belong, if you want to be healthy!" he said.

"Yes, sir."

VI

One of the bell-boys I knew in this hotel was keeping steady company with one of the Negro maids. Out of a clear sky the police descended upon his home and arrested him, accusing him of bastardy. The poor boy swore he had had no intimate relations with the girl. Nevertheless, they forced him to marry her. When the child arrived, it was found to be much lighter in complexion than either of the two supposedly legal parents. The white men around the hotel made a great joke of it. They spread the rumor that some white cow must have scared the poor girl while she was carrying the baby. If you were in their presence when this explanation was offered, you were supposed to laugh.

VII

One of the bell-boys was caught in bed with a white prostitute. He was castrated and run out of town. Immediately after this all the bell-boys and hall-boys were called together and warned. We were given to understand that the boy who had been castrated was a "mighty, mighty lucky bastard." We were impressed with the fact that next time the management of the hotel would not be responsible for the lives of "trouble-makin' niggers." We were silent.

VIII

One night, just as I was about to go home, I met one of the Negro maids. She lived in my direction, and we fell in to walk part of the way home together. As we passed the white night-watchman, he slapped the maid on her buttock. I turned around, amazed. The watchman looked at me with a long, hard, fixed-under stare. Suddenly he pulled his gun and asked:

"Nigger, don't yuh like it?"

I hesitated.

"I asked yuh don't yuh like it?" he asked again, stepping forward.

"Yes, sir," I mumbled.

"Talk like it, then!"

"Oh, yes, sir!" I said with as much heartiness as I could muster.

Outside, I walked ahead of the girl, ashamed to face her. She caught up with me and said:

"Don't be a fool! Yuh couldn't help it!"

This watchman boasted of having killed two Negroes in self-defense.

Yet, in spite of all this, the life of the hotel ran with an amazing smoothness. It would have been impossible for a stranger to detect anything. The maids, the hall-boys, and the bell-boys were all smiles. They had to be.

IX

I had learned my Jim Crow lessons so thoroughly that I kept the hotel job till I left Jackson for Memphis. It so happened that while in Memphis I applied for a job at a branch of the optical company. I was hired. And for some reason, as long as I worked there, they never brought my past against me.

Here my Jim Crow education assumed quite a different form. It was no longer brutally cruel, but subtly cruel. Here I learned to lie, to steal, to dissemble. I learned to play that dual role which every Negro must play if he wants to eat and live.

For example, it was almost impossible to get a book to read. It was assumed that after a Negro had imbibed what scanty schooling the state furnished he had no further need for books. I was always borrowing books from men on the job. One day I mustered enough courage to ask one of the men to let me get books from the library in his name. Surprisingly, he consented. I cannot help but think that he consented because he was a Roman Catholic and felt a vague sympathy for Negroes, being himself an object of hatred. Armed with a library card, I obtained books in the following manner: I would write a note to the librarian, saying: "Please let this nigger boy have the following books." I would then sign it with the white man's name.

When I went to the library, I would stand at the desk, hat in hand, looking as unbookish as possible. When I received the books desired I would take them home. If the books listed in the note happened to be out, I would sneak into the lobby and forge a new one. I never took any chances guessing with the white librarian about what the fictitious white man would want to read. No doubt if any of the white patrons had suspected that some of the volumes they enjoyed had been in the home of a Negro, they would not have tolerated it for an instant.

The factory force of the optical company in Memphis was much larger than that in Jackson, and more urbanized. At least they liked to talk, and would engage the Negro help in conversation whenever possible. By this means I found that many subjects were taboo from the white man's point of view. Among the topics they did not like to discuss with Negroes were the following: American white women; the Ku Klux Klan; France, and how Negro soldiers fared while there; French women; Jack Johnson; the entire northern part of the United States; the Civil War; Abraham Lincoln; U. S. Grant; General Sherman; Catholics; the Pope; Jews; the Republican Party; slavery; social equality; Communism; Socialism; the 13th and 14th Amendments to the Constitution; or any topic calling for positive knowledge or manly self-assertion on the part of the Negro. The most accepted topics were sex and religion.

There were many times when I had to exercise a great deal of ingenuity to keep out of trouble. It is a southern custom that all men must take off their hats when they enter an elevator. And especially did this apply to us blacks with rigid force. One day I stepped into an elevator with my arms full of packages. I was forced to ride with my hat on. Two white men stared at me coldly. Then one of them very kindly lifted my hat and placed it upon my armful of packages. Now the most accepted response for a Negro to make under such circumstances is to look at the white man out of the corner of his eye and grin. To have said: "Thank you!" would have made the white man *think* that you *thought* you were receiving from him a personal service. For such an act I have seen Negroes take a blow in the mouth. Finding the first alternative distasteful, and the second dangerous, I hit upon an acceptable course of action which fell safely between these two poles. I immediately—no sooner than my hat was lifted—pretended that my packages were about to spill, and appeared deeply distressed with keeping them in my arms. In this fashion I evaded having to acknowledge his service, and, in spite of adverse circumstances, salvaged a slender shred of personal pride.

How do Negroes feel about the way they have to live? How do they discuss it when alone among themselves? I think this question can be answered in a single sentence. A friend of mine who ran an elevator once told me:

"Lawd, man! Ef it wuzn't fer them polices 'n' them ol' lynch-mobs, there wouldn't be nothin' but uproar down here!"

1937

A. Philip Randolph and the March on Washington Movement

Asa Philip Randolph (1889–1979), the most influential African-American labor leader of the years between the First and Second World Wars, was a lifelong champion of the working class. If Du Bois sought the leadership of a "Talented Tenth" to advance the status of African-Americans, Randolph saw the engine of progress in the remaining ninety percent, those who earned their living in factories and trades.

The son of a minister in the African Methodist Episcopal Church, Randolph was born in Crescent City, Florida. He moved to New York City in 1911 and pursued his education by working days and at night attending City College, where he read Marx and other economic thinkers. In 1917, with Chandler Owen, he founded the liberal journal *The Messenger,* which took a benevolent view of the Bolshevik revolution in the Soviet Union. In 1918, after his article "Pro-Germanism among Negroes" appeared in *The Messenger,* Randolph was sentenced to two and a half years in jail.

In the 1920s and '30s, while some unions like the United Mine Workers had welcomed blacks, many others did not, or admitted them on a segregated basis. In 1925 Randolph founded the Brotherhood of Sleeping Car Porters, the first African-American labor union, which eventually won a contract with the railroads, and in 1936 he was elected president of the newly formed National Negro Congress in Chicago, whose eight hundred members represented a variety of industries and trades. The movement soon became fractured, however, and Randolph resigned four years later as the Congress came under the influence of the American Communist Party.

Randolph's greatest achievement, however, came with the advent of World War II. As the defense industries went into a rapid expansion during the wartime economy and were in desperate need of manpower, they turned away black workers or hired them as janitors or menial laborers. In January 1941 Randolph proposed a march of 50,000 to 100,000 workers in Washington to demand an executive order to end discrimination in hiring in the defense industry, the American military, and government.

By late June the movement had outlined its program, which follows, and many thousands were preparing across the country to march on the Capitol and the White House on July 1. President Roosevelt was anxious to head off the protest, and in New York Mrs. Roosevelt and Mayor Fiorello La Guardia met with Randolph and Walter White of the NAACP. They were unable to dissuade Randolph from his goal, and the President requested that the labor leader meet with him in Washington. Randolph refused to call off the march, and seven days later, on June 25, 1941, the president issued Executive Order 8802, the first presidential decree on race relations since the Emancipation Proclamation, establishing the Fair Employment Practices Committee, signaling the first federal involvement in the economic interests of African-Americans.

Though Randolph called off the demonstration, the March on Washington Movement persisted in mass rallies and speeches. Later that year twenty thousand workers gathered in Madison Square Garden in New York, sixteen thousand met in Chicago, and nine thousand in St. Louis. Explaining the continuation of his efforts, Randolph argued that "vested political interests in race prejudice are so deeply entrenched that to them winning the war against Hitler is secondary to preventing Negros from winning democracy for themselves."

Nearly two million blacks were employed in the defense industry by the end of the war. But though Randolph's victory represented an impressive achievement, the FEPC lacked the ability to enforce the law and was disbanded altogether after the war ended. The executive order had also been limited to employment practices and said nothing about discrimination in military service, which would only be reversed with Truman's Executive Order 9981[†] to integrate the military in 1948.

Randolph remained active in labor and political organizations for the rest of his life. In 1953 he became cochairman of the American Committee on Africa, and in 1960 he headed the Negro American Labor Council. Randolph eventually did march on Washington. In 1962, in his mid-seventies, with Bayard Rustin he helped organize the March for Jobs and Freedom, and on August 28, 1963, 200,000 black and white marchers gathered peacefully on the Mall as Martin Luther King, Jr., John Lewis, and a new generation of African-Americans affirmed that their own dream would not be deferred.

Program of the March on Washington Movement

"We demand the abrogation of every law which makes a distinction in treatment between citizens. . . ."

1. WE DEMAND, IN THE INTEREST OF NATIONAL UNITY, THE ABROGATION OF every law which makes a distinction in treatment between citizens based on religion, creed, color or national origin. This means an end to Jim Crow in education, in housing, in transportation, and in every other social, economic and political privilege; and especially, we demand, in the capital of the nation, an end to all segregation in public places and in public institutions.

2. We demand legislation to enforce the Fifth and Fourteenth Amendments guaranteeing that no person shall be deprived of life, liberty or property without due process of law, so that the full weight of the national government may be used for the protection of life and thereby may end the disgrace of lynching.

3. We demand the enforcement of the Fourteenth and Fifteenth Amendments and the enactment of the Pepper Poll-Tax bill so that all barriers in the exercise of the suffrage are eliminated.

4. We demand the abolition of segregation and discrimination in the Army, Navy, Marine Corps, Air Corps and all other branches of national defense.

5. We demand an end to discrimination in jobs and job training. Further, we demand that the FEPC be made a permanent administrative agency of the U.S. Government and that it be given power to enforce its decisions based on its findings.

6. We demand that federal funds be withheld from any agency which practices discrimination in the use of such funds.

7. We demand colored and minority representation on all administrative agencies so that these groups may have recognition of their democratic right to participate in formulating policies.

8. We demand representation for the colored and minority racial groups on all missions, political and technical, which will be sent to the peace conference so that the interests of all people everywhere may be fully recognized and justly provided for in the postwar settlement.

1942

Executive Order 8802

REAFFIRMING POLICY OF FULL PARTICIPATION IN THE DEFENSE *Program by All Persons Regardless of Race, Creed, Color, or National Origin, and Directing Certain Action in Futherance of Said Policy*

Whereas it is the policy of the United States to encourage full participation in the national defense program by all citizens of the United States, regardless of race, creed, color, or national origin, in the firm belief that the democratic way of life within the Nation can be defended successfully only with the help and support of all groups within its borders; and

Whereas there is evidence that available and needed workers have been barred from employment in industries engaged in defense production solely because of consideration of race, creed, color, or national origin, to the detriment of workers' morale and of national unity:

Now, therefore, by virtue of the authority vested in me by the Constitution and the statutes, and as a prerequisite to the successful conduct of our national defense production effort, I do hereby reaffirm the policy of the United States that there shall be no discrimination in the employment of workers in defense industries or government because of race, creed, color, or national origin, and I do hereby declare that it is the duty of employers and of labor organizations, in furtherance of said policy and of this order, to provide for the full and equitable participation of all workers in defense industries, without discrimination because of race, creed, color, or national origin;

And it is hereby ordered as follows:

1. All departments and agencies of the Government of the United States concerned with vocational and training programs for defense production shall take special measure appropriate to assure that such programs are administered without discrimination because of race, creed, color, or national origin;

2. All contracting agencies of the Government of the United States shall include in all defense contracts hereafter negotiated by them a provision obligating the contractor not to discriminate against any worker because of race, creed, color, or national origin;

3. There is established in the Office of Production Management a Committee on Fair Employment Practice, which shall consist of a chairman and four other members to be appointed by the President. The Chairman and members of the Committee shall serve as such without compensation but shall be entitled to actual and necessary transportation, subsistence and other expenses incidental to the performance of their duties. The Committee shall receive and investigate complaints of discrimination in violation of the provi-

sions of this order and shall take appropriate steps to redress grievances which it finds to be valid. The Committee shall also recommend to the several departments and agencies of the Government of the United States and to the President all measures which may be deemed by it necessary or proper to effectuate the provisions of this order.

FRANKLIN D. ROOSEVELT

THE WHITE HOUSE
June 25, 1941

Truman Integrates the Military

Though African-Americans had fought in every American war since the Revolution, they did so in circumstances far different from whites. Depending on the politics of the time and the exigencies of military necessity, they found themselves constantly subject to the varying policies of those who ultimately did not object to black soldiers putting themselves in front of a bullet, but who seemed unable to sanction their role with the force of policy or law.

Although Crispus Attucks was the first to die in the Boston Massacre and black soldiers fought throughout the Revolution, official policy changed only when manpower was short and the British Lord Dunmore had offered emancipation for those who joined the British troops. More than five thousand African-American soldiers fought in the war, for the most part in integrated units, but after the hostilities ended, in 1792 Congress passed legislation barring blacks from state militias.

In the early stages of the Civil War, blacks were not officially recognized as soldiers as Lincoln tried to placate the slave-holding border states; some white officers claimed that if black troops were raised behind enemy lines, they would stop fighting the rebels and start fighting *them.* In 1862, as war progressed, the Navy and War departments permitted their enlistment, and after the Emancipation Proclamation was made in January 1863, their numbers increased significantly. More than 175,000 African-American soldiers served the Union cause, and on July 28, 1866, Congress passed legislation that blacks could serve in the armed forces.

During World War II, while W. E. B. Du Bois argued in a controversial editorial, "Let us while this war lasts, forget our special grievances and close ranks with our white fellow citizens and the allied nations that are fighting for democracy," African-American soldiers faced institutionalized discrimination. Black soldiers confronted humiliating segregation and abuse in the presence of enlisted men and French troops, who had been advised in the Directive to French Troops† the proper way to regard them. Charles Hamilton Houston, who would become such an important figure in the legal strategy to dismantle segregation in the next several decades, recalled, "The hate and scorn heaped upon us as Negro officers by Americans . . . convinced me that there was no sense dying in a world ruled by them." Black troops found racism less ingrained in French officers; the men of the 370th Regiment were awarded seventy-five Croix de Guerre.

African-American troops faced similar discrimination in World War II. They were often assigned to construction jobs and manual labor and the government established separate blood banks for black and white troops (though an African-American doctor had devised the technique of extracting blood plasma). At Southern bases in the United States, black troops saw German POWs receiving better treatment, and there were outbursts of violence in army bases both in Europe and the U.S. As a manpower shortage developed as the war continued, after the Battle of the Bulge in late 1944, black troops were gradually integrated into the armed forces. About one million African-American men and women served in the war, about half overseas, and many individuals, like Benjamin O. Davis, Jr., and the Tuskegee airmen, served with distinction.

When black troops returned following the war, there was an increase in racial violence; several African-American soldiers were lynched while still in uniform. In 1946 Walter White, head of the NAACP, led a delegation to President Truman to urge an executive initiative. On December 5, 1946, the president issued Executive Order 9808, stating that "the action of individuals who take the law into their own hands and inflict summary punishment and wreak personal vengeance . . . is subversive to our democratic system of law enforcement and gravely threatens our form of government." He established the President's Committee on Civil Rights—the first ever formed by the federal government—to investigate lynchings, unfair employment practices, and voting rights limitations. Their recommendations, contained in the report *To Secure These Rights,* which cited "a moral dry rot" eating away at the bases of democratic beliefs, were ignored by Congress.

Truman's desire to improve conditions in the military was part of his larger civil rights agenda, devised, some argued, for political reasons during an election year. On February 2, 1948, Truman made a special address to Congress, observing that "the Federal Government has a clear duty to see that Constitutional guarantees of individual liberties and of equal protection under the law are not denied or abridged anywhere in our Union. . . . So long as one person walks in fear of lynching, we shall not have achieved equal justice." Expecting little support in the legislature, on July 26, 1948, Truman issued Executive Order 9981, on Equality of Treatment and Opportunity in the Armed Services, which follows. A task force was convened to study the problems of integration, and their report, *Freedom to Serve,* made numerous recommendations, most ineffectually implemented; again, a shortage of manpower in the Korean War (1950–1953) hastened the thrust toward integration. By October 1954, more than six years after the order, integration was officially "completed." An examination of how successful that integration was in putting black and white soldiers on an equal footing in the military was resumed during the Vietnam War.

Executive Order 9981

HEREAS IT IS ESSENTIAL THAT THERE BE MAINTAINED IN THE armed services of the United States the highest standards of democracy, with equality of treatment and opportunity for all those who serve in our country's defense:

Now, therefore, by virtue of the authority vested in me as President of the United States, by the Constitution and the statutes of the United States, and as Commander in Chief of the armed services, it is hereby ordered as follows:

1. It is hereby declared to be the policy of the President that there shall be equality of treatment and opportunity for all persons in the armed forces without regard to race, color, religion, or national origin. This policy shall be put into effect as rapidly as possible, having due regard to the time required to effectuate any necessary changes without impairing efficiency or morale.

2. There shall be created in the National Military Establishment an advisory committee to be known as the President's Committee on Equality of Treatment and Opportunity in the Armed Services, which shall be composed of seven members to be designed by the President.

3. The Committee is authorized on behalf of the President to examine into the rules, procedures, and practices of the armed services in order to determine in what respect such rules, procedures, and practices may be altered or improved with a view to carrying out the policy of this order. The Committee shall confer and advise with the Secretary of Defense, the Secretary of the Army, the Secretary of the Navy, and the Secretary of the Air Force, and shall make such recommendations to the President and to said Secretaries as in the judgment of the Committee will effectuate the policy hereof.

4. All executive departments and agencies of the Federal Government are authorized and directed to cooperate with the Committee in its work, and to furnish the Committee such information or the services of such persons as the Committee may require in the performance of its duties.

5. When requested by the Committee to do so, persons in the armed services or in any of the executive departments and agencies of the Federal Government shall testify before the Committee and shall make available for the use of the Committee such documents and other information as the Committee may require.

6. The Committee shall continue to exist until such time as the President shall terminate its existence by Executive order.

HARRY S. TRUMAN

THE WHITE HOUSE
July 26, 1948

Paul Robeson
(1898–1976)

During the 1930s and 1940s, Paul Robeson, an outstanding scholar, athlete, actor, singer, and an international star loved by millions of people around the world, was one of the most famous men in America; during the following decade he would become one of its most reviled. Born in Princeton, New Jersey, Robeson was the great-great-grandson of a slave who had purchased his own freedom and helped found the Free African Society in 1787. His father had escaped slavery in 1860 at the age of fifteen, traveling North along the Underground Railroad, and had served in the Union Army during the Civil War. A Presbyterian minister, he impressed on his son a strength of character born of a determination to prove that he "could take whatever they handed out."

On an academic scholarship, Robeson attended Rutgers University, where he earned twelve varsity letters and was twice named a football all-American. He was elected to Phi Beta Kappa, was class valedictorian, and after graduation earned a degree from Columbia Law School. While in law school he had continued acting and he gained recognition in 1924 and 1925 in Eugene O'Neill's *All God's Chillun Got Wings* and *The Emperor Jones.* In 1930 he starred as Othello in London and was the first African-American to play the role since the great nineteenth-century actor Ira Aldridge had done so in the 1830s. (In the 1940s Robeson's Othello would establish a record as the longest-running Shakespearean production in Broadway history.) On April 19, 1925, Robeson presented a landmark concert consisting solely of African-American music, which the New York *World* described as "a turning point, one of those thin points of time in which a star is born and not yet visible—the first appearance of this folk wealth to be made without deference or apology." At the same time that his fame grew, Robeson was denied service in hotels and restaurants throughout the country.

In 1927 he and his wife moved to London, where he lived for the next twelve years. There he became sympathetic to the condition of the British working class, and he went to Spain in 1938 in support of the anti-Fascist forces. He made several trips to Russia, where, he later said, "I felt for the first time like a full human being," and developed an appreciation for African culture; in a 1934 essay he wrote, "in my music, my plays, my films, I want to carry always this central idea: to be African." In 1937 he founded the Council on African Affairs to aid independence movements there. He continued to study, eventually becoming fluent in more than twenty languages. Ascribing his gift to the African oral tradition, he claimed, "I hear my way through the world."

Robeson returned to the United States in 1939, and while continuing to give concerts, he began speaking out about labor issues, lynching, and African independence. He developed ties with American Communists, though he never joined the party, and vocally opposed the Cold War. When he argued at a World Peace Conference in Paris on April 20, 1949, that it was "unthinkable that American Negroes could go to war on behalf of those who had oppressed them for generations . . . against a country which in one generation has raised our people to full human dignity," the backlash was swift. His appearance at two concerts in Peekskill, New York, in August-September 1949 ended in riots and his life was threatened. Though he was not charged formally with any crime, he was banned from appearances on radio, television, and the stage, and in 1950 his passport was revoked.

Robeson denounced his treatment unsparingly, testifying before the House Un-American Activities Committee on July 23, 1956, that "my father was a slave, and my people died to build this country, and I am going to stay here and have a part of it just like you. And no Fascist-minded people will drive me from it. Is that clear?" In his 1958 autobiography, *Here I Stand,* he wrote: "I care nothing—less than nothing about what the lords of the land, the Big White Folks, think of me and my ideas. For more than ten years they have persecuted me in every way they could —by slander and mob violence, by denying me the right to practice my profession as an artist, by withholding my right to travel abroad." Robeson defied the ban and in 1958 traveled to Europe. Plagued by illness, he returned five years later. Though he received numerous awards over the next few years, he continued to decline and made few public appearances before his death on January 27, 1976.

In the intervening decades, Robeson's reputation has been restored and he is now recognized as an American of rare talent, integrity, deep love of humanity, and courage, whose political activism preceded leaders of the next generation. "Paul Robeson was a brother of Malcolm X, Stokely Carmichael, Rap Brown, Huey Newton, Eldridge Cleaver," writes historian Eric Bentley, "before they were there to take his hand." Ozzie Davis, who later eulogized Malcolm X in similar terms, wrote of him, "Paul was a man and a half, and we have no category, even now, to hold the size of him."

Statement to the House Un-American Activities Committee

"It is my firm intention to continue to speak out against injustices to the Negro people. . . ."

IT IS A SAD AND BITTER COMMENTARY ON THE STATE OF CIVIL liberties in America that the very forces of reaction, typified by Representative Francis Walter and his Senate counterparts, who have denied me access to the lecture podium, the concert hall, the opera house, and the dramatic stage, now have me before a committee of inquisition in order to hear what I have to say. It is obvious that those who are trying to gag me here and abroad will scarcely grant me the freedom to express myself fully in a hearing controlled by them.

It would be more fitting for me to question Walter, Eastland and Dulles than for them to question me, for it is they who should be called to account for their conduct, not I. Why does Walter not investigate the truly "un-American" activities of Eastland and his gang, to whom the Constitution is a scrap of paper when invoked by the Negro people and to whom defiance of the Supreme Court is a racial duty? And how can Eastland pretend concern over the internal security of our country while he supports the most brutal assaults on fifteen million Americans by the white citizens councils and the Ku Klux Klan? When will Dulles explain his reckless irresponsible "brink of war" policy by which the world might have been destroyed.

And specifically, why is Dulles afraid to let me have a passport, to let me travel abroad to sing, to act, to speak my mind? This question has been practically answered by State Department lawyers who have asserted in court that the State Department claims the right to deny me a passport because of what they called my "recognized status as a spokesman for large sections of Negro Americans" and because I have "been for years extremely active in behalf of independence of colonial peoples of Africa." The State Department has also based its denial of a passport to me on the fact that I sent a message of greeting to the Bandung Conference, convened by Nehru, Sukarno and other great leaders of the colored peoples of the world. Principally, however, Dulles objects to speeches I have made abroad against the oppression suffered by my people in the United States.

I am proud that those statements can be made about me. It is my firm intention to continue to speak out against injustices to the Negro people, and I shall continue to do all within my power in behalf of independence of colonial peoples of Africa. It is for Dulles to explain why a Negro who opposes colonialism and supports the aspirations of Negro Americans should for those reasons be denied a passport.

My fight for a passport is a struggle for freedom—freedom to travel, freedom to earn a livelihood, freedom to speak, freedom to express myself artistically and culturally. I have been denied these freedoms because Dulles, Eastland, Walter and their ilk oppose my views on colonial liberation, my resistance to oppression of Negro Americans, and my burning desire for peace with all nations! But these are views which I shall proclaim whenever given the opportunity, whether before this committee or any other body.

President Eisenhower has strongly urged the desirability of international cultural exchanges. I agree with him. The American people would welcome artistic performances by the great singers, actors, ballet troupes, opera companies, symphony orchestras and virtuosos of South America, Europe, Africa and Asia, including the folk and classic art of the African peoples, the ancient culture of China, as well as the artistic works of the western world. I hope the day will come soon when Walter will consent to lowering the cruel bars which deny the American people the right to witness performances of many great foreign artists. It is certainly high time for him to drop the ridiculous "Keystone Kop" antics of fingerprinting distinguished visitors.

I find no such restrictions placed upon me abroad as Walter has had placed upon foreign artists whose performances the American people wish to see and hear. I have been invited to perform all over the world, and only the arbitrary denial of a passport has prevented realization of this particular aspect of the cultural exchange which the President favors. . . .

There is no doubt that the governments of those countries and many others where I would be invited to sing if I could travel abroad, would have no fear of what I might sing or say while there, whether such governments be allies and friends of America or neutrals or those others whose friendship for the American people is obstructed by Dulles and Walter and like-minded reactionaries.

My travels abroad to sing and act and speak cannot possibly harm the American people. In the past I have won friends for the real America among the millions before whom I have performed—not for Walter, not for Dulles, not for Eastland, not for the racists who disgrace our country's name—but friends for the American Negro, our workers, our farmers, our artists.

By continuing the struggle at home and abroad for peace and friendship with all of the world's people, for an end to colonialism, for full citizenship for Negro Americans, for a world in which art and culture may abound, I intend to continue to win friends for the best in American life.

July 13, 1956

Gwendolyn Brooks
(1917–)

Born in Topeka, Kansas, Gwendolyn Brooks grew up in the black community of Chicago that figures in much of her poetry. In 1945 her first volume, *A Street in Bronzeville,* representing a new urban poetry about life in the streets and tenements in Chicago, was published to critical acclaim and garnered her an award from the American Academy of Arts and Letters and a Guggenheim Fellowship. Her second volume, *Annie Allen,* published in 1949, received the Pulitzer Prize the following year. Her early poems, what she referred to as her "conditioned" poetry, often refer to the way political events impact on the individual, the psychological stresses of urban life, and personal loss occasioned by the constraints of social and economic circumstances. From her work of the 1960s and beyond, she responded to the Black Arts aesthetic with a "new consciousness." As she writes in "Primer for Blacks," "Blackness / is a title, / is a preoccupation / is a commitment Blacks / are to comprehend — / and in which you are / to perceive your Glory." There is in Brooks's work also a keen sense of community, continuity, and heritage and she has served as a generous advisor to younger poets, writing the introduction to Etheridge Knight's *Poems from Prison.* A prolific writer, Brooks has published more than fifteen volumes, including *Bronzeville Boys and Girls* (1956), *The Bean Eaters* (1961), *In the Mecca* (1968), *Riot* (1969), *Family Pictures* (1970), *Aloneness* (1971), *Beckonings* (1975), *The Near-Johannesburg Boy and Other Poems* (1986), *Blacks* (1987), and *Winnie* (1988). She is also the author of a novel, *Maud Martha* (1953), and the autobiography *Report from Part One* (1972).

The Mother

Abortions will not let you forget.
You remember the children you got that you did not get,
The damp small pulps with a little or with no hair,
The singers and workers that never handled the air.
You will never neglect or beat
Them, or silence or buy with a sweet.
You will never wind up the sucking-thumb
Or scuttle off ghosts that come.
You will never leave them, controlling your luscious sigh,
Return for a snack of them, with gobbling mother-eye.

I have heard in the voices of the wind the voices of my dim killed children.
I have contracted. I have eased
My dim dears at the breasts they could never suck.
I have said, Sweets, if I sinned, if I seized
Your luck
And your lives from your unfinished reach,
If I stole your births and your names,
Your straight baby tears and your games,
Your stilted or lovely loves, your tumults, your marriages, aches, and your deaths,
If I poisoned the beginnings of your breaths,
Believe that even in my deliberateness I was not deliberate.
Though why should I whine,
Whine that the crime was other than mine?—
Since anyhow you are dead.
Or rather, or instead,
You were never made.
But that too, I am afraid,
Is faulty: oh, what shall I say, how is the truth to be said?
You were born, you had body, you died.
It is just that you never giggled or planned or cried.

Believe me, I loved you all.
Believe me, I knew you, though faintly, and I loved, I loved you
All.

We Real Cool

The Pool Players
Seven at the Golden Shovel.

We real cool. We
Left school. We

Lurk late. We
Strike straight. We

Sing sin. We
Thin gin. We

Jazz June. We
Die soon.

The Chicago Defender Sends a Man to Little Rock

FALL, 1957

In Little Rock the people bear
Babes, and comb and part their hair
And watch the want ads, put repair
To roof and latch. While wheat toast burns
A woman waters multiferns.

Time upholds or overturns
The many, tight, and small concerns.

In Little Rock the people sing
Sunday hymns like anything,
Through Sunday pomp and polishing.

And after testament and tunes,
Some soften Sunday afternoons
With lemon tea and Lorna Doones.

I forecast
And I believe

Come Christmas Little Rock will cleave
To Christmas tree and trifle, weave,
From laugh and tinsel, texture fast.

In Little Rock is baseball; Barcarolle.
That hotness in July . . . the uniformed figures raw and implacable
And not intellectual,
Batting the hotness or clawing the suffering dust.
The Open Air Concert, on the special twilight green. . . .
When Beethoven is brutal or whispers to lady-like air.
Blanket-sitters are solemn, as Johann troubles to lean
To tell them what to mean. . . .

There is love, too, in Little Rock. Soft women softly
Opening themselves in kindness,
Or, pitying one's blindness,
Awaiting one's pleasure
In azure
Glory with anguished rose at the root. . . .
To wash away old semi-discomfitures.
They re-teach purple and unsullen blue.
The wispy soils go. And uncertain
Half-havings have they clarified to sures.

In Little Rock they know
Not answering the telephone is a way of rejecting life,
That it is our business to be bothered, is our business
To cherish bores or boredom, be polite
To lies and love and many-faceted fuzziness.
I scratch my head, massage the hate-I-had.
I blink across my prim and pencilled pad.
The saga I was sent for is not down.
Because there is a puzzle in this town.
The biggest News I do not dare
Telegraph to the Editor's chair:
"They are like people everywhere."

The angry Editor would reply
In hundred harryings of Why.
And true, they are hurling spittle, rock,
Garbage and fruit in Little Rock.
And I saw coiling storm a-writhe
On bright madonnas. And a scythe
Of men harassing brownish girls.
(The bows and barrettes in the curls
And braids declined away from joy.)

I saw a bleeding brownish boy. . . .

The lariat lynch-wise I deplored.

The loveliest lynchee was our Lord.

Ralph Ellison
(1914–)

Few writers' reputations have rested so securely on the basis of a single volume as Ralph Ellison's does on his only novel, *Invisible Man.* If Richard Wright's early years were almost unremittingly bleak, Ellison found in his youth a world of possibility, despite society's pervasive racism. Belonging neither to the urban North nor the rural South, he was born in Oklahoma City into a Midwestern black culture steeped in its own rhythms and legends. Influenced by his father, an avid reader who named his son Ralph Waldo Ellison, and his grandmother, a militant black woman who was a local organizer for the Socialist Party, Ellison developed the ability to see "heroes and ideals" wherever he found them, in "jazzmen and prize fighters, ballplayers and tap dancers; in gesture, inflection, intonation, timbre and phrasing. Indeed, in all those nuances of expression and attitude which reveal a culture." In this liberating environment, he developed early on his often expressed concept of the Renaissance Man. "We felt, among ourselves at least," he writes, "that we were supposed to be whoever we would and could be and do anything and everything which other boys did, and do it better. Not defensively, because we were ordered to do so; nor because it was held in the society at large that we were naturally, as Negroes, limited—but because we demanded it of ourselves. Because to measure up to our own standards was the only way of affirming our notion of manhood."

Drawn to the cadences of jazz and blues, Ellison aspired to be a musician, and in 1933 he entered Tuskegee Institute, where he began his musical training. Soon, however, he found the limited possibilities there stultifying, and after his junior year he left school and traveled North to work in New York. Through Langston Hughes, he met Richard Wright, who had moved to New York from Chicago in 1937, and Wright urged the young man to read Conrad, James, Dostoyevsky, and to study the craft of writing. Ellison began to contribute fiction and essays to Progressive journals like *New Masses, Common Ground,* and *The Negro Quarterly* and analyzed Wright's autobiography, *Black Boy,* in an article in *The Antioch*

Review in the summer of 1945. "One might say that with these thin essays," Ellison wrote later, "I was launched full flight into the dark."

Ellison continued to write while in the Merchant Marine during the Second World War, and at a publisher's encouragement he began work on a novel. Published in 1952, *Invisible Man* was quickly recognized as one of the most important American novels of the postwar era. In a narrative that mixes surrealism, naturalism, history, philosophy, and the found poetry of black folk culture and blues, Ellison's unnamed protagonist follows a trajectory from a conservative Southern college (not unlike Tuskegee) to the political and cultural ferment of the streets of Harlem. In a series of shifting scenes underscored with a tension between the literal and the figurative, literary art and the vernacular, and metaphors of sight and blindness, lightness and dark, the novel illuminates the central dramas of African-American history, from slavery to Reconstruction to the alienation of the twentieth century. Like the central figure of the slave narrative, who represented both himself and millions of his enslaved brethren, Ellison's antihero suggests in the book's epilogue, "Who knows but that, on the lower frequencies, I speak for you?" The first chapter of the book, which follows, reveals a literary landscape that takes on the mixed character of a nightmare and a dream.

In 1964, Ellison published *Shadow and Act,* a collection of his essays from the previous two decades grouped around the themes of black literature and folklore, black musical expression, and "the complex relationship between the Negro American subculture and North America as a whole." A second collection, *Going to the Territory,* was published in 1986, and since 1955 excerpts from a second novel-in-progress have been published, the most well known of which is the piece "And Hickman Arrives." A member of the American Academy of Arts, he has lectured widely in the United States and Europe, and has taught at the University of Chicago, Columbia, Princeton, Oberlin, and New York University, among other institutions, and has received the Medal of Freedom, the nation's highest civilian award.

While Ellison's output has remained rather limited—"my standards were impossibly high," he acknowledges—he stands with Wright as one of the two towering figures in African-American literature of the mid-twentieth century, and his influence is still felt in the "magical realism" of such contemporary writers as Toni Morrison, Clarence Major, and Charles Johnson.

from *Invisible Man*

"What powers of endurance I had during those days! What enthusiasm! What a belief in the rightness of things!"

CHAPTER 1

IT GOES A LONG WAY BACK, SOME TWENTY YEARS. ALL MY LIFE I had been looking for something, and everywhere I turned someone tried to tell me what it was. I accepted their answers too, though they were often in contradiction and even self-contradictory. I was naïve. I was looking for myself and asking everyone except myself questions which I, and only I, could answer. It took me a long time and much painful boomeranging of my expectations to achieve a realization everyone else appears to have been born with: That I am nobody but myself. But first I had to discover that I am an invisible man!

And yet I am no freak of nature, nor of history. I was in the cards, other things having been equal (or unequal) eighty-five years ago. I am not ashamed of my grandparents for having been slaves. I am only ashamed of myself for having at one time been ashamed. About eighty-five years ago they were told that they were free, united with others of our country in everything pertaining to the common good, and, in everything social, separate like the fingers of the hand. And they believed it. They exulted in it. They stayed in their place, worked hard, and brought up my father to do the same. But my grandfather is the one. He was an odd old guy, my grandfather, and I am told I take after him. It was he who caused the trouble. On his death-bed he called my father to him and said, "Son, after I'm gone I want you to keep up the good fight. I never told you, but our life is a war and I have been a traitor all my born days, a spy in the enemy's country ever since I give up my gun back in the Reconstruction. Live with your head in the lion's mouth. I want you to overcome 'em with yeses, undermine 'em with grins, agree 'em to death and destruction, let 'em swoller you till they vomit or bust wide open." They thought the old man had gone out of his mind. He had been the meekest of men. The younger children were rushed from the room, the shades drawn and the flame of the lamp turned so low that it sputtered on the wick like the old man's breathing. "Learn it to the younguns," he whispered fiercely; then he died.

But my folks were more alarmed over his last words than over his dying. It was as though he had not died at all, his words caused so much anxiety. I was warned emphatically to forget what he had said and, indeed, this is the first time it has been mentioned outside the family circle. It had a tremendous effect upon me, however. I could never be sure of what he meant. Grandfather had been a quiet old man who never made any trouble, yet on his deathbed he had called himself a traitor and a spy, and he had spoken of his meekness as a dangerous activity. It became a constant puzzle which lay unanswered in the back of my mind. And whenever things went well for me I remembered my grandfather and felt guilty and uncomfortable. It was as though I was carrying out his advice in spite of myself. And to make it worse, everyone loved me for it. I was praised by the most lily-white men of the town. I was considered an example of desirable conduct—just as my grandfather had been. And what puzzled me was that the old man had defined it as *treachery*. When I was praised for my conduct I felt a guilt that in some way I was doing something that was really against the wishes of the white folks, that if they had understood they would have desired me to act just the opposite, that I should have been sulky and mean, and that that really would have been what they wanted, even though they were fooled and thought they wanted me to act as I did. It made me afraid that some day they would look upon me as a traitor and I would be lost. Still I was more afraid to act any other way because they didn't like that at all. The old man's words were like a curse. On my graduation day I delivered an oration in which I showed that humility was the secret, indeed, the very essence of progress. (Not that I believed this—how could I, remembering my grandfather?—I only believed that it worked.) It was a great success. Everyone praised me and I was invited to give the speech at a gathering of the town's leading white citizens. It was a triumph for our whole community.

It was in the main ballroom of the leading hotel. When I got there I discovered that it was on the occasion of a smoker, and I was told that since I was to be there anyway I might as well take part in the battle royal to be fought by some of my schoolmates as part of the entertainment. The battle royal came first.

All of the town's big shots were there in their tuxedoes, wolfing down the buffet foods, drinking beer and whiskey and smoking black cigars. It was a large room with a high ceiling. Chairs were arranged in neat rows around three sides of a portable boxing ring. The fourth side was clear, revealing a gleaming space of polished floor. I had some misgivings over the battle royal, by the way. Not from a distaste for fighting, but because I didn't care too much for the other fellows who were to take part. They were tough guys who seemed to have no grandfather's curse worrying their minds. No one could mistake their toughness. And besides, I suspected that fighting a battle royal might detract from the dignity of my speech. In those pre-invisible days I visualized myself as a potential Booker T. Washington. But the other fellows didn't care too much for me either, and there were nine of them. I felt superior to them in my way, and I didn't like the manner in which we were all crowded together into the servants' elevator. Nor did they like my being there. In fact, as the warmly lighted floors flashed past the elevator we had words over the fact that I, by taking part in the fight, had knocked one of their friends out of a night's work.

We were led out of the elevator through a rococo hall into an anteroom and told to get into our fighting togs. Each of us was issued a pair of boxing gloves and ushered out into the big mirrored hall, which we entered looking cautiously about us and whispering, lest we might accidentally be heard above the noise of the room. It was foggy with cigar smoke. And already the whiskey was taking effect. I was shocked to see some of the most important men of the town quite tipsy. They were all there—bankers, lawyers, judges, doctors, fire chiefs, teachers, merchants. Even one of the more fashionable pastors. Something we could not see was going on up front. A clarinet was vibrating sensuously and the men were standing up and moving eagerly forward. We were a small tight group, clustered together, our bare upper bodies touching and shining with anticipatory sweat; while up front the big shots were becoming increasingly excited over something we still could not see. Suddenly I heard the school superintendent, who had told me to come, yell, "Bring up the shines, gentlemen! Bring up the little shines!"

We were rushed up to the front of the ballroom, where it smelled even more strongly of tobacco and whiskey. Then we were pushed into place. I almost wet my pants. A sea of faces, some hostile, some amused, ringed around us, and in the center, facing us, stood a magnificent blonde—stark naked. There was dead silence. I felt a blast of cold air chill me. I tried to back away, but they were behind me and around me. Some of the boys stood with lowered heads, trembling. I felt a wave of irrational guilt and fear. My teeth chattered, my skin turned to goose flesh, my knees knocked. Yet I was strongly attracted and looked in spite of myself. Had the price of looking been blindness, I would have looked. The hair was yellow like that of a circus kewpie doll, the face heavily powdered and rouged, as though to form an abstract mask, the eyes hollow and smeared a cool blue, the color of a baboon's butt. I felt a desire to spit upon her as my eyes brushed slowly over her body. Her breasts were firm and round as the domes of East Indian temples, and I stood so close as to see the fine skin texture and beads of pearly perspiration glistening like dew around the pink and erected buds of her nipples. I wanted at one and the same time to run from the room, to sink through the floor, or go to her and cover her from my eyes and the eyes of the others with my body; to feel the soft thighs, to caress her and destroy her, to love her and murder her, to hide from her, and yet to stroke where below the small American flag tattooed upon her belly her thighs formed a capital V. I had a notion that of all in the room she saw only me with her impersonal eyes.

And then she began to dance, a slow sensuous movement; the smoke of a hundred cigars clinging to her like the thinnest of veils. She seemed like a fair bird-girl girdled in veils calling to me from the angry surface of some gray and threatening sea. I was transported. Then I became aware of the clarinet playing and the big shots yelling at us. Some threatened us if we looked and others if we did not. On my right I saw one boy faint. And now a man grabbed a silver pitcher from a table and stepped close as he dashed ice water upon him and stood him up and forced two of us to support him as his head hung and moans issued from his thick bluish lips. Another boy began to plead to go home. He was the largest of the group, wearing dark red fighting trunks much too small to conceal the erection which projected from him as though in answer to the insinuating low-registered moaning of the clarinet. He tried to hide himself with his boxing gloves.

And all the while the blonde continued dancing, smiling faintly at the big shots who watched her with fascination, and faintly smiling at our fear. I noticed a certain merchant who followed her hungrily, his lips loose and drooling. He was a large man who wore diamond studs in a shirtfront which swelled with the ample paunch underneath, and each time the blonde swayed her undulating hips he ran his hand through the thin hair of his bald head and, with his arms upheld, his posture clumsy like that of an intoxicated panda, wound his belly in a slow and obscene grind. This creature was completely hypnotized. The music had quickened. As the dancer flung herself about with a detached expression on her face, the men began reaching out to touch her. I could see their beefy fingers sink into the soft flesh. Some of the others tried to stop them and she began to move around the floor in graceful circles, as they gave chase, slipping and sliding over the polished floor. It was mad. Chairs went crashing, drinks were spilt, as they ran laughing and howling after her. They caught her just as she reached a door, raised her from the floor, and tossed her as college boys are tossed at a hazing, and above her red, fixed-smiling lips I saw the terror and disgust in her eyes, almost like my own terror and that which I saw in some of the other boys. As I watched, they tossed her twice and her soft breasts seemed to flatten against the air and her legs flung wildly as she spun. Some of the more sober ones helped her to escape. And I started off the floor, heading for the anteroom with the rest of the boys.

Some were still crying and in hysteria. But as we tried to leave we were stopped and ordered to get into the ring. There was nothing to do but what we were told. All ten of us climbed under the ropes and allowed ourselves to be blindfolded with broad bands of white cloth. One of the men seemed to feel a bit sympathetic and tried to cheer us up as we stood with our backs against the ropes. Some of us tried to grin. "See that boy over there?" one of the men said. "I want you to run across at the bell and give it to him right in the belly. If you don't get him, I'm going to get you. I don't like his looks." Each of us was told the same. The blindfolds were put on. Yet even then I had been going over my speech. In my mind each word was as bright as flame. I felt the cloth pressed into place, and frowned so that it would be loosened when I relaxed.

But now I felt a sudden fit of blind terror. I was unused to darkness. It was as though I had suddenly found myself in a dark room filled with poisonous cottonmouths. I could hear the bleary voices yelling insistently for the battle royal to begin.

"Get going in there!"

"Let me at that big nigger!"

I strained to pick up the school superintendent's voice, as though to squeeze some security out of that slightly more familiar sound.

"Let me at those black sonsabitches!" someone yelled.

"No, Jackson, no!" another voice yelled. "Here, somebody, help me hold Jack."

"I want to get at that ginger-colored nigger. Tear him limb from limb," the first voice yelled.

I stood against the ropes trembling. For in those days I was what they called ginger-colored, and he sounded as though he might crunch me between his teeth like a crisp ginger cookie.

Quite a struggle was going on. Chairs were being kicked about and I could hear voices grunting as with a terrific effort. I wanted to see, to see more desperately than ever before. But the blindfold was tight as a thick skin-puckering scab and when I raised my gloved hands to push the layers of white aside a voice yelled, "Oh, no you don't, black bastard! Leave that alone!"

"Ring the bell before Jackson kills him a coon!" someone boomed in the sudden silence. And I heard the bell clang and the sound of the feet scuffling forward.

A glove smacked against my head. I pivoted, striking out stiffly as someone went past, and felt the jar ripple along the length of my arm to my shoulder. Then it seemed as though all nine of the boys had turned upon me at once. Blows pounded me from all sides while I struck out as best I could. So many blows landed upon me that I wondered if I were not the only blindfolded fighter in the ring, or if the man called Jackson hadn't succeeded in getting me after all.

Blindfolded, I could no longer control my motions. I had no dignity. I stumbled about like a baby or a drunken man. The smoke had become thicker and with each new blow it seemed to sear and further restrict my lungs. My saliva became like hot bitter glue. A glove connected with my head, filling my mouth with warm blood. It was everywhere. I could not tell if the moisture I felt upon my body was sweat or blood. A blow landed hard against the nape of my neck. I felt myself going over, my head hitting the floor. Streaks of blue light filled the black world behind the blindfold. I lay prone, pretending that I was knocked out, but felt myself seized by hands and yanked to my feet. "Get going, black boy! Mix it up!" My arms were like lead, my head smarting from blows. I managed to feel my way to the ropes and held on, trying to catch my breath. A glove landed in my midsection and I went over again, feeling as though the smoke had become a knife jabbed into my guts. Pushed this way and that by the legs milling around me, I finally pulled erect and discovered that I could see the black, sweat-washed forms weaving in the smoky-blue atmosphere like drunken dancers weaving to the rapid drum-like thuds of blows.

Everyone fought hysterically. It was complete anarchy. Everybody fought everybody else. No group fought together for long. Two, three, four, fought one, then turned to fight each other, were themselves attacked. Blows landed below the belt and in the kidney, with the gloves open as well as closed, and with my eye partly opened now there was not so much terror. I moved carefully, avoiding blows, although not too many to attract attention, fighting from group to group. The boys groped about like blind, cautious crabs crouching to protect their mid-sections, their heads pulled in short against their shoulders, their arms stretched nervously before them, with their fists testing the smoke-filled air like the knobbed feelers of hypersensitive snails. In one corner I glimpsed a boy violently punching the air and heard him scream in pain as he smashed his hand against a ring post. For a second I saw him bent over holding his hand, then going down as a blow caught his unprotected head. I played one group against the other, slipping in and throwing a punch then stepping out of range while pushing the others into the melee to take the blows blindly aimed at me. The smoke was agonizing and there were no rounds, no bells at three minute intervals to relieve our exhaustion. The room spun round me, a swirl of lights, smoke, sweating bodies surrounded by tense white faces. I bled from both nose and mouth, the blood spattering upon my chest.

The men kept yelling, "Slug him, black boy! Knock his guts out!"

"Uppercut him! Kill him! Kill that big boy!"

Taking a fake fall, I saw a boy going down heavily beside me as though we were felled by a single blow, saw a sneaker-clad foot shoot into his groin as the two who had knocked him down stumbled upon him. I rolled out of range, feeling a twinge of nausea.

The harder we fought the more threatening the men became. And yet, I had begun to worry about my speech again. How would it go? Would they recognize my ability? What would they give me?

I was fighting automatically when suddenly I noticed that one after another of the boys was leaving the ring. I was surprised, filled with panic, as though I had been left alone with an unknown danger. Then I understood. The boys had arranged it among themselves. It was the custom for the two men left in the ring to slug it out for the winner's prize. I discovered this too late. When the bell sounded two men in tuxedoes leaped into the ring and removed the blindfold. I found myself facing Tatlock, the biggest of the gang. I felt sick at my stomach. Hardly had the bell stopped ringing in my ears than it clanged again and I saw him moving swiftly toward me. Thinking of nothing else to do I hit him smash on the nose. He kept coming, bringing the rank sharp violence of stale sweat. His face was a black blank of a face, only his eyes alive—with hate of me and aglow with a feverish terror from what had happened to us all. I became anxious. I wanted to deliver my speech and he came at me as though he meant to beat it out of me. I smashed him again and again, taking his blows as they came. Then on a sudden impulse I struck him lightly and as we clinched, I whispered, "Fake like I knocked you out, you can have the prize."

"I'll break your behind," he whispered hoarsely.

"For *them?*"

"For *me*, sonofabitch!"

They were yelling for us to break it up and Tatlock spun me half around with a blow, and as a joggled camera sweeps in a reeling scene, I saw the howling red faces crouching tense beneath the cloud of blue-gray smoke. For a moment the world wavered, unraveled, flowed, then my head cleared and Tatlock bounced before me. That fluttering shadow before my eyes was his jabbing left hand. Then falling forward, my head against his damp shoulder, I whispered,

"I'll make it five dollars more."

"Go to hell!"

But his muscles relaxed a trifle beneath my pressure and I breathed, "Seven?"

"Give it to your ma," he said, ripping me beneath the heart.

And while I still held him I butted him and moved away. I felt myself bombarded with punches. I fought back with hopeless desperation. I wanted to deliver my speech more than anything else in the world, because I felt that only these men could judge truly my ability, and now this stupid clown was ruining my chances. I began fighting carefully now, moving in to punch him and out again with my greater speed. A lucky blow to his chin and I had him going too—until I heard a loud voice yell, "I got my money on the big boy."

Hearing this, I almost dropped my guard. I was confused: Should I try to win against the voice out there? Would not this go against my speech, and was not this a moment for humility, for nonresistance? A blow to my head as I danced about sent my right eye popping like a jack-in-the-box and settled my dilemma. The room went red as I fell. It was a dream fall, my body languid and fastidious as to where to land, until the floor became impatient and smashed up to meet me. A moment later I came to. An hypnotic voice said FIVE emphatically. And I lay there, hazily watching a dark red spot of my own blood shaping itself into a butterfly, glistening and soaking into the soiled gray world of the canvas.

When the voice drawled TEN I was lifted up and dragged to a chair. I sat dazed. My eye pained and swelled with each throb of my pounding heart and I wondered if now I would be allowed to speak. I was wringing wet, my mouth still bleeding. We were grouped along the wall now. The other boys ignored me as they congratulated Tatlock and speculated as to how much they would be paid. One boy whimpered over his smashed hand. Looking up front, I saw attendants in white jackets rolling the portable ring away and placing a small square rug in the vacant space surrounded by chairs. Perhaps, I thought, I will stand on the rug to deliver my speech.

Then the M.C. called to us, "Come on up here boys and get your money."

We ran forward to where the men laughed and talked in their chairs, waiting. Everyone seemed friendly now.

"There it is on the rug," the man said. I saw the rug covered with coins of all dimensions and a few crumpled bills. But what excited me, scattered here and there, were the gold pieces.

"Boys, it's all yours," the man said. "You get all you grab."

"That's right, Sambo," a blond man said, winking at me confidentially.

I trembled with excitement, forgetting my pain. I would get the gold and the bills, I thought. I would use both hands. I would throw my body against the boys nearest me to block them from the gold.

"Get down around the rug now," the man commanded, "and don't anyone touch it until I give the signal."

"This ought to be good," I heard.

As told, we got around the square rug on our knees. Slowly the man raised his freckled hand as we followed it upward with our eyes.

I heard, "These niggers look like they're about to pray!"

Then, "Ready," the man said. "Go!"

I lunged for a yellow coin lying on the blue design of the carpet, touching it and sending a surprised shriek to join those rising around me. I tried frantically to remove my hand but could not let go. A hot, violent force tore through my body, shaking me like a wet rat. The rug was electrified. The hair bristled up on my head as I shook myself free. My muscles jumped, my nerves jangled, writhed. But I saw that this was not stopping the other boys. Laughing in fear and embarrassment, some were holding back and scooping up the coins knocked off by the painful contortions of the others. The men roared above us as we struggled.

"Pick it up, goddamnit, pick it up!" someone called like a bass-voiced parrot. "Go on, get it!"

I crawled rapidly around the floor, picking up the coins, trying to avoid the coppers and to get greenbacks and the gold. Ignoring the shock by laughing, as I brushed the coins off quickly, I discovered that I could contain the electricity—a contradiction, but it works. Then the men began to push us onto the rug. Laughing embarrassedly, we struggled out of their hands and kept after the coins. We were all wet and slippery and hard to hold. Suddenly I saw a boy lifted into the air, glistening with sweat like a circus seal, and dropped, his wet back landing flush upon the charged rug, heard him yell and saw him literally dance upon his back, his elbows beating a frenzied tattoo upon the floor, his muscles twitching like the flesh of a horse stung by many flies. When he finally rolled off, his face was gray and no one stopped him when he ran from the floor amid booming laughter.

"Get the money," the M.C. called. "That's good hard American cash!"

And we snatched and grabbed, snatched and grabbed. I was careful not to come too close to the rug now, and when I felt the hot whiskey breath descend upon me like a cloud of foul air I reached out and grabbed the leg of a chair. It was occupied and I held on desperately.

"Leggo, nigger! Leggo!"

The huge face wavered down to mine as he tried to push me free. But my body was slippery and he was too drunk. It was Mr. Colcord, who owned a chain of movie houses and "entertainment palaces." Each time he grabbed me I slipped out of his hands. It became a real struggle. I feared the rug more than I did the drunk, so I held on, surprising myself for a moment by trying to topple *him* upon the rug. It was such an enormous idea that I found myself actually carrying it out. I tried not to be obvious, yet when I grabbed his leg, trying to tumble him out of the chair, he raised up roaring with laughter, and, looking at me with soberness dead in the eye, kicked me viciously in the chest: The chair leg flew out of my hand and I felt myself going and rolled. It was as though I had rolled through a bed of hot coals. It seemed a whole century would pass before I would roll free, a century in which I was seared through the deepest levels of my body to the fearful breath within me and the breath seared and heated to the point of explosion. It'll all be over in a flash, I thought as I rolled clear. It'll all be over in a flash.

But not yet, the men on the other side were waiting, red faces swollen as though from apoplexy as they bent forward in their chairs. Seeing their fingers coming toward me I rolled away as a fumbled football rolls off the receiver's fingertips, back into the coals. That time I luckily sent the rug sliding out of place and heard the coins ringing against the floor and the boys scuffling to pick them up and the M.C. calling, "All right, boys, that's all. Go get dressed and get your money."

I was limp as a dish rag. My back felt as though it had been beaten with wires.

When we had dressed the M.C. came in and gave us each five dollars, except Tatlock, who got ten for being last in the ring. Then he told us to leave. I was not to get a chance to deliver my speech, I thought. I was going out into the dim alley in despair when I was stopped and told to go back. I returned to the ballroom, where the men were pushing back their chairs and gathering in groups to talk.

The M.C. knocked on a table for quiet. "Gentlemen," he said, "we almost forgot an important part of the program. A most serious part, gentlemen. This boy was brought here to deliver a speech which he made at his graduation yesterday . . ."

"Bravo!"

"I'm told that he is the smartest boy we've got out there in Greenwood. I'm told that he knows more big words than a pocket-sized dictionary."

Much applause and laughter.

"So now, gentlemen, I want you to give him your attention."

There was still laughter as I faced them, my mouth dry, my eye throbbing. I began slowly, but evidently my throat was tense, because they began shouting, "Louder! Louder!"

"We of the younger generation extol the wisdom of that great leader and educator," I shouted, "who first spoke these flaming words of wisdom: 'A ship lost at sea for many days suddenly sighted a friendly vessel. From the mast of the unfortunate vessel was seen a signal: "Water, water; we die of thirst!" The answer from the friendly vessel came back: "Cast down your bucket where you are." The captain of the distressed vessel, at last heeding the injunction, cast down his bucket, and it came up full of fresh sparkling water from the mouth of the Amazon River.' And like him I say, and in his words, 'To those of my race who depend upon bettering their condition in a foreign land, or who underestimate the importance of cultivating friendly relations with the Southern white man, who is his next-door neighbor, I would say: "Cast down your bucket where you are"—cast it down in making friends in every manly way of the people of all races by whom we are surrounded . . .' "

I spoke automatically and with such fervor that I did not realize that the men were still talking and laughing until my dry mouth, filling up with blood from the cut, almost strangled me. I coughed, wanting to stop and go to one of the tall brass, sand-filled spittoons to relieve myself, but a few of the men, especially the superintendent, were listening and I was afraid. So I gulped it down, blood, saliva and all, and continued. (What powers of endurance I had during those days! What enthusiasm! What a belief in the rightness of things!) I spoke even louder in spite of the pain. But still they talked and still they laughed, as though deaf with cotton in dirty ears. So I spoke with greater emotional emphasis. I closed my ears and swallowed blood until I was nauseated. The speech seemed a hundred times as long as before, but I could not leave out a single word. All had to be said, each memorized nuance considered, rendered. Nor was that all. Whenever I uttered a word of three or more syllables a group of voices would yell for me to repeat it. I used the phrase "social responsibility" and they yelled:

"What's that word you say, boy?"

"Social responsibility," I said.

"What?"

"Social . . ."

"Louder."

". . . responsibility."

"More!"

"Respon—"

"Repeat!"

"—sibility."

The room filled with the uproar of laughter until, no doubt, distracted by having to gulp down my blood, I made a mistake and yelled a phrase I had often seen denounced in newspaper editorials, heard debated in private.

"Social . . ."

"What?" they yelled.

". . . equality—"

The laughter hung smokelike in the sudden stillness. I opened my eyes, puzzled. Sounds of displeasure filled the room. The M.C. rushed forward. They shouted hostile phrases at me. But I did not understand.

A small dry mustached man in the front row blared out, "Say that slowly, son!"

"What, sir?"

"What you just said!"

"Social responsibility, sir," I said.

"You weren't being smart, were you, boy?" he said, not unkindly.

"No, sir!"

"You sure that about 'equality' was a mistake?"

"Oh, yes, sir," I said. "I was swallowing blood."

"Well, you had better speak more slowly so we can understand. We mean to do right by you, but you've got to know your place at all times. All right, now, go on with your speech."

I was afraid. I wanted to leave but I wanted also to speak and I was afraid they'd snatch me down.

"Thank you, sir," I said, beginning where I had left off, and having them ignore me as before.

Yet when I finished there was a thunderous applause. I was surprised to see the superintendent come forth with a package wrapped in white tissue paper, and, gesturing for quiet, address the men.

"Gentlemen, you see that I did not overpraise this boy. He makes a good speech and some day he'll lead his people in the proper paths. And I don't have to tell you that that is important in these days and times. This is a good, smart boy, and so to encourage him in the right direction, in the name of the Board of Education I wish to present him a prize in the form of this . . ."

He paused, removing the tissue paper and revealing a gleaming calfskin brief case.

". . . in the form of this first-class article from Shad Whitmore's shop."

"Boy," he said, addressing me, "take this prize and keep it well. Consider it a badge of office. Prize it. Keep developing as you are and some day it will be filled with important papers that will help shape the destiny of your people."

I was so moved that I could hardly express my thanks. A rope of bloody saliva forming a shape like an undiscovered continent drooled upon the leather and I wiped it quickly away. I felt an importance that I had never dreamed.

"Open it and see what's inside," I was told.

My fingers a-tremble, I complied, smelling the fresh leather and finding an official-looking document inside. It was a scholarship to the state college for Negroes. My eyes filled with tears and I ran awkwardly off the floor.

I was overjoyed; I did not even mind when I discovered that the gold pieces I had scrambled for were brass pocket tokens advertising a certain make of automobile.

When I reached home everyone was excited. Next day the neighbors came to congratulate me. I even felt safe from grandfather, whose deathbed curse usually spoiled my triumphs. I stood beneath his photograph with my brief case in hand and smiled triumphantly into his stolid black peasant's face. It was a face that fascinated me. The eyes seemed to follow everywhere I went.

That night I dreamed I was at a circus with him and that he refused to laugh at the clowns no matter what they did. Then later he told me to open my brief case and read what was inside and I did, finding an official envelope stamped with the state seal; and inside the envelope I found another and another, endlessly, and I thought I would fall of weariness. "Them's years," he said. "Now open that one." And I did and in it I found an engraved document containing a short message in letters of gold. "Read it," my grandfather said. "Out loud!"

"To Whom It May Concern," I intoned. "Keep This Nigger-Boy Running."

I awoke with the old man's laughter ringing in my ears.

(It was a dream I was to remember and dream again for many years after. But at that time I had no insight into its meaning. First I had to attend college.)

1952

James Baldwin
(1924–1987)

Born in Harlem, Baldwin lived an impoverished childhood, dominated by the embittered figure of his stepfather, a minister. At the age of thirteen, he writes in *The Fire Next Time,* as he sensed his friends "settling in for the long, hard winter of life," he became a preacher. "My youth quickly made me a much bigger drawing card than my father. I pushed this advantage ruthlessly, for it was the most effective means I had found of breaking his hold over me." He became disillusioned with the Church, however, and left New York to work in New Jersey as the wartime economy heated up. Confronted with racial discrimination there, he moved to Greenwich Village and began writing articles and reviews for magazines like *The Nation, New Leader,* and *Commentary.* In 1948 he emigrated to Paris, where he wrote his first novel, *Go Tell It on the Mountain,* published in 1953, followed two years later by his important collection of essays, *Notes of a Native Son.*

As Baldwin writes of his experiences as a black American in the United States and in Europe, the essays in *Notes of a Native Son* display the author's active intelligence and the blend of personal autobiography and political critique that are characteristic of his nonfiction. In "Everybody's Protest Novel" and "Many Thousands Gone," Baldwin sharply faults Richard Wright's *Native Son* for its determinism and undervaluation of individual responsibility, arguing that "literature and sociology are not one and the same." Wright had been a mentor to Baldwin, and the criticism ended their friendship. The essay included here, the only one written especially for *Notes of a Native Son,* is one of its most personal.

Baldwin returned to the United States in 1956, and that year his novel *Giovanni's Room,* the first in which he explores the theme of homosexuality, was published, followed by *Nobody Knows My Name: More Notes of a Native Son* in 1961. His next work, *The Fire Next Time,* a sustained meditation on race relations as the civil rights movement was taking hold, fixed his reputation as an essayist. In the book, Baldwin draws parallels between the ways Christianity and Islam had been used to "defeat one's circumstances." He finds, ultimately, that both systems have failed. "In the realm of power," he writes, "Christianity has operated with an unmitigated arrogance and cruelty. . . . The spreading of the Gospel, regardless of the motives or the integrity or the heroism of some of the missionaries, was an absolutely indispensable justification for the planting of the flag." At the same time, he cannot accept the narrow, racist view of the followers of Elijah Muhammad that all white men are devils. "There is nothing new in this merciless formulation," he states, "except the explicitness of its symbols and the candor of its hatred. Its emotional tone is as familiar to me as my own skin." In both theologies, Baldwin argues, "If the concept of God has any validity or any use, it can only be to make us larger, freer, and more loving. If God cannot do this, then it is time that we got rid of Him." He demands, instead, the "transcendence of the realities of color, of nations, and of altars," and a tough kind of grace and courage. "Life is tragic," he writes, "simply because the earth turns and the sun inexorably rises and sets, and one day, for each of us, the sun will go down for the last, last time."

After the publication of these volumes, Baldwin enjoyed increasing celebrity and continued to write novels, stories, essays, and drama—his plays *Blues for Mister Charlie* and *The Amen Corner* were produced on Broadway—while he divided his time between Europe and America.

Baldwin was never comfortable with the mantle of political spokesman, however, and his contention that the races must find common—human—ground fell out of favor in the more militant 1960s; alluding to Baldwin's homosexuality, Eldridge Cleaver, in particular, excoriates Baldwin in a withering essay in *Soul on Ice.* More recently, however, new readers have "come to value just those qualities of ambivalence and equivocality," Henry Louis Gates writes in his recent essay "The Welcome Table," a poignant assessment of Baldwin's career, "just that sense of the contingency of identity, that made him useless to the ideologues of liberation and anathema to so many black nationalists. But then, even his fiercest antagonists have now welcomed him back to the fold. Like everyone else, we like our heroes dead." Baldwin's other works include *Another Country* (1962), *Tell Me How Long the Train's Been Gone* (1968), *No Name in the Streets* (1971), and the best-selling *If Beale Street Could Talk* (1974). His collected nonfiction, *The Price of the Ticket,* was published in 1985.

Notes of a Native Son

"Life and death so close together, and love and hatred, and right and wrong, said something to me which I did not want to hear concerning man, concerning the life of man."

N THE 29TH OF JULY, IN 1943, MY FATHER DIED. ON THE same day, a few hours later, his last child was born. Over a month before this, while all our energies were concentrated in waiting for these events, there had been, in Detroit, one of the bloodiest race riots of the century. A few hours after my father's funeral, while he lay in state in the undertaker's chapel, a race riot broke out in Harlem. On the morning of the 3rd of August, we drove my father to the graveyard through a wilderness of smashed plate glass.

The day of my father's funeral had also been my nineteenth birthday. As we drove him to the graveyard, the spoils of injustice, anarchy, discontent, and hatred were all around us. It seemed to me that God himself had devised, to mark my father's end, the most sustained and brutally dissonant of codas. And it seemed to me, too, that the violence which rose all about us as my father left the world had been devised as a corrective for the pride of his eldest son. I had declined to believe in that apocalypse which had been central to my father's vision; very well, life seemed to be saying, here is something that will certainly pass for an apocalypse until the real thing comes along. I had inclined to be contemptuous of my father for the conditions of his life, for the conditions of our lives. When his life had ended I began to wonder about that life and also, in a new way, to be apprehensive about my own.

I had not known my father very well. We had got on badly, partly because we shared, in our different fashions, the vice of stubborn pride. When he was dead I realized that I had hardly ever spoken to him. When he had been dead a long time I began to wish I had. It seems to be typical of life in America, where opportunities, real and fancied, are thicker than anywhere else on the globe, that the second generation has no time to talk to the first. No one, including my father, seems to have known exactly how old he was, but his mother had been born during slavery. He was of the first generation of free men. He, along with thousands of other Negroes, came North after 1919 and I was part of that generation which had never seen the landscape of what Negroes sometimes call the Old Country.

He had been born in New Orleans and had been a quite young man there during the time that Louis Armstrong, a boy, was running errands for the dives and honky-tonks of what was always presented to me as one of the most wicked of cities—to this day, whenever I think of New Orleans, I also helplessly think of Sodom and Gomorrah. My father never mentioned Louis Armstrong, except to forbid us to play his records; but there was a picture of him on our wall for a long time. One of my father's strong-willed female relatives had placed it there and forbade my father to take it down. He never did, but he eventually maneuvered her out of the house and when, some years later, she was in trouble and near death, he refused to do anything to help her.

He was, I think, very handsome. I gather this from photographs and from my own memories of him, dressed in his Sunday best and on his way to preach a sermon somewhere, when I was little. Handsome, proud, and ingrown, "like a toe-nail," somebody said. But he looked to me, as I grew older, like pictures I had seen of African tribal chieftains: he really should have been naked, with war-paint on and barbaric mementos, standing among spears. He could be chilling in the pulpit and indescribably cruel in his personal life and he was certainly the most bitter man I have ever met; yet it must be said that there was something else in him, buried in him, which lent him his tremendous power and, even, a rather crushing charm. It had something to do with his blackness, I think—he was very black—with his blackness and his beauty, and with the fact that he knew that he was black but did not know that he was beautiful. He claimed to be proud of his blackness but it had also been the cause of much humiliation and it had fixed bleak boundaries to his life. He was not a young man when we were growing up and he had already suffered many kinds of ruin; in his outrageously demanding and protective way he loved his children, who were black like him and menaced, like him; and all these things sometimes showed in his face when he tried, never to my knowledge with any success, to establish contact with any of us. When he took one of his children on his knee to play, the child always became fretful and began to cry; when he tried to help one of us with our homework the absolutely unabating tension which emanated from him caused our minds and our tongues to become paralyzed, so that he, scarcely knowing why, flew into a rage and the child, not knowing why, was punished. If it ever entered his head to bring a surprise home for his children, it was, almost unfailingly, the wrong surprise and even the big watermelons he often brought home on his back in the summertime led to the most appalling scenes. I do not remember, in all those years, that one of his children was ever glad to see him come home. From what I was able to gather of his early life, it seemed that this inability to establish contact with other people had always marked him and had been one of the things which had driven him out of New Orleans. There was something in him, therefore, groping and tentative, which was never expressed and which was buried with him. One saw it most clearly when he was facing new people and hoping to impress them. But he never did, not for long. We went from church to smaller and more improbable church, he found himself in less and less demand as a minister, and by the time he died none of his friends had come to see him for a long time. He had lived and died in an intolerable bitterness of spirit and it frightened me, as we drove him to the graveyard through those unquiet, ruined streets, to see how powerful and overflowing this bitterness could be and to realize that this bitterness now was mine.

When he died I had been away from home for a little over a year. In that year I had had time to become aware of the meaning of all my father's bitter warnings, had discovered the secret of his proudly pursed lips and rigid carriage: I had discovered the weight of white people in the world. I saw that this had been for my ancestors and now would be for me an awful thing to live with and that the bitterness which had helped to kill my father could also kill me.

He had been ill a long time—in the mind, as we now realized, reliving instances of his fantastic intransigence in the new light of his affliction and endeavoring to feel a sorrow for him which never, quite, came true. We had not known that he was being eaten up by paranoia, and the discovery that his cruelty, to our bodies and our minds, had been one of the symptoms of his illness was not, then, enough to enable us to forgive him. The younger children felt, quite simply, relief that he would not be coming home anymore. My mother's observation that it was he, after all, who had kept them alive all these years meant nothing because the problems of keeping children alive are not real for children. The older children felt, with my father gone, that they could invite their friends to the house without fear that their friends would be insulted or, as had sometimes happened with me, being told that their friends were in league with the devil and intended to rob our family of everything we owned. (I didn't fail to wonder, and it made me hate him, what on earth we owned that anybody else would want.)

His illness was beyond all hope of healing before anyone realized that he was ill. He had always been so strange and had lived, like a prophet, in such unimaginably close communion with the Lord that his long silences which were punctuated by moans and hallelujahs and snatches of old songs while he sat at the living-room window never seemed odd to us. It was not until he refused to eat because, he said, his family was trying to poison him that my mother was forced to accept as a fact what had, until then, been only an unwilling suspicion. When he was committed, it was discovered that he had tuberculosis and, as it turned out, the disease of his mind allowed the disease of his body to destroy him. For the doctors could not force him to eat, either, and, though he was fed intravenously, it was clear from the beginning that there was no hope for him.

In my mind's eye I could see him, sitting at the window, locked up in his terrors; hating and fearing every living soul including his children who had betrayed him, too, by reaching towards the world which had despised him. There were nine of us. I began to wonder what it could have felt like for such a man to have had nine children whom he could barely feed. He used to make little jokes about our poverty, which never, of course, seemed very funny to us; they could not have seemed very funny to him, either, or else our all too feeble response to them would never have caused such rages. He spent great energy and achieved, to our chagrin, no small amount of success in keeping us away from the people who surrounded us, people who had all-night rent parties to which we listened when we should have been sleeping, people who cursed and drank and flashed razor blades on Lenox Avenue. He could not understand why, if they had so much energy to spare, they could not use it to make their lives better. He treated almost everybody on our block with a most uncharitable asperity and neither they, nor, of course, their children were slow to reciprocate.

The only white people who came to our house were welfare workers and bill collectors. It was almost always my mother who dealt with them, for my father's temper, which was at the mercy of his pride, was never to be trusted. It was clear that he felt their very presence in his home to be a violation: this was conveyed by his carriage, almost ludicrously stiff, and by his voice, harsh and vindictively polite. When I was around nine or ten I wrote a play which was directed by a young, white schoolteacher, a woman, who then took an interest in me, and gave me books to read and, in order to corroborate my theatrical bent, decided to take me to see what she somewhat tactlessly referred to as "real" plays. Theatergoing was forbidden in our house, but, with the really cruel intuitiveness of a child, I suspected that the color of this woman's skin would carry the day for me. When, at school, she suggested taking me to the theater, I did not, as I might have done if she had been a Negro, find a way of discouraging her, but agreed that she should pick me up at my house one evening. I then, very cleverly, left all the rest to my mother, who suggested to my father, as I knew she would, that it would not be very nice to let such a kind woman make the trip for nothing. Also, since it was a schoolteacher, I imagine that my mother countered the idea of sin with the idea of "education," which word, even with my father, carried a kind of bitter weight.

Before the teacher came my father took me aside to ask *why* she was coming, what *interest* she could possibly have in our house, in a boy like me. I said I didn't know but I, too, suggested that it had something to do with education. And I understood that my father was waiting for me to say something—I didn't quite know what; perhaps that I wanted his protection against this teacher and her "education." I said none of these things and the teacher came and we went out. It was clear, during the brief interview in our living room, that my father was agreeing very much against his will and that he would have refused permission if he had dared. The fact that he did not dare caused me to despise him: I had no way of knowing that he was facing in that living room a wholly unprecedented and frightening situation.

Later, when my father had been laid off from his job, this woman became very important to us. She was really a very sweet and generous woman and went to a great deal of trouble to be of help to us, particularly during one awful winter. My mother called her by the highest name she knew: she said she was a "christian." My father could scarcely disagree but during the four or five years of our relatively close association he never trusted her and was always trying to surprise in her open, Midwestern face the genuine, cunningly hidden, and hideous motivation. In later years, particularly when it began to be clear that this "education" of mine was going to lead me to perdition, he became more explicit and warned me that my white friends in high school were not really my friends and that I would see, when I was older, how white people would do anything to keep a Negro down. Some of them could be nice, he admitted, but none of them were to be trusted and most of them were not even nice. The best thing was to have as little to do with them as possible. I did not feel this way and I was certain, in my innocence, that I never would.

But the year which preceded my father's death had made a great change in my life. I had been living in New Jersey, working in defense plants, working and living among southerners, white and black. I knew about the south, of course, and about how southerners treated Negroes and how they expected them to behave, but it had never entered my mind that anyone would look at me and expect *me* to behave that way. I learned in New Jersey that to be a Negro meant, precisely, that one was never looked at but was simply at the mercy of the reflexes the color of one's skin caused in other people. I acted in New Jersey as I had always acted, that is as though I thought a great deal of myself—I had to *act* that way—with results that were, simply, unbelievable. I had scarcely arrived before I had earned the enmity, which was extraordinarily ingenious, of all my superiors and nearly all my co-workers. In the beginning, to make matters worse, I simply did not know what was happening. I did not know what I had done, and I shortly began to wonder what *anyone* could possibly do, to bring about such unanimous, active, and unbearably vocal hostility. I knew about jim-crow but I had never experienced it. I went to the same self-service restaurant three times and stood with all the Princeton boys before the counter, waiting for a hamburger and coffee; it was always an extraordinarily long time before anything was set before me; but it was not until the fourth visit that I learned that, in fact, nothing had ever been set before me: I had simply picked something up. Negroes were not served there, I was told, and they had been waiting for me to realize that I was always the only Negro present. Once I was told this, I determined to go there all the time. But now they were ready for me and, though some dreadful scenes were subsequently enacted in that restaurant, I never ate there again.

It was the same story all over New Jersey, in bars, bowling alleys, diners, places to live. I was always being forced to leave, silently, or with mutual imprecations. I very shortly became notorious and children giggled behind me when I passed and their elders whispered or shouted—they really believed that I was mad. And it did begin to work on my mind, of course; I began to be afraid to go anywhere and to compensate for this I went places to which I really should not have gone and where, God knows, I had no desire to be. My reputation in town naturally enhanced my reputation at work and my working day became one long series of acrobatics designed to keep me out of trouble. I cannot say that these acrobatics succeeded. It began to seem that the machinery of the organization I worked for was turning over, day and night, with but one aim: to eject me. I was fired once, and contrived, with the aid of a friend from New York, to get back on the payroll; was fired again, and bounced back again. It took a while to fire me for the third time, but the third time took. There were no loopholes anywhere. There was not even any way of getting back inside the gates.

That year in New Jersey lives in my mind as though it were the year during which, having an unsuspected predilection for it, I first contracted some dread, chronic disease, the unfailing symptom of which is a kind of blind fever, a pounding in the skull and fire in the bowels. Once this disease is contracted, one can never be really carefree again, for the fever, without an instant's warning, can recur at any moment. It can wreck more important things than race relations. There is not a Negro alive who does not have this rage in his blood—one has the choice, merely, of living with it consciously or surrendering to it. As for me, this fever has recurred in me, and does, and will until the day I die.

My last night in New Jersey, a white friend from New York took me to the nearest big town, Trenton, to go to the movies and have a few drinks. As it turned out, he also saved me from, at the very least, a violent whipping. Almost every detail of that night stands out very clearly in my memory. I even remember the name of the movie we saw because its title impressed me as being so patly ironical. It was a movie about the German occupation of France, starring Maureen O'Hara and Charles Laughton and called *This Land Is Mine.* I remember the name of the diner we walked into when the movie ended: it was the "American Diner." When we walked in the counterman asked what we wanted and I remember answering with the casual sharpness which had become my habit: "We want a hamburger and a cup of coffee, what do you think we want?" I do not know why, after a year of such rebuffs, I so completely failed to anticipate his answer, which was, of course, "We don't serve Negroes here." This reply failed to discompose me, at least for the moment. I made some sardonic comment about the name of the diner and we walked out into the streets.

This was the time of what was called the "brown-out," when the lights in all American cities were very dim. When we re-entered the streets something happened to me which had the force of an optical illusion, or a nightmare. The streets were very crowded and I was facing north. People were moving in every direction but it seemed to me, in that instant, that all of the people I could see, and many more than that, were moving toward me, against me, and that everyone was white. I remember how their faces gleamed. And I felt, like a physical sensation, a *click* at the nape of my neck as though some interior string connecting my head to my body had been cut. I began to walk. I heard my friend call after me, but I ignored him. Heaven only knows what was going on in his mind, but he had the good sense not to touch me—I don't know what would have happened if he had—and to keep me in sight. I don't know what was going on in my mind, either; I certainly had no conscious plan. I wanted to do something to crush these white faces, which were crushing me. I walked for perhaps a block or two until I came to an enormous, glittering, and fashionable restaurant in which I knew not even the intercession of the Virgin would cause me to be served. I pushed through the doors and took the first vacant seat I saw, at a table for two, and waited.

I do not know how long I waited and I rather wonder, until today, what I could possibly have looked like. Whatever I looked like, I frightened the waitress who shortly appeared, and the moment she appeared all of my fury flowed towards her. I hated her for her white face, and for her great, astounded, frightened eyes. I felt that if she found a black man so frightening I would make her fright worth-while.

She did not ask me what I wanted, but repeated, as though she had learned it somewhere, "We don't serve Negroes here." She did not say it with the blunt, derisive hostility to which I had grown so accustomed, but, rather, with a note of apology in her voice, and fear. This made me colder and more murderous than ever. I felt I had to do something with my hands. I wanted her to come close enough for me to get her neck between my hands.

So I pretended not to have understood her, hoping to draw her closer. And she did step a very short step closer, with her pencil poised incongruously over her pad, and repeated the formula: ". . . don't serve Negroes here."

Somehow, with the repetition of that phrase, which was already ringing in my head like a thousand bells of a nightmare, I realized that she would never come any closer and that I would have to strike from a distance. There was nothing on the table but an ordinary water-mug half full of water, and I picked this up and hurled it with all my strength at her. She ducked and it missed her and shattered against the mirror behind the bar. And, with that sound, my frozen blood abruptly thawed, I returned from wherever I had been, I *saw*, for the first time, the restaurant, the people with their mouths open, already, as it seemed to me, rising as one man, and I realized what I had done, and where I was, and I was frightened. I rose and began running for the door. A round, potbellied man grabbed me by the nape of the neck just as I reached the doors and began to beat me about the face. I kicked him and got loose and ran into the streets. My friend whispered, *"Run!"* and I ran.

My friend stayed outside the restaurant long enough to misdirect my pursuers and the police, who arrived, he told me, at once. I do not know what I said to him when he came to my room that night. I could not have said much. I felt, in the oddest, most awful way, that I had somehow betrayed him. I lived it over and over and over again, the way one relives an automobile accident after it has happened and one finds oneself alone and safe. I could not get over two facts, both equally difficult for the imagination to grasp, and one was that I could have been murdered. But the other was that I had been ready to commit murder. I saw nothing very clearly but I did see this: that my life, my *real* life, was in danger, and not from anything other people might do but from the hatred I carried in my own heart.

II

I had returned home around the second week in June—in great haste because it seemed that my father's death and my mother's confinement were both but a matter of hours. In the case of my mother, it soon became clear that she had simply made a miscalculation. This had always been her tendency and I don't believe that a single one of us arrived in the world, or has since arrived anywhere else, on time. But none of us dawdled so intolerably about the business of being born as did my baby sister. We sometimes amused ourselves, during those endless, stifling weeks, by picturing the baby sitting within in the safe, warm dark, bitterly regretting the necessity of becoming a part of our chaos and stubbornly putting it off as long as possible. I understood her perfectly and congratulated her on showing such good sense so soon. Death, however, sat as purposefully at my father's bedside as life stirred within my mother's womb and it was harder to understand why he so lingered in that long shadow. It seemed that he had bent, and for a long time, too, all of his energies towards dying. Now death was ready for him but my father held back.

All of Harlem, indeed, seemed to be infected by waiting. I had never before known it to be so violently still. Racial tensions throughout this country were exacerbated during the early years of the war, partly because the labor market brought together hundreds of thousands of ill-prepared people and partly because Negro soldiers, regardless of where they were born, received their military training in the south. What happened in defense plants and army camps had repercussions, naturally, in every Negro ghetto. The situation in Harlem had grown bad enough for clergymen, policemen, educators, politicians, and social workers to assert in one breath that there was no "crime wave" and to offer, in the very next breath, suggestions as to how to combat it. These suggestions always seemed to involve playgrounds, despite the fact that racial skirmishes were occurring in the playgrounds, too. Playground or not, crime wave or not, the Harlem police force had been augmented in March, and the unrest grew—perhaps, in fact, partly as a result of the ghetto's instinctive hatred of policemen. Perhaps the most revealing news item, out of the steady parade of reports of muggings, stabbings, shootings, assaults, gang wars, and accusations of police brutality, is the item concerning six Negro girls who set upon a white girl in the subway because, as they all too accurately put it, she was stepping on their toes. Indeed she was, all over the nation.

I had never before been so aware of policemen, on foot, on horseback, on corners, everywhere, always two by two. Nor had I ever been so aware of small knots of people. They were on stoops and on corners and in doorways, and what was striking about them, I think, was that they did not seem to be talking. Never, when I passed these groups, did the usual sound of a curse or a laugh ring out and neither did there seem to be any hum of gossip. There was certainly, on the other hand, occurring between them communication extraordinarily intense. Another thing that was striking was the unexpected diversity of the people who made up these groups. Usually, for example, one would see a group of sharpies standing on the street corner, jiving the passing chicks; or a group of older men, usually, for some reason, in the vicinity of a barber shop, discussing baseball scores, or the numbers, or making rather chilling observations about women they had known. Women, in a general way, tended to be seen less often together—unless they were church women, or very young girls, or prostitutes met together for an unprofessional instant. But that summer I saw the strangest combinations: large, respectable, churchly matrons standing on the stoops or the corners with their hair tied up, together with a girl in sleazy satin whose face bore the marks of gin and the razor, or heavy-set, abrupt, no-nonsense older men, in company with the most disreputable and fanatical "race" men, or these same "race" men with the sharpies, or these sharpies with the churchly women. Seventh Day Adventists and Methodists and Spiritualists seemed to be hobnobbing with Holyrollers and they were all, alike, entangled with the most flagrant disbelievers; something heavy in their stance seemed to indicate that they had all, incredibly, seen a common vision, and on each face there seemed to be the same strange, bitter shadow.

The churchly women and the matter-of-fact, no-nonsense men had children in the Army. The sleazy girls they talked to had lovers there, the sharpies and the "race" men had friends and brothers there. It would have demanded an unquestioning patriotism, happily as uncommon in this country as it is undesirable, for these people not to have been disturbed by the bitter letters they received, by the newspaper stories they read, not to have been enraged by the posters, then to be found all over New York, which described the Japanese as "yellow-bellied Japs." It was only the "race" men, to be sure, who spoke ceaselessly of being revenged—how this vengeance was to be exacted was not clear—for the indignities and dangers suffered by Negro boys in uniform; but everybody felt a directionless, hopeless bitterness, as well as that panic which can scarcely be suppressed when one knows that a human being one loves is beyond one's reach, and in danger. This helplessness and this gnawing uneasiness does something, at length, to even the toughest mind. Perhaps the best way to sum all this up is to say that the people I knew felt, mainly, a peculiar kind of relief when they knew that their boys were being shipped out of the south, to do battle overseas. It was, perhaps, like feeling that the most dangerous part of a dangerous journey had been passed and that now, even if death should come, it would come with honor and without the complicity of their countrymen. Such a death would be, in short, a fact with which one could hope to live.

It was on the 28th of July, which I believe was a Wednesday, that I visited my father for the first time during his illness and for the last time in his life. The moment I saw him I knew why I had put off this visit so long. I had told my mother that I did not want to see him because I hated him. But this was not true. It was only that I *had* hated him and I wanted to hold on to this hatred. I did not want to look on him as a ruin: it was not a ruin I had hated. I imagine that one of the reasons people cling to their hates so stubbornly is because they sense, once hate is gone, that they will be forced to deal with pain.

We traveled out to him, his older sister and myself, to what seemed to be the very end of a very Long Island. It was hot and dusty and we wrangled, my aunt and I, all the way out, over the fact that I had recently begun to smoke and, as she said, to give myself airs. But I knew that she wrangled with me because she could not bear to face the fact of her brother's dying. Neither could I endure the reality of her despair, her unstated bafflement as to what had happened to her brother's life, and her own. So we wrangled and I smoked and from time to time she fell into a heavy reverie. Covertly, I watched her face, which was the face of an old woman; it had fallen in, the eyes were sunken and lightless; soon she would be dying, too.

In my childhood—it had not been so long ago—I had thought her beautiful. She had been quick-witted and quick-moving and very generous with all the children and each of her visits had been an event. At one time one of my brothers and myself had thought of running away to live with her. Now she could no longer produce out of her handbag some unexpected and yet familiar delight. She made me feel pity and revulsion and fear. It was awful to realize that she no longer caused me to feel affection. The closer we came to the hospital the more querulous she became and at the same time, naturally, grew more dependent on me. Between pity and guilt and fear I began to feel that there was another me trapped in my skull like a jack-in-the-box who might escape my control at any moment and fill the air with screaming.

She began to cry the moment we entered the room and she saw him lying there, all shriveled and still, like a little black monkey. The great, gleaming apparatus which fed him and would have compelled him to be still even if he had been able to move brought to mind, not beneficence, but torture; the tubes entering his arm made me think of pictures I had seen when a child, of Gulliver, tied down by the pygmies on that island. My aunt wept and wept, there was a whistling sound in my father's throat; nothing was said; he could not speak. I wanted to take his hand, to say something. But I do not know what I could have said, even if he could have heard me. He was not really in that room with us, he had at last really embarked on his journey; and though my aunt told me that he said he was going to meet Jesus, I did not hear anything except that whistling in his throat. The doctor came back and we left, into that unbearable train again, and home. In the morning came the telegram saying that he was dead. Then the house was suddenly full of relatives, friends, hysteria, and confusion and I quickly left my mother and the children to the care of those impressive women, who, in Negro communities at least, automatically appear at times of bereavement armed with lotions, proverbs, and patience, and an ability to cook. I went downtown. By the time I returned, later the same day, my mother had been carried to the hospital and the baby had been born.

III

For my father's funeral I had nothing black to wear and this posed a nagging problem all day long. It was one of those problems, simple, or impossible of solution, to which the mind insanely clings in order to avoid the mind's real trouble. I spent most of that day at the downtown apartment of a girl I knew, celebrating my birthday with whiskey and wondering what to wear that night. When planning a birthday celebration one naturally does not expect that it will be up against competition from a funeral and this girl had anticipated taking me out that night, for a big dinner and a night club afterwards. Sometime during the course of that long day we decided that we would go out anyway, when my father's funeral service was over. I imagine *I* decided it, since, as the funeral hour approached, it became clearer and clearer to me that I would not know what to do with myself when it was over. The girl, stifling her very lively concern as to the possible effects of the whiskey on one of my father's chief mourners, concentrated on being conciliatory and practically helpful. She found a black shirt for me somewhere and ironed it and, dressed in the darkest pants and jacket I owned, and slightly drunk, I made my way to my father's funeral.

The chapel was full, but not packed, and very quiet. There were, mainly, my father's relatives, and his children, and here and there I saw faces I had not seen since childhood, the faces of my father's one-time friends. They were very dark and solemn now, seeming somehow to suggest that they had known all along that something like this would happen. Chief among the mourners was my aunt, who had quarreled with my father all his life; by which I do not mean to suggest that her mourning was insincere or that she had not loved him. I suppose that she was one of the few people in the world who had, and their incessant quarreling proved precisely the strength of the tie that bound them. The only other person in the world, as far as I knew, whose relationship to my father rivaled my aunt's in depth was my mother, who was not there.

It seemed to me, of course, that it was a very long funeral. But it was, if anything, a rather shorter funeral than most, nor, since there were no overwhelming, uncontrollable expressions of grief, could it be called—if I dare to use the word—successful. The minister who preached my father's funeral sermon was one of the few my father had still been seeing as he neared his end. He presented to us in his sermon a man whom none of us had ever seen —a man thoughtful, patient, and forbearing, a Christian inspiration to all who knew him, and a model for his children. And no doubt the children, in their disturbed and guilty state, were almost ready to believe this; he had been remote enough to be anything and, anyway, the shock of the incontrovertible, that it was really our father lying up there in that casket, prepared the mind for anything. His sister moaned and this grief-stricken moaning was taken as corroboration. The other faces held a dark, non-committal thoughtfulness. This was not the man they had known, but they had scarcely expected to be confronted with *him;* this was, in a sense deeper than questions of fact, the man they had not known, and the man they had not known may have been the real one. The real man, whoever he had been, had suffered and now he was dead: this was all that was sure and all that mattered now. Every man in the chapel hoped that when his hour came he, too, would be eulogized, which is to say forgiven, and that all of his lapses, greeds, errors, and strayings from the truth would be invested with coherence and looked upon with charity. This was perhaps the last thing human beings could give each other and it was what they demanded, after all, of the Lord. Only the Lord saw the midnight tears, only He was present when one of His children, moaning and wringing hands, paced up and down the room. When one slapped one's child in anger the recoil in the heart reverberated through heaven and became part of the pain of the universe. And when the children were hungry and sullen and distrustful and one watched them, daily, growing wilder, and further away, and running headlong into danger, it was the Lord who knew what the charged heart endured as the strap was laid to the backside; the Lord alone who knew what one *would* have said if one had had, like the Lord, the gift of the living word. It was the Lord who knew of the impossibility every parent in that room faced: how to prepare the child for the day when the child would be despised and how to *create* in the child—by what means?—a stronger antidote to this poison than one had found for oneself. The avenues, side streets, bars, billiard halls, hospitals, police stations, and even the playgrounds of Harlem—not to mention the houses of correction, the jails, and the morgue—testified to the potency of the poison while remaining silent as to the efficacy of whatever antidote, irresistibly raising the question of whether or not such an antidote existed; raising, which was worse, the question of whether or not an antidote was desirable; perhaps poison should be fought with poison. With these several schisms in the mind and with more terrors in the heart than could be named, it was better not to judge the man who had gone down under an impossible burden. It was better to remember: *Thou knowest this man's fall; but thou knowest not his wrassling.*

While the preacher talked and I watched the children—years of changing their diapers, scrubbing them, slapping them, taking them to school, and scolding them had had the perhaps inevitable result of making me love them, though I am not sure I knew this then—my mind was busily breaking out with a rash of disconnected impressions. Snatches of popular songs, indecent jokes, bits of books I had read, movie sequences, faces, voices, political issues—I thought I was going mad; all these impressions suspended, as it were, in the solution of the faint nausea produced in me by the heat and liquor. For a moment I had the impression that my alcoholic breath, inefficiently disguised with chewing gum, filled the entire chapel. Then someone began singing one of my father's favorite songs and, abruptly, I was with him, sitting on his knee, in the hot, enormous, crowded church which was the first church we attended. It was the Abyssinia Baptist Church on 138th Street. We had not gone there long. With this image, a host of others came. I had forgotten, in the rage of my growing up, how proud my father had been of me when I was little. Apparently, I had had a voice and my father had liked to show me off before the members of the church. I had forgotten what he had looked like when he was pleased but now I remembered that he had always been grinning with pleasure when my solos ended. I even remembered certain expressions on his face when he teased my mother—had he loved her? I would never know. And when had it all begun to change? For now it seemed that he had not always been cruel. I remembered being taken for a haircut and scraping my knee on the footrest of the barber's chair and I remembered my father's face as he soothed my crying and applied the stinging iodine. Then I remembered our fights, fights which had been of the worst possible kind because my technique had been silence.

I remembered the one time in all our life together when we had really spoken to each other.

It was on a Sunday and it must have been shortly before I left home. We were walking, just the two of us, in our usual silence, to or from church. I was in high school and had been doing a lot of writing and I was, at about this time, the editor of the high school magazine. But I had also been a

Young Minister and had been preaching from the pulpit. Lately, I had been taking fewer engagements and preached as rarely as possible. It was said in the church, quite truthfully, that I was "cooling off."

My father asked me abruptly, "You'd rather write than preach, wouldn't you?"

I was astonished at his question—because it was a real question. I answered, "Yes."

That was all we said. It was awful to remember that that was all we had *ever* said.

The casket now was opened and the mourners were being led up the aisle to look for the last time on the deceased. The assumption was that the family was too overcome with grief to be allowed to make this journey alone and I watched while my aunt was led to the casket and, muffled in black, and shaking, led back to her seat. I disapproved of forcing the children to look on their dead father, considering that the shock of his death, or, more truthfully, the shock of death as a reality, was already a little more than a child could bear, but my judgment in this matter had been overruled and there they were, bewildered and frightened and very small, being led, one by one, to the casket. But there is also something very gallant about children at such moments. It has something to do with their silence and gravity and with the fact that one cannot help them. Their legs, somehow, seem *exposed*, so that it is at once incredible and terribly clear that their legs are all they have to hold them up.

I had not wanted to go to the casket myself and I certainly had not wished to be led there, but there was no way of avoiding either of these forms. One of the deacons led me up and I looked on my father's face. I cannot say that it looked like him at all. His blackness had been equivocated by powder and there was no suggestion in that casket of what his power had or could have been. He was simply an old man dead, and it was hard to believe that he had ever given anyone either joy or pain. Yet, his life filled that room. Further up the avenue his wife was holding his newborn child. Life and death so close together, and love and hatred, and right and wrong, said something to me which I did not want to hear concerning man, concerning the life of man.

After the funeral, while I was downtown desperately celebrating my birthday, a Negro soldier, in the lobby of the Hotel Braddock, got into a fight with a white policeman over a Negro girl. Negro girls, white policemen, in or out of uniform, and Negro males—in or out of uniform—were part of the furniture of the lobby of the Hotel Braddock and this was certainly not the first time such an incident had occurred. It was destined, however, to receive an unprecedented publicity, for the fight between the policeman and the soldier ended with the shooting of the soldier. Rumor, flowing immediately to the streets outside, stated that the soldier had been shot in the back, an instantaneous and revealing invention, and that the soldier had died protecting a Negro woman. The facts were somewhat different—for example, the soldier had not been shot in the back, and was not dead, and the girl seems to have been as dubious a symbol of womanhood as her white counterpart in Georgia usually is, but no one was interested in the facts. They preferred the invention because this invention expressed and corroborated their hates and fears so perfectly. It is just as well to remember that people are always doing this. Perhaps many of those legends, including Christianity, to which the world clings began their conquest of the world with just some such concerted surrender to distortion. The effect, in Harlem, of this particular legend was like the effect of a lit match in a tin of gasoline. The mob gathered before the doors of the Hotel Braddock simply began to swell and to spread in every direction, and Harlem exploded.

The mob did not cross the ghetto lines. It would have been easy, for example, to have gone over Morningside Park on the west side or to have crossed the Grand Central railroad tracks at 125th Street on the east side, to wreak havoc in white neighborhoods. The mob seems to have been mainly interested in something more potent and real than the white face, that is, in white power, and the principal damage done during the riot of the summer of 1943 was to white business establishments in Harlem. It might have been a far bloodier story, of course, if, at the hour the riot began, these establishments had still been open. From the Hotel Braddock the mob fanned out, east and west along 125th Street, and for the entire length of Lenox, Seventh, and Eighth avenues. Along each of these avenues, and along each major side street—116th, 125th, 135th, and so on—bars, stores, pawnshops, restaurants, even little luncheonettes had been smashed open and entered and looted—looted, it might be added, with more haste than efficiency. The shelves really looked as though a bomb had struck them. Cans of beans and soup and dog food, along with toilet paper, corn flakes, sardines and milk tumbled every which way, and abandoned cash registers and cases of beer leaned crazily out of the splintered windows and were strewn along the avenues. Sheets, blankets, and clothing of every description formed a kind of path, as though people had dropped them while running. I truly had not realized that Harlem *had* so many stores until I saw them all smashed open; the first time the word *wealth* ever entered my mind in relation to Harlem was when I saw it scattered in the streets. But one's first, incongruous impression of plenty was countered immediately by an impression of waste. None of this was doing anybody any good. It would have been better to have left the plate glass as it had been and the goods lying in the stores.

It would have been better, but it would also have been intolerable, for Harlem had needed something to smash. To smash something is the ghetto's chronic need. Most of the time it is the members of the ghetto who smash each other, and themselves. But as long as the ghetto walls are standing there will always come a moment when these outlets do not work. That summer, for example, it was not enough to get into a fight on Lenox Avenue, or curse out one's cronies in the barber shops. If ever, indeed, the violence which fills Harlem's churches, pool halls, and bars erupts outward in a more direct fashion, Harlem and its citizens are likely to vanish in an apocalyptic flood. That this is not likely to happen is due to a great many reasons, most hidden and powerful among them the Negro's real relation to the white American. This relation prohibits, simply, anything as uncomplicated and satisfactory as pure hatred. In order really to hate white people, one has to blot so much out of the mind—and the heart—that this hatred itself becomes an exhausting and self-destructive pose. But this does not mean, on the other hand, that love comes easily: the white world is too powerful, too complacent, too ready with gratuitous humiliation, and, above all, too ignorant and too innocent for that. One is absolutely forced to make perpetual qualifications and one's own reactions are always canceling each other out. It is this, really, which has driven so many people mad, both white and black. One is always in the position of having to decide between amputation and gangrene. Amputation is swift but time may prove that the amputation was not necessary—or one may delay the amputation too long. Gangrene is slow, but it is impossible to be sure that one is reading one's symptoms right. The idea of going through life as a cripple is more than one can bear, and equally unbearable is the risk of swelling up slowly, in agony, with poison. And the trouble, finally, is that the risks are real even if the choices do not exist.

"But as for me and my house," my father had said, "we will serve the Lord." I wondered, as we drove him to his resting place, what this line had meant for him. I had heard him preach it many times. I had preached it once myself, proudly giving it an interpretation different from my father's. Now the whole thing came back to me, as though my father and I were on our way to Sunday school and I were memorizing the golden text: *And if it seem evil unto you to serve the Lord, choose you this day whom you will serve; whether the gods which your fathers served that were on the other side of the flood, or the gods of the Amorites, in whose land ye dwell: but as for me and my house, we will serve the Lord.* I suspected in these familiar lines a meaning which had never been there for me before. All of my father's texts and songs, which I had decided were meaningless, were arranged before me at his death like empty bottles, waiting to hold the meaning which life would give them for me. This was his legacy: nothing is ever escaped. That bleakly memorable morning I hated the unbelievable streets and the Negroes and whites who had, equally, made them that way. But I knew that it was folly, as my father would have said, this bitterness was folly. It was necessary to hold on to the things that mattered. The dead man mattered, the new life mattered; blackness and whiteness did not matter; to believe that they did was to acquiesce in one's own destruction.

Hatred, which could destroy so much, never failed to destroy the man who hated and this was an immutable law.

It began to seem that one would have to hold in the mind forever two ideas which seemed to be in opposition. The first idea was acceptance, the acceptance, totally without rancor, of life as it is, and men as they are: in the light of this idea, it goes without saying that injustice is a commonplace. But this did not mean that one could be complacent, for the second idea was of equal power: that one must never, in one's own life, accept these injustices as commonplace but must fight them with all one's strength. This fight begins, however, in the heart and it now had been laid to my charge to keep my own heart free of hatred and despair. This intimation made my heart heavy and, now that my father was irrecoverable, I wished that he had been beside me so that I could have searched his face for the answers which only the future would give me now.

1955

Brown v. Board of Education of Topeka

In one of the most significant rulings in its history, on May 17, 1954, the Supreme Court handed down a unanimous decision that the doctrine of "separate but equal," established in the 1896 case of *Plessy* v. *Ferguson,*† "has no place" in public education. This landmark decision, centering on the "equal protection" clause of the Fourteenth Amendment,† would not only culminate a lengthy, intricate battle for equal access to educational opportunities waged by Charles Hamilton Houston and Thurgood Marshall of the NAACP, but would lead to greater freedoms in all areas of public life.

The Court had begun to recognize in a number of cases prior to *Brown* the difficulty of comparing the facilities afforded to black and white students. In the most important case, *Sweatt* v. *Painter* (1950), the Court argued that establishing similar institutions was not enough, but that intangible benefits, "those qualities which are incapable of objective measurement but which make for greatness"—reputation, experience, influence, standing in the community, tradition, and prestige—could not be discounted. Without these assets, the Court ruled, "few students and no one who has practiced law would choose to study in an academic vacuum." But while the Court had concerned itself in these cases with the *equality* of the separate facilities, the plaintiffs in *Brown* focused on their *separateness*. "It seems more fitting to meet the *Plessy* doctrine head-on," argued the NAACP in its brief, which follows, "and to declare that doctrine erroneous."

Brown was actually comprised of five cases launched by the NAACP at the same time in different states. Two of the cases reached the Court at the beginning of the 1952 term, and were consolidated with the remaining three. In agreeing to hear the cases, the Supreme Court asked that the counsels consider a number of legal questions regarding the intent of Congress and the state legislators in ratifying the Fourteenth Amendment. From December 7 to December 9, Thurgood Marshall argued the cases as chief counsel of the NAACP. In opposing *Plessy* v. *Ferguson,* Marshall claimed that he "was merely asking for what was ours by right—it was simple justice."

In its verdict, the Court asked, "Does segregation of children in public schools solely on the basis of race, even though the physical facilities and other 'tangible' factors may be equal, deprive the children of the minority group of equal opportunities? We believe that it does." The Court did not indicate, however, how its verdict was to be implemented, and a year later, stating that "the vitality of these constitutional principles cannot be allowed to yield simply because of disagreement with them," it ordered the states to proceed with compliance "with all deliberate speed."

When the *Brown* decision was handed down, school segregation was legally entrenched in seventeen states and the District of Columbia. On March 12, 1956, Senator Sam J. Ervin, Jr., and legislators from the eleven former Confederate states issued the "South Manifesto," arguing that the *Brown* decision was "a clear abuse of judicial power": "The unwarranted decision of the Supreme Court in the public school cases is now bearing the fruit always produced when men substitute naked power for established law." The senators claimed that the decision was "destroying the amicable relations between the white and Negro races" and that "outside agitators" were threatening "immediate and revolutionary changes." It was clear, however, that the mobs that confronted nine African-American students as they attempted to enter Central High School in Little Rock, Arkansas, were entirely homegrown. It was Orval Faubus, the governor of Arkansas, who argued that "blood will run in the streets" if the students tried to enter the school in September 1957.

Many of the school systems affected were slow in complying, and even ten years later the Court found that integration was proceeding neither deliberately nor speedily. Congress strengthened the *Brown* verdict by including its mandate in the Civil Rights Act of 1964. And while *Brown* had addressed only the issue of equality in education, the case started the Court on its way to reasoning that segregation, per se, was a doctrine inherently flawed.

NAACP Brief

"Whatever other purposes the Fourteenth Amendment may have had, it is indisputable that its primary purpose was to complete the emancipation provided by the Thirteenth Amendment by ensuring to the Negro equality before the law."

SUMMARY OF ARGUMENT

HESE CASES CONSOLIDATED FOR ARGUMENT BEFORE THIS Court present in different factual contexts essentially the same ultimate legal questions.

The substantive question common to all is whether a state can, consistently with the Constitution, exclude children, solely on the ground that they are Negroes, from public schools which otherwise they would be qualified to attend. It is the thesis of this brief, submitted on behalf of the excluded children, that the answer to the question is in the negative: the Fourteenth Amendment prevents states from according differential treatment to American children on the basis of their color or race. Both the legal precedents and the judicial theories, discussed in Part I hereof, and the evidence concerning the intent of the framers of the Fourteenth Amendment and the understanding of the Congress and the ratifying states, developed in Part II hereof, support this proposition.

Denying this thesis, the school authorities, relying in part on language originating in this Court's opinion in *Plessy* v. *Ferguson,* 163 U.S. 537, urge that exclusion of Negroes, *qua* Negroes, from designated public schools is permissible when the excluded children are afforded admittance to other schools especially reserved for Negroes, *qua* Negroes, if such schools are equal.

The procedural question common to all the cases is the role to be played, and the time-table to be followed, by this Court and the lower courts in directing an end to the challenged exclusion, in the event that this Court determines, with respect to the substantive question, that exclusion of Negroes, *qua* Negroes, from public schools contravenes the Constitution.

The importance to our American democracy of the substantive question can hardly be overstated. The question is whether a nation founded on the proposition that "all men are created equal" is honoring its commitments to grant "due process of law" and "the equal protection of the laws" to all within its borders when it, or one of its constituent states, confers or denies benefits on the basis of color or race.

1. Distinctions drawn by state authorities on the basis of color or race violate the Fourteenth Amendment. . . . Whatever other purposes the Fourteenth Amendment may have had, it is indisputable that its primary

purpose was to complete the emancipation provided by the Thirteenth Amendment by ensuring to the Negro equality before the law. . . .

2. Even if the Fourteenth Amendment did not *per se* invalidate racial distinctions as a matter of law, the racial segregation challenged in the instant cases would run afoul of the conventional test established for application of the equal protection clause because the racial classifications here have no reasonable relation to any valid legislative purpose. . . .

3. Appraisal of the facts requires rejection of the contention of the school authorities. The educational detriment involved in racially constricting a student's associations has already been recognized by this Court. . . .

4. The argument that the requirements of the Fourteenth Amendment are met by providing alternative schools rests, finally, on reiteration of the separate but equal doctrine enunciated in *Plessy* v. *Ferguson.*

Were these ordinary cases, it might be enough to say that the *Plessy* case can be distinguished—that it involved only segregation in transportation. But these are not ordinary cases, and in deference to their importance it seems more fitting to meet the *Plessy* doctrine head-on and to declare that doctrine erroneous.

Candor requires recognition that the plain purpose and effect of segregated education is to perpetuate an inferior status for Negroes which is America's sorry heritage from slavery. But the primary purpose of the Fourteenth Amendment was to deprive the states of *all* power to perpetuate such a caste system.

5. The first and second of the five questions propounded by this Court requested enlightenment as to whether the Congress which submitted, and the state legislatures and conventions which ratified, the Fourteenth Amendment contemplated or understood that it would prohibit segregation in public schools, either of its own force or through subsequent legislative or judicial action. The evidence, both in Congress and in the legislatures of the ratifying states, reflects the substantial intent of the Amendment's proponents and the substantial understanding of its opponents that the Fourteenth Amendment would, of its own force, proscribe all forms of state-imposed racial distinctions, thus necessarily including all racial segregation in public education.

The Fourteenth Amendment was actually the culmination of the determined efforts of the Radical Republican majority in Congress to incorporate into our fundamental law the well-defined equalitarian principle of complete equality for all without regard to race or color. The debates in the 39th Congress and succeeding Congresses clearly reveal the intention that the Fourteenth Amendment would work a revolutionary change in our state-federal relationship by denying to the states the power to distinguish on the basis of race.

The Civil Rights Bill of 1866, as originally proposed, possessed scope sufficiently broad in the opinion of many Congressmen to entirely destroy all state legislation based on race. A great majority of the Republican Radicals—who later formulated the Fourteenth Amendment—understood and intended that the Bill would prohibit segregated schools. Opponents of the measure shared this understanding. The scope of this legislation was narrowed because it was known that the Fourteenth Amendment was in process of preparation and would itself have scope exceeding that of the original draft of the Civil Rights Bill.

6. The evidence makes clear that it was the intent of the proponents of the Fourteenth Amendment, and the substantial understanding of its opponents, that it would, of its own force, prohibit all state action predicated upon race or color. The intention of the framers with respect to any specific example of caste state action—in the instant cases, segregated education—cannot be determined solely on the basis of a tabulation of contemporaneous statements mentioning the specific practice. The framers were formulating a constitutional provision setting broad standards for determination of the relationship of the state to the individual. In the nature of things they could not list all the specific categories of existing and prospective state activity which were to come within the constitutional prohibitions. The broad general purpose of the Amendment—obliteration of race and color distinctions—is clearly established by the evidence. So far as there was consideration of the Amendment's impact upon the undeveloped educational systems then existing, both proponents and opponents of the Amendment understood that it would proscribe all racial segregation in public education.

7. While the Amendment conferred upon Congress the power to enforce its prohibitions, members of the 39th Congress and those of subsequent Congresses made it clear that the framers understood and intended that the Fourteenth Amendment was self-executing and particularly pointed out that the federal judiciary had authority to enforce its prohibitions without Congressional implementation.

8. The evidence as to the understanding of the states is equally convincing. Each of the eleven states that had seceded from the Union ratified the Amendment, and concurrently eliminated racial distinctions from its laws, and adopted a constitution free of requirement or specific authorization of segregated schools. Many rejected proposals for segregated schools, and none enacted a school segregation law until after readmission. The significance of these facts is manifest from the consideration that ten of these states, which were required, as a condition of readmission, to ratify the Amendment and to modify their constitutions and laws in conformity therewith, considered that the Amendment required them to remove all racial distinctions from their existing and prospective laws, including those pertaining to public education.

Twenty-two of the twenty-six Union states also ratified the Amendment. Although unfettered by congressional surveillance, the overwhelming majority of the Union states acted with an understanding that it prohibited racially segregated schools and necessitated conformity of their school laws to secure consistency with that understanding.

9. In short, the historical evidence fully sustains this Court's conclusion in the *Slaughter Houses Cases,* 16 Wall. 36, 81, that the Fourteenth Amendment was designed to take from the states all power to enforce caste or class distinctions.

10. The Court in its fourth and fifth questions assumes that segregation is declared unconstitutional and inquires as to whether relief should be granted immediately or gradually. Appellants, recognizing the possibility of delay of a purely administrative character, do not ask for the impossible. No cogent reasons justifying further exercise of equitable discretion, however, have as yet been produced.

It has been indirectly suggested in the briefs and oral argument of appellees that some such reasons exist. Two plans were suggested by the United States in its Brief as *Amicus Curiae.* We have analyzed each of these plans as well as appellees' briefs and oral argument and find nothing there of sufficient merit on which this Court, in the exercise of its equity power, could predicate a decree permitting an effective gradual adjustment from segregated to non-segregated school systems. Nor have we been able to find any other reasons or plans sufficient to warrant the exercise of such equitable discretion in these cases. Therefore, in the present posture of these cases, appellants are unable to suggest any compelling reasons for this Court to postpone relief.

October 1953

Brown v. *Board of Education of Topeka*

"We conclude that in the field of public education the doctrine of 'separate but equal' has no place."

Opinion on Segregation Laws

No. 1. Appeal from the United States District Court
for the District of Kansas.

MR. CHIEF JUSTICE WARREN delivered the opinion of the Court.

These cases come to us from the States of Kansas, South Carolina, Virginia, and Delaware. They are premised on different facts and different local conditions, but a common legal question justifies their consideration together in this consolidated opinion.

In each of the cases, minors of the Negro race, through their legal representatives, seek the aid of the courts in obtaining admission to the public schools of their community on a nonsegregated basis. In each instance, they have been denied admission to schools attended by white children under laws requiring or permitting segregation according to race. This segregation was alleged to deprive the plaintiffs of the equal protection of the laws under the Fourteenth Amendment. In each of the cases other than the Delaware case, a three-judge federal district court denied relief to the plaintiffs on the so-called "separate but equal" doctrine announced by this Court in *Plessy* v. *Ferguson*, 163 U.S. 537. . . . Under that doctrine, equality of treatment is accorded when the races are provided substantially equal facilities, even though these facilities be separate. In the Delaware case, the Supreme Court of Delaware adhered to that doctrine, but ordered that the plaintiffs be admitted to the white schools because of their superiority to the Negro schools.

The plaintiffs contend that segregated public schools are not "equal" and cannot be made "equal," and that hence they are deprived of the equal protection of the laws. Because of the obvious importance of the question presented, the Court took jurisdiction. Argument was heard in the 1952 Term, and reargument was heard this Term on certain questions propounded by the Court.

Reargument was largely devoted to the circumstances surrounding the adoption of the Fourteenth Amendment in 1868. It covered exhaustively consideration of the Amendment in Congress, ratification by the states, then existing practices in racial segregation, and the views of proponents and opponents of the Amendment. This discussion and our own investigation convince us that, although these sources cast some light, it is not enough to resolve the problem with which we are faced. At best, they are inconclusive. The most avid proponents of the post-War Amendments undoubtedly intended them to remove all legal distinctions among "all persons born or naturalized in the United States." Their opponents, just as certainly, were antagonistic to both the letter and the spirit of the Amendments and wished them to have the most limited effect. What others in Congress and the state legislatures had in mind cannot be determined with any degree of certainty.

An additional reason for the inconclusive nature of the Amendment's history, with respect to segregated schools, is the status of public education at that time. In the South, the movement toward free common schools, supported by general taxation, had not yet taken hold. Education of white children was largely in the hands of private groups. Education of Negroes was almost nonexistent, and practically all of the race were illiterate. In fact, any education of Negroes was forbidden by law in some states. Today, in contrast, many Negroes have achieved outstanding success in the arts and sciences as well as in the business and professional world. It is true that public school education at the time of the Amendment had advanced further in the North, but the effect of the Amendment on Northern States was generally ignored in the congressional debates. Even in the North, the conditions of public education did not approximate those existing today. The curriculum was usually rudimentary; ungraded schools were common in rural areas; the school term was but three months a year in many states; and compulsory school attendance was virtually unknown. As a consequence, it is not surprising that there should be so little in the history of the Fourteenth Amendment relating to its intended effect on public education.

In the first cases in this Court construing the Fourteenth Amendment, decided shortly after its adoption, the Court interpreted it as proscribing all state-imposed discriminations against the Negro race. The doctrine of "separate but equal" did not make its appearance in this Court until 1896 in the case of *Plessy* v. *Ferguson, supra,* involving not education but transportation. American courts have since labored with the doctrine for over half a century. In this Court, there have been six cases involving the "separate but equal" doctrine in the field of public education. In *Cumming* v. *County Board of Education,* 175 U.S. 528, and *Gong Lum* v. *Rice,* 275 U.S. 78, the validity of the doctrine itself was not challenged. In more recent cases, all on the graduate school level, inequality was found in that specific benefits enjoyed by white students were denied to Negro students of the same educational qualifications. *Missouri ex rel. Gaines* v. *Canada,* 305 U.S. 337; *Sipuel* v. *Oklahoma,* 332 U.S. 631; *Sweatt* v. *Painter,* 339 U.S. 629; *McLaurin* v. *Oklahoma State Regents,* 339 U.S. 637. In none of these cases was it necessary to re-examine the doctrine to grant relief to the Negro plaintiff. And in *Sweatt* v. *Painter, supra,* the Court expressly reserved decision on the question whether *Plessy* v. *Ferguson* should be held inapplicable to public education.

In the instant cases, that question is directly presented. Here, unlike *Sweatt* v. *Painter*, there are findings below that the Negro and white schools involved have been equalized, or are being equalized, with respect to buildings, curricula, qualifications and salaries of teachers, and other "tangible" factors. Our decision, therefore, cannot turn on merely a comparison of these tangible factors in the Negro and white schools involved in each of the cases. We must look instead to the effect of segregation itself on public education.

In approaching this problem, we cannot turn the clock back to 1868 when the Amendment was adopted, or even to 1896 when *Plessy* v. *Ferguson* was written. We must consider public education in the light of its full development and its present place in American life throughout the Nation. Only in this way can it be determined if segregation in public schools deprives these plaintiffs of the equal protection of the laws.

Today, education is perhaps the most important function of state and local governments. Compulsory school attendance laws and the great expenditures for education both demonstrate our recognition of the importance of education to our democratic society. It is required in the performance of our most basic public responsibilities, even service in the armed forces. It is the very foundation of good citizenship. Today it is a principal instrument in awakening the child to cultural values, in preparing him for later professional training, and in helping him to adjust normally to his environment. In these days, it is doubtful that any child may reasonably be expected to succeed in life if he is denied the opportunity of an education. Such an opportunity, where the state has undertaken to provide it, is a right which must be made available to all on equal terms.

We come then to the question presented: Does segregation of children in public schools solely on the basis of race, even though the physical facilities and other "tangible" factors may be equal, deprive the children of the minority group of equal education opportunities? We believe that it does.

In *Sweatt* v. *Painter, supra*, in finding that a segregated law school for Negroes could not provide them equal educational opportunities, this Court relied in large part on "those qualities which are incapable of objective measurement but which make for greatness in a law school." In *McLaurin* v. *Oklahoma State Regents, supra*, the Court, in requiring that a Negro admitted to a white graduate school be treated like all other students, again resorted to intangible considerations: ". . . his ability to study, to engage in discussions and exchange views with other students, and, in general, to learn his profession." Such considerations apply with added force to children in grade and high schools. To separate them from others of similar age and qualifications solely because of their race generates a feeling of inferiority as to their status in the community that may affect their hearts and minds in a way unlikely ever to be undone. The effect of this separation on their educational opportunities was well stated by a finding in the Kansas case by a court which nevertheless felt compelled to rule against the Negro plaintiffs:

> Segregation of white and colored children in public schools has a detrimental effect upon the colored children. The impact is greater when it has the sanction of the law; for the policy of separating the races is usually interpreted as denoting the inferiority of the negro group. A sense of inferiority affects the motivation of the child to learn. Segregation with the sanction of law, therefore, has a tendency to [retard] the educational and mental development of negro children and to deprive them of some of the benefits they would receive in a racial[ly] integrated school system.

Whatever may have been the extent of psychological knowledge at the time of *Plessy* v. *Ferguson,* this finding is amply supported by modern authority. Any language in *Plessy* v. *Ferguson* contrary to this finding is rejected.

We conclude that in the field of public education the doctrine of "separate but equal" has no place. Separate educational facilities are inherently unequal. Therefore, we hold that the plaintiffs and others similarly situated for whom the actions have been brought are, by reason of the segregation complained of, deprived of the equal protection of the laws guaranteed by the Fourteenth Amendment. . . .

May 17, 1954

Martin Luther King, Jr.
(1929–1968)

The grandson of a slave, and the son and grandson of Baptist ministers, Martin Luther King, Jr., rose to international prominence during the civil rights era of the 1950s and 1960s. King was born in Atlanta and entered Morehouse College there at the age of fifteen. Ordained at eighteen, he continued his education at Crozer Theological Seminary in Pennsylvania and at Boston University. In 1953, he married Coretta Scott, a student at the New England Conservatory of Music, and in 1955 he received a Ph.D. in theology. King was the new pastor of the Dexter Avenue Baptist Church in Montgomery, Alabama, when Rosa Parks refused to yield her seat to a white passenger on a public bus in Montgomery in December 1955, and the destiny of the twenty-six-year-old minister took shape.

Elected president of the Montgomery Improvement Association, King directed the year-long boycott of public transportation, already demonstrating his rare personal courage and skills as an orator and leader. After the house where he lived with his wife and two-month-old baby was bombed, he dispersed an angry crowd gathered outside his home with the challenge that they meet violence with nonviolence. Appealing to a sense of justice that he would rely on throughout his career, King argued that victory would be achieved "because the arm of the moral universe is long, but it bends to justice." In November 1956 the Supreme Court ruled that the city's segregation laws were unconstitutional. In 1957 King visited India, where he continued to study the philosophy of nonviolence espoused by Mahatma Gandhi, whose writings he had first been drawn to in the seminary. Later that year, King and other activist black ministers organized the Southern Christian Leadership Conference, which would be at the forefront of social protest throughout the next decade.

It was during the massive desegration campaign in 1963 in Birmingham, Alabama, that King's role as a leader in the civil rights struggle was firmly established. When King and hundreds of other protestors were arrested, a group of eight local white clergymen characterized their efforts as "unwise and untimely." But as television cameras framed the standoff between demonstrators and police officials armed with fire hoses and trained dogs, the moral weight of King's cause became evident. Over Easter weekend, Dr. King wrote his now famous "Letter from Birmingham City Jail" included here, an extraordinarily well-reasoned expression of the doctrine of nonviolent resistance. King then helped organize the March on Washington for Freedom and Jobs, and on August 28, 1963, more than twenty years after A. Philip Randolph had launched his own March on Washington movement,† 250,000 activists gathered peacefully in the nation's capital. The "I Have a Dream" speech that follows was delivered on the steps of the Lincoln Memorial and has become one of the most well known orations of the twentieth century. King continued his work in the March from Selma to Montgomery, the Chicago Freedom Movement, and in dozens of speeches and numerous volumes, including *Stride to Freedom* (1958), *Strength of Love* (1963), *Trumpet of Conscience* (1967), and *Why We Can't Wait* (1967), King sought to persuade his critics of the rightness of his cause. In 1964 he was awarded the Nobel Peace Prize. Citing the distance he felt America still must travel, he said in his acceptance speech, "I feel as though this prize has been given to me for something that has really *not* yet been done."

King's leadership of the civil rights movement was not entirely unchallenged, however, and his methods and goals were less successful in attracting followers and achieving results in the urban North. And at the same time that disenchanted activists looked to the more militant philosophies of Malcolm X and the Black Panther Party,† King himself began to focus on a larger agenda after the passage of the Voting Rights Act in 1965. In early 1968 he launched the Poor People's Campaign, which sought to include lower-income whites and minorities in the nation's economic prosperity. His outspokenness against the Vietnam War—prompted, he argued, "because my conscience leaves me no other choice"—dismayed some of his followers who saw the focus of the civil rights movement diluted. The shift also troubled the Johnson administration, and J. Edgar Hoover's FBI took to bugging King's phone conversations and attempted to openly discredit him.

In the summer of 1967, major riots broke out in Newark and Detroit and the movement became increasingly fractured. When King supported a sanitation workers' strike in Memphis the next year that turned violent, his detractors pounced. In a speech delivered April 3 at the Mason Temple, he argued: "Well, I don't know what will happen now. We've got some difficult days ahead. But it doesn't really matter with me now. Because I've been to the mountaintop. And I don't mind. Like anybody, I would like to live a long life. Longevity has its place. But I'm not concerned about that now. I just want to do God's will. And He's allowed me to go up to the mountain. And I've looked over. And I've seen the promised land. I may not get there with you. But I want you to know tonight, that we, as a people, will get to the promised land." "And I'm happy, tonight," he concluded. "I'm not worried about anything. I'm not fearing any man. Mine eyes have seen the glory of the coming of the Lord." The following day, King was shot by James Earl Ray as he stood on the balcony of the Lorraine Motel. He died hours later, at the age of thirty-nine.

King's death was profoundly felt throughout the nation and marked a turning point in race relations. While tens of thousands of mourners followed his simple coffin, led through the streets of Atlanta by a team of Georgia mules, riots erupted in more than a hundred cities across the nation. "The murder of King changed the whole dynamic of the country," activist Kathleen Neal Cleaver recalled. "Because once King was murdered, in April '68, that kind of ended any public commitment to nonviolent change. It was like 'Well, we tried that, and that's what happened.' " Others, like King's colleagues Ralph Abernathy and Jesse Jackson, were determined that the dream would not die with the dreamer, but King's death, writes Michael Harrington, nonetheless represented "the end of the beloved community."

Because of the repeated threats of violence he faced, King had seemed to make peace with his own death. Two months before he was assassinated, he preached to his congregation at Ebenezer Baptist Church in Atlanta of how he wanted to be remembered. "Yes, if you want to say that I was a drum major, say that I was a drum major for justice; say that I was a drum major for peace; I was a drum major for righteousness. And all of the other shallow things will not matter. I won't have any money to leave behind. I won't have the fine and luxurious things of life to leave behind. But I just want to leave a committed life behind."

In November 1983, the anniversary of the birth of Martin Luther King, Jr., in January, became a national holiday by federal law.

Letter from Birmingham City Jail

"We have waited for more than 340 years for our constitutional and God-given rights. . . ."

Y DEAR FELLOW CLERGYMEN,

While confined here in the Birmingham city jail, I came across your recent statement calling our present activities "unwise and untimely." Seldom, if ever, do I pause to answer criticism of my work and ideas. If I sought to answer all of the criticisms that cross my desk, my secretaries would be engaged in little else in the course of the day, and I would have no time for constructive work. But since I feel that you are men of genuine good will and your criticisms are sincerely set forth, I would like to answer your statement in what I hope will be patient and reasonable terms.

I think I should give the reason for my being in Birmingham, since you have been influenced by the argument of "outsiders coming in." I have the honor of serving as president of the Southern Christian Leadership Conference, an organization operating in every southern state, with headquarters in Atlanta, Georgia. We have sought some eighty-five affiliate organizations all across the South—one being the Alabama Christian Movement for Human Rights. Whenever necessary and possible we share staff, educational and financial resources with our affiliates. Several months ago our local affiliate here in Birmingham invited us to be on call to engage in a nonviolent direct-action program if such were deemed necessary. We readily consented and when the hour came we lived up to our promises. So I am here, along with several members of my staff, because we were invited here. I am here because I have basic organizational ties here.

Beyond this, I am in Birmingham because injustice is here. Just as the eighth century prophets left their little villages and carried their "thus saith the Lord" far beyond the boundaries of their hometowns; and just as the Apostle Paul left his little village of Tarsus and carried the gospel of Jesus Christ to practically every hamlet and city of the Graeco-Roman world, I too am compelled to carry the gospel of freedom beyond my particular hometown. Like Paul, I must constantly respond to the Macedonian call for aid.

Moreover, I am cognizant of the interrelatedness of all communities and states. I cannot sit idly by in Atlanta and not be concerned about what happens in Birmingham. Injustice anywhere is a threat to justice everywhere. We are caught in an inescapable network of mutuality, tied in a single garment of destiny. Whatever affects one directly affects all indirectly. Never again can we afford to live with the narrow, provincial "outside agitator" idea. Anyone who lives in the United States can never be considered an outsider anywhere in this country.

You deplore the demonstrations that are presently taking place in Birmingham. But I am sorry that your statement did not express a similar concern for the conditions that brought the demonstrations into being. I am sure that each of you would want to go beyond the superficial social analyst who looks merely at effects, and does not grapple with underlying causes. I would not hesitate to say that it is unfortunate that so-called demonstrations are taking place in Birmingham at this time, but I would say in more emphatic terms that it is even more unfortunate that the white power structure of this city left the Negro community with no other alternative.

In any nonviolent campaign there are four basic steps: (1) collection of the facts to determine whether injustices are alive, (2) negotiation, (3) self-purification, and (4) direct action. We have gone through all of these steps in Birmingham. There can be no gainsaying of the fact that racial injustice engulfs this community.

Birmingham is probably the most thoroughly segregated city in the United States. Its ugly record of police brutality is known in every section of this country. Its injust treatment of Negroes in the courts is a notorious reality. There have been more unsolved bombings of Negro homes and churches in Birmingham than any city in this nation. These are the hard, brutal and unbelievable facts. On the basis of these conditions Negro leaders sought to negotiate with the city fathers. But the political leaders consistently refused to engage in good faith negotiation.

Then came the opportunity last September to talk with some of the leaders of the economic community. In these negotiating sessions certain promises were made by the merchants—such as the promise to remove the humiliating racial signs from the stores. On the basis of these promises, Rev. Shuttlesworth and the leaders of the Alabama Christian Movement for Human Rights agreed to call a moratorium on any type of demonstrations. As the weeks and months unfolded we realized that we were the victims of a broken promise. The signs remained. Like so many experiences of the past we were confronted with blasted hopes, and the dark shadow of a deep disappointment settled upon us. So we had no alternative except that of preparing for direct action, whereby we would present our very bodies as a means of laying our case before the conscience of the local and national community. We were not unmindful of the difficulties involved. So we decided to go through a process of self-purification. We started having workshops on nonviolence and repeatedly asked ourselves the questions, "Are you able to accept blows without retaliating?" "Are you able to endure the ordeals of jail?" We decided to set our direct-action program around the Easter season, realizing that with the exception of Christmas, this was the largest shopping period of the year. Knowing that a strong economic withdrawal program would be the byproduct of direct action, we felt that this was the best time to bring pressure on the merchants for the needed changes. Then it occurred to us that the March election was ahead and so we speedily decided to postpone action until after election day. When we discovered that Mr. Connor was in the run-off, we decided again to postpone action so that the demonstrations could not be used to cloud the issues. At this time we agreed to begin our nonviolent witness the day after the run-off.

This reveals that we did not move irresponsibly into direct action. We too wanted to see Mr. Connor defeated; so we went through postponement after postponement to aid in this community need. After this we felt that direct action could be delayed no longer.

You may well ask, "Why direct action? Why sit-ins, marches, etc.? Isn't negotiation a better path?" You are exactly right in your call for negotiation. Indeed, this is the purpose of direct action. Nonviolent direct action seeks to create such a crisis and establish such creative tension that a community that has constantly refused to negotiate is forced to confront the issue. It seeks so to dramatize the issue that it can no longer be ignored. I just referred to the creation of tension as a part of the work of the nonviolent resister. This may sound rather shocking. But I must confess that I am not afraid of the word tension. I have earnestly worked and preached against violent tension, but there is a type of constructive nonviolent tension that is necessary for growth. Just as Socrates felt that it was necessary to create a tension in the mind so that individuals could rise from the bondage of myths and half-truths to the unfettered realm of creative analysis and objective appraisal, we must see the need of having nonviolent gadflies to create the kind of tension in society that will help men to rise from the dark depths of prejudice and racism to the majestic heights of understanding and brotherhood. So the purpose of the direct action is to create a situation so crisis-packed that it will inevitably open the door to negotiation. We, therefore, concur with you in your call for negotiation. Too long has our beloved Southland been bogged down in the tragic attempt to live in monologue rather than dialogue.

One of the basic points in your statement is that our acts are untimely. Some have asked, "Why didn't you give the new administration time to act?" The only answer that I can give to this inquiry is that the new administration must be prodded about as much as the outgoing one before it acts. We will be sadly mistaken if we feel that the election of Mr. Boutwell will bring the millennium to Birmingham. While Mr. Boutwell is much more articulate and gentle than Mr. Connor, they are both segregationists, dedicated to the task of maintaining the status quo. The hope I see in Mr. Boutwell is that he will be reasonable enough to see the futility of massive resistance to desegregation. But he will not see this without pressure from the devotees of civil rights. My friends, I must say to you that we have not made a single gain in civil rights without determined legal and nonviolent pressure. History is the long and tragic story of the fact that privileged groups seldom give up their privileges voluntarily. Individuals may see the moral light and voluntarily give up their unjust posture; but as Reinhold Niebuhr has reminded us, groups are more immoral than individuals.

We know through painful experience that freedom is never voluntarily given by the oppressor; it must be demanded by the oppressed. Frankly, I have never yet engaged in a direct action movement that was "well-timed," according to the timetable of those who have not suffered unduly from the disease of segregation. For years now I have heard the word "Wait!" It rings in the ear of every Negro with a piercing familiarity. This "Wait" has almost always meant "Never." It has been a tranquilizing thalidomide, relieving the emotional stress for a moment, only to give birth to an ill-formed infant of frustration. We must come to see with the distinguished jurist of yesterday that "justice too long delayed is justice denied." We have waited for more than 340 years for our constitutional and God-given rights. The nations of Asia and Africa are moving with jetlike speed toward the goal of political independence, and we still creep at horse and buggy pace toward the gaining of a cup of coffee at a lunch counter. I guess it is easy for those who have never felt the stinging darts of segregation to say, "Wait." But when you have seen vicious mobs lynch your mothers and fathers at will and drown your sisters and brothers at whim; when you have seen hate-filled policemen curse, kick, brutalize and even kill your black brothers and sisters with impunity; when you see the vast majority of your twenty million Negro brothers smothering in an airtight cage of poverty in the midst of an affluent society; when you suddenly find your tongue twisted and your speech stammering as you seek to explain to your six-year-old daughter why she can't go to the public amusement park that has just been advertised on television, and see tears welling up in her little eyes when she is told that Funtown is closed to colored children, and see the depressing clouds of inferiority begin to form in her little mental sky, and see her begin to distort her little personality by unconsciously developing a bitterness toward white people; when you have to concoct an answer for a five-year-old son asking in agonizing pathos: "Daddy, why do white people treat colored people so mean?"; when you take a cross-country drive and find it necessary to sleep night after night in the uncomfortable corners of your automobile because no motel will accept you; when you are humiliated day in and day out by nagging signs reading "white" and "colored"; when your first name becomes "nigger" and your middle name becomes "boy" (however old you are) and your last name becomes "John," and when your wife and mother are never given the respected title "Mrs."; when you are harried by day and haunted by night by the fact that you are a Negro, living constantly at tiptoe stance never quite knowing what to expect next, and plagued with inner fears and resentments; when you are forever fighting a degenerating sense of "nobodiness"; then you will understand why we find it difficult to wait. There comes a time when the cup of endurance runs over, and men are no longer willing to be plunged into an abyss of injustice where they experience the blackness of corroding despair. I hope, sirs, you can understand our legitimate and unavoidable impatience.

You express a great deal of anxiety over our willingness to break laws. This is certainly a legitimate concern. Since we so diligently urge people to obey the Supreme Court's decision of 1954 outlawing segregation in the public schools, it is rather strange and paradoxical to find us consciously breaking laws. One may well ask, "How can you advocate breaking some laws and obeying others?" The answer is found in the fact that there are two types of laws: there are *just* and there are *unjust* laws. I would agree with Saint Augustine that "An unjust law is no law at all."

Now what is the difference between the two? How does one determine when a law is just or unjust? A just law is a man-made code that squares with the moral law or the law of God. An unjust law is a code that is out of harmony with the moral law. To put it in the terms of Saint Thomas Aquinas, an unjust law is a human law that is not rooted in eternal and natural law. Any law that uplifts human personality is just. Any law that degrades human personality is unjust. All segregation statutes are unjust because segregation distorts the soul and damages the personality. It gives the segregator a false sense of superiority, and the segregated a false sense of inferiority. To use the words of Martin Buber, the great Jewish philosopher, segregation substitutes an "I-it" relationship for the "I-thou" relationship, and ends up relegating persons to the status of things. So segregation is not only politically, economically and sociologically unsound, but it is morally wrong and sinful. Paul Tillich has said that sin is separation. Isn't segregation an existential expression of man's tragic separation, an expression of his awful estrangement, his terrible sinfulness? So I can urge men to disobey segregation ordinances because they are morally wrong.

Let us turn to a more concrete example of just and unjust laws. An unjust law is a code that a majority inflicts on a minority that is not binding on itself. This is difference made legal. On the other hand a just law is a code that a majority compels a minority to follow that it is willing to follow itself. This is sameness made legal.

Let me give another explanation. An unjust law is a code inflicted upon a minority which that minority had no part in enacting or creating because they did not have the unhampered right to vote. Who can say that the legislature of Alabama which set up the segregation laws was democratically elected? Throughout the state of Alabama all types of conniving methods are used to prevent Negroes from becoming registered voters and there are some counties without a single Negro registered to vote despite the fact that the Negro constitutes a majority of the population. Can any law set up in such a state be considered democratically structured?

These are just a few examples of unjust and just laws. There are some instances when a law is just on its face and unjust on its application. For instance, I was arrested Friday on a charge of parading without a permit. Now there is nothing wrong with an ordinance which requires a permit for a parade, but when the ordinance is used to preserve segregation and to deny citizens the First Amendment privilege of peaceful assembly and peaceful protest, then it becomes unjust.

I hope you can see the distinction I am trying to point out. In no sense do I advocate evading or defying the law as the rabid segregationist would do. This would lead to anarchy. One who breaks an unjust law must do it *openly*, *lovingly* (not hatefully as the white mothers did in New Orleans when they were seen on television screaming, "nigger, nigger, nigger"), and with a willingness to accept the penalty. I submit that an individual who breaks a law that conscience tells him is unjust, and willingly accepts the penalty by staying in jail to arouse the conscience of the community over its injustice, is in reality expressing the very highest respect for law.

Of course, there is nothing new about this kind of civil disobedience. It was seen sublimely in the refusal of Shadrach, Meshach and Abednego to obey the laws of Nebuchadnezzer because a higher moral law was involved. It was practiced superbly by the early Christians who were willing to face hungry lions and the excruciating pain of chopping blocks, before submitting to certain unjust laws of the Roman Empire. To a degree academic freedom is a reality today because Socrates practiced civil disobedience.

We can never forget that everything Hitler did in Germany was "legal" and everything the Hungarian freedom fighters did in Hungary was "illegal." It was "illegal" to aid and comfort a Jew in Hitler's Germany. But I am sure that if I had lived in Germany during that time I would have aided and comforted my Jewish brothers even though it was illegal. If I lived in a Communist country today where certain principles dear to the Christian faith are suppressed, I believe I would openly advocate disobeying these anti-religious laws. I must make two honest confessions to you, my Christian and Jewish brothers. First I must confess that over the last few years I have been gravely disappointed with the white moderate. I have almost reached the regrettable conclusion that the Negro's great stumbling block in the stride toward freedom is not the White Citizen's Counciler or the Ku Klux Klanner, but the white moderate who is more devoted to "order" than to justice; who prefers a negative peace which is the absence of tension to a positive peace which is the presence of justice; who constantly says, "I agree with you in the goal you seek, but I can't agree with your methods of direct action"; who paternalistically feels that he can set the timetable for another man's freedom; who lives by the myth of time and who constantly advises the Negro to wait until a "more convenient season." Shallow understanding from people of good will is more frustrating than absolute misunderstanding from people of ill will. Lukewarm acceptance is much more bewildering than outright rejection.

I had hoped that the white moderate would understand that law and order exist for the purpose of establishing justice, and that when they fail to do this they become dangerously structured dams that block the flow of social progress. I had hoped that the white moderate would understand that the present tension of the South is merely a necessary phase of the transition from an obnoxious negative peace, where the Negro passively accepted his unjust plight, to a substance-filled positive peace, where all men will respect the dignity and worth of human personality. Actually, we who engage in nonviolent direct action are not the creators of tension. We merely bring to the surface the hidden tension that is already alive. We bring it out in the open where it can be seen and dealt with. Like a boil that can never be cured as long as it is covered up but must be opened with all its pus-flowing ugliness to the natural medicines of air and light, injustice must likewise be exposed, with all of the tension its exposing creates, to the light of human conscience and the air of national opinion before it can be cured.

In your statement you asserted that our actions, even though peaceful, must be condemned because they precipitate violence. But can this assertion be logically made? Isn't this like condemning the robbed man because his possession of money precipitated the evil act of robbery? Isn't this like condemning Socrates because his unswerving commitment to truth and his philosophical delvings precipitated the misguided popular mind to make him drink the hemlock? Isn't this like condemning Jesus because His unique God-consciousness and never-ceasing devotion to his will precipitated the evil act of crucifixion? We must come to see, as federal courts have consistently affirmed, that it is immoral to urge an individual to withdraw his efforts to gain his basic constitutional rights because the quest precipitates violence. Society must protect the robbed and punish the robber.

I had also hoped that the white moderate would reject the myth of time. I received a letter this morning from a white brother in Texas which said: "All Christians know that the colored people will receive equal rights eventually, but it is possible that you are in too great of a religious hurry. It has taken Christianity almost two thousand years to accomplish what it has. The teachings of Christ take time to come to earth." All that is said here grows out of a tragic misconception of time. It is the strangely irrational notion that there is something in the very flow of time that will inevitably cure all ills. Actually time is neutral. It can be used either destructively or constructively. I am coming to feel that the people of ill will have used time much more effectively than the people of good will. We will have to repent in this generation not merely for the vitriolic words and actions of the bad people, but for the appalling silence of the good people. We must come to see that human progress never rolls in on wheels of inevitability. It comes through the tireless efforts and persistent work of men willing to be co-workers with God, and within this hard work time itself becomes an ally of the forces of social stagnation. We must use time creatively, and forever realize that the time is always ripe to do right. Now is the time to make real the promise of democracy, and transform our pending national elegy into a creative psalm of brotherhood. Now is the time to lift our national policy from the quicksand of racial injustice to the solid rock of human dignity.

You spoke of our activity in Birmingham as extreme. At first I was rather disappointed that fellow clergymen would see my nonviolent efforts as those of an extremist. I started thinking about the fact that I stand in the middle of two opposing forces in the Negro community. One is a force of complacency made up of Negroes who, as a result of long years of oppression, have been so completely drained of self-respect and a sense of "somebodiness" that they have adjusted to segregation, and of a few Negroes in the middle class who, because of a degree of academic and economic security, and because at points they profit by segregation, have unconsciously become insensitive to the problems of the masses. The other force is one of bitterness and hatred, and comes perilously close to advocating violence. It is expressed in the various black nationalist groups that are springing up over the nation, the largest and best known being Elijah Muhammad's Muslim movement. This movement is nourished by the contemporary frustration over the continued existence of racial discrimination. It is made up of people who have lost faith in America, who have absolutely repudiated Christianity, and who have concluded that the white man is an incurable "devil." I have tried to stand between these two forces, saying that we need not follow the "do-nothingism" of the complacent or the hatred and despair of the black nationalist. There is the more excellent way of love and nonviolent protest. I'm grateful to God that, through the Negro church, the dimension of nonviolence entered our struggle. If this philosophy had not emerged, I am convinced that by now many streets of the South would be flowing with floods of blood. And I am further convinced that if our white brothers dismiss as "rabble-rousers" and "outside agitators" those of us who are working through the channels of nonviolent direct action and refuse to support our nonviolent efforts, millions of Negroes, out of frustration and despair, will seek solace and security in black nationalist ideologies, a development that will lead inevitably to a frightening racial nightmare.

Oppressed people cannot remain oppressed forever. The urge for freedom will eventually come. This is what happened to the American Negro. Something within has reminded him of his birthright of freedom; something without has reminded him that he can gain it. Consciously and unconsciously, he has been swept in by what the Germans call the *Zeitgeist*, and with his black brothers of Africa, and his brown and yellow brothers of Asia, South America and the Caribbean, he is moving with a sense of cosmic urgency toward the promised land of racial justice. Recognizing this vital urge that has engulfed the Negro community has many pent-up resentments and latent frustrations. He has to get them out. So let him march sometime; let him have his prayer pilgrimages to the city hall; understand why he must have sit-ins and freedom rides. If his repressed emotions do not come out in these nonviolent ways, they will come out in ominous expressions of violence. This is not a threat; it is a fact of history. So I have not said to my people "get rid of your discontent." But I have tried to say that this normal and healthy discontent can be channelized through the creative outlet of nonviolent direct action. Now this approach is being dismissed as extremist. I must admit that I was initially disappointed to be so categorized.

But as I continued to think about the matter I gradually gained a bit of satisfaction from being considered an extremist. Was not Jesus an extremist in love—"Love your enemies, bless them that curse you, pray for them that despitefully sue you." Was not Amos an extremist for justice—"Let justice roll down like waters and righteousness like a mighty stream." Was not Paul an extremist for the gospel of Jesus Christ—"I bear in my body the marks of the Lord Jesus." Was not Martin Luther an extremist—"Here I stand; I can do none other so help me God." Was not John Bunyan an extremist—"I will stay in jail to the end of my days before I make a butchery of my conscience." Was not Abraham Lincoln an extremist—"This nation cannot survive half slave and half free." Was not Thomas Jefferson an extremist—"We hold these truths to be self-evident, that all men are created equal." So the question is not whether we will be extremist but what kind of extremist will we be? Will we be extremists for hate or will we be extremists for love? Will we be extremists for the preservation of injustice—or will we be extremists for the cause of justice? In that dramatic scene on Calvary's hill, three men were crucified. We must not forget that all three were crucified for the same crime—the crime of extremism. Two were extremists for immorality, and thusly fell below their environment. The other, Jesus Christ, was an extremist for love, truth and goodness, and thereby rose above his environment. So, after all, maybe the South, the nation and the world are in dire need of creative extremists.

I had hoped that the white moderate would see this. Maybe I was too optimistic. Maybe I expected too much. I guess I should have realized that few members of a race that has oppressed another race can understand or appreciate the deep groans and passionate yearnings of those that have been oppressed and still fewer have the vision to see that injustice must be rooted out by strong, persistent and determined action. I am thankful, however, that some of our white brothers have grasped the meaning of this social revolution and committed themselves to it. They are still too small in quantity, but they are big in quality. Some like Ralph McGill, Lillian Smith, Harry Golden and James Dabbs have written about our struggle in eloquent, prophetic and understanding terms. Others have marched with us down nameless streets of the South. They have languished in filthy roach-infested jails, suffering the abuse and brutality of angry policemen who see them as "dirty nigger-lovers." They, unlike so many of their moderate brothers and sisters, have recognized the urgency of the moment and sensed the need for powerful "action" antidotes to combat the disease of segregation.

Let me rush on to mention my other disappointment. I have been so greatly disappointed with the white church and its leadership. Of course, there are some notable exceptions. I am not unmindful of the fact that each of you has taken some significant stands on this issue. I commend you, Rev. Stallings, for your Christian stance on this past Sunday, in welcoming Negroes to your worship service on a non-segregated basis. I commend the Catholic leaders of this state for integrating Springhill College several years ago.

But despite these notable exceptions I must honestly reiterate that I have been disappointed with the church. I do not say that as one of the negative critics who can always find something wrong with the church. I say it as a minister of the gospel, who loves the church: who was nurtured in its bosom; who has been sustained by its spiritual blessings and who will remain true to it as long as the cord of life shall lengthen.

I had the strange feeling when I was suddenly catapulted into the leadership of the bus protest in Montgomery several years ago that we would have the support of the white church. I felt that the white ministers, priests and rabbis of the South would be some of our strongest allies. Instead, some have been outright opponents, refusing to understand the freedom movement and misrepresenting its leaders; all too many others have been more cautious than courageous and have remained silent behind the anesthetizing security of the stained-glass windows.

In spite of my shattered dreams of the past, I came to Birmingham with the hope that the white religious leadership of this community would see the justice of our cause, and with deep moral concern, serve as the channel through which our just grievances would get to the power structure. I had hoped that each of you would understand. But again I have been disappointed. I have heard numerous religious leaders of the South call upon their worshippers to comply with a desegregation decision because it is the *law*, but I have longed to hear white ministers say, "Follow this decree because integration is morally *right* and the Negro is your brother." In the midst of blatant injustices inflicted upon the Negro, I have watched white churches stand on the sideline and merely mouth pious irrelevancies and sanctimonious trivialities. In the midst of a mighty struggle to rid our nation of racial and economic injustice, I have heard so many ministers say, "Those are social issues with which the gospel has no real concern," and I have watched so many churches commit themselves to a completely other-worldly religion which made a strange distinction between body and soul, the sacred and the secular.

So here we are moving toward the exit of the twentieth century with a religious community largely adjusted to the status quo, standing as a tail light behind other community agencies rather than a headlight leading men to higher levels of justice.

I have traveled the length and breadth of Alabama, Mississippi and all the other Southern states. On sweltering summer days and crisp autumn mornings I have looked at her beautiful churches with their lofty spires pointing heavenward. I have beheld the impressive outlay of her massive religious education buildings. Over and over again I have found myself asking: "What kind of people worship here? Who is their God? Where were their voices when the lips of Governor Barnett dripped with words of interposition and nullification? Where were they when Governor Wallace gave the clarion call for defiance and hatred? Where were their voices of support when tired, bruised and weary Negro men and women decided to rise from the dark dungeons of complacency to the bright hills of creative protest?"

Yes, these questions are still in my mind. In deep disappointment, I have wept over the laxity of the church. But be assured that my tears have been tears of love. There can be no deep disappointment where there is not deep love. Yes, I love the church. I love her sacred walls. How could I do otherwise? I am in the rather unique position of being the son, the grandson and the great-grandson of preachers. Yes, I see the church as the body of Christ. But, oh! How we have blemished and scarred that body through social neglect and fear of being nonconformists.

There was a time when the church was very powerful. It was during that period when the early Christians rejoiced when they were deemed worthy to suffer for what they believed. In those days the church was not merely a thermometer that recorded the ideas and principles of popular opinion; it was a thermostat that transformed the mores of society. Wherever the early Christians entered a town the power structure got disturbed and immediately sought to convict them for being "disturbers of the peace" and "outside agitators." But they went on with the conviction that they were a "colony of heaven," and had to obey God rather than man. They were small in number but big in commitment. They were too God-intoxicated to be "astronomically intimidated." They brought an end to such ancient evils as infanticide and gladiatorial contest.

Things are different now. The contemporary church is often a weak, ineffectual voice with an uncertain sound. It is so often the arch-supporter of the status quo. Far from being disturbed by the presence of the church, the power structure of the average community is consoled by the church's silent and often vocal sanction of things as they are.

But the judgment of God is upon the church as never before. If the church of today does not recapture the sacrificial spirit of the early church, it will lose its authentic ring, forfeit the loyalty of millions, and be dismissed as an irrelevant social club with no meaning for the twentieth century. I am meeting young people every day whose disappointment with the church has risen to outright disgust.

Maybe again I have been too optimistic. Is organized religion too inextricably bound to the status quo to save our nation and the world? Maybe I must turn my faith to the inner spiritual church, the church within the church, as the true *ecclesia* and the hope of the world. But again I am thankful to God that some noble souls from the ranks of organized religion have broken loose from the paralyzing chains of conformity and joined us as active partners in the struggle for freedom. They have left their secure congregations and walked the streets of Albany, Georgia, with us. They have gone through the highways of the South on tortuous rides for freedom. Yes, they have gone to jail with us. Some have been kicked out of their churches, and lost support of their bishops and fellow ministers. But they have gone with the faith that right defeated is stronger than evil triumphant. These men have been the leaven in the lump of the race. Their witness has been the spiritual salt that has preserved the true meaning of the gospel in these troubled times. They have carved a tunnel of hope through the dark mountain of disappointment.

I hope the church as a whole will meet the challenge of this decisive hour. But even if the church does not come to the aid of justice, I have no despair about the future. I have no fear about the outcome of our struggle in Birmingham, even if our motives are presently misunderstood. We will reach the goal of freedom in Birmingham and all over the nation, because the goal of America is freedom. Abused and scorned though we may be, our destiny is tied up with the destiny of America. Before the Pilgrims landed at Plymouth we were here. Before the pen of Jefferson etched across the pages of history the majestic words of the Declaration of Independence, we were here. For more than two centuries our foreparents labored in this country without wages; they made cotton king; and they built the homes of their masters in the midst of brutal injustice and shameful humiliation—and yet out of a bottomless vitality they continued to thrive and develop. If the inexpressible cruelties of slavery could not stop us, the opposition we now face will surely fail. We will win our freedom because the sacred heritage of our nation and the eternal will of God are embodied in our echoing demands.

I must close now. But before closing I am impelled to mention one other point in your statement that troubled me profoundly. You warmly commended the Birmingham police force for keeping "order" and "preventing violence." I don't believe you would have so warmly commended the police force if you had seen its angry violent dogs literally biting six unarmed, nonviolent Negroes. I don't believe you would so quickly commend the policemen if you would observe their ugly and inhuman treatment of Negroes here in the city jail; if you would watch them push and curse old Negro women and young Negro girls; if you would see them slap and kick old Negro men and young boys; if you will observe them, as they did on two occasions, refuse to give us food because we wanted to sing our grace together. I'm sorry that I can't join you in your praise for the police department.

It is true that they have been rather disciplined in their public handling of the demonstrators. In this sense, they have been rather publicly "nonviolent." But for what purpose? To preserve the evil system of segregation. Over the last few years I have consistently preached that nonviolence demands that the means we use must be as pure as the ends we seek. So I have tried to make it clear that it is wrong to use immoral means to attain moral ends. But now I must affirm that it is just as wrong, or even more so, to use moral means to preserve immoral ends. Maybe Mr. Connor and his policemen have been rather publicly nonviolent, as Chief Pritchett was in Albany, Georgia, but they have used the moral means of nonviolence to maintain the immoral end of flagrant racial injustice. T. S. Eliot has said that there is no greater treason than to do the right deed for the wrong reason.

I wish you had commended the Negro sit-inners and demonstrators of Birmingham for their sublime courage, their willingness to suffer and their amazing discipline in the midst of the most inhuman provocation. One day the South will recognize its real heroes. They will be the James Merediths, courageously and with a majestic sense of purpose facing jeering and hostile mobs and the agonizing loneliness that characterizes the life of the pioneer. They will be old, oppressed, battered Negro women, symbolized in a seventy-two-year-old woman of Montgomery, Alabama, who rose up with a sense of dignity and with her people decided not to ride the segregated buses, and responded to one who inquired about her tiredness with ungrammatical profundity: "My feet is tired, but my soul is rested." They will be the young high school and college students, young ministers of the gospel and a host of their elders courageously and nonviolently sitting-in at lunch counters and willingly going to jail for conscience's sake. One day the South will know that when these disinherited children of God sat down at lunch counters they were in reality standing up for the best in the American dream and the most sacred values in our Judeo-Christian heritage, and thusly, carrying our whole nation back to those great wells of democracy which were dug deep by the Founding Fathers in the formulation of the Constitution and the Declaration of Independence.

Never before have I written a letter this long (or should I say a book?). I'm afraid that it is much too long to take your precious time. I can assure you that it would have been much shorter if I had been writing from a comfortable desk, but what else is there to do when you are alone for days in the dull monotony of a narrow jail cell other than write long letters, think strange thoughts, and pray long prayers?

If I have said anything in this letter that is an overstatement of the truth and is indicative of an unreasonable impatience, I beg you to forgive me. If I have said anything in this letter that is an understatement of the truth and is indicative of my having a patience that makes me patient with anything less than brotherhood, I beg God to forgive me.

I hope this letter finds you strong in the faith. I also hope that circumstances will soon make it possible for me to meet each of you, not as an integrationist or a civil rights leader, but as a fellow clergyman and a Christian brother. Let us all hope that the dark clouds of racial prejudice will soon pass away and the deep fog of misunderstanding will be lifted from our fear-drenched communities and in some not too distant tomorrow the radiant stars of love and brotherhood will shine over our great nation with all of their scintillating beauty.

Yours for the cause of Peace and Brotherhood,
Martin Luther King, Jr.

April 16, 1963

I Have a Dream

"*Now *is the time to make real the promises of Democracy."

IVE SCORE YEARS AGO, A GREAT AMERICAN, IN WHOSE symbolic shadow we stand, signed the Emancipation Proclamation. This momentous decree came as a great beacon light of hope to millions of Negro slaves who had been seared in the flames of withering injustice. It came as a joyous daybreak to end the long night of captivity.

But one hundred years later, we must face the tragic fact that the Negro is still not free. One hundred years later, the life of the Negro is still sadly crippled by the manacles of segregation and the chains of discrimination. One hundred years later, the Negro lives on a lonely island of poverty in the midst of a vast ocean of material prosperity. One hundred years later the Negro is still languished in the corners of American society and finds himself an exile in his own land. So we have come here today to dramatize an appalling condition.

In a sense we have come to our nation's Capital to cash a check. When the architects of our republic wrote the magnificent words of the Constitution and the Declaration of Independence, they were signing a promissory note to which every American was to fall heir. This note was a promise that all men would be guaranteed the unalienable rights of life, liberty, and the pursuit of happiness.

It is obvious today that America has defaulted on this promissory note insofar as her citizens of color are concerned. Instead of honoring this sacred obligation, America has given the Negro people a bad check; a check which has come back marked "insufficient funds." But we refuse to believe that the bank of justice is bankrupt. We refuse to believe that there are insufficient funds in the great vaults of opportunity of this nation. So we have come to cash this check—a check that will give us upon demand the riches of freedom and the security of justice.

We have also come to this hallowed spot to remind America of the fierce urgency of *now*. This is not time to engage in the luxury of cooling off or to take the tranquilizing drug of gradualism. *Now* is the time to make real the promises of Democracy. *Now* is the time to rise from the dark and desolate valley of segregation to the sunlit path of racial justice. *Now* is the time to open the doors of opportunity to all of God's children. *Now* is the time to lift our nation from the quicksands of racial injustice to the solid rock of brotherhood.

It would be fatal for the nation to overlook the urgency of the moment and to underestimate the determination of the Negro. This sweltering summer of the Negro's legitimate discontent will not pass until there is an invigorating autumn of freedom and equality. Nineteen sixty-three is not an end, but a beginning. Those who hope that the Negro needed to blow off steam and will now be content will have a rude awakening if the Nation returns to business as usual. There will be neither rest nor tranquility in America until the Negro is granted his citizenship rights. The whirlwinds of revolt will continue to shake the foundations of our Nation until the bright day of justice emerges.

But there is something that I must say to my people who stand on the warm threshold which leads into the palace of justice. In the process of gaining our rightful place we must not be guilty of wrongful deeds. Let us not seek to satisfy our thirst for freedom by drinking from the cup of bitterness and hatred. We must forever conduct our struggle on the high plane of dignity and discipline. We must not allow our creative protest to degenerate into physical violence. Again and again we must rise to the majestic heights of meeting physical force with soul force.

The marvelous new militancy which has engulfed the Negro community must not lead us to a distrust of all white people, for many of our white brothers, as evidenced by their presence here today, have come to realize that their destiny is tied up with our destiny and their freedom is inextricably bound to our freedom. We cannot walk alone.

And as we walk, we must make the pledge that we shall march ahead. We cannot turn back. There are those who are asking the devotees of civil rights, "When will you be satisfied?"

We can never be satisfied as long as the Negro is the victim of the unspeakable horrors of police brutality. We can never be satisfied as long as our bodies, heavy with the fatigue of travel, cannot gain lodging in the motels of the highways and the hotels of the cities.

We cannot be satisfied as long as the Negro's basic mobility is from a smaller ghetto to a larger one.

We can never be satisfied as long as a Negro in Mississippi cannot vote and a Negro in New York believes he has nothing for which to vote.

No, no we are not satisfied, and we will not be satisfied until justice rolls down like waters and righteousness like a mighty stream.

I am not unmindful that some of you have come here out of great trials and tribulations. Some of you have come fresh from narrow jail cells. Some of you have come from areas where your quest for freedom left you battered by the storm of persecution and staggered by the winds of police brutality. Continue to work with the faith that unearned suffering is redemptive.

Go back to Mississippi, go back to Alabama, go back to South Carolina, go back to Georgia, go back to Louisiana, go back to the slums and ghettos of our modern cities, knowing that somehow this situation can and will be changed. Let us not wallow in the valley of despair.

I say to you today, my friends, that in spite of the difficulties and frustrations of the moment I still have a dream. It is a dream deeply rooted in the American dream.

I have a dream that one day this nation will rise up and live out the true meaning of its creed: "We hold these truths to be self-evident; that all men are created equal."

I have a dream that one day on the red hills of Georgia the sons of former slaves and the sons of former slaveowners will be able to sit down together at the table of brotherhood.

I have a dream that one day even the state of Mississippi, a desert state sweltering with the heat of injustice and oppression, will be transformed into an oasis of freedom and justice.

I have a dream that my four little children will one day live in a nation where they will not be judged by the color of their skin but by the content of their character.

I have a dream today.

I have a dream that one day the state of Alabama, whose governor's lips are presently dripping with the words of interposition and nullification, will be transformed into a situation where little black boys and black girls will be able to join hands with little white boys and white girls and walk together as sisters and brothers.

I have a dream today.

I have a dream that one day every valley shall be exalted, every hill and mountain shall be made low, the rough places will be made plains, and the crooked places will be made straight, and the glory of the Lord shall be revealed, and all flesh shall see it together.

This is our hope. This is the faith with which I return to the South. With this faith we will be able to hew out of the mountain of despair a stone of hope. With this faith we will be able to transform the jangling discords of our nation into a beautiful symphony of brotherhood.

With this faith we will be able to work together, to pray together, to struggle together, to go to jail together, to stand up for freedom together, knowing that we will be free one day.

This will be the day when all of God's children will be able to sing with new meaning, "My country 'tis of thee, sweet land of liberty of thee I sing. Land where my fathers died, land of the pilgrim's pride, from every mountainside, let freedom ring."

And if America is to be a great nation this must become true. So let freedom ring from the prodigious hilltops of New Hampshire. Let freedom ring from the mighty mountains of New York. Let freedom ring from the heightening Alleghenies of Pennsylvania!

Let freedom ring from the snowcapped Rockies of Colorado!

Let freedom ring from the curvacious peaks of California!

But not only that; let freedom ring from Stone Mountain of Georgia!

Let freedom ring from Lookout Mountain of Tennessee!

Let freedom ring from every hill and mole hill of Mississippi. From every mountainside, let freedom ring.

When we let freedom ring, when we let it ring from every village and every hamlet, from every state and every city, we will be able to speed up that day when all of God's children, black men and white men, Jews and Gentiles, Protestants and Catholics, will be able to join hands and sing in the words of the old Negro spiritual, "Free at last! free at last! thank God almighty, we are free at last!"

August 28, 1963

Songs of the Civil Rights Movement

As slaves relied on spirituals for sustenance until the day of freedom came a hundred years before, during the civil rights movement of the 1960s protestors looked to the power of communal song to uphold them during the continued struggle for social progress. Combining the healing comfort of faith with the force of social protest, the songs of the sixties sprang directly from the old spirituals, as well as from work and protest songs of the 1930s and 1940s. Some spirituals, like "O Freedom" and "Free at Last," survived virtually intact, while the lyrics of others were updated ("I'm travelin' to Mississippi on the Greyhound Bus line," "No more jail house over me") to reflect the nature of the mass meetings, sit-ins, and demonstrations taking place throughout the South. "We Shall Overcome" became the virtual anthem of the movement. Based on the song "I'll Be Alright," sung in slavery times in the Sea Islands of South Carolina, and the religious song "I'll Overcome Some Day," it was first used as a form of social protest by striking tobacco workers in the 1940s and was adapted by the folk singer Pete Seeger in the 1960s. It gained widespread recognition when television cameras brought sit-ins and demonstrations to audiences around the world and President Lyndon Johnson alluded to the song when he signed the historic Voting Rights Act of 1965. "Keep Your Eyes on the Prize" is based on a traditional gospel song, "Keep Your Hand on the Plow," and the Reverend Ralph Abernathy first popularized the song "Ain't Gonna Let Nobody Turn Me 'Round" at a church rally in Albany, Georgia. Sung on the streets in the face of hostile crowds and in jail cells until bail was paid, "the Freedom songs," wrote Martin Luther King, Jr., played "a strong and vital role in our struggle . . . I think they keep alive a faith, a radiant hope in the future." Just as the songs of the civil rights movement had their origins in earlier periods of crisis, they have proved to be enormously enduring and continue to be heard anywhere in the world today where there is struggle.

We Shall Overcome

We shall overcome,
We shall overcome.
We shall overcome,
Someday.
Oh, deep in my heart,
I do believe, that
We shall overcome
Someday.

We'll walk hand in hand,
We'll walk hand in hand,
We'll walk hand in hand,
Someday.
Oh, deep in my heart,
I do believe, that
We shall overcome
Someday.

We are not afraid,
We are not afraid,
We are not afraid,
Oh, no, no, no,
'Cause deep in my heart,
I do believe that
We shall overcome,
Someday.

O Freedom

O Freedom!
O Freedom!
O Freedom over me!
And before I'd be a slave,
I'd be buried in my grave,
And go home to my Lord and be free!

No more mournin'
No more weepin'
No more misery over me.
And before I'd be a slave,
I'd be buried in my grave,
And go home to my Lord and be free.

Keep Your Eyes on the Prize

Paul and Silas bound in jail,
Had no money for to go their bail.
Keep your eyes on the prize,
Hold on, hold on.
  Hold on, hold on.
Keep your eyes on the prize,
  Hold on, hold on.

Paul and Silas begin to shout,
The jail door open and they walked out.
Keep your eyes on the prize,
Hold on, hold on.

Freedom's name is mighty sweet,
Soon one day we're gonna meet.
Keep your eyes on the prize,
Hold on, hold on.

Got my hand on the Gospel plow,
I wouldn't take nothing for my journey now.
Keep your eyes on the prize,
Hold on, hold on.

The only chain that a man can stand,
Is that chain of hand in hand.
Keep your eyes on the prize,
Hold on, hold on.

The only thing that we did wrong,
Stayed in the wilderness a day too long.
Keep your eyes on the prize,
Hold on, hold on.

But the one thing we did right,
Was the day we started to fight.
Keep your eyes on the prize,
Hold on, hold on.

We're gonna board that big Greyhound,
Carryin' love from town to town.
Keep your eyes on the prize,
Hold on, hold on.

We're gonna ride for civil rights,
We're gonna ride both black and white.

Keep your eyes on the prize,
Hold on, hold on.

We've met jail and violence too,
But God's love has seen us through.
Keep your eyes on the prize,
Hold on, hold on.

Haven't been to Heaven but I've been told,
Streets up there are paved with gold.
Keep your eyes on the prize,
Hold on, hold on.

Ain't Gonna Let Nobody Turn Me 'Round

Ain't gonna let nobody, Lordy, turn me 'round,
   Turn me 'round, turn me 'round,
Ain't gonna let nobody turn me 'round,
   I'm gonna keep on a-walkin',
Keep on a-talkin',
Marching up to freedom land.

Ain't gonna let no jail house turn me 'round,
   Turn me 'round, turn me 'round,
Ain't gonna let no jail house turn me 'round,
   I'm gonna keep on a-walkin',
Keep on a-talkin',
Marching up to freedom land.

Ain't gonna let no sheriff turn me 'round,
   Turn me 'round, turn me 'round,
Ain't gonna let no sheriff turn me 'round,
   Turn me 'round, turn me 'round,
Keep on a-talkin',
Marching up to freedom land.

Kwanzaa

Celebrated from December 26 through January 1, Kwanzaa is a uniquely African-American holiday begun in 1966 in Los Angeles by Dr. Maulana Karenga, the chairman of the black studies department at the University of California. "Kwanzaa" is adapted from the Iskwahili words *Matunda Ya Kwanza,* meaning "first fruits," acknowledging its roots in the traditional harvest celebrations in Africa. It is a nonpolitical, nonreligious, nonhistoric holiday meant to emphasize the connection with African culture while recognizing the unique history of African-Americans.

Every aspect of Kwanzaa is imbued with ritual meaning. The holiday takes place over seven days, seven symbols are used to represent its tenets, and the holiday is ordered by the *Nguzo Saba,* or seven principles.

Before the first day of Kwanzaa, the site of the celebration is prepared with the following articles:

Mkeka—A straw mat signifying tradition serves as a backdrop for the other articles.

Kinara—a branched holder for seven candles

Mishumaa Saba—the seven candles in the red, black, and green colors chosen by Marcus Garvey to symbolize African peoples around the world. In the center of the holder is placed a black candle, representing the people. To the left are three green candles, representing the bounty of Africa, and to the right three red candles, which signify the blood ties of the people and the blood shed by black nations in their struggle for independence.

Mazao—the "first fruits." The fruits and vegetables placed in a simple bowl on the Mkeka commemorate traditional African harvest ceremonies and represent the fruits of collective labor.

Muhindi—Each child in the family is represented by an ear of corn—a traditional symbol of fertility—placed on the Mkeka. In homes without children, a single ear is used to represent a connection with the next generation.

Kikombe Cha Umoja—A libation cup, from which all participants will drink, is placed on the Mkeka. Water, the essence of life, is poured to remember ancestors.

Zawadi—Gifts, preferably handmade and of cultural significance or practical use, are given, usually on the last day of Kwanzaa. They may be given to recognize a personal achievement.

On the first night of Kwanzaa, after an evening meal that may include traditional African dishes, the black candle in the center of the Mishumaa Saba is lit, and on each subsequent night another candle is lit, alternating from left to right. As each candle is lit, in the presence of family and friends, one of the seven principles of Kwanzaa is recalled:

Umoja symbolizes the unity of the family, the community, and the black nation.

Kujichagulia represents self-reliance and an expression of black identity that comes from within the community, rather than from outside the cultural group.

Ujima denotes shared goals and a collective responsibility for others in the black community.

Ujamaa symbolizes economic cooperation and support of black business enterprises.

Nia indicates a shared sense of purpose in honoring black traditions and cultures.

Kuumba depicts creativity in all aspects of life.

Imani represents a righteous faith in the history and future of black cultures.

The holiday may culminate with the Kwanzaa Karamu, a feast and cultural celebration of black culture that may include songs, dancing, poetry reading, or other cultural expressions. Guests are ritually welcomed, the past is remembered and celebrated, and commitments are renewed.

Though Kwanzaa has not replaced the Christmas holiday—nor was it meant to—many families, schools, and communities in New York, Washington, Los Angeles, Chicago, Philadelphia, and New Orleans now celebrate the holiday. Additional information about Kwanzaa and other black holidays may be obtained from the African-American Holidays Foundation in Washington, D.C. (202-310-1430) or from the African-American Cultural Center in Los Angeles (213-299-6124), among other resources.

Malcolm X
(1925–1965)

Toward the end of his autobiography, Malcolm X states, "My life has always been one of change," and, indeed, this most charismatic of black leaders assumed and discarded three names and no fewer ideologies as he traced his powerful intellectual and spiritual journey. He was born Malcolm Little in Omaha, Nebraska, the son of a Baptist preacher and Garveyite who believed that the black man would never find justice in America. After a white mob burned down his home, Earl Little moved his family to Lansing, Michigan. When Malcolm was six, his father was murdered by a white mob—his body cut nearly in half—in a death the authorities termed a suicide. His mother suffered a nervous breakdown from which she never recovered, and Malcolm and his seven siblings were separated by caseworkers.

An excellent student, Malcolm nonetheless left school after completing the eighth grade when a white teacher advised him that his aspiration to become a lawyer wasn't a "realistic goal for a nigger." He moved to Boston to live with an older stepsister and got a job on the railroad between Boston and New York, where he was exposed to the Harlem of Duke Ellington and Lionel Hampton, Billie Holiday and Ella Fitzgerald. He became a waiter in a popular club and began playing the numbers, dealing "reefer," and acting as a pimp. Known on the street as "Detroit Red," he later wrote, "Every word I spoke was hip or profane. I would bet that my working vocabulary wasn't two hundred words." At the age of twenty-one, he was convicted of armed robbery and was sent to prison, where he was called Satan by the other inmates because of his sullen behavior and irreligion. In prison he first became acquainted with the writings of Elijah Muhammad, the leader of the "Lost-Found Nation of Islam here in this wilderness of North America." He wrote in his autobiography of this period, "I had sunk to the very bottom of the American white man's society when, soon now, in prison—I found Allah and the religion of Islam and it completely transformed my life." The first excerpt from his autobiography that follows recounts the process of his conversion.

He began to read voraciously, first copying down a dictionary page by page, and then quickly moving on to works by Will Durant, H. G. Wells, W. E. B. Du Bois, Mahatma Gandhi, Herodotus, Schopenhauer, Kant, Nietzsche, and Spinoza. He began debating with other inmates the teachings of Elijah Muhammad, and he wrote to the spiritual leader in Chicago. In 1952 he was paroled and moved to Detroit to live with his brother's family, taking the name Malcolm X: "The Muslim's 'X' symbolized the true African family name that he never could know. For me, my 'X' replaced the white slavemaster name of 'Little' which some blue-eyed devil named Little had imposed upon my paternal forebears. . . . Mr. Muhammad taught that we would keep this 'X' until God Himself returned and gave us a Holy Name from His own mouth." He became one of the most successful of the young ministers, "fishing" for converts among "the twenty-two million black brothers who were brainwashed and sleeping in the cities of North America." During this time, he espoused the Muslims' view that the white man was a "devil," that integration was impossible because the white man would never cede power, that separation was the only way the black man could fulfill his own identity, and that Christianity was the religion of slaves. He founded the newspaper *Muhammad Speaks* and was Elijah Muhammad's emissary on missions to Africa.

Malcolm observed an uneasy truce with more conservative black leaders. In one of his most public rifts with Martin Luther King, Jr., he criticized what he called the "Farce on Washington," led by "integration-mad Negroes." "What that March on Washington did do was lull Negroes for a while. But inevitably, the black masses started realizing they had been smoothly hoaxed again by the white man. And, inevitably, the black man's anger rekindled, deeper than ever, and there began bursting out in different cities, in the 'long, hot summer' of 1964, unprecedented racial crises."

"The American black man," he argued, "should be focusing his every effort toward building his *own* businesses, and decent homes for himself." The white press began portraying him as a "black supremacist" and a "messenger of hate." In response, Malcolm replied, "When all of my ancestors are snake-bitten, and I'm snake-bitten . . . I warn my children to avoid snakes." Arguing that blacks had the right to defend themselves "by any means necessary," he stated, "We have never initiated any violence against anyone, but we do believe that when violence is practiced against us we should be able to defend ourselves. We don't believe in turning the other cheek." In his private life, Malcolm X was abstemious, shunning drugs, alcohol, and tobacco, and maintaining a disciplined daily life with his wife Betty Shabazz and their four daughters.

In time, however, a rift grew between Elijah Muhammad and his disciple. Malcolm came into greater contact with white students and intellectuals, many of whom responded positively to his speeches and lectures. He began to doubt both Elijah Muhammad's teachings and the morality of the older man's personal life, and his own prominence seemed to incite jealousies within the temple. At the same time, he began to believe that the Nation of Islam should relax its nonengagement policy and become more activist. "I felt that, wherever black people committed themselves, in the Little Rocks and Birminghams and other places, militantly disciplined Muslims should also be there—for all the world to see." The final break with Elijah Muhammad came when, after the assassination of President Kennedy in November 1963, he expressed the opinion that in the culture of violence that existed in America "the chickens had come home to roost." He was "silenced" by Elijah Muhammad and a few months later left for a pilgrimage to Mecca, which represented another major turning point in his life, as he recounts in the second excerpt from his autobiography that follows. He returned from Mecca bearing the name El-Hajj Malik El-Shabazz, the sign of one who has made the holy pilgrimage.

In June 1964 he founded the Organization of Afro-American Unity, meant to "embrace all faiths of black men" and to solidify ties with Africans and other peoples of color throughout the world. He now sought to frame injustice against African-Americans not as an issue of "civil rights," but as a denial of "human rights," to be debated in the court of nations. His new organization faltered, however. "One of the major troubles," he wrote, "that I was having in building the organization that I wanted—an all-black organization whose ultimate objective was to help create a society in which there could exist honest white-black brotherhood—was that my earlier public image, my old so-called 'Black Muslim' image, kept blocking me. I was trying to turn a corner, into a new regard by the public, especially Negroes; I was not less angry than I had been, but at the same time the true brotherhood I had seen in the Holy World had influenced me to recognize that anger can blind human vision."

Always convinced that he would die by violence—on February 14, 1965, his house in Queens was bombed and he told Alex Haley while they worked on his autobiography that he would not see its publication—Malcolm X was assassinated by members of the Nation of Islam at the Audubon Ballroom in New York on February 21, 1965. Elijah Muhammad said of the man who had vowed he would give his life for his leader and who for twelve years had been his most effective disciple, "Malcolm died according to his preaching." Twenty-two thousand people viewed his body, laid out in the traditional Muslim burial shrouds. In Malcolm's eulogy, Ozzie Davis recalled, "Many will ask what Harlem finds to honor in this stormy, controversial and bold young captain—and we will smile . . . They will say that he is of hate—a fanatic, a racist—who can only bring evil to the cause for which you struggle! And we will answer and say unto them: Did you ever talk to Brother Malcolm? . . . if you knew him you would know why we must honor him: Malcolm was our manhood, our living, black manhood! This was his meaning to his people. And, in honoring him, we honor the best in ourselves. . . . And we will know him then for what he was and is—a Prince—our own black shining Prince!—who didn't hesitate to die, because he loved us so."

After spending so many months working with Malcolm X on his autobiography, Alex Haley wrote, as the book was completed, "He was the most electric personality I have ever met, and I still can't quite conceive him dead. It still feels to me as if he has just gone into some next chapter, to be written by historians."

from *The Autobiography of Malcolm X*

"You have been a victim of the evil of the devil white man ever since he murdered and raped and stole you from your native land in the seeds of your forefathers. . . ."

NE DAY IN 1948, AFTER I HAD BEEN TRANSFERRED TO Concord Prison, my brother Philbert, who was forever joining something, wrote me this time that he had discovered the "natural religion for the black man." He belonged now, he said, to something called "the Nation of Islam." He said I should "pray to Allah for deliverance." I wrote Philbert a letter which, although in improved English, was worse than my earlier reply to his news that I was being prayed for by his "holiness" church. . . .

My brothers and sisters in Detroit and Chicago had all become converted to what they were being taught was the "natural religion for the black man" of which Philbert had written to me. They all prayed for me to become converted while I was in prison. But after Philbert reported my vicious reply, they discussed what was the best thing to do. They had decided that Reginald, the latest convert, the one to whom I felt closest, would best know how to approach me, since he knew me so well in the street life . . . and now, when he came to visit . . . he talked about the family, what was happening in Detroit, Harlem the last time he was there. I have never pushed anyone to tell me anything before he is ready. The offhand way Reginald talked and acted made me know that something big was coming.

He said, finally, as though it had just happened to come into his mind, "Malcolm, if a man knew every imaginable thing that there is to know, who would he be?"

Back in Harlem, he had often liked to get at something through this kind of indirection. It had often irritated me, because my way had always been direct. I looked at him. "Well, he would have to be some kind of a god—"

Reginald said, "There's a *man* who knows everything."

I asked, "Who is that?"

"God is a man," Reginald said. "His real name is Allah."

Allah. That word came back to me from Philbert's letter; it was my first hint of any connection. But Reginald went on. He said that God had 360 degrees of knowledge. He said that 360 degrees represented "the sum total of knowledge." To say I was confused is an understatement. I don't have to remind you of the background against which I sat hearing my brother Reginald talk like this. I just listened, knowing he was taking his time in putting me onto something. And if somebody is trying to put you onto something, you need to listen. . . .

Reginald, when he came to visit me again in a few days, could gauge from my attitude the effect that his talking had had upon me. He seemed very pleasant. Then, very seriously, he talked for two solid hours about "the devil white man" and "the brainwashed black man."

When Reginald left, he left me rocking with some of the first serious thoughts I had ever had in my life: that the white man was fast losing his power to oppress and exploit the dark world; that the dark world was starting to rise to rule the world again, as it had before; that the white man's world was on the way down, it was on the way out.

"You don't even know who you are," Reginald had said. "You don't even know, the white devil has hidden it from you, that you are of a race of people of ancient civilizations, and riches in gold and kings. You don't even know your true family name, you wouldn't recognize your true language if you heard it. You have been cut off by the devil white man from all true knowledge of your own kind. You have been a victim of the evil of the devil white man ever since he murdered and raped and stole you from your native land in the seeds of your forefathers. . . ."

I began to receive at least two letters every day from my brothers and sisters in Detroit. . . . They were all Muslims, followers of a man they described to me as "The Honorable Elijah Muhammad," a small, gentle man, who they sometimes referred to as "The Messenger of Allah." He was, they said, "a black man, like us." He had been born in America on a farm in Georgia. He had moved with his family to Detroit, and there had met a Mr. Wallace D. Fard who he claimed was "God in person." Mr. Wallace D. Fard had given to Elijah Muhammad Allah's message for the black people who were "the Lost-Found Nation of Islam here in this wilderness of North America."

All of them urged me to "accept the teachings of The Honorable Elijah Muhammad." Reginald explained that pork was not eaten by those who worshipped in the religion of Islam, and not smoking cigarettes was a rule of the followers of The Honorable Elijah Muhammad, because they did not take injurious things such as narcotics, tobacco, or liquor into their bodies. Over and over, I read, and heard, "The key to a Muslim is submission, the attunement of one toward Allah."

And what they termed "the true knowledge of the black man" that was possessed by the followers of The Honorable Elijah Muhammad was given shape for me in their lengthy letters, sometimes containing printed literature.

"The true knowledge," reconstructed much more briefly than I received it, was that history had been "whitened" in the white man's history books, and that the black man had been "brainwashed for hundreds of years." Original Man was black, in the continent called Africa where the human race had emerged on the planet Earth.

The black man, original man, built great empires and civilizations and cultures while the white man was still living on all fours in caves. "The devil white man," down through history, out of his devilish nature, had pillaged, murdered, raped, and exploited every race of man not white.

Human history's greatest crime was the traffic in black flesh when the devil white man went into Africa and murdered and kidnapped to bring to the West in chains, in slave ships, millions of black men, women, and children, who were worked and beaten and tortured as slaves.

The devil white man cut these black people off from all knowledge of their own kind, and cut them off from any knowledge of their own language, religion, and past culture, until the black man in America was the earth's only race of people who had absolutely no knowledge of his true identity.

In one generation, black slave women in America had been raped by the slavemaster white man until there had begun to emerge a homemade, handmade, brainwashed race that was no longer even of its true color, that no longer even knew its true family names. The slavemaster forced his family name upon this rape-mixed race, which the slavemaster began to call "the Negro."

This "Negro" was taught of his native Africa that it was peopled by heathen, black savages, swinging like monkeys from trees. This "Negro" accepted this along with every other teaching of the slavemaster that was designed to make him accept and obey and worship the white man.

And where the religion of every other people on earth taught its believers of a God with whom they could identify, a God who at least looked like one of their own kind, the slavemaster injected his Christian religion into this "Negro." This "Negro" was taught to worship an alien God having the same blond hair, pale skin, and blue eyes as the slavemaster.

This religion taught the "Negro" that black was a curse. It taught him to hate everything black, including himself. It taught him that everything white was good, to be admired, respected, and loved. It brainwashed this "Negro" to think he was superior if his complexion showed more of the white pollution of the slavemaster. This white man's Christian religion further deceived and brainwashed this "Negro" to always turn the other cheek, and grin, and scrape, and bow, and be humble, and to sing, and to pray, and to take whatever was dished out by the devilish white man; and to look for his pie in the sky, and for his heaven in the hereafter, while right here on earth the slavemaster white man enjoyed *his* heaven.

Many a time, I have looked back, trying to assess, just for myself, my first reactions to all this. Every instinct of the ghetto jungle streets, every hustling fox and criminal wolf instinct in me, which would have scoffed at and rejected anything else, was struck numb. It was as though all of that life merely was back there, without any remaining effect, or influence. I remember how, some time later, reading the Bible in the Norfolk Prison Colony library, I came upon, then I read, over and over, how Paul on the road to Damascus, upon hearing the voice of Christ, was so smitten that he was knocked off his horse, in a daze. I do not now, and I did not then, liken myself to Paul. But I do understand his experience.

I have since learned—helping me to understand what then began to happen within me—that the truth can be quickly received, or received at all, only by the sinner who knows and admits that he is guilty of having sinned much. Stated another way: only guilt admitted accepts truth. The Bible again: the one people whom Jesus could not help were the Pharisees; they didn't feel they needed any help.

The very enormity of my previous life's guilt prepared me to accept the truth.

Not for weeks yet would I deal with the direct, personal application to myself, as a black man, of the truth. It still was like a blinding light.

Reginald left Boston and went back to Detroit. I would sit in my room and stare. At the dining-room table, I would hardly eat, only drink the water. I nearly starved. Fellow inmates, concerned, and guards, apprehensive, asked what was wrong with me. It was suggested that I visit the doctor, and I didn't. The doctor, advised, visited me. I don't know what his diagnosis was, probably that I was working on some act.

I was going through the hardest thing, also the greatest thing, for any human being to do; to accept that which is already within you, and around you. . . .

I knew that when my letter became public knowledge back in America, many would be astounded—loved ones, friends, and enemies alike. And no less astounded would be millions whom I did not know—who had gained during my twelve years with Elijah Muhammad a "hate" image of Malcolm X.

Even I was myself astounded. But there was precedent in my life for this letter. My whole life had been a chronology of—*changes.*

Here is what I wrote . . . from my heart:

"Never have I witnessed such sincere hospitality and the overwhelming spirit of true brotherhood as is practiced by people of all colors and races here in this Ancient Holy Land, the home of Abraham, Muhammad, and all the other prophets of the Holy Scriptures. For the past week, I have been utterly speechless and spellbound by the graciousness I see displayed all around me by people *of all colors.*

"I have been blessed to visit the Holy City of Mecca. I have made my seven circuits around the Ka'ba, led by a young *Mutawaf* named Muhammad. I drank water from the well of Zem Zem. I ran seven times back and forth between the hills of Mt. Al-Safa and Al-Marwah. I have prayed in the ancient city of Mina, and I have prayed on Mt. Arafat.

"There were tens of thousands of pilgrims, from all over the world. They were of all colors, from blue-eyed blonds to black-skinned Africans.

But we were all participating in the same ritual, displaying a spirit of unity and brotherhood that my experiences in America had led me to believe never could exist between the whitie and the non-white.

"America needs to understand Islam, because this is the one religion that erases from its society the race problem. Throughout my travels in the Muslim world, I have met, talked to, and even eaten with people who in America would have been considered 'white'—but the 'white' attitude was removed from their minds by the religion of Islam. I have never before seen *sincere* and *true* brotherhood practiced by all colors together, irrespective of their color.

"You may be shocked by these words coming from me. But on this pilgrimage, what I have seen, and experienced has forced me to *re-arrange* much of my thought-patterns previously held, and to *toss aside* some of my previous conclusions. This was not too difficult for me. Despite my firm convictions, I have been always a man who tries to face facts, and to accept the reality of life as new experience and new knowledge unfolds it. I have always kept an open mind, which is necessary to the flexibility that must go hand in hand with every form of intelligent search for truth.

"During the past eleven days here in the Muslim world, I have eaten from the same plate, drunk from the same glass, and slept in the same bed (or on the same rug)—while praying to the *same God*—with fellow Muslims, whose eyes were the bluest of blue, whose hair was the blondest of blond, and whose skin was the whitest of white. And in the *words* and in the *actions* and in the *deeds* of the 'white' Muslims, I felt the same sincerity that I felt among the black African Muslims of Nigeria, Sudan, and Ghana.

"We were *truly* all the same (brothers)—because their belief in one God had removed the 'white' from their *minds*, the 'white' from their *behavior*, and the 'white' from their *attitude*.

"I could see from this, that perhaps if white Americans could accept the Oneness of God, then perhaps, too, they could accept *in reality* the Oneness of Man—and cease to measure, and hinder, and harm others in terms of their 'differences' in color.

"With racism plaguing America like an incurable cancer, the so-called 'Christian' white American heart should be more receptive to a proven solution to such a destructive problem. Perhaps it could be in time to save America from imminent disaster—the same destruction brought upon Germany by racism that eventually destroyed the Germans themselves.

Each hour here in the Holy Land enables me to have greater spiritual insights into what is happening in America between black and white. The American Negro never can be blamed for his racial animosities—he is only reacting to four hundred years of the conscious racism of the American whites. But as racism leads America up the suicide path, I do believe, from the experiences that I have had with them, that the whites of the younger generation, the colleges and universities, will see the handwriting on the wall and many of them will turn to the *spiritual* path of *truth*—the *only* way left to America to ward off the disaster that racism inevitably must lead to.

"Never have I been so highly honored. Never have I been made to feel more humble and unworthy. Who would believe the blessings that have been heaped upon an *American Negro*? A few nights ago, a man who would be called in America a 'white' man, a United Nations diplomat, an ambassador, a companion of kings, gave me *his* hotel suite, *his* bed. By this man, His Excellency Prince Faisal, who rules this Holy Land, was made aware of my presence here in Jedda. The very next morning, Prince Faisal's son, in person, informed me that by the will and decree of his esteemed father, I was to be a State Guest.

"The Deputy Chief of Protocol himself took me before the Hajj Court. His Holiness Sheikh Muhammad Harkon himself okayed my visit to Mecca. His Holiness gave me two books on Islam, with his personal seal and autograph, and he told me that he prayed that I would be a successful preacher of Islam in America. A car, a driver, and a guide, have been placed at my disposal, making it possible for me to travel about this Holy Land almost at will. The government provides air-conditioned quarters and servants in each city that I visit. Never would I have even thought of dreaming that I would ever be a recipient of such honors—honors that in America would be bestowed upon a King—not a Negro.

"All praise is due to Allah, Lord of all the Worlds."

"Sincerely,
"El-Hajj Malik El-Shabazz
"(Malcolm X)"

1965

Eldridge Cleaver
(1935–)

One of the most influential personal histories of the 1960s, Eldridge Cleaver's best-selling *Soul on Ice,* like Malcolm X's *Autobiography,*† recounts one man's personal and political odyssey from streethood to black culturalist, Muslim, and political activist. Born in Little Rock, Arkansas, and raised in Los Angeles, Cleaver first went to juvenile prison at the age of twelve. After several more juvenile offenses, in 1954 he was sent to Soledad Prison for possession of a shopping bag full of marijuana. In prison, Cleaver read "to save himself," his program including works by Rousseau, Voltaire, Machiavelli, Thomas Paine, Freud, Jung, Karl Marx, Frantz Fanon, Jack Kerouac, Richard Wright, and James Baldwin. He successfully challenged prison officials for the right of inmates to hold black history courses and Muslim services, and he began to write, his pieces appearing in *Esquire, Negro History Bulletin,* and *Ramparts.*

Written while Cleaver was in prison, from the opening pages of its first chapter, "On Becoming," *Soul on Ice* is an unusually revealing account of a personality in transition. The powerful essays, letters, and fragments that follow probe the psychological depths of sexuality, racism, and political and religious commitment. "Letters from Prison" delineates Cleaver's spiritual journey. In "Blood of the Beast," he analyzes white heroes and black athletes, the world of James Baldwin, the war in Vietnam, and the solidarity of people of color around the world. In "White Woman/Black Man," he examines the stereotypes of white and black sexuality, arguing that black men and white women, white men and black women, have been disastrously joined throughout our history with "two sets of handcuffs that have all four of us tied up together." As he began the book with an exploration of his obsession with white women, he ends it with a tribute to "All Black Women," "Queen/Mother/Daughter of Africa/Sister of My Soul/Black Bride of My Passion/My Eternal Love." Reflecting on the path that he has traced, Cleaver writes, "I was very familiar with the Eldridge who came to prison, but that Eldridge no longer exists. And the one I am now is in some ways a stranger to me. . . . Of course I want to get out of prison, badly, but I shall get out some day. I am more concerned with what I am going to be after I get out. I know that by following the course which I have charted I will find my salvation."

By the time of his release on parole in December 1966, Cleaver had spent nearly twenty years in prison. He moved to San Francisco, and, with other activist writers, founded the Black House, a cultural center not unlike Amiri Baraka's Black Arts Repertory Theater or those organized by Malcolm X's Organization of Afro-American Unity. Soon after, he met Huey P. Newton and Bobby Seale and joined the Black Panthers, becoming their minister of information, making speeches about the movement, and editing their journal, *The Black Panther.* The Panthers proved very adept at capturing media attention; in May 1967, to protest the killing of a black youth by police, they descended on the California legislature in military regalia and armed. A state law was soon passed forbidding weapons in public places.

In the wake of numerous clashes between the Panthers and the police, on April 4, 1968, two days after the death of Martin Luther King, Jr., Cleaver was wounded in a shoot-out with police that killed a seventeen-year-old comrade. A few hours later, Cleaver's parole was revoked, and though he challenged the ruling, he was ordered to return to prison in November. In the interim, he organized a political campaign and ran for president of the United States for the Peace and Freedom Party. Before he was due to report to prison, he fled the country, traveling to Cuba and then to Algeria, where he gave numerous interviews which ran, rather incongruously in this era of radical chic, in places like *Life* and *Look,* among others. In 1969 he published *Post-Prison Writings and Speeches.* He returned to the United States in 1975.

In the excerpt from *Soul on Ice* that follows, Cleaver talks about the death and significance of Malcolm X.

from *Soul on Ice*

"We shall have our manhood. We shall have it or the earth will be leveled by our attempts to gain it."

Initial Reactions on the Assassination of Malcolm X

SUNDAY IS MOVIE DAY AT FOLSOM PRISON AND I WAS SITTING in the darkened hulk of Mess Hall No. 1—which convicts call "The Folsom Theatre"—watching Victor Buono in a movie called *The Strangler*, when a convict known as Silly Willie came over to where I was sitting and whispered into my ear:

"Brother J sent me in to tell you it just came over the TV that Malcolm X was shot as he addressed a rally in New York."

For a moment the earth seemed to reel in orbit. The skin all over my body tightened up. "How bad?" I asked.

"The TV didn't say," answered Silly Willie. The distress was obvious in his voice. "We was around back in Pipe Alley checking TV when a special bulletin came on. All they said was Malcolm X was shot and they were rushing him to the hospital."

"Thanks," I said to Silly Willie. I felt his reassuring hand on my shoulder as he faded away in the darkness. For a moment I pondered whether to go outside and get more information, but something made me hang back. I remember distinctly thinking that I would know soon enough. On the screen before me, Victor Buono had a woman by the throat and was frantically choking the last gasping twitches of life out of her slumping body. I was thinking that if Malcolm's wounds were not too serious, that if he recovered, the shooting might prove to be a blessing in disguise: it would focus more intensified attention on him and create a windfall of sympathy and support for him throughout America's black ghettos, and so put more power into his hands. The possibility that the wounds may have been fatal, that as I sat there Malcolm was lying already dead, was excluded from my mind.

After the movie ended, as I filed outside in the long line of convicts and saw the shocked, wild expression on Brother J's face, I still could not believe that Malcolm X was dead. We mingled in the crowd of convicts milling around in the yard and were immediately surrounded by a group of Muslims, all of whom, like myself, were firm supporters of Malcolm X. He's dead, their faces said, although not one of them spoke a word. As we stood there in silence, two Negro inmates walked by and one of them said to us,

"That's a goddam shame how they killed that man! Of all people, why'd they kill Malcolm? Why'n't they kill some of them Uncle-Tomming m.f.'s? I wish I could get my hands on whoever did it." And he walked away, talking and cursing to his buddy.

What does one say to his comrades at the moment when The Leader falls? All comment seems irrelevant. If the source of death is so-called natural causes, or an accident, the reaction is predictable, a feeling of impotence, humbleness, helplessness before the forces of the universe. But when the cause of death is an assassin's bullet, the overpowering desire is for vengeance. One wants to strike out, to kill, crush, destroy, to deliver a telling counterblow, to inflict upon the enemy a reciprocal, equivalent loss. But whom does one strike down at such a time if one happens to be in an anonymous, amorphous crowd of convicts in Folsom Prison and The Leader lies dead thousands of miles away across the continent?

"I'm going to my cell," I told the tight little knot of Muslims. "Allah is the Best Knower. Everything will be made manifest in time. Give it a little time. *As-Salaam Aliakum.*"

"Wa-Aliakum Salaam," the Brothers returned the salutation and we shook hands all around, the double handshake which is very popular among Muslims in California prisons. (It is so popular that one sometimes grows weary of shaking hands. If a Muslim leaves a group for a minute to go get a drink of water, he is not unlikely to shake hands all around before he leaves and again when he returns. But no one complains and the convention is respected as a gesture of unity, brotherly love, and solidarity—so meaningful in a situation where Muslims are persecuted and denied recognition and the right to function as a legitimate religion.) I headed for my cell. I lived in No. 5 Building, which is Folsom's Honor Unit, reserved for those who have maintained a clean record for at least six months. Advantages: a larger cell, TV every Wednesday, Saturday, and Sunday night, less custodial supervision, easier ingress and egress. If while living in the Honor Unit you get into a "beef" which results in action against you by the disciplinary committee, one of the certain penalties is that you are immediately kicked out of No. 5 Building.

As I walked along the first tier toward my cell, I ran into Red, who lived near me on the tier.

"I guess you heard about Malcolm?"

"Yeah," I said. "They say he got wasted."

Red, who is white, knew from our many discussions that I was extremely partial to Malcolm, and he himself, being thoroughly alienated from the *status quo,* recognized the assassination for what it was: a negative blow against a positive force. Red's questions were the obvious ones: Who? Why? The questions were advanced tentatively, cautiously, because of the treacherous ground he was on: a red-headed, blue-eyed white man concerned by an event which so many others greeted with smiles and sighs. I went into my cell.

Although I heard it blared over the radio constantly and read about it in all the newspapers, days passed during which my mind continued to reject the fact of Malcolm's death. I existed in a dazed state, wandering in a trance around Folsom, drifting through the working hours in the prison bakery; and yet I was keen to observe the effect of the assassination on my fellow inmates. From most of the whites there was a leer and a hint of a smile in the eyes. They seemed anxious to see a war break out between the followers of Elijah and the followers of Malcolm.

There are only a few whites in Folsom with whom I would ever discuss the death of Malcolm or anything else besides baseball, or the weather. Many of the Mexican-Americans were sympathetic, although some of them made a point, when being observed by whites, of letting drop sly remarks indicating they were glad Malcolm was gone. Among the Negroes there was mass mourning for Malcolm X. Nobody talked much for a few days. The only Negroes who were not indignant were a few of the Muslims who remained loyal to Elijah Muhammad. They interpreted Malcolm's assassination as the will of Allah descending upon his head for having gone astray. To them, it was Divine chastisement and a warning to those whom Malcolm had tempted. It was not so much Malcolm's death that made them glad; but in their eyes it now seemed possible to heal the schism in the movement and restore the monolithic unity of the Nation of Islam, a unity they looked back on with some nostalgia.

Many Negro convicts saw Malcolm's assassination as a historic turning point in black America. Whereas Negroes often talk heatedly about wiping out all the so-called Negro leaders whom they do not happen to like or agree with, this was the first significant case of Negro leader-killing that anyone could remember. What struck me is that the Negro convicts welcomed the new era. If a man as valuable to us as Malcolm could go down, then as far as I was concerned so could any other man—myself included. Coming a week after the alleged exposé of the alleged plot to dynamite the Statue of Liberty, Washington Monument, and the Liberty Bell, a plot supposedly hatched by discontented blacks, the assassination of Malcolm X had put new ideas in the wind with implications for the future of black struggle in America.

I suppose that like many of the brothers and sisters in the Nation of Islam movement, I also had clung to the hope that, somehow, the rift between Malcolm X and Elijah Muhammad would be mended. As long as Brother Malcolm was alive, many Muslims could maintain this hope, neatly overlooking the increasing bitterness of their rivalry. But death made the split final and sealed it for history. These events caused a profound personal crisis in my life and beliefs, as it did for other Muslims. During the bitter time of his suspension and prior to his break with Elijah Muhammad, we had watched Malcolm X as he sought frantically to reorient himself and establish a new platform. It was like watching a master do a dance with death on a highstrung tightrope. He pirouetted, twirled, turned somersaults in the air—but he landed firmly on his feet and was off and running. We watched it all, seeking a cause to condemn Malcolm X and cast him out of our hearts. We read all the charges and countercharges. I found Malcolm X blameless.

It had been my experience that the quickest way to become hated by the Muslims was to criticize Elijah Muhammad or disagree with something he wrote or said. If Elijah wrote, as he has done, that the swine is a poison creature composed of 1/3 rat, 1/3 cat, and 1/3 dog and you attempted to cite scientific facts to challenge this, you had sinned against the light, that was all there was to it. How much more unlikely was it, therefore, that Muslims would stand up and denounce Elijah himself, repudiate his authority and his theology, deny his revelation, and take sides against him, the Messenger of Almighty God Allah? I never dreamed that someday I would be cast in that hapless role.

After Malcolm made his pilgrimage to Mecca, completing a triumphal tour of Africa and the Near East, during which he received the high honors of a visiting dignitary, he returned to the U.S.A. and set about building his newly founded Organization of Afro-American Unity. He also established the Muslim Mosque, Inc., to receive the Muslims he thought would pull away from Elijah. The Muslim Mosque would teach Orthodox Islam, under the direction of Sheikh Ahmed Hassoun from the Holy City of Mecca. Grand Sheik Muhammad Sarur Al-Sabban, secretary-general of the Muslim World League, had offered the services of Sheik Ahmed, according to the Los Angeles *Herald-Dispatch,* to "help Malcolm X in his efforts to correct the distorted image that the religion of Islam has been given by hate groups in this country."

I began defending Malcolm X. At a secret meeting of the Muslims in Folsom, I announced that I was no longer a follower of Elijah Muhammad, that I was throwing my support behind Brother Malcolm. I urged everyone there to think the matter over and make a choice, because it was no longer possible to ride two horses at the same time. On the wall of my cell I had a large, framed picture of Elijah Muhammad which I had had for years. I took it down, destroyed it, and in its place put up, in the same frame, a beautiful picture of Malcolm X kneeling down in the Mohammad Ali Mosque in Cairo, which I clipped from the *Saturday Evening Post.* At first the other Muslims in Folsom denounced me; some I'd known intimately for years stopped speaking to me or even looking at me. When we met, they averted their eyes. To them the choice was simple: Elijah Muhammad is the hand picked Messenger of Allah, the instrument of Allah's will. All who oppose him are aiding Allah's enemies, the White Devils. Whom do you choose, God or the Devil? Malcolm X, in the eyes of Elijah's followers, had committed the unforgivable heresy when, changing his views and abandoning the racist position, he admitted the possibility of brotherhood between blacks and whites. In a letter sent back to the U.S. from the Holy Land, Malcolm X had stated:

> You may be shocked by these words coming from me, but I have always been a man who tries to face facts and to accept the reality of life as new experiences and knowledge unfold it. The experiences of this pilgrimage have taught me much and each hour in the Holy Land opens my eyes even more. . . . I have eaten from the same plate with people whose eyes were the bluest of blue, whose hair was the blondest of blond and whose skin was the whitest of white . . . and I felt the sincerity in the words and deeds of these "white" Muslims that I felt among the African Muslims of Nigeria, Sudan and Ghanan.

Many of us were shocked and outraged by these words from Malcolm X, who had been a major influence upon us all and the main factor in many of our conversions to the Black Muslims. But there were those of us who were glad to be liberated from a doctrine of hate and racial supremacy. The onus of teaching racial supremacy and hate, which is the white man's burden, is pretty hard to bear. Asked if he would accept whites as members of his Organization of Afro-American Unity, Malcolm said he would accept John Brown if he were around today—which certainly is setting the standard high.

At the moment I declared myself for Malcolm X, I had some prestige among the Muslims in the prisons of California, because of my active role in proselytizing new converts and campaigning for religious freedom for Muslim convicts. We sent a barrage of letters and petitions to the courts, government officials, even the United Nations.

After the death of Brother Booker T. X, who was shot dead by a San Quentin prison guard, and who at the time had been my cell partner and the inmate Minister of the Muslims of San Quentin, my leadership of the Muslims of San Quentin had been publicly endorsed by Elijah Muhammad's west coast representative, Minister John Shabazz of Muhammad's Los Angeles Mosque. This was done because of the explosive conditions in San Quentin at the time. Muslim officials wanted to avert any Muslim-initiated violence, which had become a distinct possibility in the aftermath of Brother Booker's death. I was instructed to impose an iron discipline upon the San Quentin Mosque, which had continued to exist despite the unending efforts of prison authorities to stamp it out. Most of the Muslims who were in prison during those days have since been released. I was one of the few remaining, and I was therefore looked upon by the other Muslims as one who had sacrificed and invested much in the struggle to advance the teachings of Elijah Muhammad. For that reason, my defection to Malcolm X caused a great deal of consternation among the Muslims of Folsom. But slowly, Malcolm was getting his machine together and it was obvious to me that his influence was growing. Negro inmates who had had reservations about Malcolm while he was under Elijah's authority now embraced him, and it was clear that they accepted Malcolm's leadership. Negroes whom we had tried in vain for years to convert to Elijah's fold now lined up with enthusiasm behind Malcolm.

I ran a regular public relations campaign for Malcolm in Folsom. I saw to it that copies of his speeches were made and circulated among Negro inmates. I never missed a chance to speak favorably about Malcolm, to quote him, to explain and justify what he was trying to do. Soon I had the ear of the Muslims, and it was not long before Malcolm had other ardent defenders in Folsom. In a very short time Malcolm became the hero of the vast majority of Negro inmates. Elijah Muhammad was quickly becoming irrelevant, passé.

Malcolm X had a special meaning for black convicts. A former prisoner himself, he had risen from the lowest depths to great heights. For this reason he was a symbol of hope, a model for thousands of black convicts who found themselves trapped in the vicious PPP cycle: prison-parole-prison. One thing that the judges, policemen, and administrators of prisons seem never to have understood, and for which they certainly do not make any allowances, is that Negro convicts, basically, rather than see themselves as criminals and perpetrators of misdeeds, look upon themselves as prisoners of war, the victims of a vicious, dog-eat-dog social system that is so heinous as to cancel out their own malefactions: in the jungle there is no right or wrong.

Rather than owing and paying a debt to society, Negro prisoners feel that they are being abused, that their imprisonment is simply another form of the oppression which they have known all their lives. Negro inmates feel that they are being robbed, that it is "society" that owes them, that should be paying them, a debt.

America's penology does not take this into account. Malcolm X did, and black convicts know that the ascension to power of Malcolm X or a man like him would eventually have revolutionized penology in America. Malcolm delivered a merciless and damning indictment of prevailing penology. It is only a matter of time until the question of the prisoner's debt to society versus society's debt to the prisoner is injected forcefully into national and state politics, into the civil and human rights struggle, and into the consciousness of the body politic. It is an explosive issue which goes to the very root of America's system of justice, the structure of criminal law, the prevailing beliefs and attitudes toward the convicted felon. While it is easier to make out a case for black convicts, the same principles apply to white and Mexican-American convicts as well. They too are victimized, albeit a little more subtly, by "society." When black convicts start demanding a new dispensation and definition of justice, naturally the white and Mexican-

American convicts will demand equality of treatment. Malcolm X was a focus for these aspirations.

The Black Muslim movement was destroyed the moment Elijah cracked the whip over Malcolm's head, because it was not the Black Muslim movement itself that was so irresistibly appealing to the true believers. It was the awakening into self-consciousness of twenty million Negroes which was so compelling. Malcolm X articulated their aspirations better than any other man of our time. When he spoke under the banner of Elijah Muhammad he was irresistible. When he spoke under his own banner he was still irresistible. If he had become a Quaker, a Catholic, or a Seventh-Day Adventist, or a Sammy Davis–style Jew, and if he had continued to give voice to the mute ambitions in the black man's soul, his message would still have been triumphant: because what was great was not Malcolm X but the truth he uttered.

The truth which Malcolm uttered had vanquished the whole passel of so-called Negro leaders and spokesmen who trifle with the white power structure. He was stopped in the only way such a man can be stopped, in the same way that the enemies of the Congolese people had to stop Lumumba, by the same method that exploiters, tyrants, and parasitical oppressors have always crushed the legitimate strivings of people for freedom, justice, and equality—by murder, assassination, and mad-dog butchery.

What provoked the assassins to murder? Did it bother them that Malcolm was elevating our struggle into the international arena through his campaign to carry it before the United Nations? Well, by murdering him they only hastened the process, because we certainly are going to take our cause before a sympathetic world. Did it bother the assassins that Malcolm denounced the racist strait-jacket demonology of Elijah Muhammad? Well, we certainly do denounce it and will continue to do so. Did it bother the assassins that Malcolm taught us to defend ourselves? We shall not remain a defenseless prey to the murderer, to the sniper and the bomber. Insofar as Malcolm spoke the truth, the truth will triumph and prevail and his name shall live; and insofar as those who opposed him lied, to that extent will their names become curses. Because "truth crushed to earth shall rise again."

So now Malcolm is no more. The bootlicker, Uncle Toms, lackeys, and stooges of the white power structure have done their best to denigrate Malcolm, to root him out of his people's heart, to tarnish his memory. But their million-worded lies fall on deaf ears. As Ossie Davis so eloquently expressed it in his immortal eulogy of Malcolm:

> If you knew him you would know why we must honor him: Malcolm was our manhood, our living black manhood! This was his meaning to his people. And, in honoring him, we honor the best in ourselves. . . . However much we may have differed with him—or with each other about him and his value as a man, let his going from us serve only to bring us

> together, now. Consigning these mortal remains to earth, the common mother of all, secure in the knowledge that what we place in the ground is no more now a man—but a seed—which, after the winter of our discontent will come forth again to meet us. And we will know him then for what he was and is —a Prince—our own black shining Prince!—who didn't hesitate to die, because he loved us so.

We shall have our manhood. We shall have it or the earth will be leveled by our attempts to gain it.

Folsom Prison
June 19, 1965

The Black Panther Party

Toward the end of the sixties, the Black Panther Party briefly articulated the strongest expression of black nationalism since Marcus Garvey's Back to Africa movement of the twenties. After the riots of the "long, hot summer" of 1964 and the death of Malcolm X in early 1965, the nonviolent civil rights movement began to dissolve and the pendulum of black activism swung from alliance and integration to political and economic self-empowerment. On one front, African-Americans moved "from protest to politics," as Bayard Rustin put it, and in the fall of 1967, candidates Richard Hatcher in Gary, Indiana, and Carl Stokes in Cleveland, Ohio, successfully campaigned for mayor. New economic organizations and cooperatives also developed, and in this context the Black Panther Party emerged.

Taking its name from the Lowndes County, Alabama, Freedom Party, which had mobilized black voters with the slogan "Vote for the Panther," the BPP started in California in the aftermath of the Watts rebellion in August 1965. Inspired by Marx, Lenin, Frantz Fanon, and Mao Tse-tung, twenty-four-year-old Huey P. Newton, the son of a Baptist preacher and a part-time law student, and twenty-nine-year-old Bobby Seale, who worked with Newton at the North Oakland Neighborhood Anti-Poverty Center, issued the ten-point platform of demands included here, arguing for "land, bread, housing, education, clothing, justice, and peace."

Significantly, the group called themselves the Black Panther Party for Self-Defense. Representing a strain of militant thinking that extended from the early slave rebels who had armed themselves, to eighteenth-century activists Henry Highland Garnet and Frederick Douglass, to Malcolm X, the BPP argued that, like other American citizens, they had the right to bear arms and to defend themselves from physical violence. Adopting military-style garb, and carrying openly displayed weapons, they guarded street rallies, patrolled black communities, and provided legal assistance to police detainees. At the specter of "Negroes with guns," a California assemblyman introduced gun-control legislation, and on May 2, 1967, thirty male and female Panthers marched upon the state capitol in protest, ending up on the floor of the chamber before they were issued out. On the steps of the building Bobby Seale read Panther "Executive Mandate Number One," protesting "racist police agencies throughout the country [that] are intensifying the terror, brutality, murder, and repression of black people." Putting their complaints in a world-historical context, they argued, "Toward people of color the racist power structure of America has but one policy: repression, genocide, terror, and the big stick. Black people have begged, prayed, petitioned, demonstrated, and everything else to get the racist power structure of America to right the wrongs which have historically been perpetrated against the black people." Ending on a defiant note, they decreed, "the time has come for black people to arm themselves against this terror before it is too late. . . . A people who have suffered so much for so long at the hands of a racist society, must draw the line somewhere. We believe that the black communities of America must rise up as one man to halt the progression of a trend that leads inevitably to their total destruction."

The televised event brought the group to national attention, and with Eldridge Cleaver as minister of information, word was spread through the newspaper, *The Black Panther,* and Cleaver's bestselling *Soul on Ice.*† Local chapters were organized in twenty-five cities across the country, including Los Angeles, New York, and Chicago, where the group was led by twenty-one-year-old Fred Hampton, who couched his powerful speeches in the rhetoric of class struggle. Despite their destructive discourse, the group engaged in constructive activities like the free-breakfast programs for children, black historical and cultural centers, and health clinics. "We're not gonna fight fire with fire," Hampton argued, "we're gonna fight fire with water. We're not gonna fight racism with racism, we're gonna fight racism with solidarity." Martin Luther King said of these angry young men, "Were I able to co-opt these minds into my cause, there is no question that victory would be swift and eternal."

Before long, J. Edgar Hoover targeted the BPP, calling it "the greatest threat to the internal security of the country," and the FBI mobilized to "expose, disrupt, misdirect, discredit, or otherwise neutralize" them. As informants infiltrated the party and the FBI sent anonymous letters to encourage violence between the Panthers and youth gangs, a series of explosive confrontations with the police signaled their eventual demise. In 1967 Huey Newton was arrested for the October 28 killing of a police officer, and the Panthers launched their "Free Huey" protest. Convicted of voluntary manslaughter and given a two-to-fifteen-year sentence, he spent twenty-two months in jail before his conviction was reversed by the California State Court of Appeals. In April 1968 Cleaver was involved in a shoot-out in Oakland that killed seventeen-year-old Panther Bobby Hutton, and as one of the Chicago Eight, Bobby Seale was tried for disrupting the Democratic National Convention. In May 1969 Fred Hampton was convicted for stealing ice cream from a Good Humor vendor; he was released four months later on a $10,000 appeal bond.

Then, on December 4, 1969, Panthers Fred Hampton and Mark

Clark were killed by Chicago police in a predawn raid, ostensibly conducted to seize illegal weapons. Nearly a hundred shots were fired, most likely only one of them by Clark. When a federal grand jury acquitted the officers involved, NAACP Executive Secretary Roy Wilkins and former Attorney General Ramsey Clark, hardly radical voices, wrote in an investigative-commission report that "the planning of the raid was so inadequate as to constitute criminal conduct." Arguing that "summary execution is not tolerable," they wrote, "Of all violence, official violence is the most destructive. It not only takes life, but it does so in the name of the people and as the agent of society. It says, therefore, this is our way, this is what we believe, we stand for nothing better."

In 1982, after the longest civil rights trial in this nation's history, the survivors and families of Hampton and Clark were awarded a $1.85 million settlement.

Black Panther Party Platform

"We want land, bread, housing, education, clothing, justice and peace. . . ."

1. *We want freedom. We want power to determine the destiny of our Black Community.*

We believe that black people will not be free until we are able to determine our destiny.

2. *We want full employment for our people.*

We believe that the federal government is responsible and obligated to give every man employment or a guaranteed income. We believe that if the white American businessmen will not give full employment, then the means of production should be taken from the businessmen and placed in the community so that the people of the community can organize and employ all of its people and give a high standard of living.

3. *We want an end to the robbery by the white man of our Black Community.*

We believe that this racist government has robbed us and now we are demanding the overdue debt of forty acres and two mules. Forty acres and two mules was promised 100 years ago as restitution for slave labor and mass murder of black people. We will accept the payment in currency which will be distributed to our many communities. The Germans are now aiding the Jews in Israel for the genocide of the Jewish people. The Germans murdered six million Jews. The American racist has taken part in the slaughter of over fifty million black people; therefore, we feel that this is a modest demand that we make.

4. *We want decent housing, fit for shelter of human beings.*

We believe that if the white landlords will not give decent housing to our black community, then the housing and the land should be made into cooperatives so that our community, with government aid, can build and make decent housing for its people.

5. *We want education for our people that exposes the true nature of this decadent American society. We want education that teaches us our true history and our role in the present-day society.*

We believe in an education system that will give to our people a knowledge of self. If a man does not have knowledge of himself and his position in society and the world, then he has little chance to relate to anything else.

6. *We want all black men to be exempt from military service.*

We believe that black people should not be forced to fight in the military service to defend a racist government that does not protect us. We will not fight and kill other people of color in the world who, like the black people, are being victimized by the white racist government of America. We will protect ourselves from the force and violence of the racist police and the racist military, by whatever means necessary.

7. *We want an immediate end to POLICE BRUTALITY and MURDER of black people.*

We believe we can end police brutality in our black community by organizing black self-defense groups that are dedicated to defending our black community from racist police oppression and brutality. The Second Amendment to the Constitution of the United States gives us a right to bear arms. We therefore believe that all black people should arm themselves for self-defense.

8. *We want freedom for all black men held in federal, state, county and city prisons and jails.*

We believe that all black people should be released from the many jails and prisons because they have not received a fair and impartial trial.

9. *We want all black people when brought to trial to be tried in court by a jury of their peer group or people from their black communities, as defined by the Constitution of the United States.*

We believe that the courts should follow the United States Constitution so that black people will receive fair trials. The 14th Amendment of the U.S. Constitution gives a man a right to be tried by his peer group. A peer is a person from a similar economic, social, religious, geographical, environmental, historical and racial background. To do this the court will be forced to select a jury from the black community from which the black defendant came. We have been, and are being tried by all-white juries that have no understanding of the "average reasoning man" of the black community.

10. *We want land, bread, housing, education, clothing, justice and peace. And as our major political objective, a United Nations–supervised plebiscite to be held throughout the black colony in which only black colonial subjects will be allowed to participate, for the purpose of determining the will of black people as to their national destiny.*

When, in the course of human events, it becomes necessary for one people to dissolve the political bands which have connected them with another, and to assume, among the powers of the earth, the separate and equal station to which the laws of nature and nature's God entitle them, a decent respect to the opinions of mankind requires that they should declare the causes which impel them to the separation.

We hold these truths to be self-evident, that all men are created equal; that they are endowed by their Creator with certain unalienable rights; that among these are life, liberty, and the pursuit of happiness. *That, to secure these rights, governments are instituted among men, deriving their just powers from the consent of the governed; that, whenever any form of government becomes destructive of these ends, it is the right of the people to alter or to abolish it, and to institute a new government, laying its foundation on such principles, and organizing its powers in such form, as to them shall seem most likely to effect their safety and happiness.* Prudence, indeed, will dictate that governments long established should not be changed for light and transient causes; and accordingly, all experience hath shown, that mankind are more disposed to suffer, while evils are sufferable, than to right themselves by abolishing the forms to which they are accustomed. *But, when a long train of abuses and usurpations pursuing invariably the same object, evinces a design to reduce them under absolute despotism, it is their right, it is their duty, to throw off such government, and to provide new guards for their future security.*

October 1966

Amiri Baraka
(1934–)

The author of more than twenty volumes, Amiri Baraka has embraced a number of forms—poetry, fiction, drama, autobiography, criticism—in a career marked by continual thematic and formal change. Baraka was born Everett LeRoy Jones in Newark, New Jersey, on October 7, 1934. He attended Rutgers and then Howard University (now using the name LeRoi Jones), which he left with failing grades, and spent three years in the Air Force, where he was stationed in Europe, Africa, and the Middle East. In the late 1950s he became part of the Greenwich Village avant-garde and studied at the New School for Social Research and received a master's degree from Columbia University. In 1958 he married Hettie Cohen, with whom he edited the avant-garde journal *Yugen,* and, while teaching at the New School, the University of Buffalo, and Columbia, was also a jazz critic, contributor, and editor of numerous beat magazines, as well as more established publications like *The Nation* and *The Massachusetts Review.* His early volumes of poetry, *Preface to a Twenty Volume Suicide Note* (1961) and *Dead Lecturer* (1964), quickly established his reputation as a poet.

In 1960 Baraka visited Cuba, and his art took on a more political and racial edge. In 1965, after the death of Malcolm X, he left his wife and moved to Harlem, where he established the Black Arts Repertory Theatre School. In 1963 he published his classic study, *Blues People: Negro Music in White America,* which traces African-American music from slavery to the age of Coltrane; and in 1964 his most well-known play, *Dutchman,* a highly stylized, abstract drama that seethes with racial anger, won the Obie Award for the best off-Broadway play.

Baraka soon returned to Newark, his own "New Ark," where he started Spirit House and the Spirit House Movers, a theater group. During the riots in Newark in 1967, Jones was injured by a policeman and sentenced to more than two and a half years for illegal possession of a gun by a judge who expressed his dislike of Baraka's poetry; the decision was reversed on appeal. The trial further estranged Jones from white society. In 1966 he married Sylvia Robinson, later called Amini Baraka, and the next year he founded the Black Community Development (BCD) and assumed the name Imamu (spiritual leader), Ameer (prince), Baraka (blessed).

Throughout this period, Baraka's work moved from poetry with a highly personal voice to more overtly political manifestos in which he does not shrink from images of symbolic violence and apocalyptic doom (as in "The Last Days of the American Empire"), seeking to create, he writes in "Black Art," "poems that kill." In 1966 he published his important collection *Home: Social Essays,* and in 1969 the volume of poetry *Black Magic.* Together with Don Lee and Larry Neal, Baraka emerged as a leader in what became known as the Black Arts Movement as artists and writers sought forms and themes that arose from the context of black culture and were their own frame of reference. "Baraka dominated the Black Arts period of the late 1960s," writes critic William Harris, "both as a theorist and artist. He was the main artist-intellectual responsible for shifting the emphasis of contemporary black literature from an integrationist art conveying a raceless and classless vision to a literature rooted in the black experience. The Black Arts Era, both in terms of creative and theoretical writing, is the most important one in black literature since the Harlem Renaissance. No post–Black Arts artist thinks of himself or herself as simply a human being who happens to be black."

From the 1970s onward, Baraka abandoned black cultural nationalism for a political vision based on Marxist theories, while continuing to exploit the revolutionary potential of art. His later works include the poems in *It's Nation Time* (1970), *Hard Facts* (1975), *Daggers and Javelins: Essays, 1974–1979* (1984) and *The Autobiography of LeRoi Jones.* He is now at work on an epic poem on African-American history, *Why's/Wise,* which appears in progress in *The Amiri Baraka Reader,* published in 1992.

In his preface to that volume, Baraka writes of those who would classify him: "The typology that lists my ideological changes and so forth as 'Beat-Black Nationalist-Communist' has brevity going for it, and there's something to be said for that, but, like notations of Monk, it doesn't show the complexity of life." "All of the oaths I swore," he continues, "were reflections of what I felt—what I thought I knew and understood. But these beliefs change, and the work shows this too. From the cultural nationalist steeped in violent bitterness against the 'white eyes' there was yet a deeper commitment that could be harnessed as organization. I joined and helped create organizations, political and cultural, to work at the social transformations I sought. I wrote poetry and essays and plays and stories towards this end as well. It was, and I am still certain of this, part of the same work."

Preface to a Twenty Volume Suicide Note

(for Kellie Jones, born 16 May 1959)

Lately, I've become accustomed to the way
The ground opens up and envelopes me
Each time I go out to walk the dog.
Or the broad edged silly music the wind
Makes when I run for a bus . . .

Things have come to that.

And now, each night I count the stars,
And each night I get the same number.
And when they will not come to be counted,
I count the holes they leave.

Nobody sings anymore.

And then last night, I tiptoed up
To my daughter's room and heard her
Talking to someone, and when I opened
The door, there was no one there . . .
Only she on her knees, peeking into

Her own clasped hands.

from *Preface to a Twenty Volume Suicide Note*, 1961

State/meant

T HE BLACK ARTIST'S ROLE IN AMERICA IS TO AID IN THE destruction of America as he knows it. His role is to report and reflect so precisely the nature of the society, and of himself in that society, that other men will be moved by the exactness of his rendering and, if they are black men, grow strong through this moving, having seen their own strength, and weakness; and if they are white men, tremble, curse, and go mad, because they will be drenched with the filth of their evil.

The Black Artist must draw out of his soul the correct image of the world. He must use this image to band his brothers and sisters together in common understanding of the nature of the world (and the nature of America) and the nature of the human soul.

The Black Artist must demonstrate sweet life, how it differs from the deathly grip of the White Eyes. The Black Artist must teach the White Eyes their deaths, and teach the black man how to bring those deaths about.

We are unfair, and unfair.
We are black magicians, black art
s we make in black labs of the heart.

The fair are
fair, and death
ly white.

The day will not save them
and we own
the night.

from *Home,* 1966

Ka 'Ba

A closed window looks down
on a dirty courtyard, and black people
call across or scream across or walk across
defying physics in the stream of their will

Our world is full of sound
Our world is more lovely than anyone's

tho we suffer, and kill each other
and sometimes fail to walk the air

We are beautiful people
with african imaginations
full of masks and dances and swelling chants
with african eyes, and noses, and arms,
though we sprawl in grey chains in a place
full of winters, when what we want is sun.

We have been captured,
brothers. And we labor
to make our getaway, not
the ancient image, into a new

correspondence with ourselves
and our black family. We need magic
now we need the spells, to raise up
return, destroy, and create. What will be

the sacred words?

from *Black Magic,* 1969

The Kerner Commission

In the first nine months of 1967, as the civil rights movement was evolving from its moderate integrationist program to an increasingly fractious agenda, 164 violent protests broke out across America. The worst of these took place in July in Newark, New Jersey, where twenty-three people were killed, and in Detroit, where forty-three people died. These protests were only the culmination of a violent strain in race relations that led from the six-day riot in Watts in August 1965, to the disturbances that broke out in Omaha, Chicago, Dayton, Cleveland, Philadelphia, Atlanta, and more than thirty other cities in 1966, to the long hot summer of '67. On July 27, 1967, President Lyndon Johnson addressed a public that was becoming increasingly alarmed. While Johnson stressed the need to restore public order, he also forced the nation to confront the long-range issues that had bred despair and violence. "We should attack these conditions," he urged, "not because we are frightened by conflict, but because we are fired by conscience. We should attack them because there is simply no other way to achieve a decent and orderly society in America."

In response, the president established the Advisory Commission on Civil Disorders whose eleven members included Governor Otto Kerner of Illinois, Mayor John Lindsay of New York, Senator Edward W. Brooke, an African-American legislator from Massachusetts, and Roy Wilkins of the NAACP, and charged them to address three fundamental questions: What happened? Why did it happen? and What could be done to prevent it from happening again? The Kerner Commission spent seven months conducting research, hearing countless witnesses and experts, and visiting the sites of the major riots. In words that would soon echo in public debate, the commission's report was issued on February 29, 1968. "This is our basic conclusion," it stated. "Our nation is moving toward two societies, one black, one white—separate and unequal. . . . Discrimination and segregation have long permeated much of American life; they now threaten the future of every American." Because the panel was composed of moderates, rather than members of more radical organizations, its findings were profoundly disturbing.

Arguing that the riots of the previous summer were "the culmination of 300 years of racial prejudice," the commission's report was a stunning indictment of the pervasiveness of white racism in American society. Briefly outlining the march of African-American history from the seventeenth century to the present, the commission highlighted the chronic lack of adequate housing, education and employment opportunities, and political influence, and cited discriminatory consumer credit practices and a double standard in the administration of justice. The commission took particular aim at the frequent comparison made between African-Americans and recent immigrants "unburdened by color." "What white Americans have never fully understood," it argued, "but what the Negro can never forget—is that white society is deeply implicated in the ghetto. White institutions created it, white institutions maintain it, and white society condones it."

One of the most volatile triggers of violence, the commission found, was the bitterness of the relationship between African-American communities and the police, often viewed as an "occupying force." One witness noted that many departments instituted patrol practices that "replaced harassment by individual patrolmen with harassment by entire departments." Another observed that it was a "department's worst members, not its best, who were assigned to minority group neighborhoods." This longstanding antagonism made the matter of public arrests, random searches, and excessive force the catalyst that set disorder in motion.

In its report, which ran to more than four hundred pages, the commission made specific recommendations in the areas of jobs, housing, schools, police procedures, and media attitudes toward blacks. What remained to be seen was how effectively these suggestions would be put in place. Dr. Kenneth B. Clark, the prominent psychologist whose studies of the effects of racism on black children had played an important role in the *Brown* v. *Board of Education of Topeka*† decision, stated: "I read that report . . . of the 1919 riot in Chicago, and it is as if I were reading the report of the investigating committee on the Harlem riot of '35, the report of the investigating committee on the Harlem riot of '43, the report of the McCone Commission on the Watts riot. I must again in candor say to you members of this Commission—it is a kind of Alice in Wonderland—with the same moving picture re-shown over and over again, the same analysis, the same recommendations, and the same inaction." Many observers would recall these dispiriting words as South-Central Los Angeles burst into flames in the spring of 1992.

from The Kerner Commission Report

"This is our basic conclusion: Our nation is moving toward two societies, one black, one white—separate and unequal."

INTRODUCTION

HE SUMMER OF 1967 AGAIN BROUGHT RACIAL DISORDERS TO American cities, and with them shock, fear and bewilderment to the nation.

The worst came during a two-week period in July, first in Newark and then in Detroit. Each set off a chain reaction in neighboring communities.

On July 28, 1967, the President of the United States established this Commission and directed us to answer three basic questions:

What happened?

Why did it happen?

What can be done to prevent it from happening again?

To respond to these questions, we have undertaken a broad range of studies and investigations. We have visited the riot cities; we have heard many witnesses; we have sought the counsel of experts across the country.

This is our basic conclusion: Our nation is moving toward two societies, one black, one white—separate and unequal.

Reaction to last summer's disorders has quickened the movement and deepened the division. Discrimination and segregation have long permeated much of American life; they now threaten the future of every American.

This deepening racial division is not inevitable. The movement apart can be reversed. Choice is still possible. Our principal task is to define that choice and to press for a national resolution.

To pursue our present course will involve the continuing polarization of the American community and, ultimately, the destruction of basic democratic values.

The alternative is not blind repression or capitulation to lawlessness. It is the realization of common opportunities for all within a single society.

This alternative will require a commitment to national action—compassionate, massive and sustained, backed by the resources of the most powerful and the richest nation on this earth. From every American it will require new attitudes, new understanding, and, above all, new will.

The vital needs of the nation must be met; hard choices must be made, and if necessary, new taxes enacted.

Violence cannot build a better society. Disruption and disorder nourish repression, not justice. They strike at the freedom of every citizen. The community cannot—it will not—tolerate coercion and mob rule.

Violence and destruction must be ended—in the streets of the ghetto and in the lives of people.

Segregation and poverty have created in the racial ghetto a destructive environment totally unknown to most white Americans.

What white Americans have never fully understood—but what the Negro can never forget—is that white society is deeply implicated in the ghetto. White institutions created it, white institutions maintain it, and white society condones it.

It is time now to turn with all the purpose at our command to the major unfinished business of this nation. It is time to adopt strategies for action that will produce quick and visible progress. It is time to make good the promises of American democracy to all citizens—urban and rural, white and black, Spanish-surname, American Indian, and every minority group.

Our recommendations embrace three basic principles:

- To mount programs on a scale equal to the dimension of the problems;
- To aim these programs for high impact in the immediate future in order to close the gap between promise and performance;
- To undertake new initiatives and experiments that can change the system of failure and frustration that now dominates the ghetto and weakens our society.

These programs will require unprecedented levels of funding and performance, but they neither probe deeper nor demand more than the problems which called them forth. There can be no higher priority for national action and no higher claim on the nation's conscience.

We issue this Report now, four months before the date called for by the President. Much remains that can be learned. Continued study is essential.

As Commissioners we have worked together with a sense of the greatest urgency and have sought to compose whatever differences exist among us. Some differences remain. But the gravity of the problem and the pressing need for action are too clear to allow further delay in the issuance of this Report. . . .

CHAPTER 4 / THE BASIC CAUSES

We have seen what happened. Why did it happen?

In addressing this question we shift our focus from the local to the national scene, from the particular events of the summer of 1967 to the factors within the society at large which have brought about the sudden violent mood of so many urban Negroes.

The record before this Commission reveals that the causes of recent racial disorders are imbedded in a massive tangle of issues and circumstances —social, economic, political, and psychological—which arise out of the historical pattern of Negro-white relations in America.

These factors are both complex and interacting; they vary significantly in their effect from city to city and from year to year; and the consequences of one disorder, generating new grievances and new demands, become the causes of the next. It is this which creates the "thicket of tension, conflicting evidence and extreme opinions" cited by the President.

Despite these complexities, certain fundamental matters are clear. Of these, the most fundamental is the racial attitude and behavior of white Americans toward black Americans. Race prejudice has shaped our history decisively in the past; it now threatens to do so again. White racism is essentially responsible for the explosive mixture which has been accumulating in our cities since the end of World War II. At the base of this mixture are three of the most bitter fruits of white racial attitudes:

Pervasive discrimination and segregation. The first is surely the continuing exclusion of great numbers of Negroes from the benefits of economic progress through discrimination in employment and education, and their enforced confinement in segregated housing and schools. The corrosive and degrading effects of this condition and the attitudes that underlie it are the source of the deepest bitterness and at the center of the problem of racial disorder.

Black migration and white exodus. The second is the massive and growing concentration of impoverished Negroes in our major cities resulting from Negro migration from the rural South, rapid population growth and the continuing movement of the white middle-class to the suburbs. The consequence is a greatly increased burden on the already depleted resources of cities, creating a growing crisis of deteriorating facilities and services and unmet human needs.

Black ghettos. Third, in the teeming racial ghettos, segregation and poverty have intersected to destroy opportunity and hope and to enforce failure. The ghettos too often mean men and women without jobs, families without men, and schools where children are processed instead of educated, until they return to the street—to crime, to narcotics, to dependency on welfare, and to bitterness and resentment against society in general and white society in particular.

These three forces have converged on the inner city in recent years and on the people who inhabit it. At the same time, most whites and many Negroes outside the ghetto have prospered to a degree unparalleled in the history of civilization. Through television—the universal appliance in the ghetto—and the other media of mass communications, this affluence has been endlessly flaunted before the eyes of the Negro poor and the jobless youth.

As Americans, most Negro citizens carry within themselves two basic aspirations of our society. They seek to share in both the material resources of our system and its intangible benefits—dignity, respect and acceptance. Outside the ghetto many have succeeded in achieving a decent standard of life, and in developing the inner resources which give life meaning and direction. Within the ghetto, however, it is rare that either aspiration is achieved.

Yet these facts alone—fundamental as they are—cannot be said to have caused the disorders. Other and more immediate factors help explain why these events happened now.

Recently, three powerful ingredients have begun to catalyze the mixture.

Frustrated hopes. The expectations aroused by the great judicial and legislative victories of the civil rights movement have led to frustration, hostility and cynicism in the face of the persistent gap between promise and fulfillment. The dramatic struggle for equal rights in the South has sensitized Northern Negroes to the economic inequalities reflected in the deprivations of ghetto life.

Legitimation of violence. A climate that tends toward the approval and encouragement of violence as a form of protest has been created by white terrorism directed against nonviolent protest, including instances of abuse and even murder of some civil rights workers in the South; by the open defiance of law and federal authority by state and local officials resisting desegregation; and by some protest groups engaging in civil disobedience who turn their backs on nonviolence, go beyond the Constitutionally protected rights of petition and free assembly, and resort to violence to attempt to compel alteration of laws and policies with which they disagree. This condition has been reinforced by a general erosion of respect for authority in American society and reduced effectiveness of social standards and community restraints on violence and crime. This in turn has largely resulted from rapid urbanization and the dramatic reduction in the average age of the total population.

Powerlessness. Finally, many Negroes have come to believe that they are being exploited politically and economically by the white "power structure."

Negroes, like people in poverty everywhere, in fact lack the channels of communication, influence and appeal that traditionally have been available to ethnic minorities within the city and which enabled them—unburdened by color—to scale the walls of the white ghettos in an earlier era. The frustrations of powerlessness have led some to the conviction that there is no effective alternative to violence as a means of expression and redress, as a way of "moving the system." More generally, the result is alienation and hostility toward the institutions of law and government and the white society which controls them. This is reflected in the reach toward racial consciousness and solidarity reflected in the slogan "Black Power."

These facts have combined to inspire a new mood among Negroes, particularly among the young. Self-esteem and enhanced racial pride are replacing apathy and submission to "the system." Moreover, Negro youth, who make up over half of the ghetto population, share the growing sense of alienation felt by many white youth in our country. Thus, their role in recent civil disorders reflects not only a shared sense of deprivation and victimization by white society but also the rising incidence of disruptive conduct by a segment of American youth throughout the society.

Incitement and encouragement of violence. These conditions have created a volatile mixture of attitudes and beliefs which needs only a spark to ignite mass violence. Strident appeals to violence, first heard from white racists, were echoed and reinforced last summer in the inflammatory rhetoric of black racists and militants. Throughout the year, extremists crisscrossed the country preaching a doctrine of black power and violence. Their rhetoric was widely reported in the mass media; it was echoed by local "militants" and organizations; it became the ugly background noise of the violent summer.

We cannot measure with any precision the influence of these organizations and individuals in the ghetto, but we think it clear that the intolerable and unconscionable encouragement of violence heightened tensions, created a mood of acceptance and an expectation of violence, and thus contributed to the eruption of the disorders last summer.

The Police. It is the convergence of all these factors that makes the role of the police so difficult and so significant. Almost invariably the incident that ignites disorder arises from police action. Harlem, Watts, Newark and Detroit—all the major outbursts of recent years—were precipitated by routine arrests of Negroes for minor offenses by white police.

But the police are not merely the spark. In discharge of their obligation to maintain order and insure public safety in the disruptive conditions of ghetto life, they are inevitably involved in sharper and more frequent conflicts with ghetto residents than with the residents of other areas. Thus, to many Negroes police have come to symbolize white power, white racism and white repression. And the fact is that many police do reflect and express these white attitudes. The atmosphere of hostility and cynicism is reinforced by a widespread perception among Negroes of the existence of police brutality and corruption, and of a "double standard" of justice and protection—one for Negroes and one for whites.

To this point, we have attempted only to identify the prime components of the "explosive mixture." In the chapters that follow we seek to analyze them in the perspective of history. Their meaning, however, is already clear:

In the summer of 1967, we have seen in our cities a chain reaction of racial violence. If we are heedless, we shall none of us escape the consequences.

CHAPTER 11 / THE POLICE AND THE COMMUNITY

Introduction

We have cited deep hostility between police and ghetto communities as a primary cause of the disorders surveyed by the Commission. In Newark, in Detroit, in Watts, in Harlem—in practically every city that has experienced racial disruption since the summer of 1964—abrasive relationships between police and Negroes and other minority groups have been a major source of grievance, tension and, ultimately, disorder.

In a fundamental sense, however, it is wrong to define the problem solely as hostility to police. In many ways the policeman only symbolizes much deeper problems.

The policeman in the ghetto is a symbol not only of law, but of the entire system of law enforcement and criminal justice.

As such, he becomes the tangible target for grievances against shortcomings throughout that system: against assembly-line justice in teeming lower courts; against wide disparities in sentences; against antiquated corrections facilities; against the basic inequities imposed by the system on the poor—to whom, for example, the option of bail means only jail.

The policeman in the ghetto is a symbol of increasingly bitter social debate over law enforcement.

One side, disturbed and perplexed by sharp rises in crime and urban violence, exerts extreme pressure on police for tougher law enforcement. Another group, inflamed against police as agents of repression, tends toward defiance of what it regards as order maintained at the expense of justice.

The policeman in the ghetto is a symbol, finally, of a society from which many ghetto Negroes are increasingly alienated.

At the same time, police responsibilities in the ghetto have grown as other institutions of social control have lost much of their authority: the schools, because so many are segregated, old, and inferior; religion, which has become irrelevant to those who lost faith as they lost hope; career aspirations, which for many young Negroes are totally lacking; the family, because its bonds are so often snapped. It is the policeman who must fill this institutional vacuum, and is then resented for the presence this effort demands.

Alone, the policeman in the ghetto cannot solve these problems. His role is already one of the most difficult in our society. He must deal daily with a range of problems and people that test his patience, ingenuity, character, and courage in ways that few of us are ever tested. Without positive leadership, goals, operational guidance, and public support, the individual policeman can only feel victimized. Nor are these problems the responsibility only of police administrators; they are deep enough to tax the courage, intelligence, and leadership of mayors, city officials, and community leaders. As Dr. Kenneth B. Clark told the Commission:

> This society knows . . . that if human beings are confined in ghetto compounds of our cities, are subjected to criminally inferior education, pervasive economic and job discrimination, committed to houses unfit for human habitation, subjected to unspeakable conditions of municipal services, such as sanitation, that such human beings are not likely to be responsive to appeals to be lawful, to be respectful, to be concerned with property of others.

And yet, precisely because the policeman in the ghetto *is* a symbol—precisely because he symbolizes so much—it is of critical importance that the police and society take every possible step to allay grievances that flow from a sense of injustice and increased tension and turmoil.

In this work, the police bear a major responsibility for making needed changes. In the first instance, they have the prime responsibility for safeguarding the minimum goal of any civilized society—security of life and property. To do so, they are given society's maximum power—discretion in the use of force. Second, it is axiomatic that effective law enforcement require the support of the community. Such support will not be present when a substantial segment of the community feels threatened by the police and regards the police as an occupying force.

At the same time, public officials also have a clear duty to help the police make any necessary changes to minimize so far as possible the risk of further disorder.

We see five basic problem areas:

- The need for change in police operations in the ghetto to ensure proper individual conduct and to eliminate abrasive practices.

- The need for more adequate police protection of ghetto residents to eliminate the present high sense of insecurity to person and property.
- The need for effective mechanisms through which the citizen can have his grievances handled.
- The need for policy guidelines to assist police in areas where police conduct can create tension.
- The need to develop community support for law enforcement.

Our discussion of each of these problem areas is followed by specific recommendations which relate directly to more effective law enforcement and to the prevention and control of civil disorders.[1]

I. Police Conduct and Patrol Practices

In an earlier era third-degree interrogations were wide-spread, indiscriminate arrests on suspicion were generally accepted, and "alley justice" dispensed with the nightstick was common. Yet there were few riots, and the riots which did occur generally did not arise from a police incident.

Today, many disturbances studied by the Commission began with a police incident. But these incidents were not, for the most part, the crude acts of an earlier time. They were routine, proper police actions such as stopping a motorist or raiding an illegal business. Indeed, many of the serious disturbances took place in cities whose police are among the best led, best organized, best trained and most professional in the country.

Yet some activities of even the most professional police department may heighten tension and enhance the potential for civil disorder. An increase in complaints of police misconduct, for example, may in fact be a reflection of professionalism; the department may simply be using law enforcement methods which increase the total volume of police contacts with the public. The number of charges of police misconduct may be greater simply because the volume of police-citizen contacts is higher.

Here we examine two aspects of police activities that have great tension-creating potential. Our objective is to provide recommendations to assist city and police officials in developing practices which can allay rather than contribute to tension.

[1] In performing this task we wish to acknowledge our indebtedness to and reliance upon the extensive work done by the President's Commission on Law Enforcement and Administration of Justice (The "Crime Commission"). The reports, studies, surveys, and analyses of the Crime Commission have contributed to many of our conclusions and recommendations.

Police Conduct

Negroes firmly believe that police brutality and harassment occur repeatedly in Negro neighborhoods. This belief is unquestionably one of the major reasons for intense Negro resentment against the police.

The extent of this belief is suggested by attitude surveys. In 1964, a New York Times study of Harlem showed that 43 percent of those questioned believed in the existence of police "brutality."[2] In 1965, a nationwide Gallup Poll found that 35 percent of Negro men believed there was police brutality in their areas; 7 percent of white men thought so. In 1966, a survey conducted for the Senate Subcommittee on Executive Reorganization found that 60 percent of Watts Negroes aged 15 to 19 believed there was some police brutality. Half said they had witnessed such conduct. A University of California at Los Angeles study of the Watts area found that 79 percent of the Negro males believed police lack respect for or use insulting language to Negroes and 74 percent believed police use unnecessary force in making arrests. In 1967, an Urban League study in Detroit found that 82 percent believed there was some form of police brutality.

The true extent of excessive and unjustified use of force is difficult to determine. One survey done for the Crime Commission suggests that when police-citizen contacts are systematically observed, the vast majority are handled without antagonism or incident. Of 5,339 police-citizen contacts observed in slum precincts in three large cities, in the opinion of the observer, only 20—about three-tenths of 1 percent—involved excessive or unnecessary force. And although almost all of those subjected to such force were poor, more than half were white. Verbal discourtesy was more common—15 percent of all such contacts began with a "brusque or nasty command" on the part of the officer. Again, however, the objects of such command were more likely to be white than Negro.

Such "observer" surveys may not fully reflect the normal pattern of police conduct. The Crime Commission Task Force concluded that although the study gave "no basis for stating the extent to which police officers used force, it did confirm that such conduct still exists in the cities where observations were made."

Physical abuse is only one source of aggravation in the ghetto. In nearly every city surveyed, the Commission heard complaints of harassment of interracial couples, dispersal of social street gatherings, and the stopping of Negroes on foot or in cars without obvious basis. These, together with contemptuous and degrading verbal abuse, have great impact in the ghetto. As one Commission witness said, these strip the Negro of the one thing that he may have left—his dignity, "the question of being a man."

Some conduct—breaking up of street groups, indiscriminate stops and

[2] The "brutality" referred to in this and other surveys is often not precisely defined, and covers conduct ranging from use of insulting language to excessive and unjustified force.

searches—is frequently directed at youths, creating special tensions in the ghetto where the average age is generally under 21. Ghetto youths, often without work and with homes that may be nearly uninhabitable, particularly in the summer, commonly spend much time on the street. Characteristically, they are not only hostile to police, but eager to demonstrate their own masculinity and courage. The police, therefore, are often subject to taunts and provocations, testing their self-control and, probably, for some, reinforcing their hostility to Negroes in general. Because youths commit a large and increasing proportion of crime, police are under growing pressure from their supervisors—and from the community—to deal with them forcefully. "Harassment of youths" may therefore be viewed by some police departments—and members even of the Negro community—as a proper crime prevention technique.

In a number of cities the Commission heard complaints of abuse from Negro adults of all social and economic classes. Particular resentment is aroused by harassing Negro men in the company of white women—often their light-skinned Negro wives.

"Harassment" or discourtesy may not be the result of malicious or discriminatory intent of police officers. Many officers simply fail to understand the effects of their actions because of their limited knowledge of the Negro community. Calling a Negro teenager by his first name may arouse resentment because many whites still refuse to extend to adult Negroes the courtesy of the title, "Mister." A patrolman may take the arm of a person he is leading to the police car. Negroes are more likely to resent this than whites because the action implies that they are on the verge of flight and may degrade them in the eyes of friends or onlookers.

In assessing the impact of police misconduct we emphasize that the improper acts of a relatively few officers may create severe tensions between the department and the entire Negro community. Whatever the actual extent of such conduct, we concur in the Crime Commission's conclusion that:

> . . . all such behavior is obviously and totally reprehensible, and when it is directed against minority-group citizens it is particularly likely to lead, for quite obvious reasons, to bitterness in the community.

Police Patrol Practices

Although police administrators may take steps to attempt to eliminate misconduct by individual police officers, many departments have adopted patrol practices which in the words of one commentator, have ". . . replaced harassment by individual patrolmen with harassment by entire departments."

These practices, sometimes known as "aggressive preventive patrol," take a number of forms, but invariably they involve a large number of police-citizen contacts initiated by police rather than in response to a call for help or service. One such practice utilizes a roving task force which moves into high-crime districts without prior notice, and conducts intensive, often indiscriminate, street stops and searches. A number of persons who might legitimately be described as suspicious are stopped. But so also are persons whom the beat patrolman would know are respected members of the community. Such task forces are often deliberately moved from place to place making it impossible for its members to know the people with whom they come in contact.

In some cities aggressive patrol is not limited to special task forces. The beat patrolman himself is expected to participate and to file a minimum number of stop-and-frisk or field interrogations reports for each tour of duty. This pressure to produce, or a lack of familiarity with the neighborhood and its people, may lead to widespread use of these techniques without adequate differentiation between genuinely suspicious behavior, and behavior which is suspicious to a particular officer merely because it is unfamiliar.

Police administrators, pressed by public concern about crime, have instituted such patrol practices often without weighing their tension-creating effects and the resulting relationship to civil disorder.

Motorization of police is another aspect of patrol that has affected law enforcement in the ghetto. The patrolman comes to see the city through a windshield and hear about it over a police radio. To him, the area increasingly comes to consist only of law breakers. To the ghetto resident, the policeman comes increasingly to be only an enforcer.

Loss of contact between the police officer and the community he serves adversely affects law enforcement. If an officer has never met, does not know, and cannot understand the language and habits of the people in the area he patrols, he cannot do an effective police job. His ability to detect truly suspicious behavior is impaired. He deprives himself of important sources of information. He fails to know those persons with an "equity" in the community—homeowners, small businessmen, professional men, persons who are anxious to support proper law enforcement—and thus sacrifices the contributions they can make to maintaining community order.

Recommendations

Police misconduct—whether described as brutality, harassment, verbal abuse, or discourtesy—cannot be tolerated even if it is infrequent. It contributes directly to the risk of civil disorder. It is inconsistent with the basic responsibility and function of a police force in a democracy. Police departments must have rules prohibiting such misconduct and enforce them vigorously. Police commanders must be aware of what takes place in the field, and take firm steps to correct abuses. We consider this matter further in the section on policy guidelines.

Elimination of misconduct also requires care in selecting police for ghetto areas, for there the police responsibility is particularly sensitive, demanding and often dangerous. The highest caliber of personnel is required if police are to overcome feelings within the ghetto community of inadequate protection and unfair, discriminatory treatment. Despite this need, data from Commission investigators and from the Crime Commission disclose that often a department's worst, not its best, are assigned to minority group neighborhoods As Professor Albert Reiss, Director of the Center for Research on Social Organization, University of Michigan, testified before the Commission:

> . . . I think we confront in modern urban police departments in large cities much of what we encounter in our schools, in these cities. The slum police precinct is like the slum school. It gets, with few exceptions, the worst in the system.

Referring to extensive studies in one city, Professor Reiss concluded:

> In predominantly Negro precincts, over three-fourths of the white policemen expressed prejudice or highly prejudiced attitudes towards Negroes. Only one percent of the officers expressed attitudes which could be described as sympathetic towards Negroes. Indeed, close to one-half of all the police officers in predominantly Negro high crime rate areas showed extreme prejudice against Negroes. What do I mean by extreme racial prejudice? I mean that they describe Negroes in terms that are not people terms. They describe them in terms of the animal kingdom. . . .

CONCLUSION

One of the first witnesses to be invited to appear before this Commission was Dr. Kenneth B. Clark, a distinguished and perceptive scholar. Referring to the reports of earlier riot commissions, he said:

> I read that report . . . of the 1919 riot in Chicago, and it is as if I were reading the report of the investigating committee on the Harlem riot of '35, the report of the investigating committee on the Harlem riot of '43, the report of the McCone Commission on the Watts riot.
>
> I must again in candor say to you members of this Commission—it is a kind of Alice in Wonderland—with the same moving picture re-shown over and over again, the same analysis, the same recommendations, and the same inaction.

These words come to our minds as we conclude this Report.

We have provided an honest beginning. We have learned much. But we have uncovered no startling truths, no unique insights, no simple solutions. The destruction and the bitterness of racial disorder, the harsh polemics of black revolt and white repression have been seen and heard before in this country.

It is time now to end the destruction and the violence, not only in the streets of the ghetto but in the lives of people.

February 29, 1968

African-Americans in the Vietnam War

One of the most powerful expressions of the complex role African-Americans played during the Vietnam War can be found in Wallace Terry's oral history, *Bloods.* By the time Terry went to Vietnam as a correspondent for *Time* in 1967, the nation was already deeply divided over the course and justification for the war. To the dismay of many in the civil rights movement, Martin Luther King, Jr., had openly opposed the war, while Cassius Clay (Muhammad Ali) had been stripped of his boxing title for refusing to enlist in the draft for reasons of personal conscience. Since President Truman's Executive Order 9981† to end segregation in the armed forces, the American military had become one of the most integrated institutions in American society, and yet subtle and not-so-subtle forms of discrimination persisted. Regardless of their aptitudes or limitations, a large percentage of African-Americans ended up with the worst job in the war, assignment to the infantry. And though they represented only 11 percent of the American population, Terry argues, African-Americans accounted for 23 percent of the fatalities.

When Wallace Terry first went to Vietnam in May 1967, he found that most African-Americans supported the war. He returned later that year for a two-year stint during which he found a wider divergence of opinion. By that stage of the war, many of the professional soldiers who had sought out careers in the military because of the opportunities it represented had been replaced by draftees, many already influenced by and involved in political activism at home, where a wave of urban revolts had ignited. These Bloods, as they called themselves, were outspoken about the discrimination they experienced in uniform. "The war," writes Terry, "which had bitterly divided America like no other issue since the Civil War, had become a double battleground, pitting American soldier against American soldier. The spirit of foxhole brotherhood I found in 1967 had evaporated." Or as one soldier put it, "I wasn't fighting the enemy. I was fighting the white man."

Of the many soldiers Terry interviewed, twenty are profiled in his volume. Enlisted men and officers from all branches of service, they were pilots, electronics engineers, LURPs, corpsmen, paratroopers, and others. Some embraced religion or politics in Vietnam, while others abandoned them. Some formed deep friendships with white soldiers, while others found themselves fighting alongside members of the Ku Klux Klan. Some depended on drugs to get by, some became prisoners of war, many were wounded and killed.

Upon their return from Vietnam, black veterans experienced the same profound alienation that greeted other vets, reviled by those on the right for "losing" the war, by those on the left for killing innocents fighting the white man's battle. At the same time, they faced social circumstances in which the gains of the Great Society had been wiped out by the costs of the war. "I remember pounding the pavement for about a year looking for work," explains one vet. "I could not get a job because I was not an ex–drug addict. I was not an ex-convict. I was not an ex-Vietnamese. I had to be an ex-something before I could get work." The rate of unemployment among black veterans was more than double that of whites.

Terry writes in the introduction to his extraordinarily moving volume, "These stories are not to be found in the expanding body of Vietnam literature; they deservedly belong in the forefront because of the unique experience of the black Vietnam veteran. He fought at a time when his sisters and brothers were fighting and dying at home for equal rights and greater opportunities, for a color-blind nation promised to him in the Constitution he swore to defend. He fought at a time when some of his leaders chastised him for waging war against a people of color, and when his Communist foe appealed to him to take up arms instead against the forces of racism in America. The loyalty of the black Vietnam War veteran stood a greater test on the battleground than did the loyalty of any other American soldier in Vietnam."

Finally, though there is enormous variety in the histories recounted in Terry's eloquent volume, the chorus of their voices is added to the tale of the universal soldier. "We were programmed," one vet recalls, "for the fact as American fighting men that we were still fighting a civilized war. And you don't fight a civilized war. It's nothing civilized about—about war."

Selections from *Bloods*

I WENT TO VIETNAM AS A BASIC NAIVE YOUNG MAN OF eighteen. Before I reached my nineteenth birthday, I was an animal. When I went home three months later, even my mother was scared of me.

It began on my fourteenth day in country. The first time I was ever in a combat situation at all. We was in VC Valley, south of Pleiku.

I was a cherry boy. Most cherry boys went on point in the LURP team. I adapted so well to bein' a point man that that became my permanent position after this first mission.

We was in very thick elephant grass. We had sat down for a ten-minute break. And we heard the Vietn'ese talking, coming through the elephant grass. So we all sat ready for bein' attacked.

I heard this individual walking. He came through the elephant grass, and I let loose on my M-16 and hit him directly in his face. Sixteen rounds. The whole clip. And his face disappeared. From the chin up. Nothing left. And his body stood there for 'proximately somewhere around ten, fifteen seconds. And it shivers. And it scared me beyond anyone's imagination.

Then it was chaos from then on. Shooting all over. We had a approximate body count of five VC. Then we broke camp and head for safer ground.

After thinkin' about that guy with no face I broke into a cold sweat. I knew it could've been me that was in his place instead of me in my place. But it changed me. Back home I had to defend myself in the streets, with my fist, with bottles, or whatever. But you don't go around shooting people. As physical as I had been as a teenager, there were never life-threatening situations. I had never experienced anything quite as horrible as seeing a human being with his face blown apart. I cried. I cried because I killed somebody.

—Specialist 4 Arthur E. "Gene" Woodley, Jr.
Combat Paratrooper

I could smell the hate.

Some of them had pistols. Some guns. Some shook knives at me, shovels, even hoes. They motioned for me to stand up. Then they inched forward. About 50 of them. Communist militia, like popular forces. And just plain folk, too. All pointing guns at me.

They looked to see what I had and took my .38. They made me strip down to shorts and T-shirt. They took off my boots. They tied my hands behind me.

Then they marched me about a 100 yards, right down this hill to this hut. Then around to the backyard. There was a large hole, like a pit. They motioned for me to get into that. I hesitated. Then they pushed and shoved me into it.

I thought I was going to be executed.

I said to myself, This is it.

I guess I was in a state of shock. I wasn't afraid. I just thought my time had come.

It was July 20, 1966. Just seven days short of my twenty-ninth birthday. I had come a half world away from Fayetteville, North Carolina—the son of sharecroppers—to die in North Vietnam at the hands of peasants.

—Captain Norman Alexander McDaniel
Electronics Weapons Officer

The racial incidents didn't happen in the field. Just when we went to the back. It wasn't so much that they were against us. It was just that we felt that we were being taken advantage of, 'cause it seemed like more blacks in the field than in the rear.

In the rear we saw a bunch of rebel flags. They didn't mean nothing by the rebel flag. It was just saying we for the South. It didn't mean that they hated blacks. But after you in the field, you took the flags very personally.

One time we saw these flags in Nha Trang on the MP barracks. They was playing hillbilly music. Had their shoes off dancing. Had nice, pretty bunks. Mosquito nets over top the bunks. And had the nerve to have this camouflaged covers. Air conditioning. Cement floors. We just came out the jungles. We dirty, we smelly, hadn't shaved. We just went off. Said, "Y'all the real enemy. We stayin' here." We turned the bunks over, started tearing up the stereo. They just ran out. Next morning, they shipped us back up.

In the field, we had the utmost respect for each other, because when a fire fight is going on and everybody is facing north, you don't want to see nobody looking around south. If you was a member of the Ku Klux Klan, you didn't tell nobody.

Take them guys from West Virginia, Kentucky. First time they ever seen blacks was when they went in the service. . . . Those guys were dumb, strong, but with no problems about us blacks. Matter of fact, the whites catered to the black in the infantry in the field.

Captain one time asked Davis what kind of car he gonna have when he get back in the States. Davis told him, "I'm not gonna get a car, sir, I'm gonna get me a Exxon station and give gas away to the brothers. Let them finish burnin' down what they leave." It wasn't funny if he said it in the stateside. But all of 'em burst out laughing.

Right after Tet, the mail chopper got shot down. We moved to Tam Ky. We didn't have any mail in about three weeks. Then this lady by the name of Hanoi Helen come on the radio. She had a letter that belong to Sir Drawers. From the chopper that was shot down. She read the letter from his wife about how she miss him. But that didn't unsettle the brothers as much as when she got on the air after Martin Luther King died, and they was rioting back home. She was saying, "Soul brothers, go home. Whitey raping your mothers and your daughters, burning down your homes. What you over here for? This isn't your war. The war is a trick of the Capitalist empire to get rid of the blacks." I really thought—I really started believing it, because it was too many blacks than there should be in infantry.

—Specialist 4 Richard J. Ford III
LURP

When I heard that Martin Luther King was assassinated, my first inclination was to run out and punch the first white guy I saw. I was very hurt. All I wanted to do was to go home. I even wrote Lyndon Johnson a letter. I said that I didn't understand how I could be trying to protect foreigners in their country with the possibility of losing my life wherin in my own country people who are my hero, like Martin Luther King, can't even walk the streets in a safe manner. I didn't get an answer from the President, but I got an answer from the White House. It was a wonderful letter, wonderful in terms of the way it looked. It wanted to assure me that the President was doing everything in his power to bring about racial equality, especially in the armed forces. A typical bureaucratic answer.

A few days after the assassination, some of the white guys got a little sick and tired of seeing Dr. King's picture on the TV screen. Like a memorial. It really got to one guy. He said, "I wish they'd take that nigger's picture off." He was a fool to begin with, because there were three black guys sitting in the living room when he said it. And we commenced to give him a lesson in when to use that word and when you should not use that word. A physical lesson.

With the world focused on the King assassination and the riots that followed in the United States, the North Vietnamese, being politically astute, schooled the Viet Cong to go on a campaign of psychological warfare against the American forces.

At the time, more blacks were dying in combat than whites, proportionately, mainly because more blacks were in combat-oriented units, proportionately, than whites. To play on the sympathy of the black soldier, the Viet Cong would shoot at a white guy, then let the black guy behind him go through, then shoot at the next white guy.

It didn't take long for that kind of word to get out. And the reaction in some companies was to arrange your personnel where you had an all-black or nearly all-black unit to send out.

—Staff Sergeant Don F. Brown
Security Policeman

I didn't come home the way I went. I went a tall, slim, healthy fella. You could look at me now and tell something had happened. I was either born like that, or I was in the war. I'm scarred all over. It ain't no way you can hide it.

After six months, I started goin' to school at Northwestern Business College. Using the GI benefits. I got a associate arts degree in accounting, and they sent me all over lookin' for a job.

I tried maybe 40 places in two years. But I never did get hired.

They would say I didn't have experience. Or they would make excuses like, "You think not having that hand would interfere with your doing this kind of work?" I thought, How would that interfere sittin' there at a desk? Or they would tell me they would let me know, but nobody never did call me back.

I got discouraged. I guess I just gave up, because I kept gettin' turned down. Nobody never really wanted to give me a break. I was black. A amputee. And it was an unpopular war. Maybe they didn't like the idea nobody from Vietnam workin' in they profession.

In 1981 Social Security stopped sending me checks. . . . This lady, she said, "What do you expect, Mr. Daniels? To receive Social Security for the rest of your life?"

I started to tell her, "Yeah. My hand is gonna be missin' for the rest of my life." But I didn't say anything. Maybe Social Security thinks I've lived too long.

It's funny. When I see the Vietnamese who came over here, I just wonder how they start so fast. Get businesses and stuff. Somebody helpin' 'em. But the ones that fought for they country, been livin' here all along, we get treated like dirt.

I know you gotta help yourself, but you can't do everything. I can't hire me.

When I was nineteen, I know I didn't know too much about what's goin' on. Except you s'posed to fight for your country. And you come home. But where is my country when I come home?

But I wish I—I would've—I would've came back the way, you know, I went.

—Sergeant Robert L. Daniels
Radio Wireman, Howitzer Gunner

Maya Angelou
(1928–)

One of the most popular African-American writers of the last two decades, Maya Angelou was born Marguerite Johnson in St. Louis, Missouri. Her parents separated, and at the age of three she and her brother Bailey were sent to live with her grandmother in Stamps, Arkansas, at the center of the black community there, which often gathered at her grandmother's general store. (She was called Maya after her brother began to address her as "mya sister.") She moved to St. Louis when she was eight to live with her mother, whose lover sexually abused her, and then returned to Stamps, where she refused to speak for five years.

"I began to listen to everything," she writes in her first volume of autobiography, *I Know Why the Caged Bird Sings,* published in 1970. "I probably hoped that after I had heard all the sounds, really heard them and packed them down, deep in my ears, the world would be quiet around me. I walked into rooms where people were laughing, their voices hitting the walls like stones, and I simply stood still—in the midst of the riot of sound. After a minute or two, silence would rush into the room from its hiding place because I had eaten up all the sounds." A sympathetic neighbor, "our side's answer to the richest white woman in town," began to take an interest in her and introduced her to books, which would profoundly affect her. "She had given me her secret word," Angelou writes, "which called forth a djinn who was to serve me all my life." Her unusually brave and intimate memoir, written in a beautifully lyrical prose, heralded the debut of a writer in possession of enormous gifts and was an immediate popular and critical success; its publication marked the first time that a book by an African-American author appeared on national best-seller lists.

Maya Angelou continued her autobiography in *Gather Together in My Name* (1974) and *Singin' and Swingin' and Gettin' Merry Like Christmas* (1976), in which she describes her life with her mother in San Francisco and her growing career as a dancer and singer. She continued to work in theater, as an actress, screenwriter, composer, and director. Later volumes of autobiography include *The Heart of a Woman* (1981) and *All God's Children Need Traveling Shoes* (1984), which tells of her experiences in Ghana and the coming of age of her seventeen-year-old son, born when she was sixteen, who first appears on the closing pages of *I Know Why the Caged Bird Sings.* Angelou is the author as well of several volumes of poetry, including *Just Give Me a Cool Drink of Water 'fore I Diiie* (1973), *Oh Pray My Wings Are Gonna Fit Me Well* (1975), *And Still I Rise* (1978), *Shaker, Why Don't You Sing* (1983), *Now Sheba Sings the Song* (1987), and *I Shall Not Be Moved* (1990). Like Toni Morrison, Angelou is a mesmerizing speaker with a physical presence that is both commanding and graceful. In the fall of 1992, she composed the poem "On the Pulse of Morning" for the inauguration of President Bill Clinton.

from *I Know Why the Caged Bird Sings*

THE SCHOOL BAND STRUCK UP A MARCH AND ALL CLASSES filed in as had been rehearsed. We stood in front of our seats, as assigned, and on a signal from the choir director, we sat. No sooner had this been accomplished than the band started to play the national anthem. We rose again and sang the song, after which we recited the pledge of allegiance. We remained standing for a brief minute before the choir director and the principal signaled to us, rather desperately I thought, to take our seats. The command was so unusual that our carefully rehearsed and smooth-running machine was thrown off. For a full minute we fumbled for our chairs and bumped into each other awkwardly. Habits change or solidify under pressure, so in our state of nervous tension we had been ready to follow our usual assembly pattern; the American national anthem, then the pledge of allegiance, then the song every Black person I knew called the Negro National Anthem. All done in the same key, with the same passion and most often standing on the same foot.

Finding my seat at last, I was overcome with a presentiment of worse things to come. Something unrehearsed, unplanned, was going to happen, and we were going to be made to look bad. I distinctly remember being explicit in the choice of pronoun. It was "we," the graduating class, the unit, that concerned me then.

The principal welcomed "parents and friends" and asked the Baptist minister to lead us in prayer. His invocation was brief and punchy, and for a second I thought we were getting back on the high road to right action. When the principal came back to the dais, however, his voice had changed. Sounds always affected me profoundly and the principal's voice was one of my favorites. During assembly it melted and lowed weakly into the audience. It had not been in my plan to listen to him, but my curiosity was piqued and I straightened up to give him my attention.

He was talking about Booker T. Washington, our "late great leader," who said we can be as close as the fingers on the hand, etc. . . . Then he said a few vague things about friendship and the friendship of kindly people to those less fortunate than themselves. With that his voice nearly faded, thin, away. Like a river diminishing to a stream and then to a trickle. But he cleared his throat and said, "Our speaker tonight, who is also our friend, came from Texarkana to deliver the commencement address, but due to the irregularity of the train schedule, he's going to, as they say, 'speak and run.' " He said that we understood and wanted the man to know that we were most grateful for the time he was able to give us and then something about how we were willing always to adjust to another's program, and without more ado— "I give you Mr. Edward Donleavy."

Not one but two white men came through the door offstage.. The shorter one walked to the speaker's platform, and the tall one moved over to the center seat and sat down. But that was our principal's seat, and already occupied. The dislodged gentleman bounced around for a long breath or two before the Baptist minister gave him his chair, then with more dignity than the situation deserved, the minister walked off the stage.

Donleavy looked at the audience once (on reflection, I'm sure that he wanted only to reassure himself that we were really there), adjusted his glasses and began to read from a sheaf of papers.

He was glad "to be here and to see the work going on just as it was in the other schools."

At the first "Amen" from the audience I willed the offender to immediate death by choking on the word. But Amens and Yes, sir's began to fall around the room like rain through a ragged umbrella.

He told us of the wonderful changes we children in Stamps had in store. The Central School (naturally, the white school was Central) had already been granted improvements that would be in use in the fall. A well-known artist was coming from Little Rock to teach art to them. They were going to have the newest microscopes and chemistry equipment for their laboratory. Mr. Donleavy didn't leave us long in the dark over who made these improvements available to Central High. Nor were we to be ignored in the general betterment scheme he had in mind.

He said that he had pointed out to people at a very high level that one of the first-line football tacklers at Arkansas Agricultural and Mechanical College had graduated from good old Lafayette County Training School. Here fewer Amen's were heard. Those few that did break through lay dully in the air with the heaviness of habit.

He went on to praise us. He went on to say how he had bragged that "one of the best basketball players at Fisk sank his first ball right here at Lafayette County Training School."

The white kids were going to have a chance to become Galileos and Madame Curies and Edisons and Gauguins, and our boys (the girls weren't even in on it) would try to be Jesse Owenses and Joe Louises.

Owens and the Brown Bomber were great heroes in our world, but what school official in the white-goddom of Little Rock had the right to decide that those two men must be our only heroes? Who decided that for Henry Reed to become a scientist he had to work like George Washington Carver, as a bootblack, to buy a lousy microscope? Bailey was obviously always going to be too small to be an athlete, so which concrete angel glued to what country seat had decided that if my brother wanted to become a lawyer he had to first pay penance for his skin by picking cotton and hoeing corn and studying correspondence books at night for twenty years?

The man's dead words fell like bricks around the auditorium and too many settled in my belly. Constrained by hard-learned manners I couldn't look behind me, but to my left and right the proud graduating class of 1940 had dropped their heads. Every girl in my row had found something new to do with her handkerchief. Some folded the tiny squares into love knots, some into triangles, but most were wadding them, then pressing them flat on their yellow laps.

On the dais, the ancient tragedy was being replayed. Professor Parsons sat, a sculptor's reject, rigid. His large, heavy body seemed devoid of will or willingness, and his eyes said he was no longer with us. The other teachers examined the flag (which was draped stage right) or their notes, or the windows which opened on our now-famous playing diamond.

Graduation, the hush-hush magic time of frills and gifts and congratulations and diplomas, was finished for me before my name was called. The accomplishment was nothing. The meticulous maps, drawn in three colors of ink, learning and spelling decasyllabic words, memorizing the whole of *The Rape of Lucrece*—it was for nothing. Donleavy had exposed us.

We were maids and farmers, handymen and washerwomen, and anything higher that we aspired to was farcical and presumptuous.

Then I wished that Gabriel Prosser and Nat Turner had killed all whitefolks in their beds and that Abraham Lincoln had been assassinated before the signing of the Emancipation Proclamation, and that Harriet Tubman had been killed by that blow on her head and Christopher Columbus had drowned in the *Santa María.*

It was awful to be Negro and have no control over my life. It was brutal to be young and already trained to sit quietly and listen to charges brought against my color with no chance of defense. We should all be dead. I thought I should like to see us all dead, one on top of the other. A pyramid of flesh with the whitefolks on the bottom, as the broad base, then the Indians with their silly tomahawks and teepees and wigwams and treaties, the Negroes with their mops and recipes and cotton sacks and spirituals sticking out of their mouths. The Dutch children should all stumble in their wooden shoes and break their necks. The French should choke to death on the Louisiana Purchase (1803) while silkworms ate all the Chinese with their stupid pigtails. As a species, we were an abomination. All of us.

Donleavy was running for election, and assured our parents that if he won we could count on having the only colored paved playing field in that part of Arkansas. Also—he never looked up to acknowledge the grunts of acceptance—also, we were bound to get some new equipment for the home economics building and the workshop.

He finished, and since there was no need to give any more than the most perfunctory thank-you's, he nodded to the men on the stage, and the tall white man who was never introduced joined him at the door. They left with the attitude that now they were off to something really important. (The graduation ceremonies at Lafayette County Training School had been a mere preliminary.)

The ugliness they left was palpable. An uninvited guest who wouldn't leave. The choir was summoned and sang a modern arrangement of "Onward, Christian Soldiers," with new words pertaining to graduates seeking their place in the world. But it didn't work. Elouise, the daughter of the Baptist minister, recited "Invictus," and I could have cried at the impertinence of "I am the master of my fate, I am the captain of my soul."

My name had lost its ring of familiarity and I had to be nudged to go and receive my diploma. All my preparations had fled. I neither marched up to the stage like a conquering Amazon, nor did I look in the audience for Bailey's nod of approval. Marguerite Johnson, I heard the name again, my honors were read, there were noises in the audience of appreciation, and I took my place on the stage as rehearsed.

I thought about colors I hated: ecru, puce, lavender, beige and black.

There was shuffling and rustling around me, then Henry Reed was giving his valedictory address, "To Be or Not to Be." Hadn't he heard the whitefolks? We couldn't *be,* so the question was a waste of time. Henry's voice came out clear and strong. I feared to look at him. Hadn't he got the message? There was no "nobler in the mind" for Negroes because the world didn't think we had minds, and they let us know it. "Outrageous fortune"? Now, that was a joke. When the ceremony was over I had to tell Henry Reed some things. That is, if I still cared. Not "rub," Henry, "erase." "Ah, there's the erase." Us.

Henry had been a good student in elocution. His voice rose on tides of promise and fell on waves of warnings. The English teacher had helped him to create a sermon winging through Hamlet's soliloquy. To be a man, a doer, a builder, a leader, or to be a tool, an unfunny joke, a crusher of funky toadstools. I marveled that Henry could go through with the speech as if we had a choice.

I had been listening and silently rebutting each sentence with my eyes closed; then there was a hush, which in an audience warns that something unplanned is happening. I looked up and saw Henry Reed, the conservative, the proper, the A student, turn his back to the audience and turn to us (the proud graduating class of 1940) and sing, nearly speaking,

"Lift ev'ry voice and sing
Till earth and heaven ring
Ring with the harmonies of Liberty . . ."

It was the poem written by James Weldon Johnson. It was the music composed by J. Rosamond Johnson. It was the Negro national anthem. Out of habit we were singing it.

Our mothers and fathers stood in the dark hall and joined the hymn of encouragement. A kindergarten teacher led the small children onto the stage and the buttercups and daisies and bunny rabbits marked time and tried to follow:

> "Stony the road we trod
> Bitter the chastening rod
> Felt in the days when hope, unborn, had died.
> Yet with a steady beat
> Have not our weary feet
> Come to the place for which our fathers sighed?"

Every child I knew had learned that song with his ABC's and along with "Jesus Loves Me This I Know." But I personally had never heard it before. Never heard the words, despite the thousands of times I had sung them. Never thought they had anything to do with me.

On the other hand, the words of Patrick Henry had made such an impression on me that I had been able to stretch myself tall and trembling and say, "I know not what course others may take, but as for me, give me liberty or give me death."

And now I heard, really for the first time:

> "We have come over a way that with tears
> has been watered,
> We have come, treading our path through
> the blood of the slaughtered."

While echoes of the song shivered in the air, Henry Reed bowed his head, said "Thank you," and returned to his place in the line. The tears that slipped down many faces were not wiped away in shame.

We were on top again. As always, again. We survived. The depths had been icy and dark, but now a bright sun spoke to our souls. I was no longer simply a member of the proud graduating class of 1940; I was a proud member of the wonderful, beautiful Negro race.

Oh, Black known and unknown poets, how often have your auctioned pains sustained us? Who will compute the lonely nights made less lonely by your songs, or by the empty pots made less tragic by your tales?

If we were a people much given to revealing secrets, we might raise monuments and sacrifice to the memories of our poets, but slavery cured us of that weakness. It may be enough, however, to have it said that we survive in exact relationship to the dedication of our poets (include preachers, musicians and blues singers).

1970

Alice Walker
(1944–)

Now one of America's most notable contemporary writers, Alice Walker distinguished herself early in her career as a poet, essayist, novelist, and editor. Born the daughter of a sharecropper in Eatonton, Georgia, she experienced the strong family ties, a sense of heritage, that informs much of her work, and she credits her mother for "the three magic gifts I needed to escape the poverty of my hometown. . . . a sewing machine, a typewriter, and a suitcase, all on less than twenty dollars a week." She attended Spelman College, then Sarah Lawrence, and in 1966 left New York for Mississippi and became active in the civil rights movement. In Mississippi, where she lived for the next seven years, she met and married a Jewish civil rights attorney with whom she had a daughter.

In 1968, at the age of twenty-three, Walker published her first collection of poems, *Once,* which recounts her impressions of Africa and her experiences in the South, and in 1970 she published her first novel, *The Third Life of Grange Copeland,* which depicts three generations of the Copeland family as it migrates from the South to the North. Her next collection of poems, *Revolutionary Petunias* (1973), continues to explore the theme of love found even in a withering and turbulent landscape, but also the growing dissension and distrust among various members of the movement. Already, Walker had begun to analyze and refute taboos, the "forbidden things" denied a woman, especially a black woman, and did not hesitate to point out the sexism that was prevalent even in the movement: "He said come," she writes, "Let me exploit you; / Somebody must do it / And wouldn't you / Prefer a brother?" Her next collection of poems, *Good Night Willie Lee: I'll See You in the Morning,* published in 1979, is full of the sense of loss, occasioned by the death of her father, the dissolution of her marriage, and the murders of Malcolm X, Martin Luther King, Jr., and other comrades in the civil rights struggle. Yet the book is also imbued with the healing recompense of love and forgiveness that characterize much of Walker's work. Walker's next novel, *The Color Purple,* brought her national attention. A moving story of the bonds formed among three women, it became controversial for its depiction of abusive black men, its use of dialect, and its freewheeling sexuality. The book became a best-seller, was made into a film, and was awarded the Pulitzer Prize in 1985.

In 1978 Walker left New York for California, a move she found liberating to her craft. "My spirit," she claims, "which had felt so cramped on the East Coast, expanded fully, and I found as many presences to explore within my psyche as I was beginning to recognize in the world. I could, for the first time, admit and express my grief over the ongoing assassination of the earth, even as I accepted all the parts, good and bad, of my own heritage." Always a thematic note in her work, Walker's sense of animism becomes more explicit in her later poems and the novel *The Temple of My Familiar* (1989).

Walker has also been an important force as a critic, and as contributing editor to *Freedomways* and *Ms.* Her 1975 essay "In Search of Zora," which recounts her pilgrimage to Florida to find the unmarked grave of Zora Neale Hurston, and the Hurston anthology *I Love Myself When I Am Laughing . . .* (1979), which Walker edited, did much to revive interest in a writer whose work had been nearly forgotten. Walker has also written on the theoretical basis of African-American women's literature, often employing the metaphor of a quilt, a beautiful yet functional work of art created from the bits and pieces of everyday life that reflects the artistry of its maker. Her famous essay "In Search of Our Mothers' Gardens," which follows, argues that while Virginia Woolf suggested that women writers needed "a room of their own," African-American women have had to overcome far greater obstacles; denied the opportunity and freedom to express themselves artistically, they have constructed *lives* that are a monument to their creativity. In her essays, Walker prefers to use the term "womanist" rather than "feminist" to describe a woman "wanting to know more and in greater depth than is considered 'good' for one."

Walker is also the author of the novels *Meridian* (1976) and *Possessing the Secret of Joy* (1992), and two collections of short stories, *In Love and Trouble* (1973) and *You Can't Keep a Good Woman Down* (1981), and her essays have been collected in *In Search of Our Mothers' Gardens: Womanist Prose* (1983) and *Living by the Word: Selected Writings, 1973–1987* (1988). She has received a grant from the National Endowment for the Arts and a Guggenheim Fellowship, among other honors, and has lectured at the University of Massachusetts, Wellesley College, Yale University, the University of California, and elsewhere.

Reassessing her career in the preface to her collected poems, *Her Blue Body Everything We Know* (1991), Walker writes, "It surprises me to see I have been writing and publishing poetry for twenty-five years. For which I have Poetry itself to thank. Because I was so often filled with despair over my own and the world's shortcomings, especially during childhood, adolescence, and young adulthood, I assumed I would be a suicide by the age of thirty. Not so, I am happy to report. . . . I have climbed back into life over and over on a ladder made of words, but knitted, truly, by the Unknowable. Through Poetry I have lived to find within myself my own 'invincible sun.' "

from *In Search of Our Mothers' Gardens: Womanist Prose*

Womanist 1. From *womanish.* (Opp. of "girlish," i.e., frivolous, irresponsible, not serious.) A black feminist or feminist of color. From the black folk expression of mothers to female children, "You acting womanish," i.e., like a woman. Usually referring to outrageous, audacious, courageous or *willful* behavior. Wanting to know more and in greater depth than is considered "good" for one. Interested in grown-up doings. Acting grown up. Being grown up. Interchangeable with another black folk expression: "You trying to be grown." Responsible. In charge. *Serious.*

2. *Also:* A woman who loves other women, sexually and/or nonsexually. Appreciates and prefers women's culture, women's emotional flexibility (values tears as natural counterbalance of laughter), and women's strength. Sometimes loves individual men, sexually and/or nonsexually. Committed to survival and wholeness of entire people, male *and* female. Not a separatist, except periodically, for health. Traditionally universalist, as in: "Mama, why are we brown, pink, and yellow, and our cousins are white, beige, and black?" Ans.: "Well, you know the colored race is just like a flower garden, with every color flower represented." Traditionally capable, as in: "Mama, I'm walking to Canada and I'm taking you and a bunch of other slaves with me." Reply: "It wouldn't be the first time."

3. Loves music. Loves dance. Loves the moon. *Loves* the Spirit. Loves love and food and roundness. Loves struggle. *Loves* the Folk. Loves herself. *Regardless.*

4. Womanist is to feminist as purple to lavender.

"But this is not the end of the story, for all the young women —our mothers and grandmothers, ourselves*—have not perished in the wilderness."*

IN SEARCH OF OUR MOTHERS' GARDENS

> I described her own nature and temperament. Told how they needed a larger life for their expression. . . . I pointed out that in lieu of proper channels, her emotions had overflowed into paths that dissipated them. I talked, beautifully I thought, about an art that would be born, an art that would open the way for women the likes of her. I asked her to hope, and build up an inner life against the coming of that day. . . . I sang, with a strange quiver in my voice, a promise song.
>
> *Jean Toomer, "Avey,"*
> CANE

The poet speaking to a prostitute who falls asleep while he's talking—

When the poet Jean Toomer walked through the South in the early twenties, he discovered a curious thing: black women whose spirituality was so intense, so deep, so *unconscious,* that they were themselves unaware of the richness they held. They stumbled blindly through their lives: creatures so abused and mutilated in body, so dimmed and confused by pain, that they considered themselves unworthy even of hope. In the selfless abstractions their bodies became to the men who used them, they became more than "sexual objects," more even than mere women: they became "Saints." Instead of being perceived as whole persons, their bodies became shrines: what was thought to be their minds became temples suitable for worship. These crazy Saints stared out at the world, wildly, like lunatics—or quietly, like suicides; and the "God" that was in their gaze was as mute as a great stone.

Who were these Saints? These crazy, loony, pitiful women?

Some of them, without a doubt, were our mothers and grandmothers.

In the still heat of the post-Reconstruction South, this is how they seemed to Jean Toomer: exquisite butterflies trapped in an evil honey, toiling away their lives in an era, a century, that did not acknowledge them, except as "the *mule* of the world." They dreamed dreams that no one knew—not even themselves, in any coherent fashion—and saw visions no one could understand. They wandered or sat about the countryside crooning lullabies to ghosts, and drawing the mother of Christ in charcoal on courthouse walls.

They forced their minds to desert their bodies and their striving spirits sought to rise, like frail whirlwinds from the hard red clay. And when those frail whirlwinds fell, in scattered particles, upon the ground, no one mourned. Instead, men lit candles to celebrate the emptiness that remained, as people do who enter a beautiful but vacant space to resurrect a God.

Our mothers and grandmothers, some of them: moving to music not yet written. And they waited.

They waited for a day when the unknown thing that was in them would be made known; but guessed, somehow in their darkness, that on the day of their revelation they would be long dead. Therefore to Toomer they walked, and even ran, in slow motion. For they were going nowhere immediate, and the future was not yet within their grasp. And men took our mothers and grandmothers, "but got no pleasure from it." So complex was their passion and their calm.

To Toomer, they lay vacant and fallow as autumn fields, with harvest time never in sight: and he saw them enter loveless marriages, without joy; and become prostitutes, without resistance; and become mothers of children, without fulfillment.

For these grandmothers and mothers of ours were not Saints, but Artists; driven to a numb and bleeding madness by the springs of creativity in them for which there was no release. They were Creators, who lived lives of spiritual waste, because they were so rich in spirituality—which is the basis of Art—that the strain of enduring their unused and unwanted talent drove them insane. Throwing away this spirituality was their pathetic attempt to lighten the soul to a weight their work-worn, sexually abused bodies could bear.

What did it mean for a black woman to be an artist in our grandmothers' time? In our great-grandmothers' day? It is a question with an answer cruel enough to stop the blood.

Did you have a genius of a great-great-grandmother who died under some ignorant and depraved white overseer's lash? Or was she required to bake biscuits for a lazy backwater tramp, when she cried out in her soul to paint watercolors of sunsets, or the rain falling on the green and peaceful pasturelands? Or was her body broken and forced to bear children (who were more often than not sold away from her)—eight, ten, fifteen, twenty children—when her one joy was the thought of modeling heroic figures of rebellion, in stone or clay?

How was the creativity of the black woman kept alive, year after year and century after century, when for most of the years black people have been in America, it was a punishable crime for a black person to read or write? And the freedom to paint, to sculpt, to expand the mind with action did not exist. Consider, if you can bear to imagine it, what might have been the result if singing, too, had been forbidden by law. Listen to the voices of Bessie Smith, Billie Holiday, Nina Simone, Roberta Flack, and Aretha Franklin, among others, and imagine those voices muzzled for life. Then you may begin to comprehend the lives of our "crazy," "Sainted" mothers and grandmothers. The agony of the lives of women who might have been Poets, Novelists, Essayists, and Short-Story Writers (over a period of centuries), who died with their real gifts stifled within them.

And, if this were the end of the story, we would have cause to cry out in my paraphrase of Okot p'Bitek's great poem:

> O, my clanswomen
> Let us all cry together!
> Come,
> Let us mourn the death of our mother,
> The death of a Queen
> The ash that was produced
> By a great fire!
> O, this homestead is utterly dead
> Close the gates
> With *lacari* thorns,
> For our mother
> The creator of the Stool is lost!
> And all the young women
> Have perished in the wilderness!

But this is not the end of the story, for all the young women—our mothers and grandmothers, *ourselves*—have not perished in the wilderness. And if we ask ourselves why, and search for and find the answer, we will know beyond all efforts to erase it from our minds, just exactly who, and of what, we black American women are.

One example, perhaps the most pathetic, most misunderstood one, can provide a backdrop for our mothers' work: Phillis Wheatley, a slave in the 1700s.

Virginia Woolf, in her book *A Room of One's Own,* wrote that in order for a woman to write fiction she must have two things, certainly: a room of her own (with key and lock) and enough money to support herself.

What then are we to make of Phillis Wheatley, a slave, who owned not even herself? This sickly, frail black girl who required a servant of her own at times—her health was so precarious—and who, had she been white, would have been easily considered the intellectual superior of all the women and most of the men in the society of her day.

Virginia Woolf wrote further, speaking of course not of our Phillis, that "any woman born with a great gift in the sixteenth century [insert "eighteenth century," insert "black woman," insert "born or made a slave"] would certainly have gone crazed, shot herself, or ended her days in some lonely cottage outside the village, half witch, half wizard [insert "Saint"], feared and mocked at. For it needs little skill and psychology to be sure that a highly gifted girl who had tried to use her gift for poetry would have been so thwarted and hindered by contrary instincts [add "chains, guns, the lash, the ownership of one's body by someone else, submission to an alien religion"], that she must have lost her health and sanity to a certainty."

The key words, as they relate to Phillis, are "contrary instincts." For when we read the poetry of Phillis Wheatley—as when we read the novels of Nella Larsen or the oddly false-sounding autobiography of that freest of all black women writers, Zora Hurston—evidence of "contrary instincts" is everywhere. Her loyalties were completely divided, as was, without question, her mind.

But how could this be otherwise? Captured at seven, a slave of wealthy, doting whites who instilled in her the "savagery" of the Africa they "rescued" her from . . . one wonders if she was even able to remember her homeland as she had known it, or as it really was.

Yet, because she did try to use her gift for poetry in a world that made her a slave, she was "so thwarted and hindered by . . . contrary instincts, that she . . . lost her health. . . ." In the last years of her brief life, burdened not only with the need to express her gift but also with a penniless, friendless "freedom" and several small children for whom she was forced to do strenuous work to feed, she lost her health, certainly. Suffering from malnutrition and neglect and who knows what mental agonies, Phillis Wheatley died.

So torn by "contrary instincts" was black, kidnapped, enslaved Phillis that her description of "the Goddess"—as she poetically called the Liberty she did not have—is ironically, cruelly humorous. And, in fact, has held Phillis up to ridicule for more than a century. It is usually read prior to hanging Phillis's memory as that of a fool. She wrote:

> The Goddess comes, she moves divinely fair,
> Olive and laurel binds her *golden* hair.
> Wherever shines this native of the skies,
> Unnumber'd charms and recent graces rise. [My italics]

It is obvious that Phillis, the slave, combed the "Goddess's" hair every morning; prior, perhaps, to bringing in the milk, or fixing her mistress's lunch. She took her imagery from the one thing she saw elevated above all others.

With the benefit of hindsight we ask, "How could she?"

But at last, Phillis, we understand. No more snickering when your stiff, struggling, ambivalent lines are forced on us. We know now that you were not an idiot or a traitor; only a sickly little black girl, snatched from your home and country and made a slave; a woman who still struggled to sing the song that was your gift, although in a land of barbarians who praised you for your bewildered tongue. It is not so much what you sang, as that you kept alive, in so many of our ancestors, *the notion of song.*

Black women are called, in the folklore that so aptly identifies one's status in society, "the *mule* of the world," because we have been handed the burdens that everyone else—*everyone* else—refused to carry. We have also been called "Matriarchs," "Superwomen," and "Mean and Evil Bitches." Not to mention "Castraters" and "Sapphire's Mama." When we have pleaded for understanding, our character has been distorted; when we have asked for simple caring, we have been handed empty inspirational appellations, then stuck in the farthest corner. When we have asked for love, we have been given children. In short, even our plainer gifts, our labors of fidelity and love, have been knocked down our throats. To be an artist and a black woman, even today, lowers our status in many respects, rather than raises it: and yet, artists we will be.

Therefore we must fearlessly pull out of ourselves and look at and identify with our lives the living creativity some of our great-grandmothers were not allowed to know. I stress *some* of them because it is well known that the majority of our great-grandmothers knew, even without "knowing" it, the reality of their spirituality, even if they didn't recognize it beyond what happened in the singing at church—and they never had any intention of giving it up.

How they did it—those millions of black women who were not Phillis Wheatley, or Lucy Terry or Frances Harper or Zora Hurston or Nella Larsen or Bessie Smith; or Elizabeth Catlett, or Katherine Dunham, either—brings me to the title of this essay, "In Search of Our Mothers' Gardens," which is a personal account that is yet shared, in its theme and its meaning, by all of us. I found, while thinking about the far-reaching world of the creative black woman, that often the truest answer to a question that really matters can be found very close.

In the late 1920s my mother ran away from home to marry my father. Marriage, if not running away, was expected of seventeen-year-old girls. By the time she was twenty, she had two children and was pregnant with a third. Five children later, I was born. And this is how I came to know my mother: she seemed a large, soft, loving-eyed woman who was rarely impatient in our home. Her quick, violent temper was on view only a few times a year, when she battled with the white landlord who had the misfortune to suggest to her that her children did not need to go to school.

She made all the clothes we wore, even my brothers' overalls. She made all the towels and sheets we used. She spent the summers canning vegetables and fruits. She spent the winter evenings making quilts enough to cover all our beds.

During the "working" day, she labored beside—not behind—my father in the fields. Her day began before sunup, and did not end until late at night. There was never a moment for her to sit down, undisturbed, to unravel her own private thoughts; never a time free from interruption—by work or the noisy inquiries of her many children. And yet, it is to my mother—and all our mothers who were not famous—that I went in search of the secret of what has fed that muzzled and often mutilated, but vibrant, creative spirit that the black woman has inherited, and that pops out in wild and unlikely places to this day.

But when, you will ask, did my overworked mother have time to know or care about feeding the creative spirit?

The answer is so simple that many of us have spent years discovering it. We have constantly looked high, when we should have looked high—and low.

For example: in the Smithsonian Institution in Washington, D.C., there hangs a quilt unlike any other in the world. In fanciful, inspired, and yet simple and identifiable figures, it portrays the story of the Crucifixion. It is considered rare, beyond price. Though it follows no known pattern of quilt-making, and though it is made of bits and pieces of worthless rags, it is obviously the work of a person of powerful imagination and deep spiritual feeling. Below this quilt I saw a note that says it was made by "an anonymous Black woman in Alabama, a hundred years ago."

If we could locate this "anonymous" black woman from Alabama, she would turn out to be one of our grandmothers—an artist who left her mark in the only materials she could afford, and in the only medium her position in society allowed her to use.

As Virginia Woolf wrote further, in *A Room of One's Own:*

> Yet genius of a sort must have existed among women as it must have existed among the working class. [Change this to "slaves" and "the wives and daughters of sharecroppers."] Now and again an Emily Brontë or a Robert Burns [change this to "a Zora Hurston or a Richard Wright"] blazes out and proves its presence. But certainly it never got itself on to paper. When, however, one reads of a witch being ducked, of a woman possessed by devils [or "Sainthood"], of a wise woman selling herbs [our root workers], or even a very remarkable man who had a mother, then I think we are on the track of a lost novelist, a suppressed poet, of some mute and inglorious Jane Austen. . . . Indeed, I would venture to guess that Anon,

> who wrote so many poems without signing them, was often a woman. . . .

And so our mothers and grandmothers have, more often than not anonymously, handed on the creative spark, the seed of the flower they themselves never hoped to see: or like a sealed letter they could not plainly read.

And so it is, certainly, with my own mother. Unlike "Ma" Rainey's songs, which retained their creator's name even while blasting forth from Bessie Smith's mouth, no song or poem will bear my mother's name. Yet so many of the stories that I write, that we all write, are my mother's stories. Only recently did I fully realize this: that through years of listening to my mother's stories of her life, I have absorbed not only the stories themselves, but something of the manner in which she spoke, something of the urgency that involves the knowledge that her stories—like her life—must be recorded. It is probably for this reason that so much of what I have written is about characters whose counterparts in real life are so much older than I am.

But the telling of these stories, which came from my mother's lips as naturally as breathing, was not the only way my mother showed herself as an artist. For stories, too, were subject to being distracted, to dying without conclusion. Dinners must be started, and cotton must be gathered before the big rains. The artist that was and is my mother showed itself to me only after many years. This is what I finally noticed:

Like Mem, a character in *The Third Life of Grange Copeland*, my mother adorned with flowers whatever shabby house we were forced to live in. And not just your typical straggly country stand of zinnias, either. She planted ambitious gardens—and still does—with over fifty different varieties of plants that bloom profusely from early March until late November. Before she left home for the fields, she watered her flowers, chopped up the grass, and laid out new beds. When she returned from the fields she might divide clumps of bulbs, dig a cold pit, uproot and replant roses, or prune branches from her taller bushes or trees—until night came and it was too dark to see.

Whatever she planted grew as if by magic, and her fame as a grower of flowers spread over three counties. Because of her creativity with her flowers, even my memories of poverty are seen through a screen of blooms—sunflowers, petunias, roses, dahlias, forsythia, spirea, delphiniums, verbena . . . and on and on.

And I remember people coming to my mother's yard to be given cuttings from her flowers; I hear again the praise showered on her because whatever rocky soil she landed on, she turned into a garden. A garden so brilliant with colors, so original in its design, so magnificent with life and creativity, that to this day people drive by our house in Georgia—perfect strangers and imperfect strangers—and ask to stand or walk among my mother's art.

I notice that it is only when my mother is working in her flowers that she is radiant, almost to the point of being invisible—except as Creator: hand and eye. She is involved in work her soul must have. Ordering the universe in the image of her personal conception of Beauty.

Her face, as she prepares the Art that is her gift, is a legacy of respect she leaves to me, for all that illuminates and cherishes life. She has handed down respect for the possibilities—and the will to grasp them.

For her, so hindered and intruded upon in so many ways, being an artist has still been a daily part of her life. This ability to hold on, even in very simple ways, is work black women have done for a very long time.

This poem is not enough, but it is something, for the woman who literally covered the holes in our walls with sunflowers:

They were women then
My mama's generation
Husky of voice—Stout of
Step
With fists as well as
Hands
How they battered down
Doors
And ironed
Starched white
Shirts
How they led
Armies
Headragged Generals
Across mined
Fields
Booby-trapped
Kitchens
To discover books
Desks
A place for us
How they knew what we
Must know
Without knowing a page
Of it
Themselves.

Guided by my heritage of a love of beauty and a respect for strength—in search of my mother's garden, I found my own.

And perhaps in Africa over two hundred years ago, there was just such a mother; perhaps she painted vivid and daring decorations in oranges and yellows and greens on the walls of her hut; perhaps she sang—in a voice like Roberta Flack's—*sweetly* over the compounds of her village; perhaps she wove the most stunning mats or told the most ingenious stories of all the village storytellers. Perhaps she was herself a poet—though only her daughter's name is signed to the poems that we know.

Perhaps Phillis Wheatley's mother was also an artist.

Perhaps in more than Phillis Wheatley's biological life is her mother's signature made clear.

1974

Jesse Jackson

(1941–)

The great-grandson of slaves, Jesse Jackson was born to a single mother in Greenville, South Carolina. He earned an athletic scholarship to the University of Illinois, but when he was denied a fair opportunity to participate in sports, he transferred to North Carolina Agricultural and Technical College, and then attended Chicago Theological Seminary, where he was ordained a Baptist minister in 1968.

In the 1960s Jackson became active in the civil rights movement and participated in the Selma-to-Montgomery march in the spring of 1965. Though still in his early twenties, he became a highly valued colleague of Dr. Martin Luther King, Jr., helping to bring the movement from the rural South to the urban North; he was with Dr. King when he was shot in Memphis in April 1968. In Chicago, Jackson spearheaded Operation Breadbasket, an initiative to encourage minority jobs, and in 1966 became a leader of the Chicago Freedom Movement. As the destination of tens of thousands of blacks who had come North in the Great Migration† of the early twentieth century, Chicago remained, according to the 1959 U.S. Commission on Civil Rights, "the most residentially segregated large city in the nation" (James Baldwin referred to Chicago's South Side as "a million in captivity"), and its residents were crowded into inadequate space and deteriorating buildings and manipulated by redlining, gerrymandering, and disenfranchisement. Jackson also participated in Resurrection City in Washington, D.C., in the summer of 1968, and when the settlement was dismantled by authorities, his presence did much to stem violence in the city.

Moving beyond the political gains of the Civil Rights Act of 1964 and the Voting Rights Act of 1965, Jackson pursued the goal of "economic justice." In 1971 he founded Operation PUSH (People United to Serve Humanity), which sought to provide jobs and economic opportunities to minorities, and he was a keynote speaker at the National Black Political Convention in Gary, Indiana, in March 1972. As the convention was virtually on the point of organizing a strong third national party, Jackson, borrowing a phrase from the work of poet Amiri Baraka, argued, "It's

Nationtime, it's time to come together. It's time to organize politically. It's time for partnership. It's time for blacks to enter into the equation, it is indeed, whether you're in California or Mississippi, it is Nationtime."

In the late 1970s and early 1980s Jackson became a politician with enormous national—and international—influence. In 1983 he secured the release of a captured American navy pilot in Syria, and in 1984 he undertook a campaign for the presidency. A rousing speaker who uses alliteration and the repetition of a memorable refrain particularly effectively—"I *am* somebody." "Keep hope alive."—Jackson delivered the following address at the Democratic National Convention in San Francisco on July 17, 1984.

Though not the first African-American to run for the executive office (Eldridge Cleaver and Shirley Chisholm ran for president in 1972), he received much mainstream support and won as many as three million votes, attracting many whites as well as blacks. His effort might have been even more effective had he not offended many voters with a disparaging anti-Semitic comment, which he retracted. Four years later, Jackson ran another strong campaign, winning six million votes in the primaries. Though he was unsuccessful in both cases in winning the Democratic Party's nomination, his role as a power broker led the media to repeatedly question, "What Does Jesse Want?" "Within my lifetime," he has said, "this ongoing struggle will have an African-American as nominee of a major political party. Indeed, as president of the United States of America."

As other black politicians—notably Virginia Governor L. Douglas Wilder and Commerce Secretary Ron Brown—have gained national prominence "within the system," Jackson's role as a political gadfly has become somewhat less clear. He remains, however, an enormously popular and dedicated black leader, visible most recently in South-Central Los Angeles after the revolt in the spring of 1992.

Address to the Democratic National Convention

"We must seek a revival of the spirit, inspired by a new vision and new possibilities. We must return to higher ground."

TONIGHT WE COME TOGETHER BOUND BY OUR FAITH, IN A mighty God, with genuine respect for our country, and inheriting the legacy of a great party—a Democratic party—which is the best hope for redirecting our nation on a more humane, just and peaceful course.

This is not a perfect party. We are not perfect people. Yet, we are called to a perfect mission: our mission, to feed the hungry, to clothe the naked, to house the homeless, to teach the illiterate, to provide jobs for the jobless, and to choose the human race over the nuclear race.

We are gathered here this week to nominate a candidate and write a platform which will expand, unify, direct and inspire our party and the nation to fulfill this mission.

My constituency is the damned, disinherited, disrespected and the despised.

They are restless and seek relief. They've voted in record numbers. They have invested the faith, hope and trust that they have in us. The Democratic Party must send them a signal that we care. I pledge my best not to let them down.

There is the call of conscience: redemption, expansion, healing and unity. Leadership must heed the call of conscience, redemption, expansion, healing and unity, for they are the key to achieving our mission.

Time is neutral and does not change things.

With courage and initiative leaders change things. No generation can choose the age or circumstances in which it is born, but through leadership it can choose to make the age in which it is born an age of enlightenment—an age of jobs, and peace, and justice.

Only leadership—that intangible combination of gifts, discipline, information, circumstance, courage, timing, will and divine inspiration—can lead us out of the crisis in which we find ourselves.

Leadership can mitigate the misery of our nation. Leadership can part the waters and lead our nation in the direction of the Promised Land. Leadership can lift the boats stuck at the bottom.

I have had the rare opportunity to watch seven men, and then two, pour out their souls, offer their service and heed the call of duty to direct the course of our nation.

There is a proper season for everything. There is a time to sow and a time to reap. There is a time to compete, and a time to cooperate.

I ask for your vote on the first ballot as a vote for a new direction for this party and this nation; a vote for conviction, a vote for conscience.

But I will be proud to support the nomination of this convention for the president of the United States of America. . . .

Throughout this campaign, I have tried to offer leadership to the Democratic Party and the nation.

If in my high moments, I have done some good, offered some service, shed some light, healed some wounds, rekindled some hope or stirred someone from apathy and indifference, or in any way along the way helped somebody, then this campaign has not been in vain.

For friends who loved and cared for me, and for a God who spared me, and for a family who understood, I am eternally grateful.

If in my low moments, in word, deed or attitude, through some error of temper, taste or tone, I have caused anyone discomfort, created pain, or revived someone's fears, that was not my truest self.

If there were occasions when my grape turned into a raisin and my joy bell lost its resonance, please forgive me. Charge it to my head and not to my heart. My head is so limited in its finitude; my heart is boundless in its love for the human family. I am not a perfect servant. I am a public servant. I'm doing my best against the odds. As I develop and serve, be patient. God is not finished with me yet.

This campaign has taught me much: that leaders must be tough enough to fight, tender enough to cry, human enough to make mistakes, humble enough to admit them, strong enough to absorb the pain, and resilient enough to bounce back and keep on moving. For leaders, the pain is often intense. But you must smile through your tears and keep moving with the faith that there is a brighter side somewhere.

I went to see Hubert Humphrey three days before he died. He had just called Richard Nixon from his dying bed, and many people wondered why. And, I asked him.

He said, "Jesse, from this vantage point, with the sun setting in my life, all of the speeches, the political conventions, the crowds and the great fights are behind me now. At a time like this you are forced to deal with your irreducible essence, forced to grapple with that which is really important to you. And what I have concluded about life," Hubert Humphrey said, "when all is said and done, we must forgive each other, and redeem each other, and move on."

Our party is emerging from one of its most hard-fought battles for the Democratic Party's presidential nomination in our history. But our healthy competition should make us better, not bitter. We must use the insight, wisdom and experience of the late Hubert Humphrey as a balm for the wounds in our party, this nation and the world. We must forgive each other, redeem each other, regroup and move on.

Our flag is red, white and blue, but our nation is rainbow—red, yellow, brown, black and white—we're all precious in God's sight. America is not like a blanket—one piece of unbroken cloth, the same color, the same texture, the same size. America is more like a quilt—many patches, many pieces, many colors, many sizes, all woven and held together by a common thread.

The white, the Hispanic, the black, the Arab, the Jew, the woman, the Native American, the small farmer, the businessperson, the environmentalist, the peace activist, the young, the old, the lesbian, the gay, and the disabled make up the American quilt.

Even in our fractured state, all of us count and fit somewhere. We have proven that we can survive without each other. But we have not proven that we can win or make progress without each other. We must come together.

From Fannie Lou Hamer in Atlantic City in 1964 to the Rainbow Coalition in San Francisco today; from the Atlantic to the Pacific, we have experienced pain but progress as we ended American apartheid laws: we got public accommodations; we secured voting rights; we obtained open housing; as young people got the right to vote; we lost Malcolm, Martin, Medgar, Bobby and John and Viola.

The team that got us here must be expanded, not abandoned. Twenty years ago, tears welled up in our eyes as the bodies of Schwerner, Goodman and Chaney were dredged from the depths of a river in Mississippi. Twenty years later, our communities, black and Jewish, are in anguish, anger and pain.

Feelings have been hurt on both sides. There is a crisis in communications. Confusion is in the air. We cannot afford to lose our way. We may agree to agree, or agree to disagree on isssues; we must bring back civility to these tensions.

We are co-partners in a long and rich religious history—the Judeo-Christian traditions. Many blacks and Jews have a shared passion for social justice at home and peace abroad. We must seek a revival of the spirit, inspired by a new vision and new possibilities. We must return to higher ground. We are bound by Moses and Jesus, but also connected to Islam and Mohammed.

These three great religions—Judaism, Christianity and Islam—were all born in the revered and holy city of Jerusalem. We are bound by Dr. Martin Luther King, Jr., and Rabbi Abraham Heschel, crying out from their graves for us to reach common ground. We are bound by shared blood and shared sacrifices. We are much too intelligent; much too bound by our Judeo-Christian heritage; much too victimized by racism, sexism, militarism and anti-Semitism; much too threatened as historical scapegoats to go on divided one from another. We must turn from finger-pointing to clasped hands. We must share our burdens and our joys with each other once again. We must turn to each other and not on each other and choose higher ground.

Twenty years later, we cannot be satisfied by just restoring the old coalition. Old wine skins must make room for new wine. We must heal and expand. The Rainbow Coalition is making room for Arab-Americans. They too know the pain and hurt of racial and religious rejection. They must not continue to be made pariahs. . . .

The Rainbow is making room for the Native Americans, the most exploited people of all, a people with the greatest moral claim amongst us. We support them as they seek the restoration of their ancient land and claim amongst us. We support them as they seek the restoration of land and water rights, as they seek to preserve their ancestral homelands and the beauty of a land that was once all theirs. They can never receive a fair share for all that they have given us, but they must finally have a fair chance to develop their great resources and to preserve their people and their culture.

The Rainbow Coalition includes Asian-Americans, now being killed in our streets—scapegoats for the failures of corporate, industrial and economic policies. The Rainbow is making room for the young Americans. Twenty years ago, our young people were dying in a war for which they could not even vote. But 20 years later, Young America has the power to stop a war in Central America and the responsibility to vote in great numbers. Young America must be politically active in 1984. The choice is war or peace. We must make room for Young America.

The Rainbow includes disabled veterans. The color scheme fits in the Rainbow. The disabled have their handicap revealed and their genius concealed; while the able-bodied have their genius revealed and their disability concealed. But ultimately we must judge people by their values and their contribution. Don't leave anybody out. I would rather have Roosevelt in a wheelchair than Reagan on a horse.

The Rainbow is making room for small farmers. They have suffered tremendously under the Reagan regime. They will either receive 90 percent parity or 100 percent charity. We must address their concerns and make room for them. The Rainbow includes lesbians and gays. No American citizen ought be denied equal protection under the law.

We must be unusually committed and caring as we expand our family to include new members. All of us must be tolerant and understanding as the fears and anxieties of the rejected and of the party leadership express themselves in many different ways. Too often what we call hate—as if it were deeply rooted in some philosophy or strategy—is simply ignorance, anxiety, paranoia, fear and insecurity. To be strong leaders, we must be long-suffering as we seek to right the wrongs of our party and our nation. We must expand our party, heal our party and unify our party. That is our mission in 1984.

We are often reminded that we live in a great nation—and we do. But it can be greater still. The Rainbow is mandating a new definition of greatness. We must not measure greatness from the mansion down, but the manger up.

Jesus said that we should not be judged by the bark we wear but by the fruit we bear. Jesus said that we must measure greatness by how we treat the least of these. . . .

We have a challenge as Democrats: support a way out. Democracy guarantees opportunity, not success. Democracy guarantees the right to participate, not a license for either the majority or a minority to dominate. The victory for the Rainbow Coalition in the platform debates today was not whether we won or lost; but that we raised the right issues. We can afford to lose the vote; issues are negotiable. We cannot afford to avoid raising the right questions. Our self respect and our moral integrity were at stake. Our heads are perhaps bloodied but not bowed. Our backs are straight. When we think, on this journey from slaveship to championship, we've gone from the planks of the boardwalk in Atlantic City in 1964 to fighting to have the right planks in the platform in San Francisco in '83. There is a deep and abiding sense of joy in our soul, despite the tears in our eyes. For while there are missing planks, there is a solid foundation upon which to build. Our party can win. But we must provide hope that will inspire people to struggle and achieve; provide a plan to show the way out of our dilemma, and then lead the way.

In 1984, my heart is made to feel glad because I know there is a way out. Justice. The requirement for rebuilding America is justice. The linchpin of progressive politics in our nation will not come from the North; they in fact will come from the South. That is why I argue over and over again—from Lynchburg, Va., down to Texas, there is only one black congressperson out of 115. Nineteen years later, we're locked out of the Congress, the Senate and the governor's mansion. What does this large black vote mean? Why do I fight to end second primaries and fight gerrymandering. . . . Why do we fight over that? Because I tell you, you cannot hold someone in the ditch and linger there with them. If we want a change in this nation, reinforce that Voting Rights Act—we'll get 12 to 20 black, Hispanic, female and progressive congresspersons from the South. We can save the cotton, but we've got to fight the boll weevil—we've got to make a judgment.

It's not enough to hope ERA will pass; how can we pass ERA? If blacks vote in great numbers, progressive whites win. It's the only way progressive whites win. If blacks vote in great numbers, Hispanics win. If blacks, Hispanics and progressive whites vote, women win. When women win, children win. When women and children win, workers win. We must all come up together. We must come up together.

I tell you, with all of our joy and excitement, we must not save the world and lose our souls; we should never short-circuit enforcement of the Voting Rights Act at every level. If one of us rises, all of us must rise. Justice is the way out. Peace is a way out. We should not act as if nuclear weaponry is negotiable and debatable. In this world in which we live, we dropped the bomb on Japan and felt guilty. But in 1984, other folks also got bombs. This time, if we drop the bomb, six minutes later, we, too, will be destroyed. It's not about dropping the bomb on somebody; it's about dropping the bomb on everybody. We must choose developed minds over guided missiles, and think it out and not fight it out. It's time for a change.

Our foreign policy must be characterized by mutual respect not by gunboat diplomacy, big stick diplomacy and threats. Our nation at its best feeds the hungry. Our nation at its worst will mine the harbors of Nicaragua; at its worst, will try to overthrow that government; at its worst, will cut aid to American education and increase aid to El Salvador; at its worst our nation will have partnership with South Africa. That's a moral disgrace. It's a moral disgrace. It's a moral disgrace.

When we look at Africa, we cannot just focus on apartheid in southern Africa. We must fight for trade with Africa, and not just aid to Africa. We cannot stand idly by and say we will not relate to Nicaragua unless they have elections there and then embrace military regimes in Africa, overthrowing Democratic governments in Nigeria and Liberia and Ghana. We must fight for democracy all around the world, and play the game by one set of rules.

Peace in this world. Our present formula for peace in the Middle East is inadequate; it will not work. There are 22 nations in the Middle East. Our nation must be able to talk and act and influence all of them. We must build upon Camp David and measure human rights by one yardstick. . . .

There is a way out. Jobs. Put America back to work. When I was a child growing up in Greenville, S.C., the Rev. ——— who used to preach every so often a sermon about Jesus. He said, if I be lifted up, I'll draw all men unto me. I didn't quite understand what he meant as a child growing up. But I understand a little better now. If you raise up truth, it's magnetic. It has a way of drawing people. With all this confusion in this convention—there is bright lights and parties and big fun—we must raise up the simple proposition: if we lift up a program to feed the hungry, they'll come running. If we lift up a program to study war no more, our youth will come running. If we lift up a program to put America back to work, an alternative to welfare and despair, they will come working. If we cut that military budget without cutting our defense, and use that money to rebuild bridges and put steelworkers back to work, and use that money, and provide jobs for our citizens, and use that money to build schools and train teachers and educate our children, and build hospitals and train doctors and train nurses, the whole nation will come running to us.

As I leave you now, vote in this convention and get ready to go back across this nation in a couple of days, in this campaign, I'll try to be faithful by my promise. I'll live in the old barrios, and ghettos and reservations, and housing projects. I have a message for our youth. I challenge them to put hope in their brains, and not dope in their veins. I told them like Jesus, I, too, was born in a slum, but just because you're born in a slum, does not mean the slum is born in you, and you can rise above it if your mind is made up. I told them in every slum, there are two sides. When I see a broken window, that's the slummy side. Train that youth to be a glazier, that's the sunny side. When I see a missing brick, that's the slummy side. Let that child in the union, become a brickmason, and build, that's the sunny side. When I see a missing door, that's the slummy side. Train some youth to become a carpenter, that's the sunny side. When I see the vulgar words and hieroglyphics of destitution on the walls, that's the slummy side. Train some youth to be a painter, an artist—that's the sunny side. We need this place looking for the sunny side because there's a brighter side somewhere. I am more convinced than ever that we can win. We'll vault up the rough side of the mountain; we can win. I just want young America to do me one favor.

Exercise the right to dream. You must face reality—that which is. But then dream of the reality that ought to be, that must be. Live beyond the pain of reality with the dream of a bright tomorrow. Use hope and imagination as weapons of survival and progress. Use love to motivate you and obligate you to serve the human family.

Young America, dream. Choose the human race over the nuclear race. Bury the weapons and don't burn the people. Dream of a new value system. Teachers, who teach for life, and not just for a living, teach because they can't help it. Dream of lawyers more concerned with justice than a judgeship. Dream of doctors more concerned with public health than personal wealth. Dream preachers and priests who will prophesy and not just profiteer. Preach and dream. Our time has come.

Our time has come. Suffering breeds character. Character breeds faith. And in the end, faith will not disappoint.

Our time has come. Our faith, hope and dreams will prevail. Our time has come. Weeping has endured for the night. And, now joy cometh in the morning.

Our time has come. No graves can hold our body down.

Our time has come. No lie can live forever.

Our time has come. We must leave racial battleground and come to economic common ground and moral higher ground. America, our time has come.

We've come from disgrace to Amazing Grace, our time has come.

Give me your tired, give me your poor, your huddled masses who yearn to breathe free and come November, there will be a change because our time has come.

Thank you and God bless you.

July 17, 1984

Rap Music

From the streets of New York in the late 1970s to MTV in the 1990s, rap culture has entered the American mainstream. Rap emerged in New York when DJs like Afrika Bambaataa and Grandmaster Flash began to create a new kind of urban blues in the city's parks and neighborhoods, embracing the found noise around them and manipulating sound to produce a music that is part entertainment, part political protest. While the DJs perfected the characteristic scratching and sampling techniques, MCs overlaid the music with rapid-fire lyrics full of bravado, anger, and pride.

The first record of this new music to reach a sizable audience was *Rapper's Delight,* by the Sugarhill Gang, appearing in 1980. While the music caught on in the black community, Fab Five Freddy, now host of *Yo! MTV Raps,* helped introduce rap—"a cultural battering ram"—to the downtown New York club scene. By the mid-1980s, rap had gone beyond the ultimate dance beat to take in the reality of, among other things, the crack epidemic that started in 1985 and the growing indifference of politicians to cities in crisis. Although rap continued to use highly provocative sexual wordplay, it also began to fuel narratives of urban life. "It's like a jungle sometimes," writes Grandmaster Flash, while Naughty by Nature challenges the argument that rap lyrics are overly negative, saying, "Well positive ain't where I live." Lyrically, says writer Jefferson Morley, rap derives from an oral tradition extending all the way back to the African griot, to doing the Dozens, to the rhyming boasts of Muhammad Ali. It recalls, too, the rhetoric of Amiri Baraka ("will the machine gunners please get ready") and militant black activists of the 1960s. Ice-T has drawn on the black oral tradition to call himself a "rap trickster."

One of the most successful early groups was Public Enemy, termed the Black Panthers of rap. From their first album, *Yo! Bum Rush the Show* (1987), their "noise manifestos" tended toward apocalyptic themes, as in "Riotstarter: Message to a Black Man," "Black Steel in the Hour of Chaos," and "Welcome to the Terrordome," and their rap anthem "Fight the Power" opened Spike Lee's film *Do the Right Thing* (1989). For many rap groups, the music's foils include the police (as in Boogie Down Productions' "Illegal Business"), the media (Public Enemy's "Don't Believe the Hype"), drug dealers (Big Daddy Kane's "Another Victory"), and politicians "living large while the people starve" (Laquan's "Imprison the President"). At the same time, rap lyrics are often positively Afrocentric, recalling black heroes and stressing self-education (Kool Moe Dee's "Knowledge Is King").

The lyrics of hip-hop have proven highly controversial. In June 1990 members of 2 Live Crew were arrested on obscenity charges in Broward County, Florida, escalating the debate about rap to a struggle over First Amendment rights; in October 1990 the singers were acquitted. Ice-T, who had released the album *Freedom of Speech* in 1989, also got some heat for the record "Cop Killer," which was eventually withdrawn by Warner Records. To those who would argue that rap incites violence, Ice-T contends that rap reflects very real existing attitudes shaped by the conditions on the street, not words to music, attitudes that the prevailing culture has long ignored. "I'm going to tell you what you need to hear, not what you want to hear," Ice-T told one interviewer, and after the L.A. riots† Ice-T remarked, "I gave you a warning, that record was a warning. . . . but now you've seen it's real." In fact, instead of inciting violence, many rappers talk about using their music as a weapon (using "lyrics of ammo" writes Eric B. & Rakim) to promote unity and pride. The role of women in rap has also been widely debated. Though some songs describe women as sexual objects, strong female singers like Queen Latifah, Salt-n-Pepa, Yo-Yo, and Roxanne Shante—"Drugs is not the only thing a girl can say no to"—have responded with outspoken, self-confident raps of their own.

Now clearly one of the dominant expressions of popular culture, rap reflects, finally, a search for affirmation, pride, and a strong sense of black community, issues often ignored by the mainstream. As Chuck D of Public Enemy says, "Rap music is like CNN for black people." And while white performers have adopted hip-hop style and major record labels have seen its commercial potential, rap artists insist that they be met on their terms. "Don't be down with anybody," writes Heavy D and the Boyz in "We've Got Our Own Thang," "let them all be down with you." Two recent surveys of the origin and significance of rap are *Bring the Noise* by Havelock Nelson and Michael A. Gonzales, and *Rap Lyrics*, edited by Lawrence A. Stanley.

The Clarence Thomas Confirmation Hearings

On July 2, 1991, to fill the vacancy left on the Supreme Court by the retirement of Thurgood Marshall, President George Bush nominated newly appointed appeals court judge Clarence Thomas as "the best person" for the job, thereby beginning one of the most disturbing public dramas in recent memory.

The Clarence Thomas story would be told many times in the months before his confirmation hearings began in September. Born to very modest circumstance in Pin Point, Georgia, Thomas was raised by strict grandparents and schooled by stern but supportive Catholic nuns. He attended Holy Cross University in Boston and then Yale Law School, where he was recommended by the dean to Senator John Danforth, who would become his political patron. For eight years under Republican presidents Reagan and Bush, Thomas was a political appointee, first serving as chairman of the Equal Employment Opportunity Commission and then as assistant secretary of education. His record was marked by open criticism of traditional civil rights programs and leaders, including Justice Marshall, and an unimpressive body of writings and speeches. Remarkably, he claimed to have never discussed with friends or colleagues one of the most pressing and controversial political and judicial matters of the day, the landmark 1973 Supreme Court decision in *Roe* v. *Wade* that legalized abortion.

Once the Thomas nomination was offered, defenders and critics came forward. Staunchly supported by his educational and political mentors, Thomas was criticized by historian John Hope Franklin and others as a latter-day Booker T. Washington. Others argued that while Thomas did not espouse the liberal philosophies of the great Justice Marshall, it was important to maintain a black presence on the Court. In the African-American community, his nomination was opposed by both the Congressional Black Caucus and the NAACP, though supported by the Urban League and the Southern Christian Leadership Conference. Even his supporters, however, were highly ambivalent. Maya Angelou argued that despite his "lamentable reputation," she supported him because he was "young enough to be won over again," and John E. Jacob of the Urban League wrote, "Obviously, Judge Thomas is no Justice Marshall." On September 27 the Senate Judiciary Committee, split 7–7, sent Thomas's nomination to the full Senate, without a recommendation. Black lawyer Charles Bowser later stated, "I'd be willing to bet . . . that not one of the senators who voted to confirm Clarence Thomas would hire him as their lawyer."

Despite the ambivalence his credentials inspired, Thomas's nomination seemed secure, until, on October 6, charges of sexual harassment made previously to the Judiciary Committee by Oklahoma law professor Anita Hill, a colleague of Thomas's at EEOC and Education, were made public by *Newsday* and National Public Radio. The allegations set off shockwaves across deep fault lines of gender and race. Many women were angered that the original charges had not been made public by the all-male Judiciary Committee, which "just didn't get it," and that, if they were true, Thomas was unfit to serve on the Court. To others, despite Hill's statement that "I felt that I had to tell the truth. I could not keep silent," her assertions were a betrayal of her race, an airing of "dirty linen" in public. The divisions in many ways recalled the debates that swirled around the adoption of the Fifteenth Amendment† and the sexism found in the black activism of the sixties, arguments concerning whether a "race first" philosophy that supported tangible advances for blacks took precedence over gains for women, many of whom, of course, were black. For Anita Hill, writes Paula Giddings, "It was an act of great inner courage and conviction, to turn back the veil of our Du Boisian double consciousness. It was an act that provided clarity about our new status in the late twentieth century."

In an unprecedented series of events, from October 11 to 14, the Thomas hearings were reopened and carried on all three national television networks during prime time. In calm, measured tones, Anita Hill revealed the circumstances during which the alleged incidents took place, providing, when pressed, the sometimes ribald details as the Judiciary Committee, indeed the nation, proceeded to dissect one of the most volatile of racial stereotypes, the sexuality of the black male. On October 11, Clarence Thomas responded with the statement included here, accusing the senators of conducting a "high-tech lynching." Though his critics quickly accused Thomas of "selective blackness," of co-opting the issue of race when he had previously sought to banish it, one wonders if the national battle staged between Hill and Thomas would have taken place if the participants had been white.

Ultimately, writes Toni Morrison, "In these hearings data, not to mention knowledge, had no place. The deliberations became a contest and the point was to win." On October 16 the Senate voted 52–48 to confirm Clarence Thomas as the 106th associate justice of the Supreme Court, but the controversy was far from over. Anger at Anita Hill's treatment by the Judiciary Committee was at least in part responsible for the numerous gains women made in state and national elections in 1992. A majority of

Americans have now reversed themselves and believe that Anita Hill spoke truthfully, and with his early decisions Thomas has proven as conservative as his ideological detractors had feared, leading the *New York Times* to describe him as "the youngest and cruelest judge."

"Yet regardless of political alliances," writes Morrison, "something positive and liberating has already surfaced. In matters of race and gender, it is now possible and necessary, as it seemed never to have been before, to speak about these matters without the barriers, the silences, the embarrassing gaps in discourse. It is clear to the most reductionist intellect that black people think differently from one another; it is also clear that the time for undiscriminating racial unity has passed. A conversation, a serious exchange between black men and women, has begun in a new arena, and the contestants defy the mold."

Clarence Thomas's Second Statement to the Senate Judiciary Committee

SENATOR, I WOULD LIKE TO START BY SAYING UNEQUIVOCALLY, uncategorically, that I deny each and every single allegation against me today that suggested in any way that I had conversations of a sexual nature or about pornographic material with Anita Hill, that I ever attempted to date her, that I ever had any personal sexual interest in her, or that I in any way ever harassed her.

The second and I think more important point, I think that this today is a travesty. I think that it is disgusting. I think that this hearing should never occur in America. This is a case in which this sleaze, this dirt was searched for by staffers of members of this committee, was then leaked to the media, and this committee and this body validated it and displayed it at prime time, over our entire nation.

How would any member on this committee, any person in this room, or any person in this country like sleaze said about him or her in this fashion? Or this dirt dredged up and this gossip and these lies displayed in this manner, how would any person like it?

The Supreme Court is not worth it. No job is worth it. I am not here for that. I am here for my name, my family, my life, and my integrity. I think something is dreadfully wrong with this country when any person, any person in this free country would be subjected to this.

This is not a closed room. There was an FBI investigation. This is not an opportunity to talk about difficult matters privately or in a closed environment. This is a circus. It's a national disgrace.

And from my standpoint, as a black American, it is a high-tech lynching for uppity blacks who in any way deign to think for themselves, to do for themselves, to have different ideas, and it is a message that unless you kowtow to an old order, this is what will happen to you. You will be lynched, destroyed, caricatured by a committee of the U.S. Senate rather than hung from a tree.

October 11, 1991

The L.A. Riots

On April 29, 1992, hours after an all-white jury in Simi Valley, California, acquitted four LAPD officers of using excessive force in the arrest of black motorist Rodney King, Los Angeles exploded in the most destructive urban revolt in the United States in the twentieth century. For thirty-six hours, looting, burning, and violence continued in what one observer called this country's first "multicultural riot." When it was over, more than fifty people had lost their lives and the city had suffered almost a billion dollars in damage.

What had made the verdict—which the moderate Jesse Jackson termed "this generation's Dred Scott"—incomprehensible to many Americans was that they had seen the videotape of the police beating filmed by a bystander and had been exposed to apparently incriminating details that came out of the transcripts of the trial. The testimony of one of the officers that Rodney King had been trying to get up on "all fours," recalls language cited by a witness before the Kerner Commission in the 1960s: "What do I mean by extreme racial prejudice? I mean that [the police] describe Negroes in terms that are not people terms. They describe them in terms of the animal kingdom." As historian Nell Painter put it, "an old story reached a wide audience."

But the riot wasn't, of course, just about the perceived injustice of the Rodney King verdict. The outbreak was preceded by what Manning Marable calls "institutional violence." "The unanticipated eruption of rage stripped away the facade of black progress in the central cities," he writes, "which are boiling with the problems of poverty, drugs, gang violence, unemployment, poor schools and deteriorating public housing. . . . the King verdict was like a fireball in the night." The contributing factors went beyond the issue of black and white to encompass the frustrations of an underclass comprised as well of thousands of Latinos and others. The Los Angeles Community Reinvestment Committee determined that the median household net worth of Anglos in Los Angeles in 1991 was $31,904, that of non-Anglos $1,353. Maxine Waters, who has represented South-Central Los Angeles in the California state assembly and the U.S. House of Representatives for twenty years, describes in the testimony included here some of the economic, political, and social elements that contributed to the violence.

Much of the media coverage of the L.A. riots—reminiscent of the omnipresent helicopters strafing black neighborhoods with floodlights in John Singleton's *Boyz in the Hood*—was delivered from the air, giving them a sort of surreal, cinematic quality; they quickly became the most-watched news footage since the Persian Gulf War. In the ten days after the riots, California residents purchased 20,578 guns, many of them upgrading to a better class of weaponry, and with rumors spreading about the potential for violence in other cities (small clashes did take place in Atlanta, Seattle, San Francisco, and Las Vegas in the next few days), viewers remained glued to television sets. "There is a window of opportunity right now," commented the president of the Ad Council, which geared up for a big antiviolence PR campaign, "insofar as media acceptance is concerned."

As has been the case with every major civil disturbance this century, politicians, community leaders, sociologists, and others quickly began to assess the causes and solutions to the problem. But, as Jesse Jackson commented a month later, "So far, the response to the crisis from both political parties has been limited to arguments about how to rearrange the furniture." "What did we learn from LA, where the system of justice collapsed?" he asks. "The price of neglect is expensive." In early 1993, the four defendants in the original case were tried in federal court for violating Rodney King's civil rights. In a split verdict, two of the officers were found guilty and await sentencing. Meanwhile, South-Central Los Angeles has only begun to rebuild.

Congresswoman Maxine Waters's Testimony Before the Senate Banking Committee

"The riots in Los Angeles and in other cities shocked the world. They shouldn't have."

R. CHAIRMAN, MEMBERS OF THE COMMITTEE, IT IS A PRIVILEGE to be here today. The riots in Los Angeles and in other cities shocked the world. They shouldn't have. Many of us have watched our country—including our government—neglect the problems, indeed the people, of our inner-cities for years—even as matters reached a crisis stage.

The verdict in the Rodney King case did not cause what happened in Los Angeles. It was only the most recent injustice—piled upon many other injustices—suffered by the poor, minorities and the hopeless people living in this nation's cities. For years, they have been crying out for help. For years, their cries have not been heard.

I recently came across a statement made more than 25 years ago by Robert Kennedy, just two months before his violent death. He was talking about the violence that had erupted in cities across America. His words were wise and thoughtful: "There is another kind of violence in America, slower but just as deadly, destructive as the shot or bomb in the night. . . . This is the violence of institutions; indifference and inaction and slow decay. This is the violence that afflicts the poor, that poisons relations between men and women because their skin is different colors. This is the slow destruction of a child by hunger, and schools without books and homes without heat in the winter."

What a tragedy it is that America has still, in 1992, not learned such an important lesson.

I have represented the people of South Central Los Angeles in the U.S. Congress and the California state Assembly for close to 20 years. I have seen our community continually and systematically ravaged by banks who would not lend to us, by governments which abandoned us or punished us for our poverty, and by big businesses who exported our jobs to Third-World countries for cheap labor.

In LA, between 40 and 50 percent of all African-American men are unemployed. The poverty rate is 32.9 percent. According to the most recent census, 40,000 teenagers—that is 20 percent of the city's 16 to 19 year olds—are both out of school and unemployed.

An estimated 40,000 additional jobs were just lost as a result of the civil unrest the last two weeks. The LA Chamber of Commerce has said that at least 15,000 of these job losses will be permanent. This represents another

10 to 20 percent of South-Central LA's entire workforce permanently unemployed. Keep in mind, our region had one of the country's highest unemployment rates before the recent unrest. It is hard to imagine how our community will cope with the additional devastation.

We have created in many areas of this country a breeding ground for hopelessness, anger and despair. All the traditional mechanisms for empowerment, opportunity and self-improvement have been closed.

We are in the midst of a grand economic experiment that suggests that if we "get the government off people's backs," and let the economy grow, everyone, including the poor, will somehow be better off. So what have we done the last 12 years?

- We eliminated the Comprehensive Employment Training Act (CETA) and replaced it with the Job Training Partnership Act. In this transition, the federal commitment to job training has shrunk from $23 billion in 1980 to $8 billion now.
- General Revenue Sharing, a program designed to assist local governments to cope with their own problems, was eliminated entirely. Another $6-billion abandonment.
- Community Development Block Grants (CDBG), a building block program for local economic development, was also severely cut. In 1980 the program sent $21 billion to localities; it's now less than $14 billion.

In housing, the federal government virtually walked away from the table. Overall federal support for housing programs was cut by 80 percent.

And Reagan-Bush tried to do more—by trying to eliminate the Job Corps, VISTA and Trade Adjustment Assistance.

The results of this experiment have been devastating. Today, more than 12 million children live in poverty, despite a decade of "economic growth," the precise mechanism we were told would reduce poverty. Today, one in five children in America lives in poverty.

The number of children in poverty increased by 2.2 million from 1979 to 1989. This was true for every sub-group of America's children. White child poverty increased from 11.8 percent to 14.8 percent. Latino children's poverty went from 28 percent to 36.2 percent. And black child poverty increased from 41.2 percent to 43.7 percent.

While the budget cuts of the eighties were literally forcing millions of Americans into poverty, there were other social and economic trends destroying inner-city communities at the same time.

I'm sure everyone in this room has read the results of the Federal Reserve Board's study on mortgage discrimination that demonstrates African-Americans and Latinos are twice as likely as whites of the same income to be denied mortgages.

High-income blacks are more likely to be turned down for a mortgage than low-income whites. These trends were true in all regions of the country and in every bank surveyed.

In Los Angeles, a group called the Greenlining Coalition did its own study of the Bank of America—the area's largest bank and the primary financial institution in South Central Los Angeles. As you know, the Fed recently approved the merger of Bank of America and Security Pacific—the largest bank merger in history. One of the criteria for approval of that merger was the CRA rating of the Bank of America. BofA had earned an "outstanding" CRA rating. Despite this, the Greenlining Coalition's study revealed some startling figures:

- Only 2 percent of all of BofA's loans were made to California's 2.5 million African-Americans.
- Of these, only a trivial number, 156 loans, were made to low-income African-Americans. That comes to only one-fifth of 1 percent of all loans for low-income African-Americans.
- It is estimated that as little as $8 million was loaned to low-income African-Americans, or one-tenth of 1 percent of the $8 billion in home mortgages lent by the bank.
- Only $20 million was loaned to low-income Latinos, and one-fourth of 1 percent of Bank of America's loans went to low-income Asian-Americans.
- In total, only 4 percent of all Bank of America loans were made to low-income Californians.

In law enforcement, the problems are longstanding and well-documented as well:

- In a system where judges and lawyers remain overwhelmingly white, blacks account for a share of the prison population that far outstrips their presence in the population as a whole. According to The Sentencing Project, black men make up 6 percent of the population, but 44 percent of inmates.
- A *USA Today* analysis of 1989 drug-arrest statistics found that 41 percent of those arrested on drug charges were black, although blacks are estimated to be only 15 percent of the drug-using population.
- A *San Jose Mercury News* investigation last year of almost 700,000 criminal cases found that "at virtually every stage of pre-trial negotiation, whites are more successful than non-whites." Of the 71,000 adults with no prior criminal record,

one-third of the whites had their charges reduced, compared to only one-fourth of blacks and Hispanics.

- A Federal Judicial Center study this year of federal sentences for drug trafficking and firearms offenses found that the average sentence for blacks was 49 percent higher than for whites in 1990, compared to 28 percent in 1984.

Is it any wonder our children have no hope?

The systems are failing us. I could go on and on. All we can hope for is that the President, his Cabinet and Congress understand what is happening. We simply cannot afford the continued terror and oppression of benign neglect—the type of inaction that has characterized the federal government's response to the cities since the late 1970s.

In conclusion, I congratulate this Committee for having this hearing. We're all working overtime trying to formulate a quick and effective response to the crisis that engulfs us. With leadership and commitment, I hope we can succeed.

May 14, 1992

Selected Bibliography

Adero, Malaika, ed. *Up South: Stories and Letters of This Century's African-American Migrations.* New York: The New Press, 1993.

Angelou, Maya. *I Know Why the Caged Bird Sings.* New York: Random House, 1970.

Apetheker, Herbert. *American Negro Slave Revolts.* New York: 1943.

———. *A Documentary History of the Negro People in the United States.* 4 volumes. New York: Citadel Press, 1951–1974.

———. *One Continual Cry: David Walker's Appeal to the Colored Citizens of the World.* New York: Humanities Press, 1965.

Baldwin, James. *Notes of a Native Son.* Boston: Beacon Press, 1955.

Baraka, Amiri. *Amiri Baraka Reader.* William J. Harris, ed. New York: Thunder's Mouth Press, 1992.

Bennett, Lerone, Jr. *Before the Mayflower.* 5th rev. ed. Chicago: Johnson, 1982.

Black Scholar, The, ed. *Court of Appeal: The Black Community Speaks out on the Racial and Sexual Politics of Thomas* vs. *Hill.* New York: Ballantine Books, 1992.

Black Women in Nineteenth-Century American Life: Their Words, Their Thoughts, Their Feelings. Bert James Loewenberg and Ruth Bogin, eds. University Park: Pennsylvania State University Press, 1976.

Blaustein, Albert P., and Robert L. Zangrando, eds. *Civil Rights and African Americans.* Evanston, Ill.: Northwestern University Press, 1991; originally published by Simon & Schuster, 1968.

Bradford, Sarah. *Harriet Tubman: The Moses of Her People.* [1886]. New York: Citadel Press, 1991.

Brown, Sterling. *The Collected Poems of A. Sterling Brown.* New York: Harper & Row, 1980.

Brown, Sterling, et al., eds. *The Negro Caravan.* New York: Dryden Press, 1941.

Cantor, George. *Historic Black Landmarks: A Traveler's Guide.* Detroit: Gale Research, 1991.

Carmichael, Stokely, and Charles V. Hamilton. *Black Power: The Politics of Liberation in America.* New York: Vintage Books, 1967.

Chapman, Abraham, ed. *Black Voices: An Anthology of Afro-American Literature.* New York: New American Library, 1968.

Chesnutt, Charles W. *The Collected Stories of Charles W. Chesnutt.* [1899]. William L. Andrews, ed. New York: New American Library, 1992.

———. *The Marrow of Tradition.* [1901]. Eric J. Sundquist, ed. New York: Penguin, 1993.

The Chicago Commission on Race Relations. *The Negro in Chicago: A Study of Race Relations and a Race Riot.* Chicago: The University of Chicago Press, 1920.

Cleaver, Eldridge. *Soul on Ice.* New York: McGraw Hill, 1968.

Cooper, Anna Julia. *A Voice from the South.* [1892]. New York: Oxford University Press, 1988.

Cullen, Countee. *My Soul's High Song: The Collected Writings of Countee Cullen.* Gerald Early, ed. New York: Anchor/Doubleday, 1991.

Douglass, Frederick. *Narrative of the Life of Frederick Douglass.* [1845]. New York: Signet, 1968.

Du Bois, W. E. B. *Writings: The Suppression of the African Slave-Trade; The Souls of Black Folk; Dusk of Dawn; Essays and Articles.* Nathan Huggins, ed. New York: Literary Classics of the United States, 1986.

Dunbar, Paul. *The Complete Poems of Paul Laurence Dunbar.* New York: Dodd, Mead, 1905.

Duster, Alfreda M., ed. *Crusade for Justice: The Autobiography of Ida B. Wells.* Chicago and London: The University of Chicago Press, 1970.

Ellison, Ralph. *Invisible Man.* New York: Random House, 1952.

———. *Shadow and Act.* New York: Random House, 1964.

Evans, Mari, ed. *Black Women Writers: 1950–1980*New York: Doubleday, 1984.

The Eyes on the Prize Civil Rights Reader. Clayborne Carson, David J. Garrow, Gerald Gill, Vincent Harding, and Darlene Clark Hine, eds. New York: Viking Penguin, 1991.

Ferguson, Leland. *Uncommon Ground: Archaeology and Colonial African America.* Washington, D.C.: Smithsonian, 1992.

Freedom's Journals: A History of the Black Press in New York State. Gretchen Sullivan, Guest Curator. New York: The New York Public Library, 1986.

Garvey, Marcus. *The Philosophy and Opinions of Marcus Garvey.* New York: Atheneum, 1991.

Gates, Henry Louis, ed. *The Classic Slave Narratives.* New York: Penguin, 1987.

Giddings, Paula. *Where and When I Enter: The Impact of Black Women on Race and Sex in America.* New York: William Morrow, 1984.

Goss, Linda, and Marian E. Barnes, eds. *Talk That Talk: An Anthology of African-American Storytelling.* New York: Simon and Schuster, 1989.

Grant, Joanne. *Black Protest.* New York: Ballantine Books, 1968.

Hampton, Henry, and Steve Fayer. *Voices of Freedom.* New York: Bantam, 1990.

Handy, W. C., ed. *Blues: An Anthology.* [1926]. New York: Da Capo, 1990.

Harding, Vincent. *There Is a River.* New York: Harcourt Brace Jovanovich, 1981.

Higginson, Thomas Wentworth. *Army Life in a Black Regiment.* [1869]. New York: Norton, 1984.

Huggins, Nathan. *Harlem Renaissance.* New York: Oxford University Press, 1971.

Hughes, Langston. *Langston Hughes Reader.* New York: George Braziller, 1958.

Hurston, Zora Neale. *I Love Myself When I Am Laughing . . .* New York: The Feminist Press, 1979.

Johnson, James Weldon. *Autobiography of an Ex-Coloured Man.* [1912]. New York: Vintage, 1989.

———. *Black Manhattan.* [1930]. New York: Da Capo, 1991.

———. *The Book of American Negro Poetry.* [1922] Rev. ed. New York: Harcourt Brace, 1931.

———. *The Books of American Negro Spirituals.* [1925, 1926]. New York: Da Capo, 1977.

Kaplan, Sidney, and Emma Nogrady Kaplan. *The Black Presence in the Era of the American Revolution.* 2nd ed. Amherst, Mass.: The University of Massachusetts Press, 1989.

King, Martin Luther, Jr. *Testament of Hope: The Essential Writings of Martin Luther King, Jr.* James M. Washington, ed. New York: Harper & Row, 1986.

Lerner, Gerda, ed. *Black Women in White America: A Documentary History.* New York: Pantheon, 1972.

Levine, Lawrence W. *Black Culture and Black Consciousness: Afro-American Folk Thought from Slavery to Freedom.* New York: Oxford University Press, 1977.

Locke, Alain, ed. *The New Negro.* [1925]. New York: Macmillan, 1992.

Morrison, Toni, ed. *Race-ing Justice, En-gendering Power: Essays on Anita Hill, Clarence Thomas, and the Construction of Social Reality.* New York: Pantheon, 1992.

Penn, I. Garland. *The Afro-American Press and Its Editors.* [1891]. New York: The New York Times Publishing Company, 1969.

Quarles, Benjamin. *The Negro in the American Revolution.* Chapel Hill: University of North Carolina Press, 1961.

Randall, Dudley, ed. *The Black Poets.* New York: Bantam, 1971.

Report of the National Advisory Commission on Civil Disorders. New York: Bantam, 1968.

Robeson, Paul. *Here I Stand.* [1958]. Boston: Beacon, 1988.

———. *Paul Robeson Speaks.* Philip S. Foner, ed. New York: Citadel, 1978.

Shockley, Ann Allen. *Afro-American Women Writers 1746–1933.*[1988]. New York: New American Library, 1989.

Stanley, Lawrence A., ed. *Rap: The Lyrics.* New York: Penguin, 1992.

Stanton, Elizabeth Cady, et al. *History of American Woman Suffrage.* Vol. 1. New York: Fowler and Wells, 1881–1922.

Stepto, Robert B. *From Behind the Veil: A Study of Afro-American Narrative.* Urbana, Ill.: University of Illinois Press, 1979.

Terry, Wallace. *Bloods: An Oral History of the Vietnam War by Black Veterans.* New York: Random House, 1984.

Toomer, Jean. *Cane.* [1923]. New York: Liveright, 1975.

Truth, Sojourner. *The Narrative of Sojourner Truth.* [1850]. Margaret Washington, ed. New York: Vintage, 1993.

Van Sertima, Ivan. *They Came Before Columbus: The African Presence in Ancient America.* New York: Random House, 1976.

Walker, Alice. *Her Blue Body Everything We Know: Earthling Poems 1965–1990 Complete.* San Diego: Harcourt, Brace, Jovanovich, 1991.

———. *In Search of Our Mothers' Gardens.* San Diego: Harcourt, Brace, Jovanovich, 1983.

Washington, Booker T. *Up from Slavery.* [1901]. New York: Penguin, 1986.

Wheatley, Phillis. *The Collected Works of Phillis Wheatley.* John Shields, ed. New York: Oxford University Press, 1988.

White, Walter. *Rope and Faggot.* New York: Alfred A. Knopf, 1929.

Wilson, Harriet E. *Our Nig: or, Sketches from the Life of a Free Black.* [1859]. Henry Louis Gates, Jr., ed. New York: Random House, 1983.

Woodson, Carter G. *The Mis-Education of the Negro.* Washington, D.C.: Associated Publishers, 1933.

Wright, Richard. *Early Works: Lawd Today!; Uncle Tom's Children; Native Son.* Arnold Rampersad, ed. New York: Literary Classics of the United States, 1991.

Malcolm X. *The Autobiography of Malcolm X.* Alex Haley, ed. New York: Grove, 1965.

———. *By Any Means Necessary.* George Breitman, ed. New York: Pathfinder, 1970.

———. *Malcolm X Speaks.* New York: Merit, 1965.

Acknowledgments

Angelou, Maya: from *I Know Why the Caged Bird Sings* by Maya Angelou. Copyright © 1969 by Maya Angelou. Reprinted by permission of Random House, Inc.

Baldwin, James: "Notes of a Native Son" from *Notes of a Native Son* by James Baldwin. Copyright © 1955, copyright renewed 1983 by James Baldwin. Reprinted by permission of Beacon Press.

Baraka, Amiri: "State/meant" from *Home: Social Essays* by LeRoi Jones. Copyright © 1961, 1962, 1963, 1964, 1965, 1966, by Amiri Baraka/LeRoi Jones. Reprinted by permission of William Morrow & Company, Inc. "Preface to a Twenty Volume Suicide Note" and "Ka 'Ba" from *The LeRoi Jones/Amiri Baraka Reader*, published by Thunder's Mouth Press. Copyright © 1991 by Amiri Baraka. Used by permission of Thunder's Mouth Press.

Brooks, Gwendolyn: "The Mother," "We Real Cool," "The Chicago *Defender* Sends a Reporter to Little Rock" from *Blacks* by Gwendolyn Brooks. Reissued 1991 by Third World Press, Chicago. Reprinted by permission of the author.

Brown, Sterling: "Strong Men" from *Southern Road* by Sterling Brown. Copyright 1932 by Sterling Brown. Reprinted by permission of the author.

Cleaver, Eldridge: "Initial Reactions on the Assassination of Malcolm X" from *Soul on Ice* by Eldridge Cleaver. Copyright © 1968 by Eldridge Cleaver. Reprinted by permission of McGraw Hill, Inc.

Countee Cullen: "Heritage" and "Yet Do I Marvel" from *Color* by Countee Cullen. Copyright 1925 by Harper & Brothers, copyright © renewed 1953 by Ida M. Cullen. "From the Dark Tower" from *Copper Sun* by Countee Cullen. Copyright by Harper & Brothers, copyright © renewed 1955 by Ida M. Cullen. Reprinted by permission of GRM Associates, Inc., agents for the estate of Ida M. Cullen.

Ellison, Ralph: from *Invisible Man* by Ralph Ellison. Copyright 1947, 1948, 1952, 1975, 1976, 1980 by Ralph Ellison. Reprinted by permission of Random House, Inc.

Hayden, Robert: "Frederick Douglass" and "Middle Passage" from *Angle of Ascent: New and Selected Poems* by Robert Hayden. Copyright ©

1975, 1972, 1970, 1966, by Robert Hayden. Reprinted by permission of Liveright Publishing Corporation.

Hughes, Langston: "The Negro Speaks of Rivers" from *Selected Poems* by Langston Hughes. Copyright © 1959 by Langston Hughes. Reprinted by permission of Alfred A. Knopf, Inc. "I, Too" from *Selected Poems* by Langston Hughes. Copyright 1926 by Alfred A. Knopf, Inc., copyright renewed 1954 by Langston Hughes. Reprinted by permission of the publisher. "Dream Deferred" ("Harlem") from *The Panther and the Lash* by Langston Hughes. Copyright 1951 by Langston Hughes. Reprinted by permission of Alfred A. Knopf, Inc.

King, Martin Luther, Jr.: "Letter from Birmingham Jail" from *Why We Can't Wait* by Martin Luther King, Jr. Copyright © 1963, 1964, by Martin Luther King, Jr. Reprinted by permission of HarperCollins Publishers. "I Have a Dream" copyright © 1963 by Martin Luther King, copyright renewed 1991 by Coretta Scott King. Reprinted by arrangement with the Heirs to the Estate of Martin Luther King, Jr., c/o Joan Daves as agent for the proprietor.

McKay, Claude: "The Harlem Dancer," "If We Must Die," "Spring in New Hampshire," "The Tropics in New York," "The White City," "Tiger," and "The Lynching" from *Selected Poems of Claude McKay.* Copyright © 1981 by Harcourt Brace. Reprinted by permission of the Archives of Claude McKay, Carl Cowl, Administrator.

Malcolm X: from *The Autobiography of Malcolm X* by Malcolm X with Alex Haley. Copyright © 1964 by Alex Haley and Malcolm X. Copyright © 1965 by Alex Haley and Betty Shabazz. Reprinted by permission of Random House, Inc.

Terry, Wallace: from *Bloods: An Oral History of the Vietnam War by Black Veterans* by Wallace Terry. Copyright © 1984 by Wallace Terry. Reprinted by permission of Random House, Inc.

Toomer, Jean: "Karintha" and "Song of the Son" from *Cane* by Jean Toomer. Copyright 1923 by Boni & Liveright, copyright renewed 1951 by Jean Toomer. Reprinted by permission of Liveright Publishing Corporation.

Van Sertima, Ivan: from *They Came Before Columbus* by Ivan Van Sertima. Copyright © 1976 by Ivan Van Sertima. Reprinted by permission of Random House, Inc.

Walker, Alice: "In Search of Our Mothers' Gardens" from *In Search of Our Mothers' Gardens: Womanist Prose* by Alice Walker. Copyright © 1974 by Alice Walker. Reprinted by permission of Harcourt Brace & Company. Definition of Womanist from *In Search of Our Mothers' Gardens: Womanist Prose.* Copyright © 1983 by Alice Walker, reprinted by permission of Harcourt Brace & Company. "Women" from *Revolutionary Petunias & Other Poems,* copyright © 1970 by Alice Walker, reprinted by permission of Harcourt Brace & Company.

Wright, Richard. "The Ethics of Living Jim Crow" from *Uncle Tom's Children* by Richard Wright. Copyright 1937 by Richard Wright, copyright © renewed 1965 by Ellen Wright. Reprinted by permission of HarperCollins Publishers, Inc.

Selected Index

About the Editor

DEIRDRE MULLANE, who has worked in publishing for more than ten years, has edited numerous books on African and African-American subjects, including *Woza Afrika!*, a collection of plays by South African playwrights; *Apartheid: A History;* the biography *Winnie Mandela;* the collected speeches and writings of Oliver Tambo; and novels by Nigerian writer Buchi Emecheta. She is the editor of a forthcoming collection of African-American quotations, also from Anchor Books, and she lives in New York.